MAGIC, SCIENCE, AND HEALTH

MAGIC, SCIENCE, AND HEALTH

The Aims and Achievements of Medical Anthropology

Robert Anderson

Mills College

Harcourt Brace College Publishers

Fort Worth   Philadelphia   San Diego   New York   Orlando   Austin   San Antonio

Toronto   Montreal   London   Sydney   Tokyo

Publisher	Ted Buchholz
Editor in Chief	Christopher P. Klein
Senior Acquisitions Editor	Stephen T. Jordan
Assistant Editor	Linda Wiley/Margaret McAndrew Beasley
Project Editor	Aimé Merizon/Warren K. Ludwig
Production Manager	Serena B. Manning
Senior Art Director	David A. Day
Digital Composition	Kim Standish

Address for Editorial Correspondence: Harcourt Brace College Publishers, 301 Commerce Street, Suite 3700, Fort Worth, TX 76102.

Address for Orders: Harcourt Brace & Company, 6277 Sea Harbor Drive, Orlando, FL 32887-6777. 1-800-782-4479, or 1-800-433-0001 (in Florida).

ISBN: 0-15-500828-5

Library of Congress Card Number: 95-77909

Printed in the United States of America.

5 6 7 8 9 0 1 2 3 4   016   10 9 8 7 6 5 4 3 2 1

PREFACE

Anthropologists characteristically move back and forth between local or delimited in-depth research and wide-ranging, comparative studies that frame their more specialized interests. I began the preparation of this book after spending twenty years in a sharply circumscribed in-depth mode, investing an enormous amount of work on the seemingly narrow problem of painful disorders of the spine. The time came to orient that research, which tended to be heavily focused on how best to diagnose and treat people in severe pain, to the more wide-ranging interests of medical anthropology, my home discipline. It takes time to review a field as lively, diverse, and complex as medical anthropology, but I loved every minute of it. It gave me the opportunity to pull together for myself and to share with others what I learned about the aims and achievements of medical anthropology.

Since medical anthropology is often taught without a prerequisite anthropology course, I tried to ensure that all discussions of method, theory, and findings were comprehensible to an educated person who has had no specific preparation in anthropology. I have attempted to accomplish that without sacrificing either sophistication or a rethinking of the field in ways that will be of interest to other professional medical anthropologists as well as to students who have had other courses in anthropology.

In order to describe the aims and achievements of medical anthropology, the book consists of three major parts. Part I, Paradigms of Medical Anthropology, offers nine chapters that explore the major theoretical orientations and research methods of the field. As an organizing principle, I took advantage of the persistence of older approaches that survive as useful in our time. Thus, after two chapters that define an overall orientation to a holistic, biocultural approach, chapters three through nine detail a historical sequence of paradigms that shape anthropological approaches to health issues in the present. In this way, the student is introduced to evolutionary theory, diffusionism, functionalism, culture change theory, critical anthropology, discourse analysis, postmodernism, medical ecology, and the biocultural model as they are relevant to contemporary medical anthropology. For those for whom this is a first and perhaps only course in anthropology, Part I ensures that the way anthropologists conceptualize problems and search for solutions is clarified in the context of medical issues. Those who are already well-grounded in anthropology will learn in these chapters how what they know is put to use by specialists in medical anthropology.

Part II, Health Issues in Perspective, consists of four chapters that bring together what we now know about human illness as a result of anthropological investigations. Attention to race, ethnicity, and class highlight aspects of health that are especially relevant to a current awareness of the importance of cultural diversity. Similarly, attention is directed to the age dimensions of health, to what anthropologists have contributed to an understanding of the problems of the disabled, and to the relationship between health and gay and lesbian lifestyles. This book is distinctive for including in Part II a whole chapter on the health of women.

Part III, Health Practitioners in Perspective, shifts the perspective from those who are ill to those who provide care. Health providers who primarily confront problems of the mind are described in Chapter 14. In this chapter the reader is introduced to shamans as psychiatrists and to psychiatrists as shamans. Chapter 15 focuses on practitioners who are more oriented to bodily complaints, from doctors of traditional Chinese medicine to bonesetters, herbalists, and homeopaths. The last chapter of the book shifts from how anthropologists study the medical systems of other societies to how they study the biomedical system. Medical anthropologists themselves become a topic of discussion, while studies of midwives and nurses are given equal billing with studies of physicians and surgeons. Ethics and public policy are featured topics.

It is my hope that this book will help to redefine the dimensions of the field by framing it as more open and receptive to diversity than is the case in other books on the subject. No other text attempts to incorporate as completely the comprehensive, wide-ranging interests of anthropology as a interdisciplinarity of four fields (cultural anthropology, biological anthropology, archeology, and linguistics). It is not wrong to define the field more narrowly, but it is incomplete. Further, no other book attempts so consistently to obliterate a false and pernicious preference for theoretical as opposed to applied anthropology. The theme here is that medical anthropology must be an applied field—it must address health concerns with a commitment to finding solutions—and by virtue of that very effort, it should continue to stand in the front lines of theoretical advancement. Finally, no other book identifies so clearly the need for medical anthropologists to be skilled in multidisciplinary research as they work closely with other health professionals, whether humanistic, scientific, or clinical.

The illustrations, which are valuable teaching documents in their own right, were obtained by asking some of the anthropologists whose publications are discussed to contribute photographs of themselves at work. The result constitutes a portfolio of environmental portraits showing many of the activities medical anthropologists engage in as part of earning a living. As can be seen, these activities are highly diverse. I am very grateful to the three-score colleagues who contributed pictures to serve this purpose. They lead fascinating lives, and I want the readers of this book to catch a glimpse of them.

Acknowledgments

It has been my good fortune to have good friends and colleagues who have enriched my life as a scientist. I owe so much to fellow anthropologists that it is quite distortive to single out only a few. However, for this book, I have especially appreciated George and Louise Spindler, Cliff Barnett, and my colleague at Mills, Ann Metcalf.

The following professors served as academic reviewers: Clifford Barnett of Stanford University, Dorothy Cattle of Wake Forest University, Kathleen DeWalt of the University of Pittsburgh, Jill Dubisch of Northern Arizona University, Eugenia Georges of Rice University, Ellen Gruenbaum of California State University, and Holly F. Mathews of East Carolina University. None of them is responsible for things I say and positions I take, of course, but insofar as the book has merit, it reflects their influence.

My approach to medical anthropology is greatly shaped by what I learned in medical school and chiropractic college about how to care for people who are sick. I worked as an anthropologist for many years before I sought clinical training, which I did in part as a way to study these fields by means of participant observation, but also in part to acquire knowledge and skills that would make me a more effective anthropologist. I was granted a Ph.D. in anthropology in 1956. I earned an M.D. in 1986, exactly 30 years later.

It was exhilarating to be a student again, and particularly at a time when chiropractic was starting up its highly successful research programs and medical science was exploding with new techniques and discoveries at the submolecular level. Experience and training in clinical settings shaped how I now do medical anthropology. Of all of the physicians who had a hand in my education, Arthur White exercised the most pervasive influence. Art is an orthopedic surgeon specializing in the spine. As a medical student under his supervision, and later as his colleague at the San Francisco Spine Institute, I learned to appreciate the importance of conservative approaches in medicine and surgery, of alternative medicine as beneficial for many conditions, and of an approach to team work (multidisciplinarity) that acknowledges that no one specialist can do everything that may be necessary for a good outcome, but each has something valuable to contribute.

My training in chiropractic led to a highly detailed knowledge of the anatomy and physiology of the spine as well as how to use my own body, especially my hands, to evaluate and manipulate (adjust) the joints and muscles of a body in pain. The chiropractor who taught me the most about the diagnosis and treatment of back pain would be hard to identify, for there were many, but certainly two of the most important were Scott Haldeman and James Cox. In addition, I acquired experience in designing and administering clinical research, partly from Scott Haldeman, but above all by collaborating at times with William Meeker.

Clinical science and practice are very distant from philosophy. The one area of knowledge is not easier than the other, but they certainly are very different. I struggle still with philosophers who seem to have something to say that may be relevant to medical anthropology, but couched in often convoluted and obscure language. An important part of my education during the last few years has been a faculty development seminar on philosophy at Mills College conducted by Don Beggs, a philosopher, and enlivened by faculty colleagues in literature, music, theology, art history, communication theory, education, and chemistry. One of the benefits of teaching in a small college is the opportunity it provides for multidisciplinary conversations in various contexts, and not the least, every day over lunch in the faculty dining room.

One fellow professor at Mills has put me in her debt above every other person mentioned. She took time from her own heavy responsibilities to read, correct, and comment on every chapter in this book. She and I have been partners for over twenty years now. We share six children and step-children as well as five lively young grandchildren. We have supported each other in fieldwork such that much of my research in far away places was designed around commitments she had to work in those places; but the converse has also been true. She has counseled me on how to be a more sensitive and responsive teacher. She models a strong feminist lifestyle for me and our children. She enriches our lives with her ability to find the good in every person and the beauty in every culture. She is generous to a fault, and her smile can melt a glacier or light up the darkest night. This book is dedicated to Edna Mitchell.

CONTENTS

PART ONE
The Paradigms of Medical Anthropology   1

Chapter 1
GETTING TO KNOW MARY AND KAREN   3

Chapter 2
MEDICAL ANTHROPOLOGY IN OUR TIME   17

Chapter 3
THE TIME DIMENSION   45

Chapter 4
THE SPACE DIMENSION   73

Chapter 5
ETHNOGRAPHIC METHODS   100

Chapter 6
STRUCTURAL AND FUNCTIONAL THEORY   129

Chapter 7
CULTURE CHANGE THEORY   154

Chapter 8
MEDICAL ECOLOGY   180

Chapter 9
THE BIOCULTURAL MODEL   204

PART II
Health Issues in Perspective   231

Chapter 10
MENTAL CONDITIONS   232

Chapter 11
RACE, ETHNICITY, AND CLASS   259

Chapter 12
AGE, ABLENESS, AND LIFESTYLE   286

Chapter 13
THE HEALTH OF WOMEN   314

PART III
Health Practitioners in Perspective   343

Chapter 14
MIND-ORIENTED HEALERS   344

Chapter 15
BODY-ORIENTED HEALERS   371

Chapter 16
THE ANTHROPOLOGY OF MEDICINE   403

PART ONE

The Paradigms of
Medical Anthropology

Chapter 1

GETTING TO KNOW MARY AND KAREN

MARY: THE PATIENT WITH A PAINFUL LIMP

Mary was a fourteen-year-old African adolescent, just the kind of teenager Margaret Mead interviewed in the South Seas when she was gathering data for her book, *Coming of Age in Samoa.* Although I refer to her by the fictitious name of Mary in order to protect her privacy, the events I relate really happened. I got to know her and her family in southern Africa two years ago when my work brought me to Zimbabwe to do some preliminary ethnographic research among the Shona. At the time we met, Mary was a source of concern because severe pain had recently made it unbearable for her to stand on her right leg.

From a strictly biomedical point of view, Mary's limp was a kind of problem doctors usually treat with considerable success. Quite unexpectedly, her right hip joint had begun to hurt. A physical examination, followed by Xrays and blood and urine tests, showed only that she was in pain, demonstrated some swelling in the area, and was running a temperature. Taking all of the evidence into consideration, her doctors were able to rule out every other likely cause except an infection, probably bacterial. Since it is not uncommon in growing children for blood-borne bacteria to infect the hip, that presumptive diagnosis made good sense. Powerful antibiotics were prescribed. Within the next couple of days her temperature returned to normal, she began to feel somewhat better, and her doctors concluded it would probably be only a matter of time before she would be fully restored to health, able again to attend classes and to play netball, the sport she loved.

When a physician interrogates a patient it is spoken of as "taking a history," but the demands of daily practice are without remorse. A medical history must usually be constructed rapidly—in Mary's case, within a matter of ten to twenty minutes. It typically results in just enough information to carry out the essential task of arriving at a medical diagnosis.

Medical anthropologists work very differently. They see people in the contexts of their lives rather than in the confines of an examination room. One of their most important skills is to draw people out about themselves in a holistic way. They typically spend hours talking with informants. Where the physician rapidly conducts a physical examination and orders tests, the anthropologist commits long periods of time to close observation of people in their daily lives, checking out what people say against what can be seen and experienced. Ultimately, an anthropologist will often shift from these personalized and individualized methods to statistical explorations based on household surveys or experimental tasks. As a way to introduce readers to the field of medical anthropology, this book will gently but firmly lead them into an understanding of how medical anthropologists arrive at their understandings by means of fieldwork and cross–cultural comparative studies.

Getting to know Mary made it seem that far more was going on with this young woman than was apparent in the hospital and the doctor's office. It is the thesis of this book that physicians and surgeons do not fully succeed in preventing disease and restoring health to complex human beings like Mary solely by doing what they do best, and what we respect them for. When an individual with a health problem is transformed into a patient in a white gown, it allows the doctor to zero in on a potentially treatable problem, but the wholeness of that person is diminished. When a painful condition is reduced to a diagnosis of organic disease, an acute and even life-threatening problem may be identified, but the embeddedness of that disease in problems of life gets lost. When a cure of medicine is prescribed, it will often succeed in a gratifying way, but will frequently leave untouched all of the suffering that does not manifest as pathophysiology responsive to biomedical treatment. Getting to know Mary illustrates what I mean.

THE TROUBLED ADOLESCENT

Mary fell ill the day after she returned to boarding school following summer vacation. It began with feeling dizzy, which continued until her mother brought her to a hospital five days later. During those days she became anxious, weepy, and unable to sleep. Her hip hurt. The only way she could move was to be carried.

When I talked with Mary about her first days back in school, she assured me that she liked school, had many friends from the previous year, and was happy with her classes, especially geography. But she also communicated a sense of being anxious and homesick. Her dormitory room was shared with twenty-one other girls, each with a bed, a hanger for clothes, and an open shelf for books and personal belongings. This spartan dormitory bore no resemblance to the large English-style family home she left the day before she became ill. There, she shared a well furnished bedroom with her sister. It seemed to me telling, and unusual for a fourteen–year–old girl, that what she liked best about school was neither friends, sports, teachers, nor classes. It was going to chapel.

From talking with Mary, I felt that she was not merely suffering from a painful infection. She seemed psychologically troubled. Her disease seemed invited, somehow, by a lingering anxiety, perhaps despair. To explore that hunch, I wish I had been able to travel to her school to talk with her teachers and friends. Even better, I wish I could have collaborated with a Shona colleague, preferably a woman, who would undoubtedly have succeeded better than I in talking with these women and young girls. Fieldwork takes time, energy, money, colleagues, a willing society, and commitment. I was not able to follow up on this important lead. Fortunately, I encountered an unexpected colleague who provided important evidence that Mary probably was emotionally troubled. That colleague was a traditional healer, a shaman.

THE AFRICAN SHAMAN

In a darkened and incense-suffused room, the ordinary voice of the traditional doctor was suddenly replaced by a distant-sounding, high-pitched moan that articulated a strange and unintelligible tongue. Mary was hearing the voice of a spirit who had taken possession of the shaman's body. When translated, the voice provided a diagnosis very different from that of her medical doctors. Mary's painful hip, she was told, was a punishment sent by her family ancestors, who were angry that her father had neglected them by failing to sponsor dance rituals in their honor. As a consequence, she had become possessed by a witch and would have to undergo an exorcism ritual.

This is a common kind of diagnosis widely encountered in southern Africa. It is believed that sickness may afflict an innocent party as punishment for a moral delict perpetrated by some other member of the family. Angry ancestors and evil witches cause illness. One task for medical anthropologists is to determine how people in diverse cultures make sense of illness experiences. Mary had her illness explained in terms of two thoroughly different explanatory models: the medical model and the shamanic model. Later in this book we will look closely at healing systems around the world, exploring how diseases are explained and treated (including more detail about Mary and the shaman).

A few days later, sitting easily across from each other at the kitchen table, Mary's mother filled me in on what lay behind the shaman's revelations about the ancestors. Mary is one of seven children, all of whom attend school, including the two oldest daughters studying at the university. Her mother is employed as an English teacher while her father has a job in another city, and therein lies the problem. Her mother's eyes sought out her feet as she quietly murmured, "He spends for unnecessary things. At times, I don't have enough money, yet he spends." The appearance of prosperity is misleading. This overworked and harried mother is barely able to pay her bills and keep her children in school. Sending Mary to boarding school stretched family

Traditional Doctor (TDr) Wadi Gomiwa ready to attend a meeting of the Zimbabwe Traditional Healers Association.
(Photo, Robert Anderson)

resources to the limit, and now the illness itself added an additional financial and emotional strain.

From a medical anthropological point of view, several issues were raised by this conversation with Mary's mother. There are the large political and economic issues of how health can be maintained in a nation that is so poor that even good jobs pay very little. These critical problems will be discussed later in this book. Psychological issues become apparent, which this book will also investigate. Not the least, gender issues come to the fore as we get to know Mary. A whole chapter is devoted to how medical anthropologists concern themselves with the health of women.

TDr Wadi Gomiwa, who has an excellent record of success, assumed this formal pose just before beginning the shamanic seance for Mary.

(Photo, Robert Anderson)

THE CHILD OF CULTURAL DIVERSITY

Mary felt much improved after a dramatic ritual in which shrill screams from deep inside her accompanied a struggle between the shaman and the witch over possession of Mary's body. The shaman (and Mary) won. In that same week, Mary's healing was assured by prayers offered in the Methodist church of which she and her family are devout members. Later, after I was gone, she obtained further treatment from a homeopathic doctor who practices a form of alternative medicine that originated in Germany at the beginning of the nineteenth century.

Medical anthropologists attempt to make sense out of health issues by studying how cultural complexity is managed. That is, they try to figure out how all the parts of a culture hold together when, on the face of it, they seem to clash in irreconcilable ways. How functional integration can be identified and evaluated will be described later in this book.

How did Mary and her family make sense out of this incongruous mixture of health philosophies and practices: biomedical, shamanic, Christian, and homeopathic? Her mother told me she believes that the traditional doctor "chased away the bad spirit which caused the doctors at the hospital not to know the cause of the illness." Before the exorcism, their private doctor "tried his best to cure the child. He lessened the pain, but it could not stop. Even the doctors at the hospital were treating an unknown disease. Then, after visiting the traditional doctor, everything went on smoothly." Mary's twenty-year-old sister, whose university course load that semester included an introduction to social anthropology, separately told me much the same thing, and I agreed, except that I would attribute the benefits of the shaman's treatment to his skill as a traditional psychiatrist and family counselor. Later, I will devote a chapter to mind–oriented healers of various kinds.

KAREN: THE PATIENT WITH INCURABLE PAIN

Getting to know Karen Barrett (a pseudonym) brings us to the great divide that separates short–term (acute) health problems from long–term, degenerative (chronic) disorders. The physical, mental, social, cultural, and treatment issues are usually very different across this divide, as will become clear in later chapters. Medical anthropologists must be prepared to work on both sides of the divide.

Getting to know Karen, as in getting to know Mary, also brings us to an organizing theme that permeates this book. Health is a matter for physicians and surgeons, but it is more than that. It is equally a matter for other health scientists, including anthropologists. Medical anthropology can succeed only if medical anthropologists are trained to work with other scholars and clinicians. Given the image of the heroic field ethnographer who works alone deep in the forest or far out on an isolated island, this stance may seem like a sharp break with the history of the discipline. It is not so much a break as a shift in emphasis. One major theme that is enunciated early in this book is that medical anthropology has grown by a process of maturation (dropping concepts and methods that became obsolete), consolidation (identifying what has durable value), and growth (discovering and creating new concepts and methods) rather than by a series of disconnected paradigm shifts.

This book is oriented to medical anthropology as a comprehensive, holistic discipline that is both interdisciplinary and multidisciplinary. I will explain exactly what I mean by these terms in the next chapter. For now, I want to illustrate what I mean by getting to know Karen. Her personal history illustrates how medicine and anthropology write very different narratives about illness. This is to say that they investigate issues from very different perspectives. One perspective is not necessarily better than the other, but none is complete (holistic) without the other. Multidisciplinarity builds on the high potential of holism conceptualized in this way. Examples of how this is true will become clear as we proceed. But for now, let us see how important it can be in the case of one unfortunate woman with a severe, degenerative condition.

THE MEDICAL NARRATIVE

Incapacitated by a dull, persistent ache in her lower back that radiated excruciatingly along one leg from hip to foot, Karen was admitted to the orthopedics ward of Western Regional Medical Center one Sunday evening in 1986. It was not her first experience with severe and unremitting pain. Some years earlier she had twice gotten so bad that spinal surgeries were performed. Did she need yet another major surgery of this kind?

On Monday and Tuesday she submitted to diagnostic testing that included a CAT scan, the probing of some of her spinal nerve roots with a large needle (under fluoroscopic guidance), evaluation of the pain she reported when asked to move in prescribed ways, and interviews and questionnaires to explore her psychological state in the presence of intense chronic pain. On Wednesday morning the multidisciplinary team held its regular weekly conference in which the results of all tests and examinations were reviewed. The team was made up of physicians, surgeons, psychologists, physical therapists, nurses, and one medical anthropologist (myself). After reviewing all possible alternatives, the team concluded that the patient should be scheduled to undergo her third major operation for back and leg pain on Friday. Karen consented, and two days later the operation was performed by the world-famous spinal surgeon who headed the team.

Within a week it became apparent that the surgery had made her worse, not better. She spent the years that followed encased in a cumbersome plastic body brace, half sick from powerful (but for her ineffective) narcotics. Her body, ponderous and punitive, became foreign to her. Only on rare occasions did she venture away from her apartment, her prison.

Four years after being discharged from Western, a different but equally famous spinal surgeon operated again. This, too, was a failure, leading to a fifth surgery the following year when a neurosurgeon at State University Medical School implanted a dorsal column stimulator (electrical wires attached to the spinal cord and a control box implanted in her abdomen) designed to stop pain by interfering with nerve transmission to the brain. Very little improvement was noted. In addition, the patient was increasingly distressed by related, non-spinal symptoms that had been getting worse for several years. To ameliorate these painful and dehumanizing symptoms, she underwent major surgery by a urologist to repair pelvic damage caused by her disease and the multiple surgeries. The urologic/gynecologic surgery was successful, but she remained incapacitated by back and leg pain. In 1992 she was evaluated again by the neurosurgeon to see if it was possible that she might get relief from a surgery in which he would implant electrical wires deep in the brain itself—brain surgery for low back pain. That operation, which would have been her sixth, was scrubbed because the surgeon concluded it was inadvisable. Now sixty years old, Karen is totally disabled and in constant pain. She was twenty–four years old when her back pain first occurred as the result of an automobile accident.

This is the medical narrative of Karen, her case history. In other words, this is how a physician might summarize the medical condition of Karen when speaking as a physician to nonphysicians. The description incorporates much more jargon when the audience is made up of other doctors, and is reduced to a few lines of abbreviations and curt statements when it is written into hospital charts. Common to all of these forms of medical narrative, however, is distancing language. She is Karen Barrett, the patient, a failed back surgery, a complex but interesting case.

In this book about medical anthropology, we will look at approaches to health that bring out issues of discourse, narrative, and culture analyzed as if they were literary texts. In medical narratives, the focus is on biotechnology. Discussion for the most part narrows down to herniated intervertebral discs, edematous and inflamed spinal nerve roots, laminectomies (cutting away parts of spinal vertebrae), and surgical fusions, although psychosocial factors also constitute part of the discourse. As Mary-Jo Good and Byron Good put it in their research on medical students, "sufferers are reconstructed as cases," and cases are constructed "with minimal social and personal characteristics and great physiological detail" (Good & Good, 1989, p. 306).

The medical narrative is hegemonic, authoritative, or controlling in the sense that it reflects a viewpoint (what Michel Foucault called "the medical gaze") that incorporates a good deal of power, direct and indirect, over what happens to the patient (Foucault, 1975; Frankenberg, 1988). At the same time, it is dedicated to making the patient well, and a carefully selected patient with severe back and leg pain of a particular sort has a 95 percent chance of being restored to health by spinal surgery, in spite of the biotechnical, hegemonic quality of discourse. Karen's first operation in 1961 resulted in pain relief and good movement that lasted until she was reinjured in a job-related accident six years later. Her spinal disease became chronic at that time, shortly after her thirty-second birthday.

THE EPIDEMIOLOGIC NARRATIVE

Medicine does not speak with a single voice. In fact, many voices can be heard, one of which is that of epidemiologists. The narrative of epidemiology is oriented to prevention rather than cure, to public health measures, and to population characteristics and risk groups. Epidemiologists attempt to identify social practices that result in disease, which brings them far closer to the approach of social scientists and humanists than is the case for clinicians as such (Fraser, 1987). When they publish their reports, however, they produce narratives that greatly distance an individual such as Karen, who for them becomes a number, a mere cipher in a display of aggregate numbers. She nearly drops out of sight in the following text.

Many people experience the kind of back pain that our subject suffered when she was twenty-six years old. Low back pain often begins in the third decade of life. From surveys of various populations in different parts of the world it appears that 60 to 80 percent of the adult population will suffer at least one episode of painful, debilitating back pain during a lifetime. Between 20 to 80 percent will be suffering from back pain at any one moment in time. However, when the figure surpasses 30 percent it derives from studies that include mild to moderate pain no worse than an occasional headache, which also records high prevalence counts. Karen falls into a very small subcategory of 10 percent or less of the population with moderate to severe low back pain that has become chronic and intense.

Continuing in the epidemiologic style, Karen is typical in some ways but not in others. Whether for good or for ill, her lifestyle impacts on her disease in ways epidemiologists think of as risk factors. Obesity is a known risk factor for the onset of low back pain and for a poor outcome from spinal surgery; however, Karen was never obese. On the other hand, for twenty years she was a two-pack-a-day smoker. Cigarettes put one at risk for low back pain, as well as a failure to improve after surgery. Also, she suffered a major reinjury in a work-related accident; more than half of all working people at some time experience low back pain that has occurred on the job. She also meets risk criteria for those who have two or more spinal surgeries. Studies document that the success rate drops precipitously for multi-operated backs (Cassidy & Wedge, 1988; Anderson, 1984; Anderson, 1992; White & Hsu, 1987).

THE NARRATIVE OF MEDICAL ANTHROPOLOGY

Unlike the physician or epidemiologist (who usually is also a physician), it is the job of the anthropologist to explore thoroughly the experience of a chronic illness, helping the ill person articulate feelings perhaps never identified before; and to recount a personal narrative no physician (except perhaps a psychiatrist) would want to elicit. The illness experience can be approached through discourse analysis, and one's life can be interpreted as a text. What follows is Karen's story as recorded by an anthropologist, though not by means of discourse or textual analysis, which I will explain later in the book.

When Karen was first severely injured in an auto accident she was twenty-four years old and the single parent of two small children. She supported herself and her children by full-time employment as a mid-level professional administrator. Her medical treatment was only minimally effective, and for two years she kept working in spite of daily pain and impaired movement. She struggled on because she had no medical insurance, because she had children to take care of, and because she was afraid she might lose her job if she underwent a surgery that could require several months of recuperation. Ultimately, however, a disc ruptured causing a sudden loss of reflexes in one leg. To avoid permanent paralysis she was left with no other options. She submitted to her first operation.

Karen was very pleased with the result, dismissing as unpleasant or uncomfortable but not disabling an area of extreme skin tenderness that resulted from a permanent and incurable inflammation of the lining of the

Spine surgeon Arthur White, who has an excellent record of success, reviews computerized images of the spine just before scrubbing in to operate.

spinal cord (arachnoiditis). In her words, "I returned to a normal life." An area of extremely sensitive skin painful to the touch and to contact with clothing was a not infrequent reaction to pantopaque, the oily substance injected in those days into the spinal fluid in order to x-ray spinal nerve roots (a myelogram) before doing surgery.

Speaking of the back pain that recurred six years later, she recalls how that happened. "I grabbed at, and hung on to, a file drawer that fell. I had absorbed the fusion. Holding on to the file drawer resulted in a herniated disc with leg pain. Also, I was rolling a cart from one department to another. It was moving to the side. I tried to catch it. Those two events were close. The leg pain was bad and I was really hanging on. I didn't think it was my back, which was denial. I kept thinking, 'It must be phlebitis.' I didn't want to have another surgery." But she did, and it, too, was considered a success, since it eliminated her leg pain. However, to the skin sensitivity of arachnoiditis was now added postsurgical mild to moderate low back pain that was distressing but did not keep her from her "normal life."

At this point in her narrative—now the anthropologist's narrative—we learn something not found in her medical charts and not known to her doctors. At the age of forty-one, after years of nagging pain, she spent a month in the Philippines where she was operated on forty-four times by psychic surgeons. (These surgeries are described in a later chapter.) Her pain lessened, and she returned to the United States feeling much improved until two years later when she was thrown through the windshield of her car in a rear-end collision. Her vulnerable spine was severely reinjured. During the next half-dozen years of coping with pain she tried several other forms of alternative healing: acupuncture, acupressure, Feldenkreis, Trager, and chiropractic, the latter proving particularly effective in keeping her on her feet, as she put it.

Alternative medicine is a major field of anthropological investigation. We encountered one example in passing insofar as Mary sought care from a homeopath in addition to that of a traditional doctor. However, people with incurable conditions are far more likely than those with time-limited diseases to try unorthodox or nonmainstream forms of treatment. Karen illustrates that pattern. As will be discussed in a later chapter, anthropologists have a special obligation to document and make sense of little-known or untested medical systems.

Success in treatment cannot be measured only in terms of improved function and diminished pain. In what is one of the most distinguishing aspects of an anthropological approach to health, measures of success are defined in holistic terms that include psychosocial benefits. For example, what also is not apparent in the medical or epidemiologic narratives of Karen's life and suffering is her spiritual odyssey. She ardently pursued a career as a semiprofessional choir singer until she could no longer travel or stay on her feet for a concert. She became an intuitive consultant, earning her living as a spiritual counselor energized by paranormal powers. She had been a devout Catholic. After her second back operation she entered a convent to dedicate herself for a year to Christian austerities. During that year it became increasingly clear to her that she had a gift for knowing things intuitively. After much soul-searching, she left the convent and the church to become a Jew by conversion. Meanwhile, she recalls that the high point of her treatment by psychic surgeons in the Philippines was not the amelioriation of her residual back pain, as such, but the spiritual experience of participating in the religious rituals of these healers. On learning of these experiences, one begins to appreciate Karen's illness as a richly laden odyssey of personal meaning and cultural involvement.

Today, financially destitute, spending day after day flat on her back in unending discomfort, often in agony, she insists that her disease has not made her angry, disillusioned, or without hope. She readily acknowledges that not a day goes by without thoughts of how much she would like to be healed. At the same time, she believes her suffering has a spiritual purpose. She finds solace and strength in her conviction that through her suffering she has developed compassion, insight, and spiritual blessings she can share with others who seem led to her for solace and guidance. I do not want to dismiss or minimize her physical suffering, but in documenting how Karen endures incurable pain and confinement, it is absolutely essential that these personal and cultural dimensions be elicited as part of her health equation.

Did it make a difference to Mary and Karen that a medical anthropologist got involved in their health problems? An answer to this question requires attention to the institutional base from which the anthropologist works. In Mary's case, I participated as a caring and knowledgeable outsider who was on the scene only for a short time. I accompanied Mary and her mother and sisters on visits to her doctors and the shaman. I held unhurried conversations with each and all of them about their problems. They seemed to appreciate that I was able to answer some of the questions their physicians had failed to address. Merely articulating problems in talking with me probably helped, independently of whatever I might have said (the friendly ear effect). However, I was not present during the first two weeks when Mary's condition was most problematic and when patient and family distress was at its highest. As a general rule, for a medical anthropologist to function effectively as an interpreter or mediator between the subcultures of patient, physician, traditional doctor, alternative practitioner, minister, and so on, I would have needed an institutional base not available to me in Zimbabwe. The situation was different as concerns Karen.

As a member of the multidisciplinary team at Western Regional Center, my responsibilities were divided. In part, I designed, sought funding for, and administered a research program that was intended to explore ways in which patient care could be improved (a never–ending challenge). My two main projects at that time were to investigate the possible benefits and problems involved in adding some alternative health care providers to our team, but, of course, many other kinds of research might have been planned.

In addition to research, I also participated in weekly team meetings (see Corbett, 1986). We were experimenting at that time with the hoped for benefits of adding my in–depth ethnographic health interviews as supplements to the usual medical histories. Based on those interviews, I was able to share in the give-and-take of making tough decisions about what to do in the highly problematic cases that came to our center. In the meeting before her third surgery, the critical issue for the team evaluating Karen was whether to operate. It was a tough call, because the chance of failure when doing a third surgery is about 35 percent. We discussed the possibility of referral for one of several options in alternative medicine. My findings that she had already exhausted those options confirmed the opinion of the surgeons that only major surgery had a chance to succeed. However, because the possibility of a failed surgery was so significant, it was also essential to evaluate her capacity to cope with failure should it occur, as, in fact, it did. The psychologist and the psychiatrist, as well as the nurse and the physical therapist who had worked with her, felt that she could. I contributed to that consensus, confirming their impressions and adding what the others did not know about her remarkable spirituality. Ultimately, key members of the team, including the chief surgeon and myself, met with Karen for a give-and-take, pros-and-cons discussion in which the bottom line was that the surgeons were willing to operate, but the ultimate decision was up to her. You know the rest, including that she did demonstrate remarkable resiliency, as we had hoped.

If medical anthropologists are to realize their potential for making contributions in health care, they need to have jobs in academic or health care facilities. Medical anthropologists whose experience includes work with people such as Mary and Karen also have much to contribute to policy on governmental and institutional levels where decisions relating to health care objectives are defined.

In the last chapter of the book we will look at the job market for medical anthropologists, including medical anthropology as a policy science. It was a matter of ethics that Karen was fully informed of the possible benefits and harm of a third surgery and that the final decision was hers. In the final chapter, we will also examine ethical issues as problems especially suitable for the employment of medical anthropologists.

Beyond this book, and beyond this moment in time, medical anthropologists expect to continue to contribute to an understanding of humanity in the broadest sense. As George and Louise Spindler reminded me recently, the more we learn about health, illness, and health care, the more we learn about the human condition in the broadest sense. Feedback loops, tie-ins, and multiple interconnections between health, sickness, and context that we only dimly apprehend at present may ultimately become specific and secure. It is the attention we give to context, to holism, that makes every research project and every personal history, such as that of Mary and of Karen, an exploration into possible interconnections and complexities not presently known about people, cultures, and societies. These interactive effects are important to discover if our species is to survive and prosper on Planet Earth (Spindler & Spindler, 1994).

CONCLUSION

The aim of this book is to describe the work of medical anthropologists and to provide an overview of what they have accomplished so far in this still young and vital discipline. The book is divided into three parts. Research methods and anthropological theory relating to health are explained in Part I by taking an historical approach. Starting from the early years of anthropology allows the reader to build up an understanding of complex issues by taking them a step at a time just as they were developed by several generations of scholars. Over the years, anthropologists winnowed out what did not work or make sense, kept what was valuable, and creatively added on new ideas and approaches. That process brought them to where they are today, with a toolbox of research methods and a body of theory characterized as a biocultural model.

In Part II, the book shifts from method and theory, as such, to what we have learned by applying these methods and theories. To this end, one chapter explores mental health against an awareness of the complexity of the body/mind entity as it is embedded in culture and society. Other chapters explore interactions of health with race, ethnicity, class, age, ableness, lifestyles, and gender.

The last part of the book, Part III, shifts attention from health problems to health practitioners. Taking what may be considered a somewhat unusual approach, but one which seems to reflect a widespread distinction in how healers work, one chapter describes mind-oriented healers (including shamans and psychiatrists), while a separate chapter describes body-oriented healers, a category of health care providers generally neglected in the anthropological literature.

Finally, in a concluding chapter, "The Anthropology of Medicine," the work of medical anthropologists employed in Western medicine is summarized. Consistent with the holistic and multidisciplinary orientation of the book, attention to physicians and surgeons is balanced by equal attention to nurses (and nurse anthropologists) as well as to traditional healers (such as the African shaman) and alternative healers (such as chiropractors and homeopaths) in biomedical settings. Ethics and public policy will concern us here. The challenge of the future is for medical anthropologists to position themselves so that their work can contribute to the betterment of health at that decisive moment in time when the world must face both the enormous threats and the great potentialities inherent in beginning the third millennium of the Common Era.

REFERENCES

Anderson, R. (1984). An orthopedic ethnography in rural Nepal. *Medical Anthropology, 8,* 46-59.

Anderson, R. (1992). Back pain of bus drivers: Prevalence in an urban area of California. *Spine, 17,* 1481-1488.

Cassidy, J. D., & Wedge, J. H. (1988). The epidemiology and natural history of back pain and spinal degeneration. In W. H. Kirkaldy-Willis (Ed.), *Managing low back pain* (2nd ed., pp. 3-14). New York: Churchill Livingstone.

Corbett, K. K. (1986). *Adding insult to injury: Cultural dimensions of frustration in the management of chronic back pain.* Unpublished doctoral dissertation, Joint doctoral program of the University of California, Berkeley, and the University of California, San Francisco.

Foucault, M. (1975). *The birth of the clinic: The archaeology of medical perception.* New York: Vintage Books.

Frankenberg, R. (1988). Gramsci, culture, and medical anthropology: Kundry and Parsifal? or rat's tail to sea serpent? *Medical Anthropology Quarterly, 2,* 324-337.

Fraser, D.W. (1987). Epidemiology as a liberal art. *New England Journal of Medicine, 316,* 309-314.

Good, M. J. D., & Good, B. J. (1989). Disabling practitioners: Hazards of learning to be a doctor in American medical education. *American Journal of Orthopsychiatry, 59,* 303-309.

Spindler, G., & Spindler, L. (1994). Personal communication.

White, A. H., & Hsu, K. (1987). Failed posterior spine surgery. In White, A. H., Rothman, R. H., & Ray, C. D. (Eds.), *Lumbar spine surgery: Techniques and complications* (pp. 187-194). St. Louis: C. V. Mosby Co.

Chapter 2

MEDICAL ANTHROPOLOGY IN OUR TIME

INTRODUCTION

Medical anthropology is a subfield of general anthropology dedicated to research, teaching, and practice relating to health and all of the ways in which health is maintained, experienced, promoted, and threatened in societies everywhere, including our own now and in the past. Health in this perspective is an enormously comprehensive field which medical anthropologists approach in holistic ways. Consistent with this broad commitment, even though medical anthropologists all tend to be alike in some ways, they also differ a lot among themselves in the work they do. Compare and contrast Brigitte Jordan, Joan Cassell, and Merrill Singer, to pick just three from the almost two thousand members of the Society for Medical Anthropology.

Over a period of many months Brigitte Jordan spent her days and nights in the company of peasant midwives on the Yucatan Peninsula of Mexico. Her goal was to document low-tech methods of delivering babies in a traditional Mayan setting. Working in the field with Nancy Fuller, she recalls:

> Doña Juana was pleased with the interest we took in her profession and was always ready to talk about el trabajo (the work). We, in turn, explained our own work to the women as wanting to find out how people in different countries do certain kinds of things (such as having babies or weaving hammocks).... However,.... they began to treat us, in many ways, as if we were learning to become midwives.... "You know how to do everything now. The only thing you still have to do is catch the baby." (Jordan & Davis-Floyd, 1993, pp. 17, 19)

Joan Cassell spent eighteen months in the company of surgeons during their long days of work with fellow professionals and patients in the United States. Her goal was to contribute to an understanding of the human element in high-tech medicine. Just to get started was a challenge, although finally she was able to carry out her research in a suburban hospital. She recalls her initial discouragement:

Wearing village-appropriate apparel, Sandra Lane carried out semi-structured, day-long observations of the daily life activities of women and children in their homes and at work in a village in Egypt.

> After more than a year of letters, introductory interviews, and phone calls, I had still not managed to find a group of surgeons that would agree to be studied. One chief assented, but his senior surgeons refused; the seconds in command at two departments of surgery were unable to convince their chiefs to let me in; several chiefs did not respond to my letters or phone calls....I did not want to confine my research solely to interviews; the surgeons refused to be observed; the project appeared doomed. (Cassell, 1991, p. 221)

Merrill Singer, as director of a research project on AIDS in urban America, employs anthropologists to hang out in shooting galleries. The purpose is to study the culture of injection drug use so that strategies for the prevention of AIDS can be designed and implemented. It can be dangerous work, as Singer recalls:

> Street ethnographers in various cities have had to take cover as shots were fired by rival gangs or rival dealers, they have had contracts put out on them because it was assumed (wrongly) that they had divulged information that led to a police raid, offered shelter to informants who were being sought for deadly retribution from their enemies, witnessed various illegal activites (for which they cannot claim protection from subpoena)...., and they have

dodged streams of blood and the sharpened points of dirty needles in close quarters. (Singer, 1994, p. 30)

Although the work they do is quite variable, Jordan, Cassell, and Singer all work fundamentally in the same way, in spite of obvious differences. As George Spindler noted when he read these vignettes, all three "got close to their people—they achieved the intimacy that anthropologists depend upon for insight and accuracy" (Spindler, Letter of 9/9/94).

Jordan, Cassell, and Singer are also alike in being American-trained. So am I. At the risk of seeming chauvinistic or parochial, I have taken the liberty of writing here about medical anthropology as it is done in the United States. It goes without saying that American anthropologists draw freely on contributions from all over the world. However, the way most Americans define the field is distinctively "very American," if you will. In many other parts of the world, anthropologists approach the field with narrower limits on what they attempt to do. Characteristically, these anthropologists do social anthropology or physical anthropology quite independently of one another, and they admit to no professional ties with either archeologists or linguists. American anthropologists, in contrast, typically struggle to achieve a broader purpose that can only be done on an interdisciplinary and multidisciplinary basis.

INTERDISCIPLINARITY

Although it is common in academe to speak of interdisciplinarity and multidisciplinarity as though they are synonyms, it can be helpful to contrast them in a precise way. I take my lead here from Julie Klein (1990). For Klein, multidisciplinarity implies collaboration among scholars, scientists, and technicians who are very different in what they do. They work together, however, because each has certain skills to contribute toward achieving success in a joint enterprise. Medical anthropologists do this a lot.

To illustrate, multidisciplinarity was demonstrated in a research project on blindness that was carried out in an impoverished hamlet in Egypt. The anthropologist, Sandra Lane, functioned as part of a team that included nurses, ophthalmologists, and epidemiologists. Lane's contribution included living in the hamlet to do interviews and to interact "with both low vision and normal vision individuals, observing how the visually impaired villagers coped with their daily activities and how others treated them." The nurses and ophthalmologists documented general health conditions and performed necessary eye examinations. Epidemiologists assisted in designing the research strategy that was essential in early planning (Lane et al., 1993).

Interdisciplinarity goes beyond multidisciplinary teamwork in that the involved disciplines achieve a degree of mutuality that includes some organizing concepts, beliefs, understandings, and methods held in common. It takes place when individuals from different disciplines share at least in part a common or overlapping set of disciplinary goals. They approach these goals, however, using different methods and technologies and they also perpetuate important disciplinary goals that are not shared. It is customary in anthropology to speak of interdisciplinarity in this sense as four-field anthropology, which unites sociocultural anthropology, biological anthropology, prehistoric archeology, and anthropological linguistics.

Four-Field Anthropology

As William Adams points out, the four fields originally existed quite separately from one another. They developed in an interdisciplinary direction in part because each had something to contribute to an understanding of human evolution.

The subfields were swept into the net of emergent anthropology after 1860, because all of them provided support for an evolutionary perspective.

Adams continues, noting that in his opinion, "anthropology is probably unique among the social and natural sciences in this respect; it is not a group of increasingly divergent specialties but an uncomfortable and possibly unstable confederation of older, previously existing parts."

I have to say "unstable" because in Europe the package came unstuck around 1900, when evolution ceased to be anthropology's central organizing concept. Thereafter [in Europe, but not in North America] prehistory, ethnology, linguistics, and physical anthropology returned to their separate ways, which they have pursued down to the present day. (Adams, 1993)

Evolutionary theory has always been central to biological anthropology. Evolutionary thinking in sociocultural anthropology underwent trials and tribulations during the first half of the twentieth century that diminished and almost extinguished its shaping power. Eventually it revived, however, and in our time it serves as a central organizing concept for medical anthropology.

Medical anthropology is an interdisciplinary field that currently unites biological and sociocultural anthropology in terms of a biocultural evolutionary model, as we shall see. Most medical anthropologists are either sociocultural or biological anthropologists, so the interdisciplinarity of these two disciplines largely defines the field. Archeology is also oriented to evolutionary reconstructions and the biocultural model. It, too, can be pursued as a way to learn more about health issues, but fewer individuals are involved in these efforts.

Linguistic anthropology persists as a major part of the interdisciplinarity of medical anthropology, but on the whole not for its work on the evolution of language. Rather, in striking ways, linguists—and sociocultural anthropologists influenced by linguistic theory—have contributed to theory development and field methodology relating to the study of culture.

Evolution as an interdisciplinarity of four fields took shape as the study of culture. One might well paraphrase Adams saying that

> *the subfields were swept into the net of emergent anthropology after 1860, because all of them provided support for the study of culture.*

The concept of culture contributed the keystone to the anthropological edifice. The central importance of the concept of culture grew out of the mind-shaking realization that the incredible variety of human lifestyles cannot be explained adequately in terms of biological factors alone, as once was thought. On the contrary, social inheritance (culture) is so influential that how people live their lives can be understood only as a combination of cultural and biological interactions.

Although culture serves as a major framing concept, it does so in large part because it inspires holistic thinking. One might well say that

> *the subfields were swept into the net of emergent anthropology after 1860, because all of them provided support for holism.*

During the first half of the twentieth century, when almost every anthropologist eschewed any theory of cultural evolution, the four-field approach held firm in North America as a comprehensive approach to the study of culture. Now we speak of this approach as holism, a term that did not emerge in the literature of medicine and anthropology until 1926, when Jan-Christian Smuts, a South African biologist-philosopher-statesman, wrote his book, *Holism and Evolution.* The holistic model proposes that whole organisms and entire ecological systems are greater than the sum of their parts. Holism was urged as an alternative to scientific reductionism, which had a track record of sacrificing organismic/systemic understandings for more circumscribed research goals (Gordon, 1994, pp. 60–61).

Andrew Miracle, commenting on four-field anthropology, makes this point, stating that "holism is the strength of anthropology" (Miracle, 1993). Sue Parker makes the same point in her own way. "Of all the disciplines in the university, only anthropology studies human beings simultaneously as biological species and cultural beings using a broadly comparative approach across species, across cultures, through history, through prehistory and through paleohistory" (Parker, 1993).

In this statement, Parker refers to what can be considered another shared feature of anthropological interdisciplinarity, the comparative method. Julie Marcus, for her part, notes that "anthropology is defined as the comparative study of social systems and cultures, which makes the task of comparison explicit" (Marcus, 1992, p. 59, her italics). One might reasonably say that

> *the subfields were swept into the net of emergent anthropology after 1860, because all of them provided support for the comparative method.*

Each of the four disciplines developed its own methodology for identifying both the similarities and the differences that characterize Homo sapiens and human societies and cultures across expanses of space as well as in evolutionary approaches through time. Alone among the sciences, the four fields of anthropology in their collaborative interdisciplinarity include studies that compare and contrast languages, societies, cultures, cultural traits, and biological (racial) characteristics on a worldwide basis.

Good cross-cultural comparisons require good field data from every part of the world as well as from historic and prehistoric documents and excavations. Anthropological interdisciplinarity is based ultimately on field research carried out with meticulous care utilizing both qualitative methods (observing, photographing, talking) and quantitative methods (measuring, doing statistics). One might well say that

> *the subfields were swept into the net of emergent anthropology after 1860, because all of them provided support for fieldwork.*

In sum, the idea of four-field anthropology provides a way to talk about and carry out an interdisciplinarity of shared concepts and methods. Anthropologists from the four fields rely on one another as each needs the other in order to achieve a holistic approach to humanity, and more specifically to an understanding of human health. The shared concepts and methods include:

- an evolutionary perspective
- the concept of culture
- holistic thinking
- comparative studies
- intense field research
- multidisciplinarity

MULTIDISCIPLINARITY

Because the goals of anthropology are so all-inclusive, anthropologists long ago learned to get and use help from specialists in nonanthropological fields. Certainly as concerns medical anthropology, multidisciplinarity has been as essential as interdisciplinarity to the pursuit of its goals. Many allied fields in the social sciences, the natural sciences, and the humanities have entered into multidisciplinary relations with medical anthropology at one time or another, but none has been more consistently involved since the 1950s than biomedicine, at first primarily in the fields of psychiatry, public health, and epidemiology, but now in every field of medicine and surgery (Caudill, 1953).

Writing at length about "areas of interest common to the social and medical sciences," Steven Polgar listed many achievements that had already derived from collaboration when he wrote in 1962. However, he also made it clear that multidisciplinarity benefits came at a price. Teamwork requires resolving problems relating to who should be in charge, reaching agreement when scientific and clinical goals are in conflict, and giving professional recognition to social scientists when they work in clinical settings where they are in danger of being thought of as paramedical technicians rather than professional colleagues (Polgar, 1962, pp. 178, 186).

Multidisciplinarity also requires that one surrender a certain amount of autonomy in order to work collaboratively: "That is to say, the best methods to deal with a chosen problem must be selected, regardless of which discipline or combination of disciplines gave rise to them." Robert Rapoport expanded that observation:

> Anthropologists in medicine are, by and large, associated with other social scientists as well as with medical people. The literature around their research problem tends to be heavy with writings from disciplinary perspectives other than anthropology; the standards of their research colleagues and their research-application review boards tend to be actively eclectic (not merely tolerant, as in much traditional anthropology). (Rapoport, 1962)

During the first half of the nineteenth century, when anthropology was more embryo than baby, since it was not yet clearly separated out as a scholarly discipline, Auguste Comte provided an orientation to multidisciplinarity that shaped the field in ways we still feel (Lewes, 1887; Lévy-Bruhl, 1903). According to Comte, the fundamental law of evolution shaped up as three ways of making sense of what the senses perceive:

Theological (supernatural)

In this way of thinking, people regard themselves in important ways as pawns on a gameboard of powers unseen and unpredictable. The relationship between cause and effect is not clearly perceived because the interpretation of events is suffused with magical and religious thinking or distorted by ill-founded beliefs. For example, Comte classified as theological thinking the belief of many nineteenth century Europeans that a person bitten by a dog would fall ill with hydrophobia (rabies) if the attacking dog subsequently was itself bitten and contracted the disease. This would happen, it was thought, even though the sick dog was completely healthy at the time when it sank its fangs into its victim. Contageous magic was taken for granted in this illustration in which a traumatic moment of contact was thought to establish an enduring fatal tie between two lives, that of the animal with that of the human being.

Metaphysical (transitional)

One has entered this stage of thinking when one concludes without empirical testing that healing should be credited to some entity or principle that explains without recourse to capricious divinities (theology) on the one hand or to scientifically identified regularities (positivism) on the other. For example, metaphysics is implicit in the widespread and ancient belief in an inherent curative principle, dignified with a Latin designation as *vis medicatrix naturæ.* According to this belief, the body gets rid of noxious substances and undertakes repairs because that is its nature.

Positive (scientific)

When cause and effect are thought of in terms of observable sequences that have been proven to take place in a predictable manner, they constitute what Comte regarded as laws of nature (which today would be considered an archaic terminology for characterizing regularities or probabilities). For example, in the positive stage it was discovered that a dog bite can function as a direct mechanism for the transmission of a rabies infection, but only if the dog is infected to begin with. Again, we have learned that *vis medicatrix naturæ* can be reinterpreted to designate complex homeostatic mechanisms we now speak of as psychoneuroimmunological processes.

Although Comte regarded these three stages as an evolutionary sequence, he also insisted that the three were not mutually exclusive or completely separate, because they coexisted from the start. His stages describe emphases rather than exclusivities. Positivism and metaphysics can be identified even in the earliest theological stage, when the dominant mode of thinking was fetishistic (i.e., supernatural). A single individual, even in our time, can be expected to use all three ways of reasoning at one time or another. A modern American may pray to God, Allah, or the Great Spirit for recovery from a grave illness (Theological Stage), believe that a chiropractic spinal adjustment will free the innate intelligence of the body (also known as Innate) to permit healing as a process of *vis medicatrix naturæ* (Metaphysical Stage), and trust the representatives of medical science to provide the latest in antibiotic medications to eliminate a bacterial pathology (Positive Stage).

The three coexist in our own time, constituting what Comte considered to be intellectual anarchy, an anarchy that he believed must be surmounted. Comte explained what he meant by anarchy when he taught his Course in Positive Philosophy *(Cours de Philosophie Positive)* around 1840. He regarded it as anarchy that physics was in the Positive Stage, biology in the Metaphysical Stage, and sociology in the Theological Stage. Ultimately, to end conceptual anarchy, all must rely solely upon the positive method, and it should be our task as social scientists to fulfill that destiny. Now, a century and a half later, if Comte were alive again he would no doubt be cheered to note that biology is practiced according to positivist principles, but he would have to conclude that sociology and anthropology are not. In Comte's terms we will never escape intellectual anarchy. Fortunately, we have abandoned Comte's concept of anarchy, which assumes that all of the sciences must be rigorously positivist, an impossible and meaningless goal, as will become clear when we examine the limitations of positivism later in this chapter.

Against this larger reconstruction of human intellectual evolution, Comte spelled out his version of a hierarchy of sciences beginning with the oldest and most positivistic and culminating in the latest and least positivistic (reading from the bottom up):

- Sociology
- Physiology
- Chemistry
- Physics
- Astronomy
- Mathematics

Comte created the term *sociology,* defining it broadly to include all of the human sciences. In an 1852 revision of his work he placed anthropology above sociology in this hierarchy of sciences because he believed that it alone could organize the systematic study of moral laws. I personally like the idea of locating anthropology at the top (Urbanowicz, 1993). However, that designation of subject matter would scarcely define anthropology now, and candor compels me to note that sociology and anthropology are at the same level in terms of the Comtean hierarchy.

In all events, Comte taught that these approaches to human knowledge constitute the totality of the theoretical and abstract sciences. They were said to be fundamental or purely theoretical in the sense that their sole purpose was to identify laws of nature. The so-called concrete sciences, such as zoology, mineralogy, or geography, were described as derivative. They are applied sciences, Comte asserted, because they build upon laws of nature for practical and technical purposes. They use the laws of nature, but do not discover them.

THE POSITIVIST AGENDA

This Comtean view of the sciences was to have enormous consequences for anthropology because it established a status hierarchy within the sciences. One consequence was that higher status was accorded those who do abstract and theoretical research. For more than a century, anthropologists identified themselves as pure theoretical scientists, leaving applied anthropology to linger interminably in a purgatory of institutional prejudice and neglect.

That prejudice still exists. Academic recognition is still granted primarily to those who make contributions that advance either method or theory, if not both. Medical anthropology as a recognized field in the subspecialty of applied anthropology is quite young in part because of this prejudice against applied science as a field of expertise. Comte's long shadow still darkens part of anthropology in this sense. Yet, according to Thomas Johnson, probably most contemporary medical anthropologists work in applied rather than academic fields (Johnson, 1994).

It is an unwanted and counterproductive shadow. The distinction between theoretical and applied sciences is a construction based on an archaic philosophy of evolution and a mistaken notion about the relationship between method and theory. Only mathematics can be purely theoretical and abstract. It alone can be pursued independently of a subject matter. All of the other sciences must take account of empirical realities. Those realities are part of the real world, but it is impossible to describe any aspect of the real world in the absence of theory. In other words, the very choice of what to describe, how to characterize it, and what to ignore is a choice based on theory. Often such theory is unexamined and out of awareness, but it is inevitably present. Further, theory, and methods for exploring and developing theory, can originate in applied as well as in pure research. Referring specifically to anthropology, Rapoport saw this more than thirty years ago.

> More generally, the collaboration with medical personnel involves the further possibility of conducting "action research," through which experimentation with change goes hand in hand with *theoretical reformulation.* This new prospect, which is only now taking shape in numerous projects, provides promise for stimulating *theory-development* in the larger fields of interest in social process and social change. (Rapoport, 1962, p. 190, italics added)

At an extreme, Anthony Wilden asserts that pure knowledge as such has no value. All knowledge, without exception, is instrumental" (Wilden, 1972, p. xxii).

A second major consequence of the Comtean view was to distort the fundamental theoretical and methodological paradigm of the human sciences. The remarkable predictive capabilities of the older fields of mathematics, astronomy, physics, and chemistry convinced Comte that these physical sciences ought to serve as models for all of the sciences that emerged later in time. This is what positivism means. It is also what is meant when social science is described as reductionist.

Modernism

Comte's premodern theological or supernatural mode of thinking at one time did, indeed, more or less characterize humankind everywhere, particularly if one keeps in mind Comte's insistence that metaphysical and positivist thinking were present as well, it being a matter of emphasis. With the maturation of complex societies, supernaturalism began to yield to naturalism or empiricism as the preferred way to seek understanding in some realms of culture. In the Western tradition of medicine and science, this occurred for the first time in Ancient Greece around the fifth century BCE (Before the Common Era).

This approach to knowledge nearly died out in Europe during the Middle Ages, a sharp reminder that evolution is not the same as progress. Fortunately, Greek objectivism had spread to the Middle East, where it thrived and grew in the care of Arabic, Persian, Jewish, and other scholars, an equally important reminder that advances in knowledge have been contributed by all of the races and ethnicities of the world. At last, naturalism was borrowed back by Europeans as an intellectual movement known as the Renaissance, the "Rebirth" of classical knowledge.

Empiricism came increasingly to replace premodern and medieval supernaturalism as the dominant intellectual approach to coping with reality. Positivism gradually shaped up as the dominant paradigm for empiricism during the so-called Modern Period that began with the Enlightenment in the eighteenth century and extends to our time. Mathematics, astronomy, physics, chemistry, and physiology thrived. Anthropology, shaped by Comtean ideas, separated out from sociology on positivist philosophical grounds in the late nineteenth century.

High Modernity

At present, anthropology is struggling to redefine itself as a scientific discipline (Geertz,1984). Present-day anthropologists, like all living people, are necessarily so thoroughly caught up in their own time that it becomes difficult or impossible to be objective or dispassionate in self-assessment. Whether our time is better characterized as a phase of modernity, or whether it is one of postmodernity, is hard to say. It will take time to gain clarity on that issue.

Anthony Giddens, a sociologist, is among those who regard the turn of the twenty-first century as still oriented to modern concerns, but in a radicalized way that requires one to speak of high or late modernity (Giddens, 1991). The decline of religious convictions and the desacralization of social life have reached an extreme. Yet, the old certainties of religious conviction have not been replaced by comparable scientific certainties. Humanity turned out to be a far more complex subject for study than Enlightment philosophers ever imagined. Social scientists feel overwhelmed by their newfound awareness of greater extremes of diversity and volatility than had previously been suspected. These are radicalizing discoveries. Nonetheless, modernist anthropologists continue to assume that we live in a phenomenological world that can be described. They believe that regularities in culture and society can be identified. They adhere, to that extent, to a scientific agenda.

Some sociologists are convinced that the challenge of high modernity will be met by giving greater attention to the human body as the central object of study. They reason that a major, widespread human response to secularism and insecurity has been for people to relocate their sense of identity and purpose away from religion, community, and family, placing it instead in their own persons, their own bodies. Arthur Frank put it this way:

> Modernism, then, provides both an impetus to study the body, which is the need for some constant in a world of flux, and a problematic of that body: far from becoming a constant, it was subsumed into the flux. (Frank, 1991, p. 40)

The hand of Latu Lama, a Tibetan Buddhist priest, is seen here in the act of anointing Robert Desjarlais with a sacred piece of butter as part of a ritual blessing.

Given an unprecedented symbolic and existential focus on one's body by modern individuals, clearly, it is argued, sociologists ought to attach equal importance to research on bodies. Astonishingly, given the history of the social sciences, these sociologists for the first time are adopting an old anthropological point of view, which is that the body must be studied as a biological entity and not solely as a sociological object. "In the positivist attitude the body is knowable, and this knowledge provides some grounding" (Frank, 1991, p. 39). A person, some sociologists now acknowledge, is constituted by both a body and a mind, both of which should be subjects of sociological inquiry (Shilling, 1993; Featherstone et al., 1991).

Anthropologists for their part are also turning to the body as a central concern (Ness, 1992). Robert Desjarlais, for example, undertook the ethnography of a Yolmo Sherpa shaman in Nepal by employing a methodology of "embodied awareness." For many months, "as the shamanic apprentice to a veteran 'grandfather' healer," he took part in healing ceremonies that required him to sit, move, chant, emote, inhale incense, and experience trance. By repeatedly experiencing his own involvement with a unitary body and mind he learned, as he expressed it, to embody their cultural practices (Desjarlais, 1992; pp. 26–27).

This orientation has been couched in terms of breaking the grip of Cartesian dualism. Dualism was an Enlightenment approach to understanding individual behavior based on the assumption that the mind and the body are separate and distinct from one another and therefore can be investigated independently of one another. Late modernists challenge that old assumption. In the light of that challenge, it is imperative that one frame research and theory in terms of a unitary (monistic) mind/body entity. Nancy Scheper-Hughes and Margaret Lock propose a research agenda of the future for medical anthropology that is exactly of this sort. They characterize it as a need for a monistic approach to the mindful body (Scheper-Hughes & Lock, 1987). What will come of this proposal remains to be seen.

Postmodernism

The focus of postmodern criticism is epistemological; that is, it is based on a growing awareness that the anthropologist's understanding of another culture ("the other") must always be filtered through the observer's own mind as shaped by his or her own culture. Accomplished in this manner, how can one possibly know the true nature of the other (any other) cultural reality? The voice (or gaze) of any one anthropologist should not be privileged over that of another, or over those of nonanthropologist observers.

More broadly, some postmodernists argue that anthropology cannot be a science because the subject matter, the study of humanity, requires that anthropology become one of the humanities. Richard Schechner catches the flavor of this postmodernist critique writing, "But as Derrida and the second line of deconstructionists remind us, the boundaries between scientific thought, poetry, theatre, and literary criticism are fuzzy." He continues, "In our emergent neo-medieval world a species of religious-artistic thought is, if not replacing, then standing side-by-side with, what used to be called pure science" (Schechner, 1988, p. 10). In Comtean terms, to be postmodern is to acknowledge the failure of the positivist agenda. But is it a total failure?

ANTHROPOLOGY AS A POSITIVIST SCIENCE

The hierarchy of sciences familiar to us from positive philosophy had enormous implications for how anthropologists practiced their profession. Based on this hierarchy, the older and more basic physical sciences, particularly physics and chemistry, were thought to provide a model for the newer sciences. Anthropologists struggled for several generations to produce results comparable to those of the physical sciences. This tends to be true even today. Thomas Kuhn, a physicist and philosopher of science, discusses paradigms of science, and revolutions in these paradigms, as though physics is still the model for all of the sciences (Kuhn, 1970, p. 10). Because this kind of scientific goal has not been achieved, Kuhn speaks of the social sciences as still immature.

Stephen Kline speaks of the paradigm of the physical sciences as the capability to produce what he terms an "Entire Invariant Paradigm" (Kline, 1995). By this, Kline means that several centuries of empirical research have demonstrated that, given standardized external conditions, inert, naturally occurring objects, whether they are subatomic particles, atoms, or molecules, behave without known exception in completely predictable ways. This is true for any entire class of objects; it is "entire." It always occurs without fail; it is "invariant." Physics and chemistry produce entire invariant paradigms. Their achievements became the model for what it was thought the human sciences should produce. Anthropologists struggling to meet the goals of positive philosophy made innumerable efforts to identify a few variables that would permit them to make entire, invariant predictions for culture and society.

THE REDUCTIONIST ERROR

In discussing misdirected efforts to identify entire invariant paradigms in the human sciences, Kline sagely notes that attempting in a reductionist manner to apply the methods of the physical sciences to human systems for which they are inappropriate does not inevitably produce results that are wrong, but it does produce results that are seriously incomplete. Entire invariant paradigms, in other words, can be identified for some aspects of human behavior, but not for whole sociocultural entities or worldwide universal systems. One can produce entire paradigms, but they will not be invariant.

To demonstrate this conclusion, let us look more closely at a mental health issue, the notion that the way an infant is fondled, reprimanded, toilet-trained, fed, and so on establishes patterns of personality that persist as adult modes of behavior and, ultimately, as cultural practices. If that is true, one ought to be able to predict a person's behavior as an older child or adult based upon knowledge of how the infant was cared for. This, in fact, does not happen. Surveys "have all come to the conclusion that the available published data do not confirm the hypothesis that the pattern of child care practiced by the parent in the child's early life has a clear-cut, consistent effect on the personality of the older child or adult" (Chess et al., 1959, pp. 792–793).

Based upon their own longitudinal assessment of seventy-eight children followed for about two years plus seven additional children followed from eight to fourteen years, a team of researchers came to a startling conclusion, given the convictions of culture and personality theorists. "Our consistent finding has been that the response of the child to the parental approach in various areas and at different ages has been determined, not only by the attitude and behavior of the parent, but also by the child's own specific reaction pattern." In other words, in areas of behavior that were documented, basic temperament, that is, inborn characteristic modes of functioning that could be identified in the newborn baby, were more predictive of later personality than were parenting practices. "In all these areas [of explored behavior] there have been children who showed differing responses with parents whose approaches have been similar. There have also been children who showed similar responses with parents whose approaches have differed" (Chess et al., 1959, pp. 797-798).

The assumption that one could speak of a law "of the omnipotent role of the parent in the shaping of the child" did not hold up (Shweder, 1991, pp 284-286). Yet, a lesser kind of regularity can be identified in this longitudinal study. While the majority of the children in these series did well with diverse child care practices, a substantial minority could be predicted on the basis of congenital tendencies to encounter problems if parenting did not take into account specific circumstantial factors and parenting practices (Chess et al., 1959, p. 801).

This kind of finding falls completely short of the kind of entire invariant paradigm characteristic of physics. The power of prediction is so hedged with the need to account for social, cultural, and psychological variables that the resultant formulation has only limited explanatory power. Richard Shweder sums up the issue in no uncertain terms:

> In the last resort, a scientific theory's claim to forward our understanding of nature is dependent on its power to predict what will occur, which is based on generalizations of what regularly occurs. . . . That is, a good theory is both parsimonious (it explains a lot and does so with relatively few categories and principles) and valid (it has predictive utility). In the social sciences, however, the predictive success of culture and personality theory seems to be inversely related to its parsimony, and vice versa. Parsimony and validity cannot be simultaneously achieved. (Shweder, 1991, p. 310)

THE LIMITATIONS OF POSITIVISM

The positivist goal of ultimately devising models of human behavior in a way that would be comparable to a formula or theorem in mathematics can never be realized. Kline illustrates this by means of a complexity index of empirical systems (Kline, 1991; 1995). The complexity index (C) is defined in terms of three quantities that are required to characterize the nature of any observable system:

- Variables (V) needed to describe the state of the system;
- Parameters (P) or factors needed to distinguish the boundaries of one empirical system from another; and
- Feedback loops (L), needed to provide the different kinds of information that must be available to govern or control process or behavior within the system.

In other words, the complexity of a system is a function of the number of independent variables, independent parameters, and control feedback loops within the system and connecting the system to surroundings. The index of complexity can be quite succinctly stated as a mathematical formula:

$$C = V + P + L$$

In the hierarchy of sciences, parsimony and predictibility can be achieved only when the complexity of the system is very small, and thus only in the physical sciences in any complete way. Note how small the complexity index is for physics and chemistry, and then contrast that with the human sciences, a disparity of many orders of magnitude. We translate Kline's categories into those of Comte:

- Physics and chemistry: $C <$ (less than) 5
- Physiology (defined as a single human being): $C > 10^9$ (more than one billion)
- Sociology (defined as a human social system): $C > 10^{11}$ (more than one trillion)

The complexity index makes it clear that the problem is not that the human sciences are immature, as Kuhn says. Rather, it is that the human sciences concern themselves with extraordinarily complex systems that by no stretch of the imagination (or human ingenuity) will ever be describable in terms of simple formulae, such as Einstein's famous law of relativity.

$$E = MC^2$$

According to this formula, since the velocity of light (C) is a known constant, mass (M) is the only unknown that must be measured in order to determine the quantity of energy (E) to which mass will convert or, conversely, one only needs to know the amount of energy to determine the mass. The problem is not that the human sciences have not had Einsteins. It is that entire invariant paradigms cannot be devised for enormously complex entities. The task is impossible, unless you return to a reliance upon theology and metaphysics.

POSTPOSITIVISM AND THE CONCEPT OF DUAL-LEVEL CONTROL

Positivism was distortive for anthropological theory. It set as the research goal the identification of entire invariant paradigms for predicting human behavior. These were to be modeled on the theorems and formulae of mathematics, physics, and chemistry. This is the reductionist hypothesis. Michael Polanyi provides guidelines for moving beyond these simplistic assumptions without abandoning the larger goal of the positivist agenda, which is to identify regularities and make predictions (Polanyi, 1968; Kline, 1995).

The key to breaking out of the reductionist trap is to realize that at any level in the hierarchy of phenomenological systems two levels of structure will be involved. Let us take Polanyi's example of a machine, a structure or system that operates on two levels. On the lower level this system must obey the laws of inanimate nature if it is not to grind to a halt or self-destruct. Steel and internal combustion must be engineered in terms of physical and chemical principles. However, the engineer who designed the machine, the mechanic who constructed it, and the operator who put it to use constitute a higher level of the system that cannot be explained so simply. They have freedom to invent, experiment, and apply. They design and use the machine in terms of human values. Social, political, and economic factors shape their activity. A machine as a whole, or a body, or a society, at any one level is a process under the control of two distinct principles. It is a two-leveled structure. Let us pursue that observation a bit further.

A human being cannot be defined in terms of the physical or physiological processes which it harnesses. At each level in the hierarchy from atoms and molecules through organs and tissues to bodies and societies, boundaries separate structures/systems. At each of these boundaries, the paradigm is one of a two-leveled structure, a two-leveled system that functions under dual-control. Such a structure/system harnesses substances that compose the organism. It does so "in the service of physiological functions." Yet, these physiological functions can be understood (explained) only in biological terms that involve a higher level of complexity (variables, parameters, and feedback loops). Polanyi puts it this way, "the existence of dual control in machines and living mechanisms represents a discontinuity between machines and living things on the one hand and inanimate nature on the other hand, so that both machines and living mechanisms are irreducible to the laws of physics and chemistry" (Polanyi, 1968, p. 1310).

The bottom line is this, a lower level sets constraints on the next higher level, but it does not determine the nature of that higher level. A body/mind functions under the constraints of physical laws, but those laws are wholly (holistically) inadequate for determining the nature of body/mind systems and the activities that a person pursues. In this sense boundary conditions (the separation of hierarchies of structures/systems) require that we move beyond reductionist paradigms and learn to speak of constraints and freedoms rather than of determinants. "The theory of boundary conditions recognizes the higher levels of life as forming a hierarchy, each level of which relies for its workings on the principles of the levels below it, even while it itself is irreducible to these lower principles" (Polanyi, 1968, p. 1310). This is what is meant by dual-level control. It provides a basis for preserving what is useful in positivism without perpetuating the distortions of reductionism. It sets a postpositivist agenda.

THE HIERARCHY OF DISCIPLINES IN MEDICINE

Rudolf Virchow, the founder of modern pathology, was the founder as well of hierarchical thinking in biomedicine (Ackerknecht, 1953). Until his time, it was thought that disease involved derangements of organs and tissues. He established the importance of identifying pathology on the more basic level of the cells of which these tissues and organs are composed. Not for many decades subsequently did it begin to become possible to identify the loci of disease within cells at still deeper molecular levels. Meanwhile, physicians continued to undertake diagnostic reasoning based on physical signs and symptoms on the level of clinical anatomy and physiology. In short, for more than a century it was customary to think clinically in terms of a hierarchy that extended from the body and its various organs down to the level of physicochemical processes.

Although physicians thought in terms of a hierarchy, it was done without giving attention to hierarchy as a model or paradigm. Doctors just worked up and down in their thinking as a practical matter. Perhaps because they did not give much thought to theory of a more abstract nature, they tended to neglect consideration of social, cultural, political, and economic factors when searching for the cause and nature of a disease. Not until relatively recently did they begin to give conscious, systematic attention to these higher levels of causation. A corrective turn was triggered by George Engel's call for a new biopsychosocial model. Although Engel may be accused of overstating the case for the reductionist nature of the biomedical model, he did accurately describe the way many—indeed most—doctors probably worked in their offices and clinics. He characterizied biomedicine as trapped in a philosophy of reductionism and mind/body dualism:

> The dominant model of disease today is biomedical, with molecular biology its basic scientific discipline. It assumes disease to be fully accounted for by deviations from the norm of measurable biological (somatic) variables. It leaves no room within its framework for the social, psychological, and behavioral dimensions of illness. (Engel, 1977, p. 130)

VERTICAL REASONING

In his time (1977) Engel was a leader in the effort to make biomedicine more responsive to nonbiological factors in disease causation. A decade later, Marsden Blois further developed this approach, characterizing it as a model for vertical reasoning. His hierarchy necessarily resembles those that have been around for a long time. He lists them to make an important point—again, not original, but innovative in biomedical thinking. He characterized each level by the nature of the paradigms that could be expected (Blois, 1988).

PHYSICS

At the bottom of the hierarchy is the atom and its component parts and energies. Atoms can be described with brevity and accuracy in mathematical terms by physicists. Statements about atoms can be verified in laboratory experiments that replicate findings with a level of predictability that borders on certainty.

CHEMISTRY

When atoms combine to form molecules, the products possess properties not found in the constituent atoms as such, and not predictable from them. A different language of description, still mathematical, is needed—that of chemists.

BIOCHEMISTRY

Still higher in the hierarchy, small molecules unite into larger polymers and macromolecules, including membranes and other living tissues. Again, the objects and processes have properties not found on lower levels, not predictable from lower levels, and not discussable solely in the languages of lower levels. We have arrived at the level of biochemists.

PHYSIOLOGY

In terms of human bodies, when we arrive at the complexities of organs and physiologic systems such as the nervous system or the gastrointestinal system, we need the language of physiologists. Now it must be noted that with each step up on this hierarchy complexity increases while predictability concomitantly decreases. Mathematical equations worked very well to talk about parts and functions on the lower levels, but in the middle level we encounter a scattered range of possibilities. With complexity comes uniqueness. No two cells of the body are identical, nor are any two tissues, organs, or organ systems. Mathematics and the language of certainties decline in usefulness to be replaced by statistics and the language of probabilities.

PSYCHOLOGY AND SOCIOLOGY

This trend continues as we get to the level of individual behavior, where psychologists, sociologists, and medical anthropologists, among many others, search for regularities in the form of trends and probabilities. Mathematics is rarely involved; statistics reigns.

POLITICAL SCIENCE AND ECONOMICS

Still higher up on the scale of complexity, families, communities, and nations require social scientists such as political scientists and economists who augment statistical methods with complex cybernetic systems analyses.

AESTHETICS AND LITERATURE

At the top of the scale of human studies, civilizations and cultures yield best to specialists in aesthetics, literature, and the humanities in general. In these fields the quantitative methods of science are minimized in favor of the interpretive or intuitive methods of humanist inquiry. In place of mathematics and statistics, which have limited application, we encounter, as Blois puts it, understanding by means of empathy. Empathy is the capacity every individual has to put the self in the place of another as a way of grasping what it feels like, what it means, to experience what another experiences.

Vertical thinking, then, is an ability—as much a kind of wisdom as a professional skill—to find answers to questions by integrating input from all levels of knowledge, covering an incredible range that begins at the level of the atom and ends up embracing the planet. It is the ability to integrate physics and chemistry with anatomy and physiology, with psychology and sociology, with political science and economics, and even with aesthetics and literature. It is a capacity for bringing basic and natural sciences to bear on a problem as well as the social sciences and the humanities.

Vertical reasoning is based on an acknowledgement that human behavior is the most complex phenomenon in the universe. Paul Adelson had this extreme complexity in mind when he wrote, "I have yet to see a problem however complicated that when you look at it the right way does not become more complicated" (Adelson, 1992, pp. 1503). Kline said something similar by means of his complexity index as we saw above.

AN EXAMPLE OF VERTICAL REASONING IN MEDICINE

Vertical reasoning is best understood by looking at an example of how it can work. The following is taken directly from the field of biomedicine.

Colon Cancer

John Potter, a physician scientist, engaged in vertical thinking (without describing it as such) in a review of the causes of colon cancer. This he did by raising a question that is seldom asked: "What gets cancer—the genes, the cell, the organ, the organism, or perhaps even the population?" (Potter, 1992).

> The potential answers are not necessarily exclusive, even given reductionist tendencies and the genuine and justified excitement over discoveries in the molecular biology of cancer. Rather, these are levels of explanation that may be more or less coherent within themselves but provide even more information when they exist in a framework provided by all of the explanatory modes. For the purpose of exemplifying this framework, consider that theories of the etiology of colon cancer have been presented at a number of levels—epidemiologic, physiological, and cellular/molecular. It is proposed herein that it is worthwhile considering both the coherence and interdependence of these levels of explanation, not as a sterile exercise, but because of its heuristic value and its capacity to shape a research program. (Potter, 1992, p. 1573).

EPIDEMIOLOGIC MODEL

The fat-and-fiber or meat-and-vegetables hypotheses (take your pick) suggests that in some way a diet rich in meat, fat, protein, and total energy (all of which are highly correlated) plays a role in the cause of colon cancer. For example, in a study of Hawaiian Japanese, those who ate beef twelve times or more per month were two-and-a-half times more at risk compared with those who consumed beef fewer than eight times per month.

The possibility that low levels of dietary fiber might contribute to colon cancer came from the observation that colon cancer was uncommon among Africans who typically consumed unrefined foods. Subsequent research suggested that lower risk is associated with the consumption of vegetables even more than with fiber, cereals, or fruit. The fat-and-fiber hypothesis is therefore now referred to sometimes as the meat-and-vegetables hypothesis.

PHYSIOLOGICAL/BIOCHEMICAL MODELS

The bile acid/volatile fatty acid and cooked food hypotheses suggests that fat in the diet results in a longer and more intense exposure of the bowel lining to the toxic effects of bile acids. This exposure may contribute to the growth of cancerous cells. Incidentally, food fiber binds bile acids, increases stool bulk, speeds transit time, and results in fermentation to volatile fatty acids. Volatile fatty acids appear to be anticarcinogenic.

The fat-and-fiber and bile acid/volatile fatty acids hypotheses appear to constitute two levels of a complex causal argument, one on the epidemiologic level and the other the physiological level. However, according to the cooked food hypothesis, the association of cancer with fat may be spurious. The true cause may be the difference between cooking over high heat as opposed to lower heat. The argument is that higher temperatures are needed when cooking in fat rather than in water. Higher cooking temperatures produce carcinogenic substances. This line of reasoning leads one to conclude that the meat-and-vegetable hypothesis should actually be a high temperature/low temperature hypothesis.

Vegetables introduce an additional effect at the physiological and biochemical level. They contain many substances with potent anticarcinogenic properties. In addition, vegetables rich in calcium lower colon cancer risk because calcium binds both bile acids and harmful kinds of fatty acids. It is also possible that calcium directly inhibits cancer cell proliferation.

Potter is at pains to point out that these interpretations are not incompatible. They support a complex interpretation of cancer as a product of multiple factors that build up over time ("a multiplex/incremental view of the etiology") (Potter, 1992, p. 1574).

THE MILIEU OF COLONIC CELLS

Growth media and biological cascades theory suggests that fat, meat, bile acids, high cooking temperatures (as well as sex hormones, alcohol consumption, and exercise habits, which we have not discussed) appear to cause cancer by means of different and overlapping biochemical pathways at the level of the cells that line the gut. The final common pathway results in a moment-to-moment chemical environment that may be harmful. If and when harmful, this chemical bath can be thought of as forming growth media for cancer cells.

CELL/CRYPT MODEL

The key cell in colonic cancer is the so-called crypt epithelial cell of the colonic mucosa. It is the crypt cell that changes from being a normal part of the cell lining to a benign polyp, which in turn can transform into a cancerous cell. This polyp-to-cancer transformation justifies the practice of periodic examinations of the gut (colonoscopy) and simple surgical excision of polyps that may be encountered.

A number of genetic factors may constitute part of the ultimate cause of the changes that transform normal crypt cells into cancerous growths. In other words, cellular transformations take place under genetic control. Genetic changes on the molecular level appear to be influenced by certain foods, some of which were identified above as carcinogens. In short, research suggests that diet has effects at the molecular level within individual cells (an intracellular cascade), including specific genetic alternations.

Potter concludes by advocating what Blois refers to as vertical thinking:

> We are at a very exciting time in the understanding of the etiology of colon cancer. Although the mechanisms of colon carcinogenesis are not yet understood, the suggestion of coherence among the epidemiology, the physiology, and the molecular biology is both encouraging and challenging. Perhaps more

important, seeking integration across models of etiology provides some ideas that may be generalized to other diseases. ... Finally, on a philosophic note, it is worth bearing in mind that this does not have to be viewed as a reductionist ideology; it is rather that there are different levels of explanation that cast light, each upon the others. (Potter, 1992, p. 1576)

It is notable in this biomedical overview of what we know about one particularly serious malignancy that vertical thinking is employed, but is confined to lower levels in the hierarchy. As Kline would put it, this overview is not wrong. In fact, it is highly sophisticated and very valuable. However, it is incomplete. A medical anthropologist would want to conduct research on higher levels in order to complement and complete this effort to take a holistic view of a bad disease.

As if to prove my point, this is exactly what Thomas Csordas and John Garrity did in their assessment of a Navajo Indian being treated for colon cancer. They found that the Indian benefited psychosocially by supplementing orthodox medical treatment with traditional Navajo forms of religious healing including songs conducted by tribal medicine men and peyote prayer meetings held in the Native American Church (Csordas & Garrity, 1994).

HIERARCHIES OF DISCIPLINES IN ANTHROPOLOGY

Perhaps it is time for anthropologists to give serious attention once again to a paradigm of hierarchy. Following Comte, the concept of a hierarchy of sciences failed to have much influence on anthropology other than as an occasional, transient proposition by theoreticians such as Bronislaw Malinowski and, most recently, Roy D'Andrade and James Dow (Stocking, 1986, p. 31; D'Andrade, 1986; Dow, 1986).

AN EXAMPLE OF VERTICAL REASONING IN ANTHROPOLOGY

One of the most recent of such efforts was undertaken by Dennis Cordell, Joel Gregory, and Victor Piché. They document and analyze causes of death in two African nations: the Central African Republic and Burkina Faso. In an effort to identify reasons for the extremely high death rate in these nations, they constructed a framework for analysis that incorporates four levels of causality conceptualized as a vertical hierarchy. This hierarchy was elaborated as a way to undertake an evaluation of mortality that would allow investigators to cope with complex multicausality in a holistic way (Cordell et al., 1992).

Level I: Demographic Regime

In order to make sense of the high mortality rate, the authors begin on the assumption that demographic issues must be evaluated first, since death in a community or population cannot be understood holistically without evaluating fertility and migration as well. This is based on sound epidemiologic reasoning packed into the following formula:

Births – Deaths +/- net migration = population change

The mutual effects of births, deaths, and migration, whether for population renewal (stability), for gain in total size, or for loss, is what is meant by the concept of demographic regime. In contemporary Burkina Faso they found that levels of mortality were pathetically high.

Level II: Direct Causes of Death

They were able to identify a relatively small number of direct or proximate causes of death:

- parasitic diseases
- other infectious diseases, including viruses
- degenerative diseases
- congenital disorders
- suicide
- violence and accidents

Of these, infectious diseases accounted for the largest number of deaths, exacerbated by the effects of widespread malnutrition along with age and gender discrimination.

Level III: Health Environment

In an effort to identify social, technical, political, and economic conditions that impact locally on Level II they identified the following:

- water, both quantity and quality
- sanitation, especially waste disposal
- nutrition, both quantity and quality of food
- preventive health care practices
- illness treatment, personnel, and services
- stress

Level IV: Political Economy

Here they acknowledged ways in which local and individual health is responsive to conditions in the nation as a whole. The emphasis is on state policies and the effects of socioeconomic class discrimination as they impact on individual access to a healthy environment (although the importance of international political and economic forces is acknowledged, they are left out of the analysis).

- state policies
- social class

It is notable that, as in the case of the analysis of colon cancer, the analysis moves across levels in complex ways to identify multicausal chains, flowchart effects, and feedback loops. The hierarchy does not frame the analysis in a reductionist paradigm. It is multidisciplinary in orientation, but not in a way that is meant to suggest that one level is more important than another.

It will come as no surprise to observe that whereas the medical paradigm relating to colon cancer left out higher levels in the hierarchy of systems, this anthropological/historical paradigm left out lower levels. As concerns infectious diseases, for example, physicians expectably reach deeper into the basic medical sciences to identify vaccines, induced immunity, and drug-resistant strains of bacteria (Stoeckle & Douglas, 1994). Again, it is not wrong to limit investigations to one end or the other of the hierarchy of sciences, but it is incomplete.

An example of vertical reasoning in medicine compared with an example of similar reasoning in medical anthropology demonstrates that medicine and anthropology tend to approach shared problems with compatible but different styles of analysis and research focus. This circumstance suggests that increased multidisciplinary collaboration should hold great promise for both disciplines and, most importantly, for contributing more effectively to improvement in the health of people everywhere.

CONCLUSION

The potentiality for medical anthropology that is inherent in continuing to practice interdisciplinarity and multidisciplinarity is demonstrated in research findings already published. In the two examples of multidisciplinarity described above, one for medicine and the other for anthropology, the need of the one discipline for the other is well illustrated. On the one hand, the medical paradigm applied to colon cancer left out higher levels in the hierarchy of systems (family, community, polity, economy). This is typical of much medical research. On the other hand, the anthropological paradigm applied to death in Central Africa left out lower levels of the hierarchy (molecular, neurologic, immunologic, pathologic). This is typical of much medical anthropological research. The medical approach is not wrong. Neither is that of medical anthropology. However, each in its own way is limited or incomplete.

Physicians tend to look for causes and connections at lower levels, ranging across physics, biochemistry, anatomy, and physiology. Anthropologists are inclined to explore higher levels extending from psychology, sociology, and political economy to the humanities. Both kinds of professionals need to do some intellectual stretching in order to become more proficient at comprehensive vertical reasoning. But, whether a physician struggling to arrive at a diagnosis and treatment plan or a medical anthropologist attempting to make sense out of medical beliefs and practices, to reason vertically is to distinguish oneself from other professional scholars and scientists concerned with health and disease. Physicians and medical anthropologists on the cutting edge of science have that in common.

Interdisciplinary and multidisciplinary reasoning—working in holistic terms —brings to awareness an important realization. One cannot be an expert on every relevant subject. As concerns any single health issue, no one specialist has all of the answers. Fortunately, a holistic approach does not require universal knowledge. Rather, it requires that one act on the acknowledgement that contributions can be made by many different kinds of people: other kinds of anthropologists, clinicians, scientists, scholars, social workers, teachers, sick people... (the list is endless). Many voices need to be heard if goals are to be defined and attained.

Interdisciplinarity as a habit of thought combined with multidisciplinarity as a capacity to work with others and to orchestrate collaboration (or at the least to draw upon research in other disciplines) may in the final analysis constitute the decisive skills necessary for the successful practice of medical anthropology. This will be especially so if research is to be oriented to the mindful body (the body/mind entity) in a comprehensive way.

REFERENCES

Ackerknecht, E. (1953). *Rudolf Virchow.* Madison: University of Wisconsin Press.

Adams, W. Y. (1993). Four-field anthropology: The historical background. *American Anthropologist, 34* (1), 3.

Adelson, P. (1992). Cited in Hotchkiss, R. S., & Karl, I. E., Reevaluation of the role of cellular hypoxia and bioenergetic failure in sepsis. *Journal of the American Medical Association, 267,* 1503–1510.

Blois, M. S. (1988). Medicine and the nature of vertical reasoning. *The New England Journal of Medicine, 318,* 847–851.

Cassell, J. (1991). *Expected miracles: Surgeons at work.* Philadelphia: Temple University Press.

Caudill, W. (1953). Applied anthropology in medicine. In Kroeber, A. L. (Ed.), *Anthropology Today* (pp. 771–806). Chicago: University of Chicago Press.

Chess, S., Thomas, A., & Birch, H. (1959). Characteristics of the individual child's behavioral responses to the environment. *American Journal of Orthopsychiatry, XXIX,* 791–802.

Cordell, D. D., Gregory, J. W., & Piché, V. (1992). The demographic reproduction of health and disease: Colonial Central African Republic and contemporary Burkina Faso. In Feierman, S., & Janzen, J. M. (Eds.), *The social basis of health and healing in Africa* (pp. 39–70). Berkeley: University of California Press.

Csordas, T. J., & Garrity, J. F. (1994). Co-utilization of biomedicine and religious healing: A Navajo case study. *Yearbook of Cross-Cultural Medicine and Psychotherapy—1992*, 241-252.

D'Andrade, R. (1986). Three scientific world views and the covering law model (pp. 24-34). In Fiske, D. W., & Shweder, R. A. (Eds.), *Metatheory in social science: Puralisms and subjectivities.* Chicago: Univerity of Chicago Press:

Desjarlais, R. T. (1992). *The body and emotion: The aesthetics of illness and healing in the Nepal Himalayas.* Philadelphia: University of Pennsylvania Press.

Dow, J. (1986). Universal aspects of symbolic healing: A theoretical synthesis. *American Anthropologist, 88,* 56-69.

Engel, G. L. (1977). The need for a new medical model: A challenge for biomedicine. *Science, 196,* 129-136.

Featherstone, M., Hepworth, M., & Turner, B. (Eds.). (1991). *The body: Social process and cultural theory.* Newbury Park, CA: Sage Publications.

Frank, A. W. (1991). For a sociology of the body: An analytical review. In Featherstone, M., Hepworth, M., & Turner, B. (Eds.), *The body: Social process and cultural theory.* Newbury Park, CA: Sage Publications.

Geertz, C. (1984). Distinguished lecture: Anti anti-relativism. *American Anthropologist, 86,* 263-278.

Giddens, A. (1991). *Modernity and self-identity.* Cambridge: Polity Press.

Gordon, J. S. (1994). Holistic medicine and mental health practice: Toward a new synthesis. *Yearbook of Cross-Cultural Medicine and Psychotherapy—1992*, 59-74.

Johnson, T. M. (1994). On paradigm shifts in medical anthropology. *Anthropology Newsletter, 35* (5), 31-32.

Jordan, B., & Davis-Floyd, R. (1993). *Birth in four cultures: A crosscultural investigation of childbirth in Yucatan, Holland, Sweden, and the United States* (4th ed.). Prospect Heights, IL: Waveland Press.

Klein, J. T. (1990). *Interdisciplinarity: History, theory, and practice.* Detroit: Wayne State University Press.

Kline, S. J. (1991). A numerical index for the complexity of systems: The concept and some implications. *Proceedings of the 1990 Association for Computing Machinery Symposium: Managing complexity and modeling reality.* D. J. Frailey (Ed.) New York: Association for Computing Machinery Press.

Kline, S. J. (1995). *Conceptual foundations for multidisciplinary thinking.* Stanford, CA: Stanford University Press.

Kuhn, T. S. (1970). *The structure of scientific revolutions* (2nd ed.). Chicago: University of Chicago Press.

Lane, S. D., (1993). Sociocultural aspects of blindness in an Egyptian delta hamlet: Visual impairment vs. visual disability. *Medical Anthropology, 15,* 245-260.

Lévy-Bruhl, L. (1903). *The philosophy of August Comte* (Frederic Harrison, Trans.) New York: G. P. Putnam's Sons. (Original work published in French 1900).

Lewes, G. H. (1887). *Comte's philosophy of the sciences: Being an exposition of the principles of the cours de philosophie positive of Auguste Comte.* London: George Bell and Sons.

Marcus, J. (1992). *A world of difference: Islam and gender hierarchy in Turkey.* Women in Asia Publication Series. New Brunswick, NJ: Zed Books.

Miracle, A. W. (1993). Holism and the future of anthropology. *American Anthropologist, 34* (1), 3.

Ness, S. A. (1992). *Body, movement, and culture: Kinesthetic and visual symbolism in a Philippine community.* Philadelphia: University of Pennsylvania Press.

Parker, S. (1993). Why the four-field approach is central to our identity. *American Anthropologist, 34* (1), 3.

Polanyi, M. (1968). Life's irreducible structure. *Science, 160,* 1308-1312.

Polgar, S. (1962). Health and human behavior: Areas of interest common to the social and medical sciences. *Current Anthropology, 3,* 159-205.

Potter, J. D. (1992). Reconciling the epidemiology, physiology, and molecular biology of colon cancer. *Journal of the American Medical Association, 268,* 1573-1577.

Rapoport, R. N. (1962). Comments. *Current Anthropology, 3,* 190-191.

Schechner, R. (1988). Preface, Victor Turner, *The anthropology of performance.* New York: PAJ Publications.

Scheper-Hughes, N., & Lock, M. M. (1987). The mindful body: A prolegomena to future work in medical anthropology. *Medical Anthropological Quarterly, 1,* 6-41.

Shilling, C. (1993). *The body and social theory.* Newbury Park, CA: Sage Publications.

Shweder, R. A. (1991). *Thinking through cultures: Expeditions in cultural psychology.* Cambridge, MA: Harvard University Press.

Singer, M. (1994). Ethical challenges in street ethnography. *Anthropology Newsletter, 35* (4), 29-30.

Spindler, G. (1994). Letter of September 9 addressed to Robert Anderson.

Stocking, G. W., Jr. (1986). Anthropology and the science of the irrational: Malinowski's encounter with Freudian psychoanalysis. In G. W. Stocking, Jr. (Ed.), Malinowski, Rivers, Benedict and others: Essays on culture and personality. *History of Anthropology,* Vol. 4 (pp. 13-49). Madison: University of Wisconsin Press:

Stoeckle, M. Y., and Douglas, R. G. (1994). Infectious diseases. *Journal of the American Medical Association, 271,* 1677-1679.

Urbanowicz, C. F. (1993). Four-field commentary. *Anthropology Newsletter, 33* (9), 3.

Wilden, A. (1972). *System and structure: Essays in communication and exchange.* London: Tavistock.

Chapter 3

THE TIME DIMENSION

INTRODUCTION

Between 1860 and 1890, when anthropology emerged from its varied and scattered origins to become a definable field of expertise, practitioners of the new four-field discipline took as their task the need to describe and explain the immense and bewildering diversity of human cultures. That is still our task. However, because science is itself shaped by the cultures of scientists, what satisfied nineteenth-century European and American anthropologists as explanations of cultural diversity was strikingly culture-bound. It was thought that knowledge and understanding would reward the scientist who learned how human beliefs and practices originated and evolved, particularly if one could couch one's findings as regularities or laws of prehistoric evolution. Early cultural evolutionists concluded, not without reason, that modern complex civilizations arose during the course of many millennia from simple small-scale origins, and it became the job of anthropologists to reconstruct that enormous developmental trajectory (de Waal Malefijt, 1974; Harris, 1968).

Much of what anthropologists thought they knew in the nineteenth century had to be abandoned. Nonetheless, valuable understandings survived that theoretical debacle. It has been noted that "each of the earlier historical moments is still operating in the present, either as legacy or as a set of practices that researchers still follow or argue against"(Denzin & Lincoln, 1994, p. 11). Roy Rappaport provides a perspective on such survivals:

> I have been struck by the wastefulness of our discipline. We are ever moving on to new approaches without having assimilated the lessons of older ones. We are, I think, inclined to claim too much for new "paradigms," to expect too much of them, and then, perhaps as a consequence of our disappointment, or, possibly, in antagonistic reaction to the excessive nature of the early claims of enthusiasts, to discard them before their possibilities have been adequately explored. We are inclined to dismiss rather than modify or correct for reasons that seem to me insufficient or even wrong (Rappaport, 1984, pp. xv–xvi).

I propose to take Rappaport's statement seriously as a guideline for identifying what is valuable in medical anthropology without falling victim to outmoded ways of thinking. "It must be noted," Yvonna Lincoln and Norman Denzin warn, "that revisiting works from earlier historical moments operates at different levels of abstraction. Although colonialist, positivist ethnography may be passé, the basic strategies and techniques of case studies, ethnographies, observation, interviewing, and textual analysis still form the basis for research [at the present time]" (Lincoln & Denzin, 1994, p. 577). Early anthropological theorizing oriented to the dimension of time, and later to the dimension of space, claimed too much for their time and space models of cultural process, but when the excesses of early claims are discounted, what remains can still be put to use. Many concepts now available for contemporary purposes have roots in theories that were dismissed because too much was expected of them.

Animism and Healing

From the point of view of medical anthropology in our time, the most relevant of these early evolutionary speculations concerned religion, since it is a widespread practice for people to cope with health problems and other life-and-death issues in terms of religious beliefs and practices (Jones, 1984). Early ethnologists spilled a lot of ink speculating about primeval religions. Edward Burnett Tylor proposed animism as the primordial world religion (Tylor, 1958 [1871]). Monotheism, he observed, was unknown in most of the world. He reasoned that even where monotheism reigns, vestiges of an earlier religion might still survive. He concluded that the original religion would be that which is left among known peoples when less widespread customs are subtracted. In short, he looked for the lowest common denominator of all world religious customs. This he identified as beliefs in souls and other spiritual beings, along with beliefs that objects such as rocks and trees or phenomena such as thunder and lightning possess spiritual aliveness. He coined the term animism to mark this hypothetical ancient substratum of religious thought.

His desire to explain the origin of animism led Tylor to argue that in every society people experience the inexplicable in ways that suggest the existence of spiritual beings. They might wonder about a person who lies transformed as a corpse. What happened to the life essence? In altered states of awareness, too, thoughts about souls might emerge. After a dream, when one seems to have left one's own sleeping body, would one not evolve the idea that an incorporeal soul is involved? It followed from this line of thinking that sickness or death could result from a kidnapped or lost soul failing to get back to the body.

Extracted from assumptions about how animism was originally invented through conscious intellectual speculation, which is unlikely, and the assumption that it was the original form of all religious thought, which is unknowable, animism is still a useful way to designate supernaturalism conceived as a world inhabited by souls, spirits, and powers relevant to sickness and health. Although societies differ greatly in the specifics of such beliefs, the generic concept of animism still has a place in the anthropological vocabulary. For example, the religions of the Hmong and other new Americans who have immigrated from the mountains of Southeast Asia are usually described as animistic.

Another early contributor to the anthropology of religion was Sir James Frazer, whose book, *The Golden Bough,* went through several revisions after it was first published in 1890 (Frazer, 1951 [1922]). Eventually expanded to twelve volumes and a supplement, *The Golden Bough* exercised a pervasive and enduring influence on anthropological thinking. Some of Frazer's ideas still survive more or less hidden away in current thinking.

As Frazer saw it, despite the fact that we cannot know these things, the original human beings lived in an Age of Magic, when they defended themselves against an often hostile world by practicing magic. At a hypothetically more advanced Age of Religion, beliefs about the direct intervention of malevolent and benevolent gods supposedly shaped problem-solving behavior. Only late in human evolution, he speculated, did people progress to the Age of Science, when a belief in natural causes came into being, particularly in the West. This grand scheme of evolutionary stages, clearly derived from that of August Comte a half century earlier, is now abandoned, but not the concepts Frazer developed as tools to fabricate this theory. It is still useful to explore relationships among magic, religion, science, and sickness.

Magic, Sickness, and Healing

Drawing upon whatever scattered literary sources he could find in those decades when very few careful ethnographic studies had been published, Frazer described magic as a way in which people anywhere may attempt to cope with illness or misfortune. In the practice of magic, people believe that events in nature follow one another in an orderly and uniform manner. Human ritualists may manipulate these forces, but no godlike agency intervenes. In other words, the magician exercises a form of actual control over events. If ritual and chanting are correctly done, the desired effect must occur, just as a light will turn on if you correctly flip the right switch. When the effect does not take place, it must be because the magician made some mistake in performance or, perhaps, some other magician controlled even more powerful techniques.

When magical thinking is involved, disease is often thought to be caused by sorcery or witchcraft and cured by ritual countermeasures. Frazer described what he called sympathetic magic, which took two forms, imitative and contact. Imitative or homeopathic magic is based on what he called the law of similarity, which says that like produces like. It assumes that things that resemble each other can also influence each other.

As an illustration of how someone could get sick through imitative magic, an Ojibway Indian, we learn in *The Golden Bough,* could cause intense pain in a distant enemy if he made a small wooden statue of the victim and ran a needle into it or shot it with an arrow. If the head was pierced, it would cause headache;

if the heart, a heart attack. To kill the victim, burning or burying the image while reciting an incantation would do so.

In a similar example from Malaysia, Frazer reported that a likeness of the intended victim was molded from beeswax to cause harm. If you wanted to kill the victim, you should scorch the figure over a flame every night for seven nights while reciting, "It is not wax that I am scorching, it is the liver, heart, and spleen of So-and-so that I scorch" (Frazer, 1951, p. 15). After the seventh night, burn the image and your enemy will die. Alternatively, pierce the eye of the wax figure to cause blindness, or the head to cause headache, or some other part of the body you wish to afflict.

Frazer also provided a few illustrations of how healing might take place by using this form of magic. In the Solomon and Banks Islands of Oceania an individual reportedly could attempt to get rid of fatigue by throwing a stick, stone, or leaf on a heap that had built up over the years at a place where the path was steep and difficult. Casting away the object and saying, "There goes my fatigue," was a magical rite based on an imagery of throwing away that was thought to invoke a mystical connection between the small objects and human tiredness.

Again, Frazer recounted that a Moroccan with a headache might try to get rid of it by beating a lamb or goat, believing that the headache could be transferred from one's own aching cranium to that of the poor beast by the imitative action of battering a body.

The other major branch of sympathetic magic was contagious magic, which was based on the so-called law of contact. A mystical connection was thought to remain in force between an individual and things that had once been part of, or attached to, the body. Nail parings, bits of hair, impressions left from sitting in the sand, items of clothing, or even feces and bloody bandages could be used to cause disease if a sorcerer performed appropriate rituals over such objects. As far as health was concerned, in applying this form of magic, *The Golden Bough* for the most part described techniques of prevention but not of curing.

Frazer gave an example from Australia in which boys had their front teeth knocked out as part of the rite of passage to manhood. To prevent disease, the teeth had to be kept out of harm's way. One tribe believed that if ants ran over a tooth extracted in this manner, disease of the mouth would occur. It was reported of another tribe that the elders were sure that a boy had become sick because his extracted tooth had been injured. The elders particularly feared that the teeth of initiated boys might come into contact with quartz crystals, which they believed could cause sickness.

It is widely thought that a sympathetic union between a newborn and its placenta magically unites the two forever. Given this belief, it follows that proper preservation or disposal of the placenta should guarantee good fortune, while injury or loss should result in suffering. Frazer illustrated this kind of reasoning with an example from Berlin, where it used to be the custom for a

Loudell Snow convened a seminar at Michigan State University with Berline Williams, an expert on traditional African American medicine.

midwife to give the dried umbilical cord to the father, who was supposed to preserve it with great care in the belief that the child would live long and stay healthy as long as the "navel-string" was in good condition.

Contagious magic is often used in cures as well as prevention, even though Frazer gives no examples. This kind of magic was practiced by the African shaman in Zimbabwe, for example, when he conducted the exorcism of Mary, the adolescent with a limp. He touched a coin to her aching hip, then placed it in an empty eggshell, after which he buried the shell and coin in the ground. By touching the coin to her body and then removing it, some of the evil was transferred and rendered harmless.

To provide an example of the contemporary use of this terminology by an anthropologist, we have the example of Loudell Snow, who has devoted years to recording traditional African-American beliefs and practices relating to health, home remedies, herbalists, root doctors, spiritual healers, and medical doctors.

Speaking of the ritual manipulation of invisible forces, Snow finds the old terminology of Frazer still useful.

> Such practice is commonly divided into *imitative* and *contagious* magic. Imitative magic is based on the idea that things that are similar are somehow linked: like follows like. A wished-for outcome may be brought about, that is, by copying it. A red-colored food is eaten in the belief that it will build blood, for example, or a knife is placed under the mattress of a woman who has just delivered an infant to "cut" the pains of afterbirth. Contagious magic, in contrast, is based on the premise that things that were once joined together can never be fully put asunder: The part stands for the whole. A lock of hair or a fingernail clipping thus represents the individual from which it was taken. (Snow, 1993, p. 46)

Frazerian terms for magic (sympathetic, homeopathic, and contagious) still belong to the active vocabulary of medical anthropologists, but they are no longer meant to infer evolutionary stages or universal practices, and they are not free of ambiguities. Not infrequently it proves impossible to maintain the distinction between imitative and contact magic. The wax figure used for imitative magic in Malaysia, for example, customarily incorporated nail clippings, hair, or spittle from the intended victim, so it displayed characteristics of both imitative and contagious magic. In Zimbabwe, after burial of the coin-containing eggshell, Mary was told to spit on the burial spot, thus combining an act of contagious magic with one of imitative magic (spitting as a metaphor for getting rid of something).

Often prevention or cure is attempted by methods that are neither homeopathic nor contagious, yet reflect magical thinking. In the United States a rabbit's foot is still widely appreciated for prevention, as is holy water. A rabbit's foot or holy water is perhaps best thought of as a fetish, "an object regarded with awe as having magical qualities or as being the embodiment of some potent spiritual force" (Hunter & Whitten, 1976, p. 167).

Michael Taussig identifies origin magic as still another widespread practice, noting "that chanting or whispering or simply just thinking a thing's *origin* gives the ritualist power over it" (Taussig, 1993, p. 113). In many societies, to recite an origin history demonstrates that the magician controls the mystical secret of the object or entity and thereby can dominate or manipulate it at will. Often, it seems, just knowing the name of a person also gives one that same power, which is why in many societies true names are kept secret. Because of word magic, the true name of God was never revealed to the followers of Jehova.

If one eliminates Frazer's outmoded evolutionary interpretations along with the implication that all magic is sympathetic, his descriptions of sorcery and magic continue in our time to describe beliefs and practices that remain widespread (Wax & Wax, 1963; Goode, 1963). In addition, at least one contemporary anthropologist would add a new dimension to the concept of sympathetic magic in ethnographic description and analysis.

Taussig finds it helpful to realize, as did Frazer himself, that "in many, if not in the overwhelming majority of cases of magical practices in which the Law of Similarity is important, *it is in fact combined with the Law of Contact*" (Taussig, 1993, p. 55). He extends Frazer's concept of sympathetic magic, however, by acknowledging contact in circumstances where it would not have been apparent to Frazer.

Taussig pursues this line of reasoning based on the observation that copies used for magical purposes are not faithful copies. For example, the statuette into which a magician sticks needles in order to cause harm represents at best only a crude likeness of the intended victim. What validates this imperfect imitation is that it has, or is given, material connections to the victim. Speaking of Frazer, Taussig notes,

> What makes up for this lack of similitude, what makes it a"faithful"copy, indeed a magically powerful copy, he[Frazer] declares, are precisely the material connections—those established by attaching hair, nail cuttings, pieces of clothing, and so forth, to the likeness. Thus does the magic of Similarity become but an instance of the magic of Contact—and what I [Taussig] take to be fundamentally important is not just that a little bit of Contact makes up for lack of Similarity, or that some smattering of real substance makes up for a deficiency in the likeness of the visual image, but rather that all of these examples of (magical) realism in which image and contact interpenetrate must have the effect of making us reconsider our very notion of what it is to be an image of some thing, most especially if we wish not only to express but to manipulate reality by means of its image. (Taussig, 1993, p. 57)

At this point in his analysis, Taussig brings the body and all of the senses into the picture, just as theorists of body/mind monism would want. We must free ourselves, he insists, from "the tyranny of the visual notion of image." As an illustration, ritual healing by a Navajo singer in part requires that the priest create a myth-inspired picture with powdered colors. After hours of hard work to create this picture on a sanctified circle of ground, the effect on the patient derives not merely from looking at the pictographic text, but directly from sitting on it. Bodily contact in this case destroys in that brief ritual act the image so carefully constructed for healing purposes. Healing results from this interpenetration of imitation and contact.

As another illustration, Amazonian shamans and their clients experience hallucinogenic images in healing rituals. These images are viewed as objects to look at, but they exist simultaneously as visions that originate internally. Internal visual experiences are associated with embodied feelings of nausea, an awareness of odors, and a sensation of the rhythm of ritual chanting that is heard from an outside source, but is also experienced internally because nerve fibers in the body resonate to external stimulation. Similarity and contagion interpenetrate in these and other ways to create a kind of synesthetic body-mind awareness and response that sometimes heals.

Religion, Sickness, and Healing

"By religion," Frazer wrote, "I understand a propitiation or conciliation of powers superior to man which are believed to direct and control the course of nature and of human life" (Frazer, 1951, pp. 57–58). By this definition, one may speak of religion when natural events are believed to be influenced by the intervention of some higher power. The will of this higher power cannot be controlled directly as with magic, but can be influenced by supplication and propitiation. In the practice of religion, in other words, essentially capricious deities possess the power to do as they wish. In anger, a god or spirit can smite an offender. Conversely, the sick can hope to be cured by means of prayer and offerings. In this way, priests rather than magicians and sorcerers serve as society's practitioners of the sacred. Whereas magicians control events with charms and chants, priests lobby deities with prayerful entreaties.

Frazer discovered beliefs about spirits who could cause disease in many parts of the world. He reported that the Dyaks of Borneo believed that an epidemic of plague was caused by evil demons. A tribal people on the Malay Peninsula were said to attribute all kinds of diseases to maleficent spirits called *nyani.* A spirit of smallpox was believed to bring epidemics to some of the peoples of Africa. Nonetheless, Frazer gives very little attention to healing by divine intervention in his *magnum opus,* just as he does not discuss science in this regard. His book is primarily about magic. Evidently he felt it was not necessary to describe what would already be familiar to his readers. In his time, Christian beliefs about religious healing were widely acted upon. Most of his readers well understood what they thought of as the power of prayer to heal, based on scriptural promise as revealed, for example, in the General Epistle of James: "Is any sick among you? Let him call for the elders of the church; and let them pray over him, anointing him with oil in the name of the Lord: And the prayer of faith shall save the sick, and the Lord shall raise him up; and if he has committed sins, they shall be forgiven him" (Holy Bible, James 5:14–15; see also John 14:14; Luke 11: 9).

Personalistic Versus Naturalistic Medical Systems

Very often Frazer's mutually exclusive categories of magic and religion blend together in actual practice. As an illustration, in one community on the Indonesian island of Sulawesa, a man got sick because he became the victim of a demon. In other words, his sickness was explained in religious terms. In this Sulawesa case, friends of the victim intervened to provide a cure based clearly upon the premises of imitative magic. They moved the sick man out of his house. While the patient was then positioned to recover in a hidden place, his own bed was disguised with a mockup of the sick man constructed from a pillow and some clothes. The demon, fooled by this trick, directed his spiritual attack against the dummy, leaving the real person free to get well.

Both magic and religion can be thought of as personalistic. In the case of magic, it is widely believed that certain individuals have the power to cause and/or heal illness when they practice magic as shamans, sorcerers, and witches. As concerns religion, anthropomorphic beings in the form of deities, devils, demons, and phantoms are also said to cause or cure illness by means of their extraordinary powers.

We refer to these perpetrators of magico-religious affliction and redemption as supernatural. However, the concept of supernatural is a scientific, analytical concept, not one that is indigenous to magico-religious discourse. When used in common parlance, the term *supernatural* can be considered ethnocentric since it takes for granted that everyone should adopt an equally secular point of view. Alexander Gallus takes note of this terminological dilemma. "For the 'understanding actor,' religious and magical acts are *proper means* to control reality, according to his cognitive experiences. The notion of 'superreality' does not exist in this context" (Gallus, 1976, p. 675).

George Devereux says the same thing in his own way. "The *fact* is that the primitive acts realistically most of the time; the *trouble* is that he does not *know* that he is acting realistically when he bandages a wound but unrealistically when he tries to cure an illness by offering a sacrifice" (Devereux, 1980, p. 227). However, George Foster suggests a way out. Since magico-religious practice involves living agents, he recommends that we characterize them as personalistic medical systems that stand in contrast to naturalistic medical systems.

> A personalistic system is one in which disease is explained as due to the active, purposeful intervention of an agent, who may be human (a witch or sorcerer), nonhuman (a ghost, an ancestor, an evil spirit), or supernatural (a deity or other very powerful being). The sick person literally is a victim, the object of aggression or punishment directed specifically against him, for reasons that concern him alone. (Foster, 1976, p. 775)

Foster accomplishes more than introducing a terminological improvement allowing us better to conceptualize magico-religious disease causation and healing. He also draws attention to an area frequently neglected by medical anthropologists, the practice of naturalistic (empirical or pragmatic) healing. "In contrast to personalistic systems," he wrote, "naturalistic systems explain illness in impersonal, systemic terms." In naturalistic approaches, disease results from "such natural forces or conditions as cold, heat, winds, dampness, and, above all, by an upset in the balance of the basic body elements" (Foster, 1976, p. 775).

These two ways of thinking about disease causation are not mutually exclusive, as Foster himself is quick to point out. Typically, both occur in every society, but with one usually much favored over the other. Allan Young clarifies this point:

> While the content and organization of medical beliefs are, then, the products of both cultural and biophysical realities, it is culture—by determining which

biophysical signs are selected and which are ignored, which objects and events are implicated in disease episodes and which are dismissed as irrelevant—which dominates in traditional medicine. (Young, 1976, p. 147)

No doubt because so much ethnographic research has been devoted to medical beliefs in which cultural rather than biophysical realities have dominated, naturalism has been underreported and largely unappreciated by anthropologists. Certainly, this has been true since the time of Frazer, even though Frazer himself postulated an Age of Science as the culminating event of cultural evolution.

Science, Sickness, and Healing

Scientific medicine in *The Golden Bough* was left entirely undescribed. No inkling of how culture might shape medical science can be detected in this seminal work. It leaves largely unattended the impressive naturalistic medical systems of China, India, and the Middle East. It does not describe the pragmatic health practices of everyday life. It contains no references to Rudolf Virchow, William Osler, or any other contemporaries who were struggling to make scientific medicine effective in preventing as well as curing disease. This inherited blind spot remained with anthropologists until very recently. Medical anthropologists on the whole still fail to document and evaluate natural methods of healing that are known to occur at least to some extent in societies everywhere. Foster himself pioneered research on the naturalism of Greco-Roman medicine and of humoral medicine in Latin America. Only in the last few years have anthropologists seriously begun to explore the anthropology of Western medicine.

As we depart Sir James Frazer, a word of caution relating to magico-religious practitioners and health care is advised. In our time, given an economic system characterized by a sharply defined division of labor, we are accustomed to think about practitioners in terms of essentially discrete employment roles oriented to a complex labor market. Physicians and surgeons as well as chiropractors, dentists, physical therapists, optometrists, pharmacists, nurses, and orderlies define job categories characterized by the provision of specific health care services. In contrast, the magician and the priest exercise their roles as religious practitioners with diffuse, wide-ranging involvements not at all limited to health issues. They take responsibility for the whole panorama of cosmic and earthly events that includes worries about sickness and death, but is not limited that way.

This is illustrated by Frazer, who follows his examples of practitioners using magic to cause, prevent, or heal sick people with diverse other examples of the use of magic. Magicians in some cases were required to ensure security for towns, victory in wars, happy lives in households, success in hunting, abundance from gathering wild foods, rich harvests from cultivated gardens, ease of work in any kind of craft, consummation in the sensuousness of lovemaking, fertility in marriage, fullness of milk in nursing mothers, and sunshine or rain when unseasonal weather prevailed.

PREHISTORIC ARCHEOLOGY AND HEALTH CONDITIONS

Although some nineteenth-century evolutionary ideas remain viable as we have seen, little of use survives from early evolutionary speculations to inform us about health conditions in ancient times. Fortunately, archeologists specializing in paleopathology document health conditions both directly and indirectly (but never completely) (Wood, 1979, pp. 23–32; Wood et al. 1992). Direct signs of some diseases can be identified in ancient bones and teeth (osteology) (Zivanovic, 1982; Ortner & Putschar, 1981). Sometimes the depiction of one recognizable disease or another is discovered in old ceramic or painted portraits (Thorwald, 1963, pp. 262-267). After the invention of writing, historical documents in some times and places contribute further information (McNeill, 1977). Indirect evidence relevant to early human health conditions has resulted from studies of the diseases of living monkeys and apes (primatology) (Cockburn, 1971; Anderson & Schiller, 1991). In a comparable way, one can also make tentative assumptions about the past based on ethnographic field studies of health in contemporary bands and tribes.

Ancient ways of life were highly diverse in many ways. To put them into the venerable pigeonholes of archeological periods may seem rather arbitrary or totalizing. However, to achieve a bird's eye overview of health in antiquity it can be useful to sketch them out in very broad terms.

The Paleolithic Period

It seems likely that anatomically modern *Homo sapiens* first advanced beyond smaller-brained ancestors during the the terminal Ice Age (the Pleistocene) roughly between 200,000 and 100,000 years ago. Culturally, the earliest known modern human beings achieved an Upper Paleolithic hunting and gathering way of life by about 50,000 years ago. Social life in the Upper Paleolithic centered in small foraging bands that were heavily reliant upon tools made of stone. They probably also manufactured leather bags, plant fiber nets, and implements of bone and wood which were too perishable to survive. In addition to plant foods and smaller game and fish, large animals were clearly very important as rich sources of protein in bulk amounts. Within the animal kingdom, large prey provided the highest caloric return possible for a day of hunting. These were also the peoples who eventually left the cave art described below.

On the whole, Upper Paleolithic people were probably quite healthy. It seems that their lifestyle was quite rugged, but they appear not to have suffered anymore than later populations from trauma or degenerative diseases such as arthritis. Skeletal remains confirm that they ate well except for seasonal food shortages from time to time. They were undoubtedly pestered and sickened by parasites much as are present-day, small-scale human populations of foragers. Even chimpanzees share some of these torments, thus reflecting the great antiquity of some insect problems. However, millions of years of evolutionary coexistence can be expected to result in substantial mutual accommodation. Excessively virulent parasites kill the mammals they feed on, which is self-defeating. The tendency over a long period of time is for diseases to become less debilitating and deadly (Birdsell, 1968; Cohen, 1989; Cockburn, 1971).

The Mesolithic Period

Post-glacial foraging populations that first appeared around 12,000 years ago remained limited to Stone Age technologies. Some produced stone implements in hitherto unknown shapes by grinding, pecking, or polishing instead of chipping, but their most characteristic tools were compound implements made sharp with small flint chips (microliths) set in grooves of bone or wood. To the Upper Paleolithic spear thrower *(atlatl)* was added widespread use of the bow and arrow. They domesticated dogs, which probably helped them to hunt more effectively. The oldest known fishhooks, kitchenmiddens (mounds of discarded sea shells), and other evidence suggest a more intensive exploitation of water resources in many places. These small bands and tribes demonstrated remarkable variability over time and space. They exploited a wide range of natural resources in different parts of the world. Some established fairly large, permanent settlements. Referring to these cultures by the terms Mesolithic (Europe and Asia), Middle Stone Age (Africa), or Archaic (the Americas) perpetuates a venerable bit of archeological jargon. Many writers prefer now to speak of the Broad Spectrum Revolution that succeeded the Upper Paleolithic.

Enormous worldwide diversity makes it impossible to generalize about health conditions with certainty and completeness. Nevertheless, it is striking that many of the species of large animals hunted by Upper Paleolithic peoples became extinct. Human economies shifted from heavy reliance on large game to broad-spectrum foraging for highly variable small game, fowl, aquatic foods, and seeds that required more work while generating fewer calories of food energy.

Diverse foods provided a well-rounded diet and general good health. Because they did not usually depend on any one food resource, Upper Paleolithic peoples were on the whole less likely to suffer from seasonal undernutrition. The occurrence of dietary stress was greater in some Mesolithic populations than in some Paleolithic groups, however. Bone chemistry carried out in some Middle Eastern areas indicates that the proportion of meat in diets declined. An increase in the proportion of starchy foods was associated with occasional finds of tooth decay. Where evidence is available, the adult stature of both sexes diminished. Adults died at a younger age according to a study of Mesolithic material in India (Frayer, 1981; Cohen, 1989; Merbs, 1983; Kennedy, 1984; Dunn, 1969).

The Neolithic Period

Early in the nineteenth century archeologists defined archeological periods in terms of their stone tools, because that was almost the only evidence available to them. The Neolithic industry still included some chipped flint implements familiar from an earlier time. The most common work-a-day implements, however, were composed of granite and other noncrystalline stones that could be shaped only by pecking, grinding, and polishing. Craftspeople produced excellent tools with these techniques, including axes that were sharper and more durable than older hand axes. Apparently these early cultivators needed a superior instrument to fell trees as they cleared fields for planting. This shift to a horticulturally based economy provides the key to the Neolithic way of life. From a very old mobile lifestyle of hunting and gathering, Neolithic peoples learned to live in sedentary villages where they domesticated plants and animals for food, fiber, hides, and thongs.

Around ten thousand years ago, horticulture and animal husbandry were first practiced in only a few places. Nearly the whole of humanity lived by hunting and gathering. The spread of societies based on food production was so successful that eventually hunting and gathering societies almost disappeared. The anatomy, mind, society, and culture of the genus *Homo,* from the time of *Homo erectus,* evolved in adaptation to roughly one-and-a-half million years of foraging and hunting. Less than 1 percent of human existence has been sedentary. As a consequence, our current health is compromised because we have Paleolithic/Mesolithic bodies that were not "designed" for a sedentary existence.

The Neolithic appears to have been detrimental for human health in many but not in all places. Earlier Mesolithic peoples generally achieved better balanced diets and superior rhythms of rest and activity. Although seasonal hunger may have been a common occurrence in the Mesolithic, chronic malnutrition did not become frequent until the Neolithic. Osteological evidence confirms a decline in levels of nutrition that correlates with an increase in dental disease, infections, and epidemics. In the Mediterranean, one paleopathologist determined that early Neolithic men and women were smaller and less robust than their Mesolithic predecessors. In an Amerindian study, the Neolithic transition was associated with a fall in life expectancy. These findings need to be kept in perspective. In some cases, the immediate effect appears to have resulted in no change or even an improvement in mortality rates. But generally, the overall effect was deleterious (Roosevelt, 1984; Cohen, 1989).

The First Urban Societies

The emergence of the earliest urban centers marked a quantum leap in human evolution. Urbanism was associated with marked divisions of labor. In general, peasants supplied food and raw materials for laborers, craftspeople, priests, and the ruling class. They produced more food by applying new inventions, including plows and draft animals in the Eastern Hemisphere and irrigation in both East and West.

With urbanization, many populations declined even more in health (although some rebounded). Social change influenced pathology profoundly, according to Erwin Ackerknecht, who noted that "the densely settled empires and their large cities made it possible for the acute infections to last and for the great epidemics to spread" (Ackerknecht, 1982, p. 19). Health deteriorated under urban sanitary conditions. In the words of one biological anthropologist, "Preindustrial cities . . . often developed as market or administrative centers for a region, and their increased population size and density provided ample opportunity for epidemics of infectious disease. In addition, a number of early cities had inadequate waste disposal and contaminated water, both factors increasing the spread of epidemics" (Relethford, 1994, p. 466).

Poor diets further increased vulnerability to diseases. Replacing the diverse plant and animal resources of the Mesolithic with a heavy reliance on starchy foods resulted in the consumption of fewer nutrients other than calories. Being dependent on a few stable crops made people vulnerable to famines and chronic malnutrition on a scale unprecedented in the past. Generally, these early complex societies experienced extremely high rates of infant and child mortality. In many populations, stature declined still more from prehistoric forebears. The hardest hit were the poor (Newman et al., 1990). Mark Cohen, attempting to summarize an extremely heterogenous mass of information, describes class stratified differences in health status.

> What we seem to be seeing is not an improvement in human health and nutrition but rather a partitioning of stress such that some privileged classes or successful communities enjoyed good health and nutrition but others suffered unprecedented degrees of stress associated with low social status, unfavorable trade balance, and the parasite loads of dense settled communities engaged in trade. (Cohen, 1989, p. 127)

APPLIED EVOLUTIONARY THEORY

Can we learn anything from prehistoric archeology and evolutionary theory that is relevant to our own well-being today? We have just seen that health responds to differences in ecology, technology, communal organization, and settlement patterns. The fundamental importance of proper resource management, adequate diet, social responsibility, and public hygiene is demonstrated in these archeological findings. However, one can also offer more precise recommendations based on research into the past.

The Vitamin C Hypothesis

Probably every reader has heard claims for the value of taking daily doses of vitamin C (ascorbic acid), particularly to prevent, ameliorate, or cure virus infections, cancer, and coronary heart disease (Cameron & Pauling, 1979). Two-time Nobel laureate Linus Pauling, a scientist-humanitarian honored throughout the world, in the last decades of his career challenged medical orthodoxy on this issue. Pauling was a laboratory scientist, not a physician. Very few are aware, I am sure, that one major part of his justification for taking vitamin C is based upon an evolutionary hypothesis. It is this hypothesis we can productively explore.

In order to understand how evolutionary thinking was employed, we must begin with the lowly bacterium *Bacillus subtilis*. At some time in the past, one strain of the bacterium lost the ability to manufacture tryptophan, an amino acid essential to cellular life, while another strain retained that ability. Let us call them the Can and the Cannot strains. When the two are cultured in a medium that contains tryptophan they do not reproduce equally well. The Cannot strain takes over and the other becomes extinct. The probable reason is that the Cannot thrives and reproduces better because it can use its resources more effectively. It does not require the additional energy that the Can must have in order to produce tryptophan. It works the other way around in a medium lacking tryptophan, where the Cannot becomes extinct because it lacks this essential amino acid while the Can thrives since it is self-sufficient in this regard. Hypothesis: In an environment rich in an essential nutrient such as tryptophan (or vitamin C), being a Cannot provides a selective advantage.

The next piece of evidence in this multidisciplinary analysis comes from the study of living primates and other animals. Almost all mammals synthesize the ascorbic acid (vitamin C) they need for good health. Monkeys, apes, and humans are the most common exceptions. The ability was probably lost by their common ancestor early in the Miocene Epoch, millions of years ago. Hypothesis: At that time, ancestral primates lived in forests that provided fruits and leaves unusually rich in vitamin C. Those who were Cannot for vitamin C competed more successfully than their Can relatives who became extinct.

With the passage of time, as we have seen, primates in the human line shifted tremendously in nutritional practices. The amount of ascorbic acid in the human diet fell dramatically. Occasionally, people ingested so little vitamin C that they got sick and died from scurvy. This is where Pauling introduced the last critical piece of evolutionary thinking. He argued that human beings require vastly more than the 65 milligram (mg) recommended daily allowance (RDA) inscribed on the label of your multivitamin bottle. That is the minimal amount needed to be safe from scurvy. In order to be protected from other diseases, not usually associated with vitamin C deficiency, he recommended a megavitamin dose of several thousand milligrams per day.

His conclusion is based in part on the observation that the amount of ascorbic acid synthesized in animals that are Can for vitamin C is on the megadose level. For example, the rat synthesizes ascorbic acid at a rate of 26 to 58 mg per kilogram of body weight per day. For the average-sized human being weighing about 150 pounds that compares to 1800 to 4000 mg per day, a calculation that is only relevant, of course, if humans are ratlike in vitamin C needs.

Does megadosing with vitamin C make a difference in human health? Pauling's argument is very convincing, but no matter how impressive the logic of the argument and no matter how numerous the anecdotal reports of prevention and cures, until the hypothesis is tested in a systematic way by means of clinical trials, we cannot know if it really works as he hypothesizes. It may not be beneficial. It could be harmful. So far, the jury is still out on vitamin C. It should be noted, however, that Pauling may well win his case as concerns the benefits of this vitamin in preventing some diseases (Frei et al., 1989; Enstrom et al., 1992; Hankinson et al., 1992).

The Discordance Hypothesis

As described above, the human body was fine-tuned for hunting and gathering early in the Paleolithic period. We need to learn how to live healthy lives with bodies that were "designed" for the Stone Age. This is what the multidisciplinary team of Boyd Eaton, Marjorie Shostak, and Melvin Konner mean by the discordance hypothesis (Eaton, Shostak, & Konner, 1988).

Based on this hypothesis, good health requires that we reevaluate our sedentary way of life in terms of how it might be beneficial to modify our eating habits, movement practices, social customs, and activities of daily life. This reevaluation can be guided by what we know about our prehistoric ancestors. Eaton, Shostak, and Konner refer to this as the Paleolithic prescription. A number of recommendations have been advanced by them and by others:

- Increase your intake of vitamin C (Cameron & Pauling, 1979)
- Eat a balanced diet (Bogin, 1991; Brown & Konner, 1987)
- Exercise (Eaton, Shostak, & Konner, 1988; but note Graham, 1985)
- Sleep with your babies (McKenna & Mosko, 1990)
- Do not smoke (Eaton, Shostak, & Konner, 1988)
- Practice scrupulous restraint or abstinence in alcohol consumption (Eaton, Shostak, & Konner, 1988)

These recommendations result from data produced with the research methods of paleopathology, archeology, field ethnography among living hunting and gathering peoples, laboratory experimentation, and clinical experience. They are interpreted (made sense of) in terms of theory—in this case, an evolutionary theory of adaptation to stressors whereby some individuals do better than others in surviving and producing offspring.

By the way, if you are intrigued enough to try out the Paleolithic prescription, study the sources referred to and then discuss them with your personal health care provider. Marked changes in living habits need to be initiated in a prudent manner.

PREHISTORY, CULTURAL DIVERSITY, AND HEALTH

Based upon the mass media, it might seem that contemporary health problems can be understood mostly in terms of the recent past. True, it is now clear that health has suffered enormously during recent decades due to widespread degradation of the environment, worldwide economic exploitation of vulnerable populations, and an escalating politics of terror. However, human health problems also have roots deep in the past.

Old World Versus New World in Prehistory

Over a period of time reaching as far back as 30,000 to 50,000 years ago, small bands of Old World peoples moved repeatedly into the Americas from Asia to settle it for the first time. As far as we can see by means of the archeological record, no human beings had ever set foot in the Western Hemisphere until these Upper Paleolithic hunting and gathering bands infiltrated the icebound other half of the world. They discovered and opened up a New World in the sense that the hemisphere was discovered at this time by the ancestors of present-day Native Americans.

The Old World ancestors of these first Americans originally lived in tropical rain forests teeming with life. As these prehistoric migrants walked slowly towards what are now Siberia and Alaska they entered cooler and drier areas where the diversity of living forms diminished. Many, though not all, infectious and parasitic organisms can survive only in warm, humid environments. As small, isolated bands migrated into cooler, more temperate zones where they no longer encountered other people, they moved into healthier circumstances. Over many generations these migrants unknowingly pushed across the tundra of Siberia, across Beringia, the landbridge that formed at times during the Ice Age, and through an ice corridor into the Americas where no human beings had ever lived before. Since the process took place on a time dimension of thousands of years, it is thought that the inhabitants of the New World arrived free of many of the diseases that plagued Old World peoples. They had passed through what has been called a cold filter, an adaptive (evolutionary) process that may have cleansed them of many infectious organisms (McNeill, 1977, pp. 25–28; Jarcho, 1964; Stewart, 1960; St. Hoyme, 1969).

This interpretation of prehistory no doubt oversimplifies. One may wonder if it is truly appropriate to refer to this avenue of migration as a cold filter that killed germs. This much is clear, however. The two halves of the world differed greatly when they were brought back into contact in 1492. Europeans, Africans, Asians—all of the Old World peoples in fact—had been exposed to one another's germs for many millennia. On the whole they were well accommodated to the pathogens attacking them. Many dangerous infections were experienced as childhood diseases that people survived for the most part, and from which adults were protected by acquired immunity (McNeill, 1977).

New World populations were not prepared for infections of influenza, measles, smallpox, tuberculosis, typhoid fever, typhus, and such. When the two hemispheres were brought into intimate human contact following the voyages of Columbus, peoples of the Old World suffered little from new infectious diseases, except for a severe pandemic of syphilis that many scholars believe (but some dispute) originated in the Americas (Baker & Armelagos, 1988; Inhorn & Brown, 1990, p. 93). In the New World, sadly, the meeting of the hemispheres resulted in near-total devastation. The susceptibility of Amerindians resulted in unprecedented pandemics, contributing to political, economic, and military collapse and to horrific population loss (McNeill, 1977).

Native Americans of our time, 500 years after first contact, still embody major, measurable consequences of these ancient differences in the medical ecology of the two hemispheres. The roots of severe health problems, of social and family vulnerabilities, of psychological stress, and of political and economic exploitation and neglect date back to the European conquest that reduced healthy, thriving communities to remmant enclaves of dispossessed and oppressed survivors.

SHAMANISM IN PREHISTORY

So far I have summarized what we know about health conditions in the past. Now I propose to turn to what we know about health care. Given the presence of diseases in prehistoric populations, have archeologists uncovered objective evidence relating to ancient healing practices? The answer is yes, but it tends to be a highly equivocal yes.

The Old Stone Age in Europe

The first prehistoric evidence relating to magic and religion was discovered in 1879 in a cave located in Altamira, Spain (Kühn, 1955; Halverson, 1987). For some months the master of the local castle had been exploring the cave with a shovel, acquiring a small collection of ancient bone and stone artifacts. Amateur archeology was the "in" thing for an aristocrat in those days.

Months went by as he passed leisure hours hunting for objects in the soil. One day the squire was interrupted by his little daughter who was playing while her father spaded the soil. "Look," she said, pointing to frescos on the ceiling. Quizzically, her father stretched his back, held up his light, raised his eyes, and shared with his daughter the first view in more than ten thousand years of this art gallery created by Cro-Magnon artists during the Upper Paleolithic.

What better antidote to the often unrestrained speculations of evolutionary theorists, one might well ask, than to examine archeological remains? Cave art that survived *in situ* from some time between 28,000 and 10,000 years ago reveals a picture-book view of the past. It provides direct evidence. That evidence leaves room for dispute, unfortunately, since interpreting the evidence is fraught with possible error. Precisely because we view this ancient art in the total absence of written records and living associations, interpretations have been wildly speculative. In the absence of factual constraints, fantasy flourishes. Nevertheless, in a cautious way, we can speak of possible practices of magic, religion, and healing.

The very act of painting, engraving, or sculpting game animals and (more rarely) fish suggests that in some cases at least, magical thinking might have been involved. Keep in mind that we are discussing a wide expanse of geographical territory during the course of 18,000 years of time. It would be extraordinary if every case of artistic representation was done for a single reason. Given that caveat, many anthropologists believe that these paintings survive from their use in acts of imitative magic or animistic worship. Did the magician, by imitating mammals in paintings, magically gain control over the game for hunters? Or, did the ritual of painting expiate the killing of game? This interpretation gains credibility from the fact that most of these paintings were executed deep in the dark interiors of caves. Difficulty of access would seem to preclude their use as art for art's sake, but fits well with magical and religious thinking.

In some cases, the painting of a horse, mammoth, or other animal shows red spots painted on the animal and around it. Because the spots are not confined to the animal, they are not to be interpreted as hide markings. Perhaps they were daubed on by the community magician, each daub ensuring that a spear would reach its mark by the power of imitative magic. In other cases, the animal is portrayed with pointed arrows or spears entering its body. These examples look impressively like remnants of imitative magic.

Did the magic of the hunt include a magico-religious concern for replenishment of the herd? We do encounter paintings of pregnant mares and cows. Not infrequently, animals are shown mating.

Assumptions about magic, religion, and fertility find support in many surviving examples of human female figurines and relief carvings. However, these were carved and molded earlier in the Upper Paleolithic, predominantly between 25,000 and 20,000 years ago. The statuettes typically display only amorphous, faceless heads and rudimentary hands and feet. In contrast, secondary sexual characteristics are exaggerated. They were carved with enormous pendulous breasts, steatopygous (excessively fat) buttocks, and ponderous thighs, all suggestive of heightened fertility. In rare cases, figurines appear to have been kept erect, standing with their feet planted in the ground next to hearths. Do female figurines portray primordial goddesses, deities of the home and family, or patronesses of reproduction ensuring offspring to maintain the future survival of the community? Were they worshipped as religious icons? Where they manipulated as fetishes? Definitive answers to these questions are lost in the obscurity of time.

Last and most important, if the caves preserve evidence of imitative hunting magic, do they also tell us something about the magicians? The cave known as Les-Trois-Frères was first discovered as a mere hole in the side of a mountain in France in 1914. By that time archeologists were on the lookout for cave art, a local nobleman among them. While on a picnic jaunt with family and friends to visit a cave discovered somewhat earlier, the count was directed by a local peasant to a secret opening. After expanding the small hole with their bare hands, the adventurers borrowed a clothesline from a nearby cottager in order to lower one of the count's three sons deep into the black abyss. More than an hour passed in suspense and worry until at last the boy returned shouting out the good news. The cave was filled with hundreds of pictures.

Most of the pictures were engraved high on sheer vertical surfaces. How were they done in the darkness in such inaccessible places? The colossal Hall of Pictures is covered with images of the wildlife that populated southwestern France thousands of years ago. On it are portrayals of mammoths, rhinoceroses, bisons, wild horses, bears, wild asses, reindeer, wolverines, musk oxen, snowy owls, hares, and fishes. Some of the large animals are shown riddled with spears or arrows, their blood flowing.

In one place, a man is etched in stone, but not an ordinary man, because we can identify only his upright posture and his legs and feet as hominid. His body is covered with what appears to be a bison's skin. He seems to be playing a flute. Is he enchanting the reindeer located just in front of him? There is another, also partly disguised as a bison. Who is he? Is he a magician? A sorcerer? In the older literature, he and others like him were called wizards (defined as men skilled in magic). Is he a wizard?

More recently, influenced by customs among living or recent small-scale societies, particularly in Siberia, these costumed figures have been called shamans. Contemporary shamans frequently wear garments that are weighty with emblems and symbolism. Often they are made of animal skins, antlers, feathers, and such. Are the figures engraved on the wall of Les-Trois-Frères shamans ten or fifteen thousand years ancestral to those of our time? Is he a shaman?

High up, about twelve feet above ground, is the most remarkable of these presumed shamans, now known as the Wizard of Les-Trois-Frères. In this grotto filled with hundreds of engraved figures, the Wizard stands out because of the addition of black paint to the engraved image. He has a human body held in the strange pose of some fabulous creature or ritual dance. We clearly detect human hands and feet, arms and legs, and the genitals of a man. But his face is hidden behind a stag-mask with a long, pointed beard, large antlers, and black staring eyes. He flaunts the tail of a wild horse. Is this a religious figure, the portrait of a male deity? Is this an animistic personage, perhaps the Master of Animals? Or, is he a functionary, a priest, or a shaman?

In the cave of Lascaux, France, a prehistoric artist portrayed what could be a
shaman deep in a trance, his soul traveling, perhaps, to other realms of existence.
(© Arch. Phot. Paris / S.P.A.D.E.M. Reproduced with permission.)

Years later in 1940, the cave of Lascaux was discovered. There, too, one encounters the portrait of what we will call a shaman. His body is covered by an animal skin and he wears the mask of some fabled creature with long antlers. But while several caves picture comparable figures, only in Lascaux do we encounter a provocative scene of three figures that seem to have been painted as a single composition. The largest figure is an enormous bison, apparently killed with the spear drawn next to it, its intestines extruding from a belly wound. Toward the front of the beast is a very striking object. It seems to be a wooden pole stuck in the ground, surmounted by a well-formed bird. From contemporary studies we know that shamans often wear bird feathers to symbolize the magic flight they take to visit spirit worlds while entranced. Is this an ancient shamanic bird symbol? And, most extraordinary of all, quite without parallel in cave art, is the clear representation of a man's body with a bird's head, lying flat on his back towards the head of the bison, exposing an erect penis. This, surely, is a shaman, don't you think?

Interpreting these earliest known examples of human art as possible reflections of sympathetic magic and animistic religion in the Old Stone Age is not unreasonable, which is why these old analytic concepts from the work of Tylor and Frazer still appear in textbooks on archeology (e.g., Campbell, 1992; Staski & Marks, 1992; but note, Fagan, 1992). As for healing, the Upper Paleolithic yields not a hint. We can only surmise that if magicians were practicing imitative magic or religious ritual to ensure the fertility of hunted animals, if by magic they entranced large mammals to be successfully speared and killed, if by magical or religious use of female figurines they enhanced the pregnancy rate of their small foraging bands, then probably they used magic and religion both to prevent and to cure disease.

AZTEC MEDICINE

Archeological publications at times report information about health, especially if they describe societies for which historical documents also exist. It is exceedingly rare, however, for anyone to write a scholarly book entirely dedicated to prehistoric and early historic health issues. One recent exception was published by Bernard Ortiz de Montellano, an anthropologist biochemist (Ortiz de Montellano, 1990).

Ortiz pieced together his reconstruction of Aztec medicine from the rich resources of archeological excavations as well as from early post-Columbian writings left by conquered Aztecs and sixteenth-century Spanish rulers. The archeological and historical documentation was interpreted on the quite reasonable assumption that ancient practices survive in one form or another in many conservative Mexican villages. He acquired much field data from his own twentieth-century ethnographic fieldwork in a bilingual Chinantec-Spanish–speaking community in the remote highlands of Mexico. His book amply illustrates how certain nineteenth–century concepts remain useful to medical anthropologists when one guards against obsolete assumptions about cultural evolution.

It should be noted at the outset that Ortiz does not follow Frazer in assuming that magic, religion, and science constituted essentially separate medical systems. Quite the contrary, he acknowledges that they coexisted in a complex mixture of beliefs and practices. "Aztec religion was a state-ecclesiastical institution, that is, with priests, temples, and a formal hierarchy," Ortiz notes, "but differed from most other ecclesiastical religions in the world in its retention of shamanic elements" (Ortiz, 1990, p. 36). It also included empirical practices consistent with naturalistic and scientific assumptions.

Animism

The Aztec pantheon, described as large and confusing (to the anthropologist), included deities with human qualities. Many were also animistic, Ortiz notes, in the sense that they existed in animal forms called *nahualli*. Shamans, too, could assume animal forms and become *nahualli*. So the spiritual world was both pantheistic and animistic. Ortiz speaks also of animistic forces in the form of human souls. The three principal animistic forces were the head soul *(tonalli)*, the heart soul *(teyolia)*, and the liver soul *(ihiyotl)*, but there were others. Each soul was essential to a specific body function. Good health depended on every soul being intact and in balance with the others.

Magical Practices

Frazerian concepts serve Ortiz as organizing schemata when he writes of sorcerers and of disease causation in terms of the law of similarity (imitative magic) and the law of contact (contagious magic).

Bernard Ortiz de Montellano exploring an archeological site in Mexico.

In Aztec thought, imitative magic could both cause and cure disease. Eating seeds from a certain large bulky tree supposedly resulted in becoming morbidly obese. Eating tamales that stuck to the bottom of the pan could cause a pregnant woman to have great difficulty in her time of labor. During childbirth a woman would be given spears and a toy shield, since she was believed to be fighting a spiritual battle in which, as a brave warrior, she brought home a captive in the form of her newborn baby. In addition, to increase the flow of milk, a lactating woman was given a milk-white sap that seeped from the leaves of a certain herb.

A sorcerer could use contagious magic to harm and kill. For example, some hair acquired from an intended victim caused death when it was burned. (This simultaneously involved imitative magic, since burning the hair symbolized cremation of the resultant cadaver.) Contagious magic was also used by women who introduced menstrual blood into their husbands' food or drink. Ingestion of their blood caused husbands to exchange acts of cruelty for acts of love.

Religious Practices

Ortiz also writes of supernatural causation. It was believed that deities caused individual sickness and epidemics. The god *Titlacahuan* was considered the cause of all human ailments of supernatural origin. But he was not really alone in disease etiology, since he could delegate this harmful power to lesser gods, who in turn might send still others, including the head souls *(teyolia)* of people they had killed. The deities used sickness as a way to ensure good behavior. For example, it was forbidden to have sex during ceremonies dedicated to the gods of spring, sex, love, and dance. Sexual dalliance during that time of proscription was punished by hemorrhoids or venereal diseases. Ringworm or other skin diseases were imposed on those who failed to fast during a feast for another god. Fortunately, that festival was celebrated only once in every eight years. Afflictions attributed to deities of the Rain God Complex included drowning, gout (with its swollen joints), dropsy (characterized by swelling of the ankles and feet), and rheumatism (associated with dampness). Again we see imitative magic in religious beliefs.

As is appropriate within the category of religion, priests served as intercessors. Following an Aztec version of astrological logic, one's time of birth determined much about one's future life, including whether the infant would die young or be sickly and weak. A priest could provide a better prognosis by arranging for a change in a child's official day of birth. Moderation in sexual behavior was considered highly important for the maintenance of good health. Aztec morality taught that if you indulged in too much sex you would suffer poor health as a punishment. The priest could help. If you confessed to the god of sexual temptation and salvation and did penance in the presence of a priest, you would be cured. It was a form of cure that was not taken lightly. It could only be done once in an entire lifetime.

Naturalism

The central idea behind Frazer's concept of science was that causation was not thought of in magico-religious terms. Ortiz reflects Frazer's concept of science when he writes of natural causation in Aztec thinking, of how they recognized a natural etiology in diseases in which a relationship between empirical cause and effect was acknowledged.

Trauma, for example, could cause a fractured leg, a dislocated shoulder, or a sprained ankle in perfectly natural ways. Treatments also were based on naturalistic thinking, such as bleeding a sprained ankle to reduce the swelling. A wound, thought of as a natural result of physical trauma, was treated by first washing it with warm, fresh urine, then applying an herb to stop the bleeding, and finally, dressing the wound with an herbal juice.

As one might expect, naturalistic thinking blended easily with supernaturalistic. To treat a fractured bone, for example, in addition to applying a plaster and splint based on naturalistic concepts, one should also recite a long sacred incantation referring to a mythic event in which the god *Quetzalcoatl,* in order to recreate life, journeyed to the land of the dead to bring back the bones from men of the first creation. Is this a religious act in which a priest intercedes with prayer? Or, is this a magical act in which a shaman undertakes a mystical journey to a mythic realm in an act of imitative magic?

Nineteenth-century concepts can still be useful sometimes, often in fact, as ways to organize or classify complex observed behavior. However, when you have to puzzle out how to make the facts fit the concepts, then the concepts have become a procrustean bed. They are valuable only when they are useful. When they become merely distractive and distortive, drop them.

CONCLUSION

Early anthropologists established a beachhead in the struggle to understand the premodern condition in which theories of health and methods of care were, and still are in many places, personalistic rather than naturalistic. The approach was interdisciplinary in the sense of being done as four-field anthropology. It was not multidisciplinary at that time, particularly not as a collaboration of physicians and anthropologists. In this chapter, multidisciplinarity did contribute to archeological reconstructions of prehistoric health—the vitamin C hypothesis, the discordance hypothesis, and Aztec medicine—but all of this research is contemporary.

By the end of the century, a paradigm shift took place in anthropology. Early evolutionary theory began its sharp decline. With the new paradigm, the orientation of research shifted from the dimension of time to the dimension of space. Concurrently, some important early work was published in what was later to become the field of medical anthropology. The new work was interdisciplinary, but not yet multidisciplinary. Physicians and anthropologists were not yet ready to work together collaboratively. The new work also continued an evolutionary interest in personalistic medical systems, but not yet in naturalistic systems. Most importantly, the sophistication of anthropological research methods improved in many ways, particularly in the use of the comparative method.

REFERENCES

Ackerknecht, E. H. (1982). *A short history of medicine* (Rev. ed.). Baltimore: Johns Hopkins University Press.

Anderson, S. T., & Schiller, C. A. (1991). Rheumatoid-like arthritis in a lion tailed macaque. *Journal of Rheumatology, 18,* 1247-1250.

Baker, B. J., & Armelagos, G. J. (1988). The origin and antiquity of syphilis: Paleopathological diagnosis and interpretation. *Current Anthropology, 29,* 703-737.

The Holy Bible. Authorized King James Version. Cleveland, OH: World Publishing Company, MD.

Birdsell, J. B. (1968). Some predictions for the Pleistocene based on equilibrium systems among recent hunter-gatherers. In R. B. Lee & I. DeVore (Eds.), *Man the hunter* (pp. 229–240) Chicago: Aldine-Atherton.

Bogin, B. (1991). The evolution of human nutrition. In Ross L. Romanucci, D. E. Moerman, & L. R. Tancredi (Eds.), *The anthropology of medicine: From culture to method* (2nd ed). New York: Bergin & Garvey.

Brown, P. J., & Konner, M. (1987). An anthroplogical perspective on obesity. *Annals of the New York Academy of Sciences, 499*, 29–45.

Cameron, E., & Pauling, L. (1979). *Cancer and vitamin C*. New York: Warner Books.

Campbell, B. G. (1992). *Humankind emerging* (6th ed). (Adapted in part from materials published by Time-Life Books.) New York: HarperCollins Publishers.

Cockburn, T. A. (1971). Infectious diseases in ancient populations. *Current Anthropology, 12*, 45–62.

Cohen, M. N. (1989). *Health and the rise of civilization*. New Haven: Yale University Press.

Denzin, N. K., & Lincoln, Y. S (1994). Introduction: Entering the field of qualitative research (pp. 1–17). In N. K. Denzin & Y. S. Lincoln (Eds.), *Handbook of qualitative research*. Thousand Oaks, CA: Sage Publications.

Devereux, G. (1980). *Basic problems of ethno-psychiatry*. Chicago: University of Chicago Press.

de Waal Malefijt, A. (1974). *Images of man: A history of anthropological thought*. New York: Alfred A. Knopf.

Dunn, F. L. (1969). Epidemiological factors: Health and disease in hunter-gatherers. In R. B. Lee & I. DeVore (Eds.), *Man the Hunter.* (pp. 221–223) Chicago: Aldine-Atherton.

Eaton, S. B., Shostak, M., & Melvin, K. M. (1988). *The Paleolithic prescription: A program of diet and exercise and a design for living*. New York: Harper & Row.

Enstrom, J. E., Kanim, L. E., & Klein, M. A. (1992). Vitamin C intake and mortality among a sample of the United States population. *Epidemiology, 3*, 194–202.

Fagan, B. M. (1992). *People of the earth: An introduction to world prehistory* (7th ed.). New York: HarperCollins Publishers.

Foster, G. M. (1976). Disease etiologies in nonwestern medical systems. *American Anthropologist, 78*, 773–782.

Frayer, D. W. (1981). Body size, weapon use, and natural selection in the European Upper Paleolithic and Mesolithic. *American Anthropologist, 83,* 58.

Frazer, J. G. (1951). *The golden bough: A study in magic and religion*. New York: Macmillan Co. (Original work published 1922)

Frei, B., England, L., & Ames, B. N. (1989). Ascorbate as an outstanding antioxidant in human blood plasma. *National Academy of Science, 86*, 6377–6381.

Gallus, A. (1976). Comments. *Current Anthropology, 17*, 675–676.

Goode, W. J. (1963). Comments. *Current Anthropology, 4*, 507–508.

Graham, S. B. (1985). Running and menstrual dysfunction: Recent medical discoveries provide new insights into the human division of labor by sex. *American Anthropologist, 87*, 878–882.

Halverson, J. (1987). Art for art's sake in the Paleolithic. *Current Anthropology, 28*, 63–71.

Hankinson, S. E. et al. (1992). Nutrient intake and cataract extraction in women: A prospective study. *British Medical Journal, 305*, 335-339.

Harris, M. (1968). *The rise of anthropological theory: A history of theories of culture.* New York: Thomas Y. Crowell.

Hunter, D. E., & Whitten, P. (1976). *Encyclopedia of anthropology.* New York: Harper & Row.

Inhorn, M. C., & Brown, P. J. (1990). The anthropology of infectious disease. *Annual Review of Anthropology, 19*, 89-117.

Jarcho, Saul. (1964). Some observations on diseases in prehistoric America. *Bulletin of the History of Medicine, 38*, 1-19.

Jones, R. A. (1984). Robertson Smith and James Frazer on religion: Two traditions in British social anthropology. *History of Anthropology, 2,* 31-58.

Kennedy, K. A. R. (1984). Growth, nutrition, and pathology in changing paleodemographic settings in South Asia. In M. N. Cohen and G. Armelagos (Eds.), *Paleopathology at the Origins of Agriculture* (pp. 169-192). New York: Academic Press.

Kühn, H. (1955). *On the Track of Prehistoric Man.* New York: Vintage Books.

Lincoln, Y. S., & Denzin, N. K. (1994). The fifth moment. In N. K. Denzin, & Y. S. Lincoln. (Eds.), *Handbook of qualitative research* (pp. 575-586). Thousand Oaks, CA: Sage Publications.

McKenna, J. J., & Mosko, S. (1990). Evolution and the sudden infant death syndrome (SIDS). Part III: Infant arousal and parent-infant co-sleeping. *Human Nature, 1,* 291-324.

McNeill, W. H. (1977). *Plagues and peoples.* New York: Doubleday.

Merbs, C. F. (1983). *Patterns of activity-induced pathology in a Canadian Inuit population.* (Archaeological Survey of Canada, Paper No. 119.) Ottawa: National Museums of Canada.

Newman, L. F., Crossgrove, W., Kates, R. W., Matthews, R., & Milman, S. (Eds.) (1990). *Hunger in history: Food shortage, poverty, and deprivation.* Cambridge, MA: Basil Blackwell.

Ortiz de Montellano, B. R. (1990). *Aztec medicine, health, and nutrition.* New Brunswick, NJ: Rutgers University Press.

Ortner, D. J., & Putschar, W. G. J. (1981). *Identification of pathological conditions in human skeletal remains.* (Smithsonian Contributions to Anthropology, No. 28.) Washington, DC: Smithsonian Institution Press.

Rappaport, R. A. (1984). *Pigs for the ancestors: Ritual in the ecology of a New Guinea people* (2nd ed.). New Haven: Yale University Press.

Relethford, J. H. (1994). *The human species: An introduction to biological anthropology* (2nd ed.). Mountain View, CA: Mayfield Publishing Company.

Roosevelt, A. C. (1984). Population, health, and the evolution of subsistence: Conclusions from the conference. In M. N. Cohen, & G. J. Armelagos (Eds.), *Paleopathology and the origins of agriculture* (pp. 572-574) Orlando, FL: Academic Press.

Snow, L. F. (1993). *Walkin' over medicine.* Boulder, CO: Westview Press.

St. Hoyme, L. E. (1969). On the origins of new world paleopathology. *American Journal of Physical Anthropology, 21*, 295-302.

Staski, E., & Marks, J. (1992). *Evolutionary anthropology: An introduction to physical anthropology and archaeology.* Fort Worth, TX: Harcourt Brace Jovanovich College Publishers.

Stewart, T. D. (1960). A physical anthropologist's view of the peopling of the new world. *Southwestern Journal of Anthropology, 16,* 265-266.

Taussig, M. (1993). *Mimesis and alterity: A particular history of the senses.* New York: Routledge.

Thorwald, J. (1963). *Science and secrets of early medicine: Egypt, Mesopotamia, India, China, Mexico, Peru.* New York: Harcourt Brace & World.

Tylor, E. B. (1958). *Religion in primitive culture.* New York: Harper & Row. (Original work published 1871)

Wax, M., & Wax, R. (1963). The notion of magic. *Current Anthropology, 4,* 495-503.

Wood, C. S. (1979). *Human sickness and health: A biocultural view.* Palo Alto, CA: Mayfield Publishing Company.

Wood, J. W., Milner, G. R., Harpending, H. C., & Weiss, K.M. (1992). The osteological paradox: Problems of inferring prehistoric health from skeletal samples. *Current Anthropology, 33,* 343-370.

Young, A. (1976). Internalizing and externalizing medical belief systems: An Ethiopian example. *Social Science and Medicine, 10,* 147-156.

Zivanovic, S. (1982). *Ancient diseases: The element of palaeopathology.* New York: Pica (Universe Books).

Chapter 4

THE SPACE DIMENSION

INTRODUCTION

Writing about scientific revolutions, Thomas Kuhn concluded that the history of science repeatedly records the "rejection of one time-honored scientific theory in favor of another incompatible with it." He referred to these revolutions as "paradigm shifts," and has influenced scientists and scholars to expect that "an older paradigm [will be] replaced in whole or in part by an incompatible new one." He further concluded, "Each produced a consequent shift in the problems available for scientific scrutiny and in the standards by which the profession determined what should count as an admissible problem or as a legitimate problem-solution" (Kuhn, 1970, pp. 6, 92).

This emphasis by Kuhn on the incompatibility of paradigms and on their noncumulative character stands in striking opposition to a point of view articulated by Roy Rappaport, who urged, as we have seen, that anthropologists "modify or correct" older paradigms rather than "discard them before their possibilities have been adequately explored." In a manner contrary to the expectation engendered by Kuhn, but consistent with the programmatic recommendation of Rappaport, the history of anthropological theory documents many examples of the survival of older concepts and concerns that remained integral to, or at least supplemental to, whatever "new approaches" replaced "older ones." New paradigms, it would appear, are not as incompatible with the old as Kuhn would have us to believe (Rappaport, 1984, pp. xv–xvi).

The first paradigm shift in anthropology is said to have begun in 1899, a year when one could a detect a significant new diversity in the kinds of articles published in the *American Anthropologist* (Stern & Bohannan, 1970; Rogge, 1976, p. 836). After the turn of the century, this general shift in anthropological theory gained momentum. It took place as cultural evolutionary theory, incorporating a global dimension of time, and was abandoned in favor of historical particularism, which attempted studies of how culture traits were distributed geographically as a basis for drawing conclusions about strictly limited historical events (Harris, 1968, pp. 250–252).

In making this shift, anthropologists did not easily give up their fascination with the time dimension of culture on a worldwide totalizing scale. Early efforts to discover the origins and transformations of panhuman culture were abandoned because they were purely speculative and completely unverifiable. Nonetheless, the evolutionary perspective that was publicly disavowed by most anthropologists quietly survived.

On the surface it appeared that the time dimension was replaced by a geographic dimension. Individual traits relating to concepts of disease and healing were plotted on distribution maps to show that a trait found in one place was also found among living or historically recent peoples in many other places. By constructing maps to show where the presence of cultural traits had been located, distributions could be scrutinized to determine what their history must have been in terms of how traits must have spread or diffused. For some decades, this constituted the practice of normal science for anthropologists. They devoted themselves to "solving puzzles," as Kuhn would put it, according to the paradigm of historical particularism (Kuhn, 1970, pp. 36–37).

On the simplest and most convincing level, it was thought that a trait demonstrating a very widespread distribution was probably very old. Any trait with a worldwide distribution was probably older than one with a limited regional distribution. This became known as the age-area hypothesis, which postulated that the greater the age, the wider the area of distribution, an interpretation that still carries conviction when applied sensibly (Kroeber, 1948, pp. 561–568). The age-area hypothesis along with other principles of interpretation resulted in translations of spatial dimensions into time dimensions. Fundamental evolutionary assumptions survived this major shift in the anthropological paradigm.

THE FIRST MEDICAL ANTHROPOLOGY BOOK

Old Ideas Disguised As New

As a swashbuckling young physician, W. H. R. Rivers joined the British Torres Straits Expedition led by A. C. Haddon in 1898. He emerged from that experience as a highly influential anthropologist. During his fieldwork in Melanesia he did not particularly concentrate upon health care issues. In fact, he is best remembered for his work there on family and kinship and on native psychology. Years later, however, he drew upon Melanesian culture to lecture on primitive medicine at the Royal College of Physicians of London (Rivers, 1916). After his death, these lectures, revised and expanded, were published in 1924 as a book, *Medicine, Magic, and Religion.*

The underlying organization of the book drew heavily upon the evolutionary stages of James Frazer. Rivers believed that originally an ancient, wide dispersal

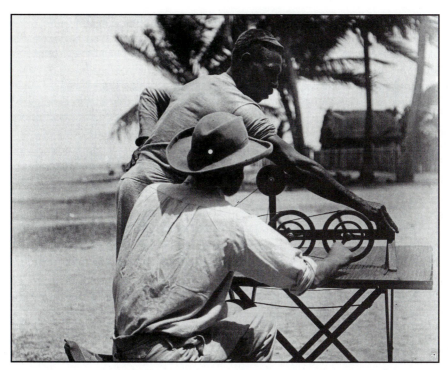

W. H. R. Rivers carrying out visual acuity tests at the turn of the century in Melanesia.

(Reproduced with permission of Cambridge University Museum of Archaeology and Anthropology.)

of early social groups over the earth ensured that all human groups began their existence with the same simple, primal culture. Subsequently, in relative isolation from each other, further independent evolution resulted in close similarities or identities of custom and belief emerging at different times in widely separated places. These similarities and identities occurred, Rivers argued, because the human mind was the same everywhere, and therefore people everywhere tended to solve problems of adaptation and survival in similar or identical ways. This quality of the human mind and experience was known in those days as the principle of psychic unity.

In his evolutionary reconstruction, Rivers differed not at all from older theorists. He defined a time sequence of three stages of evolutionary development (reading from bottom to top):

- Naturalism
- Religion
- Magic

Rivers acknowledged that much of the similarity within each sequential stage of magic, religion, and science could be explained by diffusion rather than independent invention (local evolution). In this way, much of the baggage of the older evolutionary paradigm was rationalized into the new diffusionist paradigm of historical particularlism. "Those who object to the crude evolutionary hypotheses of the last century do so," Rivers wrote, "not because they believe the hypotheses of evolution to be false, but because their advocates have treated as simple a process which has been exceedingly complex" (Rivers, 1924, pp. 112).

What was this complex process? Rivers concluded that healing traits had diffused widely, but the evolutionary stages remained valid, because when more advanced therapeutic measures were borrowed they underwent a complicated process of transformation that years later came to be called acculturation. Traits invented on an advanced naturalistic level of thinking underwent degeneration when they were borrowed by healers still functioning in the magical or religious mode. In other words, borrowed elements of scientific medicine acquired magical or religious coloration in the process of diffusion and acceptance.

The work of Rivers illustrates a recurrent reality of the sciences. Scholars tend to perpetuate anecdotal, perhaps intuitive understandings, as well as scientific conclusions from abandoned paradigms of scholarship without much awareness of the historical origins of their ideas (Anderson, 1964). The Rivers book provides a useful illustration of this process as the author struggled to keep one foot in the evolutionary school and yet place the other in the newer school of historical particularism. We have much to learn from Rivers, but it is not to be found in either the grand theory of evolution or the supposedly atheoretical pronouncements of historical particularism.

Emic and Etic Descriptions of Culture

To identify what is still useful in the old work of Rivers, it is helpful to apply a more recent theoretical construct. Many decades after Frazer, when Rivers and all of the others of their generation were gone, Kenneth Pike, an anthropologist-linguist, suggested that ethnographic descriptions of cultural traits habitually merge and confuse two very different kinds of information (Pike,1954; Fisher & Werner, 1978):

- Emic, in which indigenous practices, concepts, and worldviews of a particular culture are described as accurately as possible the way the indigenes themselves would do.
- Etic, in which the information is transformed to fit the shaping demands of cross-cultural categories or analytical concepts.

To illustrate, when I spoke recently with Karen Barrett about her psychic surgeries in the Philippines, she offered an emic description. She explained that she saw the Filipino operator push his hand into her body, she saw blood flow from between his fingers, and she felt and saw the extraction of what appeared to be diseased tissue. Miraculously, when the operation was finished and the bloody residue was wiped away, the skin was completely intact with no sign of a cut or scar. The operator was able to do this, she was told, because, being guided by powerful spirits, his fingers and hands slipped between

Philip Singer at the Pine Ridge Indian Reservation in South Dakota with his video camera at the ready.

(Photo, Todd Whitman)

molecules of the skin without disrupting the integrity of the tissue. A scalpel was not needed. This is an emic explanation because it is culture-bound. That is, it only makes sense in terms of the paradigm of spiritism that constitutes the theology of psychic surgeons and their converts.

In an etic description, the same experience must be translated into concepts and categories that constitute part of the universal discourse of science. Philip Singer, a medical anthropologist, writes in the etic mode when he describes the blood and guts display of psychic surgeons as the work of individuals who create an illusion of surgical intervention by sleight-of-hand trickery, which he has documented with videotaped evidence. This explanation leaves intact the scientific assumption that a surgeon must cut through the skin to enter the body (Singer, 1990).

In principle, etic statements are not culture-bound, but that is at best problematic. It is naive to assume that scientists in general, and anthropologists and physicians in particular, are not influenced by their own native cultures and the cultures of science (Becher, 1989; Good & Good, 1989, p. 305; McGrane, 1989, p. 119). The way in which Rivers salvaged an old evolutionary sequence of magic, religion, and naturalism in the new paradigm of diffusionism provides one example among many of how science can be deeply embedded in its own history or culture.

In spite of these philosophical cautions, however, etic descriptions cannot be avoided if one hopes to learn about general or universal characteristics of culture. They categorize human beliefs and behaviors in ways that can be applied cross-culturally, as when we speak of healers in general (etic) rather than the explanations of psychic surgeons as a culture-specific kind of healing (emic). The terminology of biomedicine is meant to be etic in this sense. *Pneumonia* is a term, for example, that refers to a deep infection of the lungs that can occur in any culture. Anthropologists employ their own vocabulary of cross-culturally valid concepts. Terms such as *animism, magic,* and *religion* are etic. Shortly I will discuss sorcery, disease object intrusion, and other widespread beliefs and practices which also serve the profession as etic categories.

To explore the field of medical anthropology we will find this distinction of emic and etic useful, beginning here as we note that both the evolutionary and the diffusionist paradigms inspired anthropologists to search for broad generalizations about culture. To arrive at generalizations requires that one work with a clearly defined etic terminology.

Translating emic to etic terms is done at a cost, however. Important kinds of information are lost. We have already seen how Frazer demonstrated that isolating medicine or sickness as discrete categories of experience (our etic categories), while often useful for analytic purposes, in fact distorts how people think and act in emic terms. It became clear in *The Golden Bough* that magic and religion, both of which are etic designations, structured how people dealt emically with the whole panoply of anxieties and disasters, of wishes and ambitions, and that health was merely one concern among many. For most preindustrial societies, health, an etic taxon, does not constitute a discrete emic category.

Rivers extended this important finding, even though the neologisms *emic* and *etic* had not yet been invented in his time. He valiantly organized his material using the accepted (etic) terms of magic and magicians as distinct from religion and priests, as distinct, again, from medicine and leeches. (He revived the old English term *leech* as a generic term to designate physicians in the widest possible sense as specialists in healing, but the revived term never caught on.) Particularly in his lectures to an audience of physicians and surgeons, he constantly bogged down in discrepancies between these (etic) categories and the unique (emic) categories of individual societies upon which they were based.

Rivers described Melanesian customs of supplicating and propitiating ancestral ghosts, activities illustrative of the (etic) category of religion and priests. They took place, however, in rites which otherwise were definitely magical in character. "Where definite rites are performed for the purpose of diagnosis," he wrote, "these often have a religious character, even when the treatment appears to be entirely of a magical order" (Rivers, 1916, p. 117). He also gave examples of the close interdependence of religion and naturalism. Even scientific medicine may incorporate some magico-religious concepts and activities. Frazer and Rivers in combination alert us to the embeddedness of health issues in all societies, including our own, in what we now would call emic patterns of thought and behavior.

Still another important contribution relates to the rationality of non-Western reasoning in health matters. The practice of ethnomedicine is neither illogical nor prelogical, as Lucien Lévy-Bruhl and other contemporaries were suggesting in those days (Lowie, 1937, 216–221). The leechcraft of ethnomedicine is not based upon disconnected and meaningless customs. It is motivated by definite beliefs about etiology and pathology. Modes of treatment make good sense in terms of those beliefs. The underlying ideas may be wrong from a scientific (etic) standpoint, Rivers acknowledged, but however wrong they may be, healing practices (emic) constitute logical consequences of those ideas. Grant the underlying premises, and ethnomedical practices follow with logical consistency. We still find this to be true. No matter how apparently bizarre or even harmful customs may seem to the naive or ethnocentric observer, anthropologists find that people everywhere are intelligent and have good reasons for what they do (Anderson, 1990).

Multidisciplinary Research Aborted

During the early twentieth century, medicine and anthropology remained distinctly isolated from one another as fields of research. Rivers pursued one career as an anthropologist and a separate career as a physician, which left no residue of multidisciplinarity. The high potential of collaboration was not thought of or explored. In lecturing to a medical audience, Rivers did introduce two etic concepts of enormous potential for the study of ethnomedicine. He spoke of diagnosis and prognosis, key organizing categories in Western medicine. He failed, however, to see how his diagnostic skills in biomedicine could be used to gain a perspective on ethnomedical beliefs and practices. Only in the last few decades have some anthropological studies been grounded in the careful diagnosis and prognosis of disease states.

One exception in the work of Rivers dramatizes this still often neglected potential. It provides the first example in the literature of an anthropologist documenting an illness with a medically confirmed diagnosis and prognosis. The case is still instructive. After a few days of illness, a man on Eddystone Island came to Dr. Rivers for treatment. Rivers made the biomedical diagnosis: pneumonia. The course of the disease was well known to every physician at that time. L. F. C. Mees, a Dutch physician, recalls from that epoch:

> In 1920 we were given a lecture on the symptoms of pneumonia. The clinical picture was very exact and minute: someone, say at 4:20 P.M., suddenly feels a sharp pain in his back; he has contracted a chill, begins to cough, and expectorates *"sputa rufa,"* brownish sputum. Blisters (herpes) develop on his lips. A high fever sets in with regular undulations: *"febris continua."* The patient feels very ill, and in the course of days, especially on the fifth and on

the sixth days, the symptoms, fever and misery, come to a climax. On the seventh day (in rare cases on the ninth day), suddenly, the fever disappears. At the same time, the patient feels quite well again, feels even reborn. The fall of temperature was called the crisis, and the increase in symptoms just before the crisis was called the ante-critical aggravation: *"perturbation ante-critica."* (Mees, 1983, p. 140)

The outcome of the disease was also very predictable at that time, as Dr. Mees reminds us many years later:

> Going back to the 1920's, I remember how our professor taught us about the prognosis for pneumonia. Babies under a year, aged people over seventy, and hunchbacks are endangered, we were informed. A healthy person, however, generally overcomes pneumonia. (Mees, 1983, 191-192)

Rivers reconstructed the following history of his patient's treatment. Rivers knew that he was second choice as a health care provider. The man's first resort was a local curer, whom he continued to see while under medical treatment. He also obtained supplemental treatment from a second local curer immediately after his first visit to Rivers. This healer carried out rubbings, spittings, and prayers to treat the chief complaint, which at that time was sweating. What Rivers learned only later was that at least a dozen other practitioners had also been involved. Three of them attempted to counteract sorcery, the presumed ultimate cause.

From an etic point of view, as we have seen, Rivers could predict that the patient would get extremely sick, reach a point of near total collapse, and then suddenly, seemingly miraculously, probably recover. (We now know that near collapse followed by sudden recovery has to do with the time it takes for the immune system to develop disease-specific antibodies.) Rivers was bringing his patient through the characteristic crisis of high fever and extreme debility, after which this particular patient recovered. At exactly that time, the family called in a magician to counter the effects of evil eye. No doubt she was credited with the recovery in emic terms. Yet, the cure was etically predictable based solely on the natural, untreated course of the disease.

A precise etic prognosis can provide a solid pathophysiologic basis for achieving a better understanding of indigenous practices evaluated in emic terms. As recently as 1994, Roderick Wilson reported a comparable sickness episode witnessed by a fellow anthropologist, Jacob Loewen, in Panama. A Christian Indian, who seemed to be dying of pneumonia, was annointed with oil and prayed for by the church elders. She was instantly healed. "Isn't it wonderful," they exclaimed, "this morning Nata was dying and now she is well. . . that Spirit of God is really powerful, when he goes after those fever spirits, they really run!" (Wilson, 1994, p. 204). What is missing in this account is a confirmed diagnosis of the pneumonia and an exact count of the number of days during which she was sick. Rivers was more thorough, and as a result, his old report is more useful. It contributes one possible response to the question asked many years later by Allan Young: Why do personalistic beliefs and practices persist if they are not actually effective as cures? (Young, 1976, p. 6). One answer is that people often get well simply as a consequence of the natural course of the disease, which is what prognosis tells you.

THE SECOND MEDICAL ANTHROPOLOGY BOOK

When Forrest Clements wrote *Primitive Concepts of Disease* in 1932 he failed to acknowledge his debt to Rivers, so I will do it for him (Clements, 1932). In writing about ethnomedicine, Rivers limited himself to one part of the world, namely, Melanesia, New Guinea, and Australia. Building in an obvious way, but without attribution, upon the geographically circumscribed research of Rivers, Clements turned his attention to a very limited number of explanatory beliefs— five to be exact. He plotted their distribution in order, as Rivers would have put it, "to see if they will apply in other parts of the world" (Rivers, 1916, p. 59). In doing that, he employed etic categories that we still use:

- sorcery
- disease-object intrusion
- spirit intrusion
- soul loss
- breach of taboo

Old Ideas Disguised As New

Edward Wellin has criticized this list as a "conceptual morass," because only sorcery and breach of taboo belong to a classification based on causes of illness. The other three are part of a different classification based on the mechanisms by which sorcerers or other personalistic agents achieve their effects (Wellin, 1977, p. 51). In truth, the five categories were not meant to constitute a proper classification as such. They were meant only to list well-known practices and beliefs. It seems obvious that they were drawn directly from the earlier writings of Rivers about magic versus religion. Extrapolating from speculation concerning the hypothetical evolutionary stage of magic, Clements plotted the distribution of (1) sorcery, and of how sorcerers caused illness in using techniques such as (2) disease-object intrusion, (3) spirit intrusion, or (4) soul loss. As for the hypothetical evolutionary stage of religion, Clements plotted the distribution of what Rivers described in his Oceanic examples as the most common form of disease causation by religious means, (5) breach of taboo, with public confession as an associated form of treatment.

Perhaps Clements neglected to make clear the extent to which his work was derivative because Rivers embedded these ethnomedical categories in a seemingly incompatible evolutionary construction that Clements and his

American colleagues had thoroughly repudiated. The five terms provide one more example of how concepts rooted in an older abandoned paradigm can survive their apparent demise to persist as hidden conceptual baggage in the paradigm that takes its place.

The Comparative Method

In the final analysis, the Clements book adds very little to our understanding of ethnomedicine. The author felt that his major achievement was to establish the antiquity of these practices based on the age-area hypothesis. Except to say that they do appear to be old and widespread, one can have but little confidence in his assumption that they can be ranked in chronological sequence, with disease-object intrusion as the oldest and breach of taboo as the most recent. As Irving Hallowell was quick to point out shortly after the book was first published, the methods of comparative research were employed in ways that were inadequate to the task. The underlying geographic documentation was seriously flawed by a failure to apply rigorous standards in defining the cross-cultural (etic) categories, by a reliance upon bibliographic sources of dubious authenticity, and by an inadequate sampling of major regions of the world (Hallowel, 1935). Against this background, the Human Relations Area Files appeared as a great leap forward.

THE HUMAN RELATIONS AREA FILES AND THEORIES OF ILLNESS

One great strength of anthropology is the practice of documenting etic categories of culture, because only by that means can commonalities be identified in societies around the world. This is the comparative method, and as a simple statistical procedure it has been part of the ethnological tool kit from the beginning. As early as 1889, believing that the methods of anthropology needed to be strengthened and systematized, Tylor wrote, "It is my aim to show that the development of institutions may be investigated on a basis of tabulation and classification" (Tylor, 1889). When Tylor developed the concept of animism as a useful etic category, he did so based upon an examination of religious practices from all of the diverse societies for which he could get information.

For many decades, comparative analysis was undertaken in a laborious fashion, as is clear in the old Clements monograph, which includes nine intense pages cryptically listing the bibliographic sources that were consulted. Clements' work is a reminder of how comparative studies were done in the nineteenth and early twentieth centuries. It required days, weeks, and months of steadfastly hunting down often obscure references searching for ethnographic statements relating to the subject under investigation. It was all done by hand, thumbing through library catalogues, tracking down references cited in articles and books, and painstakingly exploring shelves of dusty books. It was not bad, really, for those with a scholarly mind-set who derive pleasure from finding well-hidden nuggets of documentary gold. But it took a lot of time and meant that one could not get on to other projects for months and years at a time. This is where George Peter Murdock came into the picture.

Beginning in 1937 at Yale University, Murdock was instrumental in developing a tool that would permit the kind of research that Tylor and Clements carried out to be done much more rapidly and accurately. Now known as the Human Relations Area Files (HRAF), Murdock's research staff set to work on a project that continues today. Ethnographic details about hundreds of cultures from every part of the world, one by one, were compiled by means of an exhaustive investigation of all published sources. The goal was to present detailed ethnographies of each of the chosen cultures systematically organized according to a standard format.

To achieve this goal, Murdock and his collaborators developed a coding document known as the *Outline of Cultural Materials* (Murdock et al., 1950). Subsequently, Murdock published an *Atlas of World Cultures* (Murdock, 1981). Guided by these documents, researchers can organize information in terms of etic cultural categories that are the same for every society. An enormous resource of cultural documentation is now accessible for more than 700 different aspects of culture, including the food quest, clothing, building and construction, family customs, arts and crafts, and customs relating to health. This permits an investigator rapidly to obtain information on any selected aspect of culture for societies from every major part of the world. For health issues, one can consult the section on sickness. The HRAF domain of sickness makes information easily accessible on hundreds of societies relating to the following categories (Murdock et al., 1950, p. viii):

- preventive medicine
- bodily injuries
- theory of disease
- sorcery
- magical and mental therapy
- psychotherapists
- medical therapy
- medical care
- medical personnel

If this tool had been available when Clements did his study, he could have completed the job in a few weeks by just extracting data from the Theory of Disease category. It should be noted that HRAF researchers struggle hard to cope with the vexing problem of collapsing highly diverse cultural traits into the etic categories of the *Outline.* The results are inevitably only partially satisfying. They sacrifice the comprehensive, holistic approach of an ethnography in order to benefit from making cross-cultural comparisons.

In a major effort to provide an orientation to ethnomedicine by mapping the presence or absence of culture traits, Murdock, Wilson, and Frederick drew upon a sample of 186 widely dispersed cultures (known as the Standard Cross-Cultural Sample) from the HRAF to characterize the worldwide distribution of theories of illness (Murdock et al, 1978). Their findings demonstrate that Clements barely touched on the true cross-cultural diversity and complexity of such theories.

Problems in Documenting Naturalistic Medical Systems

When it comes to ethnographic studies of pragmatic, nonpersonalistic approaches to health care, Rivers took an early tentative step forward. Whereas Frazer merely alluded to naturalism, Rivers addressed it as a part of ethnomedicine, insisting that beliefs in natural causes and treatments occur in every society alongwith of magico-religious beliefs. He characterized naturalism as applying to mundane ailments that are not thought to be life-threatening. They occur with great frequency, however, and can cause great discomfort. They are discussed matter-of-factly and treated empirically in virtually all societies. Rivers failed to follow up this lead to an important area of research, however. He devoted only a few paragraphs to common ailments, what he called "domestic remedies," and left it at that.

Clements also fumbled the ball, so to speak, exactly where Frazer and Rivers failed to run with it. His work would have been much more original and stimulating if he had recorded the occurrence of naturalism free of magico-religious assumptions about etiology and treatment. Rivers provided a lead in that direction, but Clements failed to pick up on it.

Advancing beyond Tylor, Frazer, Rivers, and Clements, Murdock and his colleagues offer a perspective on naturalism as a theory of causation. Regretably, it is a flawed perspective. They conceptualized the issue badly by defining natural causation ethnocentrically as "any theory, scientific or popular, which accounts for the impairment of health as a physiological consequence of some experience of the victim in a manner that would not seem unreasonable to modern medical science" (Murdock et al., 1978, p. 451). To "not seem unreasonable to modern medical science," particularly in the 1970s, was to exclude by definition a vast number of naturalistic medical systems, including Unani, Ayurvedic, Chinese, Latin American humoral medical theory, homeopathic, and chiropractic.

Working with this distorted definition they identified five distinct ways in which people think in terms of natural causation if their concepts are translated from emic into etic:

- infection
- stress
- organic deterioration
- accident
- overt human aggression

They explain that most societies with a theory of infection conceptualize the organisms as tiny insects or worms. Stress, they indicate, can be thought of as physiological, exemplified by overexertion, prolonged hunger and thirst, or extremes of heat and cold. It can also be emotional, including worry and fear. Organic deterioration, they find, is usually associated with aging, but may manifest at other stages of life in ways that are not very clear. Accidents and overt human aggression are thought to result in suffering from physical injury.

The authors of this HRAF study concluded that theories of natural causation are very uncommon in comparison with theories of supernatural causation. This conclusion is flawed. Many naturalistic systems were excluded by definition, as we have seen. Because they worked with a Western medical definition, they were able to identify very few societies that cite infection, stress, organic deterioration, or accidents as major explanations for illness. Only aggression is commonly thought of as an explanation in and of itself.

Murdock and associates conclude with the following observation. "With the striking exception of overt human aggression, and the partial exception of stress, the natural causes of illness receive remarkably little attention in the ethnographic literature" (Murdock et al., 1978, p. 453). This sentence should heighten one's suspicion that the quantification of findings using HRAF data was subverted on this issue. Neither early ethnographers nor contemporary researchers have shown much interest in empirical practice as a part of ethnomedicine. It follows, then, that when the publications of ethnographers are summarized they produce very little information about natural causation. Given this bias in the literature, the prevalence of beliefs in natural causation cannot be determined from the HRAF.

Still one more bias detoured this study. Causation was not coded as natural if supernatural causation was also invoked. In this the HRAF theoreticians failed to acknowledge a tendency in many societies to recognize both proximate and ultimate causes. Frequently, people recognize proximate causes that are natural, such as falling out of trees, and just as frequently they treat patients on naturalistic bases, as by cleansing, massaging, and bandaging bruises. At the same time they may acknowledge an ultimate cause, perhaps an angry ghost who caused someone to fall, and they may also perform rituals, such as an appropriate sacrifice to placate a ghost.

Anthropologists often still do not look closely enough at naturalistic medical systems. "The general tendency," they wrote, "is to personalize the causation of what we term accidents and to attribute them to supernatural intervention. This presumably accounts for the rarity (only 38 of the sample societies) with which the sources cite accident as a cause of illness—and never as a major one" (Murdock et al., 1978, p. 452). It is more likely that Rivers was right. He concluded that natural causation as a theory of disease "is probably universal, though it has attracted little notice beside the more striking customs which show the relation of leechcraft with magic and religion" (Rivers, 1924, p. 40).

In our own time, Arthur Kleinman has described:

> a particular bias on the anthropological study of medicine in society. This happened because most earlier interest in this subject grew out of an anthropological study of religious systems. As a result, the non-sacred aspects of sickness and treatment received little attention until fairly recently. . . . This bias, I predict, will not be found in most future medical anthropologies. (Kleinman, 1986 [1978], p. 47)

This HRAF study is more useful in summarizing personalistic as opposed to naturalistic medical systems. It provides an expanded classification of explanatory concepts capable, they felt, of functioning as etic categories for cross-cultural research.

Theories of Mystical Causation

Bodily harm can occur without the intervention of any sorcerer or supernatural being. This kind of causation includes:

- fate
- ominous sensations (dreams, sights, feelings that cause illness)
- contagion (e.g., contact with menstrual blood or a corpse)
- mystical retribution (punishment for breaking a taboo or moral injunction)

Theories of Animistic Causation

According to these beliefs, health is impaired animistically by a hostile ghost, spirit, or god. The mechanisms are:

- soul loss (by thievery)
- spirit aggression (the attack of a malevolent or affronted being)

Ideas About Magical Causation

Harm can originate in covert magical acts of a human being who is envious, affronted, or malicious. They can accomplish their evil ends by:

- sorcery (by a person who knows magical practices)
- witchcraft (by a person endowed with evil power)

This comparative analysis of theories of disease is shot through with unresolved and unrecognized distortions. Nonetheless, the HRAF constituted an improved methodology for systematically documenting the diversity of health practices on a worldwide basis. Its usefulness has been demonstrated in correlational studies.

THE HRAF FOR CORRELATIONAL STUDIES

Historical particularism based upon distribution maps and hypothetical reconstructions of the diffusion of cultural traits based on these maps came and went as a major paradigm in anthropology. The HRAF and associated statistical techniques, however, are still used as tools of the comparative method to test hypotheses relating to how culture traits, including those relating to health, tend to coexist or to be mutually exclusive.

One enduring benefit of the HRAF is to permit the use of quantitative methods for determining how health and sickness are complexly enmeshed with other parts of culture. Functional theory, one of the mid-twentieth-century paradigms that displaced historical particularism, postulates that every culture constitutes a complex whole in which behaviors and values fit together (or fail to fit) in complex ways. The HRAF survived from one paradigm to the next to offer one way to investigate interconnections within cultures.

The first significant correlational study based on the HRAF contributing to the emerging field of medical anthropology was a monograph, *Paiute Sorcery* (1950), authored by Beatrice Blyth Whiting (Whiting, 1950). The Paiute presently live in southeastern Oregon along the northern border of California. Historically they comprised mobile hunting and gathering bands of families whose lives were oriented around a late-surviving version of a Stone Age kind of quest for food. Their ancient way of life was destroyed by the white man's takeover. After signing a treaty with the government of the United States in the nineteenth century, they were expelled from their traditional homeland. Apparently the treaty was forced on them as a way to get control of mineral resources on their terrain. Subsequent to relocation they could no longer support themselves by hunting and gathering because most of the land had come under private ownership by European-Americans. Some Indians found jobs in local industry and on ranches. In the 1920s it was recorded that they suffered from chronic hunger and disease. Many were forced to scavenge for food from garbage cans, a sad and desperate perversion of "hunting and gathering," but their religious beliefs and social values survived these tribulations. These were the Paiute Indians Whiting worked with when she carried out her field study in the mid-1930s.

The Naturalistic Medical System

Before we explore how Whiting used the HRAF for a correlational study, let us take advantage of her basic local ethnography to set the stage. First, as concerns naturalism, she confirmed that Paiute ideas about how people got sick included natural causation in cases of minor afflictions and minor therapeutic techniques. Prominent in Paiute thinking were beliefs and practices relating to rheumatic pains and headaches. These were thought to be caused by circulatory stagnation, referred to as "bad blood." It was believed that old degenerated blood turned dark red or even green, became hot, sometimes expanded too much, and might then harden inside the body. Appropriate treatment was administered by specialists in bloodletting. Herbal poultices offered an additional form of physiologically based treatment for bodily pains.

Naturalism was documented also for the treatment of infections of the eyelids (trachoma). The discomfort of a sty or a trachomatous roughness on the inner eyelid were thought of as a physiological problem that could be treated by scraping the inflamed area with rye grass. Some individuals specialized in this kind of treatment. Other diseases conceptualized in naturalistic terms included snakebites, sprains, and broken bones.

The Personalistic Medical System

In order to understand Paiute theories of disease, one must realize that they distinguished proximate from ultimate causes. For example, trachoma, an infection in which the cornea is damaged by a proliferation of diseased tissue on the inner eyelid, was treated pragmatically by scraping. The diagnosis and treatment were conceptualized in naturalistic terms. If abrasion of the cornea evolved into blindness, the explanation was switched from naturalism as a proximate cause to belief that a supernatural event was the ultimate cause. One sightless Paiute who talked with Whiting went blind, the anthropologist was told, because the eagle, a spirit helper, became angry that the man had not obeyed instructions he had been given in a dream.

Whiting found that most Paiute concepts of causation were based upon supernatural assumptions. She recorded four such categories of causation belief, corresponding to four of Murdock's eight HRAF categories: contagion, mystical retribution, spirit aggression, and sorcery.

For the Paiute, the most prominent form of contagion was contact with menstrual blood. Mystical retribution took place when someone failed to recognize or obey the demands of one's own spirit helper. One curer, for example, fell ill because she disobeyed her spirit helper who required that she never treat without getting paid, and she had scraped the trachomatous lesion of an impoverished man free of charge. Spirit aggression was thought of as being attacked by a ghost who stole one's breath. Sorcery was blamed in cases where it was believed that someone was killed or made sick by a person who used magic, usually by magically shooting a harmful substance into the victim's body (object intrusion).

The other four HRAF categories of causation were not found among these Paiute. Anyone undertaking research such as that done by Whiting would find it useful to inquire about each of the latter four as a way to make sure that one or another of the common etiological beliefs was not inadvertently overlooked: fate, ominous sensations, soul loss, and witchcraft.

Correlational Analysis and Theory

In her analysis of the Paiute, Whiting demonstrated a connection between sickness and sorcery on the one hand, and the maintenance of communal tranquility on the other. Taking note of the cultural embeddedness of health care beliefs and practices, she offered an early example of the association of health and politics. The traditional community possessed no governmental superstructure. In the face of interpersonal or factional disagreements and confrontations neither judges nor police could ensure order. Nevertheless, informal mechanisms worked effectively to place checks on antisocial behavior.

Of greatest interest was the fear of being accused of being a sorcerer. Children learned to dampen expressions of anger, always to be polite, and never to laugh at people. From childhood on, individuals were taught to avoid all actions that might lead to acquiring a reputation for sorcery, because sorcerers might be attacked, forced to flee the community, or even killed by communal vigilantes.

An equally strong sanction on behavior was the fear that forbidden behavior might result in being sorcerized. The implicit rule was, behave yourself or your enemy might make you deathly ill. Thus, Mrs. P. was said to have retaliated against a presumed thief, Mrs. S., by killing the latter's mother. Mrs. S. seems to have been in general disrepute, since it was reported that she later developed a badly swollen eye caused by a woman whose husband she had seduced. Mrs. P. for her part was equally in general disrepute. She was known to have power in snakes and was accused when Mr. M. woke up feeling ill one morning after dreaming that a snake encircled his neck and choked him. She agreed to annul the attack by bathing, which resulted in his complete recovery; but later she killed him anyway, it was said. This kind of thinking, Whiting argued, encouraged most people to behave in a circumspect fashion so that no one would want to sorcerize them or accuse them of being sorcerers.

To this point we have examined *Paiute Sorcery* as an emic case study in which the author demonstrated that a particular belief in disease causation not only shaped approaches to the treatment of disease, but also functioned in the maintenance of public order. This is an early example of a kind of anthropological understanding that only the upper part of vertical thinking can produce. Researchers in medicine and surgery do not make contributions of this sort. Anthropologists are needed if it is to be done.

An old problem for anthropologists led Whiting to the next stage in this research project. Her findings relating to health beliefs among the Paiute were of great theoretical interest, but they were of limited value if they applied only to one small population. She needed to investigate the extent to which her findings might illustrate a cross-cultural regularity. The HRAF made this possible.

The way she did it was to formulate the following hypothesis: Where political institutions authorized to administer punishment are not present, sorcery will be important in beliefs about the causes of disease and death. Conversely, where agencies such as chiefs or councils possess the authority to administer punishment, sorcery will be unimportant.

Using a worldwide sample of 50 societies, the hypothesis was confirmed: 60 percent of societies lacking judicial institutions were characterized as attaching great importance to sorcery, while 24 percent that had judicial institutions did not attach importance to sorcery. In all, 84 percent of societies for which information was available provided strong support for her hypothesis (Thomas, 1986, p. 449). Whiting had her generalization.

CHILD REARING AND BELIEFS ABOUT DISEASE CAUSATION

In research closely associated with that of Beatrice Whiting, John Whiting experienced the potential benefits of multidisciplinarity when he collaborated with a psychologist, Irvin Child, using the HRAF to explore a very different kind of possible association. Their investigation examined the relationship between beliefs about what causes disease on the one hand, and child–training practices on the other (Whiting & Child, 1953).

The hypothesis tested by Whiting and Child was based on Freudian psychoanalytic theory. Freudian theory postulates that the earliest years of an infant's experience shape its adult personality and behavior. We have already seen that this postulate has not held up well. However, it is the research methodology that concerns us here rather than the findings.

In the first year of life, according to Freud, babies experience the world with overwhelming attention to the mouth and tongue as they suckle, eat, and touch. By the second year, the focus tends to be directed heavily to excretion. The anus becomes what Freud called an erogenous zone. Later, the genitals become important. In addition, infants develop feelings about dependence versus independence and aggression versus passivity. Societies vary in how they train and nurture growing infants and children to resolve issues relating to these five systems of behavior: oral, anal, sexual, dependence, and aggression.

An important aspect of Freudian theory postulates a process referred to as fixation. Hypothetically, the fixation process occurs when an individual experiences excessive frustration or excessive gratification oriented around any of the five systems. According to this hypothesis, adult behavior will subsequently be shaped strongly by a persistence of influence from that specific erogenous zone.

Whiting and Child specifically identified negative fixations or anxieties as important for their hypothesis. Was a baby often denied the breast or weaned early or in an unfeeling manner? These experiences could result in a negative oral fixation; anxieties would tend to get embodied in motion or sensation around the lips and mouth. Was the baby subjected to early and strict toilet training that could initiate a negative anal fixation expressed as a tendency to focus anxieties on the buttocks and rectum? Was sexual indulgence frustrated or punished?

Was the infant trained to early independence, thus frustrating its unconscious wishes for dependence? Were aggressive behaviors such as temper tantrums, disobedience, and acting out of physical or verbal agonism severely forbidden? Some societies seem to be frustrating and anxiety producing in one or another of these domains while others are apparently indulgent and gratifying.

In order to explore the extent to which these areas of anxiety were correlated with beliefs about disease etiology, Whiting and Child developed a psychoanalytically based typology of the causal explanations they encountered in different societies.

Oral Explanations

Illness can be caused by eating or drinking something toxic. In addition, based upon psychoanalytic assumptions, verbal spells and incantations performed by sorcerers are considered oral causes because the mouth is used in speaking.

Anal Explanations

Constipation or diarrhea or some other circumstance affecting defecation is thought to cause sickness. One can also fall ill from smelling or having contact with feces or urine. One common kind of anal explanation is that contagious magic was performed on food leavings, nail parings, hair cuttings, sex excretions, saliva, or blood (including menstrual) as well as feces. Psychoanalytic theory would lead one to assume that individuals who were subject to severe toilet training will tend to grow up being compulsive about daily activities and reliant on ritualized behaviors. Treatments requiring the compulsive and ritualistic use of charms, curses, spells, or incantations are classified as anal explanations. Failure to perform any of these rituals will cause illness. It appears that spells and incantations can be considered either oral or anal. This ambiguity of interpretation is disturbing to scientists who always like tidy hypotheses.

Sexual Explanations

Engaging in sexual activities of specified kinds can cause sickness as can contact with sex excretions or (again) menstrual blood.

Dependence Explanations

Here one really needs to be initiated into the esoterica of psychoanalytic theory to grasp the point. Soul loss illustrates a dependence explanation because it may indicate concern about a metaphorical or supernatural dependence upon one's parents or parent surrogates. Similarly, spirit possession is a dependence explanation because it reflects concern about metaphorical or supernatural dependence, although not clearly upon parent figures.

Aggression Explanations

Sickness can occur if one is aggressive towards, or disobedient to, spirits. Illness from poison is explained as aggression if it is believed to be object intrusion rather than ingestion by mouth (another ambiguity here, this time of oral versus aggressive). One can be wounded by an imaginary spear or other invisible weapon as another form of aggression.

But let us return to the Whiting/Child hypothesis, which asserts that when a society uses repression in early socialization, the category of repression most frequently used will be highly correlated with the category used to explain adult illness.

When this hypothesis of negative fixation was tested cross-culturally it appeared to be confirmed. The most striking single confirmation emerged in the association between oral socialization anxiety and oral explanations of disease. Conformation for aggressive behavior was almost as strong. The hypothesis relating to dependence was confirmed, but not impressively. The anal and sexual systems showed no more than slight tendencies in the direction of the hypothesis. The authors concluded that customs relating to child rearing do differ from one society to another, and that customary ideas about the causes of disease also vary. Most importantly, they concluded that the two domains of custom tend to vary concordantly.

Statistical Pitfalls

A reanalysis of the Whiting and Child documentation came to my attention in a book by Richard Shweder (Shweder, 1991, pp. 281–284). He reported the findings of an unpublished secondary analysis of the original data by R. Costanzo. The reanalysis confirmed what is reported above. Oral socialization anxiety is correlated with oral explanations for the causes of sickness and the coefficient of correlation (r) is probably not just due to chance (r = .49). So far so good, but there is more! The oral explanation correlates even more strongly with anal explanations (r = .60) and sexual explanations (r = .67). As if that were not enough, the reanalysis also reveals that oral socialization anxiety predicts anal explanations (r = .60) better than do anal fixations (r = .45). Further, oral anxiety predicts sexual explanations (r= .67) better than do sexual fixations (r = .33).

In short, even the one apparently strong correlation that was predicted in the hypothesis (oral fixations with oral explanations) is disqualified. None of the strong correlations identified in secondary analysis make any sense in terms of the effects of child-rearing practices on beliefs and practices related to sickness. The proposed explanatory scheme was very convincing, but when tested statistically in a thorough way, it failed. Cause and effect in human behavior is simply not that simple.

Naturalism and Efficacy

It can be important in any effort to understand a healing system to determine if a diagnosis can be made in pathophysiologic (etic) terms or if a treatment is effective in clinical (etic) terms (Glasser, 1988: Anderson 1991). This first became a serious issue in the work of Whiting and Child.

After presenting evidence for their hypothesis of a correlation between negative fixation and beliefs about etiology, Whiting and Child presented a second hypothesis that related positive fixations with variability in treatment practices. Negative fixation and positive fixation, they argued, are distinct processes which need to be explored separately. Consistent with this observation, they hypothesized that if one of the five systems of behavior was eroticized through gratification and indulgence in infancy and childhood, it would shape not how the cause was understood, but how medicine was given or therapy applied as a culturally shaped practice of adults. For example, societies that created lasting satisfaction in oral activity would be expected to treat diseases by swallowing food, herbal teas, or other medicines while those with positive anal fixations would favor enemas and suppositories.

No general support for the hypothesis was found. Initial positive fixations maintained into adulthood were not shown to influence therapeutic practices. Why did this general hypothesis fail? Several possible explanations were offered, all couched in psychoanalytic terms. For example, they argued, perhaps a positive fixation is not intrinsically as real and lasting as a negative fixation because later, more mature experiences tend to extinguish these modes of gratification.

It is disappointing to discover that they failed to consider the possible influence of naturalistic thinking. If, on a purely pragmatic basis, people discover that a treatment works well as a palliative or a cure, that treatment will tend to be used regardless of erogenous zones and psychodynamic fixations.

Their own research offers a justification for this assumption. They provide several examples of pragmatism overriding the force of the unconscious, beginning with fractures. "Setting broken bones has an obvious reward value of a realistic character," and no history of oral fixation will divert the healer from taking that practical measure (Whiting & Child, 1953, pp. 211–212). Other examples include the ingestion of warm liquids to improve bodily comfort, poultices or skin-pricking for pain, quinine for malarial fever, and aspirin for headache.

The failure to apply biomedical etic standards was no better a quarter of a century later when Murdock, Wilson, and Frederick surveyed religious beliefs about healing. Admonishing their readers not to overlook the "substantial component of sound pragmatic knowledge" in "primitive medicine," Murdock, Wilson, and Frederick illustrated that long overdue claim by describing what they believed to be efficacious practices among the Ganda (of Uganda), Samoans, Aztecs, and Incas (Murdock, Wilson, & Frederick, 1978, pp. 449–450). Taken together, these examples of "sound pragmatic knowledge" included:

- bonesetting
- massage
- sweat baths
- blistering
- herbal remedies such as chaulmoogra oil, coca, and quinine
- washing and replacing disemboweled intestines
- sewing wounds with hair
- emetics to make one vomit
- purgatives to cause defecation
- ointments
- poultices
- cupping
- bleeding
- lancing
- bathing and bandaging cuts
- trepanation (cutting a hole in the skull)

Such treatments may or may not be beneficial. The authors offer absolutely no evidence to confirm their assumption that these treatments change pathology. In addition, no mention is made of unwanted side effects. No attention is given to indications and contraindications or when they work and when they do not. These unacknowledged issues in this HRAF study suggest that anthropologists and physicians share an important basis for multidisciplinarity in research on naturalism in ethnomedicine and the documentation of whether or not people get better with ethnotherapy.

Recent HRAF Research

HRAF-based comparative research relating to health issues continues to be done (Bourguignon & Greenbaum, 1973; Greenbaum 1973; Bourguignon, 1991). As one recent example, Michael Winkelman was able to demonstrate that shamans who diagnose and heal while in an altered state of awareness are (were) predictably found in hunting and gathering societies lacking formal class stratification and formal administrative political roles beyond the local community.

These communities closely resemble the kind of societies in which Beatrice Whiting found beliefs about sorcery functioning as a means of social control in the absence of local leadership. It is not entirely clear how one should reconcile these two studies, but apparently they are not incompatible, since small community shamans are often not particularly influential on the community level (Winkelman, 1986; Winkelman, 1990).

In terms of the attention we have given to early evolutionary theory and the ways in which that early paradigm has been carried along as hidden baggage in replacement paradigms, it is notable that it persists in the current work of Winkelman. Based on correlations identified by subjecting his data to a number of complex statistical techniques, Winkelman proposes an evolutionary model. As social and economic conditions change over time from (1) hunting and gathering (which, I would remind you, characterized the Upper Paleolithic and Mesolithic) to (2) agriculture (which would have begun with Neolithic villages) to (3) political integration and socioeconomic class stratification (which was introduced with early urban societies), the Winkelman model proposes a corresponding development from (1) shamans as the only practitioners of the sacred to (2) shamans, nontrance healers, and priests to (3) a still larger number of practitioners made up of shamans, nontrance healers, mediums, sorcerers, witches, and priests (Winkelman, 1990, p. 327).

With this model, anthropology has progressed during the course of a century of research from a nineteenth-century succession model that assumed that shamans were replaced by priests to a more complex twentieth-century additive model that on the face of it seems to fit better with what we encounter anecdotally. However, those working with HRAF data still have some "puzzle solving" to do. As Beatrice Whiting demonstrated, sorcerers are found in simple hunting, gathering, and fishing societies as agents of conflict and social control. Quite inexplicably, they are not found on this evolutionary level in the Winkelman model.

METHODOLOGICAL ISSUES

The extent to which the HRAF will be useful in the future for health-related research will depend on how flexible and adaptive it proves to be as it continues to develop as a research tool. Attention needs to be given to the information that is included in the database, to how samples are selected by researchers using the files, and to which new cultures will be added as the files continue to expand.

Information in the Database

Many topics are not adequately documented in the files. In the words of Erika Bourguignon and Lenora Greenbaum, "many vital aspects of society are not covered by the Atlas, and, therefore, extension both of ethnographic research and of Atlas coding to provide more complete data for all societies seems eminently desirable." Investigators often find it necessary to rearrange data into their own coding categories (Bourguignon & Greenbaum, 1968, pp. 8–10; Jorgensen, 1979; Dow et al., 1984). As an example, we saw in the HRAF study of illness theories that naturalistic medical practices were inadequately described.

Selecting the Cross-Cultural Sample

A fundamental assumption behind correlational studies using HRAF data is that cultures in the sample display similarities that result from the tendency for human beings anywhere in the world to respond to similar circumstances in comparable ways (psychic unity) (Cohen, 1968 pp. 402–448). If two or more societies are neighbors who could have borrowed from one another, then similarities among them can be attributed to diffusion and should not be counted for statistical purposes as separate and independent examples of the playing out of evolutionary adaptations. All societies in the sample should be historically out of touch with one another. Because Sir Francis Galton was the first to draw attention to this source of interpretive distortion, it is known as Galton's problem (Naroll and D'Andrade, 1963). On this basis, it is not acceptable that Whiting and Child counted the Hopi and Zuñi as two separate societies for statistical purposes, since they are neighbors with a long history of mutual influence.

George Murdock and Douglas White took steps to make the HRAF more user-friendly as concerns Galton's problem (Murdock & White, 1969). They proposed the Standard Cross-Cultural Sample of 186 cultures selected to represent independent cultures from every major part of the world as well as several representing past civilizations such as Babylonia and Rome. This was the sample that was selected for the illness theories study. Winkelman used a 25 percent subsample of the SCCS for his comparative analysis of shamanism.

Later a Quality Control Sample was selected, inspired by Raoul Naroll, who saw a need to differentiate files on the basis of the extent to which the field research was done well (Naroll, 1969; Legacé, 1979). Although these predrawn samples can be very useful for initial cross-cultural studies, comparativists often find that they need to select a project-specific sample based on the kinds of data they will require. The files are often not as user-friendly as was originally intended (Otterbein, 1989; White, 1990, Otterbein; 1990).

Adding New Cultures

The most common cultures in the files are those of small-scale band, tribal, and peasant communities. Most of them no longer exist as they were when the basic ethnographies were published. The influence of the urban-industrial world is usually not recorded. While useful studies can be conducted with these files, it seems clear that other valuable work is not possible because they do not include enough contemporary information. The HRAF needs to broaden its coverage to include "immigrant communities, peripatetic groups, folk cultures enmeshed in modern nations, religious groups, cultural regions, ethnic groups, and minority groups." (Levinson, 1990). Expanding the database to incorporate types of cultures not now included could enhance the theoretical and explanatory power of the HRAF and keep it viable as a research tool.

CONCLUSION

Paradigm shifts in the history of anthropology do not support Kuhn's contention that they document complete breaks of the present with the past. Rather, one encounters continuity in the guise of old ideas that resurface as new concepts and theories. This continuity included a continuing orientation to personalistic medical systems, an area of research that remains one of the strengths of medical anthropology. However, it also included a continuity of neglect well into the mid-twentieth century regarding naturalistic medical systems and a failure to appreciate the value of a multidisciplinarity of anthropologists and physicians.

Continuity did not preclude change. Important new developments did occur within a given paradigm as time passed. Methodologically, this took place with the creation of the HRAF. In terms of theory, the HRAF was first applied to older diffusionist problems, but later was seized upon for new kinds of correlational studies attempting to document the embeddedness of health behaviors and beliefs in cultures as a whole.

The paradigm shift to follow that of diffusion theory is said to have begun in 1924, based on changes that can be detected in the anthropological literature (Stern & Bohannan, 1970). The exact date is not as important as the nature of the change. Time and space dimensions expressing an etic outlook took a back seat as cultural anthropologists gave their attention to in-depth emic studies of small communities in the here and now. It was a time to perfect methods of acquiring data in the field and to develop emic-oriented theories to explicate cultural processes. With the passage of time, it led to the kind of ethnology Beatrice Whiting carried out in her theory of sorcery and social control.

REFERENCES

Anderson, R. (1964). Lapp racial classifications as scientific myths. In A. Montagu (Ed.), *The concept of race* (pp. 61-85). New York: The Free Press.

Anderson, R. (1990). Chiropractors for and against vaccines. *Medical Anthropology, 12,* 169-186.

Anderson, R. (1991). The efficacy of ethnomedicine: Research methods in trouble, *Medical Anthropology, 13,* 1-17.

Becher, T. (1989). *Academic tribes and territories: Intellectual enquiry and the cultures of disciplines.* Bristol, PA: Open University Press.

Bourguignon, E. (1991). *Possession.* Prospect Heights, IL: Waveland Press.

Bourguignon, E., & Greenbaum, L. (1968). *Diversity and homogeneity: A comparative analysis of societal characteristics based on data from the ethnographic atlas.* (Occasional Papers in Anthropology, No. l) Department of Anthropology, Ohio State University.

Bourguignon, E., & Greenbaum, L. S. (1973). *Diversity and homogeneity in world societies.* New Haven, CT:HRAF Press.

Clements, F. E. (1932). *Primitive concepts of disease. University of California Publications in American Archaeology and Ethnology, 32,* 185-252.

Cohen, Y. A. (1968). Macroethnology: Large-scale comparative studies. In Cohen, Y. Al, (Ed.), *Scope and methods of the science of man* (pp.402-448). Boston: Houghton Mifflin.

Dow, M. M., Burton, M. L., White, D. R., Reitz, K. P. (1984). Galton's problem as new-work autocorrelation. *American Ethnologist, 11,* 754-770.

Fisher, L. E., & Werner, O. (1978). Explaining explanation: Tension in American anthropology. *Journal of Anthropological Research, 34,* 194-218.

Glasser, M. (1988). Accountability of anthropologists, indigenous healers and their governments: A plea for reasonable medicine. *Social Science and Medicine, 27,* 1461-1464.

Good, M. J. D., & Good, B. J. (1989). Disabling practitioners: Hazards of learning to be a doctor in American medical education. *American Journal of Orthopsychiatry, 59,* 303-309.

Greenbaum, L. (1973). Social correlates of possession trance in sub-Saharan Africa. In E. Bourguignon, (Ed.), *Religion, altered states of consciousness, and social change.* Columbus: Ohio State University Press.

Hallowell, I. (1935). Primitive concepts of disease. *American Anthropologist, 37,* 365-368.

Harris, M. (1968). *The rise of anthropological theory.* New York: Thomas Y. Crowell.

Jorgensen, J. (1979). Cross-cultural comparisons. *Annual Review of Anthropology, 8,* 309-371.

Kleinman, A. (1986). Concepts and a model for the comparison of medical systems as cultural systems. In C. Currer, & M. Stacey, (Eds), *Concepts of health, illness and disease: A comparative perspective* (pp.27-47). Oxford: Berg (Original work published 1978).

Kroeber, A. L. (1948). *Anthropology.* New York: Harcourt, Brace and Company.

Kuhn, T. S. *The structure of scientific revolutions (2nd ed.).* Chicago: University of Chicago Press.

Legacé, R. O. (1979). The HRAF probability sample: Retrospect and prospect. *Behavior Science Research, 14,* 211-229.

Levinson, D. (1990). Comparative cross-cultural studies: A new opportunity. *Cultural Anthropology Methods Newsletter, 2* (2), 10.

Lowie, R. H. (1937). *The history of ethnological theory.* New York: Rinehart & Co.

McGrane, B. (1989). *Beyond anthropology: Society and the other.* New York: Columbia University Press.

Mees, L. F. C. (1983). *Blessed by illness.* Hudson, NY: Anthroposophic Press.

Murdock G. P. (1981). *Atlas of world cultures.* Pittsburgh: University of Pittsburgh Press.

Murdock, G. P. et al. (1950). *Outline of cultural materials* (3rd ed). New Haven: Human Relations Area Files, Inc.

Murdock, G. P., Wilson, S. F., & Frederick, V. (1978). World distribution of theories of illness. *Ethnology, XVII* (4), 449-470.

Murdock, G. P., & White, D. W. (1969). Standard cross-cultural sample. *Ethnology, 8,* 329-369.

Naroll, R., (1969). The proposed HRAF probability sample. *Behavior Science Notes, 2,* p.70-80.

Naroll, R., & D'Andrade, R. G. (1963). Two further solutions to Galton's problem. *American Anthropologist, 65,* 1053-1067.

Otterbein, K. F. (1989). Sampling and samples—An update. *Cultural Anthropology Methods Newsletter 1* (2), 4-5.

Otterbein, K. F. (1990). Two styles of cross-cultural research. *Cultural Anthropology Methods Newsletter 2* (3), 6-7.

Pike, K. (1954). *Language in relation to a unified theory of structure of human behavior* (vol. I). Glendale, CA: Summer Institute of Linguistics.

Rappaport, Roy A. (1984). Pigs for the ancestors: Ritual in the ecology of a New Guinea people (2nd ed., pp. xv-xvi.) New Haven: Yale University Press.

Rivers, W. H. R. (1916). *Medicine, magic, and religion. Lancet,* 1, 59-65. 117-123.

Rivers, W. H. R. (1924). *Medicine, magic, and religion.* London: Kegan Paul, Trench, Trubner & Co., Ltd.

Rogge, A. E. (1976). A look at academic anthropology: Through a graph darkly. *American Anthropologist, 78,* 829-843.

Shweder, R. A. (1991) *Thinking through cultures: Expeditions in cultural psychology.* Cambridge, MA: Harvard University Press,

Singer, P. (1990). "Psychic surgery": Close observation of a popular healing practice. *Medical Anthropology Quarterly, 4,* 443-451.

Stern, G., & Bohannan, P. (1970). *American Anthropologist:* The first eighty years. *Newsletter of the American Anthropological Association, 11* (10), 1, 6-12.

Thomas, D. H. (1986). *Refiguring anthropology: First principles of probability & statistics.* Prospect Heights, IL: Waveland Press.

Tylor, E. B. (1889). On a method of investigating the development of institutions; Applied to laws of marriage and descent. *Journal of the Royal Anthropological Institute, 18,* 245-269.

Wellin, E. (1977). Theoretical orientation in medical anthropology: Continuity and change over the past half-century. In D. Landy, (Ed.), *Culture, disease, and healing: Studies in medical anthropology* (pp. 47-58). New York: Macmillan.

White, D. R. (1990). Sampling and samples—Five critical issues. *Cultural Anthropology Methods Newsletter, 2* (1), 9, 11.

Whiting, B. B. (1950). *Paiute sorcery.* Viking Fund Publications in Anthropology (No. 15).

Whiting, J. W. M., & Child, I. L. (1953). *Child training and personality: A cross-cultural study.* New Haven, CT: Yale University Press.

Wilson, C. R. (1994). Seeing they see not. D. E. Young, & J. G. (Eds.) Goulet *Being changed: The anthropology of extraordinary experience* (pp. 197-208). Peterborough, Ontario, Canada: Broadview Press.

Winkelman, M. J. (1986). Magico-religious practitioner types and socioeconomic conditions. *Behavior Science Research 20* (1-4), 17-46.

Winkelman, M. J. (1990). Shamans and other "magico-religious" healers: A cross-cultural study of their origins, nature, and social transformations. *Ethos, 18,* 308-352.

Young, A. (1976). Some implications of medical beliefs and practices for social anthropology. *American Anthropologist, 78,* 5-24.

Chapter 5

ETHNOGRAPHIC METHODS

FROM GLOBAL COMPARISONS TO COMMUNITY STUDIES

A third major paradigm shift took place when anthropologists began to direct their attention away from the etic breadth of evolutionary and cross-cultural studies in order to carry out field studies of small communities in emic depth. This substitution of depth for breadth resulted in the elaboration of new theories (structural and functional, as we shall see) and in the development of new research methods. A steady improvement in research design has continued to the present.

Bronislaw Malinowski modeled a new way to do fieldwork by living among the Trobriand Islanders for a long time. He made a virtue of necessity, since his lengthy fieldwork in part was a compromise with the exigencies of World War I. The Australian government restricted his movements to a remote island as a form of internment, because technically he was considered an enemy alien. Facilitated by his long sojourn among the Trobrianders, he elaborated a practice of fieldwork based on participant observation. As Frazer saw it in rather idealized terms, "Dr. Malinowski lived as a native among the natives for many months together, watching them daily at work and at play, conversing with them in their own tongue, and deriving all of his information from the surest sources—personal observation and statements made to him directly by the natives in their own language without the intervention of an interpreter" (Frazer, 1961 [1922], pp. vii–viii). With Malinowski, the movement towards increased rigor in ethnographic research progressed considerably.

The improvement of standards of objectivity in ethnographic documentation was a gradual process. Many people as late as the eighteenth century still accepted the claim of Pliny the Elder that in remote parts of the world some people carried their faces like deep relief sculptures on their chests, or faced life with heads like dogs, swishing tails to match. Nineteenth-century anthropologists, although no longer misled by Pliny, nonetheless often constructed theoretical edifices on questionable foundations of information transmitted from unreliable sources. E. B. Tylor and James Frazer were seminal nineteenth-century theorists despite the fact that neither of them carried out field ethnography. They relied on the reports of innocents abroad: travelers, adventurers, traders, diplomatic personnel, and missionaries.

These early armchair theorists were not naive about the issue of authenticity. Eventually they took steps towards a more systematic approach. Tylor in particular corresponded with missionaries and others, encouraging them to ask about aspects of culture in which he was interested. This led to the publication in 1874 of the first edition of *Notes and Queries in Anthropology, for the Use of Travellers and Residents in Uncivilized Lands,* put together largely through the efforts of Tylor. Over the years, *Notes and Queries* was revised several times. Rivers was largely responsible for a much expanded fourth edition in 1912 (Stocking, 1983).

In those days it was thought that educated people abroad could sit down with English-speaking natives or work through translators and fill in answers to questions about any aspect of culture. Needless to say, such a procedure left much room for faulty translations and subjective distortions. To move beyond these shortcomings, some anthropologists became field-workers. Haddon, Seligman, and Rivers on the Torres Straits Expedition collected their own information. Rivers developed a particularly effective technique for working out family relationships in societies where kinship practices were greatly different from those of the English.

In the United States, Lewis Henry Morgan and other Americans took advantage of the proximity of American Indians to do fieldwork several decades before British and European ethnographers, who had to travel to distant places for their first encounters with non-Western tribal cultures. Because the theoretical orientation of these nineteenth-century American anthropologists was on the reconstruction of human cultural evolution, they tended to pay almost no attention to the contemporary scene. Before their eyes, land grabs and racial discrimination were destroying Indian societies and cultures, but on the whole they were interested in the past, not the present. They preferred to work with key informants, older individuals with good recall and excellent language skills, who would tell them about life in "the old days." Understandably, we call this "memory culture."

The significance of the Torres Straits Expedition now becomes clear. Because Haddon, Seligman, and Rivers were visiting peoples with essentially intact societies and cultures, customs as lived rather than customs as recalled became the objects of research. The attitudes of the ethnographers were still those of the authors of *Notes and Queries,* however. Although they questioned people about their present lives, they relied heavily on a standard set of questions meant to be used any place in the world. A typical day was spent on the veranda of a house at a colonial outpost quizzing natives who were invited to come to the ethnographer to be interrogated. Radcliffe-Brown worked this way on the Andaman Islands. Even Margaret Mead in the mid-1920s in Samoa did much of her work that way. She stayed in the home of a petty officer of the United States

Navy who was posted on the island. There she talked with young women and girls on his family porch (Mead, 1961). Later she recalled that experience:

> But I really did not know much about field work. The course on methods that Professor Boas taught was not about field work. It was about theory—how material could be organized to support or to call in question some theoretical point. . . . [Before leaving for Samoa] I had a half hour's instruction in which Professor Boas told me that I must be willing to seem to waste time just sitting about and listening (Mead, 1972, pp. 137–138)

PARTICIPANT OBSERVATION

This was the state of the art when Malinowski set a new standard for fieldwork, a standard that had not yet influenced American anthropologists such as Boas and Mead later in the 1920s. As a young man, while recuperating from chronic illness, Malinowski read *The Golden Bough* and experienced an intellectual conversion. This led him to change from physics and mathematics, in which he had earned a Ph.D. in Poland, to anthropology, in which he subsequently earned a D.Sc. degree in England.

Although inspired by Frazer, Malinowski moved beyond Frazer in both method and theory. He demanded better ethnographic data as an essential requirement. In doing field studies, cut yourself off from European settlements, he advised. Proper ethnographic work can be accomplished only by "remaining in as close contact with the natives as possible, which really can only be achieved by camping right in their villages." With obvious reference to how his contemporaries worked with native respondents he concluded, "And by means of this natural intercourse you learn to know him, and you become familiar with his customs and beliefs far better than when he is a paid, and often bored, informant" (Malinowski, 1961, pp. 6–7).

Later this approach came to be referred to as participant observation. At heart the method implies spending a long time in the field, living in the community, and speaking the language. It now often includes participation that would make Malinowski seem relatively standoffish, as when Michael Harner became a practicing shaman and Paul Stoller apprenticed to a sorcerer (Harner, 1973; Stoller & Olkes, 1987). It also involves checking and double-checking the correctness of what one is told in interviews. "Interview material must ultimately be taken on trust," Joan Cassel observed in her research on surgeons. Interviewing alone does not provide as good a documentation as does "extended participant observation, where the fieldworker can observe behavior as well as self-report, and check and cross-check the honesty of a particular informant and the validity of a particular account" (Cassel, 1981, p. 164).

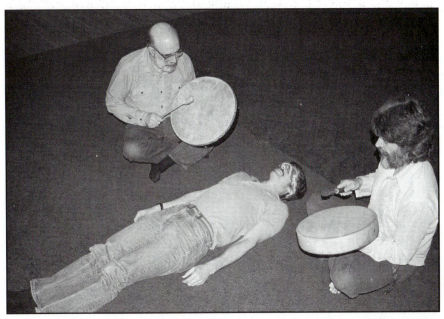

Michael Harner, aided by an assistant, introduces a student to shamanic journeying.

Robert Murphy, working with Yolanda Murphy, succeeded well as a field ethnographer. He luxuriated in no-nonsense self-awareness as he attempted to catch the spirit of the method:

> Participant observation is one of those ponderous terms that doesn't mean all that much; it refers merely to the anthropological practice of living amid the research population, taking part in their activities, watching what they do, and asking questions when one doesn't understand what's happening. This is less fancy methodology than simple necessity when studying an Indian tribe in the Amazon hinterland, where you can't pack up your notebook at 5 P.M. and go home. But it also has great methodological merit, for, unlike survey research, it allows the investigator to check statements of attitude and value against actual behavior. This is essential, as people often do not do what they say they should be doing, or even what they *think* they are doing. (Murphy, 1987, p. 174)

NEW QUESTIONING TECHNIQUE

The method of "ethnoscience" or "the new ethnography" introduced a more precise technique for conducting field ethnography, drawing its inspiration from linguistics. It was instigated by the observation that participant observation tended to result in biased descriptions. That is, in fieldwork among people of other cultures ethnologists moved all too easily (and nonreflexively) from the language or dialect of informants to that of the ethnographer. Field-workers followed no explicit rules to help them control a tendency to translate an informant's way of thinking into a culture-bound category built into the ethnographer's speech habits, as when Lévi-Strauss referred to Quesalid, a Northwest Coast Indian shaman, as a "free thinker." To be a free thinker in Europe and America implies an iconoclastic mind-set with historical roots in rebellion against family, sexual, and religious values. As will become clear later in this chapter, Quesalid appears to have been very accepting of family, sexual, and religous values in tribal life. He did believe that shamans were cheats in terms of those accepted values, but although he was a skeptic on that issue, he was not at all a free thinker in the Western sense of the term.

The Descriptive Questions Technique

The proposed solution required an unprecedented new rigor in working with informants. Let us take an early example that relates directly to medical anthropology. Charles Frake, working with Subanun informants in the Philippines, demonstrated his method of descriptive questions as he elicited an emic classification of diseases of the skin (Frake, 1961). His approach was to interview in such a way that he would be able to elicit a terminology of skin problems in their language that would not be influenced by the language of Western dermatology. To achieve this, he took advantage of the finding that in their seemingly endless discussions about sickness, one utterance invariably seemed to demand that the respondent provide a disease name, that is, a diagnostic category. All that was required was to ask a single question over and over again. The question was "What kind of illness is that?" *(dita gleruun ai run ma iin)*

To summarize in simple terms what was a complex elicitation process, and to take advantage of later thinking about ethnoscience, basically what Frake did was to select a cover term or phrase, "kind of illness," which defined the linguistic domain that he would explore (Spradley, 1979). In this early study, the question "What kind of illness is that?" was itself too inclusive, since their catalogue of human illnesses was quite enormous. For this practical reason, Frake limited this particular inquiry entirely to disorders of the skin, for which the term is *nuka* (skin disease).

The next step after selecting this domain was to collect terms. Pointing to a skin condition, he posed his question and recorded answers, including alternative terms from any one person or sometimes getting different terms from different individuals. In all, Frake identified nineteen basic terms, each specific to a skin disease in the Subanun way of thinking.

The third step was to look for contrast sets. More inclusive terms proved to be ways of talking about skin diseases at higher levels of contrast (abstraction). For example the term *meyebag* (inflammation) included three lower level terms,

FIGURE 5-1
Levels of Contrast in Skin Disease Terminology

nuka 'skin disease'														
		meyebag 'inflammation'			*beldut* 'sore'				*buni* 'ringworm'					
					telemaw 'distal ulcer'		*baga?* 'proximal ulcer'							
puga 'rash'	*nuka* 'eruption'	*pagid* 'inflamed quasi bite'	*bekukay* 'ulcerated inflammation'	*meyebag* 'inflamed wound'	*telemaw glai* 'shallow distal ulcer'	*telemaw bligun* 'deep distal ulcer'	*baga?* 'shallow proximal ulcer'	*begwak* 'deep proximal ulcer'	*beldut* 'simple sore'	*selimbunut* 'spreading sore'	*buyayag* 'exposed ringworm'	*buni* 'hidden ringworm'	*bugais* 'spreading itch'	

SOURCE: Frake, C. O., (1961). The Diagnosis of Disease among the Subanun of Mindanao. *American Anthropologist* 63: 113–132. Page 118.

pagid (inflamed quasi bite), *bekukay* (ulcerated inflammation), and *manebag* (inflamed wound). It stood in contrast to *buni* (ringworm), a higher level term that comprised *buyayag* (exposed ringworm) and *buni* (hidden ringworm). In this manner, by designating a domain, listing terms, and then looking for contrast sets, Frake identified an emic Subanun taxonomy of skin disorders undistorted by biomedical categories and concepts (fig. 5-1).

This emic classification is free of biomedical bias and is also empirically based. Nevertheless, one can do very little with it. Multidisciplinarity was subverted in this research because it leaves one with no way to know what the Subanun categories of skin lesions represent in terms of actual skin conditions. Etic equivalents were not provided. The crude clinical correlations provided by Frake were English terms such as "rashes," " ulcers," " sores," and "ring-worms." Such terms are wholly inadequate for etic purposes because each one covers a wide range of possible diseases. The term *rash,* for example, does not distinguish the red blotching of measles from the facial redness of lupus, the itchy bumps of urticaria, the raised vesicles of chicken pox, or any of the many other rashes that are identified by physicians when making a diagnosis. What Frake did, in fact, was to translate Subanun emic terms into English emic terms. A precise anthropological methodology was aborted here because the terminology was not combined with precise etic (medical) identifications.

There are other equally unsettling problems. Frake points out that the Subanun often do not agree among themselves on the nature of the lesion to which the term refers. Is it a "shallow ulcer"? Or, is it a "deep ulcer"? Not infrequently, his informants could not decide. Where informants do not agree, additional eliciting techniques and statistical calculations are needed in order to evaluate the extent of agreement within the culture. A theory and method of consensus within a culture was not available to Frake in the 1960s, but is available to us now, as we will see.

The goal of the ethnoscience eliciting procedure needs to be deconstructed. It looks suspiciously as though it incorporates an unexamined and unconscious Western assumption that people must think about diseases in very systematic ways. Does the Subanun typology really exist, or is this beautifully schematic classification of skin diseases in part, at least, an artifact of the ethnographer's effort to identify just such contrast sets and inclusive categories?

It is not unreasonable to ask. Certainly, we know that ethnoscience does not work for health concepts in some cultures and languages precisely because the people involved do not think about diseases in highly systematized ways. When John Janzen attempted to carry out an ethnoscience analysis among the Bakong people of Zaire, he concluded that he was trying to identify a level of taxonomic consistency that was not part of how they actually thought about disease. He gave up the effort as too cerebralized and idiosyncratic (Janzen, 1978, p. 34).

In spite of problems, early ethnoscience influenced research in cultural anthropology and specifically in medical anthropology. Many ethnographers now include this kind of approach to fieldwork as part of what they do. Because ethnoscience is a time-consuming procedure that produces information about limited (but often important) cultural domains, it is not a substitute for the larger enterprise of participant observation. As concerns skin disorders among the Subanun, for example, Frake's findings do not tell us how they were thought to originate, how they were treated, and what the illness experiences meant to individuals and their significant others.

The Frame Questioning Technique

The new ethnography was often referred to as cognitive analysis, since language was thought of as a way to get at how people think, in other words, at human cognition. In its earlier applications, however, ethnoscience was so focused on the structure of language domains that it seemed presumptuous to speak of research findings as cognition. Later work, building on that of Charles Frake, Duane Metzger, Gerald Williams, and others, moved beyond the patterning of elicited folk taxonomies to discover rules people possess for making decisions among alternative courses of action.

Within medical anthropology, James Young and Linda Garro demonstrated the potential for this kind of research in their study of health care decision making in Pichátaro, a rural community in Mexico (Young & Garro, 1994).

They differed from Frake in investigating the whole domain of folk medical knowledge rather than just a limited diagnostic category. Along with other eliciting practices, they identified local health-seeking beliefs and practices by using the frame questioning technique developed by Metzger and Williams (Metzger & Williams, 1963).

Question frames resemble fill-in-the-blank questions familiar to students from exams in school, except that any one question is repeated many times over with each informant in order to encourage them to provide every possible answer they can think of. For example, every subject was asked, When you leave a warm place and enter into the cold air, you can catch____? Or, Do you have to go to the doctor with____? Or, again, Do you get weak when you have____? (Young & Garro, 1994, pp. 84–85). This part of the Pichátaro study involved a difficult eight-month-long field process that required the completion of five different kinds of interviews, one of which included over two thousand questions that took several days of hourlong sessions with each of ten informants.

With such a mass of information, Young and Garro needed statistical techniques to describe their findings. They carried out cluster analyses. Cluster analysis refers to statistical manipulations that organize data such as Pichátaro illness terms and illness attributes into emic categories. Of course, cluster analysis will produce clusters only if the data are so structured. Since the Pichátareño cognitive model was well structured, these statistical techniques identified an emic taxonomy.

A cluster analysis relating to the term *pneumonia,* for example, showed that it shares many attributes with the terms *bronchopneumonia, bronchitis, and relapse.* Although fewer, it also shares attributes with *sharp headache,* and *swollen glands.* Fewer, still, are shared with *rheumatism,* and even fewer with *fever, temperature, and grippe.* This hierarchical clustering of illness terms can be diagrammed to demonstrate at a glance how illness terms in Pichátaro are clustered (fig. 5-2).

It is their work on decision making that brings us more fully into the field of cognitive anthropology. When talking about medical alternatives, Pichátareños sometimes thought in terms of a familiar contrasting set, that of folk remedies *(remedios caseros)* versus medical remedies *(remedios médicos).* However, when coping with decisions about what to do in a particular case, they weighted options in terms of a much more diverse set of treatment contrasts or alternatives:

- curers *(curanderas)*
- a woman who treated mainly burns
- a man who treated evil eye and painful joints
- specialists in witchcraft-related illnesses
- midwives *(parteras)*
- health workers *(practicantes)* who use medical remedies
- physicians

FIGURE 5-2

Hierarchical Clustering of Illness Terms

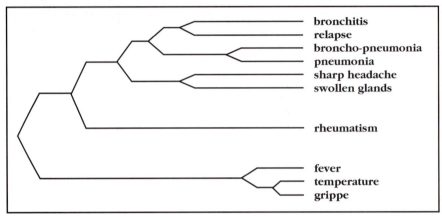

bronchitis
relapse
broncho-pneumonia
pneumonia
sharp headache
swollen glands

rheumatism

fever
temperature
grippe

SOURCE: Adapted from Young, J. C., and Garro, L., (1994). *Medical Choice in a Mexican Village.* New Brunswick, NJ: Rutgers University Press. Page 88.

- medicine vendors
- herbal remedy sellers
- Spiritual advisors who advertise over radio stations
- vows to Catholic saints

At issue for Young and Garro was this: If someone is ill, how are decisions made as to which of the healing options will be activated? Now, it is not surprising to learn that these kinds of decisions are usually made on the basis of discussions with family members, friends, neighbors, and others. Janzen explored that aspect of the healing experience in his work in Africa, when he wrote about the activities of a sick person's close kin who functioned as "the therapy managing group" (Janzen, 1981). Young and Garro moved in their own direction, however, as they applied ethnoscience methods to construct a formal model of what they refer to as the choice-making process.

As a first step in constructing this model, they needed to identify the principal decision criteria that people used. To this end, they started with the following question frame, inserting all possible contrasting pairs of alternatives:

If you or another person in your household were ill, when—for what reasons— would you (consult) (use)_____ instead of (consulting) (using)_____ ? (Young & Garro, 1994, p. 132)

The result of pursuing this line of inquiry with fifteen people was to identify the four most frequently used treatment alternatives: self-treatment, folk curers, *practicantes,* and physicians.

Further, the criteria most consistently applied in making initial decisions about treatment were also four in number: gravity or seriousness of the illness, knowledge and experience relating to an appropriate remedy, faith in the effi-cacy of folk medicine as opposed to biomedicine, and expense and ability to pay.

Moving on to questions about hypothetical situations asked of twenty infor-mants, the ways in which these criteria were applied could be explored. The results are very interesting. The perceived seriousness of the illness was the first consideration. Second, choice was influenced by whether or not a suitable home remedy was known. Third, an estimate of potential effectiveness was factored in. And fourth, cost was most often a decisive factor when medical treatment by a physician was being considered.

This model of decision making was then tested against known actual treat-ment choices that had been made when someone had fallen ill. That test indi-cated that the model correctly accounted for 91 percent of the choices that people actually made, which is very convincing indeed.

Ultimately, Young and Garro conclude, alternative forms of treatment are selected on the basis of two key considerations: their estimate of whether the treatment would effect a cure, and the estimated cost.

These findings could be represented as a flowchart that captured the basic strategy of making decisions about treatment (Young & Garro, 1981, p. 192).

It should now be clear that in fieldwork there is a trade-off of precision in identifying probabilities against the time and money it requires to do such thor-ough work. We now know a lot about how health care decisions are arrived at in Pichátero. We do not know the extent to which this model would apply to people other than the inhabitants of that one community. A wider generaliza-tion can only be investigated by replicating the study in other societies, a costly and time-consuming undertaking. For these reasons, medical anthropologists usually still rely on less rigorous research models for the study of health care–seeking behavior.

Lola Romanucci-Ross developed an early model of the impressionistic sort inherent in traditional participation observation. Based on her observa-tions among the Manus of the Admiralty Islands and elsewhere, she described what she called a hierarchy of resort. If people are influenced by international culture, they are most likely to seek biomedical care first and to resort to folk medicine only if they are not getting better. Conversely, she provided illustrations of more traditional individuals for whom the sequence is reversed (Romanucci-Ross, 1991).

The problem with the hierarchy of resort model is that it assumes an either-or dichotomy that does not allow for variability and change. It is a pattern of culture of the sort favored by Ruth Benedict and Margaret Mead in the 1920s and 1930s. The Pichátaro model of Young and Garro represents an enormous improvement in method and theory, because it takes account of individual variability and the con-siderations that influence individual decisions. It alerts us to the need in any society to think in terms of cultural criteria for decision making rather than merely to look for a pattern of presumed regularity of response to illness. It moves us away from the older assumption that in traditional societies people are unappreciative of the benefits of modern medicine because of ignorance of its benefits. In Pichátaro,

FIGURE 5-3
Decision Making in Flow Chart Form

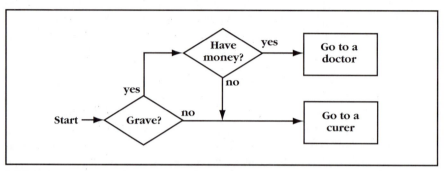

SOURCE: Young, J. C., and Garro, L., (1994). *Medical Choice in a Mexican Village.* New Brunswick, NJ: Rutgers University Press. Page 192.

people often fail to seek medical care because of poverty and isolation, not because they are locked into a traditional worldview that shapes cognition in archaic ways.

THE POSTMODERNIST CRITIQUE

The term *postmodernism* is used in various ways, so it is not always clear what is meant. In part, however, it usually refers to an attitude of reflexivity (self-awareness) based on an acknowledgment that in ethnographic reporting one always and unavoidably distorts the reality that subsequently may be thought of as factual. Postmodern sensitivity is based on the discovery that it is impossible to be completely impartial, no matter how hard one tries. How one should cope with this source of distortion is currently a hot topic in anthropological circles. As part of being reflexive about field reports, it has been argued that the anthropologist should write in a more autobiographic vein. The reader should be given enough description of the ethnographer's experience to be able to identify and evaluate the documentation that is produced (Rabinow, 1977). One postmodernist approach is to insist that anthropologists should not allow their voices alone to dominate ethnographic writing. Let people speak for themselves (incorporate multivocality into the narrative), it is urged. Do not insist on a single description or interpretation, since any so-called totalizing (hegemonic) summary is merely one interpretation among many, and all are equally valid.

Or, invalid. Informants frequently shape their statements in ways they assume will please the ethnographer. Natives also often describe their own unique experience or their versions of ideal culture in the guise of generalizations about real culture. Thus, subtle and not-so-subtle distortions survive into the literature, because every statement is molded by the anthropologist's, by the informant's, and by other natives' personal histories and individually experienced cultures (Clifford & Marcus, 1986; Jackson, 1989).

Quesalid the Shaman

Who, then, is qualified to describe health and healing in any culture? Can any one person provide an authentic description? How many voices are required to meet the demands for multivocality, since any and every version is subjective? Let us explore this issue a bit by taking the example of Quesalid, an early twentieth-century Kwakiutl shaman.

An old, influential ethnographic documentation of shamanic skulduggery concerns a Kwakiutl Indian who was called Quesalid. A fellow Indian named George Hunt transcribed Quesalid's autobiography in the Kwakiutl language using a phonetic alphabet taught him by Franz Boas. In 1930 Boas published the Quesalid account verbatim in both the Kwakiutl language and in a word-for-word translation into English. More than three decades later, Claude Lévi-Strauss used the Quesalid autobiography as key documentation for his own theory of shamanism and fraud.

From the Boas publication we learn that as a young man Quesalid figured out, rightly enough, that shamans were deceiving audiences with tricks designed to make them seem adept in supernormal ways. In order to expose the deception as well as to satisfy his curiosity, he was persuaded to apprentice to the shamans in his community. His teachers trained him in their phony methods (Boas, 1930, Part II, pp. 1–10):

- to appear to tremble and faint simulating trance and possession
- to vomit at will to produce a bloody "worm" sucked out of the patient
- to conceal eagle down under the lip and make it look like a worm
- to bite inside his mouth to make the "worm" and vomitus bloody
- to recruit a spy for information to demonstrate "mystical" knowledge
- to appear to place a quartz crystal in someone's abdomen
- to sing sacred healing songs supposedly revealed in possession
- to feel where a disease-causing intrusive object is located

Traveling among neighboring tribes he encountered still other schemes for staging seemingly miraculous events:

- A shaman's saliva is claimed to be the sickness.
- By sleight-of-hand, a rattle appears to swallow the saliva/sickness.
- A hidden pin makes a bark object appear to hover against a post.
- The death and resurrection of a shaman is faked.
- A concealed piece of tallow materializes as a lost soul.
- The tallow/soul seems to disappear into the patient's body.

In his adventures as a well-trained fraud, Quesalid described his first attempt to cure. As he tried to suck out the sickness, he recalled as follows:

Now I tasted the blood that came out of my gums. Not very long had I been sucking when I lifted my head. I spat the blood into my hand, mixed with the down intended to represent the sickness, into my right hand. Then I squeezed the blood in the water in the basin. I only squeezed the surface of the down. Then I arose and I opened my right hand and sang the sacred song. . . . Now the blood-covered down stuck on my right hand as I went around the fire in the middle of the house. . . . As soon as I came to where [the patient] was sitting I asked him to look at his former sickness. . . . Then I took off the blood covered down and wrapped it in shredded white cedar bark and I went and buried it in the hot ashes of the fire in the middle of the house. (Boas, 1930, Part II, 13)

Taking a reflexive stance, it becomes clear that every version of the life history of the shaman Quesalid is a just one view among a number of alternative and conflicting views. In this example at least five voices are involved:

■ that of Quesalid, the Kwakiutl man who apprenticed as a shaman
■ that of George Hunt, the Kwakiutl-speaking man of mixed ancestry employed as a field collaborator by Boas
■ that of Franz Boas, professor of anthropology at Columbia University
■ that of Claude Lévi-Strauss, professor of Anthropology, Collège de France
■ that of Anderson, because I am writing on the subject in this book
■ finally, put your own name here: You will have your own version as a reader

QUESALID

The protagonist in this shamanic drama is Quesalid. He describes in the first person how he was very suspicious and disdainful, and how he was taught to cheat by the shamans who trained him. Quesalid appears to have been a kind of cultural detective who identified deception through his own version of participant observation. But is this truly and completely his autobiography? Although attributed to him, it is available to us only as transcribed by Hunt.

HUNT

This remarkable man straddled two cultures, apparently with considerable dexterity. He was the son of an Indian mother and a Scottish father, but grew up in a Kwakiutl community speaking that language as his native tongue. He also spoke English, which enabled him to collaborate with Boas for over a quarter of a century. Boas taught him to record what he was told by Kwakiutl informants using a phonetic alphabet.

For most of their work together, Boas was in New York while Hunt was in the field. In the manner of old-fashioned ethnographers who organized their work by means of the *Notes and Queries in Anthropology,* Boas kept Hunt busy by supplying him with requests and questions. Through this collaboration, volumes of native texts were recorded and published in the Kwakiutl language, with direct translations into English. (It is apparent to us now, with enhanced multicultural sensitivities, that Hunt deserved to be listed as a coauthor, but that is another matter.)

Quesalid presumably represented a Kwakiutl voice. But was it actually his voice? This is the postmodernist concern. We are given no details on how Hunt encountered Quesalid, what their relationship was, or the extent to which the text was modified in the process of recording it. It is not unreasonable to suspect that Hunt may have shaped the documentation in unconscious, if not in conscious ways. He may have done this in terms of his own biases. Was shamanism acceptable to him as an alternative to Christian belief and practice? Was he inclined to denigrate it? His emphasis upon lying and cheating by shamans makes one suspect a distortive bias. Intentionally or not, did he in addition, perhaps, produce a manuscript that he believed would please Boas, his employer? In short, to some extent this is a biography by Hunt rather than an autobiography by Quesalid, but we have no basis for evaluating the existence or extent of these possibly conflicting voices.

BOAS

And what was the impact of editing and publishing by Boas? Given the postmodernist commitment to providing voices to the natives, and for other reasons as well, Boas was years ahead of his time. He records only the Quesalid-Hunt (auto)biography, completely without emendation or commentary. His only ethnographic concern was that the Kwakiutl sounds and grammar were recorded accurately. Read the English version, however, and you begin to realize that without an ethnographer's imprint, a setting of the scene, an evaluation of the data, it is very hard to know what to make of the text. Native voices alone are not anthropology. By not framing this presentation in the circumstances of Quesalid's life and times, Boas implicitly frames it as a kind of mythic heroism. He fails us in that way.

LÉVI-STRAUSS

Quesalid might have descended into ethnographic oblivion if Claude Lévi-Strauss had not found and used his life story more than thirty years after it was published. Lévi-Strauss had a theoretical orientation that clearly shaped how he interpreted the life of this shaman. The major conclusion of his article was that Quesalid eventually came to believe in his own power as a shaman in spite of knowing that he used trickery. When the Lévi-Strauss text is deconstructed by comparing it with the original publication, however, a significant distortion becomes apparent.

ANDERSON

This is where Anderson comes in, embarrassed somewhat at playing the authorial role of "the expert" who "says it like it is." (This is the hegemonic [controlling] voice that is anathema in postmodernism.) I take on that role, however, to argue that no statement in the Quesalid-Hunt text justifies the interpretation provided by Lévi-Strauss. Let us compare statements made by Lévi-Strauss with what is actually written in the Boas text.

■ *Claim by Lévi-Strauss:* In one community shamans showed the sickness as materialized in spittle on the palms of their hands. They failed to heal the patient. Quesalid outdid them when he vomited up a bloodly "worm" of bird down. This made him, as misquoted by Lévi-Strauss, "'hesitant and thinking about many things.'" Lévi-Strauss continues, "Here he encountered several varieties of a 'false supernatural,' and was led to conclude that some forms were less false than others"(Lévi-Strauss, 1967, p. 170).

■ *The Boas text:* Quesalid nowhere used the phrase "false supernatural." He did give thought to some forms of trickery as more convincing than others, but not as more powerful in supernatural terms. At that point, what he actually said is correctly quoted as follows: "And so I was sitting there for quite a while thinking about many things, for I was hesitating and was afraid of the words of the chiefs who had praised me. They had made their shamans common people. That is why I said in my mind I would go home to Fort Rupert; and so I told Great-Mountain that I would go home when day came next morning" (Boas, 1930, Part II; pp. 19–20). The reference is clearly not to a sudden belief that he had supernatural powers, but to an awkward, even dangerous situation he had created by humiliating the local shamans in a healing competition. "Now I saw that the shamans of the Koskimo, were ashamed, the four reputed ones, on account of what I had done. . . . Then I was scared of what they might say to me" (Boas, 1930, Part II; p. 18).

Further, the Quesalid-Hunt text offers no support at all for the major conclusion offered in support of the Lévi-Strauss hypothesis.

■ *Claim by Lévi-Strauss:* "Thus his original attitude has changed considerably. The radical negativism of the free thinker has given way to more moderate feelings. . . . He seems to have completely lost sight of the fallaciousness of the technique which he had so disparaged at the beginning" (Lévi-Strauss, 1967, pp. 172–173).

■ *The Boas text:* Quesalid encountered only one shaman whom he respected, not because he was a powerful healer, as Lévi-Strauss states, but because he was not greedy. He did not perform for personal profit. Quesalid concludes in his final paragraph, speaking of the last encounters of his travels as an investigative participant observer *en nature,* "all only pretend to be shamans." That is what he said, and I believe that is what he meant.

YOUR NAME HERE

It is a tenet of postmodernism that the meaning of the text resides in what the reader takes from it. That is where you come in. You will evaluate all of these other voices, including mine, in terms of your personal, family, ethnic, and educational history as well as your status in the political economy of your nation. In your own way, you will surely arrive at interpretations that are distinctive and unique.

The Method of Good Enough Ethnography

When pushed to an extreme, the postmodernist critique makes it impossible to practice anthropology as a social science. How can one make any generalizations at all if every culture, in fact, every individual experience of a culture and every written report, is unique? Uneasy with this dilemma, many anthropologists feel that they can only acknowledge the uncertainties and carry on. Donald Campbell takes this position, believing that the intensive study of single communities is an essential undertaking:

> That is not to say that such common-sense naturalistic observation is objective, dependable, or unbiased. But it is all that we have. It is the only route to knowledge—noisy, fallible, and biased though it may be. We should be aware of its weaknesses, but must still be willing to trust it if we are to go about the process of comparative (or monocultural) social science at all. (Campbell, 1979, p. 54)

As a medical anthroplogist, Nancy Scheper-Hughes reflects considerable frustration with the postmodernist challenge in the following caustic statement:

> I grow weary of these postmodernist critiques, and given the perilous times in which we and our subjects live, I am inclined towards a compromise that calls for the practice of a good enough ethnography. The anthropologist is an instrument of cultural translation that is necessarily flawed and biased. We cannot rid ourselves of the cultural self we bring with us into the field . . . . Nonetheless, . . . we struggle to do the best we can with the limited resources we have at hand—our ability to listen and observe carefully, empathically, and compassionately. (Scheper-Hughes, 1992, p. 28)

Good enough, in fact, shows promise of getting better. Ethnologists have moved beyond participant observation without abandoning this method that still basically characterizes the profession. It will never be possible to characterize a whole society with absolute precision. It is not even possible to define the personality of a single individual with precision. The purpose is too vague, societies and individuals are too complex, and both are riddled with inconsistencies and repeated changes. Given these realities, much about cultures can nonetheless often be described with confidence (Spiro, 1992).

To say "often" is to acknowledge that some cultures demonstrate more intracultural homogeneity than do others. It is also to acknowledge that an identified homogeneity will often be limited to a restricted cultural domain,

Arthur Rubel celebrating a ritual with the municipal band of a community in Mexico.

such as the domain of disease concepts or kinds of healers. Within a given domain, however, one often encounters considerable uniformity. These uniformities, that is, these probabilities of how people will reason and what they will do, can be very important for medical anthropologists when they identify values, attitudes, and practices related to health. In the absence of certainties, a lot can be accomplished if one can accurately estimate probabilities. One of the earliest of these methods was that of ethnoscience, as we have seen.

PARTICIPANT OBSERVATION AND QUANTITATIVE METHODS

According to Lise Swartz, "Anthropologists are trained to investigate, analyze and interpret data from cultures different from their own" (Swartz, 1994, p. 209). For many years, it seemed that the only method really essential for the practice of sociocultural anthropology was participant observation, or possibly ethnoscience. Anthropological field methods were almost entirely qualitative rather than quantitative. As recently as 1980 it was possible for a cultural anthropologist to say, "We need only . . . an educated person's grasp of quantitative techniques" (Vivelo, 1980, p. 346). But with the postmodernist critique, the need for quantitative skills has increased. Physical anthropologists have employed complex computations for almost a century, cultural anthropologists working with the HRAF have relied on statistics since midcentury, and many medical anthropologists have been at it in recent decades.

Earlier ethnographic fieldwork for the most part was a humanist enterprise that required very little mathematical or computational skill. Anthropologists made generalizations of an impressionistic nature. As an example, Boas was forced to confess with regret that because the bulk of the Kwakiutl texts, including Quesalid's autobiography, were obtained from a single informant, we cannot know whether we are dealing with an individual style or one that is tribal (Boas, 1930, Part I, p. xii).

To avoid these errors in generalizing about cultural traits, even within a single community, it is now customary to combine qualititative with quantitative methods (Bernard et al., 1986; Cook & Reichardt, 1979). How fieldwork of this type can build on participant observation is best understood by reviewing a specific project based on this format.

The Susto Study

It is widely believed in Mexico as well as elsewhere in Latin America that a person who experiences a sudden fright can become very ill. The victim tends to become restless, listless, debilitated, depressed, anorexic, and neglectful of appearance. "Susto is a very bad thing to get—you can die from it." This according to Alicia, one of Margaret Clark's informants when she studied the health of a Mexican-American community in California some years ago (Clark, 1970, p. 176).

To learn more about the susto phenomenon, Arthur Rubel and his collaborators, Carl O'Nell and Rolando Collado-Ardón, designed a multidisciplinary project of controlled comparisons for which they selected three culturally distinct communities speaking three mutually unintelligible languages, all in Mexico: Valley Zapotec, Chinantec, and Ladino (mestizo) (Rubel, O'Nell, & Collado-Ardón, 1984). The HRAF was not used for this purpose, but as concerns Galton's problem, it was determined that the three cultures were historically independent of one another. Above all, the three were selected to be comparable in terms of the influence of change agents such as priests or schoolteachers.

The project began with a study of the illness by means of participant observation. On the basis of this initial investigation, Rubel formulated a series of hypotheses to be tested. The investigators then translated these hypotheses into questionnaires that could be administered to representative samples in each of the three communities. One was designed to elicit information about aspects of lifestyle, another was intended to explore social stress that appeared to be related to getting sick with susto, and the third was to measure levels of psychiatric impairment. Before the full-scale investigation was undertaken, the questionnaires were pretested in a small pilot study to make sure that respondents did not have problems understanding them.

The team designed this project on the assumption that cultural factors were probably causal one way or another in the etiology of susto. They expected to find that susto would reflect the dominant values, beliefs, and normative expectations of these societies and mirror the emotions and feelings invested in social relationships. Following the research design, they identified fifty individuals said to be ill with susto and an additional fifty who were identical in every way except that they were said not to suffer from susto. The result was a sample of matched pairs that could be compared in terms of contrasts in lifestyles, social stress, and psychiatric impairment in each of the pairs.

The most comprehensive hypothesis postulated that those stricken with susto would score higher on social-stress scores derived from the questionnaire than would matched individuals who were sick, but who were not identified as being ill with susto. The experiment showed that high scores for stress were positively associated with complaints of susto in all three communities. Persons stricken with susto thought of themselves as inadequate in performing crucial social roles and were probably under stress because they sensed the discrepancy between their expectations and their actual performance.

Remember how Whiting and Child were led astray by incomplete statistics in their HRAF study of childhood experiences and health beliefs? No matter how reasonable a prediction may seem, until thoroughly tested it is only speculation. In testing this prediction, an association between stress and susto was found, yes, but the association was not very strong. Something was missing. And this is where it paid off that the experiment was multidisciplinary, because it joined anthropologists with physicians (exactly as Rivers failed to do almost a century earlier).

In addition to the ethnographic documentation and questionnaire results described above, the subjects were also examined and diagnosed by a physician, and the results of these medical evaluations were interpretated by two physician-scorers who independently assigned diagnoses, estimated levels of severity, and predicted the gravity of probable outcomes. Bringing the two kinds of documentation together, the anthropological and the medical, completely transformed the conclusions that would have resulted had the anthropologists worked alone.

It had been thought that susto was a form of unique social behavior, a culture-bound syndrome that was best explained in psychosocial terms as a way in which a socially burdened individual could get "time off." The survey research provided positive but weak evidence for that conclusion. However, the medical examinations demonstrated that those with susto carried a measurably heavier burden of biological disease than did their matched controls. Not only does life overburden those with susto, but the *asustados* (those with susto) are doubly overburdened with an excessive load of disease. The conclusion had to be significantly altered. As the researchers put it, "Rather than electing the sick role to legitimize a respite from their obligations, asustados are *forced to the sidelines* by excessive demands on their adaptive resources" (Rubel, O'Nell, & Collado-Ardón, 1984, p. 122).

This research has had an impact on research design. It demonstrates the value of designing multidisciplinary protocols to include diagnostic work by physicians. It is also a reminder that anthropologists need to break away from a Cartesian dualism that inclines them to attribute illness either to the mind or to the body. Researchers do better if they assume that it is not an issue of either/or, but of both/and. Above all, it models a distinctly anthropological methodology whereby initial participant observation provides the basis for producing emically sensitive hypotheses and questions that can be explored statistically.

STATISTICS

Participant observation often requires learning a foreign language, a task which anthropologists take on without complaint. One of the personal benefits of the profession is the joy of this accomplishment. Spanish, Chinantec, and Zapotec were the languages of the Susto study, a complex situation that required some use of interpreters. Students of anthropology also need to gain proficiency in statistics, which is the numerical language of quantitative research. Complaint and anxiety sometimes rob them of the joy of this accomplishment, which is unfortunate. Descriptive and inferential statistics empower the researcher with tools of description and analysis that broaden and deepen documentation and understanding, particularly when used in conjunction with qualitative methods in an anthropological way (Pelto & Pelto, 1978; Thomas, 1986).

Descriptive statistics is the organization of information for ready comprehension or for further analysis. It is a way to benefit from acquiring large amounts of data without being overwhelmed. The susto study employed descriptive statistics to demonstrate that a number of conditions varied together, including the correlation of complaints of susto with high scores for stress and with a high prevalence of other sicknesses. Descriptive statistics also permitted Beatrice Whiting to show a strong relationship between sorcery and social control in the absence of designated community leaders. The same kind of statistics permitted Whiting and Child to claim a correlation between erogenous zone fixations and healing practices, a claim that was also rejected years later on the same basis.

Inferential statistics allow one to go beyond description in order to identify probabilities. On this basis, calculations in the susto study included estimates of the probability that the covariations that were discovered occurred simply by chance. Using inferential statistics, it was possible to demonstrate that the major findings were significant at a probability level of at least 0.05 percent ($p < 0.05$). In other words, there were no more than five chances in a hundred that they had been misled by random associations. Beatrice Whiting's study demonstrated a statistical significance of less than one chance in a hundred ($p < 0.01$) that her findings did not support her hypothesis.

With a computer assist, more complex inferential statistics, such as cluster analysis or factor analysis, provide ways to examine more than two variables at a time. With techniques of this sort it becomes possible to identify an otherwise inapparent combination of variables that stands out as having explanatory (predictive) value.

POSTPOSITIVISM AND METHODOLOGICAL TRIANGULATION

The repertoire of the ethnographer now includes many techniques for acquiring information about one aspect or another of a culture. Each is useful in some ways if not in others. Using a mix of these techniques to get informant responses relating to any one cultural domain is a way to identify valid and reliable findings. This is what is meant by the method of triangulation (Duffy, 1987). It offers the expectation that one can greatly improve good enough ethnographies, based on the belief that

> because all methods have biases, only by using multiple techniques can the researcher triangulate on the underlying truth. Since quantitative and qualitative methods often have different biases, each can be used to check on and learn from the other. (Reichardt & Cook, 1979, p. 21)

This approach is sometimes referred to as postpositivism, or more narrowly, as the new tradition of postpositivist applied anthropology (Denzin & Lincoln, 1994, p. 207). It is based on the premise "that some form of social science is possible and desirable" (Strauss & Corbin, 1994, p. 274). Postpositivism acknowledges that it is impossible definitively to verify claims about the nature of the real world, so it settles for doing the best one can, conducting good enough ethnographies in that sense. Furthermore, it is assumed that if findings are repeated in various ways, they are more likely to be true; hence, triangulation becomes the method of choice. Postpositivist methodologists feel at home in more natural settings rather than in the experimental laboratories of positivist scientists. They attempt to incorporate emic viewpoints that include the meanings and purposes that people attribute to their actions. They situate information about humans as holistically as possible in their sociocultural and environmental contexts (Guba & Lincoln, 1994, p. 110). They tend to be more action- and activist-oriented than is true of traditional positivists. Not the least, the goal of grand theory is replaced by "more local, small-scale theories fitted to specific problems and specific situations" (Denzin & Lincoln, 1994, p. 11).

Key Informants

Field-workers usually have questions for nearly everyone they meet, and longer interviews with various individuals are common. The role of a key informant refers to an established relationship with an individual who has a talent for teaching and answering questions and who is able to find time for the ethnographer. Usually key informants learn to anticipate needs as they acquire a feel for ethnographic analysis and come to understand the reasons for questions that at first may have seemed strange or perverse. For this reason, some anthropologists feel they should be referred to as collaborators or consultants rather than informants.

The use of key informants is as old as ethnography itself. When early American anthropologists documented Native American memory culture, they relied on older key informants. George Hunt worked as a field assistant when he gathered information for Boas from other Kwakiutls, but often he simply provided explanations from his own experience, so that he functioned also as a key informant.

How can one be sure that a key informant is accurate and knowledgeable, since it is common to make the selection in terms of personal relationships and availability? In fact, it is now possible to measure the extent to which any informant, key or occasional, is likely to be an accurate reporter on beliefs and practices relevant to a particular cultural realm (Romney, Weller, & Batchelder, 1986). Before describing that methodology, I need to explain the free listing and the pile sort techniques.

The Free-Listing Technique

Rather than a key informant, one can work with a selected sample of informants. For example, Susan Weller asked twenty women in Guatemala to name and describe every illness they could think of (Weller, 1983; Weller, 1984a; Weller, 1984b). This provided her with a list of the twenty-seven most used terms that constitute the cultural domain. What is needed next is to identify contrast sets.

Pile-Sort Techniques

One way to arrive at contrast sets is to put terms or pictures on cards and ask informants to sort them in one way or another, depending on the project. In the Guatemalan research of Weller, the most frequently mentioned terms were written on cards. Each subject was asked to sort the cards into piles of disease terms that in her judgment were similar. She was told to use any criteria that came to mind and to make as many piles as she wished. This produced similarity clusters representing each woman's conceptual model of illness.

Turning to a computer and a statistical program to sort out the combined lists, Weller created a total sample cluster model that can be taken to represent

FIGURE 5-4

Multidimensional Scaling Representation of Twenty-One Diseases for Rural Guatemala

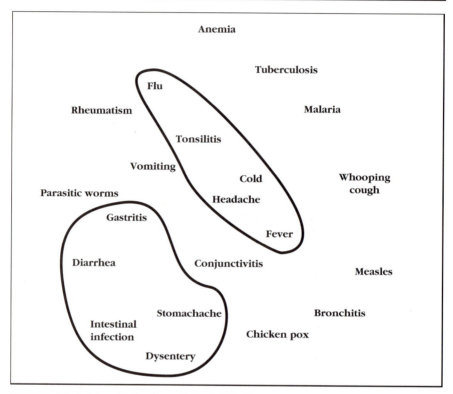

SOURCE: Adapted from Weller, Susan C. O., (1983). New Data on Intracultural Variability: The Hot-Cold Concept of Medicine and Illness. *Human Organization* 42: 249–257. Page 254.

a conceptual model of this cultural domain for the population as a whole. A visual model of these clusters was created by multidimensional scaling (MDS), which translates similarities into distances. MDS, produced a visual model in which those terms that were considered most alike appear close together, and the least alike are located elsewhere. For example, the Spanish terms for gastritis, diarrhea, stomachache, intestinal infection, and dysentery cluster in the lower left quadrant of the diagram, while flu, tonsilitis, cold, headache, and fever clustered in the upper central area.

Measures of Consensus and Expertise

Now we are in a position to discuss how the value of a key informant can be ascertained. The cluster diagram, representing the sum of responses of all informants, can be taken to represent the cultural model, but it is meaningful only if the variability from one informant to another is not very great. "It makes little sense," Weller notes, "to speak of a 'typical' pattern if the variability is extreme" (Weller, 1984, p. 341; see also Garro, 1988). To triangulate on the amount of variability that is present, a second pile-sort task was needed. To this end, a rank-order task was organized. Each subject was asked to sort the illness terms along dimensions found to be meaningful for contrast purposes. Weller asked that they be ranked in terms of certain attributes.

Of the attributes that were investigated in this study, one was how contagious each illness was thought to be and another was how they categorized illnesses in terms of the traditional hot and cold humoral qualities. Weller was able to measure intracultural variability by comparing (triangulating) the attributes identified by means of rank-order scales with the MDS-derived conceptual model of named diseases based on similarity data. Each subject's independent judgment of rank order was compared to the MDS coordinates representing the sample as a whole. To make statistical inferences from so much documentation required the use of a computer to perform a multiple regression analysis, which is a statistical technique by means of which all possible combinations of a number of independent variables can be identified.

These procedures allowed Weller to measure the fit between the rankings of each individual subject and the MDS model. For attributes of contagion she found a close fit. That is, the general unanimity identified in similarity pile sorts was also found in rank-order sorts. The model defined a high level of cultural consistency. This means that if one works with a woman in the community whose personal pile sorts match the model well, she ought to be highly reliable as a key informant for illness concepts.

On the other hand, the fit for the attributes of hot and cold was very poor. Informants were variable (unpredictable) in assigning hot or cold qualities to diseases and treatments. The lack of consensus demonstrated that these literate women of median socioeconomic status no longer think of illnesses in terms of hot and cold qualities. Since there is no cultural consistency in this area, there can be no key informant who will be dependable as a source of information on that topic. On this issue in this population, the anthropologist mires down in the postmodernist dilemma of too much diversity to permit any one voice to speak for all.

THE METHODS OF RAPID ETHNOGRAPHIC ASSESSMENT

It requires years of work and a lot of money to develop a project design, to carry out the fieldwork, to do the analysis of data, and to publish findings in the tradition of Malinowski. Medical anthropologists working on multidisciplinary teams with public health professionals often need to complete the fieldwork, finish the data analysis, and prepare a report in a short period of time with limited funding. They are asked to produce a rapid ethnographic assessment.

Under ideal circumstances, the anthropologist involved in a rapid assessment project will be working in a community already well-known from previous long-term participant observation. More commonly, the culture of the community is known in a general way from fieldwork in the culture and published ethnographies. At times the community will be studied without a good orientation from previous studies. Ethnographic studies are always context sensitive, but sometimes it is not possible for short-term, time-urgent projects to be as holistically oriented as one would wish. Good enough ethnographies must suffice.

A rapid ethnographic assessment builds on the basic strategy illustrated in the susto study in that it is a community based design. Also, as in the susto study, the projects are initiated with participant observation. In rapid, sharply delimited ethnographic studies, the ethnographer has to move fast. Dorothy Mull and Dennis Mull based their pilot study of child pneumonia in Pakistan on in-depth interviews with thirty-five mothers and grandmothers along with four health care providers (Mull & Mull, 1994). Mark Nichter and Mimi Nichter initiated their rapid assessment of acute respiratory infections in the Philippines with open-ended interviews with practitioners: physicians, pharmacists, traditional herbalists, midwives, and nurses (Nichter & Nichter, 1994).

Gretel Pelto, a medical and nutritional anthropologist, together with Sandy Gove, a physician epidemiologist, are among those who have collaborated to develop the method of focused ethnographic studies for the World Health Organization as a highly systematic way to meet the need for rapid ethnographic assessment relating to the particular categories of diarrheal and respiratory diseases (Gove & Pelto, 1994). Assigned to work on acute respiratory infections, Gove and Pelto began with a number of informants who were asked to participate in a free listing exercise as a way to identify the relevant vocabulary, in this case, of acute respiratory infections. By means of pile sorts and other techniques, contrast sets were identified and a provisional conceptual model was produced.

One key to the success of rapid ethnographic assessments is to target samples of the population representative of the community members involved. Where cultural consensus is high, samples can be relatively small (on the order of twenty to thirty individuals). In the focused ethnographic approach of Gove and Pelto, mothers of young children were interviewed in their homes and a similar sample were interviewed in a health facility where mothers bring children with respiratory symptoms. Health workers were also interviewed, including traditional healers as well as doctors. Finally, since advice and medication is often obtained from drug stores, salespeople and pharmacists were investigated.

Triangulation is the key to working with these populational samples in refining and confirming the consensus model that is identified. A number of techniques can be used (eleven are specified in the Focused Ethnographic Studies manual for acute respiratory infections). These include:

- Mothers are asked to provide narrative accounts of experiences they have had with symptomatic children.
- Hypothetical case scenarios are presented to mothers for their comments on what they would do in each case.
- Videotaped episodes of sick children are shown for comments on what they thought was wrong and what they would do.
- Pile-sorting exercises are conducted to explore their thinking about symptoms and treatment options.
- Forced-choice paired comparison tasks are presented, asking mothers to choose between two options (one health care provider versus another) and to explain their preferences.
- Inventories of medications are conducted in the home interviews as a basis for discussing beliefs and practices relating to symptomatic children.
- Structured interviews about home care and care-seeking are conducted with mothers in health facilities.
- Open-ended interviews are conducted with health care providers to document their experiences with patients.
- Hypothetical case scenarios are presented in drug stores as cases for which advice was being sought.
- Focus groups are convened in which five or six informants are guided (but not controlled) in conducting a free exchange of views and opinions about the diseases under study.
- Observed cases of sick children are documented in homes, hospitals, and other health facilities.

The goals of rapid assessment are sharply delimited. In focused ethnographic studies of acute respiratory disease, one of the main objectives was to teach caregivers how to identify infants and children who are in urgent need of medical attention. Biomedical research has demonstrated that two key signs of pneumonia and of the need for prescribing antibiotics in an appropriate manner are very rapid breathing and a drawing in of the upper abdomen and lower chest when gasping for air. It was determined that mothers usually did not recognize these signs. Children with these symptoms are in grave danger of dying, but with correct antibiotic treatment have an excellent chance for recovery. Thus, based on these findings, plans could be made to educate mothers to recognize danger signs in time to make informed decisions about the care of their children.

CONCLUSIONS

The shift to community studies and later developments to the present were associated with changes in research methodology that are best thought of as cumulative rather than as sharp breaks with the past: not a paradigm shift, but improvements based on puzzle solving. Participant observation appeared as a reasonable extension of refinements already well underway when earlier ethnographers began to investigate societies that still possessed viable nonindustrialized cultures. Efforts to improve the rigor of fieldwork grew with ethnoscience, matured with protocols that joined qualitative with quantitative methods, and continue to the present with experiments in conducting rapid ethnographic assessments.

In contrast to gradualism in the development of research methods, the community studies approach brought with it what appeared to constitute a major paradigm shift in anthropological theory. The functional and structural studies of mid-century represented a near-total break with evolutionary and diffusionist concerns. With this new paradigm it was decided that the way to understand human diversity was to investigate the cultural holism of individual bands, tribes, and villages rather than universal, cross-cultural regularities. Each ethnographer was to become an expert on one small society that, without theoretical or philosophical qualms, was taken to be somehow (hopefully) as a microcosm of the human condition. We turn, now, to this new theoretical approach.

REFERENCES

Bernard, H. R. et al., (1986). The construction of primary data in cultural anthropology. *Current Anthropology, 27*, 382–396.

Boas, F. (1930). *The religion of the Kwakiutl.* Columbia University Contributions to Anthropology (Vol. X, Part I).

Boas, F. (1930). *The religion of the Kwakiutl.* Columbia University Contributions to Anthropology (Vol. X, Part II).

Campbell, D. T. (1979). "Degrees of freedom" and the case study. In T. D. Cook & C. S. Reichardt (Eds.), *Qualitative and quantitative methods in evaluation research* (pp.49–67). Beverly Hills, CA: Sage Publications.

Cassel, J. (1981). Technical and moral error in medicine and in fieldwork. *Human Organization, 40*, 160–168.

Clark, M. (1970). *Health in the Mexican-American culture: A community study.* Berkeley: University of California Press.

Clifford, J., & Marcus, G. E. (Eds.). (1986). *Writing culture: The poetics and politics of ethnography.* Berkeley: University of California Press.

Cook, T. D., & Reichardt, C. S. (Eds.). (1979). *Qualitative and quantitative methods in evaluation research (pp. 1–17).*Beverly Hills, CA: Sage Publications.

Denzin, N. K., & Lincoln, Y. S. (1994). Introduction: Entering the field of qualitative research. In N. K. Denzin & Y. S. Lincoln (Eds.), *Handbook of qualitative research (pp. 1–17).* Thousand Oaks, CA: Sage Publications.

Duffy, M. (1987). Methodological triangulation: A vehicle for merging quantitative and qualitative research methods. *Image, 19* (3), 130–133.

Frake, C. O. (1961). The diagnosis of disease among the Subanun of Mindanao. *American Anthropologist, 63,* pp.113–132.

Frazer, J. G. (1961). Preface. In B. Malinowski (Ed.), *Argonauts of the western Pacific (pp. vii–xiv).* New York: E. P. Dutton & Co. (Original work published 1922)

Garro, L. C. (1988). Explaining high blood pressure: Variation in knowledge about illness. *American Ethnologist, 15,* 98–119.

Gove, S., & Pelto, G. H. (1994). Focused ethnographic studies in the WHO programme for the control of acute respiratory infections. *Medical Anthropology, 15,* 409–424.

Guba, E. G. & Lincoln, Y. S. (1994). Competing paradigms in qualitative research. In N. K. Denzin & Y. S. Lincoln (Eds.), *Handbook of qualitative research* (pp. 105–117). Thousand Oaks, CA: Sage Publications.

Harner, M. J. (1973). The sound of rushing water. In M. J. Harner (Ed.), *Hallucinogens and shamanism* (pp. 15–27). London: Oxford Undiversity Press.

Jackson, M. (1989). *Paths toward a clearing: Radical empiricism and ethnographic inquiry.* Bloomington: Indiana University Press.

Janzen, J. C. (1978). *The quest for therapy.* New Brunswick, NJ: Rutgers University Press.

Lévi-Strauss, C. (1967). *Structural anthropology.* Garden City, NY: Doubleday & Co., Anchor Books.

Malinowski, B. (1961) *Argonauts of the western Pacific.* New York: E. P. Dutton. (Original published 1922)

Mead, M. (1961). *Coming of age in Samoa.* New York: William Morrow & Company. (Original work published 1928)

Mead, M. (1972). *Blackberry winter: My earlier years.* New York: Simon & Schuster.

Metzger, D., & Williams, G. (1963). A formal ethnographic analysis of Tenejapa Ladino weddings. *American Anthropologist, 65,* 1076–1101.

Mull, D. S., & Mull, J. D. (1994). Insights from community-based research on child pneumonia in Pakistan. *Medical Anthropology, 15,* 335–352.

Murphy, R. F. (1987). *The body silent.* New York: Henry Holt and Co.

Nichter, M., & Nichter, M. (1994). Acute respiratory illness: Popular health culture and mother's knowledge in the Phillipines. *Medical Anthroplogy, 15,* 353–375.

Pelto, P. J., & Pelto, G. H. (1978). *Anthropological research: The structure of inquiry* (2nd ed.). Cambridge: Cambridge, MA: University Press.

Rabinow, P. (1977). *Reflections on fieldwork in Morocco.* Berkeley: University of California Press.

Reichardt, C. S., & Cook, T. D. (1979). Beyond qualitative versus quantitative methods In T. D. Cook and C. S. Reichardt (Eds.), *Qualitative and quantitative methods in evaluation research (pp. 7–32).* Beverly Hills, CA: Sage Publications.

Romanucci-Ross, L. (1991). Creativity in illness: Methodological linkages to the logic and language of science in folk pursuit of health in central Italy. In L. Romanucci-Ross, D. E. Moerman, & L. R. Tancredi (eds.). *The anthropology of medicine: From culture to method* (2nd ed., pp. 5–19). New York: Bergin & Garvey.

Romney, A. K., Weller, S., & Batchelder, W. (1986). Culture as consensus: A theory of culture and informant accuracy. *American Anthropologist, 88,* 313–338.

Rubel, A. J., O'Nell, C. W., & Collado-Ardón, C. (1984). *Susto, A folk illness.* Berkeley: University of California Press.

Scheper-Hughes, N. (1992). *Death without weeping: The violence of everyday life in Brazil.* Berkeley: University of California Press.

Spiro, M. E. (1992). *Anthropological other or Burmese brother? Studies in cultural analysis.* New Brunswick, NJ: Transaction Publishers.

Spradley, J. P. (1979). *The ethnographic interview.* New York: Holt, Rinehart and Winston.

Stocking, G. W., Jr. (1983). The ethnographer's magic: Fieldwork in British anthropology from Tylor to Malinowski. In G. W. Stocking, Jr. (Ed.), *Observers observed: Essays on ethnographic fieldwork (pp. 70-120)*. (History of Anthropology, Vol. 1). Madison, WI: University of Wisconsin Press.

Stoller, P., & Olkes, C. (1987). *In sorcery's shadow: A memoir of apprenticeship among the Songhay of Niger*. Chicago: University of Chicago Press.

Strauss, A., & Corbin, J. (1994). Grounded theory methodology: An overview. In N. K. Denzin & Y. S. Lincoln, (Eds.). *Handbook of qualitative research* (pp. 273-285). Thousand Oaks, CA: Sage Publications.

Swartz, L. (1994). Being changed by cross-cultural encounters. In D. E. Young, & J. G. Goulet (Eds.). *Being changed: The anthropology of extraordinary experience* (pp. 209-236). Peterborough, Ontario, Canada: Broadview Press.

Thomas, D. (1986). *Refiguring anthropology: First principles of probability & statistics*. Prospect Heights, IL: Waveland Press. (Original work published 1976)

Vivelo, F. R. (1980). Anthropology, applied research, and nonacademic careers: Observations and recommendations, with a personal case history. *Human Organization, 39,* 345-357.

Weller, S. C. (1983). New data on intracultural variability: The hot-cold concept of medicine and illness. *Human Organization, 42,* 249-257.

Weller, S. C. (1984a). Cross-cultural concepts of illness: Variation and validation. *American Anthropologist, 86,* 341-351.

Weller, S. C. (1984b). Consistency and consensus among informants: Disease concepts in a rural Mexican village. *American Anthropologist, 86,* 966-975.

Young, J. C., & Garro, L. (1994). *Medical choice in a Mexican village*. New Brunswick, NJ: Rutgers University Press. (Original work published 1981)

Chapter 6

STRUCTURAL AND FUNCTIONAL THEORY

FUNCTIONAL THEORY

The year 1922 stands out in the history of anthropology as a herald of change in anthropological theory. By unplanned happenstance, that was the year when Bronislaw Malinowski published *Argonauts of the Western Pacific,* describing the Trobriand Islanders, and A. R. Radcliffe-Brown published *The Andaman Islanders* (Malinowski, 1961 [1922]; Radcliffe-Brown, 1964 [1922]). Separately and together, these books broke new ground showing how to make sense of local culture by means of structural and functional theory. From an evolutionary time-scale covering the whole of human existence, or a spatial orientation to the geography of the entire world, or both, sociocultural anthropologists shifted their attention as theorists to individual small-scale communities.

To put it as plainly as possible, Malinowski found that as he learned about different aspects of the life of the Trobrianders, every custom seemed to fit jig-saw-like with every other custom in mutually interactive and supportive ways. In a comprehensive or holistic way, family practices, religious beliefs, political organization, craft production, economic exchange institutions, and so on were all mutually adapted. The best way to understand this notion of functionalism is to consider an example.

Frazer, as we have seen, gave a lot of attention to magic as a stage in cultural evolution. Malinowski documented the practice of magic with a very different kind of question in mind. How did magic support or find support in other Trobriand customs? Participant observation showed that magic pervaded all activities, so in that sense functional theory was invoked simply to describe how it was well integrated.

Malinowski also demonstrated that the function of magic included helping people to cope in psychosocial terms with the threats and uncertainties of life. "All those crises of life, which are associated with fear of danger, with the awakening of passions or of strong emotions, have also their magical accompaniment" (Malinowski 1961: p. 393). Trobrianders had magic to make gardens productive, magic to support the building of sea-going boats, magic for the prevention as well as the cure of illness, magic for success in trading, and so on.

But magic was not just pervasively present. It was present in proportion to how great were the uncertainties and threats. In effect, he identified contrast domains of naturalism versus supernaturalism. Specifically, Malinowski found that a lot of magical ritual was performed when men fished on the dangerous open sea, but very little magic was practiced when they fished on the lagoon which was protected and safe. The functional integration of fishing and magical practice was excellent. The same was true of magic in the cultivation of crops.

> Thus there is a clear-cut division: there is first the well-known set of conditions, the natural course of growth, as well as the ordinary pests and dangers to be warded off by fencing and weeding. On the other hand there is the domain of the unaccountable and adverse influences, as well as the great unearned increment of fortunate coincidence. The first conditions are coped with by knowledge and work, the second by magic. (Malinowski, 1948; 29)

It is still useful to make sense of cultural practices by documenting the extent to which they demonstrate functional integration or demonstrate failure to fit nicely together. Malinowski stressed good fit and almost changeless homeostasis on the Trobriand Islands, seemingly secure in the belief that good fit was the norm. "The main social force governing all tribal life could be described as the inertia of custom, the love of uniformity of behavior" (Malinowski, 1961, p. 326). However, ethnographic research often demonstrates poor functional integration, especially in times of social upheaval and cultural change, which is exactly why it is useful to explore the extent to which health beliefs and practices fit, for example, with family and community involvements, on-the-job activities, recreational habits, religious commitments, and so on.

Malinowski's functional theory in its simplest form merely requires that the ethnographer look for mutually reinforcing, or possibly mutually incompatible, customs. It requires holism in the cultural description of a single community, with attention to how the parts fit together. One thorough example of this sort of generic functionalism can be found in the publications of George Foster, based on his and Mary Foster's many years of fieldwork in the peasant community of Tzintzuntzan, Mexico (Foster, 1967).

Foster proposed an equilibrium model. "A striving to maintain equilibrium thus emerges as the dominant pattern in Tzintzuntzan culture, a consistent organization of beliefs and actions reiterated in the major institutions of the community." Governmental activities, religious rituals, agricultural practices, the local pottery industry, family, community, schooling, all are adapted to the "basic cognitive orientations and behavior forms" of this large village. Not the least, "health concepts and behavior conform to the equilibrium model" (Foster, 1967, p. 168).

George and Mary Foster with two friends, village priests, on the occasion of a fiesta marking fifty years of anthropological research in Tzintzuntzan, Mexico.
(Photo, Melissa Bowerman)

The peasants of Tzintzuntzan taught Foster that the community is in good shape ("healthy") if everyone is about equally well-off in economic and social status terms. If one family enjoys an excess of wealth, then others must have less than their share, an attitude Foster made famous as "the image of the limited good." In a parallel way, villagers taught him that an individual is in good health if heat is evenly distributed throughout the body. One gets sick if heat becomes excessive in any one body part, if it escapes the body, or if cold invades it. For good health, it is essential that a hot-cold homeostasis be maintained. "The steps man takes to restore the equilibrium in a 'sick' society and a sick body are similar: drain off the excess of wealth and other Good, or the excess of heat, as the case may be; or add wealth, or heat, or otherwise remedy the imbalance that produces the unhealthy condition" (Foster, 1967, pp. 184–185).

Thus, using an equilibrium (functional) model, Foster demonstrates how curing techniques make sense for these people. All foods and beverages are classified as either hot or cold. These categories are metaphoric rather than physiologic. Thus, beef and wheat are hot but rabbit and maize are cold, which makes no sense in terms of nutritional chemistry but makes a lot of sense in terms of local disease theory. This way of thinking about health and disease in terms of a hot-cold balance may be ancient in Mesoamerica, but at least in part it derives from ancient Greek medicine by way of the Spanish invasion (Ortiz de Montellano, 1990, pp. 219–221; Foster, 1987). The underlying assumption is that an equilibrium of hot and cold must be maintained for good health. For this reason, for example, a case of diarrhea that is diagnosed by family members, neighbors, or the local healer *(curandero)* as caused by cold is treated with hot herb tea. However, if it is the kind of diarrhea that is caused by too much heat, the ill person will be given a cold drink strengthened with some sugar, ashes from the stove, or bits of tomato skin, all considered to be cold substances. Incidentally, Cecil Helman has identified and described some remnants of a similar hot/cold model of disease in a contemporary English suburb (Helman, 1978).

STRUCTURAL-FUNCTIONAL THEORY

Radcliffe-Brown, on a kind of parallel but independent track, postulated a version of functionalism that is somewhat different from the generic functionalism we have just illustrated. It is referred to it as the structural-functionalist approach (Radcliffe-Brown, 1952). Like Malinowski, Radcliffe-Brown looked for cultural interconnections, but with a teleologic slant. He demonstrated how certain cultural beliefs and practices appear to support the persistence of particular aspects of culture known as the social structure. The social structure was thought of as rules of alliance (such as kinship or political institutions) that had to be obeyed if the society was to hang together as an agglomeration of people.

We need examples relevant to health. Radcliffe-Brown gave his attention to nonhealth-related aspects of culture, such as the widely found rule that a boy may have a special relationship with his mother's brother, a custom known as the avunculate. He believed that the avunculate supported the functioning of a matrilineal social structure and thus of social survival (Radcliffe-Brown, 1924).

Let us not pursue Radcliffe-Brown's reasoning on the avunculate. Rather, let me illustrate the structural-functional approach with the health-related example of Beatrice Whiting, even though her work was not directly influenced by Radcliffe-Brown. You will recall that among the Paiute, Whiting found that one aspect of culture, beliefs about sorcery as the cause of illness, functioned indirectly to support another part of the culture, a social structure lacking police and judicial institutions. It achieved this by giving indirect structure to the control of violence. Thus, illness behavior shaped by a widespread fear of sorcery contributed to group survival in those communities.

The Sick Role Concept

Probably the single most influential application of structural-functional theory in medical anthropology is known to us as the concept of the sick role. It was introduced by Talcott Parsons, also without reference to the writings of Radcliffe-Brown (Parsons, 1951; Parsons & Fox, 1952). (Parsons, by the way, was a sociologist, illustrating the fact that sociologists and anthropologists have influenced each other repeatedly over the years since the time of August Comte.)

Abstracting from observed sickness behavior in the United States, Parsons postulated the existence of a component of the social structure that he designated the sick role. He observed that the status of patient seemed consistently to define four role privileges or obligations:

Privilege: Not held guilty or responsible for having fallen sick.
Privilege: Given respite from customary work or involvements.
Demand: Psychologically must want to get well.
Demand: Should seek care and cooperate with providers.

The sick role, in other words, permits a sick individual to take time off from work and to stay in bed if it is wished, but only on the condition of wanting to get well and of faithfully seeking appropriate health care.

From a structural-functional point of view, sickness always places burdens on the individual, the family, and the society (especially in the workplace). Sick role privileges and demands function to minimize societal stress. The sick role removes the patient from normal expectations while simultaneously creating a situation and attitude of mind conducive to recovery and reentry. Both the individual and society benefit. Equilibrium is maintained.

From the point of view of medical anthropologists, the concept of the sick role provides a useful model or ideal type for comparative analysis. It should not be taken as a statement of how things are. Rather, the sick role concept directs attention to the fit or nonfit of illness behavior in other settings (Wolinsky & Wolinsky, 1981; p. 229; Levine & Kozloff, 1978). Within American and Western culture itself, for example, it led to the realization that our social structure actually includes multiple sick roles. The Parsons sick role as such is best regarded as essentially culture-bound, characterizing upper middle-class urban Americans, and even for them, describing responses to acute illness episodes but not to chronic illness (Lowenberg, 1989; pp. 116, 118).

Sixty percent of the patients in an American clinic for the treatment of chronic pain suffered from neck or back pain. From a medical and surgical point of view, these patients were treatment failures. In reporting on them, Linda Alexander notes that whether consciously or not, medical personnel, family, friends, fellow workers, and others tended to place blame on the patients for continuing to be incapacitated and express pain behavior. Indeed, to some extent patients did benefit from their chronic pain in the form of disability income payments, solicitous care by family and friends, and in having leisure time. These benefits were offset by disadvantages additional to the pain and disability. They encountered resentment on the part of many because they no longer did work or chores. On the basis of her findings, Alexander documented a sick role very different from the Parsonian model (Alexander, 1982, p. 365):

- Privilege Denied: Felt to be responsible for being sick.
- Privilege Denied: No respite from customary work or involvements.
- Demand Frustrated: Psychologically must want to get well even though this is unrealistic and self-defeating.

- Demand Frustrated: Should seek care and cooperate with providers in spite of treatment failures.

June Lowenberg identified still another American model for the sick role. Lowenberg is a sociologist who carried out what she designates as "ethnographic research" that involved "participant observation" over a period of four years (Lowenberg, 1989, p. 9). The focus of her research was holistic health practices in Southern California, surely an exotic culture area if one is given to travelogue jargon. She found that the holistic model differed from the Parsons ideal type in the demands it made on the sick person. Care providers were more willing to work with clients who did not try to get well, feeling that overcoming client negativity can form part of the challenge of helping. The holistic care version of the sick role model also gives more control to the client. The sick participate actively in all phases of care. Because every illness is interpreted as having a potential for stimulating personal growth, illness and health are less categorically differentiated than in the standard middle-class model (Lowenberg, 1989, pp. 116–120):

- Privilege: Not held guilty or responsible for having fallen sick.
- Privilege: Given respite from customary work or involvements.
- Demand Mitigated: Negativity about getting well is acceptable.
- Demand Mitigated: In cooperating with health care providers, the sick participate in making decisions and take responsibility for health-affirming behaviors.

Moving from the United States to other parts of the world, James Young and Linda Garro illustrated a use of the sick role concept for comparative research in work they carried out in a Mexican village. In that community, as in the Parsonian model, a person was held blameless for emotion-related illnesses. The victim of evil eye *(mal de ojo)*, for example, accepts the sick role free of guilt or shame. However, someone who falls ill because of carelessness relating to inclement weather or dietary indiscretion is at fault. Bundle up in cold weather and don't eat too many hot peppers or you are to blame if you get sick. "To a certain extent, then, a person is considered responsible for what happens as a result of failure to defend against known hazards" (Young & Garro, 1994; p. 60).

In Malaysia, Aihwa Ong documented still another application of the ideal type model of the sick role. In that nation, multinational corporations now employ thousands of young, unmarried women as factory workers. To the chagrin of industrial managers, when at work on the assembly line an otherwise excellent worker may suddenly hyperventilate, scream, hit, kick, convulse, and collapse. The attack may spread to others who do the same, producing chaos and, alas, production delays. What are we to make of this?

As an anthropologist contributing to feminist theory, Ong is able to show the similarity of these spirit attacks to attacks in rural circumstances among a different category of Islamic Malay women (Ong, 1988). Traditionally, the victim is a married woman who has just given birth to her first child. It almost never happens in rural areas to an unmarried woman. Now the attacks are against these younger women in factories.

Ong sees a similarity in that both categories of young women are entering new phases of their lives and are subject to male domination that leaves them vulnerable to abuse. She points out that "the modern factory is an arena constituted by a sexual division of labor and constant male surveillance of nubile women in a close, daily context" (Ong, 1988, p. 34). Following I. M. Lewis, their episodes of violent spirit possession are interpreted as "thinly disguised protest against the dominant sex" (Lewis, 1971, p. 31). Effective treatment is provided by a practitioner of folk medicine, the *bomoh,* who is qualified to exorcise the evil spirit and to purify factory areas where evil spirits are known to lurk.

In contrast to this evaluation based on anthropological and feminist theory and experience, a medical approach employed by the corporations tended to be ineffectual and to cause many of these young women to lose their jobs. Of special interest here is that Ong uses the concept of sick role to make sense of this abusive approach:

> In corporate discourse, both the biomedical and psychological interpretations of spirit possession defined the affliction as an attribute of individuals rather than stemming from the general social situation. Scientific concepts, pharmaceutical treatment, and behavioral intervention all identified and separated recalcitrant workers from "normal" ones; disruptive workers became patients. According to Parsons, the cosmopolitan medical approach tolerates illness as sanctioned social deviance; however, patients have the duty to get well. This attitude implies that those who do not get well cannot be rewarded with "the privileges of being sick." In the . . . factory, the playing out of this logic provided the rationale for dismissing workers who had had two previous experiences of spirit attacks, on the grounds of "security.". . . The sick role was reconceptualized as internally produced by outmoded thought and behavior not adequately adjusted to the demands of factory discipline. The worker-patient could have no claim on management sympathy but would have to bear responsibility for her own cultural deficiency. (Ong, 1988, p. 37)

Functional and structural-functional theory were the hottest things in town around mid-century before they, too, fell out of favor. The argument was that functionalism was merely a truism. Functional theory was stuck in a concept of culture as essentially unchanging. It was branded an equilibrium model in the sense that any changes that occurred served merely to perpetuate the cultural system as it was. Structural-functional interpretations did this with a vengeance. The concept of ideal types was an inherently static rather than dynamic concept. But while structural and functional theory were pushed out of the limelight, they continue to provide one important way among many of exploring and making sense out of health care circumstances. The work of Young and Garro in Mexico and Ong in Malaysia should serve to make this point.

STRUCTURAL THEORY

As the influence of Malinowski and Radcliffe-Brown diminished, it was to some extent replaced by that of Claude Lévi-Strauss. No purely cultural approach has had more impact on the field than some of the challenging and extremely influential methods and theories inspired by anthropological linguistics as a field of cultural studies. We have already verified this assertion in discussion of the methods of ethnoscience and cognitive anthropology. What was unanticipated, however, was the massiveness of the contribution of linguistics to the invention of new methods and theory that for a time dominated much of cultural anthropology. This influence of linguistically based theories led in several directions.

Claude Lévi-Strauss took the lead in a direction that came to be called structural anthropology. He was inspired by structural linguistics as conceptualized in the Prague School founded by N. Trubetzkoy and Roman Jacobson (Lévi-Strauss, 1967 [1945]). Jacobson developed techniques for converting the diversity of sounds recorded in phonetics, which is merely descriptive, to the identification of meaningful sound units created by phonemics.

Phonemics is a method of analysis that allows linguists to convert the hundreds of sounds of a spoken language into a smaller number of clusters of sounds. Variations within a cluster are not noticed by speakers, but contrasts between any two clusters acquire meaning. For example, the difference between the sound of [p] with a small puff of air or without that puff is so unimportant in the English phoneme [p] that most of us do not even notice or hear it. However, the difference between [p] and a very similar sound, [b], is noticed. So, we know that the word *pin* and the word *bin* have different meanings because [p] and [b] are meaningful contrasts, while the difference between the [p] in *pin* (which has a puff) and the [p] in *spin* (which has no puff) has no significance; both are merely variations of a [p]. This is what Jacobson referred to as distinctive feature analysis (Leach, 1970; p. 23).

Lévi-Strauss reasoned that a culture is similar to a language. A culture comprises a myriad of thoughts, values, behaviors, selective awarenesses, and knowledge. Typically we attach meaning to aspects of culture. They become symbols. For example, a cross or a crescent in our society is rich with meaning. Making a "V" with your fingers also conveys a meaning that we all understand. These symbols are more or less conscious, obvious, and contrived.

Somehow, at some time, meanings become attached to cultural traits. The meanings often seem to be quite arbitrary. Why should a white flag symbolize surrender or the Stars and Stripes a nation? The achievement of Lévi-Strauss was to realize that while symbols represent powerful aspects of culture, an even more powerful level of meaning is to be found in a deeper, unconscious patterning of language and thought that lies beyond awareness and that came into being without conscious contrivance. This deeper structure consists not of symbols as such, but of relations between symbols (Leach, 1970; Paz, 1970). Speaking of the symbolism of art, Anthony Forge put it this way, "Any systematic symbolism must be at the level of the relation between symbols, and at this level may not be consciously perceived by either the artist or the beholder" (Forge, 1971, p. 297). In this sense, culture is a language or code of symbols.

Binary Oppositions

The first point to make in applying the structural method is to note that the code is one of binary oppositions. This form of analysis is best understood by means of an illustration. Let us take the case of contemporary urban Japan, where Emiko Ohnuki-Tierney applied structural principles as a way to better understand Japanese beliefs and practices relating to daily hygiene (Ohnuki-Tierney, 1984).

Ohnuki-Tierney found that she could identify a number of binary oppositions in Japanese personal hygiene. For example, people are very concerned about avoiding sickness. So, one binary opposition is that of health versus illness. In spatial terms, people feel that their homes are clean places while the world beyond the home is dirty and threatening. Hence, another binary opposition is that of inside versus outside.

Time also structures their thinking and behavior relating to health, since the binary opposition of day and night relates in part to the health-preserving qualities of nighttime safe at home and the health-endangering qualities of daytime in the world outside of the home. Further, people tend to think of the body as bifurcated into the upper half, which is clean and pure, and the lower half which, by virtue of excretory and genital functions, is impure. The binary opposition of above versus below is thus also salient for health.

Japanese religious ideology attaches great importance to the maintenance of purity as a moral value. "Be pure" is a motto often seen around schools and in other public places. Purity is thought of as health preserving, so purity versus impurity is another binary opposition that is relevant. Religion also deals with profound eschatological issues, not the least of which is life versus death.

In this Japanese code of binary oppositions, the deeper symbolic meaning of any one of these terms reflects its opposite. In other words, if we look at a word on one side, its meaning is informed by the word on the other side that is its opposite. These linear or horizontal relationships are sometimes referred to as metonymic or syntagmatic, which I mention because you will encounter these usages. Thus, it is a metonymic effect that life has meaning as the opposite of death just as night has meaning as the opposite of day.

Transformations

In structural analysis, one does not stop here. In addition to looking at horizontal oppositions, one looks for vertical transformations. These can be referred to as metaphoric or paradigmatic rather than metonymic or syntagmatic relations. Transformations are easy to see if we list all of the oppositions in a vertical column as follows:

Back in the United States after field work in Japan, Emiko Ohnuki-Tierney devoted long, hard hours to library research and analysis of her original documentation before publishing her findings.

health	illness
life	death
inside	outside
night	day
purity	impurity
above	below

The symbolism of the words on the left side are influenced by other words on the same side. Thus, health and life are dimensions of each other, and reflect the benefits of being inside at night as well as the purity of the upper part of the body. Transformations on the other side are of an opposite character.

These metonymic oppositions and metaphoric transformations can be restated in a different way: Health is to illness as life is to death, as night is to day, as purity is to impurity, and as above is to below. So, when a person uses any one of these terms or concepts, it is loaded in the sense of implying meanings derived from both oppositions and transformations. The unaware mind is made vastly richer and more complex in these ways. To be able to describe cultural beliefs and practices in rich and complex ways by building up layers of meaning is to achieve what Clifford Geertz refers to as *thick description,* an appropriate goal for an ethnographer (Geertz, 1973).

Mediation

Codes of binary oppositions and transformations are pervasive (some would argue, universal) within cultures and across cultures. Where they can be identified, they probably do more than just deepen the unconscious associations of symbols, but what do they achieve? Regarding hygiene in Japan, they seem to reflect deep and largely subconscious anxieties about life and health.

These subconscious codes presumably are therapeutic to the extent that they express deep-seated fears simultaneously with acknowledgments of hope. After all, retreat to night and inside along with commitments to purity and the body "above" offer some balance to the dangers of the day spent outside in impure circumstances.

The Japanese code relating to daily health concerns does more than that. The oppositions are mediated in the sense that one can feel they are being resolved or minimized by proper actions and thoughts. One can do something to relieve anxieties. For example, the oppositions of inside/outside and night/day are acted on in an ameliorating (mediating) way by practicing the custom of maintaining a high fence or wall around the house and of taking shoes off at the door, leaving contact with the dirt below and outside as a way to preserve cleanliness and health inside and above. Similarly, night inside is kept pure and clean. Opposites are resolved by the custom of bathing immediately before going to bed with the idea that to do so will hold germs at bay and ensure that one will not catch a chill in the winter air. Subsequently, night is protected by one of the first duties of the morning, which is to fold the futon, ensure that it is clean, and hide it away in a closet where it will not get soiled.

Purity above is dramatized in the practice of washing underpants separately from other clothing when doing the family wash and in the requirement to carefully soap, wash, and rinse before getting into the hot tub for a good soak. The toilet, which is the most defiling place in the house, is closeted by itself, away from other facilities including bathroom sinks. In some houses a special pair of slippers is kept in the toilet room, to be used only there to guard feet and stockings from contamination.

In all, daily hygienic practices can be understood as expressing health anxieties in the form of a binary code of oppositions and transformations. These anxieties or dangers appear to be resolved or reduced by mediation in the form of activities that are felt to remove the dangers and resolve the tensions. However, the success of these various acts of mediation appear to be limited, judging from the observation that people feel impelled to repeat them daily in a quotidian cycle that never ends.

If only at this level, structural analysis offers one option among many for anthropologists who may be casting about for theoretical models to help them make sense out of the health-related beliefs and behaviors they encounter. But much more is at stake. Although out of conscious awareness, the structuralist code at its deepest level appears to be making important statements about fundamental eschatological issues having to do with the ultimate meaning of life and death.

Lévi-Strauss came to the conclusion that in every society people deeply fear an unavoidable danger. Every one of us eventually must die. As human beings we are conscious of this ultimate reality in that we are very different from animals. Not only do we have this awareness of ultimate demise, but we also have culture. Animals do not have culture. The awareness of death is shaped by cultural conventions having to do with ideas about life after death. Thus, both awareness and culture make us different from animals. For these reasons a universal code is expressed in every society. It shapes up as the ultimate opposition, which is the opposition of culture versus nature, along with its transformation as an opposition of life versus death.

By means of metaphoric extensions, a code such as that of Japanese hygiene often can be interpreted as as elaborate statement about culture and life versus nature and death. Ultimately the code is about individual immortality (some form of life after death) versus mortality. Animals are mortal—they die for eternity. We are different from animals, and by the logic of oppositions, we live for eternity.

In structural terms, then, the minutiae of cleanliness having to do with health, inside, night, purity, above, and life constitute a daily attempt to assuage health anxieties, including the deepest unconscious anxiety of all. The mediations encountered in Japan are assumed to help relieve these diverse anxieties, but they do so only temporarily. The next day they will need to be mediated all over again.

If this structuralist analysis is helpful in Japan, it leaves unanswered the assertion by structuralists that at a deep level, removed from cultural specifics, the code is found in every society. A contemporary poststructuralist critic would insist that the deep structure identified in Japan cannot be expected to endure forever in Japan, and certainly does not mirror a deep structure of personal hygiene that constitutes a universal grammar of human symbolic systems. The existence of, and importance of, universal, invariant, or essential structures remains, despite decades of theorizing, an issue heavily debated (Waitzkin, 1991, p. 34).

An Example from Bali

Anthropologists working in many parts of the world have found it useful to employ structural analysis to help thicken their descriptions of health and healing. One additional example will suffice. Linda Conner approached her description of the ethnomedical practitioner *(balian)* of Bali in part by taking note of a pervasive opposition, that of darkness versus light. The cosmos in Bali is conceptualized as two realms in opposition, one mystical and the other empirical.

"Darkness," the domain of mystical activity, need not have sinister connotations; rather, the term indicates that this realm is largely opaque to human understanding. "Light" is the domain of everyday life. Mystical forces constantly impinge upon the realm of human activity; darkness and light are separated only in the abstract, never in practice. (Connor, 1986, p. 27)

The balian, she finds, fights against disease, death, and other misfortunes by using spiritual powers to mediate between these opposing realms. "Balians, in their healing ceremonies, attempt to influence the condition of their patients by deploying spiritually powerful . . . medicines, offerings, and mantra syllables." Further, human health and the larger universe are thought of as dimensions of one another. She writes of several transformations, speaking of them in terms of a principle of correspondence:

small world	great world
microcosm	macrocosm
human body	all of existence (cosmos)

Just as the mediation of a balian may contribute to the resolution of an illness, "People with great spiritual power may also effect changes in the natural universe by the correct manipulation of mystical forces within their own bodies. Balinese myths and chronicles contain many stories about deities and seers whose meditations changed the course of nature" (Connor, 1986, p. 28). She notes in summary, "On behalf of individuals and communities, balians struggle with misfortune, disease, and death by deploying their spiritual powers in mediation between the domain of mystical activity (to which they have privileged access) and their clients' immediate concerns" (Connor, 1986, p. 27).

CULTURE AS A TEXT

From language and linguistics to literary theory is quite a jump. The theoretical grounding is still in linguistics, and specifically in Jacobson, who had gone well beyond his formulation of code to explore the constitutive factors of any speech event in a larger context that included the addresser, the addressee , and the message (Jacobson, 1960). The central concern of ethnologists using this theoretical approach is to interpret or explain the meaning of cultural beliefs and practices. As Michael Lambek put it, "the goal is to reduce the strangeness of other people's symbolic constructions without thereby sacrificing their richness and complexity" (Lambek, 1981, pp. 4–5). The work of Lambek is particularly appropriate for our purposes, since he uses this approach to explore the meaning of illness and treatment among the people of Mayotte Island, located between East Africa and Madagascar.

We can begin by noting how Lambek employs the kind of basic structural analysis we have just reviewed. He describes an affliction caused by spirit possession, which is usually imposed at the instigation of a sorcerer. This spirit intrusion results in long-lasting or recurring illness complicated by disturbing dreams and spontaneous episodes of trance. Most commonly, the spirit is of a kind known as *patros.*

Binary Oppositions and Transformations

What is a patros? It is conceptualized as a living humanlike being who is opposite to a human being in strange ways, particularly in food preferences.

human	patros
host (possessed)	spirit (possesser)
village on land	village under water
visible	invisible
smell cologne	consume cologne
eat cooked foods	eat raw foods
eat cooked eggs	eat raw eggs
red meat, no liver	liver, no red meat
no blood eaten	blood frequently consumed
cake as a treat	cake as a staple
sugar as luxury	sugar in large amounts

It should be noted that Lambek stresses the key significance of the contrast between a person who is ill and a patros or other spirit who causes the illness. "This opposition between two discrete identities, host and spirit, is the single most crucial element, the axiom, upon which the entire system of possession rests" (Lambek, 1981, p. 41). From a Lévi-Straussian perspective, it should also be noted that cooked foods symbolize culture, since only human beings cook their food, while raw foods symbolize nature. Symbolically, these foods incorporate the implicit opposition of culture versus nature (Lévi-Strauss, 1969).

FIGURE 6-1
The Process of Mediation as a Triad

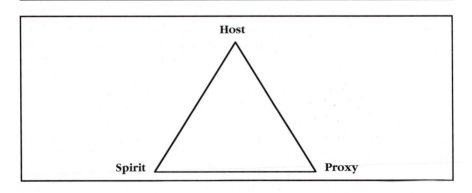

Mediation

It is the function of the curer to mediate these oppositions. The cake and cologne serve as stage props for this healing activity. Cologne is valued by both, although in different ways. Cake is the one food that is eaten by both spirit and human participants in the ritual. The cakes are divided with great care by the curer. To do so correctly is considered a difficult technique and how well it is carried out is regarded as a measure of a curer's skill. The ritual constitutes a bridge that helps to unite the sick person, the spirit, and the community as a healing communion, "performing a mediative function or transfer point between the human and spirit systems, clarifying the significance of the occasion for both sides" (Lambek, 1981, p. 39).

Triads and Triangles

With this, Lambek moves into a diagrammatic approach much liked by Lévi-Strauss, the use of triangles. To put it differently, Lambek moved beyond the dyad of host and spirit to demonstrate the importance of triads as a way to think about communication as a process of mediation. In the case of Mayotte Islanders, he identified a minimal structure of possession that is composed of three figures (fig. 6-1).

The three apices of the triangle thus represent:

- the host, that is, the individual who is possessed
- the spirit who intrudes into the host's body
- the host's proxy, e.g., spouse, relative, or curer

From his discussion of this triad as a way to talk about communication, one begins to sense how Lambek moved towards the concept of culture as a text. The curing process is one of communication. Through possession, a text is generated or transmitted. The text is made possible by this system of conventions—the triad—that structures communication in a way that permits comprehension by the participants or observers, that is, the readers of the text.

> What I wish to suggest is that the triad is the irreducible minimal structure of possession. That is to say, communication entails a minimum of three figures—sender, receiver, and intermediary . . . . A spirit that rises in a host always does so in order to make its presence known to a third party, that is, in order to speak to someone. . . . To the degree that such separation between host and spirit is maintained, the spirit can say and do things that would be impossible or unthinkable for the host (and also say things to the host), such as to make unilateral demands or to publically challenge or scorn the host's spouse, relatives, or curer. . . . Such freedom of expression is further enhanced by the fact that host and spirit are frequently of opposite sex from one another. A male spirit in a female host, by far the most frequent

combination, speaks with the authority and perogatives of a male in contexts in which it might be inappropriate for women to speak or act and in which their male listeners might otherwise lose face. (Lambek, 1981, pp. 73–74)

The text (possession ritual) has a metonymic (syntagmatic) dimension, which is to say that the meaning of the text can be extracted by following events in time sequence, lineally or horizontally, just as one follows the words of this sentence or the relationships of oppositions described above.

The text also has a metaphoric (paradigmatic) dimension, which is the vertical dimension described above, albeit less obvious because it must be teased out of the complexity of the possession events. Mediation is seen in this example as the provision of a voice of complaint for individuals who feel abused. Possession empowers subaltern members of the community, women above all, in the sense that it gives them some leverage against the oppressive hegemony of family and community authorities.

DISCOURSE ANALYSIS

I have gone to some length to indicate that literary theory shapes the work of some medical anthropologists. In addition to the term *structuralism,* as such, these theorists refer to their work as structuralist poetics, literary criticism, narrative analysis, discourse analysis, hermeneutics, or semiology. The purpose of these kinds of analysis is to ferret out meanings that cultural events such as curing rituals have for participants and observers. If you want to know why a Mayotte Islander who is possessed by a patros suddenly gives in to an urge to drink a bottle of cologne or to lap up a bowl of congealed goat's blood, this analysis will help. You will have moved from naive observation through what the French philosopher Paul Ricoeur refers to as an interpretive arc that ends in knowledgeable understanding. You will have read the events as a text.

Newer approaches derived from linguistics have given attention to the language usages of health care encounters. These are taken as oral texts that can be deconstructed to reveal hidden messages. In the interaction of doctors and nurses, for example, it has been said that language usage by physicians indicates a primary orientation to diagnosis and treatment, while that of the nurse reveals an orientation to personal and social aspects of an illness.

As an illustration, physicians use distancing terms such as "symptoms" and "diseases" while nurses speak more interactively of "patient problems" and "concerns." Vocabulary alone suggests differing professional priorities in patient care that can result in miscommunication and discord within a health care team. This divergence in professional values is suggested by such seemingly innocuous phrases as when a nurse speaks highly of a doctor because "he really knows his patients," while a physician praises a doctor on an entirely different basis because "he really knows his medicine" (Lynaugh & Bates, 1973).

Language usage among physicians has also been explored. One study focused on humor in speech play, particularly the humor that derives from breaking linguistic rules in the social contexts of patient care. Referring to Amphoteracin B, a powerful but dangerous drug, as "Amphoterrible" reflects physician anxieties about possible misprescribing as well as concern for patients who risk seizures and even death if they are intolerant of it. Again, to speak of transferring a patient to the "Expensive Care Unit" for intensive care uses punning as a way to express complex feelings about a serious decision, including an awareness of the extremely high costs, the sophistication of the technology, and, no doubt, the sense of inadequacy of a physician whose patient is failing (Burson-Tolpin, 1989).

Language usage in a cross-cultural perspective also offers a way to get at deeper understandings of health care situations. A comparison of American physicians with their counterparts in Europe and Asia reveals that cancer specialists interact with patients in contexts that are culturally and linguistically framed. Italian and Japanese physicians usually conceal a diagnosis of cancer by devious and misleading language. A generation ago, American physicians did the same. Now, the dialogue of American doctors is shaped by ethical and legal requirements that patients be told in clear, unambiguous terms if malignancy is involved.

Most discourse analysis has focused on dialogue between doctors and patients rather than among health professionals. In working with cancer patients, for example, doctors are trained to use discourse with considerable sensitivity, as appears in this interview with a cancer specialist.

QUESTION: How do you determine whether or not a patient knows their diagnosis?

DOCTOR: Well, I ask them how I can help them. It's the only question I ask to begin an interview and they have to spin it out from there.

QUESTION: If a patient comes to you not knowing their diagnosis. . . [?]

DOCTOR: I tell them that we are concerned it may be a tumor. . . I never use the word cancer, ah, it is just not in my vocabulary.

QUESTION: Why?

DOCTOR: Because that is a word that patients assume and don't want to hear you say until they work up the courage to ask "Is the tumor malignant?" or "By tumor do you mean cancer?" So I give them the—control—to decide when they want to phrase the question that way. They all do but . . . some ask immediately and others—it may be a second or third visit before they'll ultimately ask if the tumor I'm talking about is a malignant one. (Good et al.; 1990, p. 65)

As seen here, language is used to shape doctor/patient interactions. What a lot of people dislike is the sense of being subordinate to their doctors. Discourse analysis reveals what all of us have experienced at one time or another. While you think back to your experiences, let me tell about one of mine. I took time off from work one afternoon when my mother was in her eighties to take her for the first time to meet her new doctor, an internist fresh out of residency. As he phrased the usual questions in taking her medical history, I interjected a word or two when I knew my mother was uncertain or confused. He asked about her medications, and I began to list them, but was abruptly and preemptorily told to be quiet and to let Mrs. Anderson speak for herself. Chagrinned and humiliated, I never said another word.

> DOCTOR: What medications do you take?
> PATIENT: None.
> DOCTOR: Have you ever had any surgery done?
> PATIENT: No, never.

And so it went. The history was soon finished, her answers being quite short. The doctor asked me to leave while he conducted his physical examination, which revealed a large abdominal scar from an old hysterectomy and a disfiguring chest scar from a mastectomy. She had simply forgotten that years earlier she had undergone two major surgeries. For his part, he never acknowledged to me that my intercessions were actually necessary if he was to get the correct information he should have. Needless to say, once we had left we never went back again.

Having had that experience, I was pleased when I came across "The Family Caregiver as Interpreter in the Geriatric Medical Interview," a report on research by Betty Hasselkus (Hasselkus, 1992). Her research seemed to confirm my instincts as a dutiful son. She obtained permissions that allowed her to turn on a tape recorder in the room where old people, accompanied by a family member, were meeting with their doctors, documenting forty sessions in all. She herself was not present during the meetings. Meticulous thematic analysis of the audiotapes revealed three modes of discourse involving a family member.

■ Sometimes the family member functioned as a facilitator, helping the patient by prompting, correcting, and clarifying. For example,

> PATIENT [TO DOCTOR]: I take one of each. The reason why I think maybe they would've given me two uh [pause]
> CAREGIVER: Motrin.
> PATIENT: Motrin is that I have a couple bottles of Nyle [pause], Nylenol [pause]
> CAREGIVER: Tylenol.
> PATIENT: Yeah, I wanted to use them up.

■ Or, the family member might serve as an intermediary, attempting to clarify possible misunderstandings in a triadic exchange. For example:

> DOCTOR: No chest pain or anything of that sort with exercise or activity, I take it?
> PATIENT: No.
> DOCTOR: Good. [pause]
> CAREGIVER: But, he does have a cough, a dry cough.

■ Finally, the family member may act as a direct source of information for the doctor. Again, a brief example will illustrate the point:

CAREGIVER: She would like me to increase the amount that she gets, the meat and potatoes.

DOCTOR: Uh-huh. What's she been running? [blood sugars]

CAREGIVER: Uh, three to four hours after a meal it's been like 102, 103.

DOCTOR: OK. No insulin reaction, so—

CAREGIVER [TO PATIENT]: Do you want to ask him what you wanted to ask? About your meat and potatoes?

PATIENT: Oh yeah. Could I have a little more meat and potatoes for my meals?

DOCTOR: It certainly sounds that way.

Hasselkus concludes, "Mishler has contrasted statements of doctors and patients as 'the voice of medicine' and 'the voice of the lifeworld.' The findings in the present study can be interpreted in the context of the two voices. In the triadic medical interview, however, the vocal duet becomes a trio, and the caregiver-interpreter is trying to sing all three parts." Knowing more about the nature of discourse in these three-person negotiations should be helpful in efforts to improve the effectiveness of triadic medical encounters. My mother, may she rest in peace, would agree wholeheartedly, I am sure, but perhaps it is time that I stop speaking on her behalf.

Elliot Mishler concludes that doctors tend to keep interviews focused strictly on medical issues. They convey a sense of time urgency, wanting patients to get to the point and not ramble. They permit only the "voice of medicine," censoring out the "voice of the lifeworld" that reflects a patient's concerns and ways of thinking about the illness (Mishler, 1984). Patients initiate fewer questions than do doctors and they rarely interrupt, although they are more likely to interrupt female than male doctors. Physicians, for their part, often interrupt patients who digress from their agendas, steering them back by posing questions. Doctors initiate more questions than do patients, cutting off some topics and bringing in others. Important aspects of a patient's experience are dismissed and ignored (West, 1984).

Howard Waitzkin recorded this fragment of a dialogue of a thirteen-year old girl with the doctor who was giving her a medical examination as a condition of going to summer camp:

DOCTOR: Do you smoke at all?

PATIENT: Mari-

DOCTOR (INTERRUPTING): Never smoke cigarettes?

PATIENT: No.

DOCTOR: No. Good. Okay. Maybe we could bring you in here and take a look at you.

Waitzkin's analysis reveals how the doctor controlled the discourse. He did not want to hear about the illicit smoking of marijuana, so he stopped her by interrupting her before the word is fully out of her mouth. He immediately sub-stituted a leading question to limit her response clearly to cigarettes. The patient answered this in an acceptable way, after which the doctor shifted abruptly from taking her history to performing a routine physical examination. Her voice of the lifeworld—the issue of emotional importance to this young teenager who was experimenting with smoking pot—was cut out of the conversation. It sim-ply disappeared (Waitzkin, 1991, p. 235).

Doctors are able to minimize or eliminate the lifeworld because they closely control discourse. Racial, ethnic, gender, and class differences can compound the power plays of clinical language. Consider this dialogue recorded by Leslie Swartz in South Africa. It took place between an African woman who made her living in the city as a live-in domestic and the white doctor who attended her in the hospital where she was seen. She spoke English with ease, so a third-party translator was not required. The big issue in her lifeworld at that time was that she was worried about her son who lived six hundred miles away in a rural area. Her doctor believed she was depressed. The clinical interview in part went as follows (Swartz, 1991, p. 223):

CLINICIAN: You have bad dreams.
PATIENT: I do not have dreams.
CLINICIAN: You are troubled by your bad dreams.
PATIENT: I do not have bad dreams.
CLINICIAN: You have bad dreams about your son.
PATIENT: (quickly and apparently angrily) I do not have any dreams.

Out of earshot, the clinician continued to insist that this mother truly was having bad dreams. The vehemence of her denial was offered as proof. It should be noted that Western-trained physicians do not usually interview patients by making assertions that require affirmation. On the contrary, African patients are sometimes baffled by the questions medical doctors ask because the nature of Western medical discourse is so different from what they are accustomed to. Whether purposefully or not, this white doctor had conducted his interrogation in a traditional African way. The patient's experi-ence with traditional South African healers would have prepared her for that. Relying upon spiritual insight, African healers do tell a patient what is wrong and ask the patient to verify the truth of their statements. However, unlike the hegemonic dialogue recorded above, denial of the imputed symptoms is taken to mean that the doctor is on the wrong track and should immediately switch to an alternative clinical hunch or be discredited.

Let me illustrate an example of this mode of discourse that was recorded in Zimbabwe. A traditional Shona doctor (n'anga) sat next to a young woman who came to him for help. I was seated facing them both. The n'anga, possessed by an ancestral spirit, cast a handful of bones on a cloth on the ground where he was sitting. How they fell gave him the information he needed. (The following is an abbreviated version of the dialogue.)

N'ANGA: Your hips and shoulders are painful.

CLIENT: Right. Both shoulders hurt, I have stomach problems, and my right leg is painful.

N'ANGA: You have premenstrual pain and your knees get weak.

CLIENT: Yes.

N'ANGA: (unexpectedly turning to Anderson) In your earlier days you had a stomach problem.

ANDERSON (Silence. I never had a stomach problem.)

N'ANGA: (to Anderson) You have had a problem in your sex life.

ANDERSON: (Silence. Who hasn't!)

N'ANGA: (directing his attention back to the client, who asked: What should I do to get well?) You can go to a hospital and get well, or to a n'anga.

CLIENT: I want a n'anga. How much will it cost?

It should not go unnoticed that African healers may also control patients in discourse, but the force field of language and gesture is very different. When I did not pick up on his apparent effort to recruit me as a client, the n'anga turned his attention back to his client without forcing the issue.

Conversation analysis can also demonstrate helpful and supportive interactions. Consider the following dialogue, a short illustration from the records of eleven patient-doctor dyads audiotaped in an urban family practice residency in California. The doctor and the patient are both Spanish-speaking women. (The following excerpt is modifed from the author's publication to fit the format used above in recording discourse.)

DOCTOR: Regresemos a como se siente Ud. Ud. me estaba diciendo que no se sentía bien. (Let's go back to how you feel. You were telling me that you were not feeling well.)

PATIENT: Oh, sí, me siento mal ya/ no se ni como vivo/ el dolor aquí en mis riñones. (Oh, yes, I feel bad now/ I do not even know how I live/the pain here in my kidneys.)

DOCTOR: Um-hum.

PATIENT: No, no se me quita. Hay días que lo tengo tan fuerte. (It does not stop. There are days that I have it so strong.)

DOCTOR: Um-hum.

PATIENT: De hace ocho días para, para esta fecha no me he sentido nada de bien. (It has been eight days from this day that I have not felt any bit well.)

DOCTOR: Cuando Ud. dice nada de bien, qué es lo que Ud. siente que por eso se siente nada de bien? (When you say nada de bien?)

PATIENT: Siento como si me está hirviendo toda la sangre como que me siento y luego no me dan las fuerzas y me tengo que acostar. (I feel as if all my blood is boiling is how I feel and later I do not have strength and I have to lie down.)

DOCTOR: Um-hum. So, está cansada. (Um-hum. So, you are tired.)
PATIENT: Sí, muy mala. (Yes, very bad.)

Sharry Erzinger, who carried out this conversation analysis, draws attention to how the doctor helped her patient make her description clearer. Her conversation style encouraged the patient to elaborate. On occasion she used the patient's own words to facilitate dialogue. She also paraphrased the patient's description of how she felt as she worked with the patient to arrive at a meaningful statement of what the patient was feeling and wanted to express. The cultural rules of respect required this patient to defer to the conversational direction set by the doctor. The patient showed appropriate respect and deference. The doctor, however, showed respect in return, and used her language skills to encourage the patient to express herself fully (Erzinger, 1991).

So far, most published research on discourse analysis has been situated in Western medicine. "Unfortunately," Joel Kuipers observes, "as of this writing, there are no full-length, anthropologically oriented, comparative studies that examine detailed transcriptions of such interactions in relation to cultural ideologies of sociability, gender, deference, or time use in institutional encounters in non-Western countries. Such studies may significantly alter taken-for-granted assumptions about the conduct of the medical encounter" (Kuipers, 1989, p. 108). As Alan Harwood pointed out a few years ago, discourse analysis is characterized by an "apparent all-purposeness of the method" that makes it useful for anthropologists with diverse theoretical perspectives (Harwood, 1988, p. 101). We may expect to see more use of this approach in the future.

CONCLUSION

The shift from cross-cultural comparative research to fieldwork in face-to-face communities as the signature activity of anthropologists was associated with a paradigm shift in theory. It incorporated a pendulum swing from deductive to inductive reasoning, in principle if not in fact. Rather than interpret the ethnographica of cultural diversity deductively in terms of how cultural findings meshed with a theory of evolution or of diffusion, the challenge became one of constructing an inductive theoretical edifice on the basis of what one discovered in the field.

To the extent that one can consistently distinguish induction from deduction, a questionable enterprise at best, functional theory and structural-functional theory illustrate this shift to an inductive approach. So, too, does structuralism, but with more of an obvious blending of inductive and deductive reasoning, since it resulted from an attempt to apply linguistic theory to cultures and did not directly emerge from ethnographic field data unassisted.

As anthropologists further explored the potentialities of linguistic theories for cultural analysis, some experimented with interpreting cultures as texts. Others took social discourse as an aspect of culture revelatory of the power of the word, as it were. Discourse analysis revealed modes of hegemonic control of subaltern participants in many customary encounters, as between doctors and patients. It also documented language usage calculated to give voice to those who often are silenced, ignored, or controlled.

Within anthropology, field-based studies appeared to result in a paradigmatic revolution. Concordantly, functional theory in its various manifestations seemed to constitute a near total break with the past. It was incompatible with either evolutionary reconstructions or historical particularism, both of which it supplanted as the main thing cultural anthropologists did. It redefined the basis for comparative studies as a process whereby many anthropologists working through the years would gradually build up a library of studies from different parts of the world, endlessly documenting diversity to the neglect of uniformities. It led to a shift in the problems thought worthy of study and in the standards for admissible evidence and legitimate solutions. By any measure, it represented a quantum shift in what anthropology is about.

Yet, the categorical newness of this shift was an illusion. By mid-century, elements of older paradigms began to reemerge. Reaching simultaneously into the future and into the past, the next paradigm shift began with a return of the time dimension. American cultural anthropologists shifted from a synchronic perspective (this moment in time) to the diachronic—the study of culture change.

REFERENCES

Alexander, L. (1982). Illness maintenance and the new American sick role. In N. J. Chrisman & T. W. Maretzki (Eds.), *Clinically applied anthropology* (pp. 351–367). Boston: D. Reidel Publishing Co.

Burson-Tolpin, A. (1989). Fracturing the language of biomedicine: The speech play of U.S. physicians. *Medical Anthropology Quarterly, 3,* 383–393.

Conner, L. (1986). Balinese healing. In L. Conner, P. Asch, & T. Asch (Eds.), *Jero Tapakan: Balinese healer—An ethnographic film monograph* (pp. 21–53). Cambridge, MA: Cambridge University Press.

Erzinger, S. (1991). Communication between Spanish-speaking patients and their doctors in medical encounters. *Culture, Medicine, and Psychiatry, 15,* 91–110.

Forge, A. (1971). Art and environment in the Sepik. In C. F. Jopling (Ed.), *Art and aesthetics in primitive societies* (pp. 290–314). New York: E. P. Dutton & Co.

Foster, G. M. (1967). *Tzintzuntzan: Mexican peasants in a changing world.* Boston: Little, Brown and Co.

Foster, G. M. (1987). On the origin of humoral medicine in Latin America. *Medical Anthropological Quarterly, 1,* 355–393.

Geertz, E. (1973). Thick description: Toward an interpretive theory of culture. In C. Gertz (Ed.) *The interpretation of cultures* (pp. 3–30). New York: Basic Books.

Good, M. J. D., Good, B. J., Schaffer, C., & Lind, S. E. (1990). American oncology and the discourse on hope. *Culture, Medicine and Psychiatry, 14,* 59–79.

Harwood, A. (1988). A discussion about "discourse." *Medical Anthropology Quarterly, 2,* 99–101.

Hasselkus, B. R. (1992). The family caregiver as interpreter in the geriatric medical interview. *Medical Anthropology Quarterly, 6,* 288–304.

Helman, C. G. (1978). Feed a cold, starve a fever: Folk models of infection in an English suburban community, and their relation to medical treatment. *Culture, Medicine and Psychiatry, 2,* 107–37.

Jacobson, R. (1960). Linguistics and poetics. In T. Sebeok (Ed.), *Style in language.* Cambridge, MA: M.I.T. Press.

Kuipers, J. C. (1989). "Medical discourse" in anthropological context: Views of language and power. *Medical Anthropology Quarterly, 3,* 99–123.

Lambek, M. (1981). *Human spirits: A cultural account of trance in Mayotte.* Cambridge, MA: Cambridge University Press.

Leach, E. (1970). *Claude Lévi-Strauss.* New York: Viking Press.

Levine, S., & Kozloff, M. A. (1978). The sick role: Assessment and overview. *Annual Review of Sociology, 4,* 317–343.

Lévi-Strauss, C. (1967). Structural analysis in linguistics and in anthropology. In C. Lévi-Strauss, *Structural anthropology* (pp. 29–53). Garden City, NY: Doubleday & Co. (Original work published in French 1945)

Lévi-Strauss, C. (1969). *The raw and the cooked: Introduction to a science of mythology* (Vol. I). New York: Harper & Row. (Original work published in French 1964)

Lewis, I. M. (1971). *Ecstatic religion: An anthropological study of spirit possession and shamanism.* Harmondsworth, England: Penguin.

Lowenberg, J. S. (1989). *Caring and responsibility: The crossroads between holistic practice and traditional medicine.* Philadelphia: University of Pennsylvania Press.

Lynaugh, J. E., & Bates, B. (1973). The two languages of nursing and medicine. *American Journal of Nursing, 73,* 66–69. Reprinted in A. Klein (Ed.), *Culture, curers, & contagion: Readings for medical social science* (pp. 129–137). Novato, CA: Chandler & Sharp Publishers.

Malinowski, B. (1948). *Magic, science and religion and other essays.* Garden City, New York: Doubleday & Co.

Malinowski, B. (1961). *Argonauts of the Western Pacific.* New York: E. P. Dutton & Co. (Original work published 1922)

Mishler, E. G. (1984). *The discourse of medicine: Dialects of medical interviews.* Norwood, NJ: Ablex.

Ohnuki-Tierney, E. (1984). *Illness and culture in contemporary Japan: An anthropological view.* Cambridge, MA: Cambridge University Press.

Ong, A. (1988). The production of possession: Spirits and the multinational corporation in Malaysia. *American Ethnologist, 15,* 28–42.

Ortiz de Montellano, B. R. (1990) *Aztec medicine, health, and nutrition.* New Brunswick, NJ: Rutgers University Press.

Parsons, T. (1951). *The social system.* Glencoe, IL: The Free Press.

Parsons, T., & Fox, R. (1952). Illness, therapy and the modern urban American family. *Journal of Social Issues, 8,* 31–44.

Paz, O. (1970). C*laude Lévi-Strauss: An introduction.* Ithaca, NY: Cornell University Press.

Radcliffe-Brown, A. R. (1924). The mother's brother in South Africa. *South African Journal of Science, 21,* 542–555.

Radcliffe-Brown, A. R. (1952). *Structure and function in primitive society.* London: Oxford University Press.

Radcliffe-Brown, A. R. (1964). *The Andaman Islanders.* New York: The Free Press. (Original work published 1922)

Swartz, L. (1991). The politics of black patients' identity: Ward-rounds on the black side of a South African psychiatric hospital. *Culture, Medicine, and Psychiatry, 15,* 217–244.

Waitzkin, H. (1991). *The politics of medical encounters: How patients and doctors deal with social problems.* New Haven: Yale University Press.

West, C. (1984). *Routine complications: Troubles with talk between doctors and patients.* Bloomington: Indiana University Press.

Wolinsky, F. D., & Wolinsky, S. R. (1981). Expecting sick-role legitimation and getting it. *Journal of Health and Social Behavior, 11,* 229–242.

Young, J. C., & Garro, L., (1994). *Medical choice in a Mexican village.* New Brunswick, NJ: Rutgers University Press. (Original work published 1981)

Chapter 7

CULTURE CHANGE THEORY

AFTER WORLD WAR II

World War II was a rite of passage for anthropology. Anthropologists entered the war as academicians whose best-known claim to fame was that they knew a lot about tribal peoples with cultures that were very different from middle-class cultures in Europe and America. Vivid descriptions of tribal life provided an ethnographic basis for spreading a message that had enormous humanistic appeal. Anthropologists served as propagandists for the fascination of cultural diversity, the virtues of cultural relativism, and the evils of ethnocentrism. They provided evidence to support the fight against racist ideologies. In spite of some notable exceptions, however, pre-war anthropologists on the whole considered themselves theorists who observed political and social neutrality. Most of them earned their livings as university professors or museum curators who were paid to teach and do research. They left it to politicians and social workers to apply anthropological insights in real world struggles.

The war came. It must be remembered that the Western Allies who fought against Nazi Germany, Fascist Italy, and Imperialist Japan were considered "the good guys" throughout the anglophone world. In the United States, public support for the war effort was universal and largely unquestioned. Given these circumstances in the early 1940s, Anglo-American anthropologists looked for ways in which they could help to win. Coincidentally, the Society for Applied Anthropology was founded in 1941. Only much later did anthropologists raise questions about whether or not it was ethical to be involved in a war effort (Wax, 1971; Stewart, 1983).

The most direct and obvious contribution of anthropologists during the war was in places such as the Pacific Islands, the Far East, Southeast Asia, Africa, and the Middle East where those who spoke local languages, knew the people and were familiar with the terrain could provide much needed expertise. But some were recruited to investigate the national character of complex societies involved in the war, particularly of Germany and Japan (Mead & Metraux, 1953). Virtually without precedent, those anthropologists shifted their field of enquiry from small, relatively homogeneous, face-to-face communities to complex modern states. The discipline has not been the same since.

In the postwar period through the 1950s and 1960s, anthropologists expanded their newly assumed scholarly responsibility for the study of complex societies. It no longer mattered so much that the small-scale hunting, gathering, fishing, and gardening societies mourned by Malinowski were becoming extinct. They now had an enormous new field of enterprise, new kinds of small-scale societies to work with, above all those of peasant communities and, to a lesser extent, those of ethnic enclaves, urban underclasses, racial minorities, and even small towns and suburbs.

Motivated by national self-interest combined with humanitarian idealism, the most vocal American cultural anthropologists in those days defined their field as culture change. As witnesses to poverty and helplessness, they wanted to study how old tribal and peasant societies adopted new technologies in the hope that their findings would provide models for how modernization could be successful.

They undertook this while fully aware of competing functional thinking based on the asssumption that a culture normally would persist as an equilibrium system that seeks to replicate itself without change. These events took place before medical anthropology was identified as a specialty. For applied anthropologists, health was simply one important area of concern among many. Ethnologists documented the culture change process set in motion by new methods of growing crops and raising livestock, new techniques of village sanitation, literacy programs for children and adults, job opportunities through the creation of new or better village industries, increased opportunities for migration, changing attitudes and values via urbanization, and not the least, efforts to improve health by means of prevention campaigns and curative health services.

ACCULTURATION

The first theoretical concept to become widely influential in culture change circles was remarkably open and nonspecific in nature. It was meant to expand the old concept of diffusion, which came into the literature during the early twentieth-century attack on evolutionary theory. Culture change theorists noted that diffusionists were satisfied merely to record that a trait had apparently arrived in a culture by spreading from somewhere else, thus demonstrating that it had not been invented or discovered locally. The term *acculturation* was created to designate a different kind of theoretical orientation. With it, ethnographers attempted to learn how a diffused trait was welcomed or rejected by the people of a community and what happened in the subsequent process of integration and adaptation.

This turned out to be a way of partially satisfying the criticism that functional theory could not accommodate or explain change. It was assumed that a complex chain reaction might take place in response to borrowed traits and that this could result in a new equilibrium and a new version of an integrated culture. As a result, functionalists and culture change theorists got along very well in those years.

DOCUMENTING ACCULTURATION

McKim Marriott wrote about a response to culture contact in which Western medicine was introduced to a non-Western society (Marriott, 1955). The place was Kishan Garhi, a village in North India. (The name of the village is fictive to protect the privacy of those who live there.) Take note that Marriott's study may be characterized as primarily humanistic rather than scientific, because it is rich in describing the realities of a way of village life and because it recalls the experience of only one small locality, leaving the reader to assume that one can usefully extrapolate to other parts of North India, South Asia, and the rest of the world, but not indicating how this might be done.

Marriott and an English physician collaborated to introduce Western medicine as a humanitarian and exploratory effort that would help a population assailed by dysentery, malaria, cholera, smallpox, typhoid fever, tuberculosis, gonorrhea, eye and skin infections, infected cuts and bruises, general debilitation, and early death. They set up a small clinic to provide health care and learned quite a bit from the experience.

Marriott noted, for example, that local people mistook the appearance of Western medicine for its reality. This cognitive distortion was symbolized by local entrepreneurs who set up healing businesses in which they provided hypodermic injections of unsterilized water as cures for almost all conditions. They had plenty of patients, because the prestige of this aspect of the technology of Western medicine stood high.

In pragmatic (etic) terms, Western medicine was powerful when compared to indigenous forms of medicine. The English doctor, given the opportunity to provide immunizations, antimalarial tablets, penicillin, and sulfa compounds, could offer effective prevention or treatment for most of these serious conditions. One for which he did not have a cure was tuberculosis (TB). Forty years later we note with sympathy that he treated TB by prescribing calcium lactate and shark liver oil. Why not snake oil? Only later did medical science discover effective drugs such as streptomycin and pyrazinamide. Still, except for TB, a Western-trained physician at that time could achieve more than traditional physicians, priests, and healers in combating all of the serious diseases listed above that afflicted people in Kishan Garhi. Yet, in spite of the technological capabilities of Western medicine, the local clinic failed miserably. Why?

Answers were not found in strictly medical issues, the culprits usually suspected by concerned physicians, but rather in the culture of interpersonal relations having to do with trust, responsibility, charity, power, and respect. Marriott arrived at that conclusion by contrasting indigenous health practitioners with medical doctors. His findings are still quite helpful.

Who Represents the Patient?

The physician interviewed and examined patients privately. He often found that the medicines they begged for were later not used. In many cases the failure of follow-through occurred because the doctor's English ideas about privacy and individual responsibility did not apply in this kinship-based society. The doctor failed to include all important family members in his consultations, what Janzen years later was to call the therapy management group (Janzen, 1978). In the case of a girl with malarial chills and fever, for example, he prescribed quinine, which should have been quite effective. The medicine was never used. When the girl arrived back home her old widowed aunt objected to it. In family health matters, that old lady voiced more authority than the father and uncle who had gone with the girl to talk with the doctor.

Conflicting Medical Beliefs

Members of the family and community often held quite varied beliefs about how to treat illnesses. To avoid a row, it was not uncommon for several or all of the known remedies to be applied, which, taken together could make the patient worse rather than better. This practice sometimes worked against the success of medical treatment. For example, applying folk remedies to open wounds could interfere with medical attempts to clean and sterilize them with antiseptic solutions and sterile bandages. Marriott states the dilemma well:

> To the same sort of cut or boil, one man will apply a hot mango leaf; his neighbor will apply a paste of wheat flour; his father will apply a poultice of cow dung, while his wife continues to believe firmly in the efficacy of plain butter. If the wife is under the thumb of her husband's mother, then that matriarch's proposal for a magical sweeping and blowing may be added to the other treatments. In case of conflicting ideas, all advisers' suggestions for treatment may be applied in succession, or even all at once. Butter, dung, flour, and leaf may be simply laid on in successive layers—a typical solution to the problem of insistent but varied individual beliefs. (Marriott, 1955, p. 251)

Magical Medicine

Invading spirits thought to cause disease could be warded off by practices such as wearing amulets or performing exorcisms. "Most young children wear two or three charms purchased from magicians—silver moon pendants, small red beads, capsules containing written spells, tiny bags containing iron, grain, and so on tied around their necks or wrists" (Marriott, 1955, p. 252). It was believed that the threatening spirit, held at bay by amulets, might be angered if English medicine were added.

Only by being sensitive to these beliefs would it occur to the physician to explain a medication in a way that would make it desirable in terms of indigenous concepts. For example, an antiseptic might be acceptable if it were explained as a biomedical way to clean a wound that resonated with magically blowing and sweeping across it. Again, to vaccinate a child against smallpox might anger Mata, the Goddess of Smallpox, who would surely kill or disfigure the child in retaliation. To be accepted, it was essential that the vaccination be given when no active cases of poxlike disease were in the area to suggest that the goddess was lurking about. Only if she were away at the time would no harm come from accepting a vaccination.

Class and Caste

In Kishan Garhi as well as in India generally, upper-class educated people did not practice hands-on occupations such as barbering or shopkeeping, particularly when only small amounts of money were involved. Low-ranking assistants did the dirty work. In health care, the traditional herbal doctor only touched a patient to feel pulses and otherwise merely observed, asking no questions. In contrast, the English physician behaved in what was taken to be a low-caste and inept manner, because he touched the patient intimately in performing a physical examination and seemed unduly dependent on information provided by the patient when he asked that symptoms be described.

Further, he insisted that patients pay the small costs of the medicines they were given. Marriott recalls, "The doctor was obliged to spend nearly half of his clinical hours in coaxing the patients to pay the tiny amounts charged for medicines in order that the clinic might support itself" (Marriott, 1955, p. 243). Locally, it was believed that the more one paid for a magical or medicinal treatment, the more potent it was and the more certain the cure would be. The result was that the doctor's prestige and influence plummeted to a level with that of barbers and shopkeepers. Such low prestige was incompatible with the authority he needed to get patients to conform to his treatment plans.

The Duty of *Noblesse Oblige*

A practitioner of traditional medicine brought a literate, scholarly practice of medicine to the village. This kind of physician belonged to a high-ranking caste and economic class. Often he was a landlord or wealthy merchant whose medical training took him away from the village for a higher education. High birth, education, urbanism, and wealth created a gulf between the practitioner and his patients that had to be bridged. Three techniques worked especially well for this kind of traditional doctor:

- He inspired confidence by his almost magical knowledge of the body, asking no questions, getting all the information he needed by merely feeling the pulses at the wrists and asking a few indirect questions.

- He charged nothing for his services, providing them as a charity. It was customary for him to maintain a clinic that was free to all comers.
- Although he did not charge directly for his diagnosis, he actually could earn a lot of money. This was because he personally dispensed the medicines he prescribed, and did so at a high cost. After all, it was believed that expensive powders and elixirs were more powerful. Further, he guaranteed his medicines, collecting his payment only after the patient was well again. Being a local resident, he knew people well enough to be sure that they would pay their obligations.

Clearly, the temporary Western clinic failed in spite of well-intentioned efforts in part because the acculturation process was thwarted. The clinic arrived at the very doorstep of village culture, diffused that far, one might say. But successful acculturation failed for the reasons given. As Marriott put it, "In the light of this analysis, it would appear that if Western medicine is to find a firm place in the village under present conditions, its role must be defined according to village concepts and practices." Knowing about Kishan Garhi, other anthropologists in comparable situations of culture contact would be sure to recall what Marriott learned in order not to make the same kinds of mistakes.

At the time it was felt that research of this sort, multiplied by field studies all over the world, would eventually add up to widely applicable understandings that would validate culture change research as useful. Following ethnological practices of the time, the next expectable step would be to propose some regularities based upon an overview of these scattered studies. And that is exactly what happened.

APPLIED ANTHROPOLOGY

Quite a few anthropologists and anthropologically oriented sociologists took up the challenge to create the field of applied anthropology, conceived of as a broad concern with technological development (Lerner, 1958; Erasmus, 1961; Arensberg & Niehoff, 1964; Clifton, 1970). In particular, George Foster did much to inaugurate this new field in the 1960s (Foster, 1962; Foster, 1969; Foster, 1973). Foster eventually concentrated on the emerging subspecialty of medical anthropology. Indeed, he became a founder, authoring with Barbara Anderson the first widely used textbook for the newly recognized field. That text, aptly titled *Medical Anthropology*, was published in 1978 (Foster & Anderson, 1978). To be sure, since every scholar builds on the work of predecessors, it was preceded by (or was simultaneous with) other books and monographs that also contributed to creation of the new specialty:

- 1924: W. H. R. Rivers, *Medicine, Magic, and Religion*
- 1932: Forrest E. Clements, *Primitive Concepts of Disease*
- 1955: Benjamin D. Paul, Ed., *Health, Culture and Community: Case Studies of Public Reactions to Health Programs*

- 1964: Ari Kiev, Ed., *Magic, Faith, and Healing: Studies in Primitive Psychiatry Today*
- 1970: Alexander Alland, Jr., *Adaptation in Cultural Evolution: An Approach to Medical Anthropology*
- 1977: David Landy, Ed., *Culture, Disease, and Healing: Studies in Medical Anthropology*
- 1978: Michael H. Logan and Edward E. Hunt, Jr., Eds., *Health and the Human Condition: Perspectives on Medical Anthropology*
- 1979: Norman Klein, Ed., *Culture, Curers and Contagion*

In his review of cross-cultural community studies and international public health programs of the sort that Marriott had published, Foster concluded that it was helpful to organize this body of experience on the negative side in terms of cultural, social, and psychological barriers to change and on the positive side in terms of factors that promote change. What emerged was an enormous, and frankly cumbersome, list (Foster, 1962):

Cultural Barriers to Change:

- Tradition—preferring stability as a value in itself
- Cultural ethnocentrism—preferring customary ways to novelty
- Pride and dignity—fear of seeming ignorant to agents of change
- Norms of modesty—new practices may seem improper
- Relative values—the innovation may actually not be appealing
- Logical incompatibility—the new may not fit with local customs
- Unforeseen consequences—problems emerge in a chain reaction
- Posture and movement—may require difficult bodily adaptations
- Superstitions—opposed by beliefs not based on fact

Social Barriers to Change:

- Family, kin, and friendship obligations—work against change when individualism is required
- Small-group dynamics—reciprocal obligations interfere with individual autonomy
- Public opinion—an individual may not feel free to break with customary practices
- Factionalism—the innovation may get identified socially with an antagonistic group and cannot be adopted
- Vested interests—group security may seem threatened by an individual who does better than others
- Authority in the family—change may undercut the family head
- Political authority—the technician may be a threat to the established hierarchy
- Authority of others—any established authority may suffer if new leaders emerge

- Caste and class barriers—agents of change may have the wrong status affiliations
- Basic social configurations—donor and recipient of an innovation my be too distant from one another in terms of cultural understandings

Psychological Barriers to Change:

- Perception of government—recipients may be suspicious of the change agents
- Perception of gifts—recipients may suspect the motives of those offering to help
- Perception of roles—technicians may not fit preconceived notions of the kind of person a person of authority should be
- Differing perception of purpose—expectations may differ between what the agent prizes and the donor values
- Language difficulties—misunderstandings can arise from differences in dialect or styles of speech
- Demonstration dangers—the meaning of success may be understood differently

Some of the barriers listed above may seem unclear or unintelligible, but I do not want to devote space to explaining them. It is still valuable to read Foster's books, in which he spells out what is meant by these listings, along with listings relating to incentives to change. As presented here, this list serves only one purpose: It demonstrates that applied anthropology in the 1960s more or less got stuck. Information was accumulating at an unprecedented rate. Every new study, such as that of Kishan Garhi, or the Cornell-Navajo project that we will shortly examine in detail, seemed to contribute some new twist on the acculturation scenario. As a result, this approach became enormously cumbersome. Newly christened medical anthropologists at that time made themselves useful primarily because in one's memory (or one's library) was preserved this enormous checklist of things that could go wrong or practices that could help.

While many anthropologists in those days were attempting to be useful in just that way, some were using this approach as a basis for collaboration with physicians, scientists, technicians, and administrators in public health and epidemiology. A multidisciplinarity that united anthropologists and physicians as teammates on public health projects became a reality at this time.

THE PROLOGUE TO MULTIDISCIPLINARITY

Collaboration between anthropologists and physicians was slow in coming. During the second half of the nineteenth century there was medicine and there was anthropology. They were separate, unrelated fields. However, a few individuals were expert in both fields, working both as physicians and as anthropologists. We have already encountered an Englishman of this sort, W. H. R. Rivers, whose influence was not truly felt until after the turn of the century.

But the most influential individual in the second half of the nineteenth century was Rudolf Virchow (1821–1902), one of the most prominent anthropologists of his time (Ackerknecht, 1953; Silver, 1987).

Having earlier made outstanding contributions to medicine, of which more later, Virchow devoted the last thirty years of his creative life overwelmingly to anthropology, especially physical anthropology. He voyaged to Egypt to do research on mummies. He examined and evaluated (wrongly) the earliest known cranium of a prehistoric Neanderthal. He was the first German scientist to insist that all races were intrinsically equal, a highly unpopular position to espouse at that time in his native land. Also active in archeology, he made his way to Anatolia to observe Schliemann's excavations of Troy. His published output added up to a mind-boggling 1180 titles in anthropology works alone. He and another pioneer German anthropologist, Adolph Bastian (1826–1905), founded the first major museum of ethnology in Germany, the *Museum für Völkerkunde.* He and Bastian were also leaders in creating the German Society for Anthropology.

His influence as an anthropologist extended indirectly to the changes that eventually took place in the United States. Virchow was one of a small number of early anthropologists whose teaching and research directly shaped the thinking of Franz Boas when, as a young scholar, Boas shifted his field from physics, the field in which he had earned his doctorate, to anthropology (Goldschmidt, 1959). Boas, a German *emigré,* eventually dominated early twentieth-century American anthropology. Persuaded in part through mentoring by Virchow, Boas redefined anthropological methods to emphasize a meticulous dedication to factual documentation that ideally should be kept as free as possible from all excesses of theory. He turned anthropologists away from their nineteenth-century fascination with speculating about grand theoretical schemes and led them to emphasize careful ethnographic documentation oriented to strictly limited kinds of theoretical issues.

Virchow's profound influence on modern biomedicine is much more widely known than is his role in early anthropology. Pathology, until his time, was examined and conceptualized in gross anatomical terms, but new refracting lenses enlarged the capabilities of microscopy. In place of pathology on the level of different tissues and tissue changes that are visible to the naked eye, medical scientists shifted their gaze to more basic cellular structures never clearly seen before. Virchow became identified with this transition to what much later in the mid-twentieth century came to be known as biomedicine. His book, *Cellular Pathology* (1858), marked a profound paradigm shift, which still newer technology more than a century later further reduced to molecular and atomic levels.

Virchow, preeminent in applying the basic sciences to medicine, did not become so seduced by these emergent biomedical capabilities that he abandoned the holistic principles of Hippocrates. Simultaneously, and bravely, given the reactionary politics of his time, he articulated a comprehensive social theory of disease. "Mcdicine is a social science," he wrote with notable hubris, "and politics nothing but medicine on a grand scale." "The physician," he said at another time, "is the natural attorney of the poor." How did he arrive at such a radical antiestablishment social and political philosophy?

As a young physician in his twenties, Virchow was sent as a member of an official governmental commission of inquiry to investigate an epidemic of typhus in Upper Silesia, the impoverished, famine-prone Polish territory of the German Second Reich. His own words, recently translated into English, are powerful: "The logical answer to the question as to how conditions similar to those. . . in Upper Silesia can be prevented in the future is, therefore, very easy and simple: education, with its daughters, liberty and prosperity." He argued that education should be in native languages, Polish in the case of Upper Silesia. Exploitative and oppressive economic and political policies benefiting the Catholic hierarchy and the landed aristocracy should be abolished. "These are the radical methods I am suggesting as a remedy against the recurrence of famine and of great typhus epidemics in Upper Silesia. . , a lovely and rich country which, to the shame of the government, has so far been inhabited only by a poor and neglected people" (Rather, 1985).

Virchow was neither the first nor the last to talk about medicine as a social science. Few now remember the American Hermann Biggs (1859–1923), but in his lifetime he too was a physician who advocated public health and social policies to improve standards of health and the quality of life. His motto for the Board of Health brought attention to the communal and national dimensions of medicine: "Public Health is purchasable. Within natural limitations every community can determine its own death rate" (Breo, 1990).

The fields of medicine and anthropology in the nineteenth and early twentieth centuries seemed poised for fruitful collaboration. With the benefit of hindsight, it would seem that multidisciplinarity might have been attempted by Virchow. He was a physician with interests in public health. He was an anthropologist. Yet, he did nothing to unite the two fields. Many years later, as we have seen, W. H. R. Rivers, also a physician and an anthropologist, similarly failed to inaugurate multidisciplinarity.

MULTIDISCIPLINARITY: ANTHROPOLOGY AND MEDICINE

Against this background, the Navajo-Cornell project in 1955 epitomized a new kind of enterprise that joined anthropologists with public health physicians. The purpose of this research and implementation program was to find ways successfully to introduce Western medicine to the Navajo reservation based on the experience of anthropologists and public health physicians who had studied interventional culture change programs in different parts of the world (Adair, Deuschle, Barnett, & Rabin, 1970). It was organized as a collaborative effort of the Navajo Tribe and the Cornell University Medical College under the auspices of the U.S. Public Health Service.

Anthropologist demonstrations of how culture change research could identify what could go wrong, summarized in Foster's barriers to change, constituted after-the-fact (retrospective) explanations. Could anthropologists apply their methods and findings prospectively in planning and implementing health programs? If put to work as members of a multidisciplinary project, would an ability to speak local languages and an understanding of a community's social organization, value system, and religion make it possible to avoid pitfalls in designing and carrying out a medical program?

The immediate goal was to improve the health of the Navajo people. The long-range goal was to apply what was learned in carrying out this project as a basis for introducing biomedicine to comparable communities in developing nations. It was hoped that it would be possible to identify useful guidelines that would replace reliance on intuition along with the wasteful method of trial and error. The possibility of extrapolating from this experience to other parts of the world was realistic, it was thought, because the health profile of the Navajo nation in 1955 was very similar to that found in less-developed nations:

- Infectious diseases were the main causes of sickness and death.
- These included severe endemics, such as tuberculosis.
- The infant death rate was high.
- The incidence of chronic degenerative diseases was low.
- Planning was hampered by inadequate health and population statistics.
- Complications included a high birthrate combined with a falling death rate, which results in a rapid increase of the total population.
- People relied heavily on ethnomedicine for prevention and cure.

Summarizing what anthropologists had learned about successes and failures in many studies such as that of Kishan Garhi, broad guidelines for introducing Western medicine were made explicit in a number of organizational propositions.

Planners Must Begin with a Comprehensive Knowledge of the Culture of the Target Community

Four anthropologists spent two years each on the reservation doing research in collaboration with physicians and nurses. They also drew on an extensive documentation of Navajo culture published by other anthropologists not connected with the project. Ethnographic input was well-grounded in field experience.

Based on this background knowledge, anthropologists could serve as cultural translators qualified to explain Navajo beliefs about sickness and healing to their medical colleagues. These were (and still are) very religious people with a holistic view of the need to maintain a state of balance between the individual and the physical environment, other people, and spiritual beings and forces. They lived in a world populated by:

- earth surface people (ordinary human beings)
- holy people (deities)
- dangerous quasi-human forces: thunder, lightning

- beneficial quasi-human forces: rain, mountains, corn
- animals in their divine aspects
- ghosts
- witches

Believing that they were surrounded by dangers on all sides, they also believed that safety lies in observing righteous behavior. Above all, one must avoid dangerous objects and actions by observing taboos. Deserted dwellings (hogans) should be avoided out of fear of antagonizing ghosts. Nail cuttings, hair, and excreta should be carefully concealed, because witches can use them to practice contagious magic. Any object struck by lightning is dangerous to life and limb and should not be touched.

When sickness or misfortune strikes, the first requirement is to establish a diagnosis by any of several means:

- hand trembling
- gazing at the stars
- listening to night noises

In hand trembling, the diagnostician, in a trance, experiences a convulsive shaking of the hand and arm that reveals the cause of the illness, which might be that the victim used wood from a lightning-struck tree or crossed a trail left by a snake. Star gazing is done by singing ritual songs and staring at a star until the cause of the illness becomes visible. In the listening method, concentrating on sounds long enough will produce a sense of being told what is causing the sickness (Adair, Deuschle, & Barnett, 1988, pp. 162–163).

After identifying the broken taboo that caused the illness, a singer (priest) will be asked to perform a ceremony to drive out the evil, bring the danger under control, attract the good and beautiful, and thus restore harmony. The singer is a highly skilled professional who has qualified himself by devoting many years to memorizing complex rituals that keep people in tune with the cosmos. He cures by reciting elaborate prayers and chants, by preparing sacred pictures on sanctified soil using dry pigments, by administering emetics and other herbal infusions, and by conducting ceremonies that require long hours of concentration. Truly powerful ceremonies may require a faultless performance lasting as long as nine days and nights, attended by everyone in the family, by members of the clan, and by neighbors and friends, some of whom will have traveled hundreds of miles to take part.

Planners Need to Maintain Constant Awareness of Their Own Culture, Particularly Its Relevant Values and Biases

What is medically relevant is culturally determined according to project guidelines. Knowing how Navajo lives were cocooned in religion so that health was not separated out from other issues contributed importantly to the understandings required if planned acculturation was to work. Just as important, however, was for outsiders to identify how their own culture, including the subculture of medicine, was implicated. It was considered essential never to forget that acculturation is conceptualized as two cultures meeting and influencing each other, not as one culture simply giving culture traits to the other. It is harder to be objective about one's own culture than about the cultures of others.

Reservation hospitals and clinics were understaffed. Doctors and nurses faced difficulties they had not encountered in earlier training and experience:

- social isolation
- language barriers
- lack of professional contacts
- inadequate access to medical journals
- overwhelming workloads

Under these conditions professional staff felt very stressed and marginalized. Morale was low.

Many of the older physicians responded in ways that hampered their effectiveness in the community. Singers held in high esteem by Navajos were treated with disrespect and outright contempt by medical doctors who told their patients that ceremonies were without value. It was even said that the healing sessions were harmful because medicines were passed from one person to another and could spread infections. One highly respected singer reflects this arrogance in his recollection of the past:

> I have great respect for the doctors. I would not have done to them as they have done to us and try to shame many of us from practicing our own medicine. At one time the American physicians would have all of us medicine men put out of business. I have never felt that way towards the white doctors. (Adair, Deuschle, & Barnett, 1988, pp. 27-28)

The culture of medicine was neither uniform nor unchanging. Some young physicians shared values and attitudes that were more openminded, apparently influenced by exposure to psychiatry and the social sciences. A letter written by one of these young physicians contained the following reflections:

> [W]e have a deep sense of the fact that concepts of illness are more closely integrated with spiritual concepts among the Navajo than is the case in our own culture. Moreover, when one considers the more modern notions enjoying examination in our own culture with respect to environmental and emotional influences on what happens to the tuberculous patient, the concepts of the Navajo singers and of our own people are really not too far apart. . . . I am simply trying to make the point that we have sympathy and respect for the Navajo point of view, as I gather they have for ours. (Adair, Deuschle, & Barnett, 1988; p. 31)

The amelioration of bias was dramatically demonstrated on one occasion after the patients in one hospital were terrorized by lightning that struck a tree near the building. Doctors arranged for a singer to be called in and for his chanting to be heard in every room on the public address system. On another occasion a pediatrician requested that a sacred hogan be constructed near the hospital so that parents could arrange for sings to be held over babies without subjecting them to long and debilitating journeys that interrupted medical care.

This growth of understanding between some physicians and many singers created an atmosphere receptive to the new program when the medical team from Cornell University Medical College arrived to begin their work.

Baseline Cultures of Both the Donor and the Recipient Societies Are Never Static, So Knowledge and Awareness Must Be Current

Navajo methods of curing had been receptive to borrowed innovations long before Western contact. Masks, paintings, fetishes, and other ritual techniques were borrowed and adapted from Pueblo neighbors. Hand trembling diffused from the Apaches. The Native American Church, with peyote rituals and curing rites, found its way onto the reservation. Biomedicine was merely the most recent of curing innovations to be adapted and modified to meet Navajo health needs.

The history of Western medicine, for its part, documents immense change. In the late 1930s, for the first time, seriously infected wounds could be cured with the application of sulfanilamide and other sulfa compounds. By the 1940s, deadly infectious diseases such as pneumococcal pneumonia succumbed to massive injections of penicillin. Project doctors arrived shortly after the discovery in 1952 of antibiotics effective against tuberculosis, one of the most resistive and serious of all infections.

A growing sense of trust and faith between doctors and patients, as well as between doctors and medicine men, was also new. But while it is important to recognize the malleability of both cultures of healing, it is also important to recognize that many barriers to successful acculturation were still present. The project was designed to surmount those obstacles.

The Attitudes and Beliefs That Had Shaped Previous Social Relations and Had Influenced What Was Borrowed or Rejected in the Past Must Be Identified

Physicians, teachers, and government workers arriving on the reservation were often misled into thinking that the Navajo were stuck in an unchanging past, which was never true. In the eyes of the newcomer, old-fashioned culture traits gave the appearance of a very conservative society:

- the beehive shaped hogan constructed of boards and stones caulked with mud
- ankle-length velveteen dresses and long braids
- babies swaddled and carried on cradle boards
- traditional ceremonial gatherings
- monolingual Navajo language use

It must be recognized that the symbolism of these enduring practices was of enormous importance. The hogan possesses deep religious significance, the old-fashioned dress of the women indicates modesty, cradle boards ensure that babies will grow up in proper Navajo rectitude, rituals maintain the equilibrium of the cosmos, and the Navajo language was without competition in the home and community. Culture change in these areas can be expected to be resisted or to take place very slowly.

Nonetheless, the Navajo have a history of rapidly adopting major innovations in instances when they did not conflict with other cultural goals and made sense in pragmatic terms:

- the historical abandonment of hunting and gathering to take up gardening and stock raising
- the more recent addition of wage work to the pattern of self-employment
- creation of a modern Tribal Council
- bilingualism on the part of some
- automobiles to replace horses and wagons

Specifically regarding health, Navajos were exposed to physicians practicing in the area as early as 1880. Several thousand young servicemen during the World War II years experienced biomedicine in a major way, as did others who worked all over the western states in war industries. When they could, Navajos took advantage of the apparent benefits of Western medicine. As Sam Yazzi, an old singer, put it, "I have great respect for white doctors; there are things they can do that we cannot. For example, they can remove an appendix, they can take out a gall bladder, or treat a urinary tract infection" (Adair, Deuschle, & Barnett, 1988, p. 11).

Recent history shows that if medical benefits can be demonstrated in ways that are meaningful to the Navajo, they will acculturate to them. This is where the culture of the cultural donors is also implicated. Many government officials, physicians, traders, and other outsiders who worked on the reservation were unable to interact successfully because they were blinded by racial prejudice, ethnic insensitivities, and ignorance of Navajo society and culture. As noted above, some of the physicians, nurses, and administrators assigned to hospitals and clinics in previous years hindered their own efforts to provide medical care because of these shortcomings.

Proposals Must Meet Felt Needs in the Recipient Community

In the decade before the project got started, about one out of every ten people on the reservation was infected with tuberculosis. Although not all manifested severe symptoms, it was common to see people coughing, spitting, and eventually dying from TB. Almost every family had firsthand experience with the disease.

The community felt a need to have access to treatment for tuberculosis that would be more effective than herbal medicine and religious rituals. They rapidly recognized the benefits of the new antibiotics. In a very short time, medicine men who previously had attempted to treat tuberculosis themselves were sending seriously ill people for medical evaluation and treatment.

It did not follow automatically that all treatable diseases were referred to the hospitals and clinics. Congenital hip dislocations in newborn infants are unusually common on the reservation. The deformity is easily diagnosed and can be treated with success if babies simply are positioned to keep their legs in a frog-like position while the hip socket matures. Treated babies grow into adults with completely normal hip function. Undetected and untreated, however, babies grow up to experience a painful limping impairment. In field research, Clifford Barnett found that alleviation of this endemic condition was not a felt need. Impaired hip motion was not thought of as a social, personal, or economic problem. The appearance of limping was not stigmatized. In addition, the treatment was incompatible with keeping a baby on a traditional cradle board, which kept the legs aligned rather than abducted, so treatment was not felt to be worth the trouble, and efforts to introduce diagnostic and preventive practices received a very poor response.

Recipients Must Share in Making Decisions; Planning Must Take Account of Tribal Politics and Concepts of Prestige

In government and medicine, lines of authority and an authoritarian flow of information from top to bottom are so customary that they tend to be accepted without question. In a dramatic break with such practices and assumptions, collaboration replaced subordination in this program.

From the moment the team from the Cornell University Medical College arrived on the reservation an equal partnership was established. This ethos of shared responsibility and mutual respect resulted in an unprecedented collaboration of team physicians, team anthropologists, and representatives of the Navajo community.

The program started in 1952 when Cornell specialists in infectious diseases were asked by the tribe to consult on a severe outbreak of acute miliary (disseminated) tuberculosis that struck down five children. Three months after these specialists arrived they met with members of the Advisory Committee of the Navajo Tribal Council. This was the first of many meetings

Clifford Barnett (center rear) and Richard Brough, social science teacher (upper left), with Zuni high school students. Barnett teaches cultural anthropology in New Mexico every other year at the invitation of the Zuni Tribal Council and the Zuni Public School District.

over the next three years in which the medical scientists discussed their work with leaders of the Council.

The Council responded with a substantial grant of money ($10,000) to the Department of Medicine of Cornell University to be used to support this work. The grant specified that the Department of Medicine, in return, was to report back to the Council on how the money was used. The tribe wanted feedback and involvement, and it happened.

From this beginning, a long-term collaboration evolved, characterized by joint participation. Outside physicians and scientists worked together with tribal leaders to try new ways of providing for tribal health needs. When the Cornell team reported back to the tribe on how their money had been spent, not only was the importance of the tribal funds acknowledged, but also the benefits of joint activity.

Communication Among All Who Are Involved Must Be Facilitated

The style of communication helped make cooperation work. It was not easy, and it was certainly not automatic, but mutual respect and repeated dialogue smoothed the way. The leader of the medical team knew that it was important not to be patronizing. He was aware of the need to explain activities and plans in sophisticated ways while remaining warm and sympathetic. Navajo leaders responded in their own style of dialogue and of granting respect. One can sense this from the following speech by Manuelito Begay, a tribal councilman and leading singer:

> One thing we do not agree on with the doctors and myself has been discussed and I do not fully agree with them on this, and that is the question of how tuberculosis is inflicted on a person. They tell me it is inflicted by a person coughing in your face—this is the way you get tuberculosis in your system. Right away I disagree with it. A person should not be that weak to [be] susceptible to a man's cough. We have a definite point in mind and know of how a man gets to be afflicted with tuberculosis. One is the ceremony about the Wind Chant. If something goes wrong with that it is tuberculosis and, if lightening strikes you, tuberculosis is the result. I just want to bring these things out so that we would agree on how tuberculosis afflicts the Navajo. Although we do not agree on this, we do recognize one another and that is at least a step forward. (Adair, Deuschle, & Barnett, 1988, p. 42)

An important part was played by so-called health visitors, members of the community who were trained to work as paramedical intermediaries. The training and employment of paramedical personnel was an innovation at that time. Being Navajo in language and culture, health visitors were uniquely qualified to staff the field arm of the clinic. They accomplished much on the face-to-face level to ensure that the program would succeed overall.

Good interpreters were also very influential in determining success or failure. The advice of Scott Preston, the vice chairman of the Tribal Council, proved valuable:

> Do not rely on an interpreter who has had only a fifth or sixth grade education to translate a difficult message. It is most important that the intepreter have a good attitude for he must be pleasant and accommodate both parties, the doctor and the patient. (Adair, Deuschle, & Barnett, 1988, 67)

Relations Between Acculturated and Conservative Members of the Target Community Must Be Understood

Highly acculturated tribal leaders were the key link between the Cornell team and the tribe as a whole. The tribal chairman, the secretary-treasurer, and members of the Advisory Committee were better educated, more experienced in the the ways of white people, and spoke English with greater fluency than was true of members of the Tribal Council at large and of adults in general. In explaining and coordinating project activities, the key to successful communication was first to achieve an understanding with the more urbane, educated tribal leaders.

The latter could then facilitate communication between the Cornell team and monolingual Councilmen who, in turn, linked up with local leaders on the community level. In this way, more acculturated tribal members who were to some extent bicultural functioned to bring monocultural Navajos into the loop.

PUBLIC HEALTH PHYSICIANS AND ANTHROPOLOGISTS

Cornell University Medical College and the U.S. Public Health Service got involved when the Department of Health, Education and Welfare (DHEW) took on responsibility for the well-being of American Indians. It had become clear in various parts of the world that technical aid programs, including public health programs, would succeed better if the concept of culture was applied, and that concept was central to anthropology. Administrators of these technical aid programs found that anthropologists could contribute to their success by identifying linkages between the various aspects of culture, linkages that were often not apparent to practitioners of public health. Planners of the Navajo-Cornell project, aware of this kind of collaboration, built it into their program from the start.

The Navajo-Cornell project demonstrated the value of this joining of public health and applied anthropology, but it would be Pollyannish to assume that it succeeded completely. Writing about the whole field of applied anthropology in 1973, George Foster noted that by that time one could say we had learned a great deal, but, at the same time,

> we have now been sobered. We now know that what at one time seemed relatively easy to stimulate—technological and economic development—is an enormously complex and often discouragingly slow process. The right mix of money and skilled specialists in health, agriculture, and education—valuable as far as it goes—is insufficient to solve the problems that face the world. (Foster, 1973, p. viii)

Fortunately, the Navajo-Cornell project was planned to permit a long-term assessment of results. The initial program was funded for six years. Subsequent appraisals were carried out to provide in all a fifteen year overview of the process of establishing a culturally sensitive primary health care system. Did it work?

During the initial six years the innovations resulted in some important improvements:

- reduction in the spread of TB
- reduction in ear infections (otitis media)
- better referral of seriously ill individuals for hospital care
- slight reduction in death rates (crude mortality)

However, it must also be noted that some extremely important goals were not achieved:

- No reduction in active eye infections causing blindness (trachoma)
- No reduction in the single greatest cause of disease and death, the pneumonia-diarrhea complex

Clifford Barnett, now at Stanford University but at that time one of the anthropologists on the Cornell team, believes that to understand the failure to achieve these goals, it is important to make a distinction between a primary care program *as distinct from* a public health program. The Navajo-Cornell program was based on the assumption that the way to improve Navajo health was by means of primary care, that is, by providing health services. As concerns the infectious diseases that did not respond impressively to improved primary care, specifically trachoma, pneumonia, and diarrhea, it is because primary care is oriented mainly to treating diseases and their symptoms *after* people have gotten sick. The program would have been more successful in this area, Barnett points out, if it had included a public health program aimed at *prevention,* including immunization campaigns and the construction of an infrastructure to provide potable water and sanitary sewage disposal. This is not a criticism of primary care programs, but, as Barnett put it recently, "it is important to understand the kinds of policy decisions being made and the limitations of various strategies" (Barnett, 1994, personal communication).

After termination of the experimental program, Navajo health experienced a sharp upswing. Health improvement in the 1960s occurred when, in addition to public health measures, upgrading also took place in the quality of life, the home environment, and the level of formal education. This development is consistent with Foster's later observations concerning the importance of economic factors. "Cultural, social, and psychological barriers and stimulants to change exist in an economic setting," he wrote. He then went on to say, "If an economic potential does not exist or cannot be built into a program of directed change, the most careful attention to culture and society will be meaningless" (Foster, 1973, p. 78). Even in the 1960s it was clear to many that when approaching public health problems on a community and family level, wider political and economic issues must be addressed if success is to ensue. Isn't that what Virchow bravely advocated a hundred years earlier? (Adair, Deuschle, & Barnett, 1988, pp. 191–200).

Current Multidisciplinarity

Have anthropologists and public health professionals succeeded in forming multidisciplinary teams? Do they at last work well together to initiate and facilitate international health, by which we mean the diffusion of biomedical health technology from wealthier nations to poorer nations, including to internal fourth-world nations such as that of the Navajo? The answer remains problematic, so some say "no" and others say "yes." Sandra Lane and Robert Rubinstein veer towards the "no" response:

International health development work is among the most personally challenging, intellectually engaging, and potentially frustrating areas of medical anthropological practice. On a personal level, it can demand compassion and understanding in the midst of seemingly incredible amounts of disease, poverty, and suffering. Yet because an adequate understanding of the dynamics that lead to these conditions requires the integration of information from many spheres—biological, ecological, social, and cultural, for instance—using a variety of qualitative and quantitative methods, it engages the holistic commitment of anthropology as do few other anthropological activities. Notwithstanding this, it can be a frustrating area of work because the interaction of the broader political and economic contexts in which international health and development work is situated and the culture of the community of international health workers often lead to perverse outcomes. (Rubinstein & Lane, 1990, p. 367)

In their frustration with some of the attitudes and practices of international health professionals, Rubinstein and Lane admonish fellow medical anthropologists to "work to ensure that bureaucratic and ethnocentric program rationales do not blind health professionals to the critical and dynamic role that culture and political processes play in enabling people to achieve satisfactory levels of health and well-being" (Rubinstein & Lane, 1990, pp. 367, 389).

As one illustration of this frustration among several, Rubinstein and Lane cite flawed and failed efforts worldwide to introduce a medical intervention known to be effective in preventing death from diarrhea, that pernicious killer of millions of poor people every year.

Oral rehydration therapy (ORT) was originally invented to treat cholera by replacing the enormous volume of fluid loss that is the most devastating consequence of that infection. Applications to other diarrheal diseases demonstrated its wider efficacy. Rehydration requires more than just water, since the body will not function if salts (electrolytes) and sugars get out of balance, but that is easily achieved. Basically, a homemade solution of water, table salt, and granulated sugar ladled into sick people, especially malnourished infants and children, in spite of the complications of nausea and vomiting, will save lives.

One would expect such a low-cost, simple solution to be adopted rapidly and widely, but not so. "In part this failure derives from the frustrating circumstances that [anthropological] research supporting health planning is constrained by bureaucratic commitments so that it necessarily fails to discover culturally appropriate ways of integrating low-cost technologies, like ORT, into peoples' daily lives" (Rubinstein & Lane, 1990, p. 368; Foster, 1987).

But while some experienced medical anthropologists are discouraged, others apparently are not. Jeannine Coreil, working out of the College of Public Health of the University of South Florida, conducted basic acculturative research on the ORT program in Haiti with results that, while not definitive, are very promising (Coreil, 1988). Coreil carried out survey research to determine whether or not traditional healers, known to be widely available, could be trained to recommend or provide ORT. After identifying thirty-seven healers (ten midwives, ten herbalists, ten shamans, and seven injectionists) she set as her first task to determine whether

Jeannine Coreil conducting a focus group discussion with rural Haitian mothers on the topic of childhood immunizations.

(Photo, Jeannine Coreil)

or not people came to them for the treatment of diarhhea. She found that they did. The most common practice was to provide herbal teas, especially guava. I should mention parenthetically that guava tea appears to work well to stop painful peristalsis and to dry up diarrheal fluid loss. A study carried out in Mexico suggests that it is fully as effective as a widely prescribed drug, Lomotil (diphenoxylate hydrochloride with atropine sulfate), which is prohibitively expensive for poor people (E. A. Berlin & B. Berlin, personal communication, 1993).

Only three of the thirty-seven healers were not involved in diarrhea management, so the survery demonstrated that healers were strategically placed to add ORT to their treatment practices. Further, traditional healers provided herbal remedies that appear to provide some symptomatic relief. (We cannot be sure of this, because more than fifty plants were used, and we have no information on most of them.) However, to save lives it is not enough to stop diarrhea. It is also important to provide fluid, carbohydrate, and electrolyte replacement. ORT was still needed. Thus, a related question was posed: Were these healers familiar with ORT?

Coreil found that only half of the healers in her sample had heard of ORT, only one-third had actually prescribed ORT, and only one-fourth had used it themselves. This finding became the basis for a policy recommendation: Train traditional healers in the use of ORT and use them to get ORT to needy people.

Two additional findings helped to refine this policy recommendation. First, gender needed to be factored in. Female healers, especially midwives, much more than male were involved in the care of women and children. The

promotion of ORT had already reached them more effectively than male healers because the promotion of ORT had already been geared especially to those
responsible for sick children (mothers and women healers). This would suggest that it might take more effort to train male than female healers and that
men might be less effective as promulgators of ORT.

Injectionists, who tended to be men, better educated, and familiar with
biomedical medicines, presented a catch-22 as concerned public health policy.
These men actually treated a large number of children with diarrhea. Many
already were familiar with the use of ORT. For these reasons, they were strategically well positioned for the dissemination and integration of ORT. The problem was that from a biomedical standpoint they posed a danger to health since
they diagnose and treat patients without training or medical supervision, just
as the injectionists did in the village of Kishan Garhi described by McKim
Marriott. Under such circumstances, drugs are given for conditions for which
they are worthless, potentially effective drugs are not given, and insufficient
attention is directed to the harmful or deadly consequences of incorrectly
administered pharmaceuticals, or to the possibility that the chemicals were
out-of-date and decomposed. To train injectionists for ORT management
requires a trade-off, pitting their beneficial contributions in the treatment of diarrhea against the harm that would ensue if they were authenticated as biomedical practitioners. On balance, Coreil concluded that health authorities would
be unlikely to bring injectionists into the official health care sector but would be
well-disposed to make greater use of traditional female birth attendants.

Coreil's research makes good sense and seems to have produced important information for those who are responsible for implementing diarrheal control in rural Haiti. However, until such proposals are tried out it is essential that
they be considered unproven. This need-to-test attitude gets additional support
from more recent research carried out in Honduras and Mexico by Carl Kendall
and a team of investigators (Kendall, et al. 1991). The concern in this anthropological study was to take account of worldwide exponential population
growth and macro-urbanization as creating new ecologies of disease. Urbanism,
they argue, requires methods different from those that have been found to work
in rural circumstances.

> [Speaking of human adaptations to these urban environments, they note that]
> urban environments present new threats from air, water, and noise pollution,
> as well as substance abuse and violence. Poverty, crowding, lack of services,
> and frequent migration in and around urban areas have also created ideal con-
> ditions for the development of new diseases. It is likely that new diseases will
> continue to emerge in coming years as a result of environmental degradation
> and continuing sociocultural change, particularly from increased mobility.
> (Kendall et al. 1991, p. 258)

Turning specifically to infectious diseases, they note that while we continue
to think of diseases spread by insect bites as rural problems, because insects
breed well in the countryside, in fact, insects have adapted with remarkable

agility to cities and slums. The *Aedes aegypti* mosquito, for example, breeds in prodigious numbers in barrels, washbasins, bottles, tires, flowerpots, vases, and even the drinking dishes set out for cats and dogs. They explore this insight by means of surveys carried out in several Mesoamerican communities concerning the *Aedes* mosquito and the viral disease they spread, dengue and dengue hemorrhagic fever. The effects of dengue range from asymptomatic or very mild to severe pains in the head, eyes, muscles, and joints; upper respiratory distress; and sometimes skin eruptions and painful swellings.

Because neither vaccines nor cures are known, the only strategy for dengue is to attack breeding sites in and around houses. The public health approach for years has favored vertically organized programs in which the national public health service trains and orchestrates an army of hygienic workers to attack and destroy breeding sites. At best, this works only in countries that possess highly centralized, committed, and well-financed preventive health organizations. Dengue control, Kendall and colleagues argue, needs to be designed to achieve control at the household level. Prevention must be based on an awareness of what people know or believe about how the disease is spread. Anthropologists skilled in ethnographic elicitation techniques can provide the kind of community level information that is essential if good local participation and support are to be achieved.

A rapid ethnographic assessment demonstrated that many people thought that dengue was spread by "winds," particularly from the north. Further, dengue was not recognized as distinct from other such diseases. Many were unaware that mosquitoes were the vector, others were uncertain, while still others were convinced that infective mosquitoes never came from their own backyards, since these were harmless "family" insects. Clearly, then, to mobilize local families would require communication and educational approaches to mediate between folk and biomedical concepts and practices. They conclude that the first step in prevention is to carry out basic ethnographic research sensitive to ecological and biological factors.

CONCLUSION

With culture change theory and applied anthropology, the time dimension reappeared in the mainstream of ethnology as a frame for anthropological research. It reemerged, however, as part of a new and unprecedented commitment on the part of many anthropologists to make their work count in a world beset with unsolved human problems. At last, the hegemony of theory over applications gave way to a sharing of the disciplinary terrain.

Legitimizing the field of applied anthropology was an essential precondition for a multidisciplinarity that would bring anthropology and medicine together. The rapprochement of anthropology with epidemiology/public health is still a promise as much as a reality. As an exploration still in progress, professionals all over the world are experimenting with ways in which social science and medicine can achieve more by multidisciplinarity than either can hope to achieve unilaterally.

The dimension of time reappeared as part of the paradigm of cultural anthropology, but what about the dimension of space? Space for a while shriveled within the boundaries of individual face-to-face communities under the sway of functional theories. Comparative studies produced generalizations that floated over the globe, without being given anchors in named distributions. Foster's barriers to change, although worldwide in reference, are not precisely bound to any terrain in the way that HRAF studies are terrain-bound. Would geography, like time-depth, reappear in the mainstream of anthropological theory? The answer is yes. It began modestly with cultural ecology, which was the next major shift of paradigms to assume a commanding position in American anthropology.

REFERENCES

Ackerknecht, E. (1953). *Rudolf Virchow*. Madison, WI: University of Wisconsin Press.

Adair, J., Deuschle, K. W., Barnett, C. R., & Rabin, D. L. (1970). *The people's health: Medicine and anthropology in a Navajo community*. New York: Appleton-Century-Crofts.

Adair, J., Deuschle, K. W., & Barnett, C. R. (1988). *The people's health: Medicine and anthropology in a Navajo community* (Rev. and expanded ed). Albuquerque: University of New Mexico Press.

Alland, A. (1970). *Adaptation in cultural evolution: An approach to medical anthropology*. New York: Columbia University Press.

Arensberg, C. M., & Niehoff, A. H. (Eds.) (1964). *Introducing social change: A manual for community development*. Chicago: Aldine-Atherton, Inc.

Barnett, C. (1994). Personal communication.

Breo, D. L. (1990). MDs of the millennium—The dozen who made a difference. *Journal of the American Medical Association, 263,* 108–113.

Clements, F. E. (1932). *Primitive concepts of disease*. University of California Publications in American Archaeology and Ethnology 32 (2).

Clifton, A. C. (Ed.) (1970). *Applied anthropology: Readings in the uses of the science of man*. Boston: Houghton Mifflin Co.

Coreil, J. (1988). Innovation among Haitian healers: The adoption of oral rehydration therapy. *Human Organization, 47,* 48–57.

Erasmus, C. J. (1961). *Man takes control: Cultural development and American aid*. New York: The Bobbs-Merrill Co.

Foster, G. M. (1962). *Traditional cultures and the impact of technological change*. New York: Harper & Brothers.

Foster, G. M. (1969). *Applied anthropology*. Boston: Little, Brown and Co.

Foster, G. M. (1973). *Traditional societies and technological change*. New York: Harper & Row.

Foster, G. M. (1987). World Health Organization behavioral science research: Problems and prospects. *Social Science and Medicine, 24,* 709–715.

Foster, G. M., & Anderson, B. G. (1978). *Medical anthropology.* New York: John Wiley & Sons.

Goldschmidt, W. (Ed.) (1959). *The anthropology of Franz Boas.* American Anthropological Association, Memoir No. 89 (Vol. 61, No. 5, part 2).

Janzen, J. M. (1978). *The quest for therapy: Medical pluralism in lower Zaire.* Berkeley: University of California Press.

Kendall, C. et al. (1991). Urbanization, dengue, and the health transition: Anthropological contributions to international health. *Medical Anthropology Quarterly, 5,* 257-268.

Kiev, A. (1964). *Magic, faith, and healing: Studies in primitive psychiatry today.* Glencoe, IL: The Free Press.

Klein, N. (1979). *Culture, curers & contagion.* Novato, CA: Chandler & Sharp Publishers.

Landy, D. (1977). *Culture, disease, and healing: Studies in medical anthropology.* New York: Macmillan Publishing Co.

Lerner, D. (1958). *The passing of traditional society: Modernizing the Middle East.* New York: The Free Press.

Logan, M. H., & Hunt, E. E. (Eds.) (1978). *Health and the human condition: Perspectives on medical anthropology.* North Scituate, MA: Duxbury Press.

Marriott, M. (1955). Western medicine in a village of northern India. In B. D. Paul (Ed.), *Health, culture and community: Case studies of public reactions to health programs* (pp. 239-268). New York: Russell Sage Foundation.

Mead, M., & Metraux, R. (Eds.). (1953). *The study of culture at a distance.* Chicago: University of Chicago Press.

Paul, B. D. (Ed.) (1955). *Health, culture and community: Case studies of public reactions to health programs.* New York: Russell Sage Foundation.

Rather, L. J. (Ed.) (1985). *Rudolf Virchow: Collected Essays on Public Health and Epidemiology (*2 vols.) Canton, MA: Science History Publications.

Rivers, W. H. R. (1924). *Medicine, magic, and religion.* New York: Harcourt Brace & Co.

Rubinstein, R. A., & Lane, S. D. (1990). International health and development. In T. M. Johnson & C. F. Sargent (Eds.), *Medical anthropology: Contemporary theory and method* (pp. 367-390). New York: Praeger.

Silver, G. A. (1987). Virchow, the heroic model in medicine: Health policy by accolade. *American Journal of Public Health, 77,* 82-88.

Stewart, O. C. (1983). Historical notes about applied anthropology in the United States. *Human Organization, 42,* 189-194.

Wax, R. (1971). *Doing fieldwork: Warnings and advice.* Chicago: University of Chicago Press.

Chapter 8

MEDICAL ECOLOGY

THE DIMENSION OF SPACE

Culture change theory and functionalism can be looked at as efforts to move anthropological theory beyond the paradigms of earlier evolutionary reconstructions and historical particularism. However, the replacement paradigms brought with them their own frustrations. Anthropologists wanted some predictive capabilities they were not getting. The puzzles left to solve were much too confined to investigating how cultures seemed to hang together or to change in response to acculturative exposures.

That kind of puzzle solving was good, but it was not great. Perhaps, thought Julian Steward, the answer was to be found by adapting a currently hot item in biology, the paradigm of ecology. It would fit well with an old version of diffusionism that privileged the environment as a shaping force in culture history, the food areas of Clark Wissler.

To understand what happened, let us begin with two ideas that had been around for many years. You will remember that when Rivers shifted from evolutionary to diffusionist speculations, he postulated that the traits that diffused to a society would be modified as required to fit with the culture of the recipient society so that the latter remained unaltered as an evolutionary stage. An unrelated concept, also congruent with historical particularism, was essentially very similar. It drew attention to the recipient environment rather than a hypothetical cultural stage as a shaper of borrowed cultural traits. This was the culture area theory enunciated by Clark Wissler (Wissler, 1917).

Wissler noted that neighboring tribes of Indians in native North America seemed very similar to one another in culture, yet remained different from the Indians of other areas. In the American and Canadian Plains, for example, the Crow, Comanche, Assiniboin, Blackfoot, Dakota, Cheyenne, and Arapaho tribes all lived in tepees, rode horses, hunted buffalo with lances and bows and arrows, wore moccasins and tailored skin clothing, endured vision quests, and celebrated the Sun Dance. Plains Indians were culturally different from those of other culture areas, such as the Pacific Northwest extending from Northern California by way of British Columbia to Alaska. Northwest Coast Indians lived in hand-hewn cedar plank houses, erected totem poles, wore basketry hats and elaborately carved and painted wooden ritual masks, fished with lines and nets from enormous wooden boats, and practiced the potlatch in which vast wealth was distributed in competitive ritual competitions to see who could be the most generous.

Wissler proposed that similarities within a geographic region (a "food area") resulted from a process of diffusion that was shaped by the regional environment. New traits were adopted only if they fit with basic environmental (food) resources. In short, the Plains area demonstrated cultural uniformities (constituted a culture area) because new traits had to be adapted to an economy and technology based on hunting buffalo and other wild game that ranged across the wide open grasslands of that part of the world. The Northwest Coast formed a contrasting culture area because it was a food area rich in salmon and wild game abundant in the complex water ways and dense forests of the region. Obviously, this theoretical approach took as a given the shaping force of ecology in the sense that cultural characteristics were thought on the one hand to be limited by environmental resources, and on the other to be permitted by them.

Many years later, when culture change theory was in the ascendency, Julian Steward revived this old diffusionist model. He proposed that by bringing the environment more into the picture, anthropological theory could hope to obtain more explanatory power. In applying his method to South America, he stated its fundamental principle in this way:

> The potentialities [for accepting and patterning diffused sociopolitical institutions and technologies] were a function of the local ecology, that is, the interaction of environment, exploitative devices, and socioeconomic habits. In each case, the exigencies of making a living in a given environment with a specific set of devices and methods for obtaining, transporting, and preparing food and other essential goods set limits to the dispersal or grouping of the people and to the composition of settlements, and it strongly influenced many of their modes of behavior. (Steward, 1949, p. 674)

Multilinear Evolution

In elaborating the concept of cultural ecology, Steward distinguished cultural cores from the secondary features of cultures (Steward, 1955). Cores consisted of cultural traits so closely tied into subsistence activities; technology; economic practices; and environmental conditions of climate, flora, and fauna that they would be the same in any part of the world in which the basic environment and sociotechnology were the same. Secondary features were free to vary and it was these aspects of cultures that gave the appearance of unlimited diversity in cultural traits. To illustrate, Paiute Indians in the Great Basin area of California and

Nevada resembled the Australian Aborigines in core culture. Both ways of life were characterized by a combination of semi-desert conditions and simple Stone Age technologies. Therefore both had a social structure of migratory bands comprising only a few families. Both lived in temporary structures that provided only minimal protection from the elements. Both carried with them only the few material possessions that could reasonably be transported by people who had to walk long distances.

Yet, these Paiute and Australian natives seemed very different from one another in language sounds and grammar, details of house construction, bodily adornment, artistic products, folk tales, religious beliefs, and other characteristics.

Cultural ecology, then, gave new life to old anthropological interests in both time and space, in both evolution and geographic diffusion. Steward practiced a version of historical particularism. In any one region such as the Great Basin or Central Australia, cultural resemblances could be reconstructed as a product of diffusion shaped by environmental conditions. Yet Steward spoke of his approach as the method of multilinear evolution. Multilinear evolution is a way to acknowledge the unique history of each society; but it also permits one to generalize about the ways in which some of them seem to form one type or another based upon similar ecological core features.

The outcome of this speculation was to define several broad categories of organizational complexity that Steward called levels of sociocultural integration. These levels were meant to serve as guidelines (taxonomic categories) for applying the comparative method to living populations. They are still used in that way, and are often encountered in the anthropological literature without explanation or ascription.

Steward did not concern himself with health issues. More recent research, however, has used these sociocultural taxa as a way to discuss the health of small-scale societies in the modern world.

Bands

The subsistence base for this level of sociocultural integration is that of hunting wild animals, fishing, and gathering fruits, nuts, and vegetables utilizing a simple technology in a variety of climatic zones (Service, 1962). (Archeologically, Paleolithic and Mesolithic populations met these subsistence criteria.) The band is characteristically organized around family groups that stay together or split up as circumstances warrant. Consensus rather than coercion characterizes decision making in most bands, which rarely number over fifty people. The traditional Paiute of southern Oregon lived in bands of this sort.

Teams of anthropologists and physicians have studied the health of some of the few societies still living at this level of social and technological simplicity (Lee & DeVore, 1968). They report that on the whole people in bands eat a highly variable but essentially balanced diet of fresh meat and vegetables. The essential vitamins and minerals are present. The sparse distribution of wild plant and animal food keeps them from overeating and hunger is often a seasonal problem. Low caloric intake and daily activities to forage and hunt keep them lean without wearing them down from overwork. The combination of small population size and frequent moves to new campsites protects them from gastrointestinal, respiratory, and vector-borne diseases that build up in large settled environments characterized by poor sanitation. They are not untouched by epidemic diseases. In fact, infections can be deadly to them. But epidemics tend not to reach all groups, and microorganisms soon die out within any one group because the population is too small to sustain them. As noted in describing the discordance hypothesis, they are also well defended by their diet and activity levels against degenerative diseases, such as high blood pressure, stroke, heart attack, and cancer.

Given this apparently clean bill of health, why do they not all live to a ripe old age? Part of the answer lies in infant and childhood mortality. On the average, only 50 to 65 percent of all babies in hunting and gathering societies reach adulthood, which is very low. Estimates of life expectancy at birth range from only twenty years to as high as fifty years. Those who survive the first fifteen years live on the average to the age of forty-three, which is also low. It is hard to know what to make of this short life expectancy, but it must be remembered that most contemporary band societies live in extremely difficult environments. Their way of life survived precisely because farmers and industrialists were not greatly tempted to take away their barren, marginal territories. So one explanation for the relatively short life span is that it is a very demanding lifestyle for people who are aging. It should be noted, too, that numbers of healthy older people have been reported for some bands, where they may commonly reach sixty-five years of age.

Tribes and Chiefdoms

Scattered communities of settled villagers reliant on horticulture and animal husbandry (and in some places on fishing or large-scale pastoralism) frequently unite larger populational aggregates (Service, 1962). (In prehistoric times, Neolithic societies provided the prototype for this level of sociocultural integration.) The wider family-based ties of kinship can organize hundreds of people for economic cooperation, trade, ritual, or warfare. Although many of these societies trace descent matrilineally, the communities tend to subordinate women to an extent not usually found in bands.

When tribes accord leaders clear rights to make and enforce decisions relating to the maintenance of order, the management of external affairs, and the distribution of harvests, we can speak of chiefdoms. The families, lineages, and clans of chiefs usually enjoy privileges, although they tend to be privileges of prestige rather than of commodities. A chief tends to get more food and possessions than other people, but it is the same kind of food and possessions. Chiefdoms vary widely in their wealth, power, and complexity.

For convenience, we will refer to both tribes and chiefdoms as tribes.

In the academic division of labor, anthropologists acquired the task of studying the many tribes of the world. Most earlier anthropological experience was acquired among tribal (and peasant) peoples until the present generation, when even these societies are rapidly being absorbed into the global village.

The key to tribal health conditions in comparison with bands is that tribal people usually live in settled hamlets and villages. Settled populations are more susceptible to infectious diseases, especially from fecal contamination of food and water and from household vermin. The diet usually is not as good, with less meat than hunting people and a poorer balance of plant foods. Commonly, gardening tribes subsist on high-caloric crops such as taro, yams, and manioc without sufficient supplementation for protein, fatty acids, vitamins, and minerals. Finally, their activity levels are almost always lower and their fertility rates higher.

Peasants

Peasant villages differ strikingly from tribal settlements because the tribal community is characteristically self-contained and independent while the peasant community is dependent and controlled by outside powers (Redfield, 1956). Peasants differ also from farmers, whom we think of as relatively independent entrepreneurs caught up in market capitalism. Farms are a lot like small (or large) businesses in contrast to peasant family holdings and villages in which the domestication of plants and animals is much more an end in itself (a way of life) rather than a means of earning income in a rural environment.

Peasant life can be quite healthy and satisfying, an observation to be emphasized since attention here will be directed to the harmful and unhappy qualities of peasant life. Living in permanent settlements as food producers, peasant villages share a lot with tribal villages, including an almost universal acceptance of patriarchal domination. They differ, however, in substantial ways. They plow and irrigate their fields, working very hard to produce surplus crops far bigger than those of most (but not all) tribal cultivators. They are required to turn over much of their produce to money lenders, landlords, and tax collectors. As a related feature, they tend to cultivate commercial crops in order to meet their needs in a money economy, often leaving minimal resources for family support.

Because they live in the countryside distant from industrial pollution, with fresh produce and meat ready at hand, peasants ought to enjoy excellent health. Only rarely is that potential realized. In most of the world, it is common for peasants to be overworked and undernourished because they live under exploitative politico-economic systems (see Taussig, 1980).

Their health is undermined in other ways as well. As part of a large national population, they are much more exposed to infectious diseases. Every few years village children born since the last epidemic catch measles, chicken pox, and other childhood diseases. Mortality rates can be high. In every epidemic, some victims are impaired for life, although the community as a whole survives since nearly all surviving adults are protected by acquired immunity.

Villagers are also frequently debilitated by gastrointestinal and respiratory diseases. They tend to contaminate their water and food supplies by inattention to waste disposal practices. Crowded, dark, poorly heated, and poorly ventilated houses expose their inhabitants to chest infections. Many infants and children die. Daily intimacy with domestic livestock exposes people to still other diseases, such as tapeworms and lockjaw.

Not the least, permanent life in villages tends to incubate interpersonal conflict. Close living quarters result in disputes over property rights and communal obligations. Personalities clash. Anger and anxiety thrive where landlords and governmental agents exert enormous power. Disputes over inheritance and wedding exchanges become major sources of discord. Harsh conditions for women and landless field laborers often fester in the social body. Chronic stress and persistent low-grade unhappiness can thrive under these conditions.

ECOSYSTEM ECOLOGY IN ANTHROPOLOGY

Spearheaded by Steward, cultural ecology in the 1940s and 1950s moved beyond the Malinowskian version of functionalism. It required an expansion of the concept of cultural integration to include the wider environment. Yet cultural ecology offered essentially no more than a more satisfying kind of functional analysis. It still perpetuated most of the longstanding shortcomings of functionalism.

The most generic shortcoming was that cultural ecologists continued to produce field reports that were basically merely descriptive, even though more completely so than in earlier research. Cultural ecology still tended commonly to identify a structure (a static model) when what was wanted, particularly from the culture change perspective, was to identify the dynamics of systemic accommodation and mutation (a processual model). To break away from stasis and move toward process would require more rigorous quantitative (descriptive) and biological methods that would supplement the qualitative ethnographic descriptions to which anthroplogists were accustomed. The 1960s and 1970s moved the discipline in that direction.

The concept of an ecosystem, borrowed directly from biology, provided the key to this new approach. An ecosystem describes the structure and process of interrelationships among all living organisms (bacteria, plants, animals, humans) and the physical environment (including geography, topography, and climate) in which they exist (Moran, 1990, p. 3). The physical environment (consisting of abiotic factors) is identified as of fundamental importance in the study of animal and human behavior.

As conceptualized by biologists the concept of ecosystem allowed scientists to move in the direction of greater accuracy by means of very sophisticated

Emilio Federico Moran (right) employing the GPS (global positioning system) to
determine exact latitude and longitude for ecological research purposes.

(Photo, Eduardo Brondizio)

counting procedures (quantification). Experimental research in growth cham-
bers as well as large-scale deductive models could be constructed using cybernetic (systems engineering) concepts and computer simulations. As Emilio
Moran points out, in the move from these experimental procedures to the study
of real ecosystems, some readily measurable quality of these systems needed to
be identified for study. The concept of energy flow promised to meet that need,
since it should be possible, it was thought, to measure energy as it was created, exploited, and depleted in real ecosystems (Moran, 1990, pp. 5-6).

This move to take the measure of energy flow as a way to calculate ecological dynamics sounded good to anthropologists at that time. Leslie White prepared the way when he rehabilitated a formal anthropological interest in
cultural evolution by introducing the notion that one could speak of stages of
evolutionary progress that applied to world culture as a totality (universal evolution) if progress were described in terms of energy. He proposed a basic law
of cultural evolution: "Other factors remaining constant, culture evolves as the
amount of energy harnessed per capita per year is increased, or as the efficiency
of the instrumental means of putting the energy to work increased" (White,
1949, pp. 368-369).

Attention to energy flow also promised to get us by a logical hurdle. The
central dynamic of ecological processes was that of adaptation (functional integration), a concept acceptable to both biologists and cultural anthropologists
except that it was often expressed as mere circular thinking (a tautology). This

was a major complaint against functionalism: Trobriand magic was functionally related to (adapted to) gardening and fishing practices, and so on, because these customs all coexisted with one another. Note the circularity: What is functionally adapted has a place in Trobriand culture (or whatever culture you are studying) and what is in the culture is culturally adapted.

To get around this trap of circular reasoning, it is necessary to apply some measure of adaptation that is not merely the description of still one more cultural trait. Documenting energy flow provided a way to escape circularity. If energy was not depleted with the passage of time, the system was in equilibrium (homeostasis). If energy increased, the system was evolving to a new level of energy dynamics. If energy was depleted, degradation of the environment and/or the society was taking place.

Cultural anthropology was profoundly influenced by this way of thinking about ecology.

> A generation of anthropologists, trained in ecology and systems theory, went to the field to measure the flow of energy through the trophic [food utilization] levels of the ecosystems of which humans were but a part. The choice of research site was still a local community, often treated as a closed system for the purposes of analysis. (Moran, 1990a, 13–14)

Some sound ethnology documented the insights that could be gained by using this approach. However, as concerns cultural anthropology, it seemed most useful in the study of band, tribal, and peasant communities just at a time in the history of the discipline when we were encountering far more complex sociocultural entities. Two examples from this period in our history will illustrate what I mean.

The Flow of Energy in a Band

William Kemp reported on a Baffin Island Inuit village in which he measured food and fuel utilization in a challenging arctic environment. With remarkable fortitude, he measured and counted in freezing, dangerous places. Based upon his measures of the consumption of human food, dog food, snowmobile and outboard motor gasoline, ammunition, wages, and calories for heating dwellings along with careful descriptions of seasonal activities, especially hunting and trapping, Kemp was able to construct a holistically oriented flow diagram that represented the ecosystem as comprising in part a functionally integrated cultural system and also as a flow of energy acquisition and consumption.

Kemp's study demonstrated that in addition to environment and technology, culture could be accounted for in ecological research. Acculturation, for example, introduced major changes in the form of money and wages, snowmobiles, and rifles. The ecological (and cultural) balance collapsed at one point as a result of nearly exterminating the caribou herds by hunting with the new, more efficient technology (Kemp, 1971).

The Flow of Energy in a Tribe

Roy Rappaport worked under very difficult circumstances to document energy dynamics among the Tsembaga, a community of Maring people in New Guinea (Rappaport, 1971). In spite of very difficult field conditions in that hot, humid, mountainous part of the world, he calculated energy consumption as they cleared and fenced fields; planted, weeded, and harvested sweet potatoes, taros, cassavas, and yams; and slaughtered pigs. Combining all energy inputs and then comparing that figure to the total yield, also measured under trying circumstances, Rappaport demonstrated that in this village horticulturalists earned a reasonable return on their investment. The ratio of yield to input was more than 15:1. The ecosystem was stable and efficient in terms of energy flow.

Based on his analysis of energy flow, Rappaport concluded that pig husbandry failed to make good sense in purely economic terms, since pigs were kept for years rather than regularly eaten as soon as they reached maximal size. This is because Tsembaga social values required that the members of the tribe be able to make impressive ritual presentations of pig meat every decade or so. Towards the end of a decade-long cycle, about a third of all cultivated land (worked by the women) was needed just to provide feed for the increasingly immense herds of swine. Why? They explained (in emic terms) that it was the way ancestors were honored.

Rappaport concluded (in etic terms) that other important although unconscious needs were also served. The well-spaced rituals in which pigs were slaughtered and cooked in large numbers to honor dead ancestors served effectively as a mechanism to organize intervillage relations in a world without political structures. Not the least, the rituals kept a lid on mutual destruction by means of warfare, since fighting could be resumed only after the the dead from the previous battle season of a decade or so earlier had been honored.

Ecosystem research constitutes a powerful paradigm for investigators working in small-scale societies, but it will have only limited utility for most others. In order for an anthropologist working alone to accomplish careful and complete quantitative evaluations of energy flow, the ecosystem needs to be small—on the scale of a band, tribe, chiefdom, or peasant village—and it needs to be relatively homogeneous in culture. Most populations of concern to medical anthropologists are not sufficiently small, self-contained, and culturally uniform for this kind of research.

To make matters worse, the extent to which findings in any one community can be generalized to a whole category of socioeconomic integration (all bands, all tribes, all chiefdoms, all peasant communities) is very limited. Robert Netting, for example, invested enormous time and work in order to characterize the ecosystem of a Swiss Alpine village, only to find that French, Italian, and Austrian Alpine villages with comparable physical environments and peasant technologies—villages that he assumed would be very similar—turned out to be highly variable in political, economic, and cultural dimensions (Netting, 1990).

Steward's levels of sociocultural integration are meaningful only on a very abstract and epistomologically rather spongy level.

Most significantly for medical anthropologists, nobody has demonstrated that these ecosystem studies offer an efficient and informative way to get at health issues. Kemp apparently did not find it necessary to evaluate health as part of the energy equation of his arctic Inuit community. Rappaport did consider health, but in a way that is essentially tangential to his analysis.

Rappaport explicitly argued that pigs may have contributed to the recovery of health in cases of serious illness. Pigs are killed only on ritual occasions, but these include times when someone has been injured or is sick. On a daily basis, protein intake just barely meets human nutritional needs. Sickness and injuries characteristically result in nitrogen (that is protein) loss, putting a strain on already marginally nourished bodies. The immune system, including antibody production, requires good protein nutrition.

The ritual slaughter of a pig thus provides added protein precisely when it is needed most to avoid decline and death. This assumption led Rappaport to conclude, "The nutritional significance of the Tsembaga pigs thus outweighs their high cost in energy input. They provide a source of high-quality protein when it is needed most" (Rappaport, 1971, p. 128). The assumption is physiologically questionable, since one could as well speculate that it would be better to maintain a more steady intake of protein than to practice binge feeding when ill. Either way, however, the Tsembaga energy flow analysis proved to be only minimally informative about sickness and health in Maring society. It apparently did not prove necessary to identify pigs as scavengers who improve sanitation (reduce vulnerability to parasitic infections) because they feed on garbage and human fecal waste. Nor did it prove necessary to include malaria in the Tsembaga equation.

"Research on energetic efficiency among such people [as the Tsembaga] can provide answers to some questions," Andrew Vayda and Bonnie McCay concluded in their evaluation of new directions in ecological anthropology, "but not to those that are most critical for assessing their health or adaptedness. It cannot, in other words, answer questions about how effectively the hazards actually confronting people in their environments—for example, . . . malaria-transmitting anopheles mosquitoes in the case of the Marings—are dealt with" (Vayda & McCay, 1975, p. 297).

HIGHER LEVELS OF ECOLOGICAL ANALYSIS

Much confusion about the usefulness of medical ecology can be avoided if one clearly and explicitly takes account of the level of the analysis under consideration. Multiple hierarchical levels exist. In the real world of people and environments, the continuum from small local communities at the one end, through wider geographic entities across the center, to spaceship earth in its entirety at the opposite end, can be divided up (classified) in limitless ways. For heuristic purposes (teaching or overview), we can discuss this vertical range better if we arbitrarily think in terms of (impose on the continuum) a limited number of categories. Moran finds it useful to construct ecological models at three hierarchical levels: global, regional, and local or site-specific.

Anthropologists usually fail to indicate clearly which level is under investigation in their work. Moran refers to this source of confusion as the problem of level shifting, because most commonly one takes information from one level to substantiate conclusions at another.

So far I have discussed ecosystem analysis on the level of small-scale (site-specific or micro-level) communities. It is an ecological fallacy to assume that one can extrapolate from these studies to larger, more complex ecosystems. Local models are useful for dealing with site-specific resources. In such models the culture and social structure must be evaluated in communal, family, and individual terms. This contrasts with regional models which guide research for longer time periods, wider patterns of exchange, and larger political and social interactions. On a regional level cultural considerations must be reduced to partial and relatively abstract levels. Finally, global models are useful tools for dealing with many problems of pollution and toxic waste, the production and distribution of food for good health, and the spread and control of epidemic (pandemic) infections, but environmental and cultural aspects of the problem can be factored in only if they are limited to relatively few critical conditions or customs.

At each level, the designated ecosystem must be studied separately and in terms of materials and processes appropriate to its level of complexity. From a postpositivist perspective, one must keep in mind that each boundary in the hierarchy constitutes a two-leveled system that functions under dual control. The lower level sets constraints on the higher level, but it does not determine the nature of the higher level.

> It has not been sufficiently recognized that each level's structural and functional relations obscure relationships observable at other levels, particularly as one moves from micro to macro levels. The greater the scope of the level, the less visible details of group and individual behavior and ideology appear. (Moran, 1990b, p. 279)

As one moves up from micro-ecological studies, it becomes virtually impossible for field ethnographers to collect data on the ecosystem (environment) as part of their work, that is, to take direct responsiblility for identifying and evaluating culturally relevant flora, fauna, soils, and climate. To achieve the holism of medical ecology at higher levels, multidisciplinarity as well as interdisciplinarity are imperative. Research at these higher levels requires the highly technical capabilities of biological anthropologists (for genetic and physiologic documentation and analysis) in addition to that of cultural anthropologists (for social, symbolic, technological, economic, and political dimensions). Beyond anthropology, biocultural studies can be ecological only if documentation of the abiotic and nonhuman biotic environment is provided by other scientists.

Another way to explore this issue is to be aware that to speak of medical ecology is to identify the environment as a major consideration, if not the major consideration, in coping with health issues. It is a way to give attention to what in culture change theory was neglected and often ignored. Ann McElroy and Patricia Townsend explain this position as follows:

> A community's health closely reflects the nature of its adaptation to the environment. Through this emphasis on the ways ecological concepts contribute to the theoretical development of medical anthropology, we attempt to give unity to an interdisciplinary [i.e., multidisciplinary] science that uses clinical, epidemiological, and ethnographic approaches to health problems. (McElroy & Townsend, 1989, p. xix)

McElroy and Townsend are right on target when they stress the need in our time to unify "clinical, epidemiological, and ethnographic approaches to health problems." It requires a multidisciplinarity of physicians and anthropologists as well as others. No one would deny that a holistic approach requires that one take account of ecological factors. Evaluated in terms of energy flow, an ecosystem approach is particularly salient for small-scale foraging and food-producing communities, even though, as we have seen, more puzzle solving is still needed if it is properly to incorporate health issues.

The claim for ecology as the most suited of all theoretical frameworks to serve as an organizational paradigm for medical anthropology is sustained at a cost. Medical anthropologists who advocate ecosystems as workable portals of entry to research and explanation have not characteristically carried out their work in completely holistic ways. On the regional level, where most research is done, their work emphasizes epidemiologic/public health and related issues, but quite neglects a very large part of what most medical anthropologists study and consider important. Clifford Barnett, in his review of the McElroy and Townsend book, notes "that certain areas of work in medical anthropology that do not relate directly to this framework are given little or no mention—e.g., patient-practitioner relationships, professionalization, the meaning of the medicalization of social behaviors, paleopathology, the dynamics of ethnomedical systems, critical medical anthropology, etc." He continues, "These are not thoughtless gaps; they simply do not fit the framework and goals set by the authors" (Barnett, 1989). Let us keep these constraints in mind, then, as we move on to identify what is useful in the perspective of regional ecology for structuring the exploration of health issues.

REGIONAL ECOLOGY: ADAPTATION TO INFECTIOUS DISEASES

As already noted, moving up a hierarchy from a community or locality (micro-analysis) to regionwide areas (macro-analysis) forces one to abandon intimacy with the individuals and families that are encountered in site-specific work. At higher levels only parts of the environment can enter one's calculations. Individual and social dimensions must be accounted for in more abstract ways. Correspondingly, health implications must be evaluated differently. Ecology at this level is very useful in some ways, but that utility is strictly delimited. On the whole, models of regional ecosystems have been helpful in identifying human adaptive responses to three broadly characterized threats to health: infectious diseases, adaptations to extremes of climate, and environmental disasters.

Turning first to infectious diseases, Carlos Coimbra finds it descriptively and analytically useful in an ecological perspective to distinguish three categories of human responses or adaptations to diseases in which people are the prey and micro-organisms are the predators (Coimbra, 1988b): genetic, physiologic, and cultural.

These categories, as one might suspect, require a temporary suspension of a holistic orientation for the sake of facilitating discussion, since they are not completely categorical (mutually exclusive). That is, all three factors—genetic, physiologic, and cultural—may be simultaneously involved as a complex adaptive response, even though one predominates or at least strikes one's attention as more significant. It can be helpful to suspend holism when one is trying to solve complex problems, as long as it is only temporary. In fact, it is done all the time in the field as well as in the laboratory, where it is referred to as "holding other things equal."

Genetic Responses: Malaria in Africa

During World War II medical scientists stepped up their research on blood types (blood antigens) to cope with medical problems on a scale that was new and without precedent. Especially by means of airborne bombing raids, long distance artillery shelling, and rocket attacks on defenseless cities (not to mention the first use of nuclear bombs), civilian war casualties in great numbers were added to the large number of military wounded who were produced by that war. Successful storing and transfusing of blood and blood plasma was considered essential in treating these victims of warfare.

Blood research was given a high wartime priority, and we began to learn of many blood types and molecular structures other than the familiar Landsteiner ABO antigen types with which everyone was familiar. During the course of a very productive career, Linus Pauling explored the use of several valuable laboratory techniques including that of electrophoresis. By these means he was able to show in 1949 that sickle cell anemia was a molecular disease caused by the abnormal sickling (shrinking) hemoglobin which was designated hemoglobin S (Hb^s). Blood cells containing Hb^s were capable of distorting or sickling when placed under oxygen stress.

Other medical scientists, continuing to undertake research on sickle cell disease, made some startling observations about a possible relationship between the genetic factor for Hb^s, since that is an inherited trait, the disabling and deadly disease of sicklemia that is its consequence, and an infectious disease, malaria, that on the face of it seemed quite unrelated. Based upon research in Africa, where sickle cell anemia is common, a physician, A. C. Allison, published a seminal paper in the *British Medical Journal* in 1954 in which he demonstrated that individuals who inherited the Hb^s gene from one parent (were heterozygous for the gene) did not succumb to severe anemic disease the way those did who inherited the gene from both parents (were homozygous) but, and this is a very important "but," were protected to some extent from falling ill from a very severe form of malaria (falciparum malaria) that infects almost everyone in many parts of the African region in which he carried out his research. In other words, a genetic mutation may have been favored by (been adaptive for) the benefits it conferred in fighting off a dreadful parasitic infection.

A French physical anthropologist, Jean Hiernaux, was quick to see its implications for anthropologists, publishing an early study in 1955. By 1958, Frank Livingstone, an American physical anthropologist, was ready to produce his documentation and analysis of this complex genetic adaptation to an infectious disease (Livingstone, 1958).

Livingstone certainly had to account for ecological factors, which he laid out very clearly based upon well-known findings produced by entomologists (insect specialists). He did not do this work himself, but ecology was definitely central to his analysis. Falciparum malaria as a disease occurs when the blood of a human being is invaded by a microscopic single-celled parasite *Plasmodium falciparum.* The parasite gets injected into the body when a predator mosquito, *Anopheles gambiae,* in the process of claiming a blood meal, regurgitates into its prey. For this reason a key variable in determining who will get the disease is ecological, having to do with places where mosquitoes breed and humans live in substantial numbers.

Anopheline mosquitoes do not do well in unbroken tropical rain forests. They need sunny, pure, stillwater pools in which to breed. The floor of a tropical forest, being heavily shaded with very little standing water, is inhospitable. In prehistoric times, this breed of mosquitoes must have been rare or absent throughout much of west and central Africa.

When human beings cleared away the forest for planting fields the ecosystem changed dramatically. The good topsoil, no longer protected by overhanging trees, washed away, leaving areas on which daily rainwater easily collected in the presence of direct sunlight. This key ecological change took place when scattered hunting and gathering bands were supplanted by settled horticultural villagers. Tribal invaders converted vast dark tangles of rain forest into enormous expanses of breeding territory for these voracious mosquitoes.

But was this truly the scenario for malaria in Africa? Livingstone found the answer in a review of massive linguistic and archeological evidence. Drawing historical inferences from the geography of language distributions based upon principles of interpretation at home in historical particularism, Livingstone concluded that expanding populations of horticulturalists had taken over the rain forests in relatively recent times. This Bantu expansion converted territory that until then had been occupied for many millennia by short-statured peoples, of whom central African pygmies and southern African Khoisan are near-extinct remnants.

When and how did this Bantu explosion take place? This is where archeology came into play. The expansion was dependent upon a shift from foraging to field cultivation. The earliest archeological evidence for plant domestication in Africa dates to 4000 BCE in Egypt. With time—a rather long time—plant domestication spread. The limiting factor was that iron implements were required for cutting down huge trees to clear fields for planting. The iron industry originating in the Middle East (the Turkish peninsula), diffused by way of Egypt to arrive in the Sudan around 600 BCE, and then spread throughout western and central Africa. Bringing together the linguistic and archeological evidence, Livingstone was able to demonstrate that the two requirements for severe malarial endemicity were present from roughly 2500 years ago: hordes of mosquitoes and large populations of people living in the same ecosystem.

The human response included physiologic and cultural defenses, as we shall see. But, a couple of thousand years was time enough for the slower response of genetic mutation. Now we are in the realm of biological (genetic) anthropology. In a very simple mutation the DNA for hemoglobin underwent a substitution of one amino acid (valine) for another (glutamic acid) at just two places in a total DNA length of 574 amino acids. However, two molecules of glutamic acid imparted a dramatic change in the conformation of the larger molecule of hemogloben. They make it sensitive to reductions in the amount of oxygen to which it is exposed, causing the blood cell to lose its plump, round shape and deform in a way that makes it look somewhat like a microscopic harvesting sickle.

In individual inheritance, if one inherits the gene for hemoglobin Hb^s from only one parent, that individual will acquire only the sickle cell trait. That is a way of saying that such individuals do not usually suffer in any way from the mutant gene, because their nonsickling gene ensures them enough wholesome blood for normal needs. On the other hand, the trait does include enough sickling capability to at least partially kill or disarm falciparum parasites, perhaps by depriving them of the oxygen they need to survive and thrive. These individuals, in short, have acquired a genetic defense against this "greatest single destroyer of the human race," as William Osler put it a century ago.

Individuals who inherit Hb^s genes from both parents pay a terrible price for this genetic defense against malaria. They are the ones who get sick with sickle cell disease. They may suffer horrible pain, debilitating weakness, brain damage, paralysis, joint and muscle destruction, heart failure, lung disease, and kidney failure. The pain and impairment strike first in childhood. Nothing so wrenches one's heart as to care for an innocent, trusting child who suffers the agony of acute sicklemic attacks.

In health care it is not uncommon to turn down personal emotions by concentrating on the scientific aspects of disease and suffering. One can absorb only so much sadness and still function effectively as a clinician or scientist, and I think we need to do that right now. It is fascinating in terms of population genetics to realize that Livingstone provides us with the first, and still the best, characterized example of a balanced polymorphism. Balanced polymorphism?

To put it in plain language, African ecology provides an adaptive situation in which human populations benefit when they receive a partial inheritance of the gene for Hb^s. That is, when the gene for Hb^s is inherited from one parent but not from the other, a condition known as heterozygosity, the infant grows up producing enough healthy blood for normal needs, but simultaneously also produces enough Hb^s to provide protection against malaria. These are the lucky ones who have the sickle cell trait. Unlucky infants are those who inherit the gene from both parents, the condition known as homozygosity. They lack a gene from either parent to allow them to produce healthy blood cells. Protection against malaria is of minor importance for these individuals because they suffer and die young with sickle cell disease. The trait is good; the disease is bad. This situation favors keeping enough Hb^s in the gene pool so that some people will be born with the trait, but not so much that a large number of people will be homozygous and die early from the disease. Adaption, in short, favors the transmission of the gene to only about twenty percent of the population. More than that results in some who have protection against malaria, but at a cost of too many who die from the disease. This equation is what physical anthropologists have in mind when they speak of a balanced polymorphism.

Physiologic Responses: Malaria in South America

Malaria was brought to the New World by post-Columbian invaders, slaves, and colonists. With widespread, ecologically unsound destruction of the rain forest in our time through road building, mining, rubber tapping, lumber cutting, and farming, malaria has emerged as one of the most serious of all public health problems in the Amazon basin. It seems likely that because endemic malaria is recent in that region, genetic protection has not had time to evolve. The Hb^s gene introduced by African-Brazilians is rare. So, a genetic response does not constitute an important part of the epidemiologic picture.

Much of the response to malaria in Amazonia is cultural, as Coimbra demonstrates (Coimbra, 1988a). But it is neither the genetic adaptation (miniscule) nor the cultural adaptation (massive) that concerns us here. It is Amazonia as an illustration of how a physiologic response may evolve as an adaptation to an endemic infectious disease.

More or less the way annual vaccinations can confer immunity to influenza, repeated infections with *P. falciparum* can confer immunity to getting sick from falciparum malaria. The same applies to the milder disease, vivax malaria *(P. vivax),* which is also common in Amazonia. According to a medical textbook,

> infants do not become infected during the first 3 to 4 months of age because of transplacental immunity from their mothers and also because of the reduced ability of fetal hemoglobin to support development of the parasites. Thereafter, over the first few years of life, children suffer repeated infections. Without treatment, many die if *P. falciparum* is present; those who survive become immune by late childhood. The age at which immunity develops will depend upon the intensity of transmission. Malaria surveys in endemic areas will therefore disclose many individuals with parasites in the blood but with no or few clinical symptoms of malaria. (Brown & Neva, 1983, p. 97)

To develop a physiologic kind of protection the human host must be infected often enough to keep some protozoa in its system all of the time. It can take years of recurrent sickness, particularly when the invader is falciparum, to achieve this level of protection against further episodes of malarial chills, fever, weakness, and malaise (Coimbra, 1988b, p. 255).

The adaptation is physiologic in the sense that the parasite, serving as a protein antigen, elicits an immune response, including the arming of macrophages, the production of T-cell killer leucocytes, and the proliferation of B-cell antibodies specific to disarm the invader. These physiologic defenses take time to achieve what remains an often limited resistance, much longer than one would expect based on experience with other diseases. This is because plasmodia counterattacks by suppressing the immune system. The slow and inefficient development of an ability to fight off natural malarial infections by means of physiological mechanisms provides a measure of the physiologic forces arrayed against each other in this microscopic battle over ecological adaptation. The powerful immune response is counterattacked by an equally powerful malarial process of immunosuppression. Physiology can put on a very impressive show for the investigative scientist.

Cultural Responses: Malaria in Europe

Sardinia is a large island province of Italy characterized by political neglect, economic stagnation, and the worst malarial endemicity in the western Mediterrannean. Given an anthropologist's propensity for comparisons, it is interesting to keep Africa and Brazil in mind as we proceed.

First, two genetic adaptations to the disease have evolved. Both occur as DNA mutations affecting the blood, but neither one produces Hb^s (Brown, 1986a, p. 319; Inhorn & Brown, 1990, p. 92). Rather, one, known as thalassemia, results in hemoglobin with defective amino acid chains that can cause the molecule to self-destruct. The other, known by the code name G-6-Pd deficiency, interferes with the chemistry of hemoglobin, causing it to fail to produce a necessary chemical enzyme (glucose-6-phosphate dehydrogenase). Heterozygotes for the first (diagnosed as having thalassemia minor) are usually asymptomatic or only partially impaired by anemia. With T. minor these individuals have inherited a resistance to malaria. But it is a balanced polymorphism. Homozygotes (thalassemia major) inherit a bad blood-destroying disease that results in gallstone obstructions of the biliary ducts, leg ulcers, thickening of bones of the head and face, weak long bones that may break, and heart failure while still young.

G-6-Pd enzyme deficiency also protects against malaria, but since the body has an alternative, secondary chemical pathway for achieving the molecular transformation that must be carried out—breaking down one sugar molecule (glucose) to another (fructose)—homozygosity makes no difference under ordinary conditions. It is sobering to note, however, that people carrying this mutation are intolerant of meals that include fava beans, a widely consumed item of diet in the Mediterranean area. If they eat them they become acutely ill with a destructive blood disease (hemolysis) and may die. Solomon Katz and J. Schall refer to this as gene-bean interaction (Katz & Schall, 1979). It provides an unusual but instructive example of genetic and cultural coevolution relating to the environmental challenge of an infectious disease.

So, genetic responses occur in Sardinia. If we turn now to physiologic adaptations, we learn that they are rare for ecological reasons (Brown, 1981, p. 319). This is because climatically Sardinia is located in the temperate zone. The weather changes dramatically from one season to another. Mosquitoes only breed during the late summer and early fall (August through October), so Sardinia has a malaria season. For this reason the immune system fails to kick in, because acquired immunity against this immunosuppressive disease requires the kind of year-round exposure you get only in tropical regions such as parts of Africa and Amazonia.

With these observations on genetic and physiologic adaptations as background, let us look now at the cultural adaptations. What are the health beliefs and behaviors that medical anthropologist Peter Brown identified in Sardinia? I find it useful in summarizing Brown's work to organize his findings in a way suggested by a physician anthropologist, Frederick Dunn.

Dunn breaks health-related culture into four categories in terms of whether the health-related behaviors and beliefs are deliberate (intentionally concerned with health) or nondeliberate and whether they are health-beneficial or health-demoting (Dunn, 1983; Inhorn & Brown, 1990, p. 99).

DELIBERATE HEALTH-RELATED CUSTOMS THAT PROMOTE HEALTH

A purely speculative but nonetheless fascinating case can be made for fringe benefits deriving from practices relating to traditional folk beliefs about fevers and prevention. To be more convincing, it would need to be demonstrated that adherence to these customs is associated with less disease, and this was not possible. Be that as it may, Brown offers "the hypothesis that traditional

Peter Brown doing field research in a formerly malarial lowland town in Sardinia, Italy.

(Photo, Elizabeth S. Brown)

Sardinian folk theories of fever causation had adaptive value by reducing malaria relapse rates" (Brown, 1981, p. 329).

Brown reasons that a traditional emic belief about malaria, known in the nineteenth century as *Intemperie Sarda* and now only rarely mentioned, was that it was caused by too rapid a change from being hot to cold. The change of seasons *(cambiamento delle stagione)* could be dangerous to one's health. A related emic theory of disease causation that can still be encountered at times in modernizing Sardinia, is the concept of *colpo d'aria*, meaning that if you get caught in a draft you might catch a cold or experience a flare-up of rheumatism. Consistent with these once widespread beliefs, people still tend to practice general moderation in their personal habits, including the avoidance of drafts and dampness, not getting either too cold or too hot, not consuming cold drinks on a hot day, avoiding overexertion, attempting to eat well regularly, taking alcoholic drinks only in moderation, not sleeping out-of-doors, not going bare-headed, always wearing plenty of clothing, and not sleeping in a room with an open window.

To present this argument for the adapative value of these behaviors as strongly as possible, I will let Brown speak for himself:

> [C]linical observations of malaria relapses have consistently shown that certain conditions function to provoke recurrent attacks. Such conditions

include: the common cold or chills, change of climate, overexertion, heat exhaustion or exposure, alcohol abuse, surgery, trauma, and shock. . . . Since relapse rates directly affect the overall incidence of primary malaria cases during the annual summer epidemic [because only those who are acutely ill or in active relapse can provide mosquitoes with plasmodia to pass on], belief in these folk theories and adherence to the behaviors prescribed by them may have benefited the health of the entire society. (Brown, 1981, p. 332)

The location of human settlements also appears to have functioned as a preventive measure. On those parts of the island where agriculture is practiced in low elevation zones, people continue to live in nucleated settlements on hilltops, even though these settlements entail rigorous and time-consuming daily hikes downwards in the mornings and upwards in the evenings. People resist the temptation to move their homes to lowland areas because they believe that it is healthier to live where the quality of the air is good *(buon' aria)*, cleansed by healthful winds. Of course, the altitude and breezes reduce mosquito activity, so a belief in the importance of *buon' aria* has the effect of reducing malarial exposure.

CUSTOMS NOT PERCEIVED TO BE HEALTH-RELATED THAT NEVERTHELESS ENHANCE HEALTH

Brown succeeded here in demonstrating an association between folk customs and disease prevention. Shepherds in many parts of Sardinia graze their flocks on lowland areas throughout the winter, which happens to be off-season for malaria. They move to exploit mountain pastures in the summer, precisely when hoards of mosquitoes swarm in the lowlands. This transhumant calendar burdens them with winter hard work at inconvenient locations when they are away from home. "Lambing, milking, cheese making, and shearing must all be accomplished in isolated winter pastures, and this is associated with significant problems of labor recruitment." However, the seasonality of their transhumance protects them from malaria. "In short, this land use pattern allows for the exploitation of fertile but malarial lowland pastures during the 'safe' season of November to May, while it also permits shepherds to escape those high risk zones during the peak of the malarial cycle" (Brown, 1981, p. 325).

Brown found that social values relating to gender also demonstrated clear health effects for sound ecological reasons. In the Sardinian value system, it cuts down on the social prestige of the men in a family to have their women work in the fields. Men and women live in very different social worlds, with women restricted to home and neighborhood while men are entitled, indeed required, to range more freely. This gender differentiation is based on notions of honor and purity, but it contributes to better health for women because ecologically the settlements are located higher up on hilly terrain and therefore are less infested with infectious mosquitoes *(Anophelus labranchiae)* which prefer the agricultural and grazing areas situated lower down. Statistics support this hypothesis: More men than women fall ill with malaria.

This benefit extends to men of the more well-to-do classes, since these men also confine themselves to the village or town. In addition, wealthy landowners move to alternate residences in safe urban areas during the mosquito season, hiring less fortunate overseers to keep peasant laborers at their tasks in the lowlands. Again, statistics provide confirmation. Professional men, artisans, and merchants contract the disease less frequently than do agro-pastoral workers.

BEHAVIOR NOT PERCEIVED TO BE HEALTH-RELATED THAT CONTRIBUTES TO ILL HEALTH OR MORTALITY

Unfortunately, not all of the peasantry benefited as did shepherds from seasonality. Field-workers were required to be in the lowlands maximally for harvesting, which took place at the height of the annual malaria epidemic. Statistics document this effect. Agricultural workers suffered more from malaria than did shepherds.

DELIBERATE HEALTH-RELATED CUSTOMS THAT CONTRIBUTE TO ILL HEALTH OR MORTALITY

Brown describes no custom relating to malaria that fits in this category. It can be illustrated, however, from Brazil, where Millicent Fleming-Moran found that patients often stop taking their prescribed medication as soon as they feel well again. They believe it is good to save some of the medicine for future use (Fleming-Moran, 1975). Stopping treatment too soon results in the creation and spread of drug-resistant strains of the parasite. In fact, treatment-resistant strains have become a serious problem in Brazil as well as in other parts of the world (Coimbra, 1988a, p. 257).

FROM ECOLOGY TO CRITICAL MEDICAL ANTHROPOLOGY

Ecological studies of health behaviors are particularly important because they demonstrate ways in which infectious diseases have been and can be prevented by means of the folk customs of small-scale societies. In West Africa and Sardinia, these small-scale folk societies are parts of large population agglomerations with urban characteristics, but they remain small-scale in terms of their primary social involvements and their essentially preindustrial economies. To raise standards of care in any region of the world, and particularly in underdeveloped small-scale societies, prevention is more effective than attempting cures. We saw in the last part of this chapter that prevention was partially effective in Sardinia, achieved as an unintended consequence of old customs and unexamined habits. However, acknowledgement of these benefits must not blind us to larger realities. Sardinia was plagued by severe recurrent epidemics of malaria.

Brown offers Sardinia as an example of an undeveloped region in Europe, a region suffering from unremitting poverty and discontent, in which customs capable of preventing malaria protect only part of the population. Because malaria remained such a serious health problem, the prevention and eradication of malaria was targeted as a major development goal. It was advanced by economists and politicians as essential for economic growth and social success. This is the argument that the health costs of malaria constituted the main reason why the people of Sardinia remained so poor. However, peasant wisdom reminds us that larger critical issues are even more important, as clarified in this poignant paragraph in an article by Peter Brown:

> When I first arrived in the ex-malarial community of Bosa in western Sardinia in 1976, I explained to some peasant farmers about the "Malaria Blocks Development" hypothesis and how I wanted to study about the positive economic effects of malaria eradication. Some Sardinians listened politely, but most openly laughed at the argument. To them, the island's economic problems, both in the past and the present, were to be traced to problems of land ownership and other political-economic issues. From their perspective, malaria had been a consequence and *not* a cause of their poverty. Their analysis was almost always that poverty had been the result of a history of economic exploitation. Many men, retired agricultural wage laborers *(serbidores)*, told stories of 'not being able to afford having malaria,' that is, being economically compelled to spend the day in the field doing wage labor even when they were suffering an acute attack. In striking contrast to the scholarly literature, the people in Bosa did not have great expectations about the positive effects of the eradication of malaria. In fact, their attitude was that the entire malaria argument might be considered a political smokescreen. (Brown, 1987, p. 168)

In fact, it has never been demonstrated that antimalarial programs in Sardinia brought about any meaningful economic development (Brown, 1986, p. 858). The Sardinians Brown talked with offer a powerful though poignant reminder of how important it can be to listen to other voices, to put multivocality to use in the work of medical ecologists and field ethnographers.

The Sardinians also bring up a point of view known as critical medical anthropology, that is, to solve problems on the local or regional level does not bring good health and well-being to an underclass if the country is controlled by a political and economic elite that is exploitative and repressive.

CONCLUSION

The paradigm of medical ecology brought back the dimensions of time and space as key variables for cultural analysis. It demonstrated its value as a way to approach human health. Recent work has illustrated how it can be applied profitably to the study of small-scale communities as well as on regional and global levels. With a bit of stretching, it lends itself to a more completely holistic approach that incorporates cultural factors, as Brown demonstrated in his study of malaria in Sardinia. Ecology is essential for a holistic understanding of human health. In itself, however, it is not fully holistic. Complete holism was achieved with the biocultural model, to which we now turn.

REFERENCES

Barnett, C. R. (1989). Review of medical anthropology in ecological perspective by A. McElroy and P. K. Townsend. *Medical Anthropological Quarterly, 3,* 405–407.

Brown, H. W., & Neva, F. A. (1983). *Basic clinical parasitology* (5th ed.) Norwalk, CT: Appleton-Century-Crofts.

Brown, P. J. (1981). Cultural adaptations to endemic malaria in Sardinia. *Medical Anthropology, 5,* 313–339.

Brown, P. J. (1986a). Cultural and genetic adaptations to malaria: Problems of comparison. *Human Ecology, 14,* 311–332.

Brown, P. J. (1986b). Socioeconomic and demographic effects of malaria eradication: A comparison of Sri Lanka and Sardinia. *Social Science and Medicine, 22,* 847–859.

Brown, P. J. (1987). Microparasites and macroparasites. *Cultural Anthropology, 2,* 155–171.

Coimbra, C. E. A., Jr. (1988a). Human factors in the epidemiology of malaria in the Brazilian Amazon. *Human Organization, 47,* 254–260.

Coimbra, C. E. A., Jr. (1988b). Human settlements, demographic pattern, and epidemiology in lowland Amazonia: The case of Chagas's disease. *American Anthropologist, 90,* 82–93.

Dunn, F. L. (1983). Human behavioral factors in mosquito vector control. *Southeast Asian Journal of Tropical Medicine and Public Health, 14,* 86–94.

Fleming-Moran, M. (1975). *The folk view of natural causation and disease in Brazil and its relation to traditional curing practices.* Unpublished M.A. thesis in anthropology. University of Florida, Gainesville.

Hiernaux, J. (1955). Physical anthropology and the frequency of genes with a selective value: The sickle cell gene. *American Journal of Physical Anthropology, 57,* 455–472.

Inhorn, M. C., & Brown, P. J. (1990). The anthropology of infectious disease. *Annual Review of Anthropology, 19,* pp. 89–117.

Katz, S. V., & Schall, J. (1979). Fava bean consumption and biocultural evolution. *Medical Anthropology, 3,* 459–476.

Kemp, W. B. (1971). The flow of energy in a hunting society. *Scientific American, 225,* (3), 105–115.

Lee, R. B., & Irven D. (Eds.) (1968). *Man the hunter.* Chicago: Aldine–Atherton.

Livingstone, F. B. (1958). Anthropological implications of sickle cell gene distribution in West Africa. *American Anthropologist, 60,* 533–562.

McElroy, A., & Townsend, P. K. (1989). *Medical anthropology in ecological perspective* (2nd ed). Boulder, CO: Westview Press.

Moran, E. F. (1990a). Ecosystem ecology in biology and anthropology: A critical assessment. In E. F. Moran (Ed.), *The ecosystem approach in anthropology: From concept to practice* (pp. 3-40). Ann Arbor: University of Michigan Press.

Moran, E. F. (1990b). Levels of analysis and analytical level shifting: Examples from Amazonian ecosystem research. In E. F. Moran, (Ed.), *The ecosystem approach in anthropology: From concept to practice* (pp. 279-308). Ann Arbor: University of Michigan Press.

Netting, R. M. (1990). Links and boundaries: Reconsidering the alpine village as ecosystem. In E. F. Moran (Ed.), *The ecosystem approach in anthropology: From concept to practice* (pp. 229-245). Ann Arbor: University of Michigan Press.

Rappaport, R. A. (1971). The flow of energy in an agricultural society. *Scientific American, 225* (3), 117-132.

Redfield, R. (1956). *Peasant society and culture: An anthropological approach to civilization.* Chicago: University of Chicago Press.

Service, E. R. (1962). *Primitive social organization: An evolutionary perspective.* New York: Random House.

Steward, J. H. (Ed.) (1949). *Handbook of South American Indians* (Vol 5.). Smithsonian Institution Bureau of American Ethnology Bulletin 143. Washington DC: United States Government Printing Office.

Steward, J. H. (1955). *Theory of culture change: The methodology of multilinear evolution.* Urbana: University of Illinois Press.

Taussig, T. T. (1980). *The devil and commodity fetishism in South America.* Chapel Hill, NC: University of North Carolina Press.

Vayda, A. P., & McCay, B. J. (1975). New directions in ecology and ecological anthropology. *Annual Review of Anthropology, 4,* 293-306.

White, L. A. (1949). *The science of culture: A study of man and civilization.* New York: Grove Press.

Wissler, C. (1917). *The American Indian: An introduction to the anthropology of the New World.* New York: D.C., McMurtrie.

Chapter 9

THE BIOCULTURAL MODEL

FROM MEDICAL ECOLOGY TO THE BIOCULTURAL MODEL

The biocultural model is not new as a way to design research. It is merely new as the dominant paradigm of medical anthropology. To understand how this took place, let us take a second look at the immediate post–World War II years when cultural anthropologists shifted their emphasis to culture change and applied anthropology. In the late 1940s and early 1950s physical anthropology was still largely a specialty for those with skills in assessing dimensions of the human musculoskeletal system. Although physical anthropologists were well aware of the importance of cultural factors relating to the human body, and genetics was a major consideration, they nevertheless tended to concentrate their efforts on the architectonics of the body. In a typical introductory seminar on physical anthropology, students practiced how to measure various features, including:

- Skin color (look at the armpit where the effect of the sun is minimal)
- Head length and breadth (using large Swiss-made calipers)
- Stature (with an anthropometer [a very long yardstick] that was also used to measure leg length, arm length, etc.)
- Hair form (checked against drawings of straight and curly hair)
- Thickness of hair (based impressionistically on fingering the hair in the-light of one's experience)
- Width of nose (measured with small steel calipers) (Sullivan & Shapiro, 1928)

Students also learned a lot of anatomy, particularly skeletal, which is why gross anatomy to this day is sometimes taught in medical schools by physical anthropologists. In addition to these skills in anthropometry (literally, "people measuring"), students learned how to document physiological diversity. Physical anthropologists were interested in human variability in such biological functions as the following:

- body temperature
- cold or heat tolerance
- landsteiner blood types
- work capacity
- infant and childhood growth patterns
- adaptations to high altitude

Above all, students were drilled in osteology as it related to deciphering prehistoric skeletal remains in terms of the sex, age, and race of surviving bones. They were taught how to pour bird shot or grain particles through the foramen magnum (Latin for "the big hole") at the bottom of the skull in order to measure cranial capacity (as a way to estimate brain size), and even got a few lessons on how to identify diseases and trauma based on lesions visible on bony surfaces. Theodore McCown at Berkeley, where I studied, was a specialist in forensic anthropology and took pleasure in having been the scientist (a Protestant at that) who measured and authenticated the sacred skeletal relics of Junípero Serra as integral to canonization proposed by the Catholic church.

But change was in the air. The 1950s and 1960s saw people come on the scene who insisted that efforts to document human biological variability were distorted because anthropologists failed to give adequate attention to the influence of culture. Witness this clarion call from Stanley Garn:

> It would seem that the range of human capacities, including cold-tolerance, heat-tolerance, and load-carrying will have to be reinvestigated with more adequate attention to the cultural factor. As with studies involving nutrition, genetics, or human growth, these more coldly physiological aspects of human biology cannot be investigated as if the subjects lived in a cultural vacuum up to the time they were enlisted as "volunteers" for research. (Garn, 1954, p. 79)

Fifteen years later, Alexander Alland identified "the growing field of medical anthropology" as an especially appropriate field of endeavor for these more holistically aware biological anthropologists. Latching explicitly onto the Darwinian evolutionary model, he presented the idea of adaptation as a key medical-anthropological concept, recommending that biological adaptation (e.g. success in the fight against disease) be conceptualized in terms of reproductive success (Darwin's criterion) and measured in terms of population growth and expansion. Cultural adaptation was a conceptual partner in this approach to health and adaptation, thought of as a more efficient use of energy (White's evolutionary criterion) and itself also evaluated in terms of population growth (Alland, 1970, pp. 42–43). In this very early statement about medical anthropology as a specialty within anthropology, Alland identified the high potential inherent in a multidisciplinarity that would combine medicine (specifically epidemiology) with anthropology:

Medical anthropologists focus their attention on patterns of disease and treatment within a wide range of populations and environmental settings. They investigate relationships between behavior and epidemiological patterns and are frequently called upon to aid in the analysis of specific etiological problems. Many, if not all, epidemiological patterns involve complex relationships among physiological, genetic, cultural, demographic, and environmental variables. Intensive field studies as well as cross cultural analyses of behavior related to productivity on the one hand and epidemiology on the other should prove highly useful for the analysis of the adaptive process. (Alland, 1970, pp. 4-5)

In 1978, Arthur Kleinman was already insisting that medical anthropology must be multidisciplinary in the sense that practitioners "must draw from ethnographic, clinical, epidemiological and social psychological sources." "Clearly," he added, "they will require models and concepts which consider health and sickness to be the results of complex multi-factor interactions on biological, psychological and social levels, not the results of single determinants operating on only one level of analysis" (Kleinman, 1986 [1978], p. 41). In short, Kleinman described a biocultural model.

More recently in the 1990s, Ann McElroy spoke out in favor of biocultural studies as a way to achieve what she refers to as an integrative medical anthropology. "The term 'biocultural' ideally implies a model in which cultural data are systematically collected *and integrated* with biological and environmental data." (McElroy, 1990, p. 250).

In taking this stance, McElroy shares with Patricia Townsend an acknowledgment of the need to redefine the conceptual basis for research in medical anthropology. "Townsend (1989) questions why the 'dominant paradigm' (that is, medical ecology) 'does not dominate' and why, with 'the exception of excellent work in human biology, the ecological approach is not being tested much in research'." (McElroy, 1990, pp. 250, 258; Townsend, 1989).

McElroy and Townsend appear to be asking for a revitalization of the paradigm of cultural ecology which had become narrower than it needed to be as a conceptual basis for the practice of medical anthropology. "Medical ecology has been one of the dominant theoretical strands in medical anthropology since the 1960s," she wrote with Townsend in 1992. Unfortunately, they conclude, "It has come to be identified with a rather narrow range of research issues, concerning such matters as adaptation to climate and infectious disease, and has dealt with small-scale foraging societies" (Townsend & McElroy, 1992, p. 9). It can well be argued that medical ecology, with its roots in early formulations of the cultural ecology model and multilinear evolution, was as holistic in its potential as is the biocultural model. Medical ecology needed to return to its roots, and to mark that rebirth, the concept of biocultural anthropology has been proposed.

George Armelagos, Thomas Leatherman, Mary Ryan, and Lynn Sibley explain how they, too, arrived at this shift in paradigms from medical ecology to biocultural anthropology:

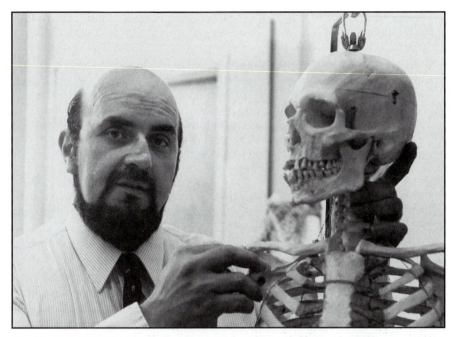

George Armelagos teaching anatomy as part of his work as a physical anthropologist.

(Photo, University of Massachusetts Photographic Services)

[W]e would argue that [an] ecological perspective did not gain the general acceptance in medical anthropology that was expected. The failure of the model to provide a synthesis of the health and disease processes may be found in the past formulations and current perceptions of medical anthropologists. Many medical anthropologists perceive the ecological approach as having a limited view of the ecosystem. (Armelagos et al., 1992, p. 38)

Armelagos and associates further explain: "We do not suggest a complete rejection of ecology and adaptation in medical anthropology, but a reformulation of this perspective into a truly biocultural model." Their "biocultural model of health and disease" moves beyond "past ecological formulations in medical anthropology" in order to examine "health systems and [the] behavior of interacting organic, inorganic, and cultural environments." The key issue in this updated formulation is to include in the model

a more complete consideration of culture as part of the human environment and, specifically, a greater attention to the impact of political-economic factors and social relations on the health process. . . . The benefit of this model lies in the ability to integrate physical, biological, and cultural components of human environments and to synthesize key aspects of ethnomedical and biomedical perspectives in medical anthropology. (Armelagos et al., 1992, pp. 39, 49)

David Landy also advises that medical anthropologists move on to a bio-cultural model:

> We should attempt to make anthropology, and especially medical anthropol-
> ogy, the kind of integrative discipline McElroy urges. What renders our species
> human are not only culture, social system, and language, but our special brains
> and bodies, our extraordinary genetic codes that make possible the human
> ways of life. Keys to understanding how humans manage to maintain health and
> react to illness lie not only in their cultural modes and social arrangements,
> but in how health and illness become the products of behavior *and* biology.
> (Landy, 1990; p. 366)

The biocultural model, then, is a holistic model. It takes culture as a cen-
tering concept that must be reconciled with the realities of human biology and
of ecosystems at all levels. The individual as a mind/body constitutes an ultimate orientation. The model also incorporates the perspective of evolutionary
adaptation, requiring attention to both time and space dimensions. In research
strategy it includes both community-based fieldwork and geographically oriented comparative studies. The strategy also requires a commitment to interdisciplinarity and multidisciplinarity, when appropriate. Ultimately, the
biocultural model requires vertical thinking that ranges in principle from the
subatomic to the cosmic.

The biocultural model is holistically inclusive, but not exclusive. It does
not exclude research that fails to actualize all of its holistic potential. On the
contrary, most research of necessity only activates a part of the phenomenological hierarchy. Most research is puzzle-solving work that takes on bits and
parts at a time of what needs eventually to be done. This means that it is congenial to work carried out according to older paradigms of all sorts. Not the
least, it is compatible with ongoing work that is basically that of medical ecology as practiced in the 1980s. For that reason, in what follows I will continue
the discussion of a biroculturally oriented regional medical ecology dedicated
to the study of three major kinds of health hazards: infectious diseases, adaptations to extremes of climate, and environmental disasters.

INFECTIOUS EPIDEMICS

The hazards most obviously and comprehensively relevant to health, treatment, and prevention are the great epidemics. For centuries that stretch back-
ward into millenia, infectious calamities have devastated humanity.
Epidemiologists and anthropologists want to know how they can be controlled. Three worldwide epidemics provide evidence for three different
ways in which they have come under control: through the natural history of
the disease in the absence of direct human intervention, by means of public
health measures based on changing human behavior, and through public
health measures based on medical technology.

Control Without Intervention: The Plague in Europe

Microscopic bacteria known as *Yersinia pestis* are so tiny and transparent that they can be seen only under a microscope after they have been stained to provide color. Then they look like small safety pins since they are short fat rods in which most of the color concentrates at the two ends, but there is nothing safe about them. They are horrible and deadly for humans. The baccilus survives well in a flea, *Xenopsylla cheopis,* which regurgitates the bacillis in the process of sucking up a blood meal. Fleas for their part get their infections from small rodent hosts, including mice, squirrels, and prairie dogs, but especially the black rat, *Rattus rattus. Yersinia* moved west from an ancient focus in rodent populations somewhere in Asia, hitchhiking with travelers along Central Asian caravan routes as far as the Crimea and then by ship throughout the Middle East and Europe (Zinsser, 1935; Langer, 1964; Eli, 1980; Twigg, 1985).

By the fourteenth century ecological conditions were right for Europe to become a sink of disease. The medieval population had grown dense. Deforestation was extensive in many areas. The climate worsened. Increasingly severe winters and repeated years of crop failure weakened people and forced hard-pressed rats with their fleas to encroach more intimately on human settlements. In crowded, unsanitary towns, fleas transferred their microscopic fellow travelers from hordes of rats to susceptible human populations. Pesky fleabites evolved year after year into horrible plagues that spread over Asia and Europe for a number of centuries.

Plague produced swollen glands (buboes, hence "bubonic plague"), sometimes black hemorrhagic skin blotches ("black plague"), or severe lung infections (pneumonic plague), along with weakness, debilitating fever, and agonizing pain. The victim was usually restless, delirious, confused, and uncoordinated. Most died in three to five days. People found it horrifying to contemplate their own disfigurement, dehumanizing prostration, and enormous pain as a prelude to almost certain death. In company with the plague, the hygienic disaster included concurrent epidemics of pneumonic anthrax (often confused with pneumonic plague, it appears) and other deadly diseases, including typhus, the very disease Virchow was to witness as the ravager of Upper Silesia many centuries later.

Spring should be the season of hope, but it became a time of anxiety as people braced for a new attack before they had fully recovered from the last. From a public health point of view, the population was completely overwhelmed. Physicians could do nothing to help and were sometimes stoned, accused of causing the disease they could not cure. Racist, sexist, and paranoid accusations led to hunting down and killing Jews, presumed witches, and others. Revenge was exacted from gravediggers in the belief that because they profited from deaths, they had a motive for causing deaths. It is true that not infrequently death workers threw the sick and the dead indiscriminately into carts to be hauled to huge burial pits.

Those who viewed the plague as punishment from God made ostentatious donations to the church and vowed do do penance if they lived. The failure of the church to turn back the terror helped to make the Protestant revolt possible in the sixteenth century. Others, numbed by despair, abandoned all moral and legal restraints, defiantly looting, thieving, and murdering or falling drunkenly into ribald orgies of forlorn sensuality.

During one three-year period (1348 through 1350), an astonishing 20 to 25 percent of the total population of large areas of Western Europe died under these gruesome conditions. Europe sank into a century or more of economic stagnation and political uncertainty. As aristocratic and village patriarchs succumbed, manors, farms, and crafts fell into the hands of people who never expected to be among the controllers. The world of wealth and power was turned topsy-turvy. Overall, Europe was ravaged almost beyond belief between the thirteenth and late seventeenth centuries, helpless and terrified by a disaster that returned again and again, out of control.

Today's newspapers almost never carry notices of the plague, which nonetheless still dangerously infects people in parts of the world where it smolders in rodent populations. In areas of endemicity, a standard plague vaccine offers protection where it is available. It is particularly recommended for use in parts of Asia. The lesson of the plague, however, is that the great pandemic of the Middle Ages was not defeated by either public health officials or medical practitioners. Yet it virtually disappeared after 1679. How could that be?

Let it be said up front that nobody knows exactly why the plague declined after centuries of recurrence. Perhaps some change in the organism itself took place, although it seems unlikely. More likely explanations have to do with the ecology of the black rat, who somewhat mysteriously declined in numbers, again for reasons not entirely clear. Did cleanliness in homes and towns make the critical difference in exposure to fleas and their hidden passengers? It is possible that human nutrition improved, although we have no direct evidence for that. Good nutrition strengthens innate immune responses. The end of the epidemics of plague demonstrates, then, that improvement in health is neither automatically nor necessarily due only to medical progress.

Control by Changing Human Behavior: Cholera in Asia

Looking through a microscope you can't mistake the short comma-shaped organism that wiggles actively as you watch. When Robert Koch first made the discovery he called it the comma bacillus, but now it is known as *Vibrio cholerae;* its cute antics are soon forgotten as you become aware of its disasterous consequences. It gets into the intestines when people drink water or eat food contaminated by the excrement of infected people. The results are catastrophic. *Vibrio* causes the inner lining of the bowels to fall apart (desquamate). Blood capillaries along the entire length of the small and large intestines dilate intensely into microscopic sieves, exuding huge quantities of fluid that get discharged as vomitus and "rice-water stool." Blood vessels rupture, discoloring the skin. Without treatment, 50 to 75 percent of cholera victims experience such a sudden and enormous loss of body fluids that within a few hours a person who was fit as a fiddle at noon is transformed into a shrunken, emaciated, blue-black corpse before nightfall. Part of the dread experienced in an epidemic was precisely that you could not know from one hour to the next whether you would be dead before the end of the day (McNeill, 1977; Barua & Greenbough, 1992). Rudyard Kipling, conveys with poetic clarity something of that dread in his verse, "Cholera Camp (Infantry in India)." I quote Kipling here as a reminder that literature can serve as a powerful ethnographic source when appropriately contextualized.

We've got the cholerer in camp—it's worse than forty fights;
We're dyin' in the wilderness the same as Isrulites;
It's before us, an' be'ind us, an' we cannot get away,
An' the doctor's just reported we've ten more to-day!

Oh, strike your camp an' go, the bugle's callin',
The Rains are fallin'—
The dead are bushed an' stoned to keep 'em safe below.
The Band's a-doin' all she knows to cheer us;
The Chaplain's gone and prayed to Gawd to 'ear us—
To ear us—
O Lord, for it's a-killin' of us so!

Since August, when it started, it's been stickin' to our tail,
Though they've 'ad us out by marches an' they've 'ad us back by
rail;
But it runs as fast as troop trains, and we cannot get away;
An' the sick-list to the Colonel makes ten more to-day.

(Kipling, 1920, p. 500)

The disease smoldered endemically in India for centuries, carried by pilgrims from populous temple cities into distant towns and villages across the subcontinent. For centuries cholera was confined mainly to Hindu nations in South Asia, with only occasional shipborne outbreaks as far away as China. After 1817, however, epidemics in Calcutta disseminated with the movements of British troops and colonial travelers by steamships and railroads. New international linkages spread the disease northward into Central Asia, southward to Sri Lanka, eastward as far as China and Japan, westward into the Middle East and, ultimately, to Europe and the Americas.

The horror of cholera led to the performance of rituals that did little or nothing to stop the disease. A Chinese-American anthropologist, Francis L. K. Hsu, encountered an epidemic of cholera associated with largely traditional responses in a community in the Yunnan Province of China in 1942 (Hsu, 1983) . The disease moved along the Burma Road with World War II refugees crowding into buses, cars, and trucks or trudging along on foot towards China. With motor vehicles, distances that once would have slowed the epidemic for days were covered in hours. Hsu's community was suddenly overwhelmed by the dread cholera.

Within the walls of the town, a death or two in the beginning escalated to six or seven per day, not counting those in the surrounding countryside. People tried vainly to treat this frightening disease with traditional herbal preparations. Poorly organized public health measures were confined largely to posting moral injunctions around town, urging the inhabitants to practice clean habits, such as not scattering night soil (human feces) or garbage. Cholera vaccinations, a product of modern science at that time still unintegrated into local health thinking, appealed to very few. Even vaccinated townspeople put their trust primarily in concomitant ritual measures. One notice from the town elders entreated: "Pray and abstain with all earnestness. Filth and uncleanliness are forbidden." The injunction to abstain meant that safety lay in avoiding prurient thoughts, sexual intercourse, and eating meat.

Coffins inflated in price and then became completely unavailable in this society where honoring one's ancestors is a powerful religious sentiment. Funeral processions became daily events, soon shorn of customary dignities. On various streets ritual platforms were erected from which prayers and incantations were led by priests, often assisted by musicians. Angry gods thought to be punishing the town for sin were given offerings. To ensure the efficacy of these ritual measures, the chief priest demanded that at the platform with its pictures of the gods, no one should indulge in profane thoughts, appear in dirty clothes, spit or blow their noses on the floor, fail to fast, recite the wrong scriptures, or play music out of key. Quoting from an ancient Ming dynasty sage, a poster captured the anguish of the moment: "If man does not repent his doom will come soon. . . .There will be no crop anywhere; no smoke from any chimney; there will be wars, looting, and unburied skeletons of the dead everywhere" (Hsu, 1983, p. 39). Such were the anxious thoughts and acts of a town where ritual purefication seemed the only promising way to fight chaos and despair.

Public health measures, however, can cut disease rates dramatically. In nineteenth-century America, cholera struck hardest in slum housing, where whole families crowded into single rooms in tenement buildings crammed with hundreds of people. Tenements lacked flush toilets and running water. They were impossible to keep rigorously clean. Kerosene lamps disseminated a dirty film that spread throughout the living area. Windows, small or absent, were often covered with broken glass or waxed paper. Heating was expensive and dangerous. Dung heaps of human excrement piled high on ground level courtyards. Towns had become cesspools of human misery.

Many early nineteenth-century Americans were convinced that cholera epidemics were sent by God as punishment for sin. "The cholera is not caused by intemperance and filth, in themselves, but it is a scourge, a rod in the hand of God" (cited in Starr, 1982, p. 36). Church pastors and their flocks believed that the threat could be turned back with prayer.

Many Americans looked for naturalistic explanations. Some believed that quarantines offered a solution, but isolating infected victims was wholly inadequate to stop a food- and water-borne disease such as cholera. What did help were sociopolitical programs of sanitation.

Nineteenth-century clean-ups on a large scale got the public health movement started. Virchow in Silesia, although by no means among the first, had shown that sanitary changes could be effective against typhus. Others in France, London, New York City, and elsewhere also demonstrated the effectiveness of cleanliness. At the end of an epidemic of yellow fever in Philadelphia in 1793, after town authorities had tried in vain to stop the devastation by firing canons into the misty miasma that was thought to spread the disease, physicians convinced fellow citizens that the cause was filth. They persuaded the town to establish a board of health. Streets were cleaned, and one of the first free public water systems was constructed (Guthrie, 1946).

An important early example of successful epidemiologic reasoning emerged out of fighting against cholera. In 1854 John Snow, a physician-scientist already well-known for his early experiments in the use of choloroform as a surgical anesthetic, struggled along with his fellow physicians against an outbreak of cholera in London. With extraordinary perspicacity, he began to realize that although his patients were diverse in social class and occupation, in one way or another they all shared one thing in common. Every one had drunk water that came from the public pump on Broad Street. This was before the modern science of bacteriology was established by Louis Pasteur in France and Robert Koch in Germany. The comma bacillus was not thought of. Nevertheless, Snow reasoned that something in the water was causing the disease. He arranged to have the pump handle removed, after which the epidemic fizzled out.

Snow's success in the absence of effective medicinal treatment provides an early classic example of the effectiveness of epidemiologic reasoning as a weapon. The real lesson, however, is less obvious. It is not enough that he acquired an important kind of understanding. He needed to succeed equally well in communication and recruitment. Snow, who died just four years later at age forty-five, was not able to convince the medical establishment that public health measures based upon the Broad Street pump kind of reasoning could serve as a powerful weapon in the fight against disease. His evidence was merely circumstantial, and the medical establishment did not think in terms of an explanatory model, a paradigm that could incorporate the concept of sanitation. The needed sanitary revolution came later, after germs were discovered by Pasteur and Koch in the late 1870s.

Cholera is still with us, even though it can be controlled by sanitary measures alone. An ongoing pandemic began in Asia around 1961, spread early to Africa, Europe, and Oceania, smoldering in those parts of the world for several decades before advancing to Latin America in 1991. Since 1961, occasional sporadic cases have been reported in the United States, mostly carried by U.S. travelers returning home from countries where the disease is prevalent

(Swerdlow & Ries, 1992; Centers for Disease Control, 1992). Why is cholera still a successful killer? A bit of basic ethnography provides the answer.

> Cholera is a disease of the poor. People in the middle and upper classes rarely contract it; those who are healthy and have access to quality health care can almost always survive. Those who live in unsanitary conditions, primarily those without clean drinking water, are most susceptible. In Central America, according to UNICEF's conservative estimates, 10 million of the region's 28.7 million—more than one third—don't have clean drinking water. (Jeffrey, 1992, p. 84)

Poor people are unable to save themselves and their children from dying because they cannot afford to boil their water. They can scarcely find enough money to pay for cooking. To boil drinking water is simply impossible.

> A collective solution to the problem, such as potable water systems for entire communities, is something U.S. citizens take for granted, but not people in the rest of the hemisphere. And when poor neighbors have organized to change their lot, local elites have resisted. Grassroots activists in places like Brazil and Guatemala have been labeled communist and murdered for sins as simple as seeking safe water for their communities. (Jeffrey, 1992, p. 85)

These observations bring us back to the Sardinian peasants who believe that malaria on their island will not be conquered until political freedom and social justice are achieved. Will it ever happen?

Control with Medical Technology: Smallpox in Africa

Unlike the plague and cholera, which are bacterial diseases, smallpox is caused by a virus. A bacterium is a complete living cell. In addition to DNA (genes) that serve as a template for reproduction in enormous numbers by cell division, bacteria contain all of the organelles in their cytoplasm that are necessary for life. All they need to thrive is a protected environment that bathes them with nutrient-rich fluids. In contrast, viruses are merely bits of protein and nucleic acid, fragments of cells, so to speak. They contain some DNA or RNA to code for reproduction, but must live in the cells they invade if they are to multiply and spread, because they lack organelles of their own. So tiny are they that no one had ever seen one until electron microscopes became available in the 1960s, yet they cause catastrophic diseases. One of these truely gruesome viral diseases is smallpox, *Variola virus.*

The onset of smallpox is rapid, unleashing high fever, disabling headache, and severe backache, compounded sometimes by stomach pains. The victim complains of feeling terrible and often collapses in sudden weakness. The diagnosis becomes unmistakable after two to four days when eruptions appear in a characteristic pattern, evolving into pustules and eventually scabs over a three- or four-week period. From 20 to 40 percent die, usually during the second week.

Those who survive are marked by pitted and scarred skin, a cosmetic disaster by the beauty standards of most societies. The worst result, however, is that the vesicles and pustules often erupt on the eyes, causing permanent blindness.

Smallpox is a severe, highly contagious, often deadly disease that caused alarm throughout Asia and Europe in the old days when epidemics were common. Smallpox ravaged Africa as well. An epidemic among the Tiv is described in an anthropological novel by Laura Bohannan, for example, under her *nom de plume,* Elenore Smith Bowen (Bohannon, 1964, pp. 264–269). However, I will take my example from the Nuer.

The Nuer are well-known to every anthropologist through field studies carried out in the 1930s by E. E. Evans-Pritchard, an English anthropologist (Evans-Pritchard, 1940). Much more recently, Hilary Harris, working with Robert Gardner, produced a film documentary which, like literature, can deepen one's ethnographic comprehension (Harris, Breidenbach, & Gardner, 1970). The disease struck while Gardner and Harris were there with their cameras. The sad hopelessness of a fulminant infection is seen in a boy so massively covered with pustules that he must surely have died within the next twenty-four hours. Others displayed less serious rashes. Most adults appear untouched, immune, no doubt, from earlier epidemics.

The Nuer are very tall, slender people living in the region of the Upper Nile where their lives are shaped by cattle herding. When the seriousness of the epidemic became apparent, a great crowd of people gathered in a field. The prophet Kirean, wearing his leopard skin emblem of office, orchestrated the ritual fight. Two by two, young men charged an unseen enemy, firing their noisy muskets into the sky, then retreating to make room for the next two.

In a ritual celebration of joy and strength, Kirean asked God to relieve them of smallpox. He then led his people to the riverbank where three goats were sacrificed to the mother of gods who lives in the river. People swarmed into the the blood-tinged water, vigorously jostling one another as they rubbed the sanctified water into their own skin and the skin of others, a clear example that belongs in Frederick Dunn's category of deliberate health-related customs that contribute to ill health or mortality.

SMALLPOX IN THE AMERICAS

The year 1492 marks the bringing together of the two halves of the world for the first time in any significant way since the original discovery of the New World tens of thousands of years earlier. The result was the most enormous cataclysm for health and happiness the world has ever known. It occurred in the dimension of a hemisphere. Disease, in combination with military cruelty and ruthless religious, political, and economic oppression, savaged Native American peoples, causing anguish, demoralization, overwhelming depopulation, and outright extinction. Surviving Native Americans have not yet recovered (Crosby, 1972).

Virgin populations in which not a single person had previously been exposed were overwhelmed by diseases never encountered before, carried by invaders from Europe. Viral diseases such as measles, influenza, mumps, and yellow fever struck hard along with bacterial and other infectious diseases, diphtheria, typhus, and malaria, among others. Measles, which can be a harmless childhood infection that causes only mild distress for most people, caused, under those circumstances prostration and death on a massive scale. No disease was more severe than smallpox, although very rarely was an epidemic limited to a single disease, and it is not always certain whether the disease referred to by the conquistadores as *viruelas* was truly smallpox or may have been confused with measles, chicken pox, or typhus.

What is clear is that smallpox was a major killer that matched and probably surpassed the plague in depopulating, demoralizing, and destroying previously healthy people. In vulnerable populations, over 90 percent succumbed to this highly infectious disease, with a case mortality rate of around 30 percent. The first recorded epidemic in the New World took place in the winter of 1518–1519 among the Indians of Santo Domingo Island in the Carribean. A few Spaniards got sick, all of whom recovered; however, it killed at least 30 percent of the native islanders. Spreading quickly along the Antilles and onto mainland Yucatan, it rapidly became a continentwide disaster.

For this population at risk, any contact with colonials resulted in catching smallpox. If the contact was peaceful trade, it killed. If it was religious conversion done with humane intent, it killed. Wars inevitably spread smallpox. The first known use of germ warfare was planned and executed in fighting Pontiac's Rebellion, in 1763, when it was arranged that two blankets and two kerchiefs purposely infected with smallpox pustules would fall into Indian hands.

The disease itself was often fatal. But whether smallpox or one of the other severe infectious diseases, infections struck so many simultaneously that almost no one was left to feed and nurse the ill. People died of exposure and neglect. Planting, gathering, hunting and fishing became impossible. Food shortages led to malnutrition and starvation. Social order was destroyed. People were psychologically shattered. Writing in 1622, one European was a witness.

> [Indians] died on heapes, as they lay in their houses; and the living, that were able to shift for themselves, would runneaway and let them dy, and let there Carkases ly above the ground without burial. . . . And the bones and skulls upon the severall places of their habitations made such a spectacle after my coming into those partes as I travailed in the Forrest nere the Massachusetts, it seemed to me a new found Golgotha. (cited in Crosby, 1972, p. 42).

The Vaccine Against Smallpox

Before the institutionalization of modern scientific medicine, rational problem solving was certainly not unknown to practioners of traditional medicine. Healers often made discoveries of great practical utility, although more commonly these were for curing rather than preventing disease. One of the most important examples of prevention in the history of ethnomedicine concerns the dreaded smallpox (Duffy, 1979; Hopkins, 1983). Some centuries ago—we do not know how distant in the past—a technique called inoculation or variolation was invented, possibly more than once, somewhere in Asia or Africa. Records do not survive to inform us with exactitude. We do know that by the eighteenth century the technique had been transported from the Middle East to England. Soon it also became known in America. This was a century before Louis Pasteur in the early 1880s developed vaccines effective against anthrax in sheep and cattle, chicken cholera, and, in 1885, the first dramatic cure of a rabies infection in a man who had been bitten by a mad dog. Untreated rabies always kills in a gruesome scenario.

By the method of inoculation, the live virus in pus or in powdered scabs from a smallpox victim was either inserted into a cut in the skin or into the mucosa of the nose to produce a mild form of the disease. Lady Montagu, an Englishwoman who learned of the technique in Turkey, was taught to do it by making a superficial incision in the arm through which a thread soaked in fluid from a pustule was drawn. Another method was to blow scab powder into the nose. After recovery, the patient was immune.

The technique was not without danger. One danger was that if the inoculate did not confine itself to the site of application as it was supposed to, it caused a sickness as horrible as the wild disease. Another danger was that inoculated patients had to be isolated for a couple of weeks because others could catch a bad case of the disease from them. In an evaluation of the technique in 1723, English investigators determined that one out of ninety-one died of inoculation (a bit over one percent). The decision to undergo this kind of prevention could be frightening. However, the danger was far less than to say no to variolation. Of those striken with smallpox in a natural way, one out of every five or six (17 to 20 percent) died. From these figures, many concluded that even though a serious danger was involved, it was safer to submit to inoculation than to take a chance on getting infected in the usual way.

The technique of inoculation, although very old, was not widely practiced to prevent terrible epidemics. Its dangers made it a great source of controversy. In England and on the continent its use was restricted to the upper class until shortly before it became obsolete. The American colonies were exceptional because inoculation was practiced there on a large scale. General Washington even ordered it for all of his troops.

Beginning in 1796, inoculation was replaced by another unique method, also invented many decades, perhaps centuries, before modern bacteriology. Dairy herding produces a rather mild disease called cowpox that gets on one's hands from handling the cow's udder when milking. English peasants, at least in Gloucestershire, were well aware that a case of cowpox made them safe in a smallpox epidemic. It was no more than a bit of folk wisdom, however, until it came to the attention of a physician, Edward Jenner. A dairymaid told him, "I can't take smallpox, for I have already had cowpox" (cited in Guthrie, 1946, p. 248).

Jenner thought about it and talked about it for twenty years until finally, in 1796, he did an experiment we now would consider worthy of a Nazi doctor. He applied pus from the hand of a dairy maid to the skin of an eight-year-old boy. Eight weeks later, he exposed the boy to smallpox. The experiment confirmed peasant wisdom. The child remained completely healthy. Because cowpox was caused by the vaccinia virus, the technique of introducing cowpox to prevent a different but related disease, smallpox, became known as vaccination.

A true cowpox vaccination is different from what we think of as a vaccination for any other disease. When Pasteur developed vaccines for anthrax and other diseases, he injected a weakened or killed strain of bacteria that resulted in creating antibodies to the powerful natural microbe of identical type, but was too weak to cause symptomatic disease. Anthrax, caused by *Bacillus anthracis* is prevented by injecting old *B. anthracis* culture of low virulence that causes only a mild attack and confers immunity. But in spite of this important difference, Pasteur was impressed with the similarity, naming his technique vaccination.

Jenner's vaccine came into wide use during the next hundred fifty years. Smallpox smoldered and flared, but became much less common in industrialized nations because of the success of vaccination campaigns. Unfortunately, many parts of the nonindustrialized world continued to experience disastrous epidemics, particularly in Africa and India.

The ending is happy, and it exemplifies how the method and theory of epidemiology/public health can work. In 1967 the World Health Organization (WHO) sponsored a global smallpox eradication program using perfected vaccines and a refined method of delivery. By then epidemiologists could demonstrate that the disease was mainly endemic in Bangladesh, India, and Ethiopia, but was not confined to those areas. International cooperation and rigorous public health intervention succeeded. The key to success was a strategy of surveillance containment. Instead of expensive mass vaccinations of entire populations, nondoctors trained by physicians and health professionals were taught to spot active cases of smallpox in their localities, search out all of the people who had come into contact with them, and vaccinate those who were unprotected. In just over a decade the disease was completely eradicated. The last person to get infected outside of a laboratory accident (because the virus was kept alive for research purposes) was a man in Somalia in 1977. This terrible disease is now extinct, based upon the medical technique of vaccination and effectuated by epidemiologic and public health methods (Chase, 1982, pp. 81–83). In retelling this story, I leave the following point of view to ponder:

> It would be nice to believe that sheer altruism was the primary or even a significant inspiration for launching the successful global smallpox eradication program. . . . The truth is that the empathy and compassion of the powerful, industralized, and, as of 1967, smallpox-free superstates—starting with the United States, the Soviet Union, England, and France—had very little if anything at all to do with the mounting of this astoundingly inexpensive effort to stamp out smallpox in

bone-poor countries. . . . The WHO program owed its political origins, its adequate funding, and its epidemiologically rational execution to the painful truth that until smallpox was eradicated everywhere in the world, no nation . . . would ever be truly free of the . . . disease. (Chase, 1982, 82)

FIGHTING EPIDEMICS

The disappearance of the plague pandemic illustrates that disasters can resolve without conscious human initiative. Because of the human tendency to hubris, we need to be reminded of this. The whole of nature is not subservient to humans. However, the time it takes to let an epidemic burn itself out can be long and the cost in human lives can be great.

Given that caution, the control of cholera epidemics illustrates that it is possible to take control by changing human behavior (culture) in strategic ways. Prevention rather than cure is the key. Epidemics once wildly out of control were contained if not conquered by the rational implementation of public hygiene measures, especially when they were based on systematic (epidemiologic) investigations into the nature of the origin and spread of disease. The example of cholera, like that of malaria, also illustrates that the ultimate solution to epidemics will require enormous political and economic changes because so many people still live in deep and widespread poverty. The AIDS epidemic, in principle, can be controlled by comparable methods, but it presents a discouragingly difficult challenge for all concerned, including medical anthropologists.

Finally, the history of smallpox is a reminder that medical technology can also be effective against epidemics. The challenge of smallpox prevention was all the greater because no medical treatment was effective. An effective vaccine was available. Social issues were understood. Political and economic forces were enlisted in the cause. Most importantly, the extermination of smallpox in a vaccination campaign was biologically and environmentally feasible, because smallpox was not reservoired by nonhuman carriers, as is the case for the plague and malaria. Only human populations were involved.

With time, circumstances change. To the extent that the plague still smolders in some places, it can now be prevented with a vaccine and treated with antibiotics. Again, hygienic measures are extremely effective against cholera, but it, too, can be prevented now with a vaccine or treated effectively with intravenous rehydration fluids if they can be made available to the population in need. AIDS research is advancing the general cause of epidemic control through experimentation with new approaches to medical treatment combined with social science and epidemiologic research oriented to prevention of further spread, but the war against epidemics will never end. Microbes are formidable enemies, infinitely capable of eluding preventative and curative technologies.

MEDICAL ECOLOGY AND ENVIRONMENTAL HAZARDS

Andrew Vayda and Bonnie McCay, writing in 1975 about new directions in ecological anthropology, advocated attention to environmental disasters characterized by large magnitude, high speed of onset, long duration, and relative novelty (to use A. H. Barton's typology of collective stress situations) (Vayda & McCay, 1975; Barton, 1969). Vayda and McCay drew on what is referred to as neo-Darwinian selection theory, which assumes that those who live out their lives to produce children are those who are best adapted to survive the hazards of life in any time and place. They are onto something that ought to occupy medical anthropologists. We should concern ourselves with sickness and death that can result from environmental catastrophes, environment taken here in a very broad sense to include: plagues (massive epidemics); earthquakes; floods; freezes; hurricanes and tornadoes; droughts and crop failures; massive and sudden toxic pollution; nuclear explosion or poisoning; warfare, plundering, and terrorism; tribute and extortion; and religious, social, or political persecution.

It is fascinating and important to engage this topic, particularly in our time—on this shrunken globe—when extraordinary disasters seem to have become almost daily events. Since Vayda and McCay proposed their agenda of environmental concern, a number of researchers have taken up the challenge. On the whole, Vayda and McCay conceptualized the field as one in which geophysical events (ecosystem or environmental dimensions) were givens for the anthropologists in the sense that they relied on the research of others (indirect multidisciplinarity). Biological anthropologists and biocultural methods were often involved (interdisciplinarity). Overwhelmingly, this field of medical ecology provides work primarily for ethnographers experienced in participant observation and the study of culture. When Vayda and McCay wrote, the conceptual framework was that of culture change theory, still widely applied at that time. Interestingly, most studies continue this traditional approach in terms of method and theory.

MEDICAL ECOLOGY IN EXTREME CLIMATES

Many human adaptability projects have now been completed, sparked by the decade-long International Biological Program begun by the International Council of Scientific Unions in 1964 and continuing since then. Each project concerns a population that lives under one form or another of environmental stress. These projects have been, as Michael Little and his associates put it, "environmentally (but *not* ecosystematically) oriented" (Little et al., 1990, p. 394) . To give a sense of how the common element of environmental stress shaped the projects undertaken by these researchers, take note of the variety of environments that have been investigated in detail:

- high altitude areas
- circumpolar and circumboreal forests
- tropical rain forests
- arid savanna environments

Currently, the concept of environmental stress is being defined in very broad terms to also include a wide array of perturbing forces that may disrupt and challenge human existence. These may include:

- new diseases (such as AIDS)
- toxic pollutants
- social change
- migration
- new foods
- breakdown of traditional values

These studies resonate well with the biocultural model of medical anthropology in that disruption and adaptation are measured in terms relevant to health conditions. In addition to studies of sociopsychological status, they include:

- reproductive success
- nutritional assessment
- child growth patterns
- physical work capacity
- disease and death rates
- substance abuse prevalence (Little et al., 1990, p. 400)

The Turkana of East Africa

The South Turkana Ecosystem Project of northwest Kenya will serve to illustrate this type of research. The region is very dry with a rugged terrain and poor soils for agriculture. Turkana nomadic pastoralists traditionally have lived there by herding cattle, camels, goats, sheep, and donkeys, moving from one area to another as grazing conditions permitted or required. Their diet varies from time to time, with periods of little or no food at all. In general they produce their own milk, meat, and blood for consumption, buy or trade for cornmeal and sugar, and round out their diet with wild plants and hunted game. In all, the diet is unusually high in protein and relatively low in carbohydrates.

Using anthropometric techniques, it was determined that Turkana children are slower than American children to attain full adult height. Eventually both men and women become tall by world standards. They always remain comparatively lean. It is reasonable to assume that genetic potential plays a role in ultimately producing tall, lean people (Bergman's rule of body linearity in hot climates), but genetics directs long-term, multigenerational evolutionary processes that are not a feature of this contemporary research in which diet and activity are the key influences on characteristics of body size during the lifetimes of individuals being measured. The tall, slender bodies of the Turkana are consistent with the diet and with activity levels that burn off a lot of calories. "Day-to-day tasks include: walking herds to distant grazing and browsing areas; milking, bleeding, and watering animals; collecting firewood and fetching water; visiting other settlements; moving and constructing new settlements; and other, more sedentary, activities" (Little et al., 1990, p. 419).

And what of their health? By the measure Alland favored many years ago, applied again in this study, they are well adapted. In other words, they produce a lot of babies, demonstrating a healthy fecundity (about seven children for each woman who reaches menopause). This is offset, however, by a relatively high rate of infant mortality. Moreover, by some but not all other measures they are less than completely well off. Although the children show no signs of severe hunger disease (marasmus or kwashiorkor), their slow growth suggests that they do feel the effects of periodic food shortages. "One of the most sensitive measures of health and adaptation in a population is the growth of its children," Michael Little and Sandra Gray report in one publication issuing from this research. "Stunting (short height for age compared to established standards) usually indicates long-term stress in children, and wasting (low body weight for height), more immediate stress." Both stunting and wasting characterize these nomadic children. "Both are indicators of poor health of children, which may then continue as poor health of adults in the next generation" (Little & Gray 1990, p. 296).

Nomadic children suffer less from gastrointestinal and systemic infections than do children in settled communities with poor sanitation. The worst disease problem is malaria, which periodically sickens from 10 to 30 percent of the children. Taking these several measures together (fecundity, neonatality, body composition, and infectious diseases) these communities seem reasonably healthy but not exuberantly so.

Interestingly, since anthropologists find that requiring pastoralists to settle down as farmers usually results in severe health problems the community did not have before, settled Turkana children actually were taller and heavier at all ages than nomadic children. The critical factors appear to have been that settled children are provided with meals by missions and schools, ensuring them a regular if minimal diet. In addition, sitting in schools probably keeps them from burning up so much energy.

To most of anthropologists it does not seem right that sedentation would correlate with improvements on these measures of health (height and weight). Perhaps that says something about an unconscious anthropological preference for a self-sufficient nomadic lifestyle rather than village domesticity. Certainly, Little and Gray struggled with their data until they could in a reasonable manner conclude that nomadic children were, after all, better off.

"In the present study," they note, "settled children had adequate protein intakes, were larger in size than nomadic children, had greater adipose and muscle tissue reserves, but had very low food energy intakes. In contrast, nomadic children were smaller at all ages, had less tissue reserves, but had high food energy and very high protein intakes." Since this is inconsistent with their expectations, the authors invoke several variables "about which we have very little information," especially noting differences in activity levels and drawing inferences from the fact that children outside of the study do not receive food supplementation at school. The latter, indeed, were found to experience stunting and wasting.

The real issue, it seems, has to do with social values and the cultural embeddedness of science. The settled children reported upon in this study depend on charity feeding while the nomads who were assessed were self-sufficient. Ultimately it is in that sense that nomadism is described as better than sedentism in this research. "We conclude, then, that Turkana children growing up as more traditional nomadic pastoralists are relatively better off than a vast majority of the settled children" (Little & Gray, 1990, pp. 309, 311). That conclusion sounds reasonable, but it was arrived at by shifting outcome measures from nutritional well-being to sociopolitical dependency. The investigators muddied the waters when they based their report on one group of subjects (children with supplemental feeding) but drew their conclusions from another (the 80 percent of the population that does not benefit from free food).

ENVIRONMENTAL DISASTERS

The following description of a research orientation for investigating disasters, although published in 1975, describes most of what is still done now:

> The important point is that in studying the responses of people to hazards or other problems, we begin to ask who is affected by the hazards and who is responding; whether individuals respond by cooperating in groups of various kinds or by leaving groups; whether enduring, widespread, and/or severe environmental hazards result in the transformation of the responding units; and perhaps whether such features of human social life as loyalty, solidarity, friendliness, and sanctity may sometimes be important either as incentives for group action that may be advantageous for members of the group or as inhibitors of ill-timed individual responses (e.g. premature withdrawal from the group). (Vayda & McCay, 1975, p. 302)

Disaster research, then, comprises part of the workload of medical anthropologists. For example, Joan Ablon did research on the response of individuals and an ethnic community to a terrible fire that trapped 250 Samoans in a church social hall in the United States, killing and maiming many (Ablon, 1973). Again, John Omohundro conducted research on the impact of a major oil spill on the St. Lawrence River in 1976 (Omohundro, 1982). However, I will confine my discussion to anthropological research relating to two major earthquakes in Latin America.

Earthquake in Peru

In 1970 a powerful earthquake (7.7 on the Richter scale) shook the nation of Peru so violently that to this day it stands in the world record book of natural disasters as the worst ever known to have destroyed and mangled human beings in the New World. It brought death to 70,000 people, injury to 140,000, homelessness to over 500,000, and significant stress to approximately 3,000,000. Every single number, reaching into the millions, stands for a person just as eager to live and enjoy good health as you or I. It was a calamity of staggering dimensions.

High and remote in the Andes, scenic but vulnerable at the foot of a massive mountain, the rural town of Yungay was normally a sleepy place during any midafternoon, especially on a Sunday. The serenity of one unforgettable afternoon exploded at 3:23 P.M. into a scene out of hell. The entire north-central region of Peru shook so violently that for forty-five seconds people fell to their knees because it was impossible to stand erect. While still reeling and dodging flying debris townspeople became aware of a great rumbling sound. In crescendo, the air carried this brief, ominous warning of an avalanche of mud that shook loose from the mountain and poured over the town like a wild, dark river. In minutes, beautiful Yungay was buried so deeply and completely that only a moonscape of mud remained visible. More than 4000 people died in those horrendous moments. Nothing was salvaged. It was a "valley of death." A mere three to five hundred shaken individuals survived (Oliver-Smith, 1992).

This small congeries of distraught, destitute survivors was to experience the anguish and hardships of recovery in diverse and complex ways. Hopefully, what they experienced and learned will benefit other victims elsewhere. The story of the death and rebirth of Yungay was transformed into a written narrative by Anthony Oliver-Smith, who recorded their voices along with his own to serve as a kind of manual of what the first year and the first decade can hold in store for survivors of an overwhelming natural disaster.

It is rare to have an anthropologist on site when a completely unpredictable disaster erupts, and no anthropologist was present on that unforgettable day in May. Fortunately, Oliver-Smith would soon arrive. He had carried out fieldwork in Yungay four years earlier and was scheduled to return to carry out doctoral research. He knew the town and its inhabitants well. Four months after the catastrophic quake and avalanche, he made his way up the mountain to help and intervene as best he could. He stayed for a year as the professional scribe of what he observed and was told.

Oliver-Smith's approach was participant observation. His theory, the kind of essentially empirical description of culture change, we became acquainted with in an earlier chapter. Oliver-Smith recorded the experiences of Indians as well as aristocrats, of women and children as well as men, of young and old, of those who were heroic, and of others who were selfish and greedy. He was aware that people survived with different perceptions of their needs and losses, and each was a voice that should be heard. His narrative of Yungay recounts how the community reconstituted itself in phoenixlike fashion. But what specifically does this story tell us about health?

THE URGENCY OF PROVIDING ACUTE MEDICAL CARE

In the immediate aftermath of the tragedy the community struggled to treat the wounded. Eventually the most seriously hurt were flown out for hospital care. Others were tended to in the refugee camp, eventually by teams of foreign doctors using donated medical supplies.

THE NEED TO BURY THE DEAD

As the mud island began to dry out, more and more corpses were revealed. It became urgent for health reasons to dispose of the dead, a grisly task directed by a grieving survivor. For some, it helped in coming to terms with the disaster.

OTHER IMMEDIATE SURVIVAL NEEDS

To prevent infectious epidemics, starvation, and exposure, clean water, decent food, clothing, and housing had to be provided.

Volunteerism and self-help carried survivors through the first week or two. After that, outside assistance became available. Ultimately the economy and government were reconstituted. Perhaps the ultimate lesson is that the utopian volunteerism and selflessness of the first few days did not last. In the end, Indians remained marginalized, poor, uneducated, and vulnerable. The old ladino elite regained their lands, businesses, social recognition, and political power. Wealth and power remained concentrated in the hands of the few, endless toil and suffering remained the lot of the many.

Earthquake in Guatemala

In 1976, a violent earthquake (also Richter 7.7) demolished parts of Guatemala, including two highland communities that had previously been studied by an American nurse-anthropologist, Jody Glittenberg. Immediately on hearing of the disaster, Glittenberg made her way back to Guatemala as a volunteer. She recalls that experience:

> Of all the possible places to which I could have been assigned in the whole country of Guatemala, I was assigned to "my" villages. The next morning twelve male volunteers and I loaded a large truck and headed into the highlands. The devastation was unbelievable. The road had diminished to crevices, and huge bridges hung in dangling pieces. . . . People were sheltered under cardboard boxes, canvas tarpaulins, or whatever covering they could find to protect them from the cold nights of winter. (Glittenberg, 1994, p. 192)

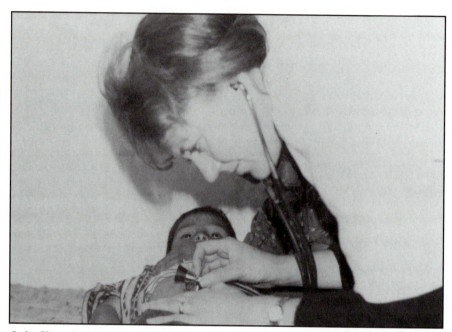

Jody Glittenberg, a nurse as well as an anthropologist, listens for abdominal sounds as she provides care for a sick boy in the clinic at Xajaxac, Guatemala.

(Photo, Dr. Eugenio Schieber)

Subsequently, Glittenberg participated in a five-year follow-up study of how communities responded to the disaster. Findings of long-term relevance for recovery and reconstruction included:

- Outside financial, organizational, and legal assistance is essential in poor communities.
- Agencies involving people who work and live in the community will be the most valued.
- Success is enhanced with shared decision making.
- The total settlement should be planned before reconstruction begins.
- In the long run, permanent, safe housing is the single most important- need. (Glittenberg, 1989)

CONCLUSION

The foremost paradigm in medical anthropology at this time is the biocultural model. It did not come into being by means of a rejection of a preceeding paradigm with which it was incompatible, as a reading of Kuhn might lead one to expect. On the contrary, it is better understood as the culmination of an additive process that has been underway since the earliest years of anthropology. The biocultural concept represents a logical extension of the paradigm of medical ecology, now revitalized to balance biological and ecological emphases with a renewed orientation to cultural and individual factors. For this reason, the biocultural model did not gain influence by means of a revolution. It was more of a gradual unfolding. It came easily and is being accepted at present without resistance by medical ecologists. However, not all medical anthropologists are enthusiasts. It has been labeled postpositivist and is considered reductionist by medical anthropologists of an extreme postmodernist persuasion.

At this time, the most influential paradigm in medical anthroplogy is fully oriented to holism. It requires vertical thinking. Medical anthropologists still tend to emphasize the upper levels of the hierarchy of sciences while physicians and laboratory scientists continue to stress lower levels. Inherent in research shaped by the biocultural paradigm of medical anthropology, then, is the need for an openness to both interdisciplinary and multidisciplinary thought and practice.

As for the future, one can expect changes in labeling (in jargon). George Marcus suggests that we have already entered a post-"post" period; a time of post-postmodernism and, I suppose, post-postpositivism (Marcus, 1994). But behind name changes, which one can expect, one should not expect to witness paradigm shifts of revolutionary dimensions. Rather, it would seem safer to predict a much more modest kind of scientific process in which anthropologists will continue a long-term trend of refining and expanding their capacity to think expansively and holistically about health and the human condition. It also seems safe to predict that as an awareness of the complexity of these conditions continues to grow, so too will an orientation to interdisciplinarity and multidisciplinarity.

REFERENCES

Ablon, J. (1973). Reactions of Samoan burn patients and families to severe burns. *Social Science and Medicine, 7,* 167–178.

Alland, A. Jr. (1970). *Adaptation in cultural evolution: An approach to medical anthropology.* New York: Columbia University Press.

Armelagos, G. J., Leatherman, T., Ryan, M., & Sibley, L. (1992). Biocultural synthesis in medical anthropology. *Medical Anthropology, 14,* 35–52.

Barton, A. H. (1969). *Communities in disaster: A sociological analysis of collective stress situations.* New York: Doubleday and Co.

Barua, D., & Greenough, W. B. (1992). *Cholera.* New York: Plenum.

Bohannan, L. (E. S. Bowen) (1964). *Return to laughter.* Published in cooperation with the American Museum of Natural History. Garden City, NY: Doubleday & Co. (Original work published 1954).

Centers for Disease Control (1992). Cholera associated with an international airline flight, 1992. *Journal of the American Medical Association 267,* 1444

Chase, A. (1982). *Magic shots: A human and scientific account of the long and continuing struggle to eradicate infectious diseases by vaccination.* New York: William Morrow.

Crosby, A. W. Jr. (1972). *The Columbian exchange: Biological and cultural consequences of 1492.* Westport, CT: Greenwood Press.

Duffy, J. (1979). *The healers: A history of American medicine.* Urbana: University of Illinois Press.

Eli, S. R. (1980). Interhuman transmission of medieval plague. *Bulletin of the History of Medicine, 54,* 497–510.

Evans-Pritchard, E. E. (1940). *The Nuer: A description of the modes of livelihood and political institutions of a Nilotic people.* Oxford: Oxford University Press.

Garn, S. M. (1954). Cultural factors affecting the study of human biology. *Human Biology, 26,* 77–79.

Glittenberg, J. A. (1989). Socioeconomic and psychological aspects of disasters. *Prehospital and disaster medicine, 4,* (1) 21–30.

Glittenberg, J. A. (1994). *To the mountain and back: The mysteries of Guatemalan highland family life.* Prospect Heights, IL: Waveland Press.

Guthrie, D. (1946). *A history of medicine.* Philadelphia: J. B. Lippincott Press.

Harris, H., Breidenbach, G., and Gardner, R. (1970). *The Nuer.* 16 mm film, color (75 min). Distributed by Phoenix Films, 470 Park Avenue S., New York, NY 10016.

Hopkins, D. R. (1983). *Princes and peasants: Smallpox in history.* Chicago: University of Chicago Press.

Hsu, F. L. K. (1983). *Exorcising the trouble makers: Magic, science, and culture.* Westport, CT: Greenwood Press.

Jeffrey, P. (1992, January 29). Cholera: Disease of the Poor. *The Christian Century pp.* 84–85.

Kipling, R. (1920). *Rudyard Kipling's verse, inclusive edition, 1885–1918.* New York: Doubleday, Page & Co.

Kleinman, A. (1986). Concepts and a model for the comparison of medical systems as cultural systems (Original work published 1978). In C. Currer, & M. Stacey, (Eds.), *Concepts of health, illness and disease: A comparative perspective* (pp. 27–47). Oxford: Berg.

Landy, D. (1990). Toward a biocultural medical anthropology. *Medical Anthropology Quarterly, 4,* 358–369.

Langer, W. L. (1964). The black death. *Scientific American, 210,* 114–121.

Little, M. A., Dyson-Hudson, N., Dyson-Hudson, R., Ellis, J. E., Galvin, K. A., Leslie, P. W., & Swift, D. M. (1990). Ecosystem approaches in human biology: Their history and a case study of the South Turkana Ecosystem Project. In E. F. Moran (Ed.), *The ecosystem approach in anthropology: From concept to practice.* Ann Arbor: University of Michigan Press.

Little, M. A., & Gray, S. J. (1990). Growth of young nomadic and settled Turkana children. *Medical Anthropology Quarterly, 4,* 296–314.

McElroy, A. (1990). Biocultural models in studies of human health and adaptation. *Medical Anthropological Quarterly, 4,* 243–265.

McNeill, W. H. (1977). *Plagues and peoples.* New York: Doubleday.

Marcus, G. E. (1994). What comes (just) after "post"? In N. K. Denzin, & Y. S. Lincoln, (Eds.), *Handbook of qualitative research* (pp. 563–574). Thousand Oaks, CA: Sage Publications.

Oliver-Smith, A. (1992). *The martyred city: Death and rebirth in the Andes.* Prospect Heights, IL: Waveland Press. (Original work published 1986).

Omohundro, J. T. (1982). The impacts of an oil spill. *Human Organization, 41,* 17–25.

Starr, P. (1982). *The social transformation of American medicine*. New York: Basic Books.

Sullivan, L. R., & Shapiro, H. L. (1928). *Essentials of anthropometry: A handbood for explorers and museum collectors*. New York: American Museum of Natural History.

Swerdlow, D. L., & Ries, A. A. (1992). Cholera in the Americas: Guidelines for the clinician. *Journal of the American Medical Association, 267,* 1495-1499.

Townsend, P. K. (1989). *Medical ecology: Whatever happened to the dominant paradigm?* Paper presented at the 88th annual meeting of the American Anthropological Association. Washington, DC. Cited in McElroy 1990.

Townsend, P. K., & McElroy A. (1992). Toward an ecology of women's reproductive health. *Medical Anthropology, 14,* 9-34.

Twigg, G. (1985). *The black death: A biological reappraisal*. New York: Schocken Books.

Vayda, A. P., & McCay, B. J. (1975). New directions in ecology and ecological anthropology. *Annual Review of Anthropology, 4,* 293-306.

Zinsser, H. (1935). *Rats, lice and history: A study in biography*. Boston: Little, Brown and Co.

PART II

Health Issues in Perspective

Chapter 10

MENTAL CONDITIONS

INTRODUCTION

Having described the various paradigms that shape the work of medical anthropologists, let us turn now to what anthropologists have learned in their research on health. This literature is large and growing. The move towards a mind/body monism in anthropological research remains an unachieved goal, so, in terms of a primary emphasis or definition of problem, most of what anthropologists have accomplished has been framed by a body/mind dualism. Having made that statement, I hasten to add that this primary emphasis has not excluded significant efforts to incorporate a biopsychosocial holism. Nonetheless, in part, much published research has been mainly about physical disorders (the body). That work will be reviewed in the three following chapters from the perspectives of race, ethnicity, socioeconomic class, age, ableness, lifestyle, and gender. In the present chapter we will review what anthropologists have had to say about psychological conditions (the mind).

Anthropologists have been interested in mental health for a long time. They have explored the common circumstances of mental life, including adolescent unhappiness and the uses of mind-altering substances such as beer or LSD. They have investigated neurotic behaviors that can be problematic in a society. And, they have carried out research on psychotic diseases that can destroy peoples' brains and lives. This highly diverse range of mental conditions is what will concern us now.

RESEARCH DESIGN: THE NATURAL EXPERIMENT

When young Margaret Mead published *Coming of Age in Samoa* in 1928 she was decades ahead of her time as a woman anthropologist undertaking research relating to women and girls (Mead, 1961 [1928]). She continued to stay at least one step ahead of most other anthropologists for all of her long and productive life. As a major contribution to what was to become medical anthropology, she demonstrated the usefulness of a design for research based on the concept of a natural experiment. A natural experiment is fully congruent with the biocultural model, since it offers a way to explore the interactions of biology and culture.

Arriving in Samoa at a time when the culture was substantially unchanged from precontact times, she had a clear agenda. She wanted to demonstrate that a person (the mind or self) was a product of social values and practices rather than of genetically determined neurology. Cultural determinism rather than biological determinism (racial legacy) lay behind the immensity of human diversity, she believed.

Using the comparative method requires that one identify similarities as well as differences. Mead found that Samoan and American girls experienced the same process of physical development: "cutting their first teeth and losing them, cutting their second teeth, growing tall and ungainly, reaching puberty with their first menstruation, gradually reaching physical maturity, and becoming ready to produce the next generation" (Mead, 1961 [1928], pp. 195–196). Comparability in development, she pointed out, constituted the conditions for a natural experiment.

Given identical physiological events, only cultural differences could explain the fact that most American girls experienced adolescence as a difficult time of psychological anxiety and personal distress while Samoan girls entered adulthood smoothly. Ideas about sexuality constituted especially important aspects of this cultural contrast. Whereas American children faced dilemmas in standards of sexual morality, including a double standard in permissive premarital sex that favored boys over girls, Samoan girls faced no such dilemmas. Premarital sex in Samoa, Mead was told, was condoned as a natural and pleasurable activity for almost all adolescents. As Mead saw it, a free and easy attitude toward sexual experimentation contributed to their apparent good psychological health.

Half a century later, even after critical scrutiny by a later generation of anthropologists, Mead's early intuition appears to have been substantially on the mark (Freeman, 1983; Brady, 1983; Holmes, 1987; Feinberg, 1988). Worldwide variability in adolescent mental health seems to correlate with diversity in cultural values and behaviors. Emotional stress in coming of age appears to be far more a cultural happenstance than a biological necessity.

Mead's programmatic field project has since been carried out in many studies throughout the world. Marjorie Shostak, for example, published the biography of an African San woman that illustrates how adolescent mental health can evolve in a very different society from that found in either the United States or Samoa. She did her fieldwork with a small hunting and gathering band in which she observed a highly nurtured childhood. This comes out in one passage describing how parents cope with the psychological presssures on a child who is weaned when a new baby was born. "But parents are aware that the tremendous outpouring of love given each child in the first few years of life produces children who are typically secure and capable of handling this period of emotional stress" (Shostak, 1983, p. 48). And they handle later stress equally

well. Girls grow up with a great deal of individual freedom in a sexually permissive and largely egalitarian atmosphere. They experience adolescence with
far less *angst* than do American middle-class girls.

ALTERED STATES OF AWARENESS

The natural experiment illustrated in early research by Mead can be usefully
applied in the cross-cultural study of any mental condition for which the biological parameters can be known, including altered states of consciousness
(ASC). Perhaps all human beings need or crave the experience of an ASC at
times. Erika Bourguignon in HRAF research, using a large sample of 488 societies
from around the world, found that "90 percent are reported to have one or more
institutionalized, culturally patterned forms of altered states of consciousness"
(Bourguignon, 1973, p. 11). That is an impressive statistic. However, an etic
category that is so all-encompassing clearly brings together highly diverse neurophysiologic events that have very little in common except that one's state of
mind is changed from that of daily living (which itself is highly diverse). It would
include the effects of meditation, medication, music, dance, drama, exercise,
physical activity, and, often, monotony. Even if ASC is taken to refer only to the
effects of hallucinogenic substances, alcoholic beverages, and tobacco, the neu-
rochemistry is not the same for all. The actual chemicals are highly variable and
the extent of inebriation ranges from barely perceptible to transcient psychosis
and coma. For many reasons, then, anthropologists still have a long way to go
in their explorations of how cultures shape the uses of intoxicants and their
behavioral effects as influenced by underlying brain chemistry.

HALLUCINOGENS IN THE AMERICAS

Weston La Barre was perplexed. Why, he asked, did the traditional cultures of
the New World (the Americas) and the Old World (Eurasia and Africa) differ so
greatly in their recourse to psychoactive plants (La Barre, 1969)? Native
Americans used eighty to a hundred different species, 90 percent more than
were used by peoples of the Old World (Furst, 1976; Harner, 1973). Yet, the
Old World constitutes a much larger land mass with at least as many hallucinogenic species. So, we begin our exploration of mind-altering substances with an
evolutionary conundrum.

   It will be recalled that the New World was settled by Upper Paleolithic
and Mesolithic bands of hunting and gathering migrants at the end of the Ice
Age. They arrived from Siberia where an ancient Eurasian shamanic religion
appears to have incorporated raptures of ecstacy attained from consuming
bright red mushrooms with white polka dots known as fly agaric *(Amanita
muscaria)*. La Barre argued persuasively that Siberians moving across Beringia

brought this religion into the New World. There, the prehistoric epistemology of the sacred persisted into modern times. This religious orientation served as the foundation for discovering and using new hallucinogens. For tens of thousands of years such plants have contributed to religious and social life.

In most of Europe, Asia, and Africa, however, psychoactive plants were not widely used. In their place, Old World alternatives were invented for achieving altered states of consciousness. Alcoholic beverages such as kumiss, mead, beer, and wine are consumed in many places. Also, since the Middle Ages, more potent distilled liquors such as arrack, *aqua vitae,* and whiskey have been favored in some societies.

Of course, this contrast of the two halves of the world must be kept in perspective. It is a matter of emphasis rather than of complete dissimilarity. On the one hand, psychoactive plants were also important to some societies in parts of the Old World. In prehistoric South Asia, for example, a mind-altering substance called soma is described in the ancient Sanskritic *Rig Veda.* Soma probably was none other than fly agaric (Wasson, 1968). Again, in late medieval and Renaissance Europe, witches are thought to have hallucinated after rubbing themselves with ointments derived from plants such as the deadly nightshade *(Atropa belladonna)* which contain atropine (Harner, 1973). In the New World, on the other hand, Lacandon Maya people in Mexico enact an old religious ritual of getting drunk on mead, a honey-based drink which contains alcohol (McGee, 1990). Whether in the Old World or the New World, however, the key to the anthropological perspective is how the experience of an altered brain physiology is always embedded in cultural practices.

Peyote

Beginning in 1935, Weston La Barre did fieldwork on the use of peyote *(Lophophora williamsii)* among the Kiowa, Oto, Wichita, and other Native American communities (La Barre, 1969). This widely used cactus bud is neither addictive nor known to be harmful. It contains strychninelike alkaloids that produce an early sense of exhilaration. A depressed mood then follows, accompanied by an uncomfortable queasy feeling, but the depression and nausea evaporate when morphinelike alkaloids take effect to produce brilliant color visions, the sought-after mental state which lasts for several hours.

Prehistorically, peyote was eaten seasonally by Aztecs, Huichols, and other Native Mexicans as a religious activity. To this day, a delegation of Huichol Indians participates in an annual pilgrimmage to a distant part of Mexico to renew their supply of peyote and to experience a sense of intimacy with god. Towards the end of the nineteenth century, the religious use of peyote spread into the United States, particularly among Plains Indians, but also among tribes in the Southwest, where the way was prepared by an anciently used psychotrophic plant, known as the mescal bean *(Sophora secundiflora).*

Plains peyote rituals took place during nightlong meetings in tepees lit by ceremonial fires. They ended in the morning with ritual curing.

> The standard ritual is an all-night meeting in a tipi around a crescent-shaped earthen mound and a ceremonially-built fire; here a special drum, gourd rattle and carved staff are passed around after smoking and purifying ceremonies, as each person sings four "peyote songs." Various water-bringing ceremonies occur at midnight and dawn, when there is a "baptism" or curing rite, followed by a special ritual breakfast of parched corn, fruit, and boneless meat. (La Barre, 1969 [1938], pp. 7–8)

Modified with the passage of time, a Christianized version was eventually established as the Native American Church (Spindler & Spindler, 1971). Still organized as a periodic all-night ritual, members consume peyote, pray, confess their sins, and heal the sick. La Barre concluded that the church was profoundly functional in providing a context for ameliorating anxiety under circumstances of poverty and discrimination. George Spindler and Louise Spindler agree, describing "how the Peyote experience helps resolve culture conflict, provides a primary group and security, cures ills, and protects against witchcraft and other evil influences through power" (Spindler & Spindler, 1971, p. 130). It should be noted that the practice of this religion has repeatedly been challenged by the U.S. government as immoral and unlawful because peyote is classified as an illegal mind-altering substance.

ALCOHOL IN THE OLD WORLD

Describing only peyote use in Native America provides no more than an anecdotal view of New World hallucinogenic practices. It provides one illustration among many of the cultural embeddedness of consuming such substances. It helps one to realize how psychosocial costs and benefits related to these customs can be explored. The same approach can be useful in the Old World.

The two global hemispheres on the whole are very different as concerns cultures of mind-altering practices. The difference is not simply in the contrast of hallucinatory plants versus alcoholic depressants. They differ also in symbols, meanings, and practices associated with achieving altered states of consciousness.

In the New World, as illustrated by the use of peyote, mind-altering substances are characteristically consumed in religious settings as sacred activities. In contrast to these symbols, meanings, and practices, the consumption of alcohol in the Old World almost always takes place in convivial secular groupings, usually with considerable ritual but little or no religion. In contrast to a Plains Indian all-night peyote meeting, let us examine how beer is consumed in two Old World communities, one in Africa and the other in Europe.

Louise and George Spindler (center and right), adapting to a time-honored custom, engage in wine tasting in the home of the local dentist while doing fieldwork in a small community in southern Germany.

(Photo, G. Spindler)

Beer in Africa

In many parts of Africa men gather frequently, in some communities daily, to drink beer. Let us pause to consider that statement, because we are not talking about the powerful brews widely consumed in the United States today. Beer produced by traditional African methods out of fermented cereals contains very little alcohol. One can get drunk on African beer, but steady drinking is required. John Middleton has described how he drank beer with the Lugbara men he worked with in Uganda around 1950 (Middleton, 1970). An important observation can be made based on his experience. While men certainly got inebriated after a day of work, we have no basis for knowing whether alcoholism contributed to social or individual problems or resulted in alcohol-related diseases. We do know, however, that beer drinking must be examined with great cultural sensitivity. Clearly, it contributed to male bonding among the Lugbara, since the calabash of beer, though brewed by the women of the house as a cottage industry, was shared only among the men. Clearly, too, it was a souplike cereal brew with significant caloric value. "Beer drinks were regular occurrences," Middleton recalled. "The consequence was that for many men life consisted of drifting from one beer-drink to another day after day and I have known men who ate virtually no solid food at all, relying for sustenance on this thick and nutritious beer" (Middleton, 1970, p. 21).

Some Lugbara men also consumed a powerful distilled liquor; this, too, was produced by women as a cottage industry. Known as *waragi* or Nubian gin, it was relatively new to the Lugbara. They drank it from glass tumblers rather than calabash cups, and thought of it as a European practice. Since it had a high alcoholic content, only a tumbler or two was enough to get thoroughly drunk. From Middleton's work, it is not clear what role *waragi* played in Lugbara life.

Beer and Whiskey in a Rural Irish Community

When Conrad Arensberg published *The Irish Countryman* in 1937, he inaugurated a tradition of community studies in complex societies that for two decades after the end of World War II provided perhaps the single most common format for research in cultural anthropology (Arensberg, 1968 [1937]). In this village ethnography, Arensberg did not show much interest in drinking habits as such, but he did mention that it smoothed the flow of work and trade. Cooperative harvesting provides an example, as told to Arensberg by a villager:

> And at the time of the saving of the hay and up to the War didn't it used to be that a man's place was done in turn and there would be fifteen or twenty men working at a time on one place. . . . Each would do as much as he could. Then the man whose field it was would have half a barrel of porter [beer] and the men would all drink. At noon and in the evening the neighboring women would come in and spread a great feed with jam and sweet breads and other things out of the ordinary, and in the evening there would be a tea for all of them in the fields. (Arensberg, 1968 [1937], p. 269)

What is missing in Arensberg references to drinking is an acknowledgment of how it might reflect upon social and psychological problems. Nancy Scheper-Hughes, a generation later in a similar community, added this dimension. She focused her attention on bachelor farmers struggling in a stagnant economy and a dying society that was marginalized in urban-industrial Great Britain. She described drinking as an escape valve for these men, since alcoholism was a more or less acceptable form of bachelor activity. Hugh Brody, writing of a similar community, describes behavior Scheper-Hughes found mirrored in her community. Bachelors spend long hours in summer drinking. They consume less in the winter, but drink hard and become exceedingly morose.

> A drunken man in winter leans more heavily on the bar. He often seeks to draw another drinker or two to his side. Such a group creates a tight circle of privacy around itself—a privacy physically expressed by the arms they lay across one another's shoulders. Then, with faces almost touching, they appear to join closely in evident despair. This despair is not expressed in discussion

among the drinkers. Rather they exchange silence as if it were words, and words in brief expressions of the lonesomeness. (Brody, 1973, pp. 32-33)

Yet, if heavy drinking relieved stress, it did so at a high cost in mental and physical health. The Irish are hospitalized for alcoholism twelve times more frequently than the English (Scheper-Hughes, 1979, pp. 53-54).

TOBACCO

Tobacco (genus *Nicotiana)* belongs to the family *Solanaceae* that includes other plants with mind-altering capabilities. From a biological perspective nicotine is an alkaloid that affects tissues and organs throughout the body, even when present in small amounts, and it does so with remarkable speed. It takes only a few seconds from the moment of the first puff of a cigarette to affect the brain, the autonomic nervous system, and the endocrine (hormonal) system. Even in small amounts, nicotine releases major neurochemicals (acetylcholine, epinephrine, norepinephrine, serotonin, and dopamine), resulting in wakefulness, excitement, dizziness, and loss of appetite. In large amounts, nicotine produces altered states of consciousness to the point of hallucinating.

The consumption of tobacco originated in the New World, where it was used in many different ways (Kroeber, 1948). Smoking was common, although sometimes instead of inhaling, the smoker blew the smoke into the nostrils of a partner. Local customs varied enormously. Many tribes used no tobacco at all. On the hemispheric level, Native Americans smoked cigars, tobacco-stuffed reed cigarettes, elbow pipes, and straight pipes. They also imbibed nicotine by chewing, sucking, licking, drinking, snuffing, and absorbing through the skin, in the eye, and by enema (Wilbert, 1987).

In the New World, tobacco usually was consumed as a religious activity. Among Indians of the North American Plains, the medicine pipe could be the principal ritual object in a warrior's sacred bundle (Lowie, 1954). Pipes were handled as sacred objects and were often offered to the four cardinal directions before smoking. Among the Blackfoot, each man took a few puffs and then passed the holy object on to the next man, the pipe being handed solemnly from person to person until the last man had his turn, after which it was returned to the host who initiated the next liturgical round.

Tobacco consumption was not inevitably sacred. In South America, Yanomami men, women, and children exemplified daily habitual use that had nothing at all to do with religious beliefs and practices. As soon as a person got up in the morning, an enormous wad of tobacco was placed behind the lower lip to be sucked steadily throughout the day. "Normally, if anyone is short of tobacco, he can request a share of someone else's already chewed wad, or simply borrow the entire wad when its owner puts it down somewhere. Tobacco is so important to them that their word for 'poverty' translates as 'being without tobacco'" (Chagnon, 1977, p. 90).

Tobacco offers a very impressive example of how a borrowed cultural trait may be adapted to other cultures in the process of acculturation. Tobacco, like other mind-altering plants, was almost always integrated into sacred religious practices in the New World. When it was transported to the Old World, it was divested of its religous associations. In Europe, Asia, and Africa, for the most part, it was consumed as a secular activity, mainly for pleasure and prestige. From occasional ritual uses among Native Americans (the Yanomami being an exception) it became a personal addiction for millions. The cultural associations that characterized tobacco use in the Old World eventually diffused back to the Western Hemisphere, where many Native Americans now consume tobacco as a daily indulgence in addition to occasional smoking for ritual purposes.

This worldwide shift in tobacco consumption had tragic consequences. Driven by aggressive promotion and distribution on the part of multinational tobacco conglomerates, worldwide tobacco use has increased 75 percent in the last two decades. Cigarette smoking is now responsible on a global basis for about 5 percent of all deaths. This is a conservative estimate (Council on Scientific Affairs, 1990). In the United States, cigarette consumption remains the single most preventable cause of sickness and premature death. According to the Centers for Disease Control and Prevention, SAM (smoking-attributable mortality) accounts for approximately 20 percent of all deaths each year in the United States (Leads from the Morbidity and Mortality Weekly Report, 1993).

Contemporary Substance Abuse

Mind-altering substances are not always benign when consumed in societies adhering to traditional cultural practices. Yanomami men who constantly have a quid of tobacco in their mouths are at risk for cancer of the mouth as well as other nicotine-related diseases. We should not assume that Lugbara men are not at risk for cirrhosis of the liver if they get intoxicated on a daily basis. Scheper-Hughes and Brody identify problem drinking in village Ireland. Ruth Boyer, Harry Basehart, and Bryce Boyer record that the Mescalero Apache have not permitted peyote rituals in their community since the early twentieth century because, under the influence of peyote, parents and siblings quarreled with one another to the point of outright fighting and feuding. (Boyer, Boyer, & Basehart, 1973, p. 58).

More broadly, substance abuse has become a health issue of enormous complexity in contemporary societies everywhere. These serious problems are not limited to any particular culture, class, or gender, although how they are experienced is shaped by culture, class, and gender. Many anthropologists have willingly applied their expertise in attempts to identify the dimensions of these problems in culturally sensitive ways. Some of these studies take a critical medical anthropology stance. For example, Kenyon Stebbins targets transnational conglomerates which, in order to offset declining tobacco sales in the urban-industrial world, turned to the Third World to promote "unhealthy products for consumers who are at best only vaguely aware of the health risks associated with cigarette smoking" (Stebbins, 1987). Others, including Livingston Sutro in a Mexican Indian village, document local efforts at the community level to solve their own addiction problems (Sutro, 1989). In an American inner-city environment, Ann Metcalf serves as a consultant and research worker for a Native American healing center that is involved in providing culturally relevant and gender-sensitive treatment for the alcohol addiction of Indian women (Metcalf, 1994).

Joan Weibel-Orlando, who has worked extensively on alcoholism in Native American communities, insists on the need for cultural sensitivity. Alcoholics Anonymous, for example, often does not work well for Native Americans, but the Indian Shaker Church or peyotism seem culturally well situated to succeed (Slagle & Weibel-Orlando, 1986; Hill, 1990). Weibel-Orlando introduces a serious caution, however. Although considerable enthusiasm has backed efforts to build on indigenous beliefs and practices in intervention programs, follow-up studies of the efficacy of these programs have been neglected or poorly done. It has not been demonstrated that they actually confer any long-term benefits. "Theory without empirical proof is simply unsubstantiated belief, a leap of faith," Weibel-Orlando regretfully but rightfully concludes. "The field of cross-cultural studies of alcohol addiction is generally guilty, even with the best of intentions, of theoretical faith leaping. . . . For that matter, we still do not know if any sort of alcoholism intervention, conventional or indigenous, works at all or for long periods of time" (Weibel-Orlando, 1989, pp. 150–151). Weibel-Orlando's commentary could just as well be applied to culturally sensitive programs in other communities and for other kinds of substances.

CULTURE-BOUND PSYCHIATRIC SYNDROMES

Margaret Mead and her early twentieth-century contemporaries opened the door to exploring how mental health could be investigated by means of natural experiments. That approach has matured in work done on a wide range of neurotic syndromes characterized as culture-bound. These syndromes manifest symptoms very different from those familiar to Western psychiatrists and psychologists. Each is found only in one or a few cultures. Susto is one example, but there are others, including pibloktoq (Simons & Hughes, 1985).

Joan Weibel-Orlando and Margaret Hardin (Curator of anthropology at the Los Angeles County Museum of Natural History) in an honoring dance at an Honoring of Elders Powwow.

(Photo, Robert A. Orlando M.D., Ph.D.)

Pibloktoq: A Culture-Bound Syndrome of the Inuit

The first attempts to gain an understanding of why people in certain societies behave in unfamiliar ways proposed cultural and psychological rather than neurophysiological explanations. For example, in the Alaskan and Canadian Arctic, *pibloktoq* seemed unique from a cross-cultural perspective. In its earliest phase, the affected individual becomes irritable and solitary. Often without warning, this withdrawing behavior explodes into shouting, reckless thrashing about, breaking anything within reach, tearing off clothing, and running nude into the icy wilderness. After being captured and returned by members of the band, sometimes after having a convulsion, the victim typically falls into a deep sleep. On awakening, the victim behaves in a normal way again and has no memory of the attack.

The earliest attempts at explanation by psychologists and anthropologists were that pibloktoq was a form of hysteria precipitated by a need for love (1913), an infantile wish to attract attention (1960), a reaction to low self-esteem

(1962), or a response to separation anxiety (1978) (Barnouw, 1985, pp. 371–375). Cartesian mind/body dualism seemed to shape our way of thinking about conditions such as this until some theorists began to wonder if biological factors might be involved. Anthony Wallace thought that pibloktoq might be caused by reduced calcium uptake in the nervous system brought on by winter foods low in calcium and enhanced by a vitamin D deficiency due to an absence of sunlight (Wallace, 1961). More recently, David Landy has suggested that the real problem may be overdosing on vitamin A from eating the livers and fat of arctic mammals (Landy, 1985).

Consistent with a biocultural orientation, a combination of cultural, psychological, and biological factors became and remains a best guess as to what happens in culture-bound psychiatric syndromes such as pibloktoq. However, no matter how reasonable an hypothesis may seem, until tested it is only speculation. In testing Wallace's calcium deficiency hypothesis, Edward Foulks, an anthropologist physician, examined thirty-one Inuit, ten of whom were known to have a history of pibloktoq and twenty-one of whom lacked such a history. The matched groups turned out not to differ in calcium status (Foulks, 1972). Perhaps physiologic causes are inherent in life-long debilitating conditions and/or with alcoholism. Eventually it will probably be possible to identify multiple factors in many if not all of these culture-specific syndromes. It is clearly simplistic to believe that for each disease a single major cause must be found.

Most recently for some theorists, strong efforts to break away from emic descriptions that highlight what is culturally unique in each society have given place to etic perspectives that interpret these syndromes as the variable expressions of underlying neurogenic processes that are the same everywhere. Ronald Simons, adopting a natural experiment design, suggests that culture-specific neuroses can be examined as emic expressions of etic categories defined in psychoneurologic terms. To this end he created a cross-cultural classification of culture-bound syndromes, as illustrated by the following three:

- The Running Taxon (running wildly into the wilderness): Greenland (pibloktoq), Alaska, Nicaragua, Honduras
- The Startle Matching Taxon (a startle reaction of compulsive imitative acts): Java, Burma, Thailand, Philippines, Siberia, Japan, Mongolia, Southwest Africa, Northern Finnoscandia
- The Sudden Mass Assault Taxon (amok): Malaysia, Indonesia, Laos, Papua, New Guinea, Canada (Simons, 1985)

Similarities that permit these local culture-bound psychiatric syndromes to be grouped into broader cross-cultural taxa draw attention to the probable origins of these conditions in complex etiologies of both mind (cultural expectations) and body (neuroendocrine physiology). We saw that this approach produced inconclusive results for the running taxon (pibloktoq). In the discussion of depression, shortly to follow, the sudden mass assault (amok) will become relevant. For the moment, let us examine the startle matching taxon.

The Startle Matching Taxon

An attack of *latah* in Southeast Asia is characterized by a sudden fright that results in strong feelings of fear and timidity simultaneously with an irresistable impulse to shout obscenities and to repeat the words (echolalia) or gestures (echopraxia) of the person who caused the fright. Since the startle reaction and the imitation (matching) of words and movements can be quite dramatic, it is not uncommon to tease people afflicted with latah by surprising them just to witness their reactions.

Following a paradigm of cultural explanation that ignored possible biological factors, latah in the past has been attributed to psychodynamic causes alone:

- repressed wishes: probably of an infantile sexual character
- stimulus generalization: nonsexual stimuli misinterpreted as sexual
- masochistic tendencies: resulting in failure to defend against stimuli
- dissociative child-rearing practices: conducive to hypersuggestibility
- rewarding hypersuggestibility: attention-getting adult behavior
- suppression of trance states: limiting those opportunities to give expression to repressed wishes
- inflexibility of impulse control: temporary suspension of inhibitions (Murphy, 1976)

Psychoanalytic speculations of this sort may well help to explain the experience of latah in some cases, but they do not offer an adequate hypothesis, since the causal factors listed above are demonstrably not always present when cross-cultural data are examined. For this reason, it is more convincing to regard latah and related phenomena as culturally, and perhaps psychodynamically, shaped responses to an involuntary neurologic reaction to sudden stimuli. The startle response appears to be a universal human or mammalian reflex. It is an instantaneous, involuntary, fixed action pattern that obliterates whatever the individual was doing by an emergency override system that includes:

- Always: an eye blink
- Usually: forward bending of the head and body in the first half-second
- Sometimes: aimless overflow phenomena (involuntary acts)

Simons favors this neurological hypothesis, arguing that "most or all human populations contain individuals who can be easily and strongly startled and whose ongoing stream of activity can be disrupted by startle" (Simons, 1985, p. 45). It becomes a form of latah when it occurs in occasional individual hyperstartlers or in societies which encourage and pattern the involuntary muscular and vocal acts that form part of a startle.

According to this line of reasoning, complex psychological, biological, and sociocultural conditions must combine for culture-specific psychiatric syndromes to occur. In some, such as the startle matching taxon, neurophysiological factors seem dominant. In others, such as the running taxon, neurophysiological factors are only suspected at this time, and psychological and sociocultural factors predominate in our explanations. This interpretation by Simons is very attractive. It makes good use of the natural experiment as a design for research. It is consistent with a biocultural model that builds on multidisciplinary input. But then, the calcium hypothesis of Wallace for pibloktoq was also very attractive. No such hypothesis can stand as more than suggestive until it has been tested by follow-up experimental research on a more detailed level. More precise experiments have not yet been done.

DEPRESSION

Depression has been explored as an example of the cultural embeddedness of a neurophysiologic disorder. Unfortunately, it is often not at all clear what is meant in referring to depression in English, including the way the term is used by physicians and surgeons. Usually, one thinks of depression as a mood or emotion that anyone may experience from time to time. Who has not at one time or another felt gloomy, pessimistic, worried, or preoccupied with personal inadequacy? Most of us get over it and it does not dominate our lives. Clinical depression, however, can be far more serious. It is extremely difficult to carry on if one experiences some or all of the following mental problems:

- sadness, hopelessness, irritability, joylessness, crying spells, mood swings
- loss of concentration, poor memory, suicidal thoughts, fear of dying
- sleep disturbances, appetite changes, fatigue, loss of sexual desire
- delusions of worthlessness, frightening hallucinations

Symptoms of depression, whether as a transient mood or as a deep psychotic illness, alternate in many people with feelings of energy and excitement. Severely disturbed people may experience uncontrolled mania in which the psychosis is experienced as grandiose delusions, racing thoughts, and fleeting hallucinations. Whether manic or depressive, at some point along a continuum from mild and common to serious and incapacitating, the biochemistry of the brain is strongly implicated. Abnormalities in levels of biogenic amine neurotransmitters (norepinephrine, dopamine, and serotonin) have been detected. This is why psychotrophic drugs such as tricyclic antidepressants or lithium are effective. They correct biochemical imbalances, at least in part (Berkow & Fletcher, 1992, p. 2657). So, as with the culture-bound syndromes, the current assessment of depression is that it too is both a psychosocial and a biochemical condition.

The cross-cultural evaluation of depression as a natural experiment is impeded, however, because identification of the brain chemistry involved is still highly tentative and, importantly, biochemical markers have not been identified to serve as clinical measures for disease assessment. There is no reliable biochemical test for the presence or absence of clinical depression. A diagnosis is still based upon subjective statements by the individual and impressionistic interpretations by the clinician, neither of which can be confirmed with confidence by laboratory tests (Blazer, 1990).

Depression and Culture

In spite of these difficulties, it has been suggested that depression can be classified as a culture-bound syndrome, "that depression, like amok, is a culturally determined variant, not of a universal form of psychopathology but of a range of alternative responses to universal antecedent life events" (Carr & Vitaliano, 1985, pp. 244–245). In all societies, independently of distortions in brain chemistry, deprivations of love and support early in life may engender a low sense of self-worth and self-confidence. Deep insecurities originating in infancy and early childhood may, according to this line of thinking, teach the individual a sense of hopelessness about relationships and safety. When a sense of hopelessness is generalized to all experiences, the individual reaches a critical level of emotional incapacitation that may find expression in a major depression or in an alternative mental and behavioral response such as going amok.

North Americans who feel that the events of their lives are beyond control only rarely go amok (the sudden mass assault taxon), although the "Calgary Mall Sniper" has been described as a Canadian case. Waving several guns, this twenty-five-year-old man with unexpected suddenness randomly shot, wounded, and killed anybody he could until he himself was shot down and subdued. Do not miss the importance of this point: What Carr and Vitaliano are suggesting is that the expression of an emotional deficit can take different forms in different individuals or societies. Amok may in part be a way to express depression, since the stricken individual often broods about the unfairness of life in a despondent way before exploding into mayhem. However, a sudden mass assault is probably best conceptualized not as depression, but as an alternative to depression in the form of a brief reactive psychosis or an isolated explosive derangement: one cause, diverse outcomes.

Far more commonly Americans learn to respond to a sense of hopelessness by experiencing depression. They may demonstrate this by engaging in blunting or distracting activities. These are the depressive people who get fat from eating too much, who become television couch potatoes, or who descend into alcoholism or other substance abuse. Other depressed Americans may cope through withdrawal behavior, becoming apathetic, slow moving (psychomotor retardation), or anorexic. Many North Americans hide their depression behind cheerful demeanors, but express their feelings of helplessness in somatization (experiencing bodily ills). They suffer the physical pain of headaches and backaches or the discomforts of digestive complaints, weaknesses and fragilities, none of which are completely organic in nature.

Neurasthenia

A century ago, depression, as an American culture-bound disorder, was experienced differently. In 1869 George Beard, a New York neurologist, described what he called the "American Disease," naming it neurasthenia (Beard, 1869). He considered it a chronic disease of the nervous system caused, he felt, by heavy expenditures of nervous energy. Its victims were disabled by feelings of profound mental weakness and physical exhaustion together with headaches, insomnia, vague pains, dyspepsia, palpitations, and flushing. He conjectured that in the United States of his time, modern changes placed too many demands on people. This drained them of nervous energy and left them with the symptoms of neurasthenia. The term is now considered obsolete by American psychiatrists, but doctors still see patients with one version or another of this composite of complaints. The symptoms suggest depression and somatization. As we have seen, depression may still be considered an American-bound syndrome.

Western-oriented Chinese psychiatists in Asia still view neurasthenia as a valid diagnosis. Arthur Kleinman, an American psychiatrist anthropologist, examined one hundred neurasthenic patients at Hunan Medical College and demonstrated that most of them could be rediagnosed as cases of major depressive disorder (Kleinman, 1980; Kleinman, 1988). What is intriguing about Kleinman's research is that neurasthenia, no longer at home in the United States, now appears to function as a Chinese culture-specific syndrome.

Chinese culture is frightful for people who suffer psychological disabilities. To have a mental illness is to be stigmatized. The diagnosis can keep a person from getting a job, finding a spouse, and gaining respect in the community. However, it is not stigmatizing to suffer from chronic aches and pains, digestive problems, or sleeplessness. Kleinman reasons that personal problems and biochemical changes causing depression result in the same emotional and mental symptoms that are prominent in Americans with depression. However, since it is not acceptable to admit to mental problems, Chinese patients commonly somatize, unconsciously masking their despair in physical complaints. Since neurasthenia is thought of as a physical disease having to do with nerve physiology, a chronic malfunction of the cerebral cortex, it is a permitted diagnosis for these sufferers. Neurasthenia explains one's disability in a socially acceptable way.

It is interesting to note that both biological and psychosocial factors are implicated in neurasthenia in China. The patients examined by Kleinman responded to antidepressant medications, which suggests that they suffered from biochemical brain disease. However, their responses were muted. They got better, but not entirely well. The illnesses ended only when, in addition to medication, work and family problems were successfully addressed. This is holism in action.

Soul Loss

Still another way to think about depression in diverse societies is put forward by Richard Shweder. His observations start with a given: In terms of individual growth and development (ontogeny), any normal child by the age of four possesses a well differentiated emotional "keyboard." From that perspective, each key is a psychoneural means for striking a specific emotion such as disgust, distress, anger, fear, guilt, and so on. As the child grows older and internalizes cultural practices, the keyboard loses keys, a process Shweder refers to as *dedifferentiation.* "What is fascinating about the ontogeny of emotions," Shweder writes, "is that, while a differentiated emotional keyboard may be available to most four-year-olds around the world, the tunes that get played and the emotional scores that are available diverge considerably for adults" (Shweder, 1991, pp. 259–260). By this means, adults end up being very different from one society to another. In situations in which adult Chinese become neurasthenic and Malays go amok, Americans suffer from depression.

Following this line of thought, Shweder returns us to an early interest of anthropologists, the finding that many people explain illness as due to soul loss. He suggests that a belief in soul loss is a way in which people may make sense out of the physical and emotional symptoms of depression. Individuals suffering from soul loss feel empty. They lose interest in food, sex, people, and projects. They lose weight. They become insomniac.

The possibility that depression is experienced (explained) as soul loss forces us to reconsider what is meant by a culture-bound syndrome, since soul loss has a very wide, panglobal distribution, as Forrest Clements, 1932 demonstrated many years ago (Clements, 1932). Many mental and physical disorders are collapsed into the diagnosis of soul loss. Depression is merely one such disorder, albeit a common one. So we are reminded that in other cultures, the idiom of distress may cluster and separate experiences in diverse ways. For many individuals around the world, then, soul loss probably serves as a label or language that provides a convincing explanation for the experience of depression as a biological state of being. It implies the presence of associated feelings and thoughts as well as physical manifestations, and it suggests a cure, namely, to find and restore the lost soul through magic or ritual.

Depression, neurasthenia, and soul loss as labels serve to remind us that how one experiences illness is shaped by personal development as this, in turn, reflects interaction between personality (or sense of self in society), culture, and the body. On the whole, psychological anthropologists are now moving away from interpreting a depressive symptomatology in terms of a monocausal concept of cultural determinism. Attempting to solve the puzzle of depression in terms of a biocultural paradigm has demonstrated that mental conditions are more complex than once was thought, but also more intriguing.

Schizophrenia

Schizophrenia can be mild and temporary, but it often manifests as a severe organic disorder that can render a person completely psychotic, totally controlled by a brain mechanism that is unable to function rationally, happily, or safely. Despite this undeniable physical pathology, the schizophrenic experience is always shaped by culture.

The Organic Pathology

Brain anatomy and chemistry make it almost possible for anthropologists to carry out a powerful natural experiment modeled on the research of Margaret Mead in Samoa. Rather than taking normal adolescent developmental physiology as the constant feature (the independent variable), the pathophysiology of a psychosis is taken as the constant feature. The experiment, then, is to see what happens in the experience of the illness in different cultures, culture and context thus serving as the experimental (dependent) variable.

The independent variable in schizophrenia appears to consist in part of small but significant features of neuroanatomy. In at least some individuals with schizophrenia the cerebral ventricles that contain cerebral spinal fluid are slightly enlarged at the expense of adjacent brain tissue. In addition, a portion of the limbic system (the hippocampus) tends to be smaller. We do not yet know how these changes impact on brain function (Suddath et al., 1990).

Biochemical differences are even more obvious in the disease, although the complexity of brain chemistry still leaves the exact mechanisms unclear. It has been noted that levels of one important neurotransmitter in particular, dopamine, appear to be unusually high in association with schizophrenia. As supportive evidence to implicate excess dopamine, it has been found that schizophrenic symptoms ameliorate with the administration of phe nothiazine drugs (such as Thorazine) or the butyrophenones (e.g., Haldol). From pharmacologic studies, it is known that these drugs block dopamine activity in the brain, so several lines of evidence come together here in an impressive way to implicate brain anatomy and chemistry (Berkow & Fletcher, 1992, p. 2657).

In addition, a genetic susceptibility appears to make some people more vulnerable than others. Twin studies have been helpful here. If one becomes severely schizophrenic, the other of two identical twins is four to five times more likely also to have schizophrenia than if the other twin is fraternal. Since identical twins are more alike genetically than are fraternal pairs, some gene or genes must play a role in the onset of the disease. Although some would dispute the very existence of a significant genetic propensity, most neuroscientists agree that close blood relatives to someone with schizophrenia are slightly more likely to succumb to the disease themselves than are

more distant blood relatives or relatives by marriage who are genetically different (Suddath et al., 1990).

We can with reasonable confidence say that whether it is a person who
has been ill with schizophrenia on a long-term basis or one momentarily caught
in the grip of a psychotic episode, a disease in which the brain is not working
right constitutes the underlying pathology. Defective brain function results in
organically based symptoms. These symptoms vary, but include one or more of
the following:

- a defective comprehension of life circumstances (delusions)
- perceptual mistakes (auditory hallucinations)
- a faulty sense of person (unrealistic self-identity)
- idiosyncratic thinking (speech that makes no sense to ordinary people)

Unfortunately, the potential power of this natural experiment is weakened
by clinical problems. It is still not possible to zero in on the exact organic
pathology in any particular individual with symptoms suggestive of
schizophrenia. A diagnosis is still based primarily on a patient's behavior and
expressed feelings. As of now, at least, it is not based on CAT scan imaging of
brain anatomy or assays of brain chemistry. (The natural experiment design
can be used with greater precision in diseases for which clinical measures
can be ascertained, as in diabetes or heart disease.) Nonetheless, important
anthropological studies of schizophrenia have been conducted, whether
explicitly or implicitly, in the knowledge that the underlying condition is
organic and found all over the world in a small percentage of people (in
Western society, around 1 percent of the total population).

The Family and Schizophrenia

In the 1950s Gregory Bateson and his colleagues carried out systematic observations of intrafamilial communication as it might relate to schizophrenia
(Bateson, 1972 [1956]). At that time, it was not clear that brain chemistry and
cerebral architecture were implicated. Bateson evolved a theory of how
schizophrenia can apparently be produced in some children by faulty patterns of
interaction with family members. Typically, he found, the mother in a schismatic
family is a troubled woman who places mutually irreconcilable demands upon
the child by initiating loving communication while simultaneously signalling
withdrawal and rejection. That is, the mother distances herself from her child by
means of hostile, anxiety-producing words and bodily movements when the
child directs loving attention to her. However, when the child withdraws, she
then counters with loving, attractive signals and words. Since it is impossible to
escape this situation, particularly when the father is weak and without insight,
the child is entrapped in unresolvable anxieties.

"To put it another way," Bateson wrote, "if the mother begins to feel
affectionate and close to her child, she begins to feel endangered and must

withdraw from him; but she cannot accept this hostile act and to deny it must simulate affection and closeness with her child" (Bateson, 1972 [1956], p. 213). This, Bateson suggested, puts the child in a double bind. No matter how it responds with emotions of love or hostility, the anxiety-provoking behavior will remain unchanged.

As an illustration, the mother may say, "Go to bed, you're very tired and I want you to get your sleep." In a normal family, this would simply communicate solicitous concern. In a schizmatic family, the child rightly senses that it simultaneously is intended to say, "Get out of my sight because I'm sick of you." In short, the mother is deceptive in her loving behavior, since it coexists with rejection. *The child is punished for discriminating accurately what she is expressing, and he is punished for discriminating inaccurately—he is caught in a double bind"* (Bateson, 1972 [1956], p. 215). Multiply this episode daily throughout childhood and the pattern of interaction will initiate or at least reinforce schizophrenia in the susceptible child.

Many since Bateson have examined the family as the source of mental derangement without emphasizing the dilemma of the double bind (Reynolds, & Farberou, 1981). It has been suggested, for example, that psychotic behavior emerges out of family myths that place a particular child in jeopardy. In proposing family myths as a model for how psychosis can develop, Antonio Ferreira has in mind disturbed kin who preserve the sanity of the family by sharing the belief within the family that one member alone is deranged and at fault. The scapegoat child becomes a vent for family friction, but at the expense of that child's mental health (Ferreira, 1963).

Labeling theory says much the same thing. So, too, does Erving Goffman's application of the term stigma (Goffman, 1963). When parents and others in the family and community agree that a child is weak, inferior, mentally deficient or psychologically strange, the child may well grow up identifying with and internalizing the qualities of that label, stigma, or myth.

In yet other research that implicated family dynamics, Nancy Scheper-Hughes studied schizophrenia in rural Ireland (Scheper-Hughes, 1979). She identified a constellation of family life incorporating a pervasive socialization to guilt and shame about sexuality that seemed to destine many young to middle-aged bachelor farmers to experience schizophrenia. As infants and toddlers, physical stimulation was consistently withheld. A crying baby was allowed to cry in vain. It was rarely rocked or held. As Scheper-Hughes notes, "rural infants and toddlers spend an inordinate amount of time by themselves, unrocked, unheld, and unreassured" (Scheper-Hughes, 1979, p. 134). Boys and men grew up so sexually fearful that they groaned in the Catholic confessional about their temptations as "shy, women-fearing bachelors," unaware that sin-free sex was possible for them then or in the future (Scheper-Hughes, 1979, p. 112). Restrained from marriage until the parents were old and willing to relinquish ownership of the family farms, these men remained subordinate to their fathers and tied to their mothers' apron strings, forever thought of as "boys." Many escaped into schizophrenic delusions.

COMMUNITY AND NATION

To understand the Irish schizmatic family, however, one needs to take a larger perspective on the political economy of rural West Ireland with its depressed farm economy. The nature of family life is importantly shaped by a traditional rural industry that has become stagnant. Poverty and listlessness pervade these small communities in the Irish-speaking areas of the west where it is common to live on welfare. Most young people emigrate. Young women, especially, find work elsewhere, unwilling to marry locally and be tied down in the parish. The men who stay on as bachelor farmers have little hope for independence and marriage. The life histories of young mental patients interviewed in hospitals revealed "the continuing dialogue between the repressed and unfulfilled wishes of childhood, and the miseries of adult life in devitalized rural Ireland" (Scheper-Hughes, 1979, p. 13).

Others, too, have urged that family life and the sociocultural causes of schizophrenia be viewed from a larger, national perspective. Richard Warner links the political economy to the prevalence of schizophrenia, noting that schizophrenia is especially a disease of the lower social classes (Warner, 1985). No one would dispute this basic observation, but scholars differ in how it should be interpreted. Some believe that schizophrenia causes downward mobility, so of course more schizophrenia is found lower down in the socioeconomic hierarchy. Others speculate that because life is difficult in the lower classes, more who are predisposed will become actively schizophrenic, what Robert Barrett terms the "social stress hypothesis" (Barrett, 1988). Barrett notes that the social stress hypothesis also fits with the finding in India that higher castes suffer more schizophrenia, perhaps because people with socioeconomic aspirations are particularly frustrated at that level in contemporary India.

Barrett also argues that schizophrenia is a product of labeling or stigma associated with a Western ideology of individualism. He argues that "whatever these patients have in common, they come to be interpreted and categorized through a culturally specific ideology of individualism as broken individuals, and that this interpretive lens informs and shapes their own experience of their disorder" (Barrett, 1988, p. 377). In the light of our previous discussion, this interpretation is interesting even if it is not entirely convincing, since it leads Barrett to conclude that schizophrenia can be completely accounted for as a culture-bound illness. "In sum I have sketched a view of schizophrenia as a culturally embedded disease category which accurately describes patients' experiences within a Western psychiatric idiom that is saturated by and constituted within symbols of individuality, chronicity, deterioration, stigma and mind/body dualism" (Barrett, 1988, p. 377).

Schizophrenia As Culture-Bound

At about the time that Bateson proposed the double-bind hypothesis to explain how schizophrenia might be engendered in pathogenic family situations, another anthropologist, Marvin Opler, carried out a natural experiment in a hospital in New York City that also examined family cultures as schizmatic (Opler , 1957). He began by conducting an ethnographic study of Irish-American and Italian-American families in the neighborhoods from which the hospital patients came. His field study revealed two contrasting patterns of family dynamics, each of which in its own way seemed capable of producing the schizophrenic men he encountered in the hospital.

> The Irish family tends to be dominated by the mother; the father is often a weak and shadowy figure. The mother, assuming most of the major responsibilities, may treat her sons as "forever boys and burdens." In the Irish home active expression of emotions is frowned upon; sexual feelings are clouded with conceptions of sin. All this is reflected in the personality of the male offspring. The Irish male is apt to be quiet, repressed, shy or fearful of women and, as his literature attests, given to fantasy as an outlet for his emotions. (Opler, 1957, p. 106)

Opler characterized the Italian families of that part of New York that he investigated in the mid-1950s as living in terms of a very different kind of family style.

> The Italian home is an almost total contrast. The dominant figure is the father. He rules the family with a sometimes benevolent, sometimes rough, hand. Emotions and passions are allowed free expression. Little or no sin or guilt is attached to sex. As a result the Italian male is proverbially excitable, given to acting out his emotions and sometimes hostile to his father and older brothers (to whom the father may delegate authority over him). (Opler, 1957: p. 108)

From the hospitalized population, Opler identified thirty Irish (or Irish-American) patients to compare with thirty Italian (or Italian-American) patients. All were diagnosed as severely schizophrenic. However, how they experienced the disease contrasted, just as their patterns of family life were highly contrasted.

Irish (n=30)	Italian (n=30)
Repressed homosexuality (n=27)	Overt homosexuality (n=20)
Guilt about sex	No guilt about sex
Passive and withdrawn (n=26)	Violent episodes (n=23)
Compliant to authority	Rebellious against authority
Elaborate delusions (n=22)	No delusions (n=20)
No hypochondria	Hypochondria (n=20)

Alcoholic (n=20)   Not alcoholic (n=29)
Dominant emotion: anxiety, fear   Dominant emotion: hostility

The overall impression one gains from comparing these two ethnic groups is that they experience schizophrenia in very different ways. On the whole, the pallidly asexual, withdrawn Irish male seemed able to express his emotions only vicariously through elaborate delusional systems. One Irish patient, for example, told the same story over and over of how his father had been killed in a terrible accident for which his mother was to blame. Investigation revealed that his father died quietly at a ripe old age. Another patient, struggling with guilt about homosexual longings, nurtured the delusion that he wore an apron that bled from time to time.

The Italian patient, by contrast, tended to be impulsive and at times assaultive and destructive. Although homosexuality was not an acceptable form of masculine behavior in the 1950s in New York's Little Italy, aggressive sexuality was, and Italian-Americans experiencing schizophrenia yielded freely to their sexual impulses, even if they were not heterosexual.

The Opler research was completed a long time ago. In recent years, the World Health Organization organized a natural experiment project in which severe schizophrenia in Ibadan, Nigeria, was compared and contrasted with the same disease in Agra, India (Katz et al., 1988). As in the pioneering work of Opler, the WHO study found that the experience of schizophrenia was shaped by cultural differences.

Schizophrenia in India appears to be a very emotional, self-centered kind of agitation. Family mechanisms are postulated to acount for how the underlying, biologically based psychosis is experienced. India is characterized by a strong pattern of subordination of the individual to communal wishes and patriarchal family control. Self-centeredness clashes with these family and community values and is normally suppressed. However, with schizophrenia the usual unconscious repression of what one thinks and does is released, giving rise to egocentricity that seems wild and dangerous.

In contrast, the Nigerian with schizophrenia behaves in a very paranoid fashion, easily becoming highly suspicious of people, and often expressing bizarre fears and thoughts. These thoughts and behaviors are interpreted as developments out of a customary Nigerian worldview of secretive distrust of others. In hallucinating, voices are interpreted as malevolent witches and enemies. Based upon systematic documentation of patients in Agra (n=93) and Ibadan (n=135), schizophrenia in the two nations can be discriminated on the basis of a number of findings.

Greater in Indian Patients Than in Those of Nigeria:

- systematization of delusions
- morbid jealousy
- olfactory hallucinations
- dissociative hallucinations

Greater in Nigerian Patients Than in Those of India:

- primary delusions
- acting out of delusions
- Visual hallucinations
- Voices speaking to subject

In short, although the major formal elements of schizophrenia are shared in both nations (i.e., disordered thought, inappropriate emotions, and psychomotor distortions), the content and quality of emotional expression and social behavior are markedly different. Schizophrenia expresses core problems of family and community. Specifically, schizophrenia in India is shaped by the suppression of self, while in Nigeria, suspiciousness of evil intent by others seems to constitute the core stressor.

CONCLUSION

The natural experiment design first demonstrated its potential many years ago. It now serves the profession better than ever, since it resonates well with a biocultural paradigm. It has permitted a reassessment of culture-bound syndromes, the result of realizing that all mental conditions based on brain alterations are subject to cultural conditioning. As Arthur Kleinman put it, "Most, and perhaps all, of the so-called culture-bound disorders can be construed as extreme examples of the general function of health care systems to culturally pattern universal diseases into culturally-specific illnesses" (Kleinman, 1986, p. 45).

As we turn now from a primary emphasis on mental conditions to an emphasis on sick bodies, we will find that the same conditions prevail. Deranged biological functioning (pathophysiology) is experienced differently by different individuals (psychlogical factors) and in different societies (cultural factors).

REFERENCES

Arensberg, C. (1968). *The Irish countryman: An anthropological study.* Garden City, NY: Natural History Press. (Original work published 1937)

Barnouw, V. (1985). *Culture and personality* (4th ed.). Homewood, IL: The Dorsey Press.

Barrett, R. J. (1988). Interpretations of schizophrenia. *Culture, Medicine and Psychiatry, 12,* 357–388.

Bateson, G. (1972). Toward a theory of schizophrenia. In *Steps to an ecology of mind* (pp. 201–227). New York: Ballantine Books. (Original work published 1956)

Beard, G. M. (1869). *American nervousness.* New York: Putnam's Publishing Co.

Berkow, R., & Fletcher, A. J. (1992). *The Merck manual of diagnosis and therapy* (16th ed.). Rahway, NJ: Merck Research Laboratories.

Blazer, D. G., II. (1990). Depression. In W. B. Abram, R. Berkow, & A. J. Fletcher (Eds.), *The Merck manual of geriatrics* (pp.1014–1018). Rahway, NJ: Merck & Co.

Bourguignon, E. (1973). *Religion, altered states of consciousness, and social change.* Columbus: Ohio State University Press.

Boyer, L. B., Boyer, R. M., & Basehart, H. W. (1973). Shamanism and peyote use among the Apaches of the Mescalero Indian reservation. In M. J. Harner (Ed.), *Hallucinogens and shamanism* (pp. 53–66). London: Oxford University Press.

Brady, I. (Ed.). (1983). Speaking in the name of the real: Freeman and Mead on Samoa (special section). *American Anthropologist, 85,* 908–947.

Brody, H. (1973). *Inishkillane: Change and decline in the west of Ireland.* Harmondsworth, Middlesex, England: Penguin.

Carr, J. E., & Vitaliano, P. P. (1985). The theoretical implications of converging research on depression and the culture-bound syndromes. In A. Kleinman & B. Good (Eds.), *Culture and depression* (pp. 244–266). Berkeley: University of California Press.

Chagnon, N. A. (1977). *Yanomamo: The fierce people* (2nd ed.). New York: Holt, Rinehart and Winston.

Clements, F. E. (1932). *Primitive Concepts of Disease.* University Publications in American Archaeology and Ethnology, 32, 185–252.

Council on Scientific Affairs. (1990). The worldwide smoking epidemic: Tobacco trade, use, and control. *Journal of the American Medical Association, 263,* 3312–3318.

Feinberg, R. (1988). Margaret Mead and Samoa: Coming of Age in fact and fiction. *American Anthropologist, 90,* 656–663.

Ferreira, A. (1963). Family myths and homeostasis. *Archives of General Psychiatry, 9,* 457–643.

Foulks, E. F. (1972). *The Arctic hysterias of the North Alaskan Eskimo.* Washington, DC: American Anthropological Association.

Freeman, D. (1983). *Margaret Mead and Samoa: The making and unmaking of an anthropological myth.* Cambridge, MA: Harvard University Press.

Furst, P. T. (1976). *Hallucinogens and culture.* San Francisco: Chandler & Sharp.

Goffman, E. (1963) *Stigma: Notes on the management of spoiled identity.* Englewood Cliffs, NJ: Prentice-Hall.

Harner, M. J. (1973). The role of hallucinogenic plants in European witchcraft. In M. J. Harner (Ed.), *Hallucinogens and shamanism* (pp. 125–150). London: Oxford University Press.

Hill, T. W. (1990). Peyotism and the control of heavy drinking: The Nebraska Winnebago in the early 1900s. *Human Organization, 49,* 255–265.

Holmes, L. D. (1987). *Quest for the real Samoa: The Mead/Freeman controversy and beyond.* South Hadley, MA: Bergin and Garvey.

Katz, M. M., Marsella, A., Dube, K. C., Olatawura, M., Takahashi, R., Nakane,Y., Wynne, L. C., Gift, T., Brennan, J., Sartorius, N., & Jablensky, A. (1988). On the expression of psychosis in different cultures: Schizophrenia in an Indian and in a Nigerian community. *Culture, Medicine and Psychiatry, 12,* 331–355.

Kleinman. A. (1980). *Patients and healers in the context of culture: An exploration of the borderland between anthropology, medicine, and psychiatry.* Berkeley: University of California Press.

Kleinman, A. (1986). *Social origins of distress and disease: Depression, neurasthenia and pain in modern China.* New Haven, CT: Yale University Press.

Kleinman, A. (1988). *Rethinking psychiatry: From cultural category to personal experience.* New York: The Free Press.

Kroeber, A. L. (1948). *Anthropology*. New York: Harcourt, Brace and Co.

La Barre, W. (1969). *The peyote cult* (2nd ed.) New York: Schocken. (Original work published 1938)

Landy, D. (1985). Pibloktoq (hysteria) and Inuit nutrition: Possible implication of hypervitaminosis A. *Social Science and Medicine, 21,* 173–185.

Leads from the Morbidity and Mortality Weekly Report. (1993). Cigarette smoking—Attributable mortality and years of potential life lost—United States, 1990. *Journal of the American Medical Association, 270,* 1408–1413.

Lowie, R. H. (1954). *Indians of the plains.* The American Museum of Natural History: Anthropological Handbook Number One. New York: McGraw-Hill Book Co.

McGee, R. J. (1990). *Life, ritual, and religion among the Lacondon Maya.* Belmont, CA: Wadsworth Publishing Company.

Mead, M. (1961). *Coming of age in Samoa.* New York: William Morrow & Co. (Original work published 1928)

Metcalf, A. (1992). *Culture-as-medicine: Relevant treatment of Native American women.* Paper presented at the annual meeting of the American Anthro-pological Association, San Francisco, CA.

Middleton, J. (1970). *The study of the Lugbara: Expectation and paradox in anthropological research.* New York: Holt, Rinehart and Winston.

Murphy, H. B. M. (1976). Notes for the theory of *Latah.* In W. P. Lebra, (Ed.), *Culture-bound syndromes, ethnopsychiatry, and alternate therapies* (Vol. IV, pp. 3–21). Honolulu: University Press of Hawaii.

Opler, M. K. (1957). Schizophrenia and culture. *Scientific American, 197,* 103–110.

Reynolds, D. K., & Farberou, N. L. (1981). *The family shadow: Sources of suicide and schizophrenia.* Berkeley: University of California Press.

Scheper-Hughes, N. (1979). *Saints, scholars, and schizophrenics: Mental illness in rural Ireland.* Berkeley: University of California Press.

Shostak, M. (1983). *Nisa: The life and words of a !Kung Woman.* New York: Random House (Vintage Books).

Shweder, R. A. (1991). *Thinking through cultures: Expeditions in cultural psychology.* Cambridge, MA: Harvard University Press.

Simons, R. C. (1985). Sorting the culture-bound syndromes. In R. C. Simons, & C. C. Hughes, (Eds.), *The culture-bound syndromes* (pp. 25–38). Dordrecht: D. Reidel.

Simons, R. C., & Hughes, C. C. (Eds.), (1985). *The culture-bound syndromes.* Dordrecht: D. Reidel.

Slagle, A. L., & Weibel-Orlando, J. (1986). The Indian Shaker church and Alcoholics Anonymous: Revitalistic curing cults. *Human Organization, 45,* 310–319.

Splindler, G., & Spindler, L. (1971). *Dreamers without power: The Menomini Indians.* New York: Holt, Rinehart and Winston.

Stebbins, K. R. (1987). Tobacco or health in the third world: A political economy perspective with emphasis on Mexico. *International Journal of Health Services, 17,* 521–536.

Suddath, R. L., Christison, G. W., Torrey, E. F., Casanova, M. F., & Weinberger, D. R. (1990). Anatomical abnormalities in the brains of monozygotic twins discordant for schizophrenia. *New England Journal of Medicine, 322,* 789–794.

Sutro, L. D. (1989). Alcoholics Anonymous in a Mexican peasant-Indian village. *Human Organization, 48,* 180–186.

Wallace, A. F. C. (1961). Mental illness, biology, and culture. In F. L. K. Hsu (Ed.), *Psychological anthropology* (pp. 255–295). New York: Dorsey Press.

Warner, R. (1985). *Recovery from schizophrenia: Psychiatry and political economy.* London: Routledge and Kegan Paul.

Wasson, R. G. (1968). *Soma: Divine mushroom of immortality.* New York: Harcourt Brace Jovanovich

Weibel-Orlando, J. (1989). Hooked on healing: Anthropologists, alcohol and intervention. *Human Organization,* pp. 148–155.

Wilbert, J. (1987). *Tobacco and shamanism in South America.* New Haven, CT: Yale University Press.

Chapter 11

RACE, ETHNICITY, AND CLASS

RACE AND ETHNICITY

Many medical anthropologists have done research on what we in the West refer to as psychological health. Many others, however, have oriented their research to biomedically defined diseases such as hypertension, diabetes, or malnutrition. In such work anthropological contributions, along with those of epidemiology and public health, are presented as correlations between health status and socio-cultural variables that include race, ethnicity, and class, as we shall see in this chapter, or age, ableness, lifestyle, and gender, as we shall see in subsequent chapters. In accordance with a biocultural approach, diseases in this correlational research are understood in terms of how human physiology and pathology interact with self, society, and culture. Taking race into account, for example, often demonstrates that racism is consistently associated with more sickness, less enjoyment of life, and earlier death for those who experience discrimination.

> Perinatal outcomes are only the tip of the iceberg of social inequity in the health status of Americans. Not only are black infants 240% more likely than whites to die in the perinatal period, but they also face a far more uncertain future if they live. A black male born today in the United States has the following excess risks of death compared with a white male: 150% for heart disease, 190% for stroke, 280% for renal disease, 340% for human immunodeficiency virus–related death, and 680% for homicide. Life expectancy for a black male at birth today is 8 years less than for a white male; for a black female, it is 6 years less. (Berwick, 1994, p. 801)

If scientists were consistent in the use of scientific terms, which is not the case, race would refer only to biological (genetic) characterizations. It is often assumed that blacks, whites, Asians, and Native Americans are uniform (each constituting a race) based on a shared and exclusive reproductive (biological) ancestry. Such assumptions are scientifically unjustified. These assumption of racial identity (uniformity, purity) have confused and misled efforts to identify correlations between race and certain diseases, disease proclivities, or resistances to diseases.

The misleading concept of large-scale, geographic races arises from the simplistic assumption that populations with the same skin color (together with hair form, shape of the nose, and a few other physically noticeable traits) represent biological categories of people (shared genotypes). Such groups are mistakenly thought to be essentially uniform within the race and clearly differentiated from other races in much of their DNA (genome).

This belief in large-scale racial uniformities is senseless when examined in the light of known evolutionary processes (Darwinism). On an evolutionary time scale, just to give a single example, variability in exposure to the sun, as modified by clothing and shelter, may correlate with differences in skin color because more exposure to sunlight selects for darker skin. However, sunshine would appear to have no direct bearing on other traits such as differences in blood types. Further, although skin color may be associated with resistance to skin cancers induced by ultraviolet rays (dark skin being more protective than light), sunlight alone seems to have no effect on whether one is more or less susceptible to an infectious disease such as, for example, malaria.

Hemoglobin S As a Racial Trait

Malaria, in fact, illustrates the point well (Edelstein, 1986). Earlier I described how an inherited trait, a gene for hemoglobin S (Hb^s), provides protection against malaria if it is inherited from one parent (heterozygous) but is lethal if inherited from both (homozygous). Often it is assumed, incorrectly, that Hb^s is a racial trait. Of course, it is a trait found in some populations and not in others. But, if it is a racial trait, how can that assumption be reconciled with the following findings:

- In African populations where Hb^s is common, it exists as a balanced polymorphism and is thus not inherited by most people (80 percent or more). Do two races coexist, one with Hb^s and one without? Obviously not.
- In those African societies where Hb^s is common, it has clearly evolved as independent mutations in different places at different times. Thus, the Benin, Senegal, and Central African Republic (CAR) haplotypes (DNA mutations), all of which result in the Hb^s blood type, are products of three different ancestries (different genotypes) within the "black race" of Western and Central Africa. Are we looking at several different black races whose separate identities are disguised by similar outward (phenotypic) appearances? Certainly not.
- None of these haplotypes characterizes blacks in South Africa where falciparum malaria is not endemic. Are these blacks not of the same race under the skin? Clearly, it depends on which traits are taken as identifiers of a race.

- Some whites, particularly in Spain, Sicily, Greece, and Turkey, inherit the Hb^s trait. This inheritance undoubtedly resulted from interracial mating as caravans moved repeatedly across the Sahara desert to the shores of the Mediterranean Sea. Not surprisingly, the sickling gene is of the Benin type that characterizes all of West Africa, much of the Sahara, and a few places in North Africa. Thus, we see that the DNA involved does not occur in all people of color but does occur in some, but not all, whites.
- Some Asians, particularly on the Arabian Peninsula, in South Asia (India), and in Southeast Asia, have the trait. They inherited the CAR type found in Central and East Africa rather than the Benin type of West Africa. The distribution of the CAR gene was probably influenced by sailing ships that moved along ancient trade routes across the Arabian Sea. So, the DNA involved also occurs in some Asians.

To summarize, the blood type Hb^s appears as a physical trait (phenotype) when one amino acid (valine) is substituted for another (glutamic acid) at position 6 on the Beta chain of amino acids of the hemoglobin molecule. Deep down in the DNA, mutations to cause that change can take place in several different ways involving different combinations of nucleic acids (i.e., as different genotypes). These genotypic and phenotypic characteristics are not found uniformly in any population, but are most frequent in black populations in or from West and Central Africa. This is a vast area in which falciparum malaria represents a serious threat to public health. The mutations appear to constitute genetic adaptations that can be protective against this dread disease. Most of the Africans who came to North America in the diaspora came from West and Central Africa. Hence, sickle cell anemia is far more likely to afflict African Americans than any other racial/ethnic group in the United States. However, most African Americans do not inherit the Hb^s trait or disease. Further, it does occur in other racial/ethnic groups. One study carried out at the Los Angeles County–University of Southern California Medical Center identified fourteen patients with sickle cell anemia. All of them had the following physical traits:

- fair skin
- straight brown or blond hair
- brown, gray, or blue eyes

Although none could identify any black ancestors, all had inherited African genes for Hb^s, mostly the Central African Republic haplotype. Sickle cell screening programs target African-American infants. It is important to do so, because prophylactic penicillin, parent education, and comprehensive medical care can significantly reduce infantile suffering and death. However, failure to think of sickle cell disease as a possible cause of anemia in nonblack individuals can result in failure to treat life-threatening complications (Rogers et al., 1989). Thinking in outdated racial terms can lead to serious errors in medical research and practice.

Race and Ethnicity As Fuzzy Categories

From observations such as these, one can conclude only that any correlation of racial identity with health status must be interpreted with enormous sensitivity to the complexities involved (Montagu, 1964; Gould, 1977, pp. 231–236). The issue is further complicated by confusing race with ethnicity. Ethnicity should refer, not to biological ancestry, but to social and cultural affiliation. But ethnicity itself is an unclear concept. Susan Keefe finds it necessary to think in terms of several different dimensions of ethnicity. She notes that ethnic culture, ethnic group membership, and ethnic identity do not necessarily coincide.

> The way in which ethnic identity is most often operationalized is to provide a list of ethnic group name labels and ask respondents to choose those labels with which they identify (such as *Mexicano* or *Hispanic*). The results of our research, however, call into question the validity of this marker of ethnic identity. . . . [V]ariation is common within any ethnic group and even among members of a single family, and at an individual level, ethnic identity can change over an individual's lifetime as well as in response to different situational contexts. (Keefe, 1992, p. 43).

Robert Hahn, trained in both anthropology and public health research, has identified serious errors deriving from ambiguities that confuse people who are questioned about their racial and ethnic identities (Hahn, 1992). He notes that the Bureau of Census found that individuals may be inconsistent in how they identify themselves to census enumerators. Thus, in one report, 26.5 million respondents identified themselves as black or Negro in one place on the questionnaire, but only an estimated 21 million matched that racial identification on another part of the questionnaire with a self-identification as being of Afro-American ancestry. In other words, approximately one in five gave an inconsistent response. In another consistency check, the United States Bureau of Census compared household responses to identical questions about race given exactly one year apart and found that one in three (34.3 percent) of the households reported what amounted to changed ethnic identities.

Clearly, respondents in survey research are confused by fuzzy criteria of group membership that leave unclear the difference between race and ethnic identity. It is true that many people are quite mixed in biological and sociocultural ancestry, and an individual's sense of identity may be situational rather than fixed. Since racial and ethnic diversities are so important in contemporary life we will want to (need to) consider them as significant variables relating to health, but always we will do so with the realization that race and ethnicity are spongy concepts that must be used with great caution.

> The concept of race is, at best, elusive. There is no accepted scientific definition of race. Racial definitions (and connotations) depend on location, social class, and nationality. Race is not a dichotomous variable such as gender or

marital status. The emphasis on racial categorization creates an illusion of mutual exclusiveness. This is one of the many reasons why race as a research category seriously compromises the objectivity of scientific inquiry. When race is a study variable, the likelihood increases that the scientific merits of the investigation will suffer. (Osborne & Feit, 1992, p. 275)

Further, what is said of race applies with equal devastation to the concept of ethnicity, since "ethnicity is used too loosely in referring variously to racial groups, nationalistic groups and cultural groups" (Jackson, 1985, p. 268). As Keefe demonstrates and recommends, because ethnic identity is shaped by complex social, psychological, and cultural factors, to avoid serious distortions in the interpretation of survey research findings will require careful interdisciplinary [i.e., multidisciplinary] study (Keefe, 1992, p. 43).

Anthropological Approaches to Diabetes

In order to illustrate how race and ethnicity are dealt with as aspects of current research, and also to demonstrate how anthropologists draw upon the many strands of their disciplinary inheritance, let us briefly look at some recent work relating to noninsulin-dependent diabetes mellitus (NIDDM). This disease is also known as Type II diabetes mellitus. It has become increasingly prevalent among the indigenous populations of Africa, Asia, Oceania, and the Americas.

Approximately 80 to 90 percent of diabetics experience NIDDM rather than early onset, insulin-dependent diabetes that includes similar symptoms but is quite different genetically, anatomically, and physiologically. NIDDM is characterized by vascular degeneration (atherosclerosis), kidney disease, high blood pressure, coronary artery disease, compromise of brain function (stroke), nerve impairment (neuropathy), ulcerations, susceptibility to severe infections, crippled feet that frequently require amputation, and blindness. It can be treated by lifestyle modification (especially weight control and dietary restrictions), oral hypoglycemic (sugar-reducing) pills with dietary control, or hypodermic insulin injections with dietary control.

Interestingly, part of an anthropological view of the disease is evolutionary. Let us focus on diabetes among Native Americans to illustrate the evolutionary dimension. Geneticists (Neel, 1962) and anthropologists (Weiss et al., 1984; Ritenbaugh & Goodby, 1989) espouse Neel's "thrifty gene" hypothesis, an idea clearly related to that of "the cold filter" discussed earlier. It is argued that the prehistoric migration across Beringia from Siberia to Alaska would have selectively favored a genotype that enhanced the migrants' ability to do well on a hunter-gatherer diet low in sugar intake, high in protein, and moderate in fat. Reduced hormonal insulin production would have favored storage of scarce carbohydrates (sugars) in fatty deposits that could be life preserving in harsh times of food scarcity.

The prehistoric migration to the New World led to the emergence of a variant form of diabetes among the Native American population that Kenneth Weiss refers to as a New World Syndrome. It is very widespread in the Western Hemisphere and in some ways is different from adult-onset diabetes in other parts of the world. He characterizes it as NIDDM with obesity and gallbladder disease (including cancer), but without cardiovascular disease, high blood pressure, and stroke. The magnitude of the problem is currently quite serious. It is estimated that on the whole about one in twenty Americans is afflicted with NIDDM. However, for Native Americans, including Mexican-Americans, that ratio approaches one out of five (Lang, 1985; p. 252; Urdaneta & Krehbiel, 1989).

Although it appears that Native Americans are predisposed to NIDDM, their identity is often problematic in racial and ethnic terms. For example, in her work on diabetes among Mexican Americans, Maria Luisa Urdaneta encountered blurred racial and ethnic characteristics, including at least four different populations collectively referred to in the United States as Mexican American even though they are remarkably diverse in racial and cultural terms. Labeled as Mexican Americans, they diverge as:

- European migrants, long-settled in the American Southwest, whose race and ethicity are Spanish in origin.
- A well-to-do elite from Mexico [whose culture and race to some extent are European-Mexican and white in character]. They have become well-assimilated to North American life styles.

- Migrant laborers from Mexico. "This group is the most 'Mexican,' as such." [As with the well-to-do elite, note how unclear it is as to whether the reference to Mexican is to racial or to ethnic identity, to biology or to culture.]

- Native Americans who speak Spanish but are essentially Indian in important ways. (Urdaneta & Krehbiel, 1989)

From the point of view of a biological anthropologist/geneticist, the four categories of Mexican Americans referred to by Urdaneta and Krehbiel are not all equally likely to be carriers of diabetes susceptibility genes. Certainly, only the last two categories would be expected to inherit the New World Syndrome.

Ethnicity is also involved in NIDDM. Whether or not the gene results in falling ill with the disease appears in part to be culturally shaped by ethnic practices. The food one eats, for example, always has profound health consequences. Among Mexican Americans, an acculturative shift to diets higher in fat and sugar content has occurred since World War II, in part characterized by an increasing reliance on convenience foods. Similar changes have been observed in Native American communities elsewhere in North America. Gretchen Lang brought this out in her study of NIDDM in a Sioux Community in North Dakota, where she made the following observation: "A distinction should be made between the wild plant and game foods that are viewed as traditional foods

Maria Luisa Urdaneta in a botanica in Miami, Florida, where religious supplies are sold for healing rituals.

(Photo, Pauline C. Keitt)

('way back') and the foods that are identified as 'Indian,' such as fry bread or rich beef stews, and often served at 'Indian' occasions" (Lang, 1985, p. 254). Shifts in food habits undoubtedly make Mexican Americans and Indians more likely to experience the disease now than in the past (Medical News & Perspectives, 1993, pp. 2617–2618).

Social and political factors should not be neglected. Trying to live in contemporary communities in which racism impairs employment opportunities, schooling and daily activities certainly increases stress, which in turn increases susceptibility to disease. Physical activity fits in here. Native populations tend to become more sedentary and obese as they acculturate and integrate with the majority society. As a consequence of increased stress and decreased mobility, glucose and stress tolerance decline. Referring to genes, diet, stress, and physical activity, Urdaneta and Krebiel arrive at an inevitable conclusion. "It appears that the interrelationship of these four factors renders the Native-American and a high percentage of the Mexican-American populations more susceptible to diabetes" (Urdaneta & Krehbiel, 1989, p. 273).

From the perspective of applied (medical) anthropologists, it is not possible to do anything about the diabetes susceptibility genes, except for the possibility of genetic counseling. However, one can contribute to the development of prevention programs targeting cultural practices that are diabetogenic (Weiss et al., 1989; Lang, 1989; Szathmary, 1989). Not that success will come easily. Lang describes how discouraging the effort often can be. Among the Sioux Indians she recorded that even though most diabetics understood the basic requirements of dietary management, they commonly failed to eat properly. When asked why, they most often spoke of how hard it is to give up foods they like that can be harmful, the high cost of a good diet, and the difficulty in finding time to prepare proper meals. In addition to these emic explanations, Lang invokes her own interpretive (etic) explanation. "The powerful symbolic dimension of foods is well known. Foods are an important element of social identity, foods play significant roles in ceremonies" (Lang, 1985, p. 255) and, one might add, in religious convictions. Foods, it is believed, are sanctified by The Great Spirit. One must add to these influences on diet an aesthetic of the body and of eating that favors obesity. "Indian people like to eat a lot," they report. They "like to feel full." A stout body offers a comforting image to those who remember food shortages in the past (Lang, 1985, p. 252).

Cardiovascular Disease Among African Americans

In the United States, the avowed national health objectives are to reduce preventable sickness and death among populations that experience harmful discrimination based on race, ethnicity, gender, age, lifestyle, and ableness. It has not happened yet, as is tragically clear when rates for death from all causes are reported by race. If one measures years of potential life lost before age 65 (YPLL-65), which is a way to emphasize the effects of preventable death among younger people, one encounters increasing (rather than decreasing) disparities between blacks and whites. During the 1980s, the YPLL-65 ratio of blacks compared with whites increased at a rate of 10 percent for females and 16 percent for males (Centers for Disease Control, 1992). Racism is the rotting underpinning for this sad statistic, but while racism is the ultimate cause of health disparities, it is shaped in many ways by social, cultural, political, and economic practices. Cultural factors have particularly attracted the interest of anthropologists.

The greatest YPLL-65 vulnerability of African Americans has been pinpointed to deaths due to homicide, HIV infection, and cerebrovascular disease (high blood pressure, heart attack, and stroke). Sociocultural factors are extremely important in all three of these causal complexes. Let us take high blood pressure as an example.

One of the most interesting and durable explanations for hypertension would locate the ultimate cause as life stresses in the contemporary urban-industrial world (Booth-Kewley & Friedman, 1987; Matthews, 1988). If one moves from this high-level politico-economic viewpoint to a more mundane sociocultural level, which is what we are interested in at the moment, it has been postulated that the type of behavior more likely to achieve success in this kind of a society (an evolutionary concept of differential selectivity) is that of the hard-driving individual characterized by the Type A behavior pattern (TABP) with the following traits:

- strong need to be the best in things
- being hard driving and competitive
- usually feeling pressed for time

- eating too fast
- being bossy or dominating
- getting upset when having to wait for things (Houston et al, 1986)

You may recognize yourself in these traits. Type A is very common in our time. The causal link between Type A behavior and coronary heart disease was first identified by two cardiologists, Friedman and Rosenman (1974). Their findings serve as a reminder that many physicians in our time are sensitive to sociocultural conditions that impact on health.

William Dressler, an anthropologist, investigated Type A behavior among African Americans. Under his direction, one adult each from a randomly selected sample of 186 rural African American households was interviewed and examined in an effort to explore the nature of Type A behavior in this community (Dressler, 1993). When Dressler's findings are compared to findings relating to white Americans, the two racially defined groups are both alike and different.

African Americans and European Americans are very similar when time urgency is measured. Being hard-driving and competitive, however, is associated in the African American community with lower rather than higher blood pressure. How can one make sense of this finding? According to Dressler, to be hard-driving is perceived differently in the two populations. In the African American community, it is valued, not for personal reasons, but as a way to contribute to the larger good of family and community. "For an individual in the black community to endorse self-descriptors concerning his or her commitment to hard work is to affirm basic socially-patterned values, values which connect the individual to a community tradition. . . . This self-perception, in turn," Dressler found, "is associated with lower blood pressure, because there exists little conflict, at least along this dimension, between the individual respondent and the social-constructed ideals of the individual" (Dressler, 1993, p. 293).

One must be cautious in generalizing from this one study. To know whether other African Americans are the same or different will need more work. The important finding here is on a different level. This research demonstrates that while Type A behavior being hard on the heart passes as an etic (scientific) generalization, in fact, the stressfulness of Type A behavior appears to be shaped by cultural values and attitudes and thus has different health effects in different ethnic/racial communities. Behavior that is unhealthy in one society may be healthy in another because of the symbolism involved (meaning on the emic level).

Type II diabetes mellitus and heart disease, then, offer two examples among many of ways in which concepts of race and ethnicity (racism and ethnic discrimination) are used in anthropological research. When used with caution and sophistication, these concepts are useful and necessary for defining problems and interpreting findings.

Socioeconomic Status

Most medical anthropologists would agree that they have focused dispropor-
tionately on ethnicity and race as major variables relating to health, to the
neglect of socioeconomic status (SAS). It is relatively unusual to encounter an
anthropological journal article such as that of Martha Balshem on cancer in a
working-class community, or of Harriet Chino and Lothar Vollweiler on beliefs
about illness among middle-income Anglo-Americans (Balshem, 1991; Chino,
& Vollweiler, 1986). Yet, as Cecil Helman, Libbet Crandon-Malamud, and others
have pointed out, when class is taken into account, it almost always demonstrates that lower socioeconomic status is associated with relatively poor health
and shorter lives (Helman, 1990; Crandon-Malamud, 1991, p. 268). It is generally agreed that more attention should be given to this issue.

Even though at times anthropologists do consider class as a variable, the
concept is often inconsistently and unclearly applied. Some ambiguity cannot
be avoided. Minority status widely overlaps low-income status and working-
class lifestyles as a result of racial and ethnic discrimination. Whether research
is framed in ethnic and racial terms or in class terms may be determined more
by the theoretical perspective of the anthropologist than by the social and cultural status of the population under study.

Critical Medical Anthropology, Class, and Alcoholism

The perspective of critical medical anthropology on alcoholism among Puerto
Ricans in New York will illustrate the preceding point. Although critical anthropology has been said to have its roots in part in Virchow's investigation of health
in East Prussia, it emerged more directly as a product of the theories of Marx and
Engels. Consequently, socioeconomic class rather than ethnicity is a key variable. The fact that Puerto Ricans can be described as an ethnic or racial group
is subordinate to this theoretical imperative (Singer et al., 1992).

The analysis of male alcoholism among Puerto Ricans in New York is
framed in terms of

- evolution of the capitalist mode of production
- the creation of a rural proletariat in Puerto Rico
- labor migration creating an urban working class in New York
- hegemony of the bourgeois class in capitalist worlds
- bourgeois medicine as a tool of the capitalist world economy

The Marxist labeling and assignment of guilt ("documenting what the West
has done to other societies" [Mintz 1989]) that is implicit in the use of terms
such as "proletariat," "bourgeois class," "bourgeois medicine," or "capitalist
worlds" has great appeal to some, but is a tremendous put-off for many. This
nomenclature derives from a nineteenth-century totalizing paradigm that sim-
plistically sorted individuals into one or another of these Marxist classes.

Would that it were so simple. However, if one thing is clear from research on social and cultural diversity, it is that human beings worldwide absolutely defy any social science effort to make sense of our differences by splitting us up into a small number of oppositional pigeonholes. Dichotomies such as bourgeois versus proletarian, capitalist versus noncapitalist, developing capitalist versus developed capitalist, and so on, are too simplistic as labels for complex human beings. It is impossible to take seriously the statement that bourgeois medicine is no more effective than any other medical tradition in curing disease, but is now the dominant medical system only because it contributed to the expansion of the capitalist world economy (and was even adopted as the official medical system of the Soviet Union as a result of a successful ideological *Anschluss*).

If such excesses of Neo-Marxist ideology are put aside, the approach of critical medical anthropology offers insights that are very helpful. It is certainly true that low-income and no-income people need support and advocacy as they struggle to achieve political and economic equality, particularly in areas of employment, food, housing, education, and health care. It is also true that the American political system has earned low marks on domestic issues in recent decades. Taxpayers have paid a lot, only to witness faltering governmental agencies and programs becoming overwhelmed by conditions that have worsened rather than improved.

It is especially helpful that critical medical anthropology strives to be holistic. Merrill Singer speaks of this as "the holistic model of critical medical anthropology" (Singer et al., 1992, p. 78). It offers an approach to vertical reasoning that attempts to understand human behavior and human events by taking into account input from multiple levels of scientific inquiry from the micro level to the macro level. This is achieved by insisting on the inclusion of political and economic forces that are often neglected, ignored, or denied by anthropologists. At the same time, in spite of good intentions, these theorists tend not to include issues at the micro level that build upon the basic sciences such as physics, chemistry, anatomy, and physiology.

> Critical medical anthropology understands health issues within the context of encompassing political and economic forces that pattern human relationships, shape social behaviors, condition collective experiences, re-order local ecologies, and situate cultural meanings, including forces of institutional, national and global scale. (Singer et al., 1992, pp. 78-79)

It has become common in American medical and social science circles to conceptualize alcoholism as an individual problem, to take the position that alcoholism is a sickness and thus should be treated under medical supervision. This is what is meant when one speaks of the medicalization of problem drinking. It is what a critical medical anthropologists has referred to as "the bourgeois construction of alcoholism as a health problem."

It should be noted in passing that medicalizing alcoholism has offered some benefits. It takes away the issue of guilt. To be sick is not exactly one's fault, as Parsons pointed out in defining his concept of the sick role. To consider chronic drunkenness as a sickness provides a rationale for providing help. In addition, the sick role requires one to try to get well and to accept treatment from qualified medical personnel. But while there are some benefits in a medicalized explanatory model (EM), there are costs as well. It is the costs that are clarified by means of critical analysis.

Puerto Rican men tend to become heavy drinkers as a concomitant of moving from agricultural communities in Puerto Rico, where heavy drinking traditionally is an indulgence of fiesta weekends, to working-class neighborhoods in New York, where daily drinking is the norm. This shift in drinking practices is supported by changed social circumstances. Barrooms serve as social and recreational centers for many Puerto Rican men.

However, although he may drink heavily, a Puerto Rican working-class man does not have a drinking problem, critical theorists insist, as long as he is employed. This is because drunkenness is not considered inappropriate behavior for a family man with a job. "Alcohol was his culturally validated reward for living up to the stringent requirements of the male role in capitalist society" (Singer et al., 1992, p. 90).

Here is where evaluation at lower micro levels is called for but not included in this example of the holistic model of critical medical anthropology. Regardless of how drinking is viewed in Puerto Rican culture, chronic heavy drinking ultimately results in severe liver disease, neurological deterioration, and cardiovascular degeneration resulting in general debility and death. These considerations on a physiologic/pathophysiologic level are hardly trivial.

Pushing still deeper in the direction of micro-level processes, it should be noted as contested but arguable that alcoholism may sometimes arise as a product of predisposing genes in certain individuals (Nogami et al., 1990; Bolos et al., 1990). A gene for alcoholism may or may not exist, but other molecular events relating to alcohol metabolism have been identified, including racial variability in the capacity to produce an enzyme molecule known as ethanol dehydrogenase, which determines how drunk one will become from a given amount of alcohol. An holistic analysis requires that this level of investigation not be excluded.

Sociocultural and politico-economic factors are surely of overwhelming importance in the vast majority of cases of alcoholism, but at least a small percentage, particularly those characterized by early onset (twenty–twenty-five years of age) and marked sociopathic behavior, may be strongly determined genetically. In a more thoroughly holistic study, one would want to rule out a genetic predisposition among at least a subset of Puerto Rican alcohol abusers.

But let us return to the critical analysis as published. The fatal flaw in this drama of migrant life is that these men find it hard to get work, are frequently fired, and readily become unemployable because of inability to speak English, lack of technological skills, increasing age, poor health, and racism. By "refocusing upstream" from alcoholism as a personal problem or sickness to alcoholism as a disease of the world economic system, anthropologists recognize that it is not enough to intervene in social welfare programs, to enroll the individual in Alcoholics Anonymous, or to provide medical evaluation, detoxification, and rehabilitation (medicalization). Individual social/medical programs are palliative, it is argued. A more basic treatment will require a change in American politico-economic culture so that working-class people, including many Puerto Rican workers, can earn honest livings in a society that will treat them fairly. Thus stated, this argument has merit.

How macro-level changes can be achieved is where differing political ideologies lead to conflicting agendas. For critical medical anthropologists, fundamental improvement cannot be met by merely developing programs within the existing political/industrial system. Revolutionary or utopian "socialist-oriented" changes will be required. "Thus we see the distortion inherent in separating problem drinking, decaying teeth, or any other health condition from its wider political-economic environment, as is routine in the medicalization of health problems" (Singer et al., 1992, p. 100; but note Singer 1995; Johnson 1995).

Class and Obesity

Critical medical anthropologists "argue for the adoption of a broad theoretical framework designed to explore and explain macro-micro linkages and to chan-nel praxis accordingly" (Singer et al., 1992, p. 101). Their work identifies power and vulnerability aspects of health at macro levels of politics, economics, and history. They describe linkages one might otherwise miss between individual, family, and community levels of working-class populations and national and international levels of the political and industrial upper classes. Others have done the same. One example is found in a publication by Jeffery Sobal in which he explores relationships between socioeconomic status and obesity (Sobal, 1991).

Sobal bases his approach on older ideas that were current during the post–World War II era when ideology seemed simple, a matter of Us (the Free World) against Them (the Communist World), of non-Marxist versus Marxist social scientists. Among the leading theoreticians of that era was Talcot Parsons, who was avowedly non-Marxist. On one occasion, having mentioned some aspect of what he referred to as "Marxist dogma," he evidently felt compelled to distance himself ideologically by cautiously reassuring his readers, "To men-tion this view is not to subscribe to it" (Parsons, 1978, p. 365). Sobal found it useful to build on the so-called "action theory framework" in which Parsons out-lined a systems model designed to guide sociologists in identifying linkages between quite distinctive social and physical (genetic/physiologic) levels of human behavior (action).

In the hands of Parsons, this approach produced a theoretical framework, "the four-function paradigm," that was highly formal and thoroughly schematic. It rigorously crammed all of the essential qualities, the uncertainties, the unpredictablities of being human into a completely symmetrical geometric matrix, as though lives were experienced like game pieces on a checkerboard.

Yet, he started off well enough with a bit of vertical thinking. He began by identifying four primary system levels, hierarchically ranked so that each succeeding level was more comprehensive ("more general") than the one that preceded it. Beginning with the least comprehensive at the bottom, the four levels can be characterized as follows:

- telic system (religion)
- action system (social sciences)
- human organic system (biology)
- physico-chemical system (chemistry and physics)

To this he added Norbert Weiner's concept of a cybernetic hierarchy, which is the idea that any one level controlled the level below it, much as Polanyi argued in his concept of dual-level control (Weiner, 1963 [1948]). In this model the telic system controls the action system, which controls the organic system, which controls the physico-chemical system (Parsons, 1978, pp. 362, 374).

At this point, frankly, Parsons fumbled the ball by advancing this insight of hierarchy and of direction of control into a dead end. So carried away was he by his penchant for geometric formalism that he ended up hopelessly quagmired in a labyrinth of his own construction. It led nowhere, as one might guess from the following quotation: "In any set of four entities [the four systems] there are six relational pairs, consisting of the relations of each of the four to each of the other three. . . . Each of the *six* sets consists of four catgegories, making twenty-four categories in all. Each set of four in turn is divided into two pairs" (Parsons, 1978, p. 405).

Time often has a way of perpetuating what remains useful from the scrappile of abandoned methods and theories. A lot of good ideas have survived from Parsons's action theory. His hierarchy of systems and control is among them. We see this in the way Sobal reconfigured the Parsonian paradigm. Taking liberties with the older geometric format, Sobal distinguishes five systems in a hierarchy of levels.

The concept of systems seemed acceptable in the third quarter of the century. Functional theory supported the notion that societies constituted entities in equilibrium. It is a bit surprising to find that way of thinking persisting in our time. Most contemporary observers are far more impressed with the nonsystemic and in some ways chaotic nature of life. But Sobal's analysis largely escapes from these anachronisms by honing in on two well-differentiated levels of analysis, the physical and the social, and in exploring how one level can effect the other.

The valuable contribution here is that Sobal demonstrates how being alert to differences in these two frames of reference, and to how each impacts on the

FIGURE 11-1
Levels of Analysis and Systems in Parsonian Action Theory

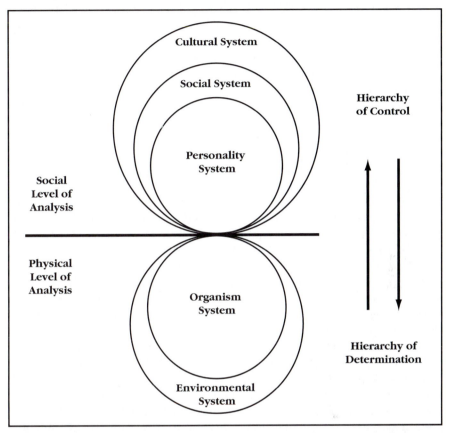

SOURCE: Sobal, Jeffery, (1991). Obesity and Socioeconomic Status: A Framework for Examining Relationships Between Physical and Social Variables. Medical Anthropology 13: 231-247. Page 234.

other, can serve as a guide to insights we might otherwise miss. We should begin by clearly recognizing that on the physical level phenomena are conceptualized as objects subject to physical, chemical, and biochemical processes. This kind of science is totally different from what is appropriate to the social level, in which the common frame of reference is that of individuals and societies shaped by cultural understandings.

Systems on the social level of analysis include the cultural, social, and personality systems. All of these systems have a common frame of reference, with many shared concepts such as identities, norms, values, etc. By contrast, the physical level of analysis shares a common frame of reference, which examines

> phenomena in the organism system and the environmental system, which are studied by the life sciences and physical sciences. . . . The physical level of analysis measures phenomena in time and space units and includes biological, physical, and chemical processes. Common concepts are shared on the physical level of analysis, such as energy, mass, etc. (Sobal, 1991, p. 233)

Either of these two levels can be understood only in terms of reference appropriate to the involved level, each of which constitutes a separate and distinct realm of action. Yet, mechanisms operate so that to understand one level in holistic terms one must take into account the other level. Specifically, the physical level sets limits that determine (constrain) what can occur as action on the social level. Conversely, mechanisms on the social level shape or control action, but only as permitted by underlying physical constraints.

To move from the abstract to the concrete, and to apply this model to medical anthropology, it will clarify what is involved if we explore obesity on the physical level as interactive with socioeconomic status (SES) on the social level. On this issue, a holistic understanding requires that both levels be taken into account. "An essential consideration in examining the SES–obesity relationship is that obesity is a physiological characteristic, while SES is a sociological characteristic" (Sobal, 1991, p. 232). On the physical level, genes and physiology are of fundamental importance as determinants of adiposity. The social level is equally important, however, since ideas about ideal body types and eating habits assert control over the kinds and amounts of foods that are consumed along with activity patterns that impact upon caloric consumption and fat residues, all conspiring to shape the body on the organic level.

From a cross-cultural perspective, many societies value plump silhouettes. Peter Brown and Melvin Konner demonstrated that in fifty-eight traditional societies described in the HRAF, 81 percent prefer physical amplitude for all ages and both sexes as evidence of good health, greater longevity, and an attractive appearance (Brown & Konner, 1987). In contrast, the pattern of SES and obesity differs by gender in urban-industrial societies. More specifically, among adult women it is common for weight and SES to be inversely correlated. The higher the status, the slimmer the ideal of womanhood. So, SES influences obesity. Consult a local newspaper, commercial television station, or any woman's magazine for documentation of the ways in which culture (body imagery) is manipulated to control the organism and its metabolic potentialities.

Conversely, obesity can determine SES. In the West we live in societies in which men of wealth and power (high SES) marry and mate preferentially with women who are thin. Thin women tend to marry up the SAS ladder while "fat" women tend to marry down. Thus, the culture-bound disorder of anorexia nervosa particularly affects high SES women who strive against heavy odds to meet this cultural ideal. In other more subtle ways, too, one's weight and future SES are interrelated:

- *Education*—with higher education comes more awareness of the need to watch one's weight for health and status reasons.

- *Income*—more money increases one's options in selecting foods and engaging in voluntary exercise.
- *Occupation*—obese employees are less likely to be promoted or to be hired in the executive ranks.
- *Family values*—members of the upper class attempt to differentiate themselves from the working class by means of dietary restraint.
- *Age*—at all SES levels, plump babies are admired, but that ends with the end of babyhood.
- *Medicine*—health professionals stigmatize obese patients. Seeing less therapeutic potential, they offer less care and counsel.
- *Lifestyle*—more smokers are lower in SES and smokers tend to be thinner, which should caution us not to forget that the interaction of SES and obesity is complex. We are in danger of distorting reality if we get too carried away with any analytical paradigm, as happened in the case of Parsons with his action theory.
- *Race*—genetic tendencies that affect the aggregation of obesity in families (racially identified communities) vary from one gene pool to another.

As concerns this last point, Sobal's study does not aggressively pursue the elucidation of genetic and metabolic issues that impact the problem of obesity. As a result, the powerful effect of innate metabolism is essentially factored out of his analysis. For example, in one informative laboratory study in which twenty-four-hour energy expenditures were measured in a respiratory chamber, it was demonstrated that a sample of ninety-five obese southwestern American Indians were distinguished from nonobese subjects by demonstrating a lower rate of total body energy expenditure. (They also were distinguished by NIDDM.) Having inherited this metabolic capacity to burn off fewer calories made the members of this race (these families) susceptible to obesity (Ravussin et al., 1988). As a consequence, to expect these individuals successfully and permanently to lose large amounts of weight for cosmetic or health reasons, or to blame them for not trying or succeeding, is unrealistic, an example of blaming the victim.

Substantial evidence makes it clear that obesity is a metabolic disorder and that both appetite (eating behavior) and the burning off of fat (metabolic levels) are set by physiologic systems that are not under voluntary control (Hirsch & Leibel, 1988; Roberts et al., 1988). Arthur Frank, a physician specialist in the treatment of obesity, admits that medicine has almost nothing to offer the distressed overweight client. He deplores the practice of blaming the victim and writes with unusual bluntness to emphasize what this condition looks like on the micro level:

> Endorphins regulate eating behavior, and thermoregulation controls the dissipation of excess calories. The regulation of body weight is at least as complex as any other biological regulatory system. It involves neurochemical,

gastrointestinal, and hepatic signals, mechanical and humoral processes, genetic factors, and the autonomic nervous system. Some of the time, some of the control can be overridden by the patients' deliberate behavior. . . . There is no reason to believe that the patients' behavior causes this disease. (Frank, 1993, p. 2133)

The point of all this is that how much one weighs is the end result of complex, multifaceted processes. Within inherited parameters, one can certainly control weight. To that extent, being thin or obese is a matter of choice. However, the basic dimension of one's weight is not a matter of choice but of inherited physiology. Physiology is what impresses Frank as overwhelmingly determinative for obese individuals, yet physiology is unexamined by Sobal. In part, these physiological processes reflect SES mediated by cultural, social, and personality factors. Sociocultural processes impress Sobal as key factors for weight control, but they are merely alluded to by Frank.

Anthropologists prefer to involve the full hierarchy of sciences in the effort to understand obesity and weight control. In the words of Cheryl Ritenbaugh, "The shape of one's body (or one's spouse's body) is widely recognized as sending a powerful cultural message which individuals often try to manage; however, human physiology is not completely compliant with such attempts" (Ritenbaugh, 1991, p. 174). As anthropologists, it is our job to tie all of these many strands together. Ritenbaugh, echoing Ann McElroy and David Landy, speaks of our task as an obligation to identify feedback loops between biology and culture. Thinking in terms of a hierarchy of determination and control is one way to characterize these feedback loops.

Socioeconomic class serves importantly as a key variable for research of this nature, as long as one remains aware of the ambiguities and ideologies inherent in conceptualizing this dimension of the human condition. In the examples just reviewed, both the Marxist and the non-Marxist paradigms helped to grasp how sociocultural forces impact on aspects of the human condition such as alcoholism or obesity. The Marxist paradigm did better in highlighting the local effects on lower classes of power and wealth possessed by the upper classes. The non-Marxist example was more explicit in incorporating biological factors. However, both took physiochemical and physiological factors as givens rather than as topics for analysis that are problematic on their own levels, as the biocultural paradigm would, in principle, require. It is not wrong to leave out the lowest micro levels of analysis, but it is incomplete. The writings of cultural anthropologists almost always are incomplete in this way.

NUTRITIONAL ANTHROPOLOGY

Having devoted considerable space to the topics of race, ethnicity, and socioeconomic class, I propose now to turn to one of the most serious health issues in the world today, malnutrition and starvation. This is a health problem for which race, ethnicity, and class have served as key orienting variables. A review of nutritional anthropology will illustrate that undernutrition afflicts people who rank low in SES or who are subject to racial and ethnic discrimination, but it is not that aspect of nutritional studies that I want to emphasize here. Rather, let us examine how it is possible to be more completely holistic in anthropological studies by means of vertical thinking and multidisciplinarity.

Starvation

Let us begin by noting that hunger is a sad reality for marginalized people throughout the world. It is all the sadder because it is completely preventable as far as modern technology is concerned. It used to be thought that starvation was the biggest challenge for those who fight hunger. Of course starvation is a serious problem. It results in infantile marasmus, a disease caused by grossly inadequate calories and protein, of total or near-total starvation. In a sensitive paragraph, George Graham describes

> a skeletal infant who at (ght months of age weighed less than when she was born. Her slow, shallow breathing was almost imperceptible, her pulse rate very slow, and her blood pressure scarcely measurable. She seemed very near death. There were no discernible movements except those of her eyes, which warily tracked anyone entering the room. Irregularly breast-fed for less than a month and weaned to teas and broths, she had survived almost total starvation by a miracle of adaptation: stopping all growth, reducing basal oxygen consumption, severely depleting her cell mass, and eliminating all physical activity. (Graham, 1993, p. 1058)

Populational starvation occurs primarily as a result of the kinds of human catastrophes we gave attention to when we discussed the current status of medical ecology, and in that way it is an issue for medical ecologists. Somalia comes to mind as an example of how famine (that is, massive food shortages within a given geographic area) can result from natural catastrophes (prolonged drought) and wartime strategies of genocide and population control. Starvation in our time is almost always a political and economic problem, not one of food production and distribution. Given the capacity of the global emergency food-aid system coordinated by the United Nations Food and Agriculture Organization (FAO), widespread starvation is preventable if power politics do not intervene.

> In all of the countries that have reported famine so far in the 1990s—Angola, Ethiopia, Liberia, Mozambique, Somalia, and Sudan [as well as Afghanistan, Azerbaijan, Bosnia-Herzegovina, Croatia, Kurdistan, Iran and Iraq]—armed conflict has been a major cause. Indeed, "food wars"—conflicts in which a principal feature has been the destruction or interdiction of civilian food supplies or of resources to produce food—became a consistent feature of the Cold War years. (Kates, 1993, p. 1056)

Mild to Moderate Malnutrition

The tragedy of starvation is known to every reader who has viewed with shock and sadness media accounts of starving adults and children. Famine, however, is merely the tip of the iceberg, threatening approximately 15 to 35 million children and adults worldwide. Mild to moderate malnutrition (MMM) is comparatively massive and persistent. It is estimated that 780 million people in developing nations do not get enough to eat and 2 billion (mostly women and children) are deficient in essential nutrients (iron, iodine, and vitamin A) (Kates, 1993; p. 1056).

Gretel Pelto, who specializes in nutritional anthropology, together with Pertii Pelto, well-known for his work in research methodology, demonstrate the benefits of collaboration and teamwork (multidisciplinarity), but also that problems can crop up. In their review of MMM, Pelto and Pelto sounded an alarm based upon an issue derived from the very fact of multidisciplinarity in nutritional research. It was triggered by the contribution of David Seckler, an economist, who interpreted MMM in terms of what may be referred to as the small but healthy hypothesis (Pelto & Pelto, 1989).

Now, it certainly seems like a good idea to include economists in the effort to make sense of MMM. Further, Seckler seemed to provide a valuable insight that could have an enormous impact on worldwide policy. He postulated:

- A growing child adapts to poor nutrition by remaining short and slender without impairment of basic health (stunted but not wasted).
- Small people as adults are better able to survive chronic food shortages because their food needs are relatively small.
- International policy need concern itself only with populations subject to serious malnutrition and not with MMM. (Seckler, 1980).

The problem with the small but healthy hypothesis is that it is too good to be true. Too good, because if true it would enormously reduce the cost and difficulty of doing something about world hunger. Only serious malnutrition would require intervention. And not true, because, contrary to the claim of the Seckler hypothesis, nutritionists, biochemists, physicians, and anthropologists provide evidence that chronic MMM during the growth years is harmful to health.

Before turning to the basic science contributions, let us draw race, ethnicity, and SES into the picture. Race has been drawn in on the assumption that the worldwide condition of short stature is not so much a product of inadequate food consumption, as it is of genes for shortness. This old idea has not stood the test of time. The children of migrants to the United States consistently become taller than their parents, whether they originated in Asia, Europe, or elsewhere. Within the urban-industrial world, particularly in the United States, Europe, and Japan, recent generations have witnessed a marked trend toward increasing tallness.

*Gretel Pelto, with (left to right) physicians David Robinson and Antoine Kaboré,
working on the control of diarrheal and respiratory diseases at WHO headquarters
in Switzerland.*

(Photo, Annabelle Haslop, WHO)

Many who are reading these words are probably taller than their parents and
grandparents. These phenotypic changes are not associated with correlated
changes in genotypes. It is most reasonable to conclude that they result at least
in part from better nutrition and better general health (particularly less debilitation from infectious diseases) (Overfield, 1985; p. 20). Race, one may conclude,
contributes very little to short stature in most developing nations or impoverished
populations.

Ethnicity and SES, on the other hand, clearly demonstrate positive
inverse correlations with short stature. The correlation is mediated by
poverty. This is why Pelto and Pelto reacted so vigorously to the small but
healthy hypothesis.

> Claims of a "no-cost adaptation" of MMM look very much like disguised argu-
> ments for continuance of "internal colonialism"—the maintenance of severe
> core-periphery socioeconomic stratification. The adoption of food policies
> based on Seckler's hypothesis would underwrite the maintenance of a status
> quo in which rural populations continue to have significant nutrition and
> health disadvantages in relation to urbanites, in addition to all the other
> socio-economic problems with which they must struggle. (Pelto & Pelto,
> 1989, pp. 13-14)

MMM and Vertical Thinking

Reynaldo Martorell concludes from his experience that "the basic cause of stunting is poverty and the effects on size are mediated through poor diets and infection" (Martorell, 1989, pp. 16–17). He finds it useful to distinguish three periods of growth in infants and children:

- The first 2 to 6 months of life. Growth in Third World children is as fast as in the First World.
- From about 6 months to about 3 years is the period of growth retardation. This is the weaning period in traditional societies when infant diets are placed in jeopardy.
- After about 3 years, growth rates generally equal those in First World populations.

Martorell singles out weaning as that period when children make the transition from consuming only mother's milk to total dependence on other foods. He believes "that almost all of the growth retardation observed in Third World populations has its origin in this stormy period of weaning" (Martorell, 1989, p. 18). Several powerful vectors come together in a final common pathway of stunted, unhealthy development during this critical period in the life cycle.

- It is a time of very rapid bodily changes which magnifies the effects of impediments to growth.
- Because of rapid growth, nutritional requirements are proportionally greater than at any other time of life, and the consequences of undernutrition are also greater.
- Diarrheal diseases and other infections are most frequent in this interim between the safety of passive immunities (antibodies) derived from the mother and the acquisition of active immunities produced by exposures and infections.

"If children survive to four or five years of age," Martorell concludes, "they will be healthier than they were earlier in life" (Martorell, 1989, p. 17). However, by the time children in developing countries reach this period of improved health they are so small for their age that they never catch up with children nurtured in more affluent circumstances. They are destined to be short as adults compared to people in wealthy nations, and the cause is poverty, not race. "Differences associated with poverty. . . are easy to demonstrate and far overshadow those which might be ascribed to race or ethnicity" (Martorell, 1989, 17).

So, MMM populations are smaller. But, they are not healthier. It takes biochemistry to understand the physiological changes that take place with undernutrition (Skrimshaw & Young, 1989). The body undergoes a constant, endless process of breakdown (catabolism) of body proteins and their resynthesis (anabolism). These rates of protein breakdown and synthesis slow down when protein consumption gets too low. In other words, with an inadequate diet, chemical activity is altered. In addition, the body experiences a loss of body mass, that is, anatomy is changed. (Note: Since proteins are large complex molecules made up of strings of tens to hundreds of small amino acid molecules, and since amino acids contain atoms of nitrogen, chemists are accustomed to speak of these changes as changes in nitrogen balance.)

The slower rate of protein turnover affects health. Individuals who are in negative nitrogen balance because of hunger are worsened by sickness and overwork. This is because infection and stress increase the requirements for protein. After all, immune responses take place by manufacturing antibodies, T-cells, and other molecules, all of which are proteins. The significance of lower protein turnover, then, is that it increases vulnerability to sickness. A complex and vicious cycle ensues. Children eat little because food is in short supply. They succumb to infections, which in turn causes them to lose their appetites. If they do eat, gastrointestinal infections diminish nutritive absorption.

Muscle mass decreases, robbed of amino acids by the need for constant catabolism and anabolism. With less muscle (protein) and less energy (carbohydrates), people are more easily fatigued. They get less done during a day of work and obligations.

Finally, underfed women produce low birth weight children whose growth during the first months of life starts from a lower baseline of size and energy. These low birth weight infants are also more likely to get sick, with resultant additional demands on nitrogen balance.

Short but healthy? Biochemical and biomedical studies say no! These children never get a fair start in life, and as adults they remain weaker and more vulnerable to sickness and stress. As Martorell put it, "A fundamental principle of pediatrics and of modern public health nutrition is the notion that a child who is growing normally is more likely to be healthy than one who is growing poorly" (Martorell, 1989, p. 18).

MMM and Dual-Level Control

Basic nutrition needs are a given in the human organism. How these needs are met can be shaped by metabolic processes which are automatic and beyond human control. However, meeting needs can also be shaped on the level of the person and the society. This is where dual-level control enters the picture, since people can make a difference on their own volition at this level higher up on the phenomenological hierarchy.

Two kinds of adaptation are involved in MMM: (1) biological, which we have just examined, and (2) behavioral and social, which we will examine now. In evaluating foods it is useful to distinguish carbohydrates and fats (the major sources of energy) from protein (the source of muscle mass and other tissues and substances). The direct responses to protein deficiency are those just discussed as failures in the maintainance of a healthy nitrogen balance.

Those responses are essentially anatomic and physiologic, and thus belong to the basic sciences.

The direct responses to carbohydrate deficiency, on the other hand, are to conserve energy. They are predominantly behavioral and social. "Apart from the basal metabolic rate, total dietary energy expenditure is determined almost entirely by the social, economic, cultural, and environmental factors that determine physical activity and the need for thermogenesis" (Skrimshaw & Young, 1989, p. 26). People cut back on activities. Take this example from Mesoamerica:

> Viteri and Torun (1975) observed that male workers on a plantation in Guatemala worked hard for the hours necessary to complete their tasks and then remained sedentary for the rest of the day and slept long hours in the afternoon and at night. When they were given food *ad libitum* [without limit] caloric intake and discretionary activity markedly increased. (Skrimshaw & Young, 1989, p. 27)

The behavioral responses of children are comparable. Undernourished children play less and sit around more. Play and alertness are so essential to learning that reduced play results in diminished intellectual ability.

Child care also suffers. Malnourished parents give less attention to their children, and this too impairs learning and intellectual maturation. There is evidence that starving children are particularly neglected by their mothers (Scheper-Hughes, 1992). Children who are underfed during the years of rapid growth and development may never catch up in mental agility with children who were well-fed.

For nutritional anthropologists to be effective in taking on hunger and health as their field of expertise, it seems clear that they have no recourse but to examine both micro levels and macro levels with all of their complex feedback loops. Whether they are physicial anthropologists with skills in the biological sciences, including anthropometry in quantifying body height and weight, archaeologist/prehistorians who evaluate the nutritional statuses of ancient populations, or cultural anthropologists oriented to behavior, society, and culture, nutritional anthropologists must practice vertical thinking and multidisciplinarity if their work is to be thorough (Messer, 1984).

CONCLUSION

Race, ethnicity, and socioeconomic class impact on health. One can evaluate this impact with enhanced sensitivity if it is carried out in terms of a biocultural model. Being holistic, this model encourages one to factor in political and economic circumstances as well as sociocultural variables. The model also encourages researchers to account for genetic and physiological factors. Without including findings from low down in the hierarchy of sciences, conclusions drawn in terms of findings higher up will often be incomplete and less than completely satisfactory. We will find that vertical thinking and multidisciplinarity are equally important when health is examined in terms of age, ableness, and lifestyle.

REFERENCES

Balshem, M. (1991). Cancer, control, and causality: Talking about cancer in a working-class community. *American Ethnologist, 19,* 152-171.

Berwick, D. M. (1994). Eleven worthy aims for clinical leadership of health system reform. *Journal of the American Medical Association, 272,* 797-802.

Bolos, A. M, Dean, M., Lucas-Derse, S., Ramsburg, M., Brown, G. L., & Goldman D. (1990). Population and pedigree studies reveal a lack of association between the dopamine D_2 receptor gene and alcoholism. *Journal of the American Medical Association, 264,* 3156-3160.

Booth-Kewley, S., & Friedman, H. S. (1987). Psychological predictors of heart disease: A quantitative review. *Psychological Bulletin, 101,* 343-345.

Brown, P. J., & Konner, M. (1987). An anthropological perspective on obesity. *Annals of the New York Academy of Sciences, 499,* 29-46.

Centers for Disease Control. (1992). Trends in years of potential life lost before age 65 among whites and blacks—1979-1989. *Journal of the American Medical Association, 268,* 3423.

Chino, H., & Vollweiler, L. G. (1986). Etiological beliefs of middle-income Anglo-Americans seeking clinical help. *Human Organization, 45,* 245-254.

Crandon-Malamud, L. (1991). *From the fat of our souls: Social change, political process, and medical pluralism in Bolivia.* Berkeley: University of California Press.

Dressler, W. (1993) Type A behavior: Contextual effects within a southern black community. *Social Science and Medicine, 36,* 289-295.

Edelstein, S. J. (1986). *The sickled cell: From myths to molecules.* Cambridge, MA: Harvard University Press.

Frank, A. (1993). Futility and avoidance: Medical professionals in the treatment of obesity. *Journal of the American Medical Association, 269,* 2132-2133.

Friedman, M., & Rosenman, R. N. (1974). *Type A behavior and your heart.* New York: Alfred A. Knopf.

Gould, S. J. (1977). Why we should not name human races: A biological view. In J. J. Gould (Ed.), *Ever since Darwin.* New York: W. W. Norton & Co., 231-236.

Graham, G. G. (1993). Starvation in the modern world. *New England Journal of Medicine, 328,* 1058-1061.

Hahn, R. A. (1992). The state of federal health statistics on racial and ethnic groups. *Journal of the American Medical Association, 267,* 269-271.

Helman, C. G. (1990). *Culture, health and illness.* London: Wright.

Hirsch, J., & Leibel, R. L. (1988). New light on obesity. *New England Journal of Medicine, 318,* 509-510.

Houston, B. K., Smith, T. W., & Zurawski, R. M. (1986). Principal dimensions of the Framingham type A scale: Differential relationships to cardiovascular reactivity and anxiety. *Journal of Human Stress, 12,* 105-111.

Jackson, J. (1985). Race, national origin, ethnicity and aging. In R. Binstock & E. Shanas (Eds.), *Handbook of aging and the social sciences* (pp. 264-303). New York: Van Nostrand Reinhold.

Johnson, T. M. (1995). Critical praxis beyond the ivory tower: A critical commentary. *Medical Antrhopology Quarterly, 9,* 107-110.

Kates, R. W. (1993). Ending deaths from famine: The opportunity in Somalia. *New England Journal of Medicine, 328,* 1055-1057.

Keefe, S. E. (1992). Ethnic identity: The domain of perceptions and of attachment to ethnic groups and cultures. *Human Organization, 51,* 35-43.

Lang, G. C. (1985). Diabetics and health care in a Sioux community. *Human Organization, 44,* 251-260.

Lang, G. C. (1989). "Making sense" about diabetes: Dakota narratives of illness. *Medical Anthropology, 11,* 305-327.

Martorell, R. (1989). Body size, adaptation and function. *Human Organization, 48,* 15-20.

Matthews, K. A. (1988). Coronary heart disease and type A behaviors: Update on and alternative to the Booth-Kewley and Friedman (1987) quantitative review. *Psychological Bulletin, 104,* 373-374.

Medical News & Perspectives. (1993). Obesity experts say less weight still best. *Journal of the American Medical Association, 269,* 2617-2618.

Messer, E. (1984). Anthropological perspectives on diet. *Annual Review of Anthropology, 13,* 205-249.

Mintz, S. (1989). The sensation of moving, while standing still. *American Ethnologist, 16,* 786-796. (Cited in Singer et al., New York, 1992, p. 77).

Montagu, A. (1964). *The concept of race.* New York: The Free Press.

Neel, J. V. (1962). Diabetes mellitus: A "thrifty" genotype rendered detrimental by "progress." *American Journal of Human Genetics, 14,* 353-362.

Nogami, A. H., Briggs, A. H., & Cohn J. B. (1990). Allelic association of human dopamine D_2 receptor gene in alcoholism. *Journal of the American Medical Association, 263,* 2055-2060.

Osborne, N. G., & Feit, M. D. (1992). The use of race in medical research. *Journal of the American Medical Association, 267,* 275-279.

Overfield, T. (1985). *Biologic variation in health and illness.* Menlo Park, CA: Addison-Wesley Publishing Co.

Parsons, T. (1978). *Action theory and the human condition.* New York: The Free Press.

Pelto, G. H., & Pelto, P. J. (1989). Small but healthy? An anthropological perspective. *Human Organization, 48,* 11-15.

Ravussin, E., Lillioja, S., Knowler, W. C., Laurent, C., Freymond, D., Abbott, W. G. H. , Boyce, V., Howard, B. V., & Bogardus, C. (1988). Reduced rate of energy expenditure as a risk factor for body-weight gain. *New England Journal of Medicine, 318,* 467-472.

Ritenbaugh, C. (1991). Body size and shape: A dialogue of culture and biology. *Medical Anthropology, 13,* 173-180.

Ritenbaugh, C., & Goodby, C. S. (1989). Beyond the thrifty gene: Metabolic implications of prehistoric migration into the new world. *Medical Anthropology, 11,* 227-236.

Roberts, S. B., Savage, J., Coward, W. A., Chew, B., & Lucas, A. (1988). Energy expenditure and intake in infants born to lean and overweight mothers. *New England Journal of Medicine, 318,* 461-466.

Rogers, Z. R., Powers, D. R., Kinney, T. R., Williams, W. D., & Schroeder, W. A. (1989). Nonblack patients with sickle cell disease have African Beta^S gene cluster haplotypes. *Journal of the American Medical Association, 261,* 2991-2994.

Scheper-Hughes, N. (1992). *Death without weeping: The violence of everyday life in Brazil.* Berkeley: University of California Press.

Seckler, D. (1980). "Malnutrition": An intellectual odyssey. *Western Journal of Agricultural Economics, 5,* 219-227.

Singer, M. (1995). Beyond the ivory tower: Critical praxis in medical anthropology. *Medical Anthropology Quarterly, 9,* 80-106.

Singer, M., Valentin, F., Baer, H., & Zhongke, J. (1992). Why does Juan García have a drinking problem? The perspective of critical medical anthropology. *Medical Anthropology, 14,* 77-108.

Skrimshaw, N. S., & Young, V. R. (1989). Adaptation to low protein and energy intakes. *Human Organization, 48,* 20-30

Sobal, J. (1991). Obesity and socioeconomic status: A framework for examining relationships between physical and social variables. *Medical Anthropology, 13,* 231-247.

Szathmary, E. J. E. (1989). The impact of low carbohydrate consumption on glucose tolerance, insulin concentration and insulin response to glucose challenge in Dogrib Indians. *Medical Anthropology, 11,* 329-350.

Urdaneta, M. L., & Krehbiel, R. (1989). Cultural heterogeneity of Mexican-Americans and its implications for the treatment of diabetes mellitus type II. *Medical Anthropology, 11,* 269-282.

Weiner, N. (1963). *Cybernetics: Or control and communication in the animal and the machine* . Cambridge, MA: MIT Press. (Original work published 1948)

Weiss, K. M., Ferrell, R. E., & Hanis, C. L. (1984). A new world syndrome of metabolic diseases with a genetic and evolutionary basis. *Yearbook of Physical Anthropology, 27,* 153-178.

Weiss, K. M., Ulbrecht, J. S., Cavanagh, P. R., & Buchanan, A. V. (1989). Diabetes mellitus in American Indians: Characteristics, origins and preventive health care implications. *Medical Anthropology, 11,* 283-30

Chapter 12

AGE, ABLENESS, AND LIFESTYLE

THE DIMENSIONS OF AGE

Epidemiologists have amply demonstrated that children, adults, and the elderly face different kinds of health problems associated with their differences in age. Anthropologists have contributed information and interpretations relating to how these health problems arise and what people do about them. To begin with infants and children, it is clear that they are particularly susceptible to the dangers of contagious diseases. Children weakened by malnutrition and starvation are at increased risk of becoming sick or dying of respiratory and gastrointestinal infections. Even when sick children are fed, they often succumb to infections because they lose nutrients through diarrhea. For many reasons, then, public health specialists attach great importance to both the provision of food for children and to the prevention of infectious diseases.

Public hygiene needs to be a number one priority if the health of children is to be protected. In much of the world people fall seriously ill because clean water and sewage disposal are not provided. These are political and economic issues that also concern medicine as a social science and anthropology as a medical science. More or less since the time of Virchow and Snow, what needs to be done has been known. Will it be done in our time?

IMMUNIZATION OF CHILDREN

Even where public sanitation is adequate, diseases threaten child health. As is clear from the history of infectious epidemics, immunization programs hold great promise. Smallpox is now out of the picture. Polio and measles could well be the next to go (Clements, 1994). At best, all infections will never be completely eliminated, but children can be spared the ravages of many of them if they are protected by immunization.

The current American vaccine policy articulates five goals:

- educate on the benefits and risks of immunization
- improve the availability of vaccines
- improve existing vaccines and develop new ones
- ensure the safety and effectiveness of vaccines
- support global disease prevention and eradication (Marwick, 1993)

Given this awareness and commitment by the National Vaccine Advisory Committee and the United States Public Health Service, why are so many children still denied the benefits of vaccines in the United States as well as in other parts of the world? Of course, the major explanation is economic, political, and organizational (administrative). Many people do not get vaccinated because vaccines are not available to them. But pockets of resistance are encountered even when vaccines are offered. It is this process of cultural resistance I want to discuss.

Paralytic polio will serve to illustrate. Polio could be rendered extinct, as was achieved with smallpox, if world leaders committed themselves to it and if the effort were not blocked by cultural barriers (Gunby, 1993). On the whole, public support is forthcoming, but some religious congregations, although small in total numbers, do raise cultural barriers. For example, it was officially announced in 1991 that polio had been eradicated in the Western Hemisphere. That achievement was put at risk about six months later. A wild poliovirus was carried to Canada (where not a single case of paralytic polio had been reported since 1988) by members of a religious community who arrived by air from the Netherlands. Members of this sect objected to vaccinations based on devoutly held religious beliefs. Being unprotected, sixty-eight members of the group in Europe were stricken with the disease. When one of them unwittingly brought the virus to an affiliated community in Alberta, the Western Hemisphere was invaded again, although the new invasion was quickly stopped (Center for Disease Control, 1993).

Chiropractors Who Oppose Vaccines

The first step in making an anthropological contribution to immunization practice requires ethnographic documentation. Only then can policy recommendations relating to cultural barriers be meaningfully made. My own experience in this area was not with a religious community, but with certain chiropractors (Anderson, 1990). I will summarize my findings, not only because they illustrate how baffling this important problem can be, but also because they demonstrate how contemporary medical anthropologists draw on a wide range of concepts available from anthropological experience.

Initially, I found the opposition of chiropractors to vaccination programs difficult to understand because those opposed are neither ignorant nor unintelligent. The chiropractors of our time receive three full years of professional education after completing a minimum of two years of undergraduate college work. In chiropractic college they are required to pass courses in all of the basic medical sciences taught in medical schools. They are taught the principles involved in preventing infectious diseases. So, why would they fight against vaccination programs with such vehemence?

In approaching this issue as a medical anthropologist, I found useful the concept of essentialism as encountered in feminist theory. When applied to a health care profession, essentialism offers a cautionary perspective. Essentialism is the mistaken or unexamined assumption that everyone who belongs to a specific sociocultural group is the same. Angela Harris, for example, points out that being a woman is very different for women of color, for women of other nations, and for the mostly white, middle-class, educated women who are prominent in the feminist movement in the West (Harris, 1990).

By extension, it would be an essentialist error to assume that all chiropractors are the same in the way they practice their specialty and in the philosophy of health that shapes their thinking. Consistent with this observation, approximately one-third to one-half of American chiropractors do counsel their patients to be immunized, in defiance of widespread opinion within their own profession.

It appears, however, that one-half to two-thirds oppose or downplay immunization publicly and in consulting with patients. A questionnaire mailed to a one percent sample of licensed chiropractors in the United States asked that respondents state whether the following statement was correct: "There is no scientific proof that immunization prevents infectious disease." Of those who responded (n=178), two-thirds (62 percent) either agreed that the statement was correct or were ambivalent about it. Consistent with that response, one-half (47 percent) of all respondants believed that the chiropractic profession should have an official policy opposed to the American Public Health Association immunization resolutions (Colley, 1994).

Since chiropractors are licensed to practice in every state in the union, are reimbursable under Medicare and many other insurance programs, and are found in most American communities as health care providers, this issue within the profession has profound implications for the American public.

Just as the concept of essentialism is helpful for an anthropologist confronting this issue, the concepts of differentiation and imitation can be applied. Cultural differentiation identifies a symbolic process whereby individuals or social entities in oppositional relationships tend to add new behaviors or modify old ones in ways that make them seem increasingly different from opposed individuals or entities (R. Anderson, 1971, pp. 16–18). Gregory Bateson, who coined the term *schismogenesis* for this human tendency, defined it *"as a process of differentiation in the norms of individual behavior resulting from cumulative interaction between individuals"* (Bateson, 1958, p. 175; Bateson, 1972, pp. 61–72).

Under acculturative circumstances, differentiation as a cultural process always implies the possibility of imitation. Imitation versus differentiation offers a way to understand what might lead chiropractors to oppose vaccination programs.

Chiropractic practice was "discovered" in 1895, after which it spread slowly but surely as an alternative to orthodox medicine. From the start, a certain amount of acculturation to biomedicine took place. By law, chiropractors could not adopt important aspects of medicine such as prescribing drugs and performing surgeries. However, where the law permitted, many did learn to use such medical techniques as x-ray imaging and the practice of physical therapy. The most obvious borrowings, however, were of purely symbolic importance. Imitation of medical doctors was apparent as they adopted:

- the title of doctor
- the architecture of a doctor's office
- appointment books and receptionists
- the physician's white clinic coat
- the stethoscope

These items of imitation occurred early in the history of the field, when the strategy for gaining acceptance among the public was to attempt to gain credence as alternative but legitimate doctors. This placed them in what, following Bateson, can be called a double bind. If they were thought of as merely another kind of medical doctor, they would place themselves at a competitive disadvantage, since they were not legally allowed to perform more dramatic medical tasks. Also, their credentials were not comparable, especially in the early decades of the century, when any high school graduate could become a chiropractor in eighteen months.

Chiropractors needed to offer reasons for thinking that they were more effective than medical doctors. This they could only hope to achieve if they could demonstrate that they were different and better. Thus, a small but significant amount of imitation was countered by a large amount of differentiation. In competing for a place in the marketplace of health care, chiropractors insisted that they were different in their theory of disease, methods of diagnosis, and techniques of treatment. Being different served as a symbol of their professional worth.

It is against the law for chiropractors to provide vaccinations. Imitation is not a possibility. Denied this opportunity to increase their scope of practice, some chiropractors turned defeat into victory by opposing vaccination programs on the grounds that they were dangerous and ineffective. In symbolic terms, chiropractors characterized themselves as different. They presented themselves as alternative practitioners who do not do what medical doctors do, but instead, offer an alternative that does not involve needles and pharmaceutical drugs.

Multidisciplinarity becomes essential at this point in the anthropological analysis, since the pathophysiology of infectious diseases is involved, a medical subject well understood by chiropractors trained after 1975. Based on fundamentals of immunology and clinical trials well described in the basic and medical science literature, some chiropractors found two important arguments that appear to support an anti-vaccine agenda:

■ A vaccination does not always work. For example, some children vaccinated against measles or whooping cough are known to have caught these diseases.

■ Vaccines are not 100 percent safe. The pertussis (whooping cough) vaccine in particular appears to have harmed some children who would have remained well had they not been vaccinated, if one also assumes they would not have been infected by the disease.

At this point the anthropological concept of an explanatory model (EM) proves useful (Kleinman, 1980, pp. 104–118). From a medical (emic) point of view, the trade-offs relating to vaccines overwhelmingly support the importance of immunization programs. The risks to children who are not vaccinated are far greater for an enormous number of children than are the dangers of a vaccination, real though they may be for a few individuals. Given the balance in this trade-off, the physician EM is unequivocal on this issue.

The chiropractor (emic) EM is different. Not only is an adjustment of the spine believed to cure backache, but it is also believed by some to strengthen the immune system. Many chiropractors argue that it provides a stronger, more reliable immunization against infections than does a vaccine. The EM in this way is used to justify hostility to vaccines, since the chiropractic spinal adjustment is thought to be both completely effective and completely safe as an alternative form of prevention.

Randomized controlled trials (RCTs) have been carried out to test the chiropractic claim that spinal adjusting is beneficial in the treatment of acute low back pain. On this basis, one can say that chiropractic treatment is effective for this kind of musculoskeletal disorder (R. Anderson et al., 1991). However, RCTs have not been conducted to test the claim that spinal adjusting builds up an immune system to fight off epidemic infections. Medical scientists have not considered it worth investigating and chiropractic scientists have not done it either. So, as concerns immunization, there is no evidence either for or against this chiropractic explanatory model.

The Theory of Focal Infection

In assessing that chiropractic claim, it is important to recognize that no matter how logical an assumption may be that is based on real or assumed physiology, no matter how elegant the theory, until it has been tested in clinical trials, epidemiologic studies, or laboratory experiments, it is a matter of faith and can be wrong. History demonstrates this important reality many times over. The case of the theory of focal infection provides one example.

The theory of focal infection appeared in the first half of the twentieth century, offering a very convincing model for the treatment of a number of diseases. Based on very little evidence but a lot of rational argument, an article

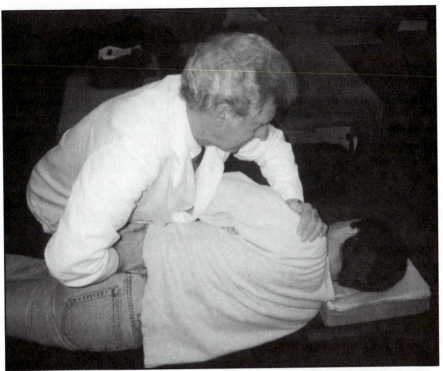

*Bob Anderson completed a full course of chiropractic training, qualified for a
license to practice, and provided patient care part-time for a year as part of his
research on chiropractors.*

(Photo, Cathleen D. Mattos, D.C.)

published in a medical journal in 1912 convinced most of the medical establishment that arthritis and many other diseases were commonly caused by a
hidden focus of low-grade, chronic infection that caused no discomfort in
itself, but resulted in disease in distant organs and joints that were silently
seeded with bacteria (Billings, 1912; Lambert, 1978, pp. 27–32). For years,
arthritis patients were subjected to extensive surgery on the assumption that
a hidden nest of infection needed to be excised. The hidden infection was so
inconsequential in itself that it was difficult to find and identify. It could be
located in a tooth, for example, or in the tonsils, or in an asymptomatic
appendix. Because it was so difficult to identify a focus of infection, many
physicians routinely ordered the removal of the teeth, tonsils, and appendices
of their arthritis patients. Men by the thousands also had their prostate glands
cut out for this reason while women surrendered their ovaries and uteri. One
surgeon believed that the whole colon needed to be removed, but fortunately
his treatment never became popular. The focus of infection theory provided a
lot of business for well-intentioned dentists and surgeons who trusted the logic
of this argument.

The point of this bit of Western medical lore is that when epidemiologic studies were finally undertaken around 1950, surgery to remove the presumed hidden causes of arthritis was shown not to work. People who had their teeth pulled, tonsils removed, or appendices excised were no less subject to arthritis than those who avoided these surgeries. With the publication of these findings, the theory of focal infection became obsolete and with it an enormous amount of surgery carried out with good intentions could no longer be justified.

The Chiropractic Explanatory Model

Chiropractors who oppose vaccinations today do so by a logic comparable to that of the theory of focal infections. They assume that an unimpeded nerve supply is the key to health, and that the primary source of nerve interference is in the spinal column where nerve roots exit from the central nervous system to supply every organ and tissue in the body, including the immune system. It follows, then, that adjusting the alignment of the spinal column, something a medical doctor is not trained to do, should clear nerve interference and improve the body's innate immunity against infectious diseases.

Now we are in a position to understand anti-vaccine chiropractors on this issue. They cannot imitate medical doctors, not only because it is against the law for them to vaccinate children (to imitate), but also because to do so would challenge their status as a distinct profession. Differentiation, not imitation, provides an effective justification in support of their separate but equal status as health care providers.

Opposing vaccination practices requires taking a position contrary to that of medical scientists, even though chiropractors are themselves trained in medical science. They are able to justify this form of differentiation because they believe firmly that spinal adjusting is safer and more effective than vaccines. That position is understandable without resorting to assumptions about limited intelligence, ignorance, or cupidity. To many chiropractors, the logic of this argument is completely convincing, and they stake their lives on it, since many of them refuse to permit even their own children to be immunized.

Given these circumstances, what is the responsibility of an applied anthropologist who believes that vaccinations are highly important for children's health? Probably nothing can be done to change the minds of those chiropractors and their clientele who oppose vaccines. In that respect, many chiropractors and their patients are not greatly different from certain religious leaders and congregations who also oppose vaccines. However, at a time when chiropractors are lobbying to have their services included under comprehensive health care schemes, planners and legislators need to be informed that chiropractic treatment of musculoskeletal disorders can be justified, whereas it cannot be justified for the prevention of infectious diseases.

CHILDHOOD TRAUMA

Continuing to examine biocultural approaches to health in childhood, let us turn from malnutrition and infectious diseases to the next most likely cause of disability and death. Until well into adulthood, the greatest danger to health in the United States is from accidents. The possibilities of trauma prevention offer an enormous challenge to anthropologists, since the key is to modify culture relating to harmful activities. Yet, childhood trauma has not attracted much attention within medical anthropology.

In American society, one thinks of what the anthropologist's role might be in developing and promoting programs of safety in home culture, automobile restraints, playground and water safety, school environments and activities, violence and gun control. In the United States as well as elsewhere, anthropologists certainly need to get more involved in the struggle against violence, now escalated to deadliness by guns, knives, and other weapons in the hands of children or directed against children. Anthropologists should concern themselves with TV and video games as cultural practices that in part are unhealthy because they foster attitudes supportive of escalating violence in our society. Obviously, TV and video games also affect health in other ways, since they encourage sedentary habits. The work of Conrad Kottak relating to TV models and foreshadows the importance of this kind of research (Kottak, 1990).

Children in traditional small-scale societies are also subject to trauma, although this problem tends not to get into the anthropological literature. In a mountain village in Nepal beyond the reach of automobiles or any machinery more elaborate than a plow, a household survey in which I participated disclosed that about one child in a hundred aged fourteen or less was suffering from some kind of orthopedic problem at the time of inquiry (R. Anderson, 1984). Almost all of them (86 percent) had fallen out of trees, which are climbed daily to harvest leaves to feed livestock. The magnitude of the problem is not great, but it deserves attention. For most parts of the world, the subject is simply not investigated.

CHILD ABUSE

Violence against children was a hidden problem until recent years. In anthropology, Raoul Naroll reviewed forty societies from the HRAF to demonstrate that in half of them children were subjected to corporal punishment, noting that "with the rise of civilization, punishment of children has tended to become harsher" (Naroll, 1983, p. 245). Somewhat later, Nancy Scheper-Hughes edited a volume that summarized current understandings of the maltreatment of children (Scheper-Hughes, 1987). The medical literature, too, has begun to spotlight child abuse, acknowledging that physicians have been reluctant to take responsibility for addressing and reporting domestic violence (American Medical Association, 1992). It is to be expected that anthropologists will devote increasing attention to child abuse in coming years on all points of the continuum from small-scale to complex societies.

HEALTH AND OLD AGE

American anthropologists who rechanneled attention from other parts of the world to our own were shocked and dismayed in 1963 when Jules Henry identified human obsolescence as a characteristic of aging in America (Henry, 1963). This finding grew out of fieldwork in three nursing homes. The worst of the three was Rosemont—a lovely name, "Rose Mountain,"—but Henry described it as the vestibule of hell.

As was characteristic of anthropological research during that era, the political/economic perspective of critical medical anthropology was absent or muted. The lives of these aged men and women were described in terms of their immediate surroundings as though their plight was purely personal and familial. Yet useful insights were achieved. "Every institution establishes a 'national character' of inmates and staff," Henry wrote, "in accordance with the remorseless requirements of the institution and in relation to the characteristics brought to it by inmates and staff" (Henry, 1963, pp. 439–440).

Rosemont was a private for-profit business. Its clients were "social security paupers," having no resources other than small monthly checks and very few family members or friends able or willing to help. Visits by relatives were rare and supplementary funds, picayune or nonexistent. In order for the owner of the business to enjoy a profit, as little as possible was spent on salaries for employees or to meet the basic needs of residents. The standard of living was set at a level just above starvation but, as Henry remarked, below that of a prison.

From Henry's field notes describing an old bedridden man who had been crippled in an automobile accident, we extract the following to illustrate conditions in Rosemont:

> He has dried feces under his fingernails and there is a bedpan almost completely full of urine setting on his bedside table. . . . He said he is constantly hungry. He said that for breakfast they had a small bowl half full of oatmeal without cream, sugar or butter, two slices of toast and coffee. Lunch wasn't bad, but not all that it should be. Supper was a small bowl of very thin soup and two slices of toast. (Henry, 1963, p. 414)

For this level of degradation to take place, personal dignity had to be sacrificed. Inmates were thought of and treated as child-animals who were no longer entitled to personal pride or individual freedom. Because American values are defined by an ability to pay, based on the performance of "the culturally necessary tasks of production, reproduction, and consumption," this American nursing home manager could rationalize heartless exploitation.

The manager also succeeded, Henry further argued, because the old people acquiesced to it. They acquiesced not only because they were old and powerless," having been abandoned by their relatives and a miserly Government," but because they too subscribed to the American value system. They acknowledged themselves as obsolete, useless, and unworthy of rights. Having nothing, they expected nothing. So, they spent their days staring into space, protecting their beds from the approach of other residents, especially those who were incontinent, staring blankly at every passerby, and waiting for the next meager, tasteless meal, obsessed by chronically unassuaged hunger (Henry, 1963, p. 440).

> Thus the "national character" of all the inmates becomes reduced to several simple components under the tyranny of the institution. These components are apathy, obsessive preoccupation with food and excreta, the adoption of the role of child-animal and defense of the bed. To this may be added general acquiescence in everything the institution does, decline of the disgust function, and preoccupation with reminiscence. (Henry, 1963, pp. 440-441)

HEALTH AND OLD AGE IN SAMOA

The depressing account of aging in America by Jules Henry, currently reinforced by public repugnance at warehousing the old, is counterbalanced in the ethnographic literature with somewhat romanticized descriptions of some traditional societies in which people seem to experience old age truly as "golden years." I refer to it as romanticized because the truth is, there is what Melvyn Goldstein and Cynthia Beall have referred to as "an amazing paucity of empirical data on the state of the elderly in traditional societies" (Goldstein & Beal, 1981, p. 48).

Lowell Holmes provides an impressionistic example in his report on elder care in American Samoa. He returned to the village on Ta'u Island, sixty miles east of Pago Pago, following up where Margaret Mead gathered data for her study of coming of age in 1925-1926. Based on his own fieldwork in 1962 and 1977, Holmes studied the elderly men and women whom Mead had studied as young people. His report, appropriately titled *Coming of Old Age in Samoa,* offers a welcome postscript to Mead's earlier work (Holmes, 1978; Holmes and Holmes, 1992).

In a traditional, small-scale Samoan community such as Ta'u village, old age on the whole is thought of as a happy time of life. High levels of personal satisfaction and security are supported by the combination of living in a large three-generational family household (averaging ten to twelve persons) that is located in a small village (of fewer than eight hundred inhabitants). Large households ensure that elders reside in contexts of familial intimacy while a small village provides community involvement since the old person knows, and is known to, everyone.

Other cultural traits reinforce these social factors. A climate warm enough to allow easy mobility also permits living in houses open on all sides. Old people can stay indoors and still exchange pleasantries with fellow villagers in the vicinity as they work or pass by. Social activities do not segregate by age, so they interact with old and young alike.

Old people are honored for their knowledge of local history and customs. Their opinions are solicited with respect. For example, when a house is under construction, an old man in the family is assigned to keep an eye on the work and to contribute by praying for success. Old men also keep busy at other work, including twisting and braiding coconut husk fibers into a sturdy twine used in building canoes and houses. Old women serve on the Women's Committee, where they perform valued social and ceremonial functions. They keep active by weaving sleeping mats, floor coverings, baskets, fans, and window coverings. They also make and decorate barkcloth (tapa cloth) tapestries. Elderly women provide valued services as midwives, body massagers, and child care workers. Men and women alike continue to work hard, albeit at age-appropriate tasks.

In sum, given basic good health, old age is a good time of life in the small-scale communities of Samoa. For many, it is the best time of life. The old are honored on social occasions, their advice on ceremonial matters is valued, and they are given priorities for food and care. "Until quite recently," Holmes learned, "Samoans were in total agreement that old age is the best time of life (Holmes, 1978; see also Holmes and Holmes, 1992, p. 96)."

ZATIONS AND ELDER NEGLECT

India, in some ways like Samoa, traditionally possessed a safety net for people who grew old. Most elders of the subcontinent also lived in small, rural communities and in large households. But times are changing. In India, Samoa, and throughout the world old age can bring abandonment and poverty. The change coincides with large-scale, politico-economic changes referred to in India as the "zations" (Cohen, 1992, p. 124): westernization, modernization, industrialization, and urbanization.

Although the crisis in elder care struck early in the United States, where it now looms as a potentially out-of-control elder boom, no part of the world is without its own version of the problem (Randall, 1993). In metropolitan Samoa, Holmes witnessed a shift in family culture that bodes ill for the aged. Urban families in Pago Pago live in European-style houses that close in rather than open out. Most able-bodied adults spend their days away from home as wage earners. Family members are too busy to cultivate gardens for food on land adjacent to the home. They supply themselves from supermarkets, driving automobiles back and forth instead of walking along village pathways. Household composition tends to be extremely fluid, as relatives and friends move back and forth among communities. The old person is marginalized under these conditions.

To reverse the trend of elder marginalization, governmental agencies supplement family resources and activities to provide for many elder needs. The Territorial Administration of Aging set up a program that pays senior citizens an hourly wage to produce wooden bowls, baskets, tapa cloth, and other craft items for sale to tourists. The administration arranges for elders to teach traditional skills to high school students. Good hospital care is available free. On the whole, one gets the sense that the shift from familial and communal to institutional and governmental care is working well.

But one also comes to a realization that the quality of life of these elder urbanites in American Samoa has declined in comparison with that of elder villagers. Attempts to provide healthy food have floundered, for example. The administration hoped to provide free well-balanced meals for needy seniors, but the Meals on Wheels program that works rather well in the United States was not successful in and around Pago Pago. Its success depends on a culture of volunteerism that is not part of traditional Samoan custom. An effort to provide hot lunches in territorial schools failed as an alternative, since elders felt it was undignified to line up to eat in a school like children. They would rather starve than diminish their personal dignity.

Zations have also impacted on Sherpas in Nepal. Goldstein and Beall found that old people were not satisfied with their lives, even though they appeared to be active, healthy, and independent.

> Despite their high level of economically productive activity, their relative physical fitness, and their ownership of agricultural land, many elderly Helambu Sherpas overtly expressed unhappiness with their lot. Several spontaneously volunteered that they wished they were dead, and others commented that their children had abandoned them and that the young in general did not care about the elderly. (Goldstein & Beall, 1981, p. 51)

Jewish old people in London's East End also appear to be less well off since the end of World War II, when family practices changed. Nuclear families now prioritize a financial commitment to educating their children. Second- and third-generation adults have adopted English values and aspirations. These changes adversely affect their aging parents. "Children tended to feel ashamed of their 'culturally deprived' parents who, in turn, developed a negative self-image, thus leaving no room for common interests and mutual regard" (Hazan, 1982, p. 355). The result is isolation. An old parent can now expect a telephone call once a week, but otherwise is left to seek companionship elsewhere.

Community as well as family changes worked against old immigrants. The size of the Jewish population declined in this multiracial working-class neighborhood.

The Jews who remain are all old, poor, and scattered. Synagogues, responding to these changes, stopped functioning as social centers, although they continue to schedule religious services. Jewish working-class clubs closed their doors. Limited now to public parks, local hospitals, and stores, community life has all but ceased to exist for older neighborhood residents.

The pattern of adaptive response resembles what we have seen elsewhere. In the London East End, common interest associations attempt to serve needs traditionally met by family and community. The Jewish Welfare Board organized and administers a day care center for these old East Enders. Haim Hazan, the anthropologist whose findings I report, found that elder culture had changed dramatically when comparisons were made to older customs. Day center old people interact on an egalitarian basis that requires them to abandon old identities centered in family affairs, job statuses, socioeconomic class, and personal interests and achievements. He sees this as a process of "irreversible disengagement and deculturation" resulting from "an increasing multifacet deterioration in social contacts, economic state, and self esteem" (Hazan, 1982, p. 358; see Anderson, 1972). Simultaneously, he regards this scenario of disengagement as a precondition to social revitalization and the development of new ways for these old Londoners to achieve self-realization. This brings us to a study of old people carried out in San Francisco in the early 1960s.

GROWING OLD IN SAN FRANCISCO

As part of a larger study of mental illness among the aged, forty residents of the San Francisco Bay Area older than sixty with no history of psychiatric hospitalization were interviewed intensively by or under the direction of two anthropologists, Margaret Clark and Barbara Anderson, assisted by a third anthropologist, Majda Turner. The work of these anthropologists represented an early effort at collaboration within a medical setting. The principal investigator, in fact, was a psychiatrist, Alexander Simon (Clark & Anderson, 1967).

This research program was hospital based, and therefore, not surprisingly, was intervention oriented. As an anthropological study it was unusual in that participant observation was not carried out. The subjects were not observed in the larger context of their lives in families and communities. However, the research questionnaire did explore issues of self-identity, needs, satisfactions, values, family and community activities, sexual relations, religious beliefs and practices, and opinions on aging. As the authors put it, "Our data, therefore, are *their* perceptions, beliefs, attitudes, and feelings, as *they* expressed them to us, in *their* own words" (Clark & Anderson, 1967, p. 77).

In a review of findings relating to these forty subjects, Clark and Anderson looked particularly at those who seemed to be happy and successful while growing older. Taught, in a sense, by these successful oldsters, they concluded that successful aging required the achievement of five adaptive tasks:

- Achieve awareness and acceptance of getting older and of no longer being able to pursue activities that were important to them earlier in life.
- Redefine the boundaries of their physical and social life space to be harmonious with the limitations of older age.
- Substitute feasible interests, activities, and relationships to replace what they must give up.
- Learn to judge themselves in the here and now rather than by measures of excellence that applied before they became old.
- Pull all of these changes together in a way that gives overall coherence to their attitudes, values, and purposes. (Clark & Anderson, 1967, pp. 402–419).

In effect, these are meant to be used as rules for success. One must succeed in achieving each of these tasks if one is to grow old successfully in terms of mental health. Basically, as Hazan was later to describe for aging Jewish East Enders, the overall requirement is one of disengagement in the sense of giving up an older identity embedded in a culture of active adulthood in order to adopt a new identity congruent with the frailties and vulnerabilities of old age.

Erik Erikson, an anthropologically informed psychologist who undoubtedly exerted an influence on Clark and Anderson, earlier arrived at a congruent way of recommending what one must do to age successfully. Based on clinical experience as a psychotherapist, Erikson introduced into anthropological discourse the concept of developmental tasks (Erikson, 1963 [1950]). At each of eight stages of life, beginning in infancy, the maturing individual must accomplish a basic task of personality development before moving on to the next stage in a way consistent with good mental health and social involvement.

In the eighth stage, that of growing old, the task identified by Erikson is to successfully achieve ego integrity as opposed to falling into despair. "It is the acceptance of one's one and only life cycle as something that had to be," he explained, "and that, by necessity, permitted of no substitutions" (Erikson, 1963, p. 268). He thought of it as requiring a renunciation that is compensated by the acquisition of wisdom. If one cannot accept one's life as it is and was, but feels that time has run out and it is too late to start again, there is no wisdom. Where there is no wisdom, there is despair.

At issue is the extent to which the developmental tasks of Erikson and of Anderson and Clark are culture and age specific. Erikson states his single task of aging in such broad terms that it would seem to apply in any culture, although each culture would shape it in its own characteristic ways. Perhaps this is so; the assumption has not been tested cross-culturally. The five tasks of aging proposed by Clark and Anderson, which have also not been subjected to rigorous cross-cultural evaluation, may or may not define a way to age successfully in other societies.

It is also not clear that the Clark and Anderson study is the best way to characterize aging in the Bay Area itself. Their findings appear to have been skewed by the way the study was designed and executed—by the nature of their questionnaire—and therefore possibly do not offer the best guidelines for successful aging. It is hard to see disengagement as making these San Franciscans any happier or better adjusted than the Jewish East Enders studied by Hazan. Disengagement as a strategy is achieved at enormous cost in terms of self-identity and social involvements. Does it really work? (Neugarten, 1968). Is that the best a middle-class California man or woman can hope for by growing old?

Sharon Kaufman offers a more hopeful scenario for late life based on her research with a similar Bay Area population a generation later. In her study she found that "when old people talk about themselves, they express a sense of self that is ageless—an identity that maintains continuity despite the physical and social changes that come with old age" (Kaufman, 1986; p. 7). Continuity, it would seem, is the way to enjoy psychological well-being in old age, not discontinuity. The fifteen informants whom she interviewed intensively found meaning in their lives in terms of values that still functioned for them as "guidelines for behavior and standards by which goals are chosen and decisions are made." She identified these values as "achievement, success, productivity, work, progress, social usefulness, independence, self-reliance, and individual initiative" (Kaufman, 1986, pp. 114, 115).

How can one reconcile two such contrasting conclusions based on anthropological research carried out with nearly identical populations? It seems unlikely that the difference between one generation and the next was that great. It is very likely, on the other hand, that the way the research was designed led to contrasting conclusions. In the Clark and Anderson study, the basis for identifying success was to correlate systematic differences in questionnaire data with differences in the amount of psychiatric treatment and hospitalization an individual had experienced. That approach demonstrated that those with fewer mental health interventions were more disengaged. Kaufman, went beyond that kind of finding. She analyzed her transcripts of conversations line by line, looking for words or phrases such as "like," "love," and "became attached," that were used over and over again. These, she identified as themes, finding that each person's life story was oriented around four to six major themes that continued to inform their lives in old age. She corroborated how these themes were expressed in their lives by the behavior she observed doing participant-observation fieldwork. Her successful informants appear to have disengaged in many ways as the Clark and Anderson model would require. They adapted to the infirmities of old age and the giving up of much that had once shaped their lives, but in their life stories they did not emphasize loss and withdrawal. Rather, they spoke in terms of personal core values that continued to give meaning to their lives. Eighty-year-old Millie, whose conversations were loaded with the terms "like," "love," and "became attached," continued to find life worth living in part because caring relationships with others shaped her daily encounters with them in the old people's home where she resided.

OLD, OLDER, AND OLDEST

From Sula Benet, one of the few American anthropologists to have done field-work in the former U.S.S.R., we are informed that Soviet scientists agreed to demarcate three differing levels of old age:

- old (60 to 75 years of age)
- older (75 to 90)
- very old or long-lived (90 and above) (Benet, 1974, p. 9; see Kaufman, 1986, pp. 4–5)

Presumably, in the experience of Soviet gerontologists, these stages of aging define significantly different ways of experiencing age. Awareness of this saves us from a kind of essentialism that fails to give attention to meaningful differences among aging people based on how the passing years require alterations in styles of living. However, by defining these categories as chronological categories, they define them in arbitrary ways that may be neccessary for large-scale statistical studies but which are distortive for holistic assessments on a person-oriented scale.

Samoans are aware that being old is not a totalizing concept. In Ta'u they think in terms of a functional definition as opposed to calendar years. People are thought to be old when they no longer can carry on as usual (which probably occurs at an age somewhere in the fifties, Holmes reports). Only later will a person be assigned to a category of weak and old (beginning at some time between ages sixty and eighty). We learn an important lesson from Samoans. Marked advantages accrue for all if old age is defined in terms of involvements and activities rather than arbitrarily as years since birth. However, these definitions are still infused with unexamined value biases, as we see when we return to Benet's research on the Abkhazians.

In Abkhazia, at the time of her research one of the Soviet Socialist Republics of the U.S.S.R., Benet found that the Russian categories did not apply. They turned out to be emic to the Soviet Union but not etic to the world. In the emic view of Abkhazians, their language did not even include a term meaning old person. A person might be called the equivalent of an elder, but this was a matter of social role and not of chronological age. Being old just was not part of their thinking, although they did recognize that some people (quite a few in fact) lived for a long time (a century or more). These they referred to as "long-living people." The labeling, you will note, is nonagist in the sense of being nonpejorative (Benet, 1974, p. 9).

What about the United States? It had become the custom to define old in important ways as beginning at sixty-five years of age. After reaching a sixty-fifth birthday, people in many jobs were labeled "senior citizens," and forced to retire. At that birthday they also became eligible for old age Social Security pensions. This practice changed in the 1980s, when federal law declared it discriminatory and made it illegal. Now, one can continue to work and earn income as long as one feels able. Americans have caught up with the Samoans and Abkhazians at last. Old ways of thinking do hang on, of course. For the purposes of demographic research, people aged sixty-five years and older are still unofficially designated by the U.S. Bureau of the Census as "the elderly."

Also in the United States, gerontological experts now agree that being old is not an all-or-none phenomenon. Although there is no overall agreement on terminology, there is general agreement that the young-old and the old-old are as different from each other as either is from the not-yet old. The young-old, although usually retired from their jobs, tend to lead active lives with multiple options for lifestyles. The old-old (for statistical purposes generally thought of as eighty or eighty-five years of age or more) are relatively restricted in their options because of what Claude Lévi-Strauss has referred to as "great age and its inconveniences" (Lévi-Strauss, 1994).

Old age, then, is wrongly thought of as a condition shaped by a single culture of aging. Multiple cultures of aging can be identified both cross-culturally and within cultures. In what society, then, and at what stage in a life trajectory, should an individual complete the five adaptive tasks of aging of Clark and Anderson if one is to maximize health and happiness?

In the world today, more and more people are surviving into old age. The United States used to be a young nation. The average age in Colonial America was sixteen years. Now it is an aging nation. The population of old people is experiencing a growth spurt that is without precedent. Not only are there more old people, but also the old are getting older. Between 1960 and 1990, the oldest-old, that is, those who were at least eighty-five years of age, increased by 232 percent (compared with a total population growth of 39 percent). Poor health and poverty in the aging population are going to become a major health challenge in the coming decades (Randall, 1993). Medical anthropologists will have a useful role to play in reseach, teaching, and applications relating to these issues.

ABLENESS AND HEALTH

In the West, with improved biomedical management and changed social attitudes, more and more individuals with impaired capacities are able to survive and remain partially (or nearly totally) functional whereas formerly they were abused, neglected, or hidden away to be treated as unwelcome or invisible in the mainstream of life. These are the children and adults who are incapacitated in some ways, but not in all. Their impairments may include vision, hearing, locomotion, neuromuscular control, chronic diseases, pain control, emotions, and cognition.

They are different from each other just as they are different from the majority population, but they all have one thing in common. Although limited in some ways that make them different, they have ability in other ways. Urban-industrial societies, in particular, have directed a gaze so focused on a disability that they failed to see all of the potential abilities. Biomedicine can often make enhanced or prolonged biological function possible, but to actualize that functionality requires supportive sociocultural understandings and practices. This is where anthropologists should be involved.

To this day, however, the differently abled remain for the most part an anthropological *terra incognita.* Their cultures are largely unexamined, although notable exceptions can be cited. Robert Edgerton, Peter Wilson, and Sue Estroff have published ethnographies of people who are mentally challenged (Edgerton, 1967) or mentally deranged (Wilson, 1992; Estroff, 1981). Joan Ablon has reported on her work with people of short stature (Ablon, 1984), while Robert Murphy documented his own progressive paralysis and what it taught him about disability in the United States (Murphy, 1987). Most recently, Susan Whyte and Benedicte Ingstad, in collaboration with ten other anthropologists, published *Disability and Culture,* in which they report on research from Indonesia, Africa, Turkey, England, Central America, and the United States (Ingstad & Whyte, 1995). This book can be expected to stimulate a marked increase in anthropological attention to impairment and disability, particularly in the non-Western world, about which very little previously has been written.

On the level of theory, the most influential work so far has been done by a sociologist, Erving Goffman. His book *Stigma* is about ableness in that it explores the issue of self-identity, attributing identity relating to three kinds of stereotypes (prejudices) that are stigmatized (considered inferior, harmful, or evil):

- abominations of the body—various deviations from physical norms
- blemishes of personality—including mental disorders, prostitution,homosexuality, alcoholism, unemployment
- assumptions about race, ethnicity, and religion (Goffman 1963)

"By definition, of course, we believe the person with a stigma is not quite human," Goffman writes. "On this assumption we exercise varieties of discrimination, through which we effectively, if often unthinkingly, reduce his life chances" (Goffman, 1963; p. 5). In *Stigma,* we catch a glimpse of the lifestyles and strategies of people who must not only cope with bodily impairment, but even more so, with unhealthy and even punitive societal reactions to impairment.

Anthropologists continue to build on the earlier work of Goffman and his effort to understand the social construction of disability. Participant observation remains the most used methodology. Shlomo Deshen, for example, carried out fieldwork in Israel on adults who had been blinded in childhood (Deshen, 1991). Based on field observations, he criticizes a form of essentialism, the widespread sociological assumption that voluntary associations of disabled people are easily established and make life better for those involved. He found that discredited people vary in the extent to which they seek the company of others similarly discredited. Those with epilepsy, for example, tend to mutually shun one another, in contrast to small people and people with hearing impairments who are prone to ingroup sociability (Schneider & Conrad, 1983; Ablon, 1984; Becker, 1981). The vision-impaired fall between these two extremes.

Deshen heard many vision-impaired individuals repeat the slogan "The blind are like anyone else, they only can't see." However, he was struck by the extent to which those same individuals, although blind themselves, perpetuated stigmatizing stereotypes of the blind. Negative self imagery among the vision-impaired in this study led his subjects to avoid friendships and associations with others who shared the discredited identity. When he did encounter an occasional small voluntary association of the blind, mutuality was always based on some other interest (such as shared ethnicity or an enthusiasm for sports), blindness being thought of as incidental rather than central to their getting together.

Ultimately, in attempting to make sense of the failure of the visually impaired to aggregate, Deshen targets Israeli social policy that includes a paternalistic condescension toward people who are disabled. This makes one unwilling to draw attention to oneself by consorting with others who are stigmatized. Thus, ideology turns the choice between common interest association or mutual rejection into an ambiguous and complex issue for those concerned. Socializing in these cases is neither automatic nor necessarily beneficial.

Carol Goldin used participant observation as well as structured interviews to study advocacy organizations for the blind in the United States. She documented the existence of extensive personal networks and organizational affiliations among vision-impaired individuals at an early stage in life before they had received vocational training (Goldin, 1984). The ideology of the civil rights movement appears to have influenced mutuality behaviors among the blind in the United States. America, far more than Israel, was found to support civil rights activism and legislation relating to ableness. Further, it was shown that the blind in this study meet together socially far more than do their Israeli counterparts. From studies such as these it is clear that ableness issues are variable and complex. They represent a fertile field for future anthropological research.

THE GAY LIFESTYLE AND HEALTH

Homophilic behavior, despite widespread social denial until recently, is quite common. In the 1950s, Alfred Kinsey and his collaborators took fifteen years to interview over 16,000 men and women about their sex lives, employing a structured interview approach (Kinsey, Pomeroy, & Martin, 1948; Kinsey et al., 1953). Subjects were recruited on the basis of a willingness or wish to talk with interviewers about their sexual experiences and habits, so it is very likely that they constituted a biased sample, as Kinsey himself realized (Frayser, 1985, p. 397). In all events, 37 percent of males and 13 percent of females in that sample had engaged at least once in a homosexual act that culminated in an orgasm.

Because the selection of respondents was not random, one cannot assume that these percentages characterized the American population at that time. Currently, the statistic that is most repeated by gay activists and others is that 10 percent of the men in the Kinsey study limited themselves completely, or almost so, to homosexual activity, at least for a minimum of three years. In other words, according to the Kinsey documentation, 10 percent of American men at that time were gay or bisexual.

More recent studies would reduce the latter figure to only 3.3 percent (Fay et al., 1989). The Kinsey counts are probably too high while the more recent count is probably too low. As anthropologist Ralph Bolton points out, it is hard to evaluate the reliability and validity of any of these studies (Bolton, 1992, pp. 163–165). This much is clear, however, homosexual behavior is far too common in American society to be dismissed as merely deviant, immoral, or pathological.

It struck me as I reread Goffman's 1963 book on discredited identities that he referred to homosexuality (male or female) as one of his examples of a stigmatized identity. Most social scientists in the 1960s accepted without question the concept of gay and lesbian behaviors as deviant (whatever "deviant" might mean). Goffman merely reflected the way social scientists and the public at large thought and felt then, and that attitude took time to change.

In 1970, the American Anthropological Association (AAA) finally acknowledged officially that homosexuality was a neglected issue that needed research attention. A symposium on homosexuality in cross-cultural perspective was organized as part of the AAA annual meeting for the first time in 1974. By the 1980s, a number of research projects had been completed and more were underway (Carrier, 1986).

The stigmatization of gay and lesbian sexuality characterized the mid-century medical sciences as well as anthropology and the social sciences. Until 1973 the official position of the American Psychiatric Association was that homosexuality constituted a mental disorder and should be treated as such by any orthodox doctor. Medicine and science, although supposedly value-neutral, in fact are shaped by culture as we have seen. No new scientific discoveries were reported in 1973 to require psychiatry to dramatically change its position on homosexuality. Nonetheless, the condition of being homosexual was changed from being a disease to being psychiatrically normal. It had become a matter of the culture and politics of medicine, and was settled by a vote.

AIDS RESEARCH

Infection with the transmissible retrovirus known as human immunodeficiency virus (HIV) usually occurs silently. Most people do not realize that their bodies have been invaded. In a minority of cases, after a latency period of two to four weeks, a recently exposed individual may experience the symptoms of primary HIV infection. This flu-like syndrome is characterized by fever, malaise, rash, painful joints, and generalized enlargement of lymph nodes (lymphadenopathy), all of which disappear after three to fourteen days except for the lymphadenopathy, which may persist. It may take as much as six months, but eventually blood tests can be expected to show conversion (seroconversion) to HIV-positive, meaning that the blood has begun to contain identifiable antibodies to HIV, a sign that the virus has invaded the body.

HIV disease is usually latent and asymptomatic for a number of years. The signs of its presence are seen in blood tests, but not in symptoms of disease. Eventually the HIV-infected person may begin to feel pretty rotten, experiencing weight loss, fever at times, fatigue, malaise, and chronic diarrhea. This constellation of chronic symptoms, the so-called AIDS-related complex (ARC), eventually transforms into full-blown AIDS.

The cumulative risk for an asymptomatic HIV-positive condition to transform into AIDS (acquired immunodeficiency syndrome) is 35 to 45 percent after the first eight to ten years. On a laboratory basis, one may be said to have AIDS when the blood T-cell count (the number of so-called CD4 lymphocytes) becomes very low (fewer than 200 per unit of measure). Clinically, however, HIV infection is said to have converted to AIDS with the first experience of any one of certain otherwise rare but serious diseases such as pneumonia caused by the bacteria *Pneumocystis carinii* (PCC), massive systemic infections by organisms that usually cause only limited damage (e.g., candidiasis, normally limited to the mouth in babies or the vagina in women), an unusual cancer known as Kaposi's sarcoma, and so on. At this point, even with treatment, the forecast is sinister. Complete recoveries are exceedingly rare, although on record, a few people, referred to as long-term survivors, have lived with AIDS for five years or more. The rest can be expected to die within one to several years of onset. There is no known cure (Berkow & Fletcher, 1992, pp. 77–86).

AIDS was unknown and unrecognized until 1981, when several gay men in California and New York were diagnosed with PCC pneumonia and Kaposi's sarcoma. With extraordinary rapidity, the disease expanded into a world pandemic. Medicine can slow down the disease and provide some symptomatic relief, but prevention, not cure, holds the most promise for success at this time. The key to prevention is to investigate how the virus spreads. Routes of transmission in the United States and Europe, characterized as Pattern I countries in epidemiologic studies, were remarkably consistent during the first decade of the pandemic. The major risk groups were.

- young—age 20 to 49 years (90 percent)
- men (93 percent)
- 94 percent in one or more of the following categories:
    - gay or bisexual men
    - injection drug users (men and women)
    - heterosexuals after unprotected sex with infected partners (mostly women)

- recipients of contaminated blood transfusions (men and women); eliminated now by careful screening of blood.
- hemophiliacs receiving blood products as treatment (boys and men); virtually eliminated now by careful processing techniques (Berkow & Fletcher, 1992, pp. 77–86)

By the early 1990s, however, it became clear that the modes of transmission in the West were shifting, and that heterosexual transmission was destined to increase in a massive way. Women became highly vulnerable. The new pattern includes babies born to infected mothers. Without preventative treatment, about 25 percent of these babies succumb to AIDS. In these ways, the pattern of HIV transmission is shifting to what epidemiologists refer to as Pattern II, which is characteristic of the Caribbean Islands and Central Africa, areas in which homosexual transmission is rare and heterosexual transmission is widespread.

Nina Schiller, Merrill Singer, and other anthropologists draw attention to problems inherent in the way the epidemic is conceptualized. This includes, for Schiller, the distinction of Pattern I and Pattern II risk groups by the World Health Organization (WHO). The WHO patterns identify cultures or subcultures at risk in a way that seems to support racist, homophobic, or elitist reactions. That is, the WHO patterns imply that homosexual and substance injector subcultures as well as African, African-American, and Hispanic cultures are in a sense reprehensible as seedbeds of risky behavior, when it would be more appropriate to accuse oppressive economic conditions and power relationships (Schiller, 1992; Singer et al., 1992).

One major thrust of anthropological research has been to identify diversity in the cultural contexts of AIDS. "Anthropology has a critical role," Janet McGrath insists, "in identifying ethnic, cultural, and class-related factors shaping different responses to HIV/AIDS" (McGrath, 1992; p. 74). A number of field anthropologists have taken on this role:

- *Brazil:* Richard Parker identified an "erotic universe focused on the transgression of public norms through a playfulness reminiscent of *carnaval"* (Parker, 1987, p. 165).
- *Haiti:* Paul Farmer elicited an evolving EM for AIDS in which "two major causal schemes, magic and germ theory, are elaborately intertwined and subject to revision." (Farmer, 1990, p. 21)
- *United States:* Norris Lang found that the AIDS epidemic contributes to "problems of stress, stigma, and rejection," which have not as yet been sufficiently studied. (Lang, 1991, p. 69)
- *U.S. Latinos:* Merrill Singer and associates argued that the medical model in most AIDS research is oriented to the individual, "while ignoring important community-level factors and political issues" (Singer et al., 1990, p. 73).
- *Mexico:* J. M. Carrier recorded that an overt gay world is almost nonexistent, but many opportunitites exist in "crowded neighborhoods as choice locations for finding sexual partners." (Carrier, 1989, p.135)

- *Zaire:* Brooke Schoepf, advocating condom use as prevention, believed that "healers may be appropriate sexual behavior change agents." (Schoepf, 1992, p. 234)
- *African-Americans:* Janis Hutchinson found that the "overrepresentation of minorities in various disease categories, including AIDS, is partially related to institutionalized racism." (Hutchinson, 1992; p. 119)

Field studies based on participant observation have allowed anthropologists to acquire basic documentation unobtainable by any other social science techniques. Even when they are done in our own society, the field situation can be very difficult, fully testing the ability and determination of ethnographers. Consider the interpersonal skills needed to carry out firsthand observations of needle-manipulation by injection drug users, as was done by Page, Chitwood, Smith, Kane, and McBride in Florida (Page et al., 1990). In another project, it took real grit for Terri Leonard to survey the clients of sex workers by allowing herself to be solicited as a presumed prostitute by men in a hardcore inner-city vice district. She managed in a remarkable way to elude danger and divert street encounters into ethnographic interviews (Leonard, 1990).

AIDS and Promiscuity

A sense of urgency impells AIDS researchers to emphasize applied anthropology dedicated to improving prevention methods. Among the many directions this has taken, one has to do with promiscuity, since statistics indicate that the risk of infection increases directly with increases in the number of sexual partners. "Promiscuity has been singled out as the primary behavioral vector of the spread of AIDS in virtually all American discourses on the subject, including those within the gay community." Having made this statement, Michael Clatts and Kevin Mutchler object that promiscuity is a pejorative metaphor, "a symbol which condenses so many anti-social metaphoric predicates of sickness and vice, insulates the virtuous, the mentally healthy, the normal, the 'average American' from contagion and concern" (Clatts & Mutchler, 1989, p. 109).

Ralph Bolton, reflecting similarly on the moral judgment implicit in the concept of promiscuity, opposes a prevention strategy that recommends to sexually active adults that they reduce or eliminate sex with multiple partners because it is dangerous. "Was this good advice then [early in the epidemic]?" he asks. "Is it good advice now?" (Bolton, 1992, p. 169). In answer to his own questions, he argues that promiscuity is a red herring. The issue is safe sex practices. "It never did matter whom one had sex with or how many people one had sex with; what mattered then and what matters now is what kind of sex one has" (Bolton, 1992, p. 177).

Bolton takes a risky stand on this issue. Of course he is right, multiple sex partners would not matter if completely safe methods were practiced. Unfortunately, he neglects to remind readers that no precaution is completely safe. Condoms fail! Above all, he implicitly plays down what he himself is aware

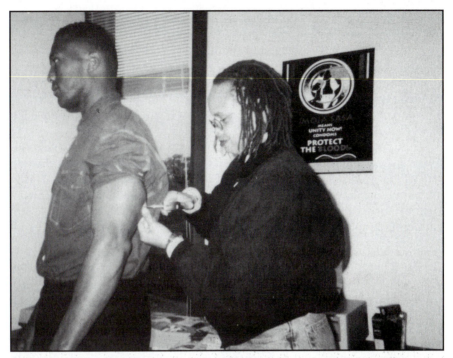

Janis Hutchinson demonstrates on her research assistant, Vernard Bonner, a technique for measuring skin thickness in studies of muscle mass and fat relationships.

of, namely, that safe sex must be negotiated, that each new partner requires new negotiations, and that negotiations often fail. As concerns gay men, Bolton describes a scenario in which an individual committed to practicing safe sex will abandon safety in order to please and keep a new partner.

But, as Bolton also points out, negotiating the details of how sexual pleasure will be given and accepted, including what safety measures will be taken, is usually done in a matter-of-fact manner by gay men in new encounters. A determined gay man has this working for him.

A woman is far more likely to be compromised, in part because she may be involved in risky behavior without consent or knowledge. Bisexual as well as heterosexual men commonly betray the trust of their paraconjugal partners. Leonard found that almost half of the men she interviewed were married. They seemed unconcerned about the risks they were taking on behalf of their primary partners. She notes that "clients infected with HIV or another sexually transmitted pathogen pose an unsuspected risk to wives, most of whom are unaware of their husbands' high risk behaviors." They also pose a risk to the babies they may father (Leonard, 1990, pp. 51–52).

The other way in which women are compromised by promiscuity derives from their vulnerability in negotiating the give-and-take of sex. Leonard found that men rather than sex workers determine whether condoms will be used.

Even if sex workers carry condoms and ask that they be used, they are often forced by clients to agree to unprotected intercourse.

This finding can be extended to all women. In summarizing relevant research, Beverly Sibthorpe reported that women consistently find it difficult to get partners to use condoms (Sibthorpe, 1992). The negotiating power of women while engaged in sexual intercourse is limited by cultural factors, including male ego needs, women's lack of power, the economic dependency of women, and their tendency to low self-esteem.

Yes, Bolton is right, promiscuity is not the direct cause of HIV infection. Unfortunately, the reality is that one must assume that multiple sexual encounters will be associated with instances of unsafe, risk-taking behavior. This is borne out by epidemiologic statistics. The greater the number of sexual partners, the higher the rates of infection. To encourage and validate multiple sex partners is to adhere to an ideal in a real world that is dangerous.

CONCLUSION

This chapter barely scratched the surface of health issues associated with diversity of age, ableness, and lifestyles. It is offered more as a sampler than as a survey, but it supports an important point of view: Health varies with one's life experiences, and anthropologists are skilled professionals precisely trained to do research and contribute to problem solving relating to diversity of life experiences.

REFERENCES

Ablon, J. (1984). *Little people in America: The social dimensions of dwarfism.* New York: Praeger.

American Medical Association, Council on Ethical and Judicial Affairs, (1992). Physicians and domestic violence: Ethical considerations. *Journal of the American Medical Association, 267,* 3190–3193.

Anderson, B. (1972). The process of deculturation—Its dynamics among United States aged. *Anthropological Quarterly, 45,* 209–216.

Anderson, R. (1971). *Traditional Europe: A study in anthropology and history.* Belmont, CA: Wadsworth Publishing Co.

Anderson, R. (1984). An orthopedic ethnography in rural Nepal. *Medical Anthropology, 8,* 47–59.

Anderson, R. (1990). Chiropractors for and against vaccines. *Medical Anthropology, 12,* 169–186.

Anderson, R., Meeker, W. C., Wirick, B. E., Mootz, R. D., Kirk, D. H., & Adams, A. (1992). A meta-analysis of clinical trials of spinal manipulation. *Journal of Manipulative and Physiological Therapeutics, 15,* 181–194.

Bateson, G. (1958). *Naven* (2nd ed.). Stanford, CA: Stanford University Press. (Original work published 1936).

Bateson, G. (1972). *Steps to an ecology of mind.* New York: Ballantine Books.

Becker, G. (1981). Coping with stigma: Lifelong adaptation of deaf people. *Social Science and Medicine, 15B,* 21-24.

Benet, S. (1974). *Abkhasians: The long-living people of the Caucasus.* New York: Holt, Rinehart and Winston, Inc.

Berkow, R., & Fletcher, A. J. (Eds.) (1992). *The Merck manual of diagnosis and therapy* (16th ed.). Rahway, NJ: Merck Research Laboratories.

Billings, F. (1912). Chronic focal infections and their etiologic relations to arthritis and nephritis. *Archives of Internal Medicine, 9,* 484-490.

Bolton, R. (1992). AIDS and promiscuity: Muddles in the models of HIV prevention. *Medical Anthropology, 14,* 145-223.

Carrier, J. M. (1986). Foreword. In E. Blackwood (Ed.), *Anthropology and homosexual behavior.* New York: The Haworth Press.

Carrier, J. M. (1989). Sexual behavior and spread of AIDS in Mexico. *Medical Anthropology, 10,* 129-142.

Centers for Disease Control. (1993). Isolation of wild poliovirus type 3 among members of a religious community objecting to vaccination—Alberta, Canada, 1993. *Journal of the American Medical Association, 270,* 3104.

Clark, M., & Anderson, B. (1967). *Culture and aging: An anthropological study of older Americans.* Springfield, IL: Charles C. Thomas.

Clatts, M. C., & Mutchler, K. M. (1989). AIDS and the dangerous other: Metaphors of sex and deviance in the representation of disease. *Medical Anthropology, 10,* 105-114.

Clements, C. J. (1994). Role of mass campaigns in global measles control. *The Lancet, 344,* 174-175.

Cohen, L. (1992). No aging in India: The uses of gerontology. *Culture, Medicine and Psychiatry, 16,* 123-161.

Colley, F. (1994). Attitudes on immunization: A survey of American chiropractors. *Journal of Manipulative and Physiological Therapeutics, 17,* 584-590.

Deshen, S. (1991). Mutual rejection and association among the discredited: The case of blind people in Israel. *Human Organization, 50,* 89-96.

Edgerton, R. B. (1967). *The cloak of competence: Stigma in the lives of the mentally retarded.* Berkeley: University of California Press.

Erikson, E. H. (1963). *Childhood and society* (2nd ed.). New York: W. W. Norton & Co. (Original work published 1950)

Estroff, S. E. (1981). *Making it crazy: An ethnography of psychiatric clients in an American community.* Berkeley: University of California Press.

Farmer, P. (1990). Sending sickness: Sorcery, politics, and changing concepts of AIDS in rural Haiti. *Medical Anthropological Quarterly, 4,* 6-27.

Fay, R. E., Turner, C. F., Klassen, A. D., & Gagnon, J. H. (1989). Prevalence and patterns of same-gender sexual contact among men. *Science, 243,* 338-348.

Frayser, S. G. (1985). *Varieties of sexual experience: An anthropological perspective on human sexuality.* New Haven, CT: HRAF Press.

Goffman, E. (1963). *Stigma: Notes on the management of spoiled identity.* Englewood Cliffs, NJ: Prentice-Hall, Inc.

Goldin, C. S. (1984). The community of the blind: Social organization, advocacy and cultural redefinition. *Human Organization, 43,* 121-131.

Goldstein, M. C., & Beall, C. M. (1981). Modernization and aging in the third and fourth world: Views from the rural hinterland in Nepal. *Human Organization, 40,* 48-55.

Gunby, P. (1993). Polio plus: Poliomyelitis eradication by year 2005. *Journal of the American Medical Association, 269,* 15-16.

Harris, A. P. (1990). Race and essentialism in feminist legal theory. *Stanford Law Review, 42,* 581-616.

Hazan, H. (1982). Beyond disengagement: A case study of segregation of the aged. *Human Organization, 41,* 355-359.

Henry, J. (1963). *Culture against man.* New York: Random House.

Holmes, L. D., & Holmes, E. R. (1992) *Samoan Village,* 2nd ed. New York: Holt, Rinehart, & Winston (first published 1974)

Holmes, L. D. (1978). *Coming of old age in Samoa.* (77 color slides, narration cassette, and script. 32 minutes). Wichita, KS: Poly Concepts.

Hutchinson, J. (1992). AIDS and racism in America. *Journal of the National Medical Association, 84,* 119-124.

Ingstad, B., & Whyte, S. R. (1995). *Disability and culture.* Berkeley: University of California Press.

Kaufman, S. R. (1986). *The ageless self: Sources of meaning in late life.* New York: New American Library (Meridian Books).

Kinsey, A. C., Pomeroy, W. B., & Martin, C. E. (1948). *Sexual behavior in the human male.* Philadelphia: Saunders.

Kinsey, A. C., Pomeroy, W. B., Martin, C. E., & Gebbard, P. H. (1953). *Sexual behavior in the human female.* Philadelphia: Saunders.

Kleinman, A. (1980). *Patients and healers in the context of culture: An exploration of the borderland between anthropology, medicine, and psychiatry.* Berkeley: University of California Press.

Kottak, C. P. (1990). *Prime-time society: An anthropological analysis of television and culture.* Belmont, CA: Wadsworth Publishing Co.

Lambert, E. D. (1978). *Modern medical mistakes.* Bloomington: Indiana University Press.

Lang, N. G. (1991). Stigma, self-esteem, and depression: Psycho-social responses to risk of AIDS. *Human Organization, 50,* 66-72.

Leonard, T. L. (1990). Male clients of female street prostitutes: Unseen partners in sexual disease transmission. *Medical Anthropology Quarterly, 4,* 41-55.

Lévi-Strauss, C. (1994). Symbolic reenactment of an earlier reception. *Anthropology Newsletter 35* (1), 3.

McGrath, J. W. (1992). The biological impact of social responses to the AIDS epidemic. *Medical Anthropology, 15,* 63-79.

Marwick, C. (1993). Vaccine program advisory committee sticks Secretary Lee with plan to fix vaccination system. *Journal of the American Medical Association, 269,* 2062-2063.

Murphy, R. F. (1987). *The body silent.* New York: Henry Holt

Naroll, R. (1983). *The moral order.* Beverly Hills, CA: Sage.

Neugarten, B. L. (Ed.). (1968). *Middle age and aging.* Chicago: University of Chicago Press.

Parker, R. (1987). Acquired immunodeficiency syndrome in urban Brazil. *Medical Anthropology Quarterly, 1,* 155-175.

Page, J. B., Chitwood, D. D., Smith, P. C., Kane, N., & McBride, D.C. (1990). Intravenous drug use and HIV infection in Miami. *Medical Anthropology Quarterly, 4,* 56-71.

Randall, T. (1993). Demographers ponder the aging of the aged and await unprecedented looming elder boom. *Journal of the American Medical Association, 269,* 2331-2332.

Scheper-Hughes, N. (Ed.). (1987). *Child survival: Anthropological perspectives on the treatment and maltreatment of children.* Dordrecht: D. Reidel.

Schiller, N. G. (1992). What's wrong with this picture? The hegemonic construction of culture in AIDS research in the United States. *Medical Anthropological Quarterly, 6,* 237–254.

Schneider, J., & Conrad, P. (1983). *Having epilepsy.* Philadelphia: Temple University Press.

Schoepf, B. G. (1992). AIDS, sex and condoms: African healers and the reinvention of tradition in Zaire. *Medical Anthropology, 14,* 225–242.

Sibthorpe, B. (1992). The social construction of sexual relationships as determinant of HIV risk perception and condom use among injection drug users. *Medical Anthropological Quarterly, 6,* 255–270.

Singer, M., Flores, C., Davison, L., Burke, G., Castillo, Z., Scanlon, K., & Rivera, M. (1990). SIDA: The economic, social, and cultural context of AIDS among Latinos. *Medical Anthropological Quarterly, 4,* 72–114.

Singer, M., Zhongke, J., Schensul, J. J., Weeks, M., & Page, J. B. (1992). AIDS and the IV drug user: The local context in prevention efforts. *Medical Anthropology, 14,* 285–306.

Wilson, P. J. (1992). *Oscar: An inquiry into the nature of sanity.* Prospect Heights, IL: Waveland Press. (Original work published 1947)

Chapter 13

THE HEALTH OF WOMEN

THE TWO CULTURES OF EVERY SOCIETY

How astonishing that until quite recently anthropologists managed to collect data and theorize in terms of an essentialist assumption that was false and misleading. The assumption was that every society had its culture, which was referred to as "the culture." Anthropologists thought and wrote about the culture of the Navajo, the Toda (a tribe in India), the Yoruba (an ethnic group in Nigeria), or Tzintzuntzan (a village in Mexico).

Incorporated into some (but not all) of these studies was some useful information about women. Many of the most important anthropologists were women who wrote at least in part about women, as did Margaret Mead in writing about girls in Samoa. A lot that is known about women's lives from a cross-cultural perspective is based on the writings of Ruth Benedict, Ruth Bunzel, Lela O'Neale, Zora Neale Hurston, Cora DuBois, Laura Thomson, Hortense Powdermaker, Ruth Landes, Monica Wilson, Irawati Karve, and many others. However, for the most part, even these anthropologists failed to communicate the extent to which women's cultures everywhere are deeply and pervasively different from those of men. It was thought that women did feminine things and men did masculine things, but the two were united by commonalities of beliefs, values, attitudes, and family life. That unexamined assumption vastly overrated the sharedness of those commonalities, real though they may be.

Not all anthropologists were equally misled, to be sure. Six decades ago, Gregory Bateson captured the essence of this difference based upon his work on the Naven ritual among the Iatmul people of New Guinea (Bateson, 1958 [1936]). He described a process of differentiation (schismogenesis) whereby male and female Iatmul not only were not the same in cultural values and behavior, but also whenever culture change took place, it took place in such a way that male and female cultures became increasingly and more deeply different.

It is now clear that even a comparatively small and homogeneous society is made up of plural cultures (also known as subcultures), of which male and female are the two most impressive components (but which include others, such as the cultures of childhood, youth, old age, sexual orientation, ableness, crafts, professions, and so on). Further, individuals vary in the extent to which they adhere to the cultural norms deemed appropriate to their assigned statuses in any given society.

A feminist sociologist, Mirra Komarovsky, looking back to Margaret Mead's *Sex and Temperament in Three Primitive Societies* (1935) as an early precursor of the new feminist scholarship, and referring to her own work since the 1950s as well, writes of how more recent feminist scholars have explored "the distinctiveness of the female worlds [in the plural] (since these differ by class, race, ethnicity, sexual preference, and other features)." "To be born a woman means to inhabit, from early infancy to the last day of life, a psychological world which differs from the world of men," Kamarovsky stated in 1953. "Much has changed since that time, but it is still unrealistic to deny that men and women continue to live in different worlds" (Komarovsky, 1991, p. 22; see also Mead, 1950 [1935]).

It is now easy to see that anthropologists understood less about the cultures of women than was thought. In spite of commonalities, women are thoroughly different from men in biology and culture. It is essential that one grasp this point in order to understand women's health issues. The biocultural perspective will guide us as we explore health from a gender perspective.

GIRLS FROM BIRTH TO PUBERTY

Just getting born is more problematic for a girl than for a boy. Abortion is practiced in many societies, often with dangerous and uncertain outcomes. However, the practice of abortion in medical offices has been blind to gender until quite recently. Abortion as a traditional means of population control contrasts with infanticide, because the latter does permit gender discrimination. The custom of killing newborn babies, or of providing so little food and care that small children die of neglect, is widespread. Where postnatal infanticide and negligent homocide are practiced, they almost invariably target girls. Using the HRAF, Marvin Harris and W. T. Divale determined that societies characterized by warfare are particularly prone to terminate girls (Divale & Harris, 1976). For children under the age of fifteen, the ratio of boys to girls is 127 to 100 in societies that attribute high status to warriors. One would expect only 106 boys to 100 girls if each sex were given equal opportunities to survive. (More boys are conceived because the natural fertilization process slightly favors the male conceptus.)

With the technology of ultrasound visualization, it is now possible to determine the sex of the embryo towards the end of the first trimester of pregnancy. Parents may elect to abort if they are not pleased with what they learn. An extreme was reached in one city in the People's Republic of China, where ultrasound testing was used to determine sex. In that city, only 25 percent of all births in 1992 were girls. Nearly half (1,006) of 2,316 pregnancies were aborted in another city that same year because the parents did not want girls (Associated Press, June 22, 1993)

MENARCHE

Every girl normally will experience a period of two or three years (puberty) when physical changes occur that transform her into an adult. The age of onset is not the same for all, since the timing of puberty is responsive to general health, nutrition, life circumstances, and genes. In urban-industrial nations, the age at which puberty begins is earlier than in more traditional societies, but everywhere, the early pubertal experience of breast budding and pubic hair is usually followed around two years later by menarche (the first experience of menstruation). Menarche on the average occurs at age sixteen-and-half among the !Kung San, for example. This is late compared to American girls at an average age of twelve-and-half years (Shostak, 1983, p. 150). Physiologically, puberty culminates processes that involve DNA, the cerebral cortex, the midbrain, the pituitary gland, many hormones, fatty acids, the mammary glands, ovaries, the uterus, and the vagina. The complexity of these changes is remarkable. Culturally, menarche is celebrated in many societies by a rite of passage that marks this stage in life as that moment when society recognizes that the girl has become a woman and will experience monthly periods for decades to come.

FEMALE CIRCUMCISION IN THE UNITED STATES

When Americans give thought to circumcision, they usually assume it is practiced only on males, and if they know something about female circumcision, they are most likely to identify it as foreign. For this reason, we need to review a bit of recent American history. Clitoridectomies (cutting off the clitoris) were in fact carried out in the English-speaking world as a way to stop masturbation, which was thought to cause a common culture-bound Victorian disorder known as hysteria. This surgery was carried out by amputating part or all of the clitoris. Although done from time to time earlier in the 1800s, the practice became more common after mid-century, popularized and practiced by Isac Baker Brown, an English gynecological surgeon (Cutner, 1985). E. Wallerstein says this about Brown and his operation on young women:

> It is not clear precisely when Dr. Brown "invented" cliteridectomy and when he began to practice the surgery. . . . It is possible that several hundred or

perhaps several thousand such surgeries were performed. What is clear is that Dr. Brown was seeking a surgical solution to the vexing mental disorders of women. According to the doctor, the main culprit was masturbation. . . . The treatment was clitoridectomy. (Wallerstein, 1980, p. 173)

In some cases girls were also infibulated (pierced) at the prepuce, again to prevent masturbation (*Infibulation*, from fibula, meaning a clasp resembling a safety pin that was used by the ancient Greeks and Romans to fasten clothing). Extremists added surgical excision of the ovaries (oöphorectomy), castrating thousands of girls before the practice was abandoned around 1880. Infibulation was not abandoned until 1905.

Clitoridectomy proved more durable, since it was thought to prevent a range of mental and physical disorders:

In 1897 a Boston surgeon maintained that contrary to men, "the sexuality of the young woman does not reside in the sexual organs." He therefore contended that orgasm in women was an ailment and removal of erectile organs like the clitoris was a necessity. A number of doctors resorted to excision for treating epilepsy, catalepsy, hysteria, melancholy, and even kleptomania. It was performed in mental hospitals until 1935. (Lightfoot-Klein, 1989, p. 180)

Excision of the clitoris was also performed by some surgeons in the 1930s and even into the 1940s as a cure for masturbation as well as to prevent what were perceived as lesbian tendencies. "My mother," as one American woman recalled about her babyhood in the late 1940s, "was fanatically obsessed with the idea that masturbation was the ultimate sin. When found guilty of this erotic pastime at the age of three, I was taken to a doctor. . . . He cut off the outer portion of my clitoris because it was 'too large' and therefore causing arousal" (cited in Lightfoot-Klein, 1989, p. 181).

Clitoridectomies are no longer authorized as a standard of practice in the United States. Some women choose to undergo piercing and infibulation of body parts, including the external genitalia, but surgeons have abandoned genital alternation. Or, have they? Hysterectomies (with or without removal of the ovaries) have almost become a stage in the contemporary woman's life cycle. By sixty years of age more than one out of every three American women will have submitted to a removal of the uterus (Carlson, Nichols, & Schiff, 1993). The justification is supposedly based upon sound medical reasoning. In most cases, however, the medical reasoning is not beyond question, since the surgeries are often performed to relieve unpleasant symptoms or to improve the quality of life, for example, as a cure for pelvic pain. One detects here a lingering vestige of antiquated thinking, as when one of my colleagues, a surgeon, advised his sister, a college professor, that since her family was complete, her severe menstrual cramps were reason enough to undergo this surgery. The uterus had become a useless organ, he believed, that could only cause trouble by permitting an unwanted pregnancy or possibly by becoming a seedbed of cancer. His attitude is not uncommon. It has been demonstrated that "in many regions of the United States more than 40 percent of the hysterectomies and oöphorectomies have involved removal of *normal* organs." One investigation concluded that, "the track record for hysterectomies was dismal. Of 148 procedures reviewed, 64, or 43 percent, were deemed unjustified" (cited in Seaman & Seaman, 1977, p. 308).

FEMALE CIRCUMCISION IN AFRICA

In a wide latitudinal band that stretches from sub-Saharan West Africa to the east and northeast parts of the continent, girls in infancy or at puberty undergo genital surgeries. The procedures range in magnitude from a mere scarring or cutting away of the prepuce to excision of the clitoris and, particularly in the Sudan, pharaonic circumcision. These procedures emerged in African history entirely without connection to female circumcision in the English-speaking world. Herodotus wrote of female genital surgery 2500 years ago as a practice of Egyptians, Phoenicians, and Hittites and its presence in the Sudan is known to us from as early as a sixteenth-century document (Lightfoot-Klein, 1989, p. 28).

Pharaonic circumcision is performed on girls usually between the ages of four and eight. Based on interviews with over three thousand women in northern Sudan, Asma El Dareer estimated that 99 percent were circumcised. Of these, approximately 83 percent had submitted to pharaonic circumcision (El Dareer, 1982).

From a surgical (etic) point of view, pharaonic circumcision is a brutal operation. Although details may vary, the following is extracted from the notes of one observer (cited in Lightfood-Klein, 1989, p. 53; see also Barclay, 1964; Hayes, 1975; Messing, 1980; Gordon, 1991). Since no anesthesia is employed, the little girl must be completely immobilized for fifteen to twenty minutes by several women who hold her as tightly as they can, her arms behind her back, her legs spread apart. The old midwife, after muttering "Allah is great and Mohammed is his Prophet, May Allah keep away all evils," swiftly cuts out the clitoris with a razor blade. She then applies the razor to the small lip (labia minora), cutting it off along one side from top to bottom after which the inner part of the vulva (labia majora) is pared down. The other side is then excised in similar fashion. The outer remnants of the two sides of the vulva are subsequently pulled together and secured. Referred to as infibulation, this pulling together is achieved by piercing the remaining labial tissue with three or four long acacia thorns held in place by winding sewing thread or horsehair around each of the ends of each thorn. The edges of the wounds eventually grow together to form a tough scar and a "clean-looking" smooth surface. A very small opening is left for the passage of urine and, eventually, of menstrual exudate.

Several health consequences derive from this practice. It can be difficult to urinate, requiring ten or fifteen minutes on the average to empty the bladder. Menstrual flow is severely impeded. The flow typically takes ten agonizing days or more to complete. Urinary tract infections, kidney disease, and pelvic inflammatory disease commonly ensue. Not infrequently, the small opening occludes and has to be cut open again. Gynecological examinations remain impossible for years at a time, including pap smears to detect early cancer of the cervix. At marriage, the husband must force open the scar of his bride. Even with the assistance of a small knife, defloration can last for painful weeks and months. Sensual response in sexual intercourse is commonly, but not always, absent or diminished. The massive scar tissue covering the outlet of the vagina makes childbirth a nightmare of tearing and episiotomies. Stillbirths and infant trauma are common. During the last generation it has become customary to reinfibulate after each birth, so that the agonies of the bridal period must be endured again after each birth when coitus is resumed (Toubia, 1994).

For most of the women involved, particularly for uneducated women, much pain, illness, and dyspareunia (painful sexual intercourse) are endured without apparent awareness that it is caused by circumcision. Women commonly seem to think of their suffering as normal, since all of the women they know have been circumcised and suffer similarly. However, educated Sudanese men and women do see the connection. They acknowledge the validity of health-related arguments against the practice. Yet, even the daughters of sociopolitical leaders continued for many years (and many still do) to be circumcised, although often at the hands of surgeons who used anesthetics and sterile technique. Urged on by an informed political elite, the pharaonic procedure was declared unlawful in 1947 in Egypt. Sudanese physicians as a body agreed to oppose it after an international conference was convened in Khartoum in 1979 to seek consensus relating to traditional practices affecting the health of women and children. Change is taking place, but it is slow and limited largely to daughters in privileged families.

The persistence of pharaonic circumcision has become a discomfiting issue for applied anthropologists. What should feminist and/or applied anthropologists do? Noting that the custom is becoming more rather than less widespread, one anthropologist wrote "Applied anthropologists, however, cannot evade the issue of such a serious and widespread problem as genital mutilation of females." Yet, what are they to do?

Daniel Gordon, at the time a medical student as well as a graduate student in anthropology, acknowledged this dilemma from both anthropological and medical perspectives. He wrote of "the ambivalence implicit in medical anthropology as both nonjudgmentally descriptive and experiential, on the one hand, and a practical adjunct to medicine and public health, on the other" (Gordon, 1991, p. 4). This is the issue of cultural relativism, which means that in order to understand a given practice, we need to view it in terms of the cultural context in which it occurs. As Clifford Barnett explains, "This does not mean that we have to 'accept' the practice as 'good' once we have achieved that understanding. After all, when anthropologists work with Western medical teams to provide those aspects of our technology which may be helpful or life-saving to people, we are saying we have something 'better' to offer than they have" (Barnett, 1994). In identifying the harmful effects of circumcision, for example, cultural relativism does not stop an anthropologist from informing people of the harm it does and to encourage them to choose to discontinue the practice.

Faye Ginsburg, an American anthropologist, points out, however, that such judgments can be more elusive than one might think. Asking for greater sensitivity to cultural contexts, she notes that the issue of female circumcision in Egypt and the Sudan poses "one of the strongest challenges to anthropology's central tenet of cultural relativism" (Ginsburg, 1991 p. 17; see Schroeder, 1994). She draws on contemporary feminist theory to make a very important point based on a critique of gender essentialism. Earlier, we saw that essentialism in Western feminist theory is the unexamined belief that women have so much in common that differences among them based on diversities of race, ethnicity, and SES are relatively unimportant. Women scholars of color have successfully challenged this unwarranted assumption (Harris, 1990; Morgan, 1989). Ginsburg adds her perspective to the anthropological debate. "[F]eminist theory has gradually shed its Eurocentric biases and expanded its own theory and practice to take into account the experience of women as socially constituted and culturally embodied agents, with different positions over the life course and with concerns that are sensitive to changing contexts" (Ginsburg, 1991, p. 18). She recommends that we document the views of the women involved and work strenuously to understand how they, the supposed victims of the practice, usually are also its strongest advocates. Anthropologists need to use their scholarship and activism in ways that will help improve dialogue among activists involved at local, national, and international levels. Anthropologists need to collaborate rather than direct, to listen rather than lecture, and to use their ethnographic skills to identify and elucidate the ethnic contexts that shape personal and societal decisions in this complex yet sensitive area of personal choice and personal hygiene.

THE BODY

The circumcised (scarified, amputated, tattooed, pierced) individual unequivocally illustrates a new and important direction taken by anthropologists in the last couple of years. In the words of two historians, Catherine Gallagher and Thomas Laqueur,

> Scholars have only recently discovered that the human body itself has a history. Not only has it been perceived, interpreted, and represented differently in different epochs, but it has also been lived differently, brought into being within widely dissimilar material cultures, subjected to various technologies and means of control, and incorporated into different rhythms of production and consumption, pleasure and pain. (Gallager & Laqueur, 1987, vii)

Anthropologists in particular have begun to think of "the body as a site on which culture and society shape ways of seeing and being" (Lock & Young, 1993, p. 24). Culture affects one's body, can be seen in one's body, and is expressed by one's body. In the seventeenth century, René Descartes introduced the notion that the body and the mind were distinct entities. "Western culture has long had a tendency to dichotomize the life of the body and the life of the mind," according to Alma Gottlieb and Thomas Buckley. "A corollary in the medical field," they add, "is the proclivity for assigning the causes of given diseases as lying in either the mind *or* the body but not in both" (Buckley & Gottlieb, 1988, p. 43). Body and mind dualism eroded for the last and current generation of physicians and scientists, however, as it became common to speculate more in terms of psychosomatic and somatopsychic connections. Nonetheless, in anthropology as an outgrowth of the 1960s (and simultaneously in other social sciences and the humanities) culture has been described and defined for the most part in mentalistic terms ("the idea that cultures were systems of symbols and meanings," as Milton Singer put it) (Singer, 1980, p. 486). Now, some anthropologists are talking about "new thinking on the body" (Sobo & Brodwin, 1993).

In an effort to turn this new line of thinking about the body-mind (the mindful body) into a comprehensive paradigm that hopefully would give structure to the field of medical anthropology, Nancy Scheper-Hughes and Margaret Lock identified three ways of conceptualizing the body as ways to frame inquiry: the social body, the body politic, and the body-self (Scheper-Hughes & Lock, 1987).

THE SOCIAL BODY

This is the symbolic body. In Western science, women historically were caught in a catch-22 (damned if you do, damned if you don't) dilemma. The woman's body and mind were regarded as inferior to those of a man. They were physically weaker, and, it seemed to follow, intellectually weaker. Men were credited with a higher capacity for reason and science, while women were limited to the realms of emotions and morality. Because they were thought to be inferior, their proper sphere of activity was said to be the home. Women were excluded from public life, and not the least from higher (especially medical and scientific) education. As a consequence (catch-22), they were not in a position to investigate and challenge the assumptions used to justify their supposed inferiority.

If we look only at recent (eighteenth- and nineteenth-century) Euro-American history, we see that scientists debated opposing views of the body social of women:

- Apart from genitalia, male and female are the same (i.e., biological differences are superficial).
- Sexual differences penetrate every part of the body. (Schiebinger, 1987, p. 51)

In the context of this debate, late eighteenth century anatomists for the first time began to produce drawings of female skeletons as different from male. The nature of these drawings had striking symbolic and political implications. As

Londa Schiebinger put it, "If sex differences could be found in the skeleton, then sexual identity would no longer be a matter of sex organs appended to a neutral human body, as Vesalius had thought, but would penetrate every muscle, vein, and organ attached to and molded by the skeleton" (Schiebinger, 1987, p. 53). As an historian, Schiebinger documents the popularity and accepted authenticity of an interpretation of the female body as incomplete and deviant compared to that of the male. The favored early nineteenth-century view depicted the female skeleton, heavily laden with cultural values, as distinguished by the following traits:

- skull and brain smaller
- hips broader
- rib cage narrower and more confined
- spine more curved
- buttocks area and pelvis larger

Some anatomists concluded that these differences were of a magnitude sufficient to demonstrate that women, together with children and "primitive" peoples, had to be regarded as representative of a lower stage of evolution. It followed, shifting not so subtly to the body politic, that women and other races were fit only for lesser roles in society. August Comte, a powerful figure in the nineteenth-century growth of sociology and anthropology, epitomized how the culturally constructed woman's body was used to justify thorough social and political inferiority to the idealized male. He argued that a healthy society demanded what biology justified and required, which is that women should be subservient to men (Schiebinger, 1987, p. 63–69).

Nineteenth-century medical and philosophical textbooks on anatomy and on the nature of womanhood followed suit. They underwrote a shift in health care from childbirth as the domain of midwives to childbirth and women's health as best achieved by men midwives and male gynecologist-obstetricians. Women were not thought capable of being trained adequately in these fields of women's health. "The 'natural' inequalities between men and women seemed to justify social inequalities between the two sexes," Schiebinger concluded. "Many believed that the social order parallels the natural order." She makes a final comment that is important always to keep in mind: The biomedical sciences are not neutral. They are not free of cultural influence. "Science too has been shaped by social forces" (Schiebinger, 1987, pp. 70–72).

THE BODY POLITIC

This is the body that matters in economic and governmental realms. Critical medical anthropologists frame research in terms of the national and international political and economic power relationships that impact on health. However, power negotiations can also be identified at the level of the body as we have just seen. Thinking along these lines owes much to French philosopher Michel Foucault. It was he who particularly indicated that

Western scholarship demonstrates a bias for visual experience and the visual authentication of experience (ocularcentrism).

Foucault described the history of European medicine and psychiatry as an emergence in modern times of what he called the clinical gaze (Foucault, 1965 [1961]; 1973 [1963]; Jay, 1986). This gaze is a way of looking that sees the patient as having a disease and as subordinate, therefore, to the authority (disciplinary power, behavioral norms) of doctors (male doctors, as we have just noted). Foucault led anthropologists into an awareness hitherto lacking of how this way of looking validated a power relationship.

THE BODY-SELF

This is the body that feels sick and in pain or well and pain-free. Anthropologists have barely begun to explore culture as bodily sensations and to do fieldwork employing a methodology of "embodied awareness," as Robert Desjarlais has put it (1992). Research on the body-self is implicit in studies of pain, since severe pain so overwhelms consciousness and so dominates psychoneuroimmunological interactions that it is almost always experienced as a monism of embodied awareness.

THE BODY-SELF IN PAIN

We have long known that the subjective experience of pain is powerfully contoured by culture. Mark Zborowski, an anthropologist, demonstrated this between 1951 and 1954 in a study of responses to pain among men in a veteran's hospital in New York (Zborowski, 1969). He found that Old Americans accepted pain without complaint. (Old Americans were defined as having lived in the New World for so many generations that they no longer had any ties with their countries of origin in the Old World.) Irish Americans in this study also accepted pain without complaint. The two groups differed greatly in how they experienced the meaning of pain, however.

To understand the pain behavior of the Old American, one needs to distinguish private from public pain. In private, an Old American left alone might collapse into tears, but never in public. The Old American tended, therefore, to withdraw in the face of strong pain. In the hands of doctors and nurses, however, to admit to pain was permitted because the professional situation transformed complaints into purposeful discussion. Possessing a mechanistic attitude to the body and its function, the Old American had considerable faith in the abilities of doctors and tended therefore to be fairly optimistic about ultimate outcomes.

Irish-American patients, equally uncomplaining when in pain, differed from Old Americans in how they felt about their illnesses. They lacked the optimism of Old Americans. In public, an Irish patient masked pain; but this was also done when talking to medical practitioners. This patient articulated pain concerns very ineptly, mumbling and bumbling along. What a surprise, since under other circumstances the Irish can be expected to display notable loquacious skill. The Irish-American felt helpless, guilty about becoming ill, and very pessimistic about the future.

Zborowski also described two kinds of patients who contrasted greatly with the stoic Old Americans and Irish. Italian-American and Jewish-American veterans tended to display highly emotional responses. They groaned and cried. They complained. They lay in wait to provide any and all a description in redundant detail of how they suffered. They shared a cultural trait that permits vivid expressions of pain, yet their pain behavior rested on very different emotional foundations.

The Jewish patient tended to experience a future-oriented anxiety. Pain was taken as a frightening warning of ultimate possible doom. This patient needed reassurance from the doctor, who found it almost impossible to evade listening to a recital of complaints that seemed endless. But this same patient was also skeptical toward the doctor and reluctant to take prescribed medications. He worried that the pills might provide only temporary improvement, but succeed in disguising symptoms in a way that could mislead the physician. He feared becoming addicted to pain-killing drugs. Experiencing pain and suffering, it was the suffering that was overwhelming. Jewish pain, as identified in this study, tended to be associated with powerful existential concerns and ultimate escatological issues.

The Italian-American was equally vocal. In place of skepticism, however, this patient showed great trust in doctors and hospitals. In place of a future orientation, the Italian experienced a present-oriented apprehension. The focus was on pain as such. In complete trust, he accepted, indeed, begged for strong analgesics to quiet the pain. As soon as the pain was gone, this patient became calm, full of smiles, and almost forgetful of the illness.

The work of Zborowski was carried out half a century ago. His characterizations resemble stereotypes rather than quantified generalizations. One would set different standards for this kind of research now, including:

- more precision about the nature and quality of the pain
- refinements in ethnic identity, since some of these veterans were immigrants while others were third-generation Americans
- search for intra-ethnic variation unbiased by prior assumptions about-expectable cultural uniformity
- control for socioeconomic status, education, age, and other possible-sources of variance that might be confused with ethnicity
- not the least, such a study should include women

In the last few years another anthropologist, Maryann Bates, has done these necessary things in several questionnaire-based research projects designed to explore the relationship between pain and ethnicity. In one of these studies, chronic pain patients from six ethnic groups were compared. The first three cohorts, it should be noted, were younger generations of three of those studied by Zborowski.

1. Old Americans (n=100)
2. Irish (n=60)
3. Italians (n=50)
4. Hispanics (n=44)
5. French Canadians (n=90)
6. Polish (n=28)

In this study, Bates, Edwards, and Anderson confirm that how people respond to pain is shaped in part by ethnic heritage. In their own words, "experiences, beliefs, attitudes and meanings derived from growing up with these social communities may affect one's reported perception of pain intensity." Consistent with that observation, they found that Hispanics and Italians reported high pain intensity, Old Americans and Irish subjects were intermediate, while Poles and French Canadians reported the lowest scores (Bates, Edwards, & Anderson, 1993, p. 106).

And what of stereotypes about men and women in pain? Are women the weaker sex who cannot take as much pain as men? Are they the stoic sex who suffer more and complain less? It is important to realize that within the ethnic categories identified in this study, Bates and associates found no variation associated with gender in reported pain intensity. In assimilating that finding, it is important to realize that one cannot generalize on the basis of one or a few research reports.

The fact is, men and women may vary, but again, based on cultural rather than biological variables. On the one hand, one study demonstrated that women showed less tolerance for experimental pain than did men (Woodrow et al., 1972). On the other hand, Bates and colleagues in recent work in Puerto Rico found that men there cope less well with pain than do women. In the Puerto Rican case, the difference appears to be related to differences in male and female cultures. Men suffer depression and a loss of self-esteem, particularly when they are unable to work or be physically active because of their pain. Several Puerto Rican chronic pain subjects attempted suicide or thought about it. Women, suffering the same severity of pain, handled it more successfully. Bates and her fellow investigators conclude that gender role expectations set by ethnic heritage make it more difficult for men than for women to cope successfully with severe chronic pain in this culture (Bates et al., 1994).

Based upon research on the body in pain as shaped by different cultures, a caution is in order:

> We stress that ethnic [and gender] stereotyping is as dangerous as inattention to cultural variables. . . . There is significant intragroup variation in our study, and others have found significant intragroup variation in other populations of pain

sufferers. Clinicians must acknowledge that not all patients are alike, that pain does not have the same meaning and significance for different patients, and that patients may exhibit different coping strategies and different responses to pain and to treatments provided. If clinicians are to treat multiethnic [and gender differentiated] chronic pain sufferers successfully, they must be able to unlock the "illness reality" of each particular patient and thereby provide more humane and personal care and treatment. (Bates & Edwards, 1992, p. 80)

MENSTRUATION

The neglect of embodied awareness in research is highlighted by Gottlieb and Buckley, who observe that actual individual physical experiences of menstruation have received very little anthropological attention (Buckley & Gottlieb, 1988, p. 40). Only occasionally does one encounter generalizations that move in the direction of body-self descriptions, and even they tend to neglect intracultural variability. In *Coming of Age in Samoa,* for example, Mead observed that it was unusual for a young woman to complain of menstrual pain, which at worst "were in no sense comparable to severe cases of menstrual cramps in our civilization" (Mead, 1961 [1928], p. 145). She also very briefly summarized cultural practices that impact on a young woman while she has her period, noting that they were minimal:

> She cannot make tafolo, a breadfruit pudding usually made by the young men in any case, nor make kava while she is menstruating. But she need retire to no special house; she need not eat alone; there is no contamination in her touch or look. (Mead, 1961 [1928], p. 81)

Marjory Shostak offers an overview for a South African people based on interviewing more than two hundred women through two menstrual cycles. Her findings are fascinating:

> The !Kung did not have any expectation or belief comparable to that held in the West of a premenstrual or menstrual syndrome. Nor did they recognize any effect of the menstrual cycle on women's moods or behavior. They were surprised when asked about it, saying that menstruation was such an unimportant event that it didn't deserve much concern. (I mentioned to one woman that women in my country are occasionally unhappy around the time of menstruation, and she suggested that it might be because their husbands were not having sex with them while they had their periods.) The women felt I was misguided: "Now, pregnancy must be what you mean; that's when a woman's behavior can turn strange." They did associate physical discomfort with menstruation, especially with its onset, but this discomfort, like the concern that others not see their menstrual blood, was described only in practical terms, not in terms of wider psychological ramifications. (Shostak, 1983, p. 353)

The biology of menstruation has also been taken for granted in most studies. Biological models are based on the Western experience. As Barbara Harrall has explained, regular menstrual periods may well be unusual urban-industrial societal effects that reflect low birthrates and short or absent interludes of nursing babies associated with the use of baby bottles (Harrell, 1981). Jane Lancaster adds to this perspective by noting that the widespread practice of nursing babies for several years, which interferes with ovulation and menstrual cycling, means that lactation rather than menstruation was probably the nearly continuous body-self experience of most women for 99 percent of human history (Lancaster, 1989, p. 99). Consider, for example, the old indigenous women of Australia, who, if we can believe what they told Diane Bell, "could remember each menstrual period of their fertile lives and count them on their fingers" (cited in Buckley & Gottlieb, 1988, p. 45). Nancy Howell found that menstruation was also rare among the !Kung San (Howell, 1979). This, however, is not consistant with what Nisa told Shostak when she reported that her mother, a !Kung San woman, "menstruated month after month, for a very long time" (Shostak, 1983, p. 78). Given this kind of inconsistency in reporting from the field, it would be prudent to wait for further studies to be carried out.

Anthropological interest in menstruation for the most part has emphasized the meanings (symbolism) attached to it. From many parts of the world we learn of rites of passage at the time of menarchy and of menstrual huts for periodic retreats. Until recently, it was assumed that taboos reflected a nearly universal sense of menstruation as polluting and dangerous. As Gottlieb and Buckley point out, we have moved away from that totalizing, monocausal assumption in favor of a far more sophisticated realization that menstrual practices are variable on both intercultural and intracultural levels, and they are multivalent, reflecting diverse causes and effects. However, menstruation as a component of the female body-self is clearly not self-evident and just begs for further study.

THE YEARS OF OVULATION-ASSOCIATED SEXUALITY

A woman's life between menarche and menopause is often referred to as her reproductive years. That phraseology is too limiting. True, in many nonindustrial societies as well as in some traditional American communities, nearly every woman gets married, has children, and confines her activities largely to the domestic sphere. Lancaster describes the reproductive strategy of women as an evolutionary force that shaped female lives and bodies around child-bearing and juvenile-nurturing roles for hundreds of thousands (millions) of years

(Lancaster, 1989). Michelle Rosaldo and Louise Lamphere took note of this some years ago, concluding that the pervasive subordination of women in societies around the world derives from their confinement to child-bearing and childrearing roles that keep them in the low-ranking domestic sphere. Under these conditions, the roles of women contrast with those of men who thrive in the powerful public sphere (Rosaldo & Lamphere, 1974). Women in the postmodern world have other options, now, so we do better to think of them in our time as hormonally but not necessarily reproductively driven.

The Body Beautiful: Corpulent or Thin?

From a cross-cultural perspective, the ideal type of female body may or may not incorporate values relating to body size. In some places where size matters, bigger women are more highly regarded. Claire Cassidy finds this ideal of beauty and appreciation so widespread that in looking at our society she wrote of "the 'thin' Anomaly" (Casidy, 1991). According to Cheryl Ritenbaugh, Americans have long thought that obesity was bad for one's health, that it was one's own fault due to overeating and lack of exercise, and that it was largely a matter of willpower to get slim and trim. That view is associated with a culture-bound disorder, anorexia/bulimia as well as health-related fads and fancies in foods and dieting (Nichter & Nichter, 1991).

On the other hand, a sedentary lifestyle in which food is consumed in excess of metabolic needs, and physical activities are insufficient to burn off excess calories, does result in excess weight. Based on interviews and medical examinations that included anthropometric measurements, height and weight were recorded for a nationally representative sample of adults twenty years of age or older (n=8260) (Kaczmarski et al., 1994). One-third of this sample was found to be overweight in a range that is at increased risk for weight-related health problems, including diabetes (NIDDM), high blood pressure, high cholesterol, heart disease, stroke, gout, sleep apnea, osteoarthritis, and some forms of cancer (Pi-Sunyer, 1994). Anthropologists and epidemiologists who attempt to frame the issue of body size and shape in biocultural terms recognize how complex the issue truly is. A multidisciplinary, holistic assessment "that can withstand the critique of each of the disciplines involved" still remains a goal rather than an achievement (Ritenbaugh, 1991).

The Woman Athlete

Very little anthropological research on the woman athlete has been published. Susan Graham, an anthropologist as well as an obstetrician-gynecologist, offers an exception. She summarized research reports since 1978 that demonstrate that strenuous exercise can result in menstrual failure (amenorrhea) and infertility. One study documented amenorrhea for women as follows:

- age-matched nonathletes, 2 percent
- runners, 26 percent
- swimmers, 12 percent
- cyclists, 12 percent (Graham, 1985)

Graham's literature summary will be useful primarily if it serves as a catalyst to medical anthropologists to design and carry out biocultural research on women in sports and physical activities.

Lesbian Health

Anthropological research on lesbian well-being is skimpy and limited to mental health. Sue-Ellen Jacobs and Christine Roberts provide a useful orientation in several ways. First, they urge that we view lesbianism not only or even primarily in sexual terms, but also in broader sociocultural terms. In addition, they find it helpful to differentiate sociocultural aspects of a lesbian identity into three categories (Jacobs & Roberts, 1989).

ADOLESCENT LESBIANS

One mental health issue concerns coming out and being publicly identified as lesbians. Getting shunned and rejected by the majority community can be psychologically painful, socially alienating, and economically devastating. Public self-identification can be especially stressful for teenage lesbians of color or ethnicity if they come out in their own communities.

MIDDLE-AGED LESBIANS

The choice of whether or not to be monogamous is conflictual. About one-fifth of lesbians are or become mothers. A lesbian family must deal with homophobia in addition to the many other problems that confront any family. Lesbians of color find prejudice compounded with racism.

OLDER LESBIANS

Homosexual women often maintain high morale and good self-esteem in old age, profiting from the support of close, enduring friendships.

Jacobs and Roberts should be given the final word:

> More research is sorely needed on lesbians. The amount and focus of the research done thus far appears to follow Western society's priorities: they focus mainly on white, able-bodied, younger middle-aged lesbians of middle- to upper-socioeconomic status. Nevertheless, lesbians of color, those with physical or other disabilities, or those who are poor or very young or elderly are especially

Claire Cassidy, her American-style grin irrepressible, dressed in appropriate "work clothes" while conducting a survey of mother and child growth in the Sahara Desert (Mauritania).

invisible to society, and they have double, triple, or more layers of discrimination with which to deal. Much more research is needed before the needs of lesbians can be responsibly dealt with by society. (Jacobs & Roberts, 1989, pp. 452–453)

The Bride and Young Wife

The young woman who marries into her husband's extended family or community (virilocality) follows a custom that is found in many parts of the world. Newly wed women in virilocal societies often suffer deprivation of food and rest, oppression within the family, and overwork, particularly early in their marriages.

Two anthropologists, John van Willigen and V. C. Channa, report that in India, the abuse of newly wed women may extend to murder. For example, one young woman accused of not bringing a large enough dowry was grabbed firmly from behind by her angry husband while her mother-in-law poured kerosene over her and set her ablaze. While dying in agony she was able to report her own murder to the police. "Bride-burning" or "dowry death" is routinely reported in newspapers of the subcontinent. It is usually claimed that the death occurred as a kitchen accident. Anthropologists need to give more attention to violence against women wherever it may occur as well as to specific issues relating to the health of recently married women (Van Willigen & Channa, 1991).

Sexually Transmitted Diseases (STDs)

To understand STDs we need to avoid essentialism. Sexuality and STD problems are obviously not the same for all women. Professional sex workers are at high risk. To a lesser extent, so are other women with multiple sex partners. Many women in stable relationships who incur no risks in their own behavior are seriously at risk without knowing it. This can happen if, without their knowledge, their partners have sex with other women, are bisexual, or are injecting drug users.

As concerns women's health issues, only tangential attention has been given to syphilis, gonorrhea, genital herpes, genital warts, chlamydia, and other sexually transmitted diseases. Yet, women are exposed differently and experience these diseases differently than men. Gonorrhea, for example, tends to be a relatively mild disease for men but can result in severe pelvic inflammatory disease and permanent infertility in women.

The risk for acquiring STDs, including AIDS, appears to be less for lesbians than for heterosexuals or bisexuals, but there is no room here for complacency. Although the numbers are relatively small, some women have been infected with HIV after having unprotected sex with other women. The total number of lesbians with AIDS appears to be seriously underreported. In part because the perceived risk is not great, very little has been done to educate lesbians about the need to adopt safe sex practices in coital activity with other women (Stevens, 1993). The need for anthropological research is great. Very little has been published by anthropologists about lesbian sex. "The role of sex toys, rough sex that damages tissue, exposure to menstrual blood, and practices such as cunnilingus in transmission of HIV between women is largely unexplored" (Cohen & Durham, 1993, p. 49).

Reproductive Health

Jane Lancaster brings a key point of view to the topic of women's reproductive health and fertility. Lancaster is a physical anthropologist whose perspective is that of evolutionary biology. She concerns herself with sexual maturation, fertility, female anatomy, and the processes of birthing, lactation, and parental investment in child care. From her biocultural perspective, it is basic to an understanding of these issues not to forget that the reproductive interests and strategies of men and women are different. I refer not merely to a male strategy biologically based on producing hundreds of thousands of sperm per ejaculation day after day in contrast with a female strategy based on producing an average of one ovum per month. Lancaster sees it as far more complex.

With regard to the reproductive strategies of female mammals, evolutionary theory predicts that since females bear the heavy biological burden of gestation, birth, and lactation, they should link their reproductive behavior to the availability of resources to carry the fertilized egg (zygote) and to care for the resultant child until it becomes an independent adult capable of reproduction when its own time arrives. The investment necessary to transform a zygote into an adult is especially heavy for female human beings, since their children are large, develop slowly, and in many societies need access to specialized resource bases (such as bride wealth, dowry, a homestead, or regular employment) in order to begin reproduction themselves. Hence, women face an even heavier burden than other female mammals in their need for reproductive resources. Lancaster records that women are characteristically active as decision makers when elemental behavioral patterns are involved, including such issues as the division of labor, family formation strategies, and parental investment patterns. In many ways they attempt to optimize their access to resources and their ability to produce healthy, competitive offspring (Lancaster, 1989, pp. 96–97).

Childbirth

By means of participant-observation, Brigitte Jordan recorded how childbirth takes place under medical management in the Netherlands, Sweden, and the United States (Jordan & Davis-Floyd, 1993). Obstetrical practices, which as scientific (culturally neutral) procedures ought to be the same in all three of these Western societies, in fact are found to differ. As concerns the use of pharmaceuticals for pain control, sedation, and speeding up of labor, for example, the Dutch use none at all in a normal birth, while in Sweden and even more so in the United States, all are used. Moreover, Swedish and American practices differ from each other in another way. The woman in Sweden has the dominant voice in deciding which medications to take and when, while in the United States the doctor is more in control. These differences and others constitute an impressive measure of how the medical management of childbirth is substantially determined by cultural beliefs, attitudes, and values.

Decisions and practices are not solely based on scientific knowledge. In the words of Faye Ginsburg and Rayna Rapp, "Strikingly different preferences with respect to labor-related anesthesia, home versus hospital births, birthing positions, and the use of neonatal intensive care make it clear that 'Western medicine' is not a monolithic category" (Ginsburg & Rapp, 1991, p. 321).

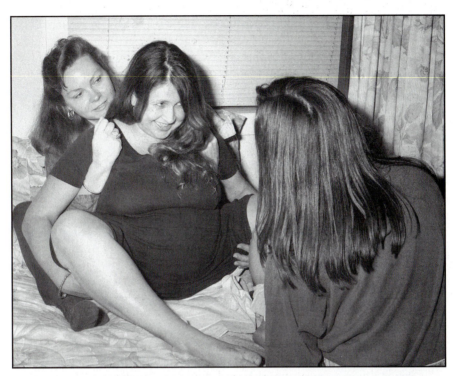

Robbie Davis-Floyd supports mother Sandie Phoenix as she prepares to push her baby out, attended by midwife Michele Fitzgerald during a home birth in Austin, Texas.

(Photo, Robert C. Steene)

Robbie Davis-Floyd pursued this impact of culture in her study of obstetrics in the United States (Davis-Floyd, 1992). Noting a massive paradigm shift signalled by the scientific revolution in the seventeenth century, she reminds us that the dominant belief system of Western society changed to the machine as a metaphor or model of the universe. This resulted in an American tendency to view the body as a machine and childbirth as a factorylike process, which is culture, not science.

Undertaking a symbolic analysis of standard obstetrical procedures, Davis-Floyd followed parturient women from the moment they reached the door of the hospital through the end of their first hour in the labor room. What follows is, in part, what she recorded.

- The woman is told she must proceed from the door of the hospital or clinic in a wheelchair. *Comment:* If she is able to walk to the door she probably can make it easily to the labor room, and almost all would prefer to walk.
- Her significant other is not permitted to be present while she changes into a hospital gown and is prepared for birth. *Comment:*

This should be her decision, since it is solely a matter of personal modesty.

- She is told to put on a hospital gown that is open at the back. *Comment:* This has a practical purpose since it is known to be clean. Also, it allows easy access to the genital area. Her own nightgown, as opposed to pajamas, actually would cause very little inconvenience to doctors and nurses, and cleanliness is easy to verify.

- Shaving the pubic hair. *Comment:* The reason usually given is that hair is hard to sterilize and vaginal surgery may be performed. This has the appearance of magical thinking, since the operative field is impossible to keep sterile no matter what is done. The woman's hair is probably no more a threat than the hair of her baby.

- She is given an enema. *Comment:* More magical thinking? It has never been demonstrated that this uncomfortable and somewhat degrading procedure confers any benefits. Fecal soiling commonly occurs whether or not an enema is given prior to delivery.

- She is confined to bed. *Comment:* It is much healthier to be up and moving about than to lie in bed while experiencing labor contractions and pain. She may be forced to lie on her back, however, because she is hooked up to a fetal monitor and an IV (intravenous) line, neither of which should be necessary in a normal birth.

- She is given nothing to eat while in labor. *Comment:* During hours of labor a woman needs nourishment, both carbohydrates and protein, to keep up her strength. That need ought to override medical concerns having to do with the remote though serious danger of inhaling vomitus in the event she is given a general anesthetic with food in her stomach.

- She is attached to an IV line for fluid replacement, sugar nutrition, and as a means for rapidly and efficiently administering tranfused blood or medications if such is required. *Comment:* A heparin lock, which is not attached to lines and equipment, would work just as well for emergency infusions, and the IV solution would not be required if she were fed.

Davis-Floyd also notes and evaluates an additional eighteen procedures followed as part of birthing and the immediate post-birth period. Her conclusion is that many of these medical procedures are difficult or impossible to justify in purely medical terms as necessary standard procedures for normal deliveries. However, in anthropological terms, Davis-Floyd demonstrates how they function as symbols that invert status relations, dramatizing that the doctor (often a man) is in charge and that the mother is made to be dependent and subordinate. Note the covert but powerful messages communicated just during the first hour in the hospital:

- *Wheelchair:* She is treated as though being pregnant has disabled her and she must be placed under the control of a hospital attendant.

- *Separation from significant other:* Her body is now claimed by the nurse on behalf of the hospital.
- *Hospital gown:* She loses a major symbol of her personal identity, her clothes. In their place the hospital gown symbolizes her loss of individual distinctiveness and of control over her most intimate private anatomy.
- *Pubic hair:* Shaving marks her further as institutional property, as a product of their technology rather than of her own body/mind.
- *Enema:* This further intensifies the symbolic conversion from private to institutional property. As is also true of her change of clothes and removal of pubic hair, the enema converts her symbolically from a woman who is dirty to an object they have made clean and suitable.
- *Bed:* Lying flat on her back, looking up at the looming figures of doctors and nurses, further intensifies unconscious messages that she is a patient and subordinate.
- *Fasting:* Food taboos are worldwide practices that symbolize the uncertain status of a person going through a rite of passage. Who is she, then, at this moment in her life? She is not even permitted to make a decision to eat food.
- *IV line:* By a kind of symbolic inversion, the woman, like her own baby, is attached by an umbilical cord to a powerful, life-giving, life-preserving source. She is made to be totally dependent on the hospital with its doctors and nurses.

The remaining eighteen procedures can be evaluated similarly in terms of medical needs and symbolic messages. In all eighteen, Davis-Floyd makes a strong case to support her contention that medical and surgical practices relating to normal birthing can be understood as metaphors of a technological or mechanistic worldview. They activate cultural attitudes that favor the subordination of women and the control of their reproductive powers.

Ginsburg and Rapp speak of hospital-based birth technologies as providing undeniable benefits, but at the expense of acquiescing to medical hegemony (Ginsburg & Rapp, 1991, p. 318). They place undeniable benefits in the balance, opposing natural birth to technological intervention. A timely obstetric intervention can stop a massive hemorrhage, salvage a disastrous delivery, or resuscitate a dying baby. The unresolved problem for American women and their newborn babies is how to make it possible for the great majority of births to take place naturally, with the woman in charge, and yet ensure access to rapid, expert medico-surgical intervention when it is urgently needed (Konner, 1987, pp. 226–228).

Midwifery offers a compromise solution. In the United States today, however, midwives face an uncertain future. Each state is different, but in general midwifery is reluctantly tolerated in mainstream medicine if it is done by certified nurse-midwives under medical supervision. It is not supposed to be done by midwives trained in apprenticeships. It is almost impossible in many places for midwives to get official certification, and often they find it hard to practice because malpractice insurance is prohibitively expensive or unavailable.

Underground practitioners abound. From time to time a midwife is hauled into court by the authorities for practicing medicine without a license. Yet, these women are capable of providing excellent care that is sensitive to women's bodies and feelings. One study reports that professional midwives in Taiwan interact well with the medical establishment in a modern context. They provide good maternity care to middle- and working-class mothers by adapting basic techniques of contemporary medical science to traditional birthing customs (Kang-Wang, 1980). If successful in Taiwan, why not in the United States?

Breast Disease

Cancer of the breast is a modern scourge of demoralizing dimensions. The incidence of breast cancer increased by 30 percent during the 1980s in the United States (Ries et al., 1991). Early detection provides some consolation. If the disease is discovered while it is still localized (nonmetastatic), the five-year survival rate is 93 percent (up from 78 percent in 1940) (Morain, 1993). Anthropologists have contributions to make. Anita Spring and Shae Kosch, for example, researched the extent to which women actually carry out recommended self-examinations of their breasts. They found that those who had been diagnosed with benign pathology were more likely to be consistent in self-examination than those with normal examinations (Spring & Kosch, 1982). Some work has been published on attitudes and practices relating to breast-feeding (Maher, 1992). Clearly, however, the opportunities and needs for anthropological research relating to the breast are enormous, including cross-cultural and class-stratified investigations to explore every aspect of mammary health and not solely the problem of early detection of cancer.

The Feminization of Poverty

Poverty is always associated with poorer health and less health care. Levels of poverty among American women are high and continue to increase. Poverty affects American women of color with an added vengeance (Mullings, 1989). It strikes harshly at immigrant women in the United States and at sweat shop workers in American-owned factories set up abroad to take advantage of low-paid labor (usually that of young women) (Ong, 1991). The health problems of poor women are multifaceted and offer many opportunities for anthropologists as ethnographic investigators, analysts, and reporters. Several studies illustrate our potential for this kind of work:

- Diana Gonzalez Kirby describes high stress and prescribed tranquilizer overuse by immigrant Cuban women in Florida (1989).

- Alicia Chavira-Prado has written about women and inadequate family health care in an undocumented Mexican migrant population in the United States (1992).
- Rebecca Doan and Barry Popkin describe how women in the Philippines whose incomes are below the median are more likely to have to work if they have several preschoolers, with deleterious consequences for family health (1993)

Women-centered research is at once a great need and an enormous opportunity. It is time that the health of women be given parity with that of men as funds are allocated for research as well as for prevention and treatment programs.

Menopause and Postmenopausal Health

Many people are confused about the technical meaning of the term *menopause*. It refers only to that time-limited process (the climacteric) when menstruation becomes irregular and then stops permanently. A woman is generally considered to have completed menopause after she has experienced one year without menses, although only if the process is age-related (or surgical) and is not a reversible amenorrhea due to other causes. We need, therefore, to distinguish two separate issues of health: menopause as a transient period in a woman's life, and postmenopausal health as distinguishing older women from younger women who are still in their fertile years.

Is menopause a condition associated with health problems? In the United States, one-half to three-fourths of all menopausal women suffer from hot flashes (a sensation of intense upper body warmth lasting from 30 seconds to 5 minutes). These uncomfortable episodes often interfere with restorative sleep, which in turn results in fatigue, irritability, and poor concentration. More than 85 percent of those who experience hot flashes complain of them for more than a year, many for as long as five years. With advancing age, hot flashes diminish in both intensity and frequency. However, until they end, many women find them so debilitating that they seek medical care. The usual treatment is hormone replacement with a regimen of estrogen and progestogen (Abrams, Berkow, & Fletcher, 1990, pp. 831–833).

The permanent cessation of ovarian function and of menses is a physiological universal for women who live long enough. How it is experienced, however, appears to be shaped culturally. Contrast the common American experience with that of an aging !Kung woman as described by her daughter Nisa:

> My mother . . . menstruated month after month, for a very long time. Then one month came and she didn't menstruate, then another and another. The months just passed her by and she was finished with the moon. (Shostak, 1983, p. 78)

Similarly, Margaret Lock reports from her fieldwork in Japan "that there was little concern about menopause until relatively recently, and the term that is used to express this concept was created at the turn of the century under the influence of German medicine" (Lock, 1988, p. 48). Since World War II, the medical and mass media in Japan have campaigned to medicalize menopause.

> However, despite the fact that the literature predicts a difficult time at menopause for many modern Japanese women, and suggests that medical treatment would be of help, its effect so far has been neither to ensure that the majority of women submit themselves to gynecological examinations, nor to stimulate a high rate of reporting of menopausal symptomatology. The mythical menopausal woman bears very little relationship to her living counterparts who, for the most part, do not find this part of the life cycle to be particularly trying (Lock, 1988, p. 44).

Postmenopausal health is another matter entirely. As far back in history as we know, the average age at menopause has apparently hovered around fifty-one years. Greater life expectancy now means that American women will spend about one-third of a lifetime after ovarian shutdown. Postmenopausal health issues will become increasingly prominant in urban-industrial societies (Abrams, Berkow & Fletcher, 1990, p. 832). These issues include:

- thinning of vaginal tissue and reduction in vaginal secretions contributing to painful sex
- osteoporosis which can progress to a broken hip (and death in some cases) as well as to spinal deformity ("the dowager's hump") or even compression fractures of spinal vertebrae (resulting in severe pain)
- atherosclerosis culminating in cardiovascular disease (heart attacks and strokes)

Aging men experience osteoporosis, but to a lesser extent. Men also experience atherosclerosis. The difference here is that women are protected against atherosclerosis-related diseases as long as they are producing estrogens, so what is a middle-aged problem for men is an old–age–related problem for women. Very little anthropological research has been devoted to these concerns of older women.

CONCLUSION

Having written this chapter on the health of women, should it be followed by a chapter on men? In fact, such a chapter would be a good thing to do if more space were available. It would include uniquely male issues such as the circumcision of boys, gay health (described in an earlier chapter), the climacteric, and prostate problems in aging men. On the whole, however, a chapter on men's health would be redundant of issues described in terms of other variables such as race, ethnicity, class, age, ableness, and so on. The fact is, most research in medicine, and most of what is published on health topics, is male-oriented and male-dominated. A special chapter on men's health is therefore optional, whereas a chapter on the health of women is virtually obligatory.

This is the last of the four chapters of Part II. They have described what anthropologists have learned about health, applying a biocultural model insofar as possible. In the three chapters of Part III, to which we now turn, interest shifts from health issues to prevention and treatment; from people who are ill, sick, or diseased (depending on the perspective) to people who are health care providers (healers in the widest sense of the term).

REFERENCES

Abrams, W. B., Berkow, R., & Fletcher, A. J. (Eds.). (1990). *The Merck manual of geriatrics.* Rahway, NJ: Merck & Co.

Associated Press, June 22, 1993.

Barclay, H. B. (1964). *Buurri al Lamaab.* Ithaca, NY: Cornell University Press.

Barnett, C. (1994). Personal communication.

Bates, M. S., & Edwards, W. T. (1992). Ethnic variations in the chronic pain experience. *Ethnicity and Disease, 2,* 63–83.

Bates, M. S., Edwards, W. T., & Anderson, K. O. (1993). Ethnocultural influences on variation in chronic pain perception. *Pain, 52,* 101–112.

Bates, M. S., Rankin-Hill, L., Sanchez-Ayendez, M., & Mendez-Bryan, R. A. (1995). Cross-cultural comparison of adaptation to chronic pain among "old Americans" and native Puerto Ricans. *Medical Anthropology, 16,* 141–173.

Bateson, G. (1958). *Naven, A survey of the problems suggested by a composite picture of the culture of a New Guinea tribe drawn from three points of view* (2nd ed.). Stanford, CA: Stanford University Press. (Original work published 1936).

Buckley, T., & Gottlieb, A. (Eds.). (1988). *Blood magic, The anthropology of menstruation.* Berkeley: University of California Press.

Carlson, K. J., Nichols, D. H., & Schiff, I. (1993). Indications for hysterectomy. *The New England Journal of Medicine, 328,* 856–860.

Cassidy, C. M. (1991). The good body: When big is better. *Medical Anthropology, 13,* 181–213.

Chavira-Prado, A. (1992). Work, health, and the family: Gender structure and women's status in an undocumented migrant population. *Human Organization, 51,* 53–64.

Cohen, F.L., & Durham, J. D. (1993). *Women, children, and HIV/AIDS.* New York: Springer Publishing Co.

Cutner, L. P. (1985). Female genital mutilation. *Obstetrical and Gynecological Survey, 40,* 437–443.

Davis-Floyd, R. E. (1992). *Birth as an American rite of passage.* Berkeley: University of California Press.

Desjarlais, R. R. (1992). *Body and emotion: The aesthetics of illness and healing in the Nepal Himalayas.* Philadelphia: University of Pennsylvania Press.

Divale, W. T., & Harris, M. (1976). Population, warfare, and the male supremacist complex. *American Anthropologist, 78,* 521–538.

Doan, R. M., & Popkin, B. M. (1993). Women's work and infant care in the Philippines. *Social Science and Medicine, 36,* 297-304

El Dareer, A. (1982). *Women, why do you weep?* London: Zed Press.

Foucault, M. (1965). *Madness and civilization* (R. Howard, Trans.) New York: Random House. (Original work published in French 1961)

Foucault, M. (1973). *The birth of the clinic: An archaeology of medical perception* (A. M. Sheridan Smith, Trans.) New York: Pantheon Books. (Original work published in French 1963)

Gallagher, C., & Laqueur, T. (Eds.). (1987). *The making of the modern body: Sexuality and society in the nineteenth century.* Berkeley: University of California Press.

Ginsburg, F. (1991). What do women want?: Feminist anthropology confronts clitoridectomy. *Medical Anthropology Quarterly, 5,* 17-19.

Ginsburg, F., & Rapp, R. (1991). The politics of reproduction. *Annual Review of Anthropology, 20,* 311-343.

Gordon, D. (1991). Female circumcision and genital operations in Egypt and the Sudan: A dilemma for medical anthropology. *Medical Anthropology Quarterly, 5,* 3-14.

Graham, S. B. (1985). Running and menstrual dysfunction: Recent medical discoveries provide new insights into the human division of labor by sex. *American Anthropologist, 87,* 878-882.

Harrell, B. B. (1981). Lactation and menstruation in cultural perspective. *American Anthropologist, 83,* 796-823.

Harris, A. P. (1990). Race and essentialism in feminist legal theory. *Stanford Law Review, 42,* 581-616.

Hayes, R. O. (1975). Female genital mutilation, fertility control, women's roles, and the patrilineage in modern Sudan: A functional analysis. *American Ethnologist, 2,* 617-633.

Howell, N. (1979). *Demography of the Dobe !Kung.* New York: Academic Press.

Jacobs, S. E. & Roberts, C. (1989). Sex, sexuality, gender, and gender variance. In S. Morgan (Ed.), *Gender and anthropology: Critical reviews for research and teaching* (pp. 438-462). Washington, DC: American Anthropological Association.

Jay, M. (1986). In the empire of the gaze: Foucault and the denigration of vision in twentieth-century French thought. In D. C. Hoy (Ed.), *Foucault: A critical reader* (pp.175-204). Oxford: Basil Blackwell,

Jordan, B., & Davis-Floyd, R. (1993). *Birth in four cultures: A crosscultural investigation of childbirth in Yucatan, Holland, Sweden, and the United States* (4th ed.). Prospect Heights, IL: Waveland Press, Inc. (Original work published 1978)

Kaczmarski, R. J., Flegal, K. M., Campbell, S. M., Johnson, C. L. (1994). Increasing prevalence of overweight among US adults: The National Health and Nutrition Examination Surveys, 1960-1991. *Journal of the American Medical Association, 272,* 206-211.

Kang-Wang, J. F. (1980). The midwife in Taiwan: An alternative model for maternity care. *Human Organization, 39,* 70-79.

Kirby, D. G. (1989). Immigration, stress, and prescription drug use among Cuban women in South Florida. *Medical Anthropology, 10,* 287-295.

Komarovsky, M. (1991). Some reflections on the feminist scholarship in sociology. *Annual Review of Sociology, 17,* 1-25.

Konner, M. (1987). *Becoming a doctor: A journey of initiation in medical school.* New York: Viking.

(1989). Women in biosocial perspective. In S. Morgan (Ed.), *Gender
: Critical reviews for research and teaching (pp. 95-115).
American Anthropological Association.

89) *Prisoners of ritual: An odyssey into female genital circum-
New York: Harrington Park Press.

Japanese mythologies: Faltering discipline and the ailing house-
Ethnologist, 15, 43-61.

(1993). Technologies as embodied power. *Anthropology Newsletter*,

92). *The anthropology of breast-feeding: Natural law or social
ord: Berg.

ex and temperament in three primitive societies. New York: The
Library. (Original work published 1935)

Coming of age in Samoa. New York: William Morrow & Co. (Original
published 1928)

80). The problem of "operations based on custom" in applied anthro-
challenge of the Hosken Report on genital and sexual mutilations of
man Organization, 39, 295-297.

3). Breast-cancer warrior: Dr. Susan Love's crusade against the killer dis-
ican Medical News, 36, 11-15.

Morgan, S. (1989). Gender and anthropology: Introductory essay. In S. Morgan (Ed.),
Gender and anthropology: Critical reviews for research and teaching (pp. 1-20).
Washington, DC: American Anthropological Association.

Mullings, L. (1989). Gender and the application of anthropological knowledge to public
policy in the United States. In S. Morgan (Ed.), *Gender and Anthropology: Critical
reviews for research and teaching* (pp. 360-381). Washington, DC: American
Anthropological Association.

Nichter, M., & Nichter M. (1991). Hype and weight. *Medical Anthropology, 13*,
249-284.

Ong, A. (1991). The gender and labor politics of postmodernity. *Annual Review of
Anthropology, 20*, 279-309.

Pi-Sunyer, F. X. (1994). The fattening of America. *Journal of the American Medical
Association, 272*, 238.

Ries, L. A. G., Hankey, B. F., Miller, B. A., Hartman, A. M., & Edwards, B. I .K. (1991).
Cancer statistics review 1973-1988. NIH Publication No. 91-2789. Bethesda, MD:
National Cancer Institute.

Ritenbaugh, C. (1991). Body size and shape: A dialogue of culture and biology. *Medical
Anthropology, 13*, 173-180.

Rosaldo, M., & Lamphere, L. (1974). *Women, culture, and society*. Stanford: Stanford
University Press.

Scheper-Hughes, N., & Lock, M. (1987). The mindful body: A prolegomenon to future
work in medical anthropology. *Medical Anthropology Quarterly, 1*, 6-41.

Schiebinger, L. (1987). Skeletons in the closet: The first illustrations of the female
skeleton in eighteenth-century anatomy. In C. Gallagher & T. Laqueur (Eds.), *The
making of the modern body: Sexuality and society in the nineteenth century*
(pp. 42-82). Berkeley: University of California Press.

Schroeder, P. (1994). Female genital mutilation—A form of child abuse. *New England
Journal of Medicine, 331* (11), 739-740.

Seaman, B., & Seaman, G. (1977). *Women and the crisis in sex hormones.* New York: Rawson Associates Publishers.

Shostak, M. (1983). *Nisa: The life and words of a !Kung woman.* New York: Vintage Books.

Singer, M. (1980). Signs of self. *American Anthropologist, 82,* 485-507.

Sobo, E., & Brodwin, P. (1993). Healing, bodily practices and Caribbean ethnicity. *Anthropology Newsletter, 34,* 25.

Spring, A., & Kosch, S. G. (1982). Breast diseases and breast self-examination: To detect or not to detect. *Human Organization, 41,* 264-268.

Stevens, P. E. (1993). Lesbians and HIV: Clinical, research, and policy issues. *American Journal of Orthopsychiatry, 63,* 289-294.

Toubia, N. (1994). Female circumcision as a public health issue. *New England Journal of Medicine, 331* (11), 712-716.

Van Willigen, J., & Channa, V. C. (1991). Law, custom, and crimes against women: The problem of dowry death in India. *Human Organization, 50,* 369-377.

Wallerstein, E. (1980). *Circumcision: An American health fallacy.* New York: Springer Publishing Co.

Woodrow, K. M., Friedman, G., Siegelaub, M., & Collen, M. (1972). Pain tolerance: Differences according to age, sex, and race. *Psychosomatic Medicine, 34,* 271-273.

Zborowski, M. (1969). *People in pain.* San Francisco: Jossey-Bass Inc. Publishers.

PART III

Health Practitioners
in Perspective

Chapter 14

Mind-Oriented Healers

INTRODUCTION

Health care providers seem on the face of it to be endlessly diverse. Not only have anthropologists described different kinds of providers in different parts of the world, but they have also recorded considerable diversity within single societies. In the final analysis, every individual health practitioner is unique to some extent. This enormous variability needs to be condensed into a smaller number of etic categories if we are to avoid getting lost in the richness of the health care experience through time and space.

To that end, the present chapter is devoted to healers who can reasonably be thought of, either in their own terms or in ours, as dealing primarily (but not exclusively) with issues of the mind. In most cultural traditions, these are magico-religious practitioners, including rabbis, priests, and pastors. In the Western medical tradition, they include empirically based psychiatrists, psychologists, and counselors.

This overview of mind-oriented healers is framed by a point of view as old as anthropology itself, distinguishing practitioners who base their practice on a naturalistic explanatory model and who employ empirical methods from those whose explanatory model incorporates ideas about extraordinary realities and who incorporate magico-religious methods (Neumann & Lauro, 1982; Bastien, 1992, p. 21).

It can be useful to distinguish empirical from magico-religious practitioners, but only if basic cautions are kept in mind. Above all, it must be remembered that practitioners themselves usually consider everything they do as natural. In this view, spirits and powers are simply parts of reality and would be considered extraordinary only in the sense that they are more sacred than daily reality, are perhaps not encountered on a daily or frequent basis, and/or require recourse to shamans, diviners, mediums or other specialists in occult matters.

In addition, it is essential to keep in mind that naturalistic versus personalistic is a matter of degree rather than of complete mutual exclusion. In general, we find that individual and family providers of first aid and home remedies, herbalists, body workers, and birth attendants primarily provide treatment and advice on an empirical basis. (A poultice or a massage can ease the pain of a bruised muscle.) Any empirical practitioner may, in addition, offer a prayer, apply an amulet, perform a magical gesture, or in some other way invoke spiritual beings or powers which they may consider additionally helpful or even essential. This etic category, however, permits the researcher systematically to explore and compare on a naturalistic basis without denying or degrading what is personalistic (supernatural).

Similarly, healing based on negotiations and involvements in the magico-religious realm will always include biological and psychological benefits mediated by complex psychoneuroimmunological mechanisms. In addition, physiological benefits may be more directly mediated. Consider, for example, how a shaman may include an herbal brew with pharmacologic effects or a massage delivered as a ritual of stroking.

WHO BECOMES A MIND-ORIENTED HEALER?

In *Patterns of Culture* (1934), a book still in circulation despite the passage of many years, Ruth Benedict taught that shamans experienced severe symptoms that in the United States would have landed them in mental hospitals or on the streets as homeless and sick. Yet, those very symptoms qualified these aberrant individuals for power and prestige. Speaking of their recruitment as healers, she wrote: "Some, during the period of the call, are violently insane for several years; others irresponsible to the point where they have to be constantly watched lest they wander off in the snow and freeze to death; others ill and emaciated to the point of death, sometimes with bloody sweat" (Benedict,1959 [1934], p. 268).

Benedict wrote that individuals with schizophrenic or other abnormal symptoms could live useful lives in communities that were more tolerant and supportive than our own by serving the community as shamans. In the decades that have passed since she wrote, anthropologists have described some shamans in support of that contention, but very few who are actively psychotic. To function successfully as a shaman requires an astute intelligence combined with responsive awareness that is not often encountered in individuals who meet the criteria of psychosis. On the contrary, as Eliade put it, "the shamans . . . show proof of a more than normal nervous constitution; they achieve a degree of concentration beyond the capacity of the profane; they sustain exhausting efforts; they control their ecstatic movements" (Eliade, 1964, p. 29). Based on firsthand observations in Tungus communities, S. M. Shirokogoroff pointed out that someone who is deranged cannot successfully carry out the duties of a shaman. "The shaman may begin his life career with a psychosis but cannot carry on his functions if he cannot master himself" (Shirokogoroff, 1935, p. 366; see Boyer, 1964, p. 402; Murphy, 1964, p. 76).

However, Benedict also postulated that shamans were individuals who may once have been psychotic, but were healed. Thus stated, the generalization holds up well. Entrance to the profession in many societies requires surviving a serious illness. Although it may be organic or infectious, the prodromal illness frequently is psychological. Shamanic ability is probably enhanced precisely because the practitioner has personally experienced, or been healed of, a psychological disorder. Frequently, shamans-to-be face death. Many recount how they visualized their own destruction and dismemberment, with the flesh stripped from their bones and the bones disarticulated. They recall, too, that they were reassembled and renewed. Confrontation with death and rebirth has an extraordinary power to transform an individual's sense of person and purpose in life (Walsh, 1990, p. 59). The shaman may have experienced a mystical union with God or the universe. Echoing Benedict, Eliade records that the magician or shaman "is, above all, a sick man who has been cured, who has succeeded in curing himself" (Eliade, 1964, p. 27). Becoming a shaman provides the cure, Benedict said.

WHEN IS A HEALER A SHAMAN?

Our earliest ethnographic familiarity with shamanism drew heavily on reports from various peoples in nineteenth-century Siberia. That is why Ruth Benedict had them particularly in mind. The very word came to us through Russian from the Tungusic term *šaman*. For decades anthropologists wrote about shamans having in mind only generic qualities of the profession, struck by similarities in other parts of the world, but not driven to great precision in categorizing these similarities. One cannot describe shamanism now, however, without facing up to a confusion that still obscures the issue of what we mean by the term.

It is quite frustrating to explore the literature in search of a consensus on the definition of shaman. The only way to proceed seems to be to pose a prior question, which is, why do we need a definition? The answer seems obvious, but needs to be explicit. It is to provide us with an etic category of healer that has a worldwide generalization built in. The definition, in other words, constitutes a generalization about minimal attributes (Tylor's lowest common denominator). Against that generalization, we can then explore emic characterizations from individual societies in a search for additional, more complex understandings of how shamanism can vary around a core of traits agreed upon by definition. Ultimately, then, usefulness is the criterion of importance: Is the definition helpful or is it not?

SHAMANISM AS AN ALTERED STATE OF CONSCIOUSNESS

In an often encountered but very loose definition, a shaman is taken to be any healer or seer who enters an altered state of consciousness (ASC) in the service of society rather than solely for personal reasons (Walsh, 1990, p. 11). This defines the term too broadly to be useful for most purposes of comparative analysis, even though Mircea Eliade, whose major work on shamanism is full of ambiguities of definition, includes this minimal designation. "A first definition of this complex phenomenon, and perhaps the least hazardous," he wrote, "will be: shamanism = *technique of ecstasy*" (Eliade, 1964, p. 4).

It is true that wherever shamanism is practiced, initiation requires the novice to undergo a kind of temporary induced insanity, ecstasy, or ASC. To Shirokogoroff, drawing on his ethnographic research among the Tungus, this was experienced as "a half-delirious hysterical condition—'abnormal' in European terms" (Shirokogoroff, 1935, p. 274). Used by Shirokogoroff and popularized by Eliade, the term *ecstasy* is widely said to characterize the ASC of shamanism. In the experience of most shamans, whether in their initiation or in their daily practice, ASCs are sacred and out of the ordinary, to be sure, but often they are no more than dreams, fugues, or illnesses. They are not always, or even usually, what one would call ecstatic, implying qualities of thrill, euphoria, bliss, or delirium. Perhaps we ought to down-play the term. Anthony Wallace glosses *ecstasy* as "enthusiastic" (Wallace, 1966, p. 35). It has also been defined as a state of intensified or heightened feeling (Walsh, 1990, p. 10). I prefer to speak of an ASC, or to follow Harner in speaking of a shamanic state of consciousness (SSC) (Harner, 1982, p. 26).

The ethnography of Sanapia, a Comanche doctor whose career is well known to most medical anthropologists, provides an example of a healer who has been referred to as a shaman, even though she is a shaman only by this minimal definition (Brown, 1980; p. 9). It is notable, by the way, that David Jones, the anthropologist who wrote the biography of Sanapia, refers to her as a native doctor or a medicine woman, but not to my knowledge as a shaman.

Sanapia was born in a tepee in Oklahoma in 1895. Her father was a Christian who had distanced himself from Native American culture, but her mother and mother's mother raised her in traditional Comanche ways. By heredity she acquired a likelihood of becoming a medicine woman, since both her mother and her mother's brother were eagle doctors. (Her uncle was also a very active peyotist.)

Around the age of ten she became sick with the flu. As a condition of being cured by her uncle, she was forced to agree to become a doctor. She later recalled that at the time she considered it blackmail and resisted taking up her vocation. She gave in, however, and for three years apprenticed to her mother and uncle, assisting in their labors and engaging in "long, long talks." At the end of that period, having reached the age of seventeen, she was prepared to practice, but, following Comanche custom, did not actually begin until after menopause when she was about fifty years old.

Sanapia periodically experienced ASCs in practicing the peyote religion as part of her healing vocation. Also, whenever she doctored she prayed fervently to the Holy Ghost as well as to the earth, the sun, and the eagle. By the time she finished praying she had become agitated and emotional, experiencing chills, shaking, and trembling as signs that her power had entered her and that she could carry on (Jones, 1972, pp. 76–77). In extreme cases, she would spend the day preceding a healing session meditating alone in a secluded area, and during the night would sing her medicine song until she could visualize the spirits of her mother and uncle (Jones, 1972, p. 80).

Sanapia also attached importance to dreams, although her first important healing dream did not happen until shortly after she began her career as a doctor. At that time, she dreamt of a man who would provide her with an eagle feather, which subsequently happened in real life. When she actually got the feather she used it as a powerful kind of medicine in her healing rituals.

It is not wrong to define shamanism so broadly that it includes Sanapia. At times anthropologists do so. But a curer such as she is so far removed in mindset and methods from a shaman of Siberia that it is usually not helpful to combine the two of them into a single etic category.

SHAMANISM AS TRANCE POSSESSION

A tighter definition requires that, in addition to experiencing an ASC in the service of society, the healer also must experience possession by a personality that is nonself. Most of those whom ethnologists regard as shamans come under this definition. Thus, I. M. Lewis described the shaman as "an inspired prophet and healer, a charismatic religious figure with the power to control the spirits, usually by incarnating them" (Lewis, 1986, p. 88).

An African Shaman

Under this definition a large amount of emic variation is found. There are many ways of experiencing trance possession. In Africa, for example, the shaman who exorcised Mary (as indicated Chapter 1) always enters an ASC when he sits with a client.

As I settled in one afternoon with my Shona colleague to observe the diagnostic seance held for Mary, the shadows of an unlighted room permitted us only dimly to make out an animal skin on the wall, tacked up next to a skin-covered shield, some spears, and an enormous hunting rifle. Crossing the floor in stocking feet we threaded our way over ten-foot-long snake skins, a giant sea shell, an elephant's foot, and the carapace of a tortoise. At the other side of the room we could make out half-hidden calabashes, pots, and jars of medicines that the healer would use. Sitting against the wall, regally robed in a flowing red, white, and black garment and hat, the shaman talked genially and laughed easily.

Eventually Mary and her seventeen-year-old sister entered in quiet dignity, folding themselves onto the floor next to us across from Gomiwa. After quiet conversation that put the two at their ease, the mood changed theatrically. The shaman methodically pulled a blanket-sized black wrap over his legs. Another wrap, with several large white stars, was pulled up and over his head and body, leaving only his nose and mouth darkly visible. He coiled a wicked- looking bullwhip around his neck and yawned, then yawned again. We all knew that yawning was a sign that he was becoming possessed. An enormous belch further confirmed the process.

From deep in his throat we heard strained sounds, "Ahh, ehh, ahh." He snuffed tobacco, first up one nostril, then up the other. It is well established that possessing spirits crave snuff. "Ugh-h-h." The groan seemed to come from deep in his body. Reaching forward, he put pinches of incense on the hot coals of the small urn at his feet, the smoke clouding our view of the proceedings. "Ehh . . . ahh . . . ehh . . . ahh . . . ." Then his body gave forth a voice that was strangely high-pitched. An ancestral spirit was addressing us. The shaman apparently had fallen into a trance. His consciousness, theoretically at least, was lost somewhere beyond awareness while the spirit who had taken over his body began a dialogue, which his wife translated, since the voice spoke one of the languages of Malawi, the neighboring nation from which the shaman had emigrated as a young man. After discussing the cause of the illness and what would need to be done, the spirit left. Some more groans, yawns, and belches informed us that the shaman was returning to his own body, ready to move to a different ritual area where the exorcism would take place.

A Brazilian Shaman

João Texeira is equally a shaman by this definition, yet he functions in a very different manner. Three times a week hundreds of sick people and their supporters make their way by bus, car, and train to his center located in a small rural town in an impoverished northeastern state. He begins his work alone in front of a picture of St. Ignatius and a crucifix, praying on behalf of his clients for grace and mercy. His eyes focused upward on the alter, the quality of his voice becomes grief-stricken in a crescendo of passion that suddenly evaporates in complete silence. He turns from the altar to administer to the needy. Without a sound, his face expressionless, his hands fallen to his side, he seems to have entered deeply into a trance, possessed, it is said, by a deceased physician under the guidance of St. Ignatius de Loyola. His voice, however, remains unchanged.

After hours of waiting for João to appear, selected individuals elsewhere in the center are guided into a room crowded with a score of mediums seated in rows on benches, each one deeply in trance. Strange animal-like sounds fill the air, bodies contort, and faces grimace. The mediums direct healing energy towards the client by aiming the palms of their hands. Two stand up to take positions in front of and behind the standing client, whom they now gently caress and rock. Suddenly, the client moans. The patient, the shaman, and the ritual assistants are all deeply in trance when it is time for the disincarnate physician, borrowing the body of João, to perform surgery in the large auditorium where an audience of two hundred await expectantly, bathed in the electronic tonalities of an amplified hymn.

SHAMANISM AS OUT-OF-BODY SENSATIONS

By an alternative definition, the shaman will serve others by entering a trance, but while in trance will experience out-of-body sensations. Shamans by this definition may also become possessed and speak in strange voices as mediums; however, many will not. One survey demonstrated that about half do and half do not (Peters & Price-Williams, 1980). The important generalization here is independent of, or separate from, trance-possession experiences. The central feature is that while "out-of-body" the spirit or soul of the shaman departs into extraordinary dimensions of reality. It takes off on mystical flights. The associated narration of a spiritual journey provides a powerful explanatory narrative about the cause and cure of an illness.

Eliade based this definition on findings that resulted from a worldwide survey undertaken without the convenience and rigor of the HRAF. Years of laboriously searching the literature on ethnography and religion produced evidence of practices similar to those of northern and central Asia, which he regarded as typical or archetypal forms of shamanism. In attempting to tighten up our understanding of what is meant by shamanism, he offered the concept of the magical flight as a unifying theme in an evolutionary and distributional perspective. A lack of rigor in systematically comparing cultures, however, amplified by inconsistencies in summarizing his findings and great variability in what shamans actually think and do, resulted in disturbing ambiguities in his characterization of the magical flight.

Contemporary anthropologists and others perpetuate this ambiguous generalization—ambiguous in the sense that each summary favors its own version of what is important and common. Here is my version, based especially on the writings of Eliade, Harner, Halifax, and Walsh (Eliade, 1964; Harner, 1982; Halifax, 1982; Walsh, 1990).

The Shamanic Cosmos

The universe in this belief system includes upper and lower worlds that cannot be seen when in an ordinary state of consciousness. Terrestial space that we take for granted is thought of as the middle world. The three worlds are linked by a central axis, the *axis mundi,* sometimes visualized as a tree of life, a world pillar, or a cosmic mountain. By means of the central axis, the spirit or soul of the entranced shaman can mount or descend into other worlds. This is the mystical flight or shamanic journey.

This cosmology is animistic. The universe is believed to be populated by eerie animals, magical birds, and humanoid spirits. Some are power creatures who will guide and protect the shaman. Others are troublemakers with whom the shaman must contend. The work of healing requires that the shaman travel to upper or lower worlds, stand up against or negotiate with otherworldly creatures, find lost souls, gain knowledge and information, or acquire needed powers, and then return to reoccupy his or her own body and to minister to the client.

As Harner describes it, the mystical journey begins when the shaman falls into a trance and enters a tunnel. "The Conibo Indians taught me to follow the roots of the giant *catahua* tree down into the ground to reach the Lowerworld," Harner writes, but in other societies it may be a cave, the hole of a burrowing animal, or a mere crack in the floor of a house. Alternatively, the journey may begin by climbing or flying skyward (Harner, 1982, p. 32).

Harner reports that the dark, constricted tunnel appears to open onto a brilliant landscape, where typically one may expect to encounter guardian spirits, power animals, and extraordinary Wonderland adventures. In this unseen world the shaman discovers "a whole new, and yet familiarly ancient universe that provides him with profound information about the meaning of his own life and death and his place within the totality of all existence" (Harner, 1982, p. 27). If the person being treated is sick because of soul loss, the shaman will locate the soul in this other world in order to get hold of it and carry it back to the patient's body. His or her work accomplished, the shaman returns to ordinary reality, where the steady beat of a drum was maintained by an assistant to ensure a safe return. If the patient is sick because a pain object has gotten into the body, the shaman will now suck out the object. The sacred work finished, the healer returns to an ordinary state of consciousness.

Shamanic Technology

The required ASC can be achieved in ways that range from sensory overload to sensory deprivation. It can be achieved by consuming hallucinogens or tobacco. However, it can be done without mind-altering substances. Drumming, chanting, or dancing will do it. So will repetitive or monotonous activities, fasting, going without sleep, enduring freezing cold, or sweltering in the heat of a sweat lodge. It can be achieved in meditation, prayer, or an "appropriate mind-set and environmental setting," such as that we witnessed in the case of the shaman in Africa, who simply put on a ritual gown in a darkened ceremonial chamber and inhaled snuff (which he takes all the day long anyway) (Walsh, 1990, p. 165).

Well-elaborated shamanic healing takes place as high drama. Sound is used theatrically, usually as compelling percussive rhythms. Fragrance from burning herbs or incense pervades the atmosphere. Light is dimmed and often colored or flickered. Many shamans perform at night, with only the light of candles or fires. Audiences as well as clients may be in ASCs. Often the architecture is theaterlike. João Texeira performs surgery on patients who are positioned in front of spectators in a large hall. Shamans in Zimbabwe perform in small, dark rooms richly accoutered with power objects: animal and snake skins, statuettes, paintings, or mysterious objects. The healers wear distinctive garb. Animal or bird sacrifices on occasion introduce life and death agonies. And, not the least, the shaman may amaze and bewilder with seemingly miraculous demonstrations of power.

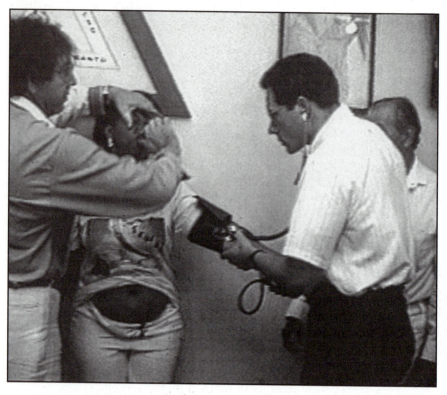

Scott Anderson, a physician as well as an anthropologist, at the request of João Texiera, the spiritist surgeon, recorded vital signs while the patient was undergoing eye, abdominal, and nasal surgeries.

From the beginning, anthropologists have struggled with a paradox. Shamans seem truly to believe in the powerful healing effects of the spirits and souls they manipulate, yet they clearly use trickery to deceive their audiences (Howells, 1948, pp. 133–134). Among the Jivaro of Amazonia, belief in sickness from object intrusion, combined with healing by sucking, is performed by a shaman under the influence of a powerful hallucinogen *(Banisteriopsis)*. The intrusive, disease-causing object, known as a *tsentsak,* can be an insect, a small plant, a worm, or almost anything small enough to be concealed in one's mouth. If in his visions the shaman determines that a witch has magically shot the sick person with a tsentsak, he will suck it out in a dark area of the house (where his sleight of hand will not easily be noticed). He allows observers to believe that the tsentsak that he spits up and gets rid of is the cause of the disease.

Harner maintains, however, that the shaman does not think of himself as lying for this reason. He sincerely believes that the supernatural essence of the object is real and does cause sickness, and his visions show him that he did suck out this essence. "To explain to the layman that he already had these objects in his mouth

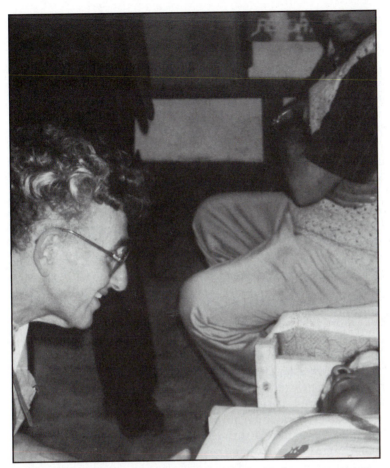

In the recovery room, Sidney Greenfield talked with the same patient to determine how she experienced the three surgeries that were performed without anesthesia.

would serve no fruitful purpose and would prevent him from displaying such an object as proof that he had effected the cure" (Harner, 1973, pp. 20, 24).

The paradox is more in the mind of the observer than in the mind of the shaman, who seems indifferent to the issue. In her early training, Sanapia, for example, acquired a special power from her mother in the form of a feather. In one important session with her mother, two eagle feathers were drawn across her mouth four times in succession. The fourth time across, one of the feathers disappeared. At this her mother said that the eagle feather had entered her body where it would stay for the rest of her life.

Sanapia was never taught how to make a feather disappear that way, and apparently gave little thought to it. When questioned she answered that her mother must have possessed powers she did not pass on to her daughter. It was not an issue for her. She explained to Jones that she never believed that the feather was literally put into her mouth. Rather, she believed it was the idea or essence of an eagle feather. In addition, she confessed that she elaborated the theatriecality of her own curing rituals. She had ways of making things appear and disappear. Her explanation was that she could bring her powers to bear without techniques of illusion, but her patients did better if they had faith that was enhanced by the drama of the encounter (Jones, 1972, pp. 33, 82-83).

Sidney Greenfield, Scott Anderson, and I encountered a similar attitude on the part of João Texeira. We had trouble understanding what he felt he was accomplishing in most of the dramatic incisions he performed. From a surgical point of view we could find no rationale for them. As an illustration, one case involved a young woman in her early twenties who traveled many miles by bus to reach his center early on a healing day. Of the hundreds present, she was among the half dozen selected that morning to be put into a trance and to stand against the wall of the auditorium where surgeries were performed. João really cuts; no false illusions at that level. On that day, while possessed, he used a surgeon's scalpel to make a two-inch-long incision in the young woman's left breast. He provided no anesthesia and demonstrated complete indifference to sterile technique, operating with bare hands still stained with blood from an earlier patient. After probing the wound with his bare finger, he sutured it with a needle and thread. In the recovery room when Greenfield asked the patient why she had come for treatment, he was told that her reason had nothing at all to do with her breast. She came because she felt she was overweight. The surgery was João's way of managing weight loss.

In trying to understand the rational for that operation, and for others equally inexplicable, we finally realized that João had told us, but we had not paid attention. He told us that the surgeries he performed on a few of his patients in front of large audiences were not really necessary. The true surgery or medication was done on the spirit plane by deceased, disembodied physicians. It was done to an invisible outer layer of the human body termed the perispirit. It did not need to be manifested on the material plane (Greenfield, 1987). The point was that cutting the visible body was done because it helped people believe and respond well to spiritist healing. That is why, of the hundreds of people who were individually seen by João, fewer than a dozen were operated on in the surgical theater.

What of the paradox, then? It is an etic, not an emic issue. On the emic level, shamans all over the world appear to believe fervently in the validity of the treatments they provide. They do not find their beliefs inconsistent with the stage management of illusion (see Joralemon, 1990).

NEOSHAMANISM

In the earlier years of anthropology, when Tylor and Fraser led the field in writing about hitherto unknown religious beliefs and practices, many readers were inspired to see their own religions in new ways. The sacred, they realized, was culture-bound. The effect on people's religiosity varied. Many found that a new cross-cultural sophistication heightened their sensitivity to the beauty and meaning of their own beliefs. The new awareness also contributed to a growing secularization. Increasingly in the urban-industrial world, the sacred and the profane were thought of as more sharply differentiated, leaving less and less in life that was subject to supernatural considerations.

By the mid-twentieth century it was easy to get seduced into thinking that God was dead, as it were. It was easy to believe that religion was becoming obsolete for educated people. Let that be a lesson against facile predictions. Contrary to what one might have expected, religion regained lost ground. With this revitalization of the sacred in modern life, a few anthropologists became religious leaders.

The flower children of the 1960s believed that they could design their own cultures. Utopian ideals led to experiments in communal living. The constraints of "middle-class morality" particularly rankled these iconoclasts, just as modern antibiotics and contraceptives freed them, so they became sexually liberated. Barefoot and vegetarian, they explored the inner world of sensations entered by meditational practices or by hallucinogens, both old herbals and new chemicals. Music, dance, incense, and art expanded their sensual awareness. They wandered the world, showing up in remote mountains, valleys, and beaches as well as in world metropolitan centers. Angry with how the industrial world shaped lives, and horrified by modern warfare, they sought ways to return to nature. Sensitive to hypocrisy in established religious institutions, they created their own religions, inspired by feelings of unity with God while tripping on LSD.

As part of this ferment of political nihilism, social millenarianism, and cultural revitalization, some of these cultural revolutionaries discovered shamanism. Their number included many university-educated enthusiasts who read the literature on anthropology and world religions. Their number also included rugged individualists who encountered shamans in remote parts of the world or in some of the ethnic enclaves of American cities. Above all, some were led to shamanic religion by anthropologists and other scholars who gave rebirth to Tylor's early search for the original religion of humankind. In the work of Eliade they encountered a facile interpretation of paleolithic religion as shamanism in the form of magical flight beliefs. This is what Eliade meant in writing of shamanism as "archaic techniques of ecstasy." Uncertainties about interpreting the evidence of paleolithic cave art became verities of hallucinogenic revelation. Eventually, many learned to be shamanists and shamans by participating in seminars, workshops, and retreats led by English-speaking shamans and, in some cases, by anthropologists.

One of the most influential anthropologists to promote neoshamanism is Michael Harner, who initially studied Jivaro and Conibo shamans in the Amazon as part of his ethnographic fieldwork. At an early stage in his career, he became an expert on traditional practices relating to hallucinogens. Eventually he wrote an unusual book, *The Way of the Shaman* (Harner, 1982). Note the subtitle: *A*

Guide to Power and Healing. This is a do-it-yourself book; how to become a shaman by practicing at home. "The main focus here," he states, "is to provide an introductory handbook of shamanic methodology for health and healing" (Harner, 1980, p. xxi). Actually, Harner would recommend that one get initiated by attending one of his weekend workshops. (Others who provide training in shamanism would recommend a much longer and more rigorous period of training.)

Harner, by the way, argues that "shamanism ultimately is only a method, not a religion with a fixed set of dogmas." He is right in denying that it is characterized by a fixed set of dogmas. Diversity is the coin word of the shamanic realm. He is right, too, if he means that it is not exclusionist. You can be a Christian, Hindu, Buddhist, or what have you, and practice shamanism as far as shamans are concerned. (Your priest, rabbi, or minister might feel differently, of course.) However, it gives one an eerie sense of disorientation to say or imply that it is only a psychobehavioral method, since it requires a belief in souls and realms of the spirit. Shamanism easily meets customary definitions of religion:

- "Religion embodies the idea of a supernatural power and of personified supernatural forces" (Winick, 1958, p. 454).
- "It is the premise of every religion—and this premise is religion's defining characteristic—that souls, supernatural beings, and supernatural forces exist" (Wallace, 1966, p. 52).

It is important to acknowledge that when anthropologists take the position that superhuman beings or extraordinary powers actually exist as empirical explanations for human events, they are, *to that extent at least,* not functioning as anthropologists. They have switched, as in the case of Larry Peters, into roles as spiritual advisors and consultants or as shamans (Peters, 1993). It is essential that one be aware of this switch, since anthropology, whether as science or humanistic scholarship, is committed to entirely naturalistic explanations, and what is considered natural must meet criteria that exclude beings and forces said to be exempt from the physical rules of nature. I do not say this in criticism of those who believe in the supernatural. It is just that as scholars and scientists we do not know how to deal with the nonordinary, so we are forced to leave it to those who do.

In recent years, several anthropologists have challenged this naturalistic posture of the profession (Young & Goulet, 1994). Edith Turner and Paul Stoller, in particular, have written of their belief in mystical powers and shamanic magic. We need to confront their challenge.

Let us look first at the assertion of Edith Turner based upon her work with a Ndembu shaman. It was her intent, she indicates, to undertake a different kind of anthropology which would have a different point to make. "When I first worked with Victor Turner," she states, "I felt there must be a more humanistic way to explain human behavior and events than the methods we were supposed to be learning in the world of anthropology. . . . I felt there was some human birthright that we possessed, which like sex in the Victorian age seemed taboo to anthropologists. But I was beginning to think that we no longer had to forego it. It was in this bold mood that I went to do my restudy of the Ndembu" (Turner, 1992, pp. xi–xiii).

Turner describes her participation in a lengthy curing ritual for a woman called Meru. She experienced at least some mild form of ASC, for she recalls that she drank a potion of leaf medicine that made her "momentarily dizzy and may have triggered and liberated a rarely-used faculty—as rarely used as childbirth muscles, but none the less real" (Turner, 1992, p. 189; Turner, 1994, p. 80). She also consumed an alcoholic beverage, experienced sleepiness, and rocked to the percussive rhythms of drums. Others around her fell into trance, but she drank some coffee to keep herself alert. As she continued to watch and take part, she had an extraordinary experience:

> I clapped like one possessed. . . . Suddenly . . . I saw with my own eyes a giant thing emerging out of the flesh of her back. This thing was a large gray blob about six inches across, a deep gray opaque thing emerging as a sphere. I was amazed—delighted. I still laugh with glee at the realization of having seen it, the ihamba [intrusive object], and so big! We were all just one in triumph. The gray thing was actually out there, visible, and you could see [the shaman] Singleton's hands working and scrabbling on the back—and then the thing was there no more. Singleton had it in his pouch, pressing it in with his other hand as well. The receiving case was ready; he transferred whatever it was into the can and capped the castor oil leaf and bark lid over it. It was done." (Turner, 1992, p. 149)

She writes of her conviction that what she saw was a paranormal event that really happened. She insists on the validity of her experience. "I repeat that I did not merely intuit the spirit form emerging from Meru's back but saw it, *saw* it with my own eyes. This is different from intuition or imagination; it is nearer to seeing a ghost" (Turner, 1992, pp. 189–190; Turner, 1994, pp. 83–84).

None of us wants to be thought of as close-minded, but we do not want to be gullible either. For that reason, when we are asked to believe that something paranormal occurred, the logic of science requires us to explore the possibility that quite ordinary events transpired and that a perfectly ordinary explanation might suffice. Now, we have abundant evidence that shamans practice legerdemain in order to create an illusion. In many places, including that part of Africa where Turner did her work, perfectly ordinary shamans can make it appear that an object was pulled out of the body. As we saw earlier, Quesalid, the Kwakiutl shaman, became quite adept at that form of deception. What Turner saw is reasonably interpreted as a well-executed example in a tradition of shamanic sleight of hand. No extraordinary explanation is required.

I am convinced that Singleton is a Quesalid among the Ndembu of south-central Africa. Take note that the reality of the spirit object remains unverified except by the testimony of Turner and her Zambian friends and collaborators, including Singleton. Note also that the object was never touched or closely observed by Turner, and it was not preserved for examination. It was immediately hidden and removed by the shaman.

Meru, by the way, was being treated for an illness that Singleton determined was caused by object intrusion; an ihamba had gotten into her body and needed to be gotten out. She experienced a cure, and when last seen was radiant, smiling, and "obviously in good fettle." I believe she was cured. It was undoubtedly a mind-oriented cure.

Let us turn next to the mystical experience of another anthropologist, also with many years of experience doing field research in Africa. When Paul Stoller writes of the Songhay people of the Republic of Niger, it is with the authority of one who learned to speak the language fluently and to know the people intimately. As part of his ethnographic research, he studied how to heal with herbs and incantations by apprenticing to a powerful magician (sorceror). Traveling to Wanzerbe, a remote, small town where he hoped to meet and talk with a powerful magician, he encountered a woman who seemed to reject and threaten him. That night, after slipping into an ASC (he fell asleep), he became the victim of an episode of paralysis he interpreted as sorcery, a true paranormal event.

> Suddenly I had the strong impression that something had entered the house. I felt its presence and I was frightened. Set to abandon the house to whatever hovered in the darkness, I started to roll off my mat. But my lower body did not budge. I pinched my leaden thighs and felt nothing. My heart raced. I couldn't flee. What could I do to save myself? Like a sorko benya [future sorceror], I began to recite the genji how, for Adamu Jenitongo had told me that if I ever felt danger I should recite this incantation until I had conquered my fear. And so I recited and recited and recited and continued to recite it until I began to feel a slight tingling in my hips. Encouraged, I continued to recite the incantation, and the tingling spread down my thighs to my legs. My voice cracked, but I continued to recite. Slowly, the tingling spread from my legs to my feet. I pinched my thigh—it hurt—and tested my response along the length of my legs. Gingerly, I rolled off the mat and stood up. The presence had left the room. Exhausted, I lay back on my straw mat and fell into a deep sleep. (Stoller & Olkes, 1987, p. 148)

Stoller recalled later how he believed that the woman had attacked him by magical means. "Before my paralysis, I *knew* there were scientific explanations of Songhay sorcery. After Wanzerbe my unwavering faith in science vanished. . . . I had crossed an invisible threshold into the Songhay world of sorcery" (Stoller & Olkes, 1987, p. 153; Stoller, 1989, pp. 52, 54, 122, 154). Stoller is on shaky ground to assert that the paralysis of his lower body was precipitated by a sorcerer who invoked magical powers.

Note the similarity here to Turner's paranormal experience in another part of Africa. First, as concerns evidence, we have only the testimony of the ethnographer. No one was present to verify Stoller's paralysis, and it never happened again. Second, a completely natural explanation, though also unprovable, is far more probable.

One of the culture-bound syndromes known to occur in several parts of the world is the sleep paralysis taxon. "The most salient symptom in this syndrome" Charles Hughes writes, "is that of the person's suddenly feeling unable to move or speak when in a borderline sleep state, although remaining fully conscious of surrounding events and people and being able to recall events after the experience. Other symptoms. . . are great agitation and anxiety. . . , followed by exhaustion" (Hughes, 1985, p. 147). It is likely that Stoller experienced sleep paralysis, a temporary effect of mind over matter. No need to invoke witches or sorcerers. Harner appears to have had a similar experience (Harner, 1982, pp. 4-6).

Shamans now constitute an increasingly widespread health care option in urban America. Several anthropologists practice as shamans. Of course, one does not have to be an anthropologist to become a neoshaman. Many nonanthropologists now engage in shamanic healing, often part-time. Phyllis Mattson notes that many holistic health advocates in the United States have eagerly studied how to become shamans (Mattson, 1982, pp. 20, 112). T. M. Luhrmann, while undertaking fieldwork among practitioners of magic and witchcraft, encountered shamanic practices in contempory England (Luhrmann, 1989, pp. 3-7; see also Oriun, 1995). The time is ripe for more field research to be carried out relating to shamanism in the modern world.

MEDICAL AND SURGICAL APPROACHES TO MENTAL HEALTH

The treatment of mental disorders in most societies, including America, relies heavily on psychological techniques, including those of shamanism. Pharmacologic or surgical approaches are also widely practiced, however. Western psychiatry above all has struggled to develop a neurophysiologic approach. Unfortunately, efforts to diagnose, treat, and prevent mental problems on a biomedical basis have proven only partly satisfactory, which is why Arthur Kleinman has written that psychiatry needs rethinking (Kleinman, 1988; Kirk & Kutchins, 1992).

A few years ago, the search for ways to ameliorate the effects of major psychoses led to a remarkable episode in the history of Western medicine. In 1949, the Nobel Prize in physiology and medicine was awarded to Egas Moniz, a neurologist, for inventing and practicing the frontal lobotomy (frontal leucotomy), a twentieth-century elaboration of a prehistoric type of surgery known as trephination.

Skull Surgery

Trephining is often incorrectly referred to as brain surgery, even by anthropologists, but it is bone surgery that only involves the skull, not the brain. Evidence that it was practiced in antiquity is not uncommon in both Old and New World prehistoric sites from as far back as 12,000 years ago. In the archeological record, the evidence survives in skeletons as holes that were cut through the skull plate. Edges of the bone usually show evidence of bony regrowth, which indicates that healing occurred. Some individuals underwent the process more than once (Ackerknecht, 1947).

In historical times, the practice was directly observed in Southeastern Europe, North Africa, Sub-Saharan Africa, Oceania, and the Americas, particularly in the Andean highlands. It has been observed and even filmed in parts of Africa and South America as recently as the 1960s and 1970s (Imperato, 1977; Bastien, 1987).

Frequently trephining was practiced for the treatment of crush injuries to the head, to relieve headaches due to pressure on the brain, and to remove splinters of bone. The explanatory theory was probably naturalistic in such cases. It was also done for the treatment of epilepsy and nontraumatic headaches, in which cases ideas about spirit intrusion were probably involved. For the most part, however, we know only that the operation was done, not why.

In East Africa, where the procedure was observed in the mid-twentieth century, a Kisii or Bakuria surgeon, usually after shaving the head, cut through the relatively thin skin, muscle, and connective tissue of the scalp to expose the surface of bone. Bleeding was controlled by pressing herbal powder or charcoal on the wound. Rather than saw or drill through the bone with flint implements, as is reported in some parts of the world, these surgeons scraped the bone away with the curved tip of a steel knife, taking care not to penetrate the membrane (dura mater) that separates bone from brain. The slow process of wearing away a circular area of bone usually lasted about four hours and was often accomplished without putting the patient under heavy restraint. Surgical patients in the Andes are reported to have chewed coca leaves to dull the pain, but these African patients depended on stoicism, and occasionally on being firmly held in place. After rinsing the wound with plain or herbally medicated water, usually spewing it from his mouth, the operator pulled the skin back over the area, covered it with butter or herbs, and allowed it to heal, often without suturing. Most patients apparently survived. Whether or not they got better cannot be said.

Brain Surgery

The frontal lobotomy of biomedicine was a surgery that destroyed parts of the frontal lobes of the cerebral cortex (Valenstein, 1986). The technique was unbelievably crude by mid-twentieth-century surgical standards. It began with trephining. Small holes were bored through the skull. A cutting instrument was inserted through these openings directly into the brain where it was rotated blindly to destroy whatever tissue it happened to contact. Brain tissue is not supplied with sensory nerves, so only the trephination and penetration of the dura mater caused pain.

Walter Freeman, who performed hundreds of these operations, usually did them under local anesthesia so that the patient could talk and respond to questions while increasingly deeper ablation was carried out. Unable to see the anatomy of the operative field, Freeman and his associates used a "disorientation yardstick" to determine how much brain tissue to destroy. By this measure, tissue destruction was halted when the patient became sleepy and disoriented.

Egaz Moniz originated this treatment of mental disorders because he believed that psychosocial approaches were ineffectual. His logic was based on the belief that all severe mental derangements, including depression and schizophrenia, resulted from "fixed thoughts" held in place by nerve pathways in the frontal lobes. It followed, then, that surgical destruction of these abnormally "stabilized" pathways would cure the disease.

The hypothesis was entirely unsupported by experimental or anatomic evidence. It is another example of how important it is not to be seduced by a logical argument without applying scientific methods of assessment. It also demonstrated how advocates of a procedure, whether willfully or by self-deception, can disregard harmful effects and failures. In spite of claims to the contrary, these patients often showed no improvement. Patients with schizophrenia who were impaired by wild, psychotic thinking remained unimproved after the surgery. Those with depression and anxiety, some of whom seemed less symptomatic postsurgically, paid dearly in pallid emotional responsiveness, lower intellectual capacity, and failure in concentration.

Between 1948 and 1952, approximately 25,000 frontal lobotomies were performed, but the heyday of that surgery passed. When Thorazine (chlorpromazine), the first of the new psychotropic drugs, became available in 1954, It was soon followed by others. It became clear that surgery was essentially worthless and harmful, a resource for doctors who at the time had nothing else to offer. Now they had the new drugs. Coincidentally, the lobotomy was abandoned at about the same time as were major abdominal and oral surgeries to treat diseases such as arthritis based on the theory of focal infections.

Psychiatric Drugs

The new psychopharmacology revolutionized the practice of psychiatry in the treatment of severe disorders. People who previously had been hidden away in insane asylums became able successfully to reenter society under medical supervision. The racing thoughts or deep depression of manic-depressive behavior or the frightening voices of schizophrenic ideation eased off. Lives were salvaged, as was confirmed by randomized controlled trials. In the case of one study of individuals with schizophrenia who were living in the community (n = 374), those receiving only a placebo experienced double the rate of relapse compared with those receiving true phenothiazine prescriptions (Hogarty et al., 1973). In another population, 71 percent on placebos relapsed compared with only 17 percent taking Prolixin (a phenothiazine). Higher success rates resulted when medications were combined with supportive care that helped in coping with psychosocial problems (Hirsch et al., 1973).

Given this dramatic turnabout in the ability of physicians to do something for severely schizophrenic and manic-depressive patients, it came as a great disappointment to find that patients all too frequently stopped taking their medicine. Of course, every doctor knew of unwanted side effects. They are part of the trade-off in the pharmacologic management of any sickness, and that basic cost-benefit equation is part of what one is taught in learning to practice medicine. For minor disorders, only minor side effects are acceptable, but for really bad diseases, serious side effects may well be a price worth paying. Psychoses are really bad diseases.

Failures in patient compliance are intensely frustrating to treating physicians and hard for them to sympathize with. This is where an anthropologist made a contribution. For two years, Sue Estroff spent her waking hours in clinical and community settings with mental patients (Estroff, 1981). To clarify that she saw the subjects of her research as individuals who were attempting to cope with serious illnesses rather than simply as submissive objects in paternalistic medical institutions, she referred to them as psychiatric clients rather than as patients. This shift in terminology is occurring in other parts of the health care system as well.

Estroff's involvement was both long and intense. She even had herself medicated with Proxilin for some weeks so that she could experience the effects of the drug subjectively. In the end she was able to propose an emic view that psychiatric personnel now find informative as they struggle to understand and respond to noncompliance. On the basis of her fieldwork, it is now known how a drug such as Prolixin impacts on the sense of self, of personhood, and on social relationships.

Estroff reports that clients were repeatedly told that they could not function without medical supervision, and that they would probably need to be on drug therapy for the rest of their lives. The implicit message "you will never get well" sinks in as a feeling of low self-esteem. Estroff concludes, "They come to see themselves caught between a nonmedicated world that is out of reach, and a medicated world that identifies them as crazy people with problems in their heads and their lives" (Estroff, 1981, p. 109). As a corollary of this identity issue, they may claim back their insane behavior by refusing medication. Being thought of as crazy creates a role that in some ways is permissive. It grants some escape from the harsh realities of being considered sane, because it grants permission to speak or shout garbled messages, to dress in bizarre ways, to "make it crazy." As Estroff sees it, "craziness provides some escape from other realities negatively perceived" (Estroff, 1981, p. 110).

But there is another, more direct reason for giving up on medications that has to do with problems of social interaction. Many of the side effects of these drugs manifest as visible behaviors that people interpret variously as signs of being mentally deranged, as evidence of being high on illicit drugs, or as behaviors that stigmatize one as wierd or strange. The medicines often cause an irresistible urge to rock or jiggle, particularly when sitting. Hands can get shaky. Sometimes eyes may roll back in their sockets. Phenothiazines can affect the muscles of the face so that in conversations a blank expression masks usually responsive facial gestures. A strange-looking, stiff, or inelegant way of walking may turn the heads of bystanders. In all, medications to keep a client from being crazy paradoxically signal a crazy identity that maintains social estrangement in an unforgiving social world.

Since the work of Estroff, others have also demonstrated the value of anthropological research relating to noncompliance. Julia Segar, for example, investigated why extremely poor South Africans with epilepsy failed to take their medicine regularly. Many of them responded so well when they took their pills regularly that they remained free of seizures and could live ordinary lives. Segar identified several impediments, including problems in communicating how and when the pills should be taken. Above all, however, she identified a social issue. In this community of high unemployment, a doctor's certification that their seizures could not be controlled made them eligible for monthly disability grants that could provide them with their only source of income. Better to have seizures than to go hungry (Segar, 1994).

The Psychopharmacology of Traditional Healers

In any community, it is one thing to live with a neurotic individual who behaves in ways deemed strange—not like other people. It is quite another thing to cope with an individual who becomes dangerous to self and others during a psychotic break with reality. What can a traditional healer do for what Benedict referred to as the "violently insane"? Their brain chemistry will not usually permit them to respond to any kind of talking cure. Psychiatry in the form of counseling will not work, but indigenous psychiatrists sometimes use herbs that appear to be helpful. Take, for example, Taiwo, a Yoruba villager whom Raymond Prince encountered in 1962 (Prince, 1964).

Taiwo was a hunter who had "run mad" for almost a week, terrorizing his fellow villagers by shooting off his rifle and wielding his machete. He was beyond reason and was himself terrorized by hallucinated voices and visions that convinced him he should kill everybody. This was a case to test the mettle of the healer who was asked to take charge. When he entered the village he found Taiwo alone in his nearly demolished house, sharpening his machete as he got ready to wreak carnage on his little world. His neighbors had fled.

The healer tried in vain to talk Taiwo into coming with him for treatment, but the distraught man flatly refused. At this point a bit of magic seemed to work. The healer touched his medicated ring to his client and recited incantations. With that, and the help of an able-bodied assistant, it became possible to grab him, tie him up, thrust him into a waiting taxi, and drive him to the healer's center.

The treatment center was actually the healer's family homestead. Clients lived in a family atmosphere while they received treatment. They got attentive day-and-night psychosocial support. Violent patients were restrained by shackling their legs, handcuffing their arms, and confining them in a locked room with iron bars over the window. Such was the treatment for Taiwo the moment he was bundled out of the taxi.

Taiwo was also immediately forced to drink a bowl of herbal liquid infused with *asofeyeje* root, a plant known to Western science as *Rauwolfia vomitoria.* The major alkaloid of rauwolfia is reserpine, which has been shown to be beneficial in relieving anxiety, promoting relaxation, and lowering arterial blood pressure. Paradoxically, it can also cause depression and despondency, at times resulting in suicide, so one has to take care in its use. The antihypertensive effects of reserpine may have been as important to Taiwo as the reduction of anxiety, since he complained of noises in his head (tinnitus) and headache, both of which often occur in severe hypertension.

Taiwo got a heavy jolt of reserpine in herbal form, and fell into a coma. He was dangerously overdosed. A major problem in herbal medication is that the amount of active ingredient is variable and to some degree unknowable, so underdosing and overdosing are common. The next day he was still asleep, unresponsive, lying in his own feces and urine, his muscles twitching. A discouraging picture to be sure, but during the next three weeks he progressed quite well. In smaller amounts, rauwolfia probably helped him.

A few weeks later, Prince found him eating and sleeping well, walking around the compound without handcuffs, although still kept in shackles as a precaution. He eventually had to be discharged before the final rituals could be carried out. His family could not afford to keep him there any longer. Traditional medical care can be very expensive. However, he seemed to be on the mend.

Prince was told that Taiwo suffered from madness caused by sorcery. He had stolen another man's wife, and the cuckolded husband was believed to have gotten back at him with black magic. Magical countermeasures were required. The treatment described by Prince, however, was pragmatic in important ways, and this is the reason for discussing his case here. Taiwo was firmly restrained until he was no longer a danger to himself and to others. He was medicated with an herb that appears to have relieved some of his distressing symptoms. Treatment was carried out in a supportive therapeutic atmosphere that could be expected to make the natural methods of restraint and medication more effective.

I give the example of Taiwo to provide a case study of how indigenous treatments addressing the symptoms of madness can be understood in part as naturalistic. I think it is important to realize that the herbal pharmacopoea of traditional psychiatrists may include many plants that contain psychoactive alkaloids.In Africa alone, healers are familiar with hundreds of herbs with stimulant, sedative, and hallucinogenic properties that can directly affect mental states.

But I conclude with a caution. Often one finds that these herbs are used in ways that cannot possibly take advantage of their mind-altering properties. Pascal Imperato, for example, found that Bambara healers applied many potentially effective remedies by rubbing them into the skin or having a client smell them. Only a few were given by mouth, which is the only way they would be effective. He also found that they were usually given for only a few days, and we know from biomedical experience that it takes longer for medication to bring brain chemistry into healthy balance (Imperato, 1977, pp. 96–97). So the caution is this: One cannot assume that treatment is effective just because herbs contain potentially active ingredients. Only after one has examined actual cases, such as that of Taiwo, to see how the indigenous psychiatrist actually uses herbs and techniques, can one draw reasonable conclusions about possible efficacy.

THE THERAPEUTIC INTERVIEW

Most people who see a mental health specialist do not require powerful drugs, and they certainly do not need incarceration or surgery. Commonly, they are provided with counseling. In Western psychiatry and clinical psychology we are accustomed to "talking cures." Comparable approaches are encountered throughout the world.

Among Native Americans, Sanapia proved to be expert in conducting therapeutic interviews. A session with a new patient began when the patient handed over small traditional gifts and they shared a few puffs of a cigarette made of leaves of the sacred tobacco plant. "Tell me your troubles," she said. That simple request often opened the floodgates of a rambling monologue that lasted for hours. On the basis of what was said, Sanapia would decide what kind of treatment might help.

Often, her patients suffered from ghost sickness, usually manifesting as a partial paralysis of the face and spasms of the hands. The patient would not feel well, it was believed, until the ghost was removed. Sanapia accomplished this by having the patient live as a guest in her home, submitting to treatment sessions three times a day for two to four days. Beginning before dawn on the first full day, they repaired to a secluded hillock, where her ministrations were carried out. Holding a Bible, she prayed to God, Jesus, and the Holy Ghost for strength to heal. Transferring a button of peyote from one hand to the other, she drew the healing power of peyote into her own body, causing her to tremble and shake. She chewed a medicine root, massaged her patient's body with it, especially the paralyzed areas, and then asked that it be swallowed down. She then sucked out the sickness, concentrating on the paralyzed areas.

At this point, her manner changed dramatically from intense agitation to a calm gentleness. Cedar incense billowed medicine smoke from hot coals. She held the patient's hands over the smoke. She then stroked the hand with her powerful medicine feather. All the while, she quietly sang her medicine songs, assuring the patient that her healing powers were strong. Between treatments, the patient was supposed to spend the day resting quietly, saying prayers, and thinking pleasant thoughts. If she felt it was necessary, at sunset of the first day she might organize a peyote meeting for the third treatment.

Sanapia was not unaware of the importance of the ritual setting. "Throughout the doctoring procedure, Sanapia continually prods the patient to have faith in her powers and the powers of the sun, earth, God, peyote, Jesus, Medicine eagle, and the Holy Ghost" (Jones, 1972, p. 82). Drawing from her father as well as her mother, she was nothing if not syncretistic (ecumenical).

The patient-doctor interaction made her a success in healing. Clients spoke explicitly of feeling better after talking with her. "The patient has a rare opportunity to speak to an old and therefore, it is assumed, wise woman and to know that her supernatural sanctions forbid her to repeat anything she has been told. They are able to gain the counsel of a woman who has had many years' experience in listening to these confidential disclosures" (Jones, 1972, p. 74). Jones adds that the psychotherapeutic quality of her doctoring became clear to him when he realized that she arrived at a diagnosis only after listening to the emotional rambling of the patient that followed her invitation, "Tell me your troubles."

THE EFFICACY OF ETHNOPSYCHIATRY

In discussing efficacy, it is useful to distinguish those common mental and social hang-ups or problems of living referred to as neuroses from severe derangements of the brain known as psychoses (Torrey, 1986). Studies of the efficacy of psychotherapy in the treatment of neuroses reveal that hundreds of schools of psychotherapy can be identified. Most readers in North America will recognize the following, but dozens more could be listed:

- psychiatry (as psychological counseling)
- psychoanalysis
- gestalt therapy
- primal scream therapy
- hypnotherapy
- biofeedback

Jerome Frank, a psychologist, asked that shamanism and other ethnomedical systems be included in this list, which would add to those discussed above:

- Siberian shamanism
- Comanche doctoring
- trance possession in Zimbabwe
- spiritist surgery in Brazil
- Kwakiutl shamanism
- Ndembu shamanism

Frank drew attention to the enormous number of different techniques used in treating problems of living. Having done that, he then made a very important point which still holds up well despite the passage of time. Insofar as efficacy has been evaluated, they all seem to work about equally well (Frank, 1961) .

- Any form of psychotherapy works better than none at all.
- In the short run, some techniques seem more effective than others.
- In the long run, patients tend to do equally well under any system.

Searching for an explanation of how therapies as diverse as psychoanalysis and shamanism can be about equally successful, Frank concluded that four factors contribute to success:

- confidence in the therapist as a caring person
- clothes and symbols that suggest competence and training
- naming and explaining the illness to confirm that it is real
- rituals demonstrating that something can be done (Frank, 1961; see Torrey, 1986)

A quick review of this chapter shows that Sanapia, the African shaman, João, and Singleton take advantage all of these ways to do therapy. So do psychiatrists.

This is not to say that all psychotherapy is the same. On the contrary, Toksoz Karasu, a psychiatrist, finds that some primarily play upon emotions, others depend heavily upon developing understanding, while still others mainly attempt to modify activities (Karusu, 1986). He refers to these techniques as:

- affective experiencing (eliciting strong emotional arousal)
- cognitive mastery (gaining insight or conscious understanding)
- behavioral regulation (learning self-regulation or control)

Psychiatrists usually emphasize cognitive mastery (especially if they are psychoanalysts) or behavioral regulation (for example, in biofeedback training). The shamans we examined depend more on affective experiencing, encouraging some behavioral regulation, but usually doing nothing to develop insight. Karasu offers reasons for believing that therapy might be more effective if it incorporated not only the four techniques outlined by Frank, but also the three approaches he has delineated. Arthur Kleinman seems unimpressed with this argument, concluding that any form of psychotherapy probably succeeds to the extent that it maximizes a placebo response, and not because some specific aspect of the technique accomplishes some specific psychological effect (Kleinman, 1988, p. 112).

CONCLUSION

It is often said that shamans and other indigenous healers can be thought of as traditional psychiatrists. Multidisciplinarity in our time supports the belief that when physicians and surgeons need help with a minority or immigrant client, it may be that the best assistance will come from a shaman. For a client brought up in a traditional culture, psychiatrists and shamans working together may achieve better success than either can achieve alone.

It is also true that psychiatrists and clinical psychologists in some ways function as though they were shamans in white coats. It should not be surprising, then, that neoshamanism is not only a viable new part of the mix of religions in the United States today, but also has curative potential for clients who need help in dealing with problems of living in our time.

REFERENCES

Ackerknecht, E. H. (1947). Primitive surgery. *American Anthropologist, 49,* 25-44.

Bastian, J. W. (1987). *Healers of the Andes: Kallawaya herbalists and their medicinal plants.* Salt Lake City: University of Utah Press.

Bastien, J. W. (1992). *Drum and stethoscope: Integrating ethnomedicine and biomedicine in Bolivia.* Salt Lake City: University of Utah Press.

Benedict, R. (1959). *Patterns of culture.* Boston: Houghton. (Original work published 1934).

Boyer, L. B. (1964). Folk psychiatry of the Apaches of the Mescalero Indian reservation. In A. Kiev (Ed.), *Magic, faith, and healing: Studies in primitive psychiatry today* (pp. 384-419). Glencoe, IL: The Free Press.

Brown, Peter J. (1980). The trial of Sanapia: A teaching aid for medical anthropology. *Medical Anthropology Newsletter, 11,* 9-10.

Eliade, M. (1964). *Shamanism: Archaic techniques of ecstacy.* Princeton, NJ: Princeton University Press. (Original work published in French 1951)

Estroff, S. E. (1981). *Making it crazy: An ethnography of psychiatric clients in an American community.* Berkeley: University of California Press.

Frank, J. D. (1961). *Persuasion and healing: A comparative study of psychotherapy.* Baltimore: Johns Hopkins Press.

Greenfield, S. M. (1987). The return of Dr. Fritz: Spiritist healing and patronage networks in urban, industrial Brazil. *Social Science & Medicine, 24,* 1095-1108.

Halifax, J. (1982). *Shaman: The wounded healer.* London: Thames and Hudson.

Harner, M. J. (1973). The sound of rushing water. In M. J. Harner (Ed.), *Hallucinogens and shamanism* (pp. 15-27). London: Oxford University Press.

Harner, M. J. (1982). *The way of the shaman: A guide to power and healing.* Toronto: Bantam Books.

Hirsch, S., Gaind, R., Rahde, P. D., Stevens, B. C., & Wing, J. K. (1973). Outpatient maintenance of chronic schizophrenics with fluphenazine decanoate injections: A double-blind placebo trial. *British Medical Journal, 1,* 633-637.

Hogarty, G. E., & Goldberg, S. C. (1973). Drug and sociotherapy in the aftercare of schizophrenic patients. *Archives of General Psychiatry, 28,* 54-64.

Howells, W. (1948). *The heathens: Primitive man and his religions.* Garden City, NY: Doubleday & Co.

Hughes, C. C. (1985). The sleep paralysis taxon—Commentary. In R. C. Simons & C. C. Hughes (Eds.), *The culture-bound syndromes: folk illnesses of psychiatric and anthropological interest* (pp. 147-148). Dordrecht: D. Reidel Publishing Company.

Imperato, P. J. (1977). *African folk medicine: Practices and beliefs of the Bambara and other peoples.* Baltimore: York Press.

Jones, D. E. (1972). *Sanapia: Comanche medicine woman.* New York: Holt, Rinehart & Winston.

Joralemon, D. (1990). The selling of the shaman and the problem of informant legitimacy. *Journal of Anthropological Research, 46,* 105-118.

Karasu, T. B. (1986). The specificity versus nonspecificity dilemma: Toward identifying therapeutic change agents. *American Journal of Psychiatry, 143,* 687-695.

Kirk, S. A., & Kutchins H. (1992). *The selling of DSM: The rhetoric of science in psychiatry.* New York: Aldine de Gruyter.

Kleinman, A. (1988). *Rethinking psychiatry: From cultural category to personal experience.* New York: The Free Press.

Lewis, I. M. (1986). *Religion in context: Cults and charisma.* Cambridge: Cambridge University Press.

Luhrmann, T. M. (1989). *Persuasions of the witch's craft: Ritual magic in contemporary England.* Cambridge, MA: Harvard University Press.

Mattson, P. H. (1982). *Holistic health in perspective.* Palo Alto, CA: Mayfield Publishing Company.

Murphy, J. M. (1964). Psychotherapeutic aspects of shamanism on St. Lawrence Island, Alaska. In A. Kiev (Ed.), *Magic, faith, and healing: Studies in primitive psychiatry today* (pp. 53-83). Glencoe, IL: The Free Press.

Neumann, A. K., & Lauro, P. (1982). Ethnomedicine and biomedicine linking. *Social Science and Medicine, 16,* 1817-1824.

Orion, L. (1995). *Never again the burning times: Paganism revisited.* Prospect Heights, IL: Waveland Press.

Peters, L. (1993). In the land of eagles: Experiences on the shamanic path in Tuva. *Shaman's Drum: A Journal of Experiential Shamanism, 33,* 42-49.

Peters, L., & Price-Williams, D. (1980) Towards an experiential analysis of shamanism. *American Ethnologist, 7,* 397-418.

Prince, R. (1964). Indigenous Yoruba psychiatry. In A. Kiev (Ed.), *Magic, faith, and healing: Studies in primitive psychiatry today* (pp. 84-120). Glencoe, IL: The Free Press.

Segar, J. (1994). Negotiating illness: Disability grants and the treatment of epilepsy. *Medical Anthropology Quarterly, 8,* 282-298.

Shirokogoroff, S. M. (1935). *The psychomental complex of the Tungus.* London: Kegan Paul.

Stoller, P. (1989). *The taste of ethnographic things: The senses in anthropology.* Philadelphia: University of Pennsylvania Press.

Stoller, P., & Olkes, C. (1987). *In sorcery's shadow: A memoir of apprenticeship among the Songhay of Niger.* Chicago: University of Chicago Press.

Torrey, E. F. (1986). *Witchdoctors and psychiatrists: The common roots of psychotherapy and its future.* New York: Harper & Row.

Turner, E. (1992). *Experiencing ritual: A new interpretation of African healing.* Philadelphia: University of Pennsylvania Press.

Turner, E. (1994). A visible spirit form in Zambia. In D. E. Young, & J. G. Goulet (Eds.), *Being changed: The anthropology of extraordinary experience* (pp. 71-95). Peterborough, Ontario, Canada: Broadview Press.

Valenstein, E. S. (1986). *Great and desperate cures: The rise and decline of psychosurgery and other radical treatments for mental illness.* New York: Basic Books.

Wallace, A. A. C. (1966). *Religion: An anthropological view.* New York: Random House.

Walsh, R. N. (1990). *The spirit of shamanism.* Los Angeles: Jeremy P. Tarcher.

Winick, C. (1958). *Dictionary of anthropology.* Ames, IA: Littlefield, Adams & Co.

Young, D. E., & Goulet, J. G. (Eds.) (1994). *Being changed: The anthropology of extraordinary experience.* Peterborough, Ontario, Canada: Broadview Press.

Chapter 15

BODY-ORIENTED HEALERS

INTRODUCTION

Healers who approach health problems on a body-oriented, pragmatic basis are found everywhere. They treat in many different ways, including the use of herbs, massage, bone setting, joint manipulation, acupuncture, or surgery. In addition, midwives and traditional birth attendants always rely importantly on empirical methods. Some of these practitioners limit themselves to body-oriented healing, but probably most also incorporate mind-oriented (including family- or community-oriented) rituals. In a Nahuat-speaking community in Mexico, for example, Brad Huber found that bonesetters *(hueseros)* set fractures, practice massage, and perform joint manipulations, but take on no other healing functions. There is nothing spiritual or overtly psychological about their approach to healing. They rely entirely on hands-on treatment to relieve joint, muscle, tendon, and ligament pain or restricted movement. However, in the same community curers *(curanderas)* engage in a synthesis of magico-religious and naturalistic practices that contrasts strikingly with what bonesetters do. Curers give no thought to the difference an anthropologist would identify as that of supernatural versus ordinary. They function as shaman-herbalist-ritualists who treat people suffering ill health and problems of living, including susto and other culture-bound syndromes (Huber & Anderson, 1996).

The same can be said of Sanapia, the Comanche medicine woman. We have already discussed her mind-oriented methods that included entering an ASC and talking with a sick or troubled person, but she also treated with herbs and other natural substances.

> Sanapia keeps the various kinds of botanical and nonbotanical medicines [such as crow feathers, charcoal from a peyote drum, the Bible, and porcupine quills] which she utilizes in a leather "travel case." . . . The medicines in the travel case are kept orderly and fully stocked at all times to facilitate speed in an emergency. (Jones, 1972, pp. 47, see also 48–51, 54–55)

HERBALISTS

The methods of preparation and use of medicinal herbs have been described by many medical anthropologists reporting from different parts of the world (Shutler, 1977, pp. 197–202; Orellana, 1987, 77–138; Vogel, 1990, pp. 162–248; Biggs, 1985, pp. 123–128; Bastien, 1987, pp. 95–170). These descriptions typically are tempting but not satisfying. David Jones, for example, listed seventeen of the plants or other substances collected by Sanapia, describing how they were prepared and the ways in which she used them. What is one to make of such a list? Of course it is useful to know the assumptions that are made about what they do and how they work, but as Pascal Imperato and others have pointed out, we need to know more (Imperato, 1977, pp. 214–217). Not the least, we need to know whether or not a particular substance, prepared and applied in a given way, confers any curative benefits or is toxic. Medical anthropologists have been very creative in approaching these issues. This becomes clear when anthropological approaches are contrasted with the ways in which pharmacological research has been done.

Biomedical Approaches

Pharmacological researchers with an interest in the possible healing benefits of traditional preparations characteristically take a direct, reductionist approach. They sometimes simply evaluate an herb in one form or another of an experiment. For example, one biomedical team carried out a laboratory procedure in which guinea pigs inflicted with full-thickness burns were treated either with the leaves of a plant, *aloe vera,* or with a synthetic chemical substance, silver sulfadiazine. This experiment demonstrated that those treated with the folk remedy healed better than those who got the high-tech drug, thus confirming a widespread belief that aloe vera works well in the treatment of burns (Rodriguez-Bigas, Cruz, & Suarez, 1988).

Some pharmaceutical firms support what they refer to as natural products programs in which they systematically examine exotic flora and bacteria for chemical compounds that might have medicinal applications (Stix, 1993). This is fairly recent. In the nineteenth century, a few valuable drugs were synthesized from herbs, including digitalis from foxglove for heart failure, quinine from cinchona bark for malaria, morphine from the poppy for pain, and aspirin from willow bark for pain, inflammation, and fever. During the first half of the twentieth century, however, chemists succeeded so well in identifying valuable pharmaceutical substances extracted from coal tar and other chemical sources that investigations of herbs and other plants fell somewhat into neglect. Sulfa drugs effective in the treatment of severe bacterial infections, including the burn medicine silver sulfadiazine mentioned above, are coal tar derivatives. Eventually, however, the synthesis of new "wonder drugs" from plants and bacteria turned this situation around. Coumarin, for example, which is highly

David Young (in hat) helps build a sweat lodge in Alberta, Canada, for use in a vision quest. Dakota healer Cliff Pompana is on the left.

(Photo provided by Steven Aung)

effective against blood clotting, was derived from sweet clover. Vincristine and vinblastine, effective against childhood leukemia and Hodgkin's disease, are derived from the rosy periwinkle of Madagascar. Penicillin is the purefied extract of a plant mold. Streptomycin comes from bacteria. The resultant beneficial drugs now include a whole array of antibiotics, anticancer agents, muscle relaxants, anti-inflammatory corticoid compounds, hypertensive agents, and anticoagulants, many of which were found in plants known to have been used by herbalists (Schultes, 1977).

Anthropologists encountering herbal medicine in field situations have almost never adopted, or adapted, biomedical research designs other than to collect plants for later laboratory analysis, hoping to identify potentially active chemicals. One informative clinical trial demonstrates why anthropologists seldom engage in this kind of work.

A multidisciplinary team led by two anthropologists, David Young and Janice Morse designed and carried out a clinical trial to test the effectiveness of Cree Indian methods of treating a common chronic skin condition (psoriasis)

(Morse, Young, & Swartz, 1991). The treatment they investigated was not simply a medication to be consumed or an ointment to be applied. It constituted a
complex mix of activities that included a ritual burning of herbal incense, the
ceremonial smoking of a sacred pipe of tobacco, offerings of tobacco and cloth,
calling upon the eagle spirit while fanning eagle wings over the body, and participating in a sweat lodge ceremony in which medicated water was sprinkled
on fire-hot rocks. Only in the context of these activities did subjects in the
experiment drink an herbal tea and soften their scaling, itching blemishes with
goose grease.

It was not feasible to conduct this research in its home setting on the Cree
reserve for several reasons. The biomedical paradigm requires that project
administrators maintain control over healers, subjects, and their interactions.
Cree Indians living on the reserve were, in the opinion of the healer, too shy
and too culturally distant from the researchers to be able to accept this kind
of intrusion into their lives. So, a sweat lodge was constructed at the home of
the anthropologist, the healer carried out his tasks in this non-traditional
environment, and the patients themselves were recruited from a population
of non-Indian Canadians. "Thus a major tenet of naturalistic research was vio-
lated—the healing did not take place in the healer's own setting with subjects
that shared his culture and his 'world view.' This disrupted the usual practice
of the healer who reported that he would have to 'pray harder' to achieve a
cure and to incorporate much English into his Cree prayers" (Morse,
McConnell, & Young, 1988, p. 91).

It is expensive, cumbersome, and time-consuming to treat psoriasis in the
Cree way. As a result, only eleven individuals with psoriasis were entered into
the study. The size and distribution of their skin lesions were measured by
physicians before and after treatment. The outcomes of treatment were as follows: One patient withdrew from the study because his condition worsened.
The remaining ten stayed with it for five months. On final assessment, four
showed no change and six were improved as documented by fewer and/or
smaller lesions (Morse, Young, Swartz, & McConnell, 1987; Young, Morse,
Swartz, & Ingram, 1988; Morse, McConnell, & Young, 1988).

These findings fail to answer the question of whether or not Cree healing
is beneficial in the treatment of psoriasis. The hypothesis (that the treatment
was beneficial) could have been demonstrated only if two conditions were met.
First, with a sample this small, success could have been recognized only if the
treatment worked so powerfully that virtually every subject was dramatically
improved or healed. The treatment did not work that well. To demonstrate a
lesser benefit would require a much larger sample, perhaps several hundred
subjects rather than only eleven. In small-scale communities, anthropologists
never encounter numbers of that magnitude.

Second, this trial could have demonstrated success only if the natural history of disease were that it was a chronic condition that never got better or
only got worse, in which case any measurable improvement could be

attributed to the treatment. However, psoriasis is a condition in which the blotches of scaling expectably get bigger and smaller from one time to another, so the changes that were recorded could merely represent the natural ups and downs of the blemishes.

Given these characteristics of the disease and the treatment, the only way to identify benefits beyond those that may occur naturally is simultaneously to enroll a control or comparison group that is identical in every way with the treatment group except that these subjects receive no treatment, are provided with a sham treatment known not to be beneficial, or are offered a different more or less beneficial treatment against which the experimental treatment can be compared. In this way, it would be possible to document improvement in the treatment group if it occurred. Young and Morse did not attempt to recruit a control or comparison group, which leaves us with no basis for confirming or disconfirming their research hypothesis.

It should be noted that a control group which receives a sham treatment is the ideal way to set up a so-called randomized controlled trial. Randomization as such can be done in various ways, but the key element is that any person in the community who has the disease is given an equal chance of being selected to participate in the study, and, if admitted to the study, has an equal chance of being assigned to either the one group or the other. Further, a comparison of control and experimental groups works best if patients do not know which of the two groups they are assigned to. In other words, they need to be blinded in this sense. Blinding permits the placebo effect to be expressed with equal likelihood in either group. Additionally, the healer should be blinded in the sense of not knowing whether a true treatment or a sham is being administered. Finally, physicians assessing original disease conditions and final outcomes should be blinded so that they evaluate the effects of treatment or sham without knowing which the subject has experienced. In short, the ideal is for the trial to be blinded in these three ways.

The procedures for carrying out a blinded study of a new pharmaceutical drug are straightforward. The key element is to provide the control group with an inert pill that looks, smells, and tastes exactly like the real medicine. Medical anthropologists are almost never in a position to organize trials that are controlled and blinded in this way. The most one can hope for, which is what Young and Morse did, is to obtain a pretreatment biomedical diagnosis for each patient in order to establish the etic category of disease under treatment—in the Cree study, that of psoriasis, and a posttreatment evaluation of outcome, preferably after the passage of some days, weeks, or months, to see if the condition is improved or cured. As the Cree research demonstrates, the biomedical experimental design has very limited potential value for those anthropologists who want to identify and measure the efficacy of highly complex, context-bound treatment practices (Anderson, 1991b).

ANTHROPOLOGICAL APPROACHES

Recognizing that they could not simply borrow research strategies from other disciplines, anthropologists have demonstrated considerable ingenuity in creating methods of their own. Daniel Moerman elaborated one such strategy. His chosen task was to evaluate the efficacy of Native American medicinal herbs (Moerman, 1983). To this end he acknowledged that, as illustrated by the Cree healer, treatment usually involves much more than simply administering some decoction of an herb. As he put it, "neither native therapists nor their patients saw pharmaceuticals as any more important in therapy than the song, dance, and din that accompanied treatment" (Moerman, 1983, p. 156). Moerman also recognized that some of the effectiveness of any medication anywhere in the world, including pharmaceutical drugs and Native American herbs, results from a psychosomatic placebo effect that is independent of any physiologically active ingredients.

Given these circumstances, would it be possible to identify the probability of herbal benefits beyond those of the placebo effects of rituals and medicines? Moerman felt that it was possible, and his strategy was as follows. He created a dictionary of Native American medicinal plants. He then was able to demonstrate that of all of the plants that grow on the North American continent, Native American herbalists tended to select those which contain bioactive chemicals. Conversely, they were much less likely to select plants made up mainly of biologically inert substances.

This evidence is highly suggestive that centuries of practical experience probably led healers to know that some plants conferred healing benefits. However, Moerman added a reminder that identifying efficacy on this basis does not permit one to draw conclusions about the value of treatment in any individual set of circumstances.

> One notes approvingly the intelligent study, the deliberate consideration, and the long empirical tradition employed as the Navaho healer gathers 30 or 40 herbal medicines—many of them "rational," "effective" drugs. But despair follows, when the subsequent infusion is fed to and washed over the patient—and a half dozen singers and friends who are participating in the ritual. What kind of effectiveness is this? (Moerman, 1983, p. 157)

Other comparable examples of the use of biologically active plants in ways that cannot be physiologically efficacious are abundant in the anthropological and ethnobotanical literature. One Mexican (Huastec) herb, for example, is known pharmacologically to function as a muscle relaxant when taken internally. "However, in the Huastec treatment of *ichich,* the leaves are not ingested but are instead crushed in water, with the diagnosis of *ichich* confirmed on observation that the liquid has gelled." Obviously, the plant results in no physiologic changes when used in this way (Etkin, 1986, pp. 15–16).

Not satisfied to approach the issue of efficacy by demonstrating that Native American medicinal herbs contain active ingredients, Moerman went on to pose this related question: "Why is it that plants have medicinal value, and how did people figure this out?" (Moerman, 1989, p. 52). He postulated probable answers by means of an exercise in evolutionary thinking. Briefly, he noted that some plants, such as edible grasses, proliferate in great abundance and succeed well even though they are heavily browsed by herbivores. Their evolutionary adaptation is one that invests very little in any particular seed, but produces huge quantities of seed so that the small percentage that survives is still ample. Because they are consumed in large amounts it seems improbable that these plants contain much in the way of bioactive substances other than carbohydrates, amino acids, fatty acids, certain vitamins, and minerals, all of which are nutrients.

In contrast, other plants reproduce in relatively small numbers, and therefore need ways to protect and support seeds, seedlings, and mature plants if they are not to become extinct. One way to gain protection against being eaten by birds and animals was to adapt to the threat of being eaten into extinction (to evolve) by producing toxic chemicals. Elderberries, for example, taste bitter and make people sick.

Toxic plants can be eaten by humans, however, if the chemicals they contain are weakened or denatured by cooking, leaching, drying, or fermenting. They can also be used as medicines, often by heating them in hot water to make herbal teas or decoctions, but also by consuming them directly, one way or another, when the toxic effect is wanted for its healing effects. The biologically active substances in elderberries, for example, include alkaloids that cause vomiting (emesis). Browsing birds, animals, and humans tend to leave these plants alone. However, herbal healers evidently discovered that elderberries and other plants of this genus could be used as medicines when they wanted to treat an illness with an emetic or a laxative.

One taste of a toxic plant may be enough to turn away hungry creatures. Often, the colors and odors associated with plant toxins serve as warnings so that a taste is not necessary. Moerman believes that human beings would have been put on the alert by bitter tastes, odd smells, or certain colors to experiment for potential medicinal benefits. "It seems plausible," Moerman notes, "to suggest that people have used these same signals as evidence of potentially valuable medicines, and over millennia, human knowledge of the subject has accumulated" (Moerman, 1989, p. 59).

Moerman's research sets the stage, so to speak, for identifying the efficacy of native North American herbs. Robert Trotter and Michael Logan have suggested ways in which one can narrow down the study of efficacy by identifying specific species with medicinal properties. They reason that one can pinpoint which herbs might be effective by identifying herbs that are used widely for a given disease either by many individuals within a society or by healers in many different societies. As they put it:

> The greater the degree of group consensus regarding the use of a plant based therapy, the greater the likelihood that the remedy in question is physiologically active or effective. (Trotter & Logan, 1986, p. 95)

The key to this kind of research is quantification. "Not having a sufficiently large and representative sample surely restricts the ability of an ethnographer to suggest which remedies enjoy a high probability of being pharmacologically active as well as therapeutically effective" (Trotter & Logan, 1986, p. 105).

Bernard Ortiz de Montellano draws attention to an important related issue when investigating the efficacy of herbs (Ortiz de Montellano, 1986; Etkin, 1988). He was able to demonstrate that Aztec herbs often did produce the effects wished for by Aztec physicians. That is, the methods demonstrated emic efficacy. For example, the administration of some herbs resulted in sneezing and hemorrhagic nosebleeds, exactly as they were meant to do. Violent sneezing and nosebleeds were desired in terms of the Aztec explanatory model because headaches were attributed to an excess of blood in the head which needed to be discharged, and these herbs were used to treat headaches. From an etic, biomedical point of view, the blood is removed from the bloodstream, but not particularly from the head, so that intracranial vasodilation, which does cause headache, would probably not be ameliorated. These herbs were probably not effective at all in the treatment of headaches except as placebos or, possibly, as counterirritants, and could, in fact, have caused harm if they resulted in excessive blood loss. Similarly, other plants met physician expectations by causing sweating or bowel movements. In all, sixteen of twenty-five herbs investigated produce most of the effects that were wanted by Aztec physicians. Many of these, such as a laxative for constipation, may have been beneficial in etic as well as emic terms (Ortiz de Montellano, 1975).

Trotter and Logan developed a statistical methodology to identify biologically active plants in part because it allows anthropologists to identify those that ought to be evaluated chemically and physiologically as possible sources of new pharmaceutic drugs. More directly relevant to the efficacy of herbalism, however, is that this kind of research provides good presumptive evidence that an herbalist using the studied herb is probably basing treatment on empirically observed results. Presumptive evidence offers a culturally sensitive, if less than fully satisfying, substitute for the randomized clinical trials that are almost impossible for medical anthropologists to conduct.

ETHNOMEDICAL MODELS AND HERBALISM

Small-Scale Communities

Herbalism in holistic perspective requires one to identify the ethnomedical models that contextualize herbal practices in small-scale oral tradition societies such as those of the Comanche medicine woman and the Cree healer. Many different explanatory schemes have been identified by anthropologists working in different parts of the world.

As an illustration, Joseph Bastien describes metaphors of anatomy and physiology explained to him by mountain-dwelling Kallawaya healers in Bolivia. In the Kallawaya model, body concepts are shaped by ideas about close connections between human bodies and local ecology. A body and a mountain are thought of as metaphoric and mystic equivalents of one another. One of Bastien's principal informants described this mountain/body metaphor as follows: "I am the same as the mountain, *Pachamama. Pachamama* has fluids which flow through her, and I have fluids which flow through me. *Pachamama* takes care of my body, and I must give food and drink to *Pachamama*" (Bastien, 1987, p. 68).

"Implicit to Kallawaya theory," Bastien notes, "are hydraulic dynamics in which liquids are concentrated or distilled by centripetal forces and dispersed to the periphery by centrifugal forces" (Bastien, 1987, p. 46). Disease results when the movement of fluids, necessary changes in fluid composition, or waste elimination are disrupted. To restore healthy function, herbs are prescribed and rituals performed bearing these and other highly elaborated concepts in mind (Bastien, 1981).

Naturopathy

Ethnomedical models to conceptualize herbal practices are found in large-scale literate societies as well. Samuel Thomson, an itinerant American herbalist, started a very popular health movement when he published his *New Guide to Health; or Botanic Family Physician* in 1822. The ethnomedical model in this case was quite simple. Thomson came to the conclusion that all diseases were caused by coldness in the body. It followed, then, that to restore heat was a cure-all. So, he recommended steam baths and "hot" herbs such as cayenne pepper (Duffy, 1976, pp. 110–111).

Old American Indian and European herbal traditions were modified in different ways to adapt to nineteenth- and twentieth-century models for the practice of medicine. One of the best known among present-day advocates of alternative medicine is naturopathy, which is still practiced in some places, often as an adjunct to chiropractic. Naturopathy is as simple in concept as was Thomsonianism, but in a different way and for a different reason. Medical politics appears to have been the critical determinant. Against a claim that medical practioners who relied on surgery and pharmaceutical drugs were dangerous, practitioners with an N.D. degree (Doctor of Naturopathy) advocated various kinds of alternative health care techniques, including some that fell out of favor after being popular in the nineteenth century. Naturopaths are nothing if they are not eclectic. They rely heavily on dietary regimens and herbs, but also advocate air and light baths, water treatments (hydrotherapy of the nineteenth century), homeopathic remedies, spinal manipulation and massage (from osteopathy and chiropractic), psychotherapy, meditation (with roots in India), acupressure (adapted from traditional Chinese medicine), and physical fitness training (Fishbein, 1932, pp. 118–125; Maretzki & Seidler, 1985; Baer, 1992).

Naturopaths were quite successful for a time. The United States alone boasted ten naturopathic schools around 1930. Several still provide training. Graduates are able to function as alternative health care practitioners in some places where the law permits. Many practice in Oregon, for example, as well as in Germany and India. Where they are permitted to practice they are appreciated for their noninvasive, nature-based, patient-oriented methods.

Homeopathy

Unlike Thomsonianism and naturopathy, homeopathy is shaped to an elegant explanatory model developed by Samuel Hahnemann (1755–1843), a highly trained physician who broke away from orthodox medicine at the end of the eighteenth century (Duffy, 1976, pp. 112–128; Blackie, 1976). Although his model became somewhat complex, it originated in the observation that an herb (or animal product or mineral) that will cure can also cause the symptoms being treated. This ballooned into the conviction that he had discovered an all-encompassing monocausal law of medicine, the principle that "like cures like," expressed in Latin as *similia similibus curantur.*

Following the rule of similia, homeopaths treat diseases such as headaches with substances that in larger amounts are known to cause headaches. This is very different from the biomedical model, Hahnemann claimed, as he turned a half-truth into an ideological maxim. Allopathic physicians in his time did and still do select some remedies that fight against the symptoms, thus illustrating an ancient axiom of contraries *(contraria contrariis curantur)*. This is the half-truth, since it correctly describes the mechanisms of many drugs. Orthodox practitioners, for example, still treat headaches with analgesics such as aspirin that oppose the pain by dulling sensation.

The other half of the truth, however, is that orthodox physicians also treat with substances that can cause symptoms that resemble those being treated. During Hahnemann's lifetime, for example, variolation for the prevention of smallpox, which was well-known in medical circles, was replaced by vaccination with cowpox. Both variolation and vaccination illustrate symptomatic similia rather than contraria. Hahnemann's mistake was to assume that allopathic medicine, which was heavily empirical in his day, was as firmly and solely deduced from a well-thought-out monocausal theory as was his own form of medicine.

Homeopathy as a form of alternative medicine is currently experiencing an upswing of popularity in the United States. It has long been a familiar part of the health care scene in Europe and India. Yet, it remains largely unstudied by anthropologists. Anthropologists willing to undertake this kind of research should design their research with a clear understanding of how homeopathy is distinctive. It is not distinctive for its principle of similia, since that principle fits easily into allopathic thinking as we have seen. A close reading of homeopathic practice will reveal that it is not even strictly opposed to the principle of contraries, despite its programmatic statements. I have never met a homeopath who would not agree with the following statement of the principle of contraries by Hippocrates:

> Diseases caused by overeating are cured by fasting; those caused by starvation are cured by feeding up. Diseases caused by exertion are cured by rest; those caused by indolence are cured by exertion. To put it briefly, the physician should treat disease by the principle of opposition to the cause of the disease according to its form, its seasonal and age incidence, countering tenseness by relaxation and *vice versa*. This will bring the patient most relief and seems to me to be the principle of healing. (Chadwick & Mann, 1950)

Homeopathic rhetoric leads one astray in the attempt to identify how it is unique. The distinction of key importance for identifying remedies and treating patients is not the deductive theory of similia, but rather, the pharmaceutical practice of compounding medicines based on the theory of minimum dose and potentization.

Hahnemann discovered how to treat diseases by conducting experiments called provings. By this method he or someone else would ingest a substance and then record what was experienced. A distillate of cinchona bark, which contains quinine, illustrates how a proving works. It causes one to experience headache, chills, and fever that resemble (but are not identical with) the symptoms of malaria. Thus, according to the similia principle, it ought to cure malaria, which, of course, it does by suppressing symptoms. Orthodox physicians in Hahnemann's day already treated malaria with quinine which is derived from cinchona bark, being quite indifferent to explanations in terms of contraries and similarities. Over time, Hahnemann did provings on hundreds of other substances, interpreting them all according to this single invariant principle, the unresearched and unproven assumption that each one ought to cure the symptoms it caused, as seemed to be the case with quinine.

Now, the next step for Hahnemann was to determine what the dosage should be. Any remedy identified in a proving was administered only in small doses. After all, a heavy dose was believed to cause the disease being treated. Following this line of thought, Hahnemann continued to experiment with reducing the amounts of these doses until he concluded as part of his explanatory scheme that the smaller the dose was, the more powerful the effect would be. This came to be known as the law of infinitesimals.

Potentization refers to his belief that each time a curative substance was diluted it became smaller in amount but more powerful in effect. Potentization, then, refers to the practice of diluting and succussing (shaking) vials of medicine. The first dilution of an herb or other substance was to dissolve one part of the remedy into nine parts of a fluid such as milk sugar (lactose). After shaking this vigorously, it was then reduced again at a rate of one part in ten. This process of diluting and shaking was not stopped until at least three serial dilutions had been carried out. However, high potency remedies were diluted from 1,000 to 50,000 times. A high potency remedy would be the equivalent of what was left if one teaspoonful of the active ingredient had been dropped into Lake Eirie and if the lake had been shaken to produce a few drops of lake water for the doctor to administer.

It is not likely that even a single atom of the original substance would be found in those few drops of remedy. Nonetheless, the remedy was considered highly potent on an intangible physical plane—one beyond the capabilities of chemistry and physics to identify. It was effective because it contributed to an equilibrium in the body of vital force. Vital force, an ancient concept in Western medicine, is also unidentifiable by scientists. In short, the homeopathic explanatory model is a naturalistic system that incorporates untestable assumptions. Potency and vital force look like secular versions of the Holy Spirit and holy water, neither of which is detectable by any of the five senses. This brings to mind Norman Klein's laconic observation in discussing the shaping power of culture that "only humans can distinguish between plain and holy water" (Klein, 1979, p. 1).

Given these beliefs and practices, one can well understand that medical and scientific critics came to the conclusion that homeopathy provides only placebo benefits and no more. The fact that patients in the care of nineteenth-century homeopathic doctors got well quicker and with fewer residual effects than did those treated by orthodox practitioners was interpreted as a measure, not of how powerful homeopathic remedies were, but of how great was the effect of mind over matter and of how ineffective and even harmful mainstream medicine was until well into the twentieth century.

Is that all there is to it for medical anthropologists? Not at all. In chapter 12 I described the focal theory of infection. The argument was that until a convincing explanatory model had been tested in practice one must assume that it might be wrong. When that theory was investigated clinically, treatment based on the focal theory of infection proved to be a failure. Now then, turn about is fair play, as they say. No matter how unconvincing an explanatory model for healing may be, if predicted health benefits occur, they need to be acknowledged and taken seriously. Surprisingly, at least for skeptics, that is the situation for homeopathy and, indeed, for the Holy Spirit. Let us take the latter as a first example.

Randolph Byrd, a physician, designed and administered a randomized, controlled, blinded trial to evaluate the efficacy of prayer as an adjunct to the medical treatment of seriously ill heart patients (Byrd, 1988; see also Dossey, 1993, pp. 169–195). The key element of this trial was that "born again" Christian believers, located outside of the hospital in a place where they could not be seen by doctors, nurses, or patients, prayed for the experimental group (n=192) but not for the control group (n=201). The results, although not unexpected by Byrd, were very surprising to many. Those who were targeted for intercessory prayer, even though they did not know they were being prayed for, did significantly better than the others in the sense that they required less ventilatory assistance, fewer antibiotics, and fewer diuretics to help them get better. It seems that prayer reduced (but did not eliminate) the need for pills and oxygen.

It is important to acknowledge that if this were a trial of a new pharmaceutical drug, the trial would probably be considered reason enough to try out the "new" treatment on a more extensive basis, or at the very least, to replicate the trial. This is because with drugs the physiologic mechanisms of action can be convincingly explained (as was the case with the theory of focal infection, of course) in terms of everything else that is known and expected in Western medicine. The findings, in other words, would fit well within the biomedical explanatory model with which physicians and scientists are familiar.

Not so intercessory prayer. We have only this study and almost no others as a scientific basis for thinking that it might work, and it flies in the face of the biomedical paradigm. When the results of a study are this surprising and require such a massive reevaluation of medical beliefs, it is prudent to check further before acting on the findings. This is what I argued when considering the extraordinary claims of Turner and Stoller relating to shamanic healing and sorcery. In this trial of healing by means of prayer, the research was flawed. Boyd reports that before initiating the experiment, "the prayer-group had less congestive heart failure, required less diuretic and antibiotic therapy, had fewer episodes of pneumonia, had fewer cardiac arrests, and were less frequently intubated and ventilated." In short, it appears that the surprising outcome occurred because the randomization procedure failed to create completely comparable groups, and that the experimental group was simply not as sick to begin with as the control group. One trial is not enough to settle the issue. It should be repeated, preferably with outcome measures of restored health rather than of the treatment interventions needed to get well (ends rather than means).

This brings us back to homeopathy, with its mystical explanatory model. A clinical trial was carried out by researchers from the Glasgow Homeopathic Hospital collaborating with members of the University Department of Medicine of the Royal Infirmary to test the effectiveness of homeopathic remedies (Gibson et al., 1980). A cohort of forty-six patients with rheumatoid arthritis (RA) were treated with one or another of the nonsteroidal anti-inflammatory drugs (NSAIDs) that are customarily used as first-line treatment for pain relief and impaired movement.

Of these forty-six, half were provided in addition with appropriate homeopathic preparations while the other half were given identical-appearing placebos. Outcome measures used to record the state of the disease demonstrated that homeopathic treatment was effective for the management of rheumatoid arthritis. In comparison with those who received the placebo, the homeopathic patients showed improvements in pain scores, grip strength, stiffness, and ability to function. The improvements were statistically significant. The investigators record, however, that the amount of improvement was small, and some would argue that they were of no clinical significance.

The results of this study of homeopathic treatment are very similar to those obtained in the trial of intercessory prayer for heart conditions, and our response should be the same. Let us take these findings seriously, but only as a stimulus to further research, which in fact is exactly what happened. A couple of years after publication of the trial just described, another collaborative team of investigators carried out a similar trial, this time in England (Shipley et al., 1983).

The design of this replicative study was rather different, which must be kept in mind as a possible explanation for why the results were so different. In this trial, the use of a single common homeopathic remedy for the treatment of osteoarthritis (OA) was uniformly administered to each patient. (The first trial had tailored the remedy to each individual case, so they were not all medicated in the same way.) Similarly, every subject was given the same NSAID (fenoprofen), rather than any one of a number of common analgesics as in the first trial. Out of a total of thirty-three patients, thirteen received additional drops of *Rhus tox* (extract of poison oak), known to produce some symptoms that mimic those of arthritis and frequently prescribed by homeopathic physicians for OA. The remedy was prepared at a potency of six, that is, as a dilution of one part per million of fluid, and was administered in the amount of five drops taken by mouth three times a day. The control group of twenty received placebo drops that were identical in appearance and taste.

The results after two weeks were not surprising for those oriented to the biomedical paradigm. *Rhus tox* did nothing to improve the condition of the patients. The collaborative team of researchers concluded "there was no significant difference between the effects of *Rhus tox* and placebo." Meanwhile, a more recent clinical trial has demonstrated a statistically significant decrease in the duration of diarrhea in children treated with a homeopathic remedy (Jacobs, 1994).

And that's how things stand at this point in time. Biomedical researchers on the whole are unimpressed and uninterested in conducting research on homeopathy. Anthropologists seem to be equally disinterested. The Congress of the United States, on the other hand, wrote into the law that established the Office of Alternative Medicine (OAM) of the National Institutes of Health that the OAM is "to facilitate the evaluation of alternative medical treatment modalities, including . . . homeopathic medicine" (AM, 1993).

The founding director of OAM, Joseph Jacobs, is a highly trained physician scientist as well as a member of the St. Regis Mohawk Tribe of upstate New York. As a child he experienced Native American healing practices in his own life. While still OAM director, he offered this advice to medical anthropologists: "We have to be more rigorous in our application of the social sciences to the study of health and medicine. The ethnographers have been studying health belief systems for a long time without being able to look at outcomes in a scientific sense, while we in medicine look at outcomes without studying the belief systems." He concludes with this admonition: "We have to get the anthropologists and the medical community together on this" (Hearn, 1993: p. 10). To this I would add that ethnographers look at far more than belief systems alone, and often are able to demonstrate that health care practices are beneficial (or harmful) in ways not anticipated by either indigenous beliefs or those of Western medicine.

OLD WORLD EMPIRICAL MEDICINE

Across the Eastern Hemisphere, from Europe to Asia, highly developed systems of medicine based on empirical reasoning arose in ancient literate societies. These medical systems resembled one another in many ways, mutually influenced as they were by diffusion over old trade, traveler, and military routes. These medical systems also differed from one another in many ways, to be sure, but all shared a methodology of cause-and-effect reasoning based upon naturalistic rather than personalistic assumptions. Because these societies had systems of writing, medical reasoning drew upon enormous data bases that accumulated over the course of hundreds and hundreds of years in the form of written records, case studies, commentaries, diagnostic and treatment manuals, and theoretical disquisitions.

Anthropologists have studied these Old World systems to some extent by means of historical research, but much more by means of ethnographic investigations in places where these traditions are still very much alive. Classical Greek medicine (also known as Galenic or Greco-Roman medicine) is no longer a living tradition in its place of origin in Europe. During the last couple of centuries it was gradually transformed out of existence, replaced by modern Western medicine to which it gave birth. The transformation began in the sixteenth century when Vesalius set new standards for the science of anatomy by undertaking and evaluating careful dissections of human cadavers. It continued in the next century as Harvey transformed physiology into a scientific pursuit when he showed by means of experiments how blood circulated through the body. By the nineteenth century, ancient concepts survived only as vestiges in the practice of parochial doctors out of touch with academic medicine in urban centers.

> The decades between 1800 and 1830 mark the decisive break with the vague "systems" of classical medicine and the formation of modern clinical methods. Combining clinical observations with pathological anatomy, the French physicians correlated the signs and symptoms of patients with the internal lesions disclosed at autopsy. In 1816 Laennac introduced the first crude stethoscope; auscultation allowed the physician to penetrate behind the externally visible to "see" into the living. As is often said, doctors previously observed patients; now they examined them. And, in a further critical step, the Paris school began to evaluate the effectiveness of therapeutic techniques statistically. (Starr, 1982, pp. 54-55).

Centuries earlier, Greco-Roman medicine diffused to the Middle East at a time when the classical world of the West was smoldering out. While medical culture stagnated and degenerated in medieval Europe, it thrived in centers of Islamic civilization, particularly as taught and elaborated by Arabic and Persian physicians. When classical Western medicine was revitalized during the Renaissance, it rediscovered its own past by translating Arabic and Persian versions of ancient Greek texts into Latin. This, in turn, withered away, as we have seen, but Greco-Roman/Arabic-Persian medicine survived to the present in the Middle East where to this day it is known as Unani Tibb (Arabic for "Greek medicine").

Unani Tibb diffused with the conquering warriors and missionaries of Islam to reach countries stretching westward across North Africa and eastward through Iran into Central Asia and India (Pugh, 1991). It did not stop until it reached seas lapping at the shores of the Philippines and Malaysia (Hilton-Simpson, 1922; Good & Good, 1992; Hart, 1969; Laderman, 1992).

Galenic medicine also survived in watered-down versions as folk medicine. By way of Islamic conquests it crossed the Sahara Desert into West Africa (Wall, 1988, p. 235). Its most impressive folk survivals, however, are to be found today in the Americas from Mexico to Argentina, brought to this vast area by post-Columbian Spanish invaders (Foster, 1978). In the New World a simplified version of humoral theory survived as ideas about hot and cold that appear to have resonated with indigenous Native American concepts of healing that in some ways were similar (Foster, 1994, pp. 165–188; see also Ortiz de Montellano, 1990, pp. 213–221).

Modern versions of the other Old World empirical medical systems are also very much alive. Ayurveda in South Asia was well developed by the beginning of the Common Era (C.E.).

The Vedas show a very primitive stage of medical and physiological lore, but the basic textbooks of Indian medicine—the compendia of Caraka (1st–2nd centuries a.d.) and Susruta (c. 4th century a.d.)—are the products of a fully evolved system which resembles those of Hippocrates and Galen in some respects, and in others was developed beyond them. (Bashram, 1959, pp. 498–499)

This ancient system of medicine underwent early exposure to Tibb-Unani on its frontiers between the sixth and ninth centuries and more massively during the sixteenth and seventeenth centuries, when the Mughal empire unified and controlled much of north and central India (Foster, 1978, pp. 7–89; Bashram, 1959, p. 480). Ayurveda was threatened with extinction in the eighteenth and nineteenth centuries when the English colonial government put its power and prestige behind its replacement by modern Western medicine. As

Charles Leslie, a founder of the International Association for the Study of Traditional Asian Medicine, discusses shared interests in medical anthropology with Aihwa Ong.

(Photo provided by Steven Aung)

Charles Leslie and others have observed, by the late twentieth century a revival of Ayurveda gained political and social momentum, not only in India, but more widely as far as Nepal in the north and Sri Lanka in the south (Leslie, 1992; Zimmermann, 1992; Obeyesekere, 1992). During the last decade, Ayurveda has also become a rising star in the melting pot of alternative medicine in the United States (Sharma & Chopra, 1991; Skolnick, 1991).

Traditional Chinese medicine (TCM) and its derivatives are alive and well from Tibet in the west, across the Peoples' Republic of China to as far east as Japan, and from Korea and Manchuria in the north to Vietnam and Indonesia in the south (Kleinman et al., 1975; Kleinman, 1980; Farquhar, 1994). In one form or another TCM also thrives in Chinese settlements all over the world, including San Francisco and New York (Flaws, 1992). Not the least, it is increasing in popularity as a component of alternative medicine in many non-Asian communities, particularly in the United States (Anderson, 1991a; Anderson, 1994).

For the purpose of introducing in summary fashion a subject that is this vast in geographic spread and historical depth, I find it useful to build on certain observations recorded by Francis Zimmermann (Zimmermann, 1992, pp. 218–220). His research reveals that in "classical India and the Western ancient world" medicine was thought of as divided into a trifunctional division of therapeutics: medicaments, manipulations, and diets. This ancient classification can be extended to include the rest of Asia in a helpful manner. I therefore propose to discuss Old World medical systems in terms of the following three subdivisions which I have modified and adapted from Zimmermann, who for his part drew upon Greek, Latin, Sanskrit, and other ancient sources:

- Medicaments—mostly herbs, but including nonvegetable substances
- Manipulations—surgery, bonesetting, and massage
- Diets and Regimens—dietary advice, but also physical and meditational exercises

Medicaments

Archeology records that the earliest complex societies to be characterized by urban centers, professional specialists, and libraries of written records appeared almost simultaneously on the horizons of history during the fourth millennium B.C.E. in the Middle East (Sumaria) and North Africa (Egypt). Egypt more than Sumaria emerged as the earliest civilization in which literate, full-time specialists worked to perfect the practices of medicine and surgery. Egyptian physicians set the stage for the great traditions of Old World medicine by developing and teaching pragmatic methods, but they were not themselves pure exponents of Old World naturalism, since they freely mixed pragmatism with magic and ritual (Breasted, 1967, pp. 85–86).

> Egyptian medical documents contain a hodge-podge of home remedies based on a lore of herbs and of sympathetic magic, outright witch-doctoring in the forms of charms and incantations, and shrewd observations on the functions of the body. (Wilson, 1951, p. 56)

The earliest records of systematic naturalism in medicine were recorded by Hippocrates, a semimythical Greek who lived in the fifth century B.C.E. When writings attributed to Hippocrates were compiled, the work of a number of physicians were included under his name. As a fundamental characteristic, these physicians were the earliest of whom we have knowledge who pervasively insisted that disease resulted from natural causes and that nothing supernatural needed to be invoked (Heidel, 1941; Temkin, 1973).

Hippocrates and his fellow physicians faced opposition even in their own time from other physicians and the priests of Aesculapius, whose temples were centers of divine healing. Aesculapius was granted immortality as the patron deity of physicians. The apotheosis of Aesculapius is a reminder that religious thinking was not totally absent from ancient Greek medicine, and that naturalism in the Hippocratic corpus was a relative matter.

As a fundamental principle, the followers of Hippocrates refused to acknowledge angry gods, evil spirits, witches, or sorcerers as causes of disease. They insisted upon an empirical, naturalistic approach that inquired into how the body was affected in anatomic and physiologic terms. In the Hippocratic treatise *On Airs, Waters and Places,* for example, the author wrote, "The still and stagnant waters of marshes are the cause of diarrhea, dysentery and intermittant fever." He went on to note, "Those cities which are favorably placed for the sun and the winds, and where the waters are of good quality, are less touched by these disadvantages" (Withington, 1928).

These are good observations, but it should be remembered that although he looked for naturalistic explanations, Hippocrates was frequently not correct in what he believed about nature. He wrote in his book *On Winds,* for example, that the cause of disease was the air, "when it enters the body in excess or in insufficient quantity or too much at a time or when tainted by morbid miasmas." Not a bad explanation for 2,500 years ago, and still a widespread folk belief in many parts of the world, but not up to contemporary scientific standards.

In order to understand these traditional Old World medical systems, we need to distinguish theory from practice. In the perspective of theory, practitioners made and make treatment decisions primarily in terms of how administering an herb seems reasonable in terms of the elegance of the overarching physiologic theory. In other words, these forms of medicine as theoretical systems remain primarily deductive sciences, enlisting inferences that follow of neccesity from premises that are not in themselves brought into question.

In Hippocratic medical theory, for example, it was taught that the body constituted a microcosm of the universe, both of which were constructed out of four primary elements: fire which was hot; earth which was dry; water which was moist; and air which was cold.

As ancient Greek theory grew more elaborate, the idea arose that good health depended upon the circulation of four humors or fluids, each of which was characterized by attributes derived from the primary elements. The four humors and their elemental qualities were: blood—hot and moist; phlegm—cold and moist; yellow bile—hot and dry; and black bile—cold and dry.

In theory, good health required that these humors with their attributes be kept in equilibrium. If one of the humors was depleted, the model called for repletion by means of herbs or diet that were suitably hot or cold, dry or moist (the principle of contraria). If too much of a humor was the cause of the disease, some form of removal was required, usually by sweating, vomiting, defecating, or bleeding.

This is deductive reasoning in that the explanatory system provides the basis for deciding what needs to be done in any specific case. In the oral tradition of Latin America, only the hot-cold dichotomy survived from the humoral theory of Spanish physicians. In folk theory, illness results from being too hot or too cold, and the treatment is to supply herbs, foods, or ambient temperatures conceptualized as caloric opposites (contraries) to the bodily excess or deficiency (Foster, 1978, pp. 4–5).

Puzzled by discrepancies in his data on folk medicine in a Mexican community, George Foster realized that it is necessary to distinguish prevention from cure if one is to understand health behavior. He noted that humoral theory customarily shapes behavior to avoid getting sick. A regular bath, for example, has a cooling effect so that one does not fall ill from getting too hot. "Bathing, therefore, is looked upon as preventive medicine, not because of cleanliness but because it keeps body temperatures within safe limits" (Foster, 1984, p. 529).

As concerns treatment, however, whereas therapy is often based on the principle of opposites (a hot remedy for a cold illness or the reverse), it also is often based solely on pragmatic experience. That is, treatment is often chosen simply and directly because it is believed to be effective. If asked, it will probably be justified (legitimated) in terms of humoral theory, but in fact it "represents the empirical application of learned, 'standard' remedies administered with little or no thought of humoral consistency" (Foster, 1988, p. 122). Thus, a tea of *flor de abrojo* serves in the community as a widely used cough medicine. When pressed for a humoral explanation, some describe it as a hot medicine suitable for a cold cough, but others characterize it as a cold medicine for a hot cough. Over all, elicited explanations have the appearance of *ex post facto* justifications thought up when the ethnographer inquired about the humoral logic of what in fact was merely a standard treatment.

Foster identified here an important reality in the practice of humoral medicine, not merely in the oral tradition of a Mexican village, but more widely when practiced as part of a literate tradition. From the beginning almost to the present, anthropologists have dismissed, ignored, or minimized naturalism in the healing arts. When they have given attention to naturalistic systems, it has mostly been directed to explanatory models, as in the case of humoral medicine. On the whole they have neglected and ignored pragmatic practices based on trial and error, on what Foster referred to as standard remedies employed because they seemed to work. Trial-and-error practices deserve careful attention. They appear to characterize the praxis of many if not most physicians in homeopathy (as in the practice of prescribing *Rhus tox* routinely for osteoarthritis), Chinese medicine (as in the case of one senior physician observed by Judith Farquhar who prescribed a liver formula for almost all of his patients), Ayurveda (in which practice at times is best described as bricolage), and, apparently, Unani Tibb (Shipley et al., 1983; Farquhar, 1994, pp. 172, 180; Beals, 1976; Obeyesekere, 1992, pp. 160, 170–171, 174; Durkin-Longley, 1982, pp. 39, 232; Good & Good, 1992, p. 265).

Manipulations

Half a century ago, Erwin Ackerknecht published a survey article in *The American Anthropologist* titled "Primitive Surgery" (Ackerknecht, 1947). In it he described worldwide practices in the suturing of wounds, the amputation of limbs, excisions (e.g., of small tumors), incisions (such as lancing boils), blood-letting, cesarean section, trephinement, and ritual or judiciary operations (such as circumcisions). He concluded that for the most part, *"Primitive surgery is indeed poor in scope and quality.* Only in the more southern parts of East Africa and in certain Polynesian localities do we encounter a relatively well-developed surgery" (Ackerknecht, 1947, p. 37 [author's italics]).

As far as medical anthropology is concerned, Ackerknecht had the first and last word on the subject. With very few exceptions, little since then has been published by anthropologists on methods of surgery and related explanatory models (Imperato, 1977, 176–199; Katz, 1981; Ward & Sadove, 1989). Here is a field worthy of attention.

Two medical advances were absolutely essential before surgery could begin to realize its potential. Most importantly, antiseptic or aseptic techniques were required. Without them, surgical patients died from uncontrolled infections. In addition, only with pain control could the surgeon operate in a time-consuming, controlled manner to undertake complex maneuvers. For these reasons alone, modern surgery was slow to develop until the second half of the nineteenth century. It seemed to be waiting for Morton in America to demonstrate the utility of ether anesthetic and for Lister in England to introduce an early method of germ control.

In light of these realities of surgery, it is quite remarkable that in some parts of the Old World, some successful surgery was done. By general agreement, the preeminent surgeons of the great civilizations of antiquity were found in India.

> The cæsarian section was known, bone-setting reached a high degree of skill, and plastic surgery was developed far beyond anything known elsewhere at the time. Ancient Indian surgeons were expert at the repair of noses, ears and lips, lost or injured in battle or by judicial mutilation. In this respect Indian surgery remained ahead of European until the 18th century, when the surgeons of the East Indian Company were not ashamed to learn the art of rhino-plasty from the Indians. (Basham, 1959, pp. 499–500)

As is clear from the old Ackerknecht article, surgical operations were and are painful and crude in most cultures. Bonesetting, on the other hand, has been and is neither rare nor crude. Only a few anthropologists, however, have described bonesetting and or massage with precision. Massage is probably a human universal in the sense that anyone can be expected purposefully to rub a part of the body to relieve pain. In many societies, but not all, some individuals are formally identified as skilled in massage. What is less obvious to the untrained eye is that some of those identified as massagers are more accurately described as bonesetters (Paul, 1976; Mull & Mull, 1983; Anderson, 1987; Schiffmann & Hernesniemi, 1989; Andritzky, 1990).

A bonesetter is someone who, in addition to soft tissue massage, moves bones and joints as part of the treatment offered. Frequently bonesetters set fractures. In traditional Chinese practice, for example, this was accomplished with splints that did not immobilize adjacent joints and was usually combined with traditional Chinese calesthentics, yielding results superior to the recent biomedical practice of encasing whole limbs in plaster casts (Horn, 1971, pp. 78-80) . Less obvious is that bonesetters also induce motion in joints that are painful or stiff, that is, they manipulate joints as well as massage them.

To understand the difference between manipulation and massage, try the following simple exercise. Using your dominant hand, rub your other hand to make the muscles, tendons, and joints feel stretched and warm. Now crack your knuckles. You have just followed a light massage with a simple joint manipulation that stretched the tendons and synovial capsules of the joints and repositioned the bones. Manipulation frequently heals by increasing joint mobility and reducing or eliminating pain. In the hands of experts it can be quite effective for the treatment of any of the joints of the upper and lower extremities as well as of the spine, benefitting associated muscle spasms, neuritis, and referred pain (Triano, 1991).

Joint manipulation is very old in Eurasia. Zimmermann describes it for Ayurveda (Zimmermann, 1989, pp. 207-231). It is at home in traditional Chinese medicine where it is known as *tui na*. It is clearly described in the Hippocratic corpus of two and a half millennia ago, and it continued to be performed by surgeons in Europe until well into the seventeenth century, when it fell into abeyance as part of formal surgical practice. However, European folk healers (traditional alternative practitioners, if you will) continued the practice until the present in some places.

By the second half of the nineteenth century unlettered bonesetters took on a small number of medical doctors as apprentices, with the result that a growing number of physicians in our time treat by means of joint manipulation. In England and on the Continent the specialty is now referred to as orthopedic medicine (or, alternatively, as manipulative or manual medicine). Bonesetting became a part of American traditional health care when a family of English bonesetters along with some others transported the practice across the Atlantic. In the United States bonesetting became the inspiration for two major healing institutions, osteopathic medicine and chiropractic, both of which originally were established to provide spinal manipulation as a way to cure any disease (Anderson, 1992).

Other kinds of body work also have tended to be undocumented and unexplored by medical anthropologists. Cupping, which is or was practiced in many places in Africa, Asia, Europe, and Latin America, is rarely mentioned in anthropological publications. It is done by heating the inside of a cup or glass (to create a vacuum). When the cup is placed on the skin it draws the covered area up, which seems to give some relief for rheumatic pain. When the cup is removed one can see a reddened circular area, which led one Israeli practitioner documented by Philip Singer to be called the Bagel-maker (Yiddish, *Bagelmacher*). (Singer, 1977)

Often cupping includes making small cuts in the skin before setting the glass or cup in place. Known as wet cupping, it draws blood, an extractive process that fits well with humoral theory, as Wall discovered in his study of Hausa medicine. Referring to low back pain, Wall writes, "Such conditions are treated by surgical cupping *(kaho)* to remove the black, dead blood—one of the routine tasks performed by village barbers *(wanzamai)"* (Wall, 1988, p. 187).

Traditional Chinese acupuncture is backed by an explanatory model oriented to returning equilibrium to the vital energy *(qi)* that courses through invisible meridians in the body. However, acupuncture is also often practiced in a rather pragmatic way, primarily for its analgesic effects, but also as a remedy for common illnesses such as constipation or chronic fatigue (Eisenberg, 1985; Flaws, 1992). Anthropologists have shown far more interest in the explanatory model than in needling as a physiologic technique with directly observable effects (Farquhar, 1994).

Diets and Regimens

In humoral medicine it can sometimes be very difficult to decide whether a substance taken orally is a medicine or a food. Eugene Anderson and Marja Anderson bring out this point as concerns Chinese folk medicine in Hong Kong. "If there is one thing universal in Chinese medicine, classical or folk, professional or self-managed," they write, "that one thing is diet therapy. Modification of food patterns is part of medication, not to be separated from the use of drugs" (Anderson & Anderson, 1975, p. 143). At times the difference between a medicine and a food is not entirely clear. Anderson and Anderson discovered that "only the thinnest of lines" separates some medicinal soups from other soups taken simply as food. Snakehead catfish soup, for example, can be eaten for nourishment, but sometimes is prescribed as a medicine, while white crane soup is always regarded as a medicine, but is prepared by boiling it to make a soup (Anderson & Anderson, 1975, p. 154).

On the whole in Hong Kong, as well as in other parts of the world where humoral concepts still shape curing efforts, food and medicine complement one another in health care. Margaret Trawick offers an illustration from the practice of an Ayurvedic physician in South India, whose advice to a patient is transcribed in the following colloquial translation:

> To keep vigorous what hunger you have, for feces to move when you have eaten, for urine to separate properly, for the body to be light, I will give medicine. You take that regularly, and with the medicine it will get better.
>
> What is called food is an important matter. . . . [I]f you eat whatever you feel like and take medicine it is useless. Therefore I will tell you a diet. If you eat according to that discipline it will become better. (Trawick, 1992, p. 139)

Foster combined examples such as these from Chinese medicine and Ayurveda, from still other parts of the world, and from his own findings in a Mexican community to identify a regularity in dietary therapy when it is informed by humoral thinking. The mainstay of the diet, he found, will usually be a food classified as neutral, one that is neither hot nor cold. In terms of Moerman's work, I would add, the food staple tends to be one of the non-medicinal plants such as rice, wheat, maize, or potatoes that do not contain bioactive substances other than nutrients.

Because the bulk of the diet is neutral not only in humoral (emic) terms, but also in biochemical (etic) terms, prevention and treatment by dietary manipulation is manageable.

> One reason, I believe, that the humoral system survives is that it is so easily controlled. Whatever the local hot/cold properties of individual herbs and foods, the fact remains that people can eat most foods at most times without having to give much thought to the problem of balance (Foster, 1984, p. 189).

Dietary aspects of prevention and healing have attracted far less attention from anthropologists than they deserve. However, the least attention of all has been given to body-mind (meditation, posture, breathing, and movement) regimens such as the hatha yoga exercises of India, Tai Chi Chuan or Qi Gong calesthentics in China, and the martial arts of diverse traditions. For information on how they may impact on health one has to turn to nonanthropologists (Iyengar, 1966; Eisenberg, 1985). More than a quarter of a century ago, Ray Birdwistell, a physical anthropologist, pointed the way in his research on kinesics (Birdwistell, 1970). More recently, some anthropologists have published studies of dance (Royce, 1980; Novack, 1990; Ness, 1992). It is rare, however, for an anthropologist to explore the health implications of dance other than as psychotherapy (Hanna, 1988).

Since the late 1980s, Michael Davis has attempted to stimulate interest in the martial arts by organizing symposia and encouraging cooperation among anthropologists, but little has been published. A book by Lowell Lewis is an exception (Lewis, 1992). His study of capoeira, the martial art of Brazil, is highly informative, but not about health benefits as such. He is primarily interested in capoeira as a cultural performance, an expressive art. Ample evidence from outside of anthropology indicates that posture and movement can impact importantly on physical and mental health (Miller, 1991). Here is a fascinating area of research up for grabs. Participant observation in this field, as Lewis demonstrated, can be rewarding as well as demanding, since the researcher will need to explore the subject with both body and mind.

Of the three areas of traditional Old World medicine identified by Zimmermann, only medicaments (herbalism), with their associated explanatory paradigms, have attracted much anthropological attention. As we have seen, the results are fascinating and valuable. The rest, with some notable exceptions, have suffered neglect. It is to be hoped that the next generation of medical anthropologists will identify this reality as rich in opportunities.

MIDWIVES AND BIRTH ATTENDANTS

Childbirth is such a dramatic personal, familial, and communal event that it almost universally is enveloped in ritual and symbolism. The event may be secular in nature, but more commonly is embellished with magical and religious practices that participants may regard as absolutely essential for health and happiness (Paul & Paul, 1975). At the same time, childbirth is always a natural and largely predictable physiologic event that requires matter-of-fact manipulations to support:

- contractions and cervical dilation
- the mother when she pushes
- that grand moment when the baby is caught
- severing the umbilical cord
- ejection or extraction of the placenta
- postpartum contraction of the uterus to stop bleeding and begin its involution
- cleaning and wrapping the baby

The kind of attention given to a parturient woman varies greatly in non-industrialized parts of the world where older traditions still prevail. It is not as uncommon as one might think for a woman to deliver herself without assistance (Shostak, 1983, pp. 205–206). Reporting on childbirth in a rural Bariba community in Africa, Carole Browner and Carolyn Sargent note that "a midwife is not usually summoned unless complications occur." They add, "Should a birth attendant be needed (many Bariba women deliver alone), elderly female kin from either side of the family may be called" (Browner & Sargent, 1990, p. 223).

In most places the birthing mother is attended by helpers, usually but not always women. Often, in addition to family members, a traditional birth attendant (TBA) assists at the time of labor and delivery. Throughout the world, the TBA is often illiterate, experienced but not trained, and low in status. In villages in North India, for example, TBAs are usually, but not always, untouchables who are thought of and treated as dirty and without worth. Birth is unclean and defiling. The work of a TBA, in addition to delivering the woman and caring for the newborn, includes cleaning feces, blood, and other dirt (Jeffery & Jeffery, 1989; Freed & Freed, 1980, pp. 359–360; Wiser & Wiser, 1971, pp. 44–45).

However, if the practitioner is a skilled midwife rather than a TBA, she may work with a woman during her pregnancy as well as at the time of delivery, and often she also provides early postpartum care of the child. She may have been thoroughly trained as an apprentice and very skilled by virtue of experience or formal education (see Bastien & Edens, 1992, p. 137; MacCormack 1994, p. 9; Kang-Wang, 1980). Brigitte Jordan documented home births managed by very skilled midwives in a Maya community of Yucatan, Mexico (Jordan & Davis-Floyd, 1993). In that small-scale, nonindustrialized society, the mother gives birth to her baby in the hammock she normally shares with her husband. It happens in the company of her family where she feels secure and at home.

Assuming a semi-upright reclining position she is partially supported at her shoulders by a helper. Her husband may do this since he is expected to be there (in part to see how a woman suffers, according to Jordan's informants). The birthing mother can move about if she wishes and may chose to be seated on a chair at the moment of delivery. Labor is allowed to unfold in an unhurried way in order to allow nature to take its course. Yet the midwife is experienced in helping the process along. If the fetus is in the breech (bottom first) position, she will use her skills in body massage to rotate it around for an uneventful delivery. That difficult maneuver was beautifully executed in a matter-of-fact way, Jordan found.

When village midwives are of the quality of those studied by Jordan, they clearly constitute a valuable health resource on a local level. Training midwives to function more effectively in biomedical terms by instructing them in modern antiseptic techniques, however, can lead to unanticipated cultural problems. This became clear in Niger, for example, where it was found that implementing new practices that were healthier in biomedical terms required midwives to violate traditional taboos relating to respect and shame. As a consequence, the introduction of improved obstetrical techniques was stalled because midwives offended and angered birthing mothers (Jaffre & Prual, 1994). Well-planned development programs therefore need to carefully investigate ways to support the work of these specialists and to add to their training (Bastien, 1992, pp. 137–169).

CONCLUSION

Naturalistic medical systems were referred to in early anthropological works, including those of Frazer, Rivers, Murdock and others, but only in passing. Magico-religious healing seemed far more interesting to those investigators. In recent decades, body-oriented healing has attracted more anthropological attention. The emphasis, however, has been on explanatory models and symbolic analysis. Except for herbalism, praxis continues to be neglected in most parts of the world. Not so, however, for Western medicine, to which we now turn.

REFERENCES

Ackerknecht, E. H. (1947). Primitive surgery. *American Anthropologist, 49, 25–42.*
AM, Bimonthly newsletter of the Office of Alternative Medicine. (1993). [Untitled], *1* (1), 1.
Anderson, E. N., & Anderson, M. L. (1975). Folk dietetics in two Chinese communities, and its implications for the study of Chinese medicine. In A. Kleinman, P. Kunstadter, E. R. Alexander & J. L. Gale (Eds.) *Medicine in Chinese cultures: Comparative studies of health care in Chinese and other societies* (pp. 143–175). DHEW Publication No. (NIH) 75-653. Washington, DC: U.S. Government Printing Office.

Anderson, R. (1987). The treatment of musculoskeletal disorders by a Mexican bonesetter *(Sobador)*. *Social Science and Medicine, 24,* 43-46.

Anderson, R. (1991a). An American clinic for traditional Chinese medicine: Comparisons
to family medicine and chiropractic. *Journal of Manipulative and Physiological
Therapeutics, 14,* 462-466.

Anderson, R. (1991b). The efficacy of ethnomedicine: Research methods in trouble.
Medical Anthropology, 13, 1-17.

Anderson, R. (1992). Spinal manipulation before chiropractic. In S. Haldeman (Ed.),
Principles and practice of chiropractic (2nd ed., pp. 3-14). Norwalk, CT:
Appleton & Lange.

Anderson, R. (1994). Unintended psychotherapy in the practice of traditional Chinese
medicine in the United States. *Jahrbuch für Transkulturelle Medizin und
Psychotherapie*—1992 (pp. 303-310). Berlin, Verlag für Wissenschaft ünd
Bildung.

Andritzky, W. (1990). Manual therapy in Andean healing (Peru) and a general outline
of concepts for research in ethnobody therapy (in German with summary in
English). *Jahrbuch für Transkulturelle Medizin und Psychotherapie*—1990 (pp.
135-162). Berlin: Verlag für Wissenschaft und Bildung.

Baer, H. A. (1992). The potential rejuvenation of American naturopathy as a consequence of the holistic health movement. *Medical Anthropology, 13,* 369-383.

Bashram, A. L. (1959). *The wonder that was India.* New York: Grove Press.

Bastien, J. W. (1981). Metaphorical relations between sickness, society, and land in a
Qollahuaya ritual. In J. W. Bastien & J. M. Donahue (Eds.), *Health in the Andes.*
(Special Publication of the American Anthropological Association, No. 12).
Washington, DC: American Anthropological Association.

Bastien, J. W. (1987). *Healers of the Andes: Kallawaya herbalists and their medicinal
plants.* Salt Lake City: University of Utah Press.

Bastien, J. W., & Edens, N. (1992). Midwives and maternal and infant health care. In J. W.
Bastien, (Ed.), *Drum and stethoscope: Integrating ethnomedicine and biomedicine in Bolivia* (pp. 137-169). Salt Lake City, UT: University of Utah Press.

Beals, A. R. (1976). Strategies of resort to curers in South India. In C. Leslie (Ed.), *Asian
medical systems: A comparative study* (pp. 184-197). Berkeley: University of
California Press.

Biggs, B. (1985). Contemporary healing practices in East Futuna. In C. D. F. Parsons
(Ed.), *Healing practices in the South Pacific* (pp. 108-128). Honolulu: The Institute
for Polynesian Studies.

Birdwhistell, R. L. (1970). *Kinesics and context: Essays on body motion.* University of
Pennsylvania Publications in Conduct and Communication, No. 2. Philadelphia:
University of Pennsylvania Press.

Blackie, M. G. (1976). *The patient, not the cure: The challenge of homoeopathy.*
London: Macdonald and Jane's.

Breasted, J. H. (1967). *A history of Egypt.* New York: Bantam Books. (Original work
published 1905)

Browner, C. H., & Sargent, C. F. (1990). Anthropology and studies of human reproduction. In T. M. Johnson & C. F. Sargent (Eds.), *Medical anthropology: Contemporary
theory and method* (pp. 215-229). New York: Praeger.

Byrd, R. C. (1988). Positive therapeutic effects of intercessory prayer in a coronary care
unit population. *Southern Medical Journal, 81,* 826-829.

Chadwick, J., & Mann, W. N. (Trans. & Eds.). (1950). *The medical works of Hippocrates.* Oxford: Blackwell Scientific Publications.

Dossey, L. (1993). *Healing words: The power of prayer and the practice of medicine.* New York: HarperCollins.

Duffy, J. (1976). *The healers.* New York: McGraw-Hill.

Durkin-Longley, M. S. (1982). *Ayurveda in Nepal: A medical belief system in action.* Unpublished doctoral dissertation, University of Wisconsin-Madison.

Eisenberg, D. (1985). *Encounters with Qi: Exploring Chinese medicine.* New York: W. W. Norton & Co.

Etkin, N. L. (1986). Multidisciplinary perspectives in the interpretation of plants used in indigenous medicine and diet. In N. L. Etkin (Ed.), *Plants in indigenous medicine & diet: Biobehavioral approaches* (pp. 2–29). Bedford Hills, NY: Redgrave Publishing Co.

Etkin, N. L. (1988). Ethnopharmacology: Biobehavioral approaches in the anthropological study of indigenous medicines. *Annual Review of Anthropology, 17,* 23–42.

Farquhar, J. (1994). *Knowing practice: The clinical encounter of Chinese medicine.* Boulder, CO: Westview Press.

Fishbein, M. (1932). *Fads and quackery in healing.* New York: Blue Ribbon Books.

Foster, G. M. (1978). Hippocrates' Latin American legacy: "Hot" and "cold" in contemporary folk medicine. In R. K. Wetherington (Ed.), *Colloquia in anthropology* (Vol. II, pp. 3–19). Dallas: Southern Methodist University, Fort Burgwin Research Center.

Foster, G. M. (1984). The concept of "neutral" in humoral medical systems. *Medical Anthropology, 8,* 180–194.

Foster, G. M. (1988). The validating role of humoral theory in traditional Spanish-American therapeutics. *American Ethnologist, 15,* 120–135.

Foster, G. M. (1994). *Hippocrates' Latin American legacy: Humoral medicine in the New World.* Langhorne, PA: Gordon and Breach Science Publishers.

Freed, R. S., & Freed, S. A. (1980). *Rites of passage in Shanti Nagar.* Anthropological Papers of the American Museum of Natural History, (Vol. 56, pt. 3). New York: American Museum of Natural History.

Gibson, R. G., Gibson, S. L. M., MacNeill, A. D., & Buchanan, W. W. (1980). Homoeopathic therapy in rheumatoid arthritis: Evaluation by double-blind clinical therapeutic trial. *British Journal of Clinical Pharmacology, 9,* 453–459.

Good, B., & Good, M. J. D. (1992). The comparative study of Greco-Islamic medicine: The integration of medical knowledge into local symbolic contexts. In C. Leslie, & A. Young, (Eds.), *Paths to Asian medical knowledge* (pp. 257–271). Berkeley: University of California Press.

Hanna, J. L. (1988). *Dance and stress: Resistance, reduction, and euphoria.* New York: AMS Press, Inc.

Hart, C. V. (1969). *Bisayan Filipino and Malayan humoral pathologies: Folk medicine and ethnohistory in Southeast Asia.* Data Paper No. 76. Ithaca, NY: Cornell University Press, Department of Asian Studies, Southeast Asia Program.

Hearn, W. (1993). Where faith meets science. *American Medical News, 36* (23), 9–10.

Heidel, W. A. (1941). *Hippocratic medicine: Its spirit and method.* New York: Columbia University Press.

Hilton-Simpson, M. W. (1922). *Arab medicine and surgery: A study of the healing art in Algeria.* London: Oxford University Press.

Horn, J. S. (1971). *Away with all pests: An English surgeon in People's China, 1954-1969.* New York: Modern Reader Paperback.

Huber, B. R., & Anderson, R. (1996) Bonesetters and curers in a Mexican community: *Conceptual models, status, and gender. Medical Anthropology 17 (1),* 1-16.

Imperato, P. J. (1977). *African folk medicine: Practices and beliefs of the Bambara and other peoples.* Baltimore: York Press.

Iyengar, B. K. S. (1966). *Light on yoga: Yoga dipika.* New York: Schocken Books.

Jacobs, J., Jiménez, L. A., Gloyd, S. S., Gale, J. L., & Crothers, D. (1994). Treatment of acute childhood diarrhea with homeopathic medicine: A randomized clinical trial in Nicaragua. *Pediatrics, 93,* 719-725.

Jaffre, Y., & Prual, A. (1994). Midwives in Niger: An uncomfortable position between social behaviours and health care constraints. *Social Science and Medicine, 38,* 1069-1073.

Jeffery, P., & Jeffery, R. (1989). *Labour pains and labour power: Women and child-bearing in India.* London: Zed Books.

Jones, D. E. (1972). *Sanapia: Comanche medicine woman.* New York: Holt, Rinehart and Winston.

Jordan, B., & Davis-Floyd, R. (1993). *Birth in four cultures: A crosscultural investigation of childbirth in Yucatan, Holland, Sweden, and the United States* (Rev. ed.). Prospect Heights, IL: Waveland Press.

Kang-Wang, J. F. (1980). The midwife in Taiwan: An alternative model for maternity care. *Human Organization, 39,* 70-79.

Katz, P. (1981). Ritual in the operating room. *Ethnology, 20,* 335-350.

Klein, N. (Ed.). (1979). *Culture, curers, and contagion: Readings for medical social science.* Novato, CA: Chandler & Sharp Publishers.

Kleinman, A. (1980). *Patients and healers in the context of culture: An exploration of the borderland between anthropology, medicine, and psychiatry.* Berkeley: University of California Press.

Kleinman, A., Kunstadter, P., Alexander, E. R., & Gale, J. L. (1975). *Medicine in Chinese cultures: Comparative studies of health care in Chinese and other societies.* DHEW Publication No. (NIH) 75-653. Washington, DC: U.S. Government Printing Office.

Laderman, C. (1992). A welcoming soil: Islamic humoralism on the Malay Peninsula. In C. Leslie & A. Young (Eds.), *Paths to Asian medical knowledge* (pp. 272-288). Berkeley: University of California Press.

Leslie, C. (1992). Interpretations of illness: Syncretism in modern Ayurveda. In C. Leslie & A. Young (Eds.), *Paths to Asian Medical Knowledge* (pp. 177-208). Berkeley: University of California Press.

Lewis, J. L. (1992). *Ring of liberation: Deceptive discourse in Brazilian Capoeira.* Chicago: University of Chicago Press.

MacCormack, C. P. (Ed). (1994). *Ethnography of fertility and birth,* (2nd ed.) Prospect Heights, IL: Waveland Press.

Maretzki, T. W., & Seidler, E. (1985). Biomedicine and naturopathic healing in West Germany: A historical and ethnomedical view of a stormy relation. *Culture, Medicine and Psychiatry, 9,* 383-421.

Miller, B. (1991). Alternative somatic therapies. In A. H. White & R. Anderson (Eds.),

Conservative care of low back pain (pp. 120–133). Baltimore: Williams and Wilkins.

Moerman, D. E. (1983). Physiology and symbols: The anthropological implications of the placebo effect. In L. Romanucci-Ross, D. E. Moerman, & L. R. Tancredi (Eds.), *The anthropology of medicine: From culture to method* (pp. 156–167). South Hadley, MA: Bergin & Garvey Publishers.

Moerman, D. E. (1989). Poisoned apples and honeysuckles: The medicinal plants of Native America. *Medical Anthropology Quarterly, 3,* 52–61.

Morse, J. M., McConnell, R., & Young, D. E. (1988). Documenting the practice of a traditional healer: Methodological problems and issues. In D. E. Young (Ed.), *Health care issues in the Canadian North* (pp. 89–94). Edmonton: Boreal Institute for Northern Studies.

Morse, J. M., Young, D. E., & Swartz, L., (1991). Cree Indian healing practices and Western health care: A comparative analysis. *Social Science and Medicine, 32,* 1361–1366.

Morse, J. M., Young, D. E., Swartz, L., & McConnell, R. (1987). A Cree Indian treatment for psoriasis: A longitudinal study. *Culture, VII,* 31–41.

Mull, J. D., & Mull, D. S., (1983). A visit with a *curandero. Western Journal of Medicine, 139,* pp. 730–736.

Ness, S. A. (1992). *Body, movement, and culture: Kinesthetic and visual symbolism in a Philippine community.* Philadelphia: University of Pennsylvania Press.

Novack, C. J. (1990). *Sharing the dance: Contact improvisation and American culture.* Madison: University of Wisconsin Press.

Obeyesekere, G. (1992). Science, experimentation, and clinical practice in Ayurveda. In C. Leslie & A. Young (Eds)., *Paths to Asian medical knowledge* (pp. 160–176). Berkeley: University of California Press.

Orellana, S. L. (1987). *Indian medicine in highland Guatemala: The pre-Hispanic and colonial periods.* Albuquerque: University of New Mexico Press.

Ortiz de Montellano, B. R. (1975). Empirical Aztec medicine. *Science, 188,* 215–220.

Ortiz de Montellano, B. R. (1986). Aztec medicinal herbs: Evaluation of therapeutic effectiveness. In N. L. Etkin (Ed.), *Plants in indigenous medicine & diet: Biobehavioral approaches* (pp. 113–127). Bedford Hills, NY: Redgrave Publishing Co.

Ortiz de Montellano, B. R. (1990). *Aztec medicine, health, and nutrition.* New Brunswick, NJ: Rutgers University Press.

Paul, B. D. (1976). The Maya bonesetter as sacred specialist. *Ethnology, 15,* 77–81.

Paul, L., & Paul, B. D. (1975). The Maya midwife as sacred specialist: A Guatemalan case. *American Ethnologist, 2,* 707–726.

Pugh, J. F. (1991) The semantics of pain in Indian culture and medicine. *Culture, Medicine and Psychiatry, 15,* 19–43.

Rodriguez-Bigas, M., Cruz, N. I., & Suarez, A. (1988). Comparative evaluation of aloe vera in the management of burn wounds in guinea pigs. *Plastic and Reconstructive Surgery, 81,* 386–389.

Royce, A. P. (1980). *The anthropology of dance.* Bloomington: Indiana University Press.

Schiffmann, A., & Hernesniemi, A. (1989). Research in the local folk bonesetting tradition at the folk medicine centre (in Finnish with summary in English). *Pohakka, 3,* 16–23.

Schultes, R. E. (1977). The future of plants as sources of new biodynamic compounds. In

T. Swain (Ed.), *Plant in the development of modern medicine* (pp. 103-124). Cambridge, MA: Harvard University Press.

Sharma, H. M., & Chopra, D. (1991). Maharishi Ayur-Veda: Modern insights into ancient medicine. *Journal of the American Medical Association, 265,* 2633-2637.

Shipley, M., Berry, H., Broster, G., Jenkins, M., Clover, A., & Williams, I. (1983). Controlled trial of homeopathic treatment of osteoarthritis. *The Lancet, 1,* (8316), 97-98.

Shostak, M. (1983). *Nisa: The life and words of a !Kung woman.* New York: Vintage Books.

Shutler, M. E. (1977). Disease and curing in a Yaqui community. In E. H. Spicer (Ed.), *Ethnic medicine in the Southwest* (pp. 169-237). Tucson: University of Arizona Press.

Singer, P. (1977). *"Cupping" for pain control—Israel* [16mm/video. Color. 22 min.] Southfield, MI: Traditional Healing Films.

Skolnick, A. A. (1991). Mahirishi Ayur-Veda: Guru's marketing scheme promises the world eternal "perfect health." *Journal of the American Medical Association, 266,* 1741-1750.

Stix, G. (1993). Back to roots: Drug companies forage for new treatments. *Scientific American, 268,* 142-143.

Starr, P. (1982). *The social transformation of American medicine.* New York: Basic Books.

Temkin, O. (1973). *Galenism: Rise and decline of a medical philosophy.* Ithaca, NY: Cornell University Press.

Trawick, M. (1992). Death and nurturance in Indian systems of healing In C. Leslie & A. Young (Eds.), *Paths to Asian medical knowledge* (pp.129-159). Berkeley: University of California Press.

Triano, J. (1991). Standards of care: Manipulative procedures. In A. H. White, & R. Anderson, (Eds.), *Conservative care of low back pain* (pp. 159-168). Baltimore: Williams and Wilkins.

Trotter, R. T., II, & Logan, M. H. (1986). Informant consensus: A new approach for identifying potentially effective medicinal plants. In N. L. Etkin (Ed.), *Plants in indigenous medicine & diet: Biobehavioral approaches* (pp. 91-112). Bedford Hills, NY: Redgrave Publishing Co.

Vogel, V. J. (1990). *American Indian medicine.* Norman: University of Oklahoma Press. (Original work published 1970)

Wall, L. L. (1988). *Hausa medicine: Illness and well-being in a West African culture.* Durham, NC: Duke University Press.

Ward, R. E., & Sadove, A. M. (1989). Biomedical anthropology and the team approach to craniofacial surgery. *Medical Anthropology Quarterly, 3,* 395-404.

Wilson, J. A. (1951). *The culture of ancient Egypt.* Chicago: University of Chicago Press.

Wiser, W., & Wiser, C. (1971). *Behind mud walls 1930-1960, with a sequel: The village in 1970.* Berkeley: University of California Press.

Withington, E. T. (1928). *Hippocrates, with an English translation.* Cambridge, MA: Harvard University Press.

Young, D. E., Morse, J. M., Swartz, L., & Ingram, G. (1988). The psoriasis research project: An overview. In D. E. Young, (Ed.), *Health care issues in the Canadian north* (pp. 76-88). Edmonton: Boreal Institute for Northern Studies.

Zimmermann, F. (1989). *Le discours des remèdes au pays des Épices: Enquete sur la médecine Hindoue.* Paris: Éditions Payot.

Zimmerman, F. (1992). Gentle purge: The flower power of Ayurveda. In C. Leslie, & A. Young (Eds.), *Paths to Asian medical knowledge* (pp. 209-223). Berkeley: University of California Press.

Chapter 16

THE ANTHROPOLOGY OF MEDICINE

A TERMINOLOGICAL PRELUDE

Deconstruction is a form of critique promoted by Jacques Derrida, a French philosopher (Hoy, 1985, pp. 41-64). He argues that words such as *anthropology* or *medicine* incorporate a powerful ability to construct or shape our understanding of reality. Built into these constructions are unexamined, often unconscious assumptions that may reflect uninformed, wrong, or biased beliefs and practices. For example, the term *anthropology* derives from two Greek roots, the—*ology* referring to knowledge and the *anthrop*—(from anthropos) referring to man. Deconstructing anthropology thus makes us aware that our subject implies a bias that favors the study of men, implicitly condoning a relative neglect of women. We used to gloss anthropology as "the study of man," assuming an equal treatment of women that in fact was not there.

In a comparable way, some observers have felt that the term *Western medicine* can be misunderstood as implying an ethnocentric bias. They argue that since it is a form of health care practiced in every country in the world, it is international rather than Western. Furthermore, they point out, and they are completely right, that some of the most valuable modern developments in medicine and surgery have been contributed by Asians, Latinos, Africans, and other non-Westerners. Several alternative terms have therefore come into use.

Cosmopolitan Medicine

The deconstructionist critique led to a search for a term that would not easily be misunderstood as ethnocentric. For Charles Leslie and Frederick Dunn, this led to the origination of an inoffensive designation, cosmopolitan medicine (Leslie, 1976, pp. 5-8). Unfortunately, although apparently value-free, it is not unambiguous. Many nonanthropologists interpret cosmopolitan to refer to urban but not rural versions of Western medicine, a limitation that is not intended. Others interpret it to mean any kind of health care practiced in sophisticated, international settings, whatever its principles of practice. Although mistaken, by this usage macrobiotic dietetics and orthomolecular medicine, for example, are cosmopolitan, even though they are not generally thought of as part of mainstream biomedicine. Most tellingly, outside of academe, and particularly outside of the United States, many people wonder what is being talked about when the term is used, even a quarter of a century after the designation was first put into sporadic use. So designating the field as cosmopolitan medicine produced a very nice word of rather limited utility.

Allopathic Medicine

In recent years, the search has led others to speak of allopathic medicine (Starr, 1982, p. 100). Physicians today sometimes refer to themselves as allopaths. *Allopathy* is a term that became popular during the nineteenth century among homeopaths as a derogation of their medical competitors. In the homeopathic view, good medical practice should be based on the similia principle. In the vitriolic political context of that century, homeopaths denigrated orthodox physicians for being commited to a theory of contraries. So deconstruction reveals a couple of problems with the term *allopathic*. First, it is inherently ethnocentric since it is demeaning of nonhomeopathic doctors by the implications of invidious comparison. Second, it implies a commitment to a monocausal theory of disease that no so-called allopathic physician in our time would agree to in such simplistic terms.

Biomedicine

As I write, *biomedicine* is the term of choice for many anthropologists, and I have used it repeatedly in my own writing, but it carries a negative connotation. In the mid-1970s, in part under the influence of an anthropological critique, leading physicians began to talk of a new paradigm, the biopsychosocial model. Disease had to be diagnosed and treated, it was argued, in a way that was responsive to the varied cultural, social, and psychological circumstances that could enhance recovery.

Currently in medical circles, the biopsychosocial model serves as the icon of good medicine. One encounters it during hospital rounds in any medical center. In the discussion of the morning report or in the parade of doctors and students looking in on each hospitalized patient, high-ranking attending physicians remind lower-ranking resident physicians of the importance of considering the full range of biopsychosocial factors, a form of wisdom that residents for their part pass on to the low-ranking medical students whom they tutor. Opposition, if it exists at all, is not vocal. Who would object to the good sense that is inherent in this model? Carryover into medical and surgical practice, unfortunately, tends to fall short of success, often with dismal consequences.

The term *biomedicine* came into widespread use in the 1970s as a way to point up the need for the biopsychosocial model proposed by George Engel. It was a straw horse. The so-called biomedical model was assumed to identify physicians and surgeons who limited themselves to molecular biology to the extent that they disregarded all of the social, psychological, and behavioral dimensions of illness (Engel, 1977). As a principle of medicine and as a standard of practice, that extreme reductionist view was not officially taught or advocated in the 1970s, when, in fact, discussions of psychosomatic mechanisms were very much in the air. It is not taught or advocated now.

Western Medicine

Let us reexamine the designation termed *Western medicine.* In the People's Republic of China it is the practice in our time to speak of Western medicine as contrasted with Chinese medicine (Leslie, 1976, pp. 6, 8, 341, 354; Unschuld, 1985, pp. 249–262). Chinese medicine, also referred to as traditional Chinese medicine (TCM), is characterized by acupuncture, herbs, and its related energetic theory. In other nations, comparable distinctions are made, as when one speaks of Unani Tibb, the medical system of the Middle East, or Ayurveda, the medical system of South Asia.

In this context, to speak of Western medicine is not really inappropriate. It is clear that the Chinese and other Asians are differentiating these various medical systems on the basis of the cultures or areas of the world in which the basic paradigms originated and from which they spread. Medical ancestry is honored in that way. It is fully understood that Chinese medicine (or Unani Tibb, or Ayurveda) in our time is not stuck in the past or excluded from other parts of the world, including the United States. It is also understood that in modern times it incorporates revolutionary changes, including some concepts and practices taken from Western medicine. The Chinese are fully aware that Western medicine is practiced all over the world and has been improved because of major contributions by Chinese and other non-Western medical scientists. The Chinese speak for about one-fourth of the population of the world. Perhaps we should let them speak for us as well in this particular matter.

Ethnomedicine

Let us extend this prelude of wordplay just a bit more. One way in which a medical anthropologist may discuss health care beliefs and practices is to refer to *ethnomedicine.* One needs to be aware that the term is used in two distinctive ways, which tends to diminish its value in discourse, since to put it in use now sometimes requires that one indicate which definition is intended.

Ethnomedicine As Ethnotherapy

The oldest and most common way in which this term was used until recently was to separate out from the wider field of medical anthropology a concentration on healing practices in cultures other than those of Western medicine. Ethnotherapy referred to studies of shamans, herbalists, massagers, spiritist curers, psychic surgeons, acupuncturists, or any health practitioners other than those of Western medicine. In the first of the modern textbooks on medical anthropology, the field of ethnomedicine was identified in this limiting way as "the lineal descendant of the early interest of anthropologists in non-Western medical systems" (Foster & Anderson, 1978, p. 5).

Ethnomedicine As Including Western Medicine

In the halls of academe, a kind of one-upmanship apparently motivated many individuals in unnumbered conversations to point out to users of the term that Western medicine is also an example of ethnomedicine. What can one say? Of course Western medicine is embedded in culture just as is any healing system. Anthropologists easily agree that it, too, is shaped by a belief system and that it is a system of practice shot through with symbolic innuendo and learned behaviors. No one would argue with these assertions. They affirm a truism. So in recent years, to avoid any implication of ethnocentrism, it has become customary to explain that ethnomedicine includes Western medicine. Unfortunately, this deprives us of a convenient, easy-to-use term to designate a more delimited reference to healing systems other than Western medicine.

The two main criteria for deciding whether a definition is good or not are clarity and utility. Often, as a medical anthropologist, one will want to refer to all healing systems other than that of Western medicine. *Ethnomedicine* in its earlier, well-established meaning was clear and useful for that purpose. In this book, ethnomedicine has been used in that original meaning.

THE ANTHROPOLOGY OF MEDICINE

We certainly want to examine Western medicine using the approach spearheaded in studies of ethnomedicine. For that purpose, when Western medicine is examined as imbedded in cultures, there is precedent for speaking of the anthropology of medicine (Romanucci-Ross et al., 1991, p. ix).

Scientific biomedicine, in principle, is value-free. Many, particularly those who work in institutional health care (whether a doctor's office or a medical center), would argue that modern medicine and surgery are only superficially shaped by the cultures of the nations of the West where they first evolved. When practiced in Japan, Mexico, or Zimbabwe, they would claim, it is still biomedicine.

Most anthropologists, on the contrary, would take the position that to be value-free is a goal that at best can be achieved only in partial and fragmented ways. The best any scientist can hope for is to control for biases by examining them, making them explicit, and having others repeat (replicate) the research independently.

Many anthropologists would argue that biomedicine is so thoroughly a product of Western cultures that in many ways it carries on in very ethnocentric and oppressive ways, since it is "pervaded by a value system characteristic of an industrial-capitalistic view of the world," as Margaret Lock put it (Lock, 1988, 3). Carol MacCormack refers disparagingly to "the rather hegemonic Western mechanistic medical world view," while Lola Romanucci-Ross and Daniel Moerman in a more moderate tone note that biomedicine constitutes an ideological system shaped by cultural values that can and do at times result in wrong ideas and poor practice (MacCormack, 1994, p. 6; Romanucci-Ross & Moerman, 1991). In the words of Arthur Kleinman, "What medicine proclaims itself to be—unified, scientific, biological and not social, non-judgmental—is shown not to resemble very much" (Kleinman, 1989, p. vii).

In what follows, we will examine Western medicine as a cultural system. Attention will not focus solely on physicians. The practice of medicine and surgery is often discussed as though only medical doctors matter. But Western health care includes other kinds of professionals equally important and worthy of attention. To be holistic and multidisciplinary in the anthropology of medicine requires that one must also give attention to dentists, chiropractors, nurses, psychologists, physical therapists, occupational therapists, midwives, alternative health care providers, traditional healers in modern settings, hospital administrators, medical economists, laboratory scientists, medical anthropologists, of course, and not the least, clients of all of these practitioners, scientists, and administrators.

PHYSICIANS AND SURGEONS

Many physicians and surgeons themselves are the first to admit that somewhere between scientific medicine and clinical intuition—that is, somewhere between a formal algorithm of decision making and the daily give and take of deciding what to do—personal and cultural forces intrude. However, it often comes to them as a surprise, even a shock, when an alert, informed observer (a medical anthropologist, for example) is able to demonstrate that culture impacts far more on how they practice than they had realized. Just how great this impact can be is variable. There are as many ways of practicing medicine and surgery as there are medical and surgical specialities and subspecialties. (Remember essentialism!)

One way to get a handle on this variability is to think of medical/surgical practice as a continuum. At one end of the continuum are doctors whose job it is to work with clients who have no disease at all, but are merely coping with problems inherent in a natural process, such as birth, adolescence, or getting old. Obstetrics is an excellent example that was discussed in the chapter on women's health. As illustrated in the research of Davis-Floyd on the practice of obstetrics, when natural processes are medicalized, culture far more than technology can impact on how medicine is practiced.

An extensive middle part of the continuum covers diseases that interfere with the naturalness of good health and for which medico-surgical intervention can be appropriate. However, in this large middle part of the continuum, the pathology is incompletely or poorly understood and/or methods of treatment are of uncertain or limited value. In addition to this kind of uncertainty, Renée Fox notes that physicians are also confronted by the uncertainties of their own imperfect mastery of medicine (Fox, 1959). Much of what doctors do in coping under these more or less anomalous conditions of uncertainty gets shaped by unconscious cultural assumptions rather than hard scientific data. Psychiatry most obviously comes to mind, but any specialty struggles at this level some of the time. As described above, Estroff demonstrated that prescribing psychotropic drugs did not benefit many mentally ill clients because physicians failed to take cultural factors adequately into account.

Finally, at the far end of the continuum are conditions that are well described and for which excellent treatment is available. In medicine, a cure for most infections is straightforward, resulting in predictable good outcomes. Surgery often can be equally successful, as in a hernia repair or an appendectomy. What needs to be stressed is that even at this end of the continuum, where cultural influences should be, and are, the least obvious, they nonetheless can shape practice.

The shaping influence tends to be tangential and minor in medico-surgical procedures. Of course, hospital care in support of the patient who is there for treatment involves meals, social interactions, religious beliefs, language usage, patient explanatory models of illness, and so on. Culture intrudes massively in this important medical arena, as Geri-Ann Galanti demonstrates in her case studies from American nursing practices. Anthropologists have a lot to contribute in this arena, as we shall see in a later section on nursing (Galanti, 1991). But let us focus for the moment on medico-surgical practices in which treatment outcomes are highly predictable and well understood.

Surgeons

When I reviewed the writings of medical anthropologists in search of examples of how they have documented surgical decisions that were shaped by culture rather than medical science, I found very little. That is, I did not find much magical thinking or many unscientific paradigms as examples of culture overriding science. The record does show errors in surgical practice. The horror stories are there. But what I found is that anthropologists usually documented mistakes made by surgeons who did not use good judgment in terms of accepted standards of practice, or who were motivated by greed.

Joan Cassell narrates one such case, a partial colon resection, in which the surgeon, knowing he was taking a chance in not using a standard approach, tried a shortcut as a matter of poor judgment, a flamboyant style, and questionable personal integrity. The patient died. His colleagues judged him harshly. That failed outcome is better thought of as malpractice than as a cultural distortion of science (Cassell, 1991, pp. 128–152).

Pearl Katz also describes a surgery that failed, in this case the repair of a hiatal hernia. The surgeon operated knowing his approach was wrong, but hoped the repair would hold for a while. He did this operation contrary to sound surgical judgment because his practice was failing and he needed the money. He was fully aware that he should have referred the patient to a different kind of surgeon (thoracic instead of general) who would have been able to do a different kind of operation that was better suited for success in this kind of case. This looks like malpractice motivated by greed rather than culture getting in the way of science (Katz, 1985).

Katz makes as strong a case as can be made for the cultural shaping of technical procedures in her description and analysis of ritual practices in the operating room. According to her analysis, nonscientific judgment is present in significant ways in the form of routine practices relating to the maintenance of a sterile operating field. In her paper she argues "that the elaborate rituals and technical procedures of the modern hospital operating room, manifestly designed to prevent infection, better serve latent functions" (Katz, 1981). She is particularly intrigued with such issues as the following:

- Blood is considered contaminated if external hemorrhage occurs before the surgery, but blood from the surgical wound is considered sterile.
- The first incision through the skin is made with a scalpel that is then discarded as nonsterile because the skin is clean but not sterile. However, all deeper cutting can be done with a single second scalpel, since all of these layers of fat, fascia, muscle, and peritoneum are considered sterile.
- If a cardiac arrest occurs, the cardiac arrest team enters the operating room and attempts resuscitation without following the strict sterile procedures that were in force until that moment.
- On closing the patient, if the surgeon's glove is contaminated by touching the face mask, it is not always the practice to reglove and regown as would have been absolutely required minutes earlier when the main work of the surgery was being done.

Do these practices represent arbitrary practices that are more important as symbolic statements in a ritual atmosphere than as efforts to reduce and eliminate infectious microbes in the high-risk presence of an open surgical wound? The answer is no, they are neither arbitrary nor of primarily symbolic value. The first two examples given above (Katz provides more in her article) all make sense in value-free, noncultural biomedical terms.

- Extravasated blood is immediately contaminated by the skin and clothes of an individual who bleeds outside of the surgical environnment. Blood in the wound is treated as though it is sterile. It may in fact carry microbes that are present in the patient's bloodstream, particularly a virus such as HIV which cannot be eliminated in advance of surgery. Nothing can be done about that. However, blood is treated as sterile relative to that patient under the aseptic conditions of surgery in the sense that one can know that the surgical personnel and their equipment are not contributing additional contaminants. This is rational in scientific terms.

- Since the skin can be cleaned but not sterilized, every effort is made to reduce contamination of the surgical site by minimizing what cannot be eliminated. Keep in mind that the danger of infection is proportional to the number of microbes introduced into the body at risk. By changing scalpels, the number of skin bacteria carried deeper into the wound is kept as small as possible. This is rational in scientific terms.

- The enormous attention given to creating and maintaining sterility can no longer be a top priority if the patient's heart suddenly fails. A trade-off is required. Since one has only a few minutes in which to save the patient's life, one does what one has to do. Afterwards, every effort will be made to return to surgical sterility and antibiotics will be administered in order to regain ascendency over microbial invasion. This is rational in scientific terms.

- The last example is a red herring. Katz reports that because closing is a relatively simple routine, and because the surgeon has the feeling that by that time the real work of the operation is done, a contaminated glove is no longer a matter of great concern. This gives the appearance that all of the practices relating to the creation and maintainance of sterility were done more for ritual than for scientific reasons. Not so. Not to reglove under these circumstances is unacceptable surgical practice. The issue is not culture overriding science; it is reprehensible surgical technique. Melvin Konner is right, doctors anguish about this kind of a problem or practice. (Konner, 1991, p. 81)

NURSES AND NURSE ANTHROPOLOGISTS

Registered nurses (RNs) constitute the single most populous profession in health care. Although some are men, 97 percent of all American nurses are women, mostly non-Hispanic white. The profession has undergone major changes in recent decades, including an increase in educational standards and a recognition of specialty qualifications within the field. The nurse as we once knew her is no more. On the one hand, much of what used to be the work of an RN has been given to others with fewer professional qualifications, including the licensed practical nurse (LPN), the licensed vocational nurse (LVN), and the orderly. On the other hand, an RN with specialty training may work as a nurse anesthetist, a nurse practitioner, an intensive care nurse specialist, and so on (Friedman, 1990).

Until the 1960s, the relationship between doctors and nurses was clearly hierarchical, with doctors being superordinant. Now nurses are trained to consider themselves status equals with all other health care professionals, including doctors, and to work in collegial rather than subservient relationships. They expect to take responsibility for their work and to make decisions on their own. Increasingly, nurses may confront and challenge physicians on issues relating to patient care. These are feminist as well as professional matters. According to an older patriarchal ethos, women are not supposed to act that way. According to that older ethos, nurses are not supposed to act that way. Many doctors still scratch their heads in puzzlement. How could doctor-nurse relations have changed so dramatically? But they have (Stein et al., 1990).

Yet, the central philosophy of nursing has not changed for the profession as a whole. Whereas physicians have always seen themselves as a curing profession, nurses still see themselves as a caring profession (Reverby, 1987). This core philosophical difference has had an enormous impact on the way the two professions have integrated with anthropology. For physicians with a biomedical orientation, the integration has been a slow and still incomplete process. Virchow's early proclamation of medicine as a social science and Engel's 1977 clarion call to shift to a biopsychosocial orientation did not bring anthropology fully into the practice of medicine and surgery. It has been different for nursing.

Oliver Osborne, a nurse anthropologist, makes the point that nursing, even though it is based on a medical model, more than any other mainstream health profession is oriented to the total care of the patient as a matter of daily work (praxis) rather than primarily as a philosophical aspiration. "The commitment of the nursing profession and nurses to total patient care parallels the anthropological tradition of the 'holistic' study of man," as Osborne put it (Osborne, 1990, pp. 9–10).

The traditional holism of nursing requires an openness to vertical thinking. Pamela Brink, also a nurse anthropologist, stresses this aspect of the holism of nursing:

> Whatever affects human behavior eventually affects nursing. For this reason, nursing involves itself with the physical sciences such as chemistry, physics and biology, since these fields are concerned with the basic parameters within which human life occurs. Other areas, equally important, include history, philosophy and the arts. The social sciences—psychology, sociology, anthropology—increase nursing's awareness of human emotions, motivations, social organization, and belief systems. . . . The nurse is expected to have a basic understanding of the norms and deviations of the norm in the human as a bio-psycho-socio-cultural being. (Brink, 1990, p. 2)

FIGURE 16-1
Leininger's Sunrise Model to Depict Theory of Cultural Care Diversity and Universality

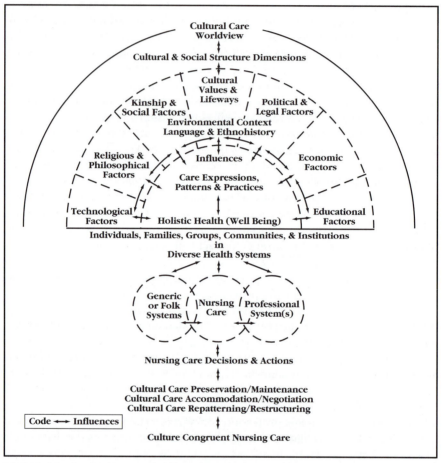

SOURCE: Leininger, Madekeine M., (Ed.), (1991). *Culture Care Diversity and Universality; A Theory of Nursing.* (1991). NY: National League for Nursing Press. Page 43.

Anyone who has worked with nurses or observed them at work will recognize Brink's description as an ideal rather than a real cultural description. Yet, nursing has moved in an impressive way to incorporate anthropological theory and practice (the practice of ethnographic eliciting techniques). Nurse anthropologist Madeleine Leininger developed an approach that has been very useful in teaching student nurses and in helping established nurses to transform the ideal of holism into the reality of nursing practice. Leininger taught nurses how to identify cultural differences that impact on patient care and how to adapt to them in ways that are sensitive and effective. She calls her approach transcultural nursing (Leininger, 1991).

The Leininger approach to transcultural nursing is succinctly laid out in a diagram that has become well-known among nurse anthropologists as the sunrise model (Leininger, 1991, p. 43). In spite of the fact that Brink states that nursing involves the physical sciences, it is notable that chemistry, physics, and biology are not in evidence in this holistic schema. One should not be surprised at holism that is not uniformly or completely whole. The model is similar to other cultural anthropological models of holism, most of which also tend to neglect the basic sciences by leaving them out or taking them for granted.

The sunrise model is refreshingly down to earth. Although referred to as a theory of nursing, the theory behind it is simply generic functionalism. The model can be used as a kind of map or checklist of cultural elements that one should look for in searching for a way to solve a clinical problem of patient care. Is there a family issue? An economic problem? A bottleneck in institutional organization? Each part of the model has the potential of alerting a nurse or any other health care professional to a troublesome cultural issue, a stumbling block to good care. Finding the cultural block may allow clinicians to respond in an effective, culturally congruent way. In a society (and world) of enormous cultural diversity, the model serves as a useful working tool.

CLINICAL ANTHROPOLOGISTS

Anthropologists who are also nurses function effectively in clinical settings. As practitioner anthropologists they are able to apply what they know of anthropology directly to their work in health care. The same is true of other anthropologists who are clinicians, including physicians. But what is the role of anthropologists in a clinical setting if they are not trained and licensed to practice one of the health care professions?

A number of medical anthropologists have struggled with this question, Noel Chrisman and Thomas Maretzki among them (Chrisman & Maretzki, 1982). Chrisman and Maretzki have taken the position that anthropologists should be useful (employable) in health care settings for their skills in teaching, research, and consulting. In a medical milieu, the bottom line is how an anthropologist can contribute to make doctors, nurses, and other clinicians more effective. Chrisman and Maretzki propose that the field be called clinically applied anthropology.

"Clinically applied anthropology" is not to be confused with "clinical anthropology," Chrisman and Maretzki insist. They got into this terminological dead-end because a few anthropologists thought that they ought to be employable as clinicians, somewhat in the manner of clinical psychologists, except that they would help people deal with problems of confusion and misunderstanding that arise from cultural barriers. Clinical anthropologists would be practitioners specializing in cultural diversity. Nothing really came of it. As Chrisman and Maretzki point out, even if that skill had potential as a commodity in the marketplace of health care, which is doubtful, it would have been blocked for legal reasons. Since anthropologists are not trained to be clinicians, no state in the union would license them to practice as health care providers. So probably we should forget about clinical anthropology in that sense, but preserve a perfectly good term. It is convenient and linguistically parsimonious to refer to those practicing what Chrisman and Maretzki refer to as clinically applied anthropology as clinical anthropologists. It should not go unnoticed that Hazel Weidman, one of the authors in the book they edited, does exactly that (Weidman, 1982).

What does clinical anthropology have to offer in a clinical setting? Chrisman and Thomas Johnson believe that it offers a valuable theoretical perspective, "an explicit rationale for how to provide culturally sensitive care" (Chrisman & Johnson, 1990, p. 104). Noting that ethnic differences within medical settings clearly require that personnel be culturally sensitive, they insist emphatically that the same sensitivity should apply to all patients, regardless of ethnicity. More specifically, they propose that clinically applied anthropologists have contributions to make in the areas of:

- ethnocentrism
- identifying patient perspectives
- differentiating disease and illness
- a holistic orientation
- differing values and beliefs
- in general, the concept of culture

In identifying the potential contribution of clinical anthropologists in this way, it is important to note that the organizing goal is to advocate and initiate "culturally sensitive care." Care, as we have already seen, is a nursing function. Indeed, in taking this position, Chrisman and Johnson cite as a main source or reference a book called *The Discipline of Nursing* (Donaldson & Crowley, 1978). What, then, does this have to do with doctors?

What does a nursing function have to do with doctoring? With curing? It should be clear by now that the opposition of nurses and doctors makes sense only in terms of a marketplace economy (capitalism in the urban-industrial world) in which people are willing to pay more for curing (doctors) but not so much for caring (nurses). The very notion of "to cure" versus "to care" constitutes a phony dichotomy. Medical and surgical procedures, as noted above, are performed in the larger context of a patient's whole life and world where that universe intersects the lives and worlds of medical personnel.

Many physicians are deeply troubled about this distressing differentiation of caring and curing. Physicians in family practice, internists, and pediatricians, those who have replaced the general practice doctors of an earlier generation, have been the most receptive to clinical anthropology. The need to truly implement a biopsychosocial model, anthropologically informed, one would hope, is clearest to them. The need is also well-known to physicians in public health. However, surgery and the subspecialties of internal medicine (cardiology, rheumatology, dermatology, and so on) "seem impermeable to anthropological

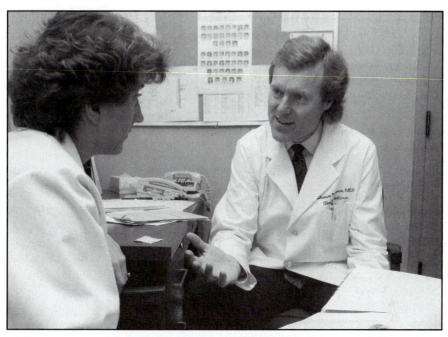

As Director of Behavioral Science for the Family Medicine Residency Program at the University of Alabama in Huntsville, Thomas Johnson, a clinical psychologist as well as an anthropologist, reviews the progress of a patient with a physician in training.

input," in the opinion of Chrisman and Maretzki, and this needs to change (Chrisman & Maretzki, 1982, p. 11).

What the clinical anthropologist can do is not a matter for complacency. It is always necessary to change and adapt. This is the experience of Janet Bronstein, an anthropologist appointed to a school of public health. She raises this question: What relevance does her training have to what she now does in a multidisciplinary setting? In searching for an answer she lists what her health service research work requires her to do:

■ She begins any project with the question: What does the policymaker, administrator, or clinician need to know?
■ She also needs to understand the social organization in terms of who makes decisions or determines constraints and incentives.
■ She will need to inform herself about content areas such as clinical medicine, epidemiology, law, economics, and so on, that take her beyond her prior experience and training.
■ She must select suitable data sources and techniques of analysis, including quantitative skills more sophisticated than those she learned as a graduate student in anthropology.

■ In each of these activites she needs to have learned how to interact with colleagues from many different fields as a multidisciplinary challenge. (Bronstein, 1993)

Every appointment as a clinical anthropologist will have its own challenges and opportunities. Any one appointment may or may not resemble the job description of Bronstein, but each anthropologist will find a potential contribution in this fact of life: Every sickness is an illness as well as a disease, and clinical anthropologists are experts on illnesses.

TRADITIONAL AND ALTERNATIVE HEALERS IN BIOMEDICAL SETTINGS

The time was 1978 and the place was Alma Ata in Central Asia. At that time and place delegates to an international WHO conference agreed to an agenda of inspiring dimensions. They proposed nothing less than to strive together to achieve "Good Health for All by the Year 2000." The goal was utopian in the extreme, but the delegates struggled to remain pragmatic, particularly as concerned curative medicine. It would be imposssible, they acknowledged, to meet health needs by attempting to pay for tens of thousands of newly recruited physicians and surgeons trained in biomedicine. However, indigenous healers constituted a resource already in place throughout the world. WHO would hope to meet their goals for 2000 in part by authenticating, encouraging, funding, and updating (in biomedical terms) the practitioners of diverse ethnomedical traditions.

With the WHO international congress, it became fashionable among health scientists to convert a hitherto rare or disputed kind of respect into a new appreciation of the benefits of traditional healing. Medical anthropologists often served an important function in this regard, for more than any other body of scientists they live and work in small-scale or impoverished urban communities where they record the practices and beliefs of world healing customs. They listen to (and hopefully hear) the voices of healers and of their clients. In many cases they apprentice to these healers and/or receive care from them. Medical anthropologists in these ways are able to serve as resources, as scientists who have studied ethnomedicine and can be consulted for information and advice.

The time was the 1960s and 1970s and the places were all over, including the Haight-Ashbury in San Francisco, Central Park in New York, and hippie communes here and there around the world where young people escaped from the reactionary ethics and politics of the Vietnam War into a New Age idealism. Conducting persistent guerilla assaults on the established values and institutions of the West, nothing was too sacred to be challenged: business, manufacturing, religion, family, politics, government, education, and, not the least, Western medicine.

Alternative health care with a stress on simple, down-to-earth remedies such as massage, herbal teas, and shamanic rituals found advocates in the sons and daughters of the entrenched middle class. Then, in 1972, the middle-aged middle class itself began a slow move toward reappraising alternative and traditional medicines when columnist James Reston, while on assignment in the People's Republic of China, experienced postsurgical pain relief by means of acupuncture, and wrote about it. Chinese medicine and many other forms of healing, some ancient, some novel, moved into contemporary American communities with unprecedented acceptance.

This ethnomedical invasion culminated in 1992 when a new office for the study of unconventional medical practices was formally installed within the bureaucracy of the National Institutes of Health. The Third World and "our" world converged toward definitions of health and health care that undercut the hitherto rarely challenged hegemony of Western medicine (Last, 1990). On the contemporary American scene as in the Third World, medical anthropologists now investigate healing and can be consulted for information and advice.

Cultural Fit

It will be expected of medical anthropologists that they provide an enumeration and evaluation of benefits in terms of cultural goals and standards. To make this contribution, anthropologists attempt to identify psychosocial benefits of treatment that are meaningful and practical in terms of culturally shaped lifestyles, ethnoeconomics, and customary beliefs and values. They elicit how health is defined and treatment evaluated from an insider's (emic) point of view.

Often it is possible to report high levels of patient satisfaction with native or counterculture healing. Whether individuals get well or not in organic terms, they are often pleased with the attention they receive. Anthropologists are particularly skilled at identifying the psychological benefits of healing, whether or not physical pain, organic dysfunction, or visceral disease are directly addressed. Much if not most of the ethnomedical literature describes ritual healing as ethnopsychology.

Although alert to these descriptions, explanations, and benefits, anthropologists still fall short of being able to identify clearly the nature and predictability of emotional, cognitive, and behavioral responses. The goal is to continue this fruitful kind of research, but in the meantime to provide information on the current state of knowledge in this area.

One can generally predict that the ritual of healing will produce health benefits regardless of whether herbs or treatment modalities provide any direct physiological benefits. Placebo-induced psychoneuroimmune responses on the average will be as effective as any medication or manipulation for about 30 percent of individuals who believe they are receiving a validated form of treatment. It can be less, but it can also measure as high as 65 percent. The benefit is often temporary, but it can be long-lasting or permanent. We do not usually have clinical studies to provide measures of this powerful effect, but in consulting one needs to provide information on this issue or admit to uncertainty.

Efficacy in Pathophysiologic Terms

People often want and need treatment for severe organic pathology. Let me try your patience with a long list (actually quite abbreviated) resembling the bibilical Book of Job, because we must never forget that ethnomedicines cope with more than personal problems, social issues, and cultural conditions. People suffer pain, disablement, and death as anatomic and physiologic realities that interfere with and destroy individual existence. These include, but are not limited to, vision impairment and blindness; psychoses such as schizophrenia and severe depression; suffocating lung diseases; infections minor and major, acute and chronic; malignant tumors; malnutrition and starvation; heart/liver/kidney/bladder/gallbladder diseases that are degenerative, autoimmune, or infectious in nature; gastroenteric problems; endocrine disorders of the thyroid, the pancreas (diabetes), and literally hundreds of other tissues and organs; crippling paralyses due to nerve, muscle, bone, and joint diseases; pelvic and genital disorders; wounds caused by violence or trauma; and birthing that can shift from a natural event to a sudden catastrophe for the parturient and/or the infant.

The job of the anthropologist consultant must include an evaluation of any evidence that relates to efficacy in pathophysiologic terms. The NIH Office of Alternative Medicine was established in order to fund research on treatments of disabling or sinister forms of visceral disease that occur commonly. The fact is, anthropologists usually cannot provide scientific evidence concerning the efficacy of ethnomedical treatments (including many used in Western medicine), because the research has not been done (Anderson, 1991).

That situation is improving, however. Mary Ryan is one of several who are presently experimenting with new approaches to the study of efficacy. Working in a Tibetan community in northern India as a medical anthropologist, she found ways to assess pain and function that made it possible to compare Western versus Tibetan treatments of arthritis. Incidentally, a preliminary report of findings suggests that the Tibetan treatment was effective for her subjects (Ryan, 1994).

Undesirable Side Effects

One frequently hears that traditional or holistic methods are natural and gentle. Whatever that may signify, it is often taken to mean that one need not worry about adverse reactions. Nothing could be further from the truth. Any category of ingested or applied substance can be toxic or caustic. For example, comfrey tea, widely advocated for pulmonary and gastrointestinal problems, is severely toxic to the liver. People have died or become extremely sick from consuming this herbal remedy (Anderson, 1992a).

It is essential that nonmainstream forms of treatment not be recommended as the primary resort for the treatment of severe and life-threatening diseases if the diseases in question can be treated successfully by Western medicine and if access to Western medicine exists as a possible avenue of recourse. The prevention or treatment of many serious infectious diseases, for example, is best achieved by vaccinations or antibiotics. As noted in discussing those chiropractors who oppose vaccination programs, lives are put at risk when unproven remedies are relied upon in the place of biomedical medical treatments that are available and known to be effective.

Multidisciplinarity is essential here. A biomedical evaluation is often required. Fortunately, most patients are self-selected in this regard. In urban-industrial settings as well as in impoverished nations, the sick usually either try medical doctors first or are experienced enough to recognize disorders that are either self-limiting or untreatable by medical doctors.

Conversely, before submitting to harsh or invasive biomedical procedures, one needs to consider the possibility that more conservative methods can be appropriate. Diet and exercise, for example, are preferred alternatives to anti-hypertensive medications in controlling borderline high blood pressure. Meditation may relieve anxiety for some individuals as effectively as valium, but without the debilitating side effects characteristic of benzodiazepines.

Justification of Cost

It is tragic that many, many people cannot afford proper health care. Part of the responsibility of anthropologists is to factor in costs and ability to pay. Well equipped hospital centers staffed by skilled specialists are too expensive for the poor of the world. It achieves nothing to make recommendations relating to the treatment of infectious diseases with antibiotics if such treatment is so expensive that the sick do not have funds enough to afford it, or if paying for such treatment results in family malnutrition and homelessness because nothing is left for food and housing. A barefoot doctor, a village health aid, or a neighborhood spiritist healer may remain as the only possible alternative in the impoverished circumstances of many deprived people.

It should also be remembered that traditional and alternative care can be very expensive, as in the case of the African psychiatrist described in Chapter 14. Particularly when the benefits are unproven, one must balance costs against the ability to pay. Individuals with severe untreatable conditions are easy recruits for untested remedies. Even if biomedicine is a complete failure in these cases, and even if the treatment is known not to cause harm, one must still consider the cost. It is unreasonable to make financial sacrifices to pay for treatments based on unproven claims and outright desperation. Good judgment is required. Well-off individuals can afford to spend a lot under these circumstances, but people with limited or low incomes should be encouraged to save their money or to spend frugally.

MEDICAL ANTHROPOLOGY AS A POLICY SCIENCE

Applied anthropologists have attempted since World War II to make anthropological methods and concepts useful in working on problems that affect people's lives. For the most part, this work has involved helping to implement programs of culture change. It was not common for anthropologists to be involved in actually determining what those programs should be. Beginning in the 1970s this began to change as some anthropologists began to think about, and get involved in, the development of public policy at state, regional, national, and international levels (Kimball, 1978).

Thomas Weaver believes that anthropologists have a contribution to make in public policy based on approaches we have discussed earlier:

- a systems-functional-holistic framework
- the cross-cultural or comparative method
- the community study method
- participant observation
- ethnographic field techniques
- an emic perspective
- an interpretive (meaning-oriented) analysis of culture (Weaver, 1985b)

Many anthropologists, Weaver included, ask if we can really succeed in this arena (Weaver, 1985a). James Lowell Gibbs, Jr. and Leith Mullings have voiced disappointment, if not despair, at the failure to truly have an impact on policy in general and health policy in particular (Gibbs, 1982; Mullings, 1989). Robert Hinshaw concludes with regret that "anthropologists have not had significant, visible impact on policy formation in any major domestic or international policy area" (Hinshaw, 1980, p. 516). Public policy clearly offers an important challenge for medical anthropologists frustrated with being asked to implement policies they do not like in the first place.

Ethics

Medical anthropology as a policy science, and applied medical anthropology more broadly, must be grounded on sound ethical principles. Nobody would disagree with that. Yet, it is difficult to decide what exactly is right or wrong, useful or harmful, as a set of ethical standards. The Society for Applied Anthropology published its first Code of Ethics in 1949. The American Anthropological Association (AAA) published its own Principles of Professional Responsibility in 1973. Yet even as I write, the profession still cannot agree and is still not sure what the code or principles should be.

When the AAA amended the Principles of Professional Responsibility in 1990, two sentences set the tone of these ethical principles:

As Dean of Undergraduate Studies at Stanford University in the 1970s, James Gibbs was an ex-officio member of the faculty senate. He also served as a trustee of Mills College.

(Photo, Stanford University News Service)

1. Anthropologists must respect, protect, and promote the rights and the welfare of all those affected by their work.

2. Anthropologists' first responsibility is to those whose lives and cultures they study.

So far so good, but no sooner were the revised principles made public than difficult questions were raised by members of the association, the public, and the media about how to apply them in specific situations. Four of these challenges can be summarized as follows (and I quote directly from the *Anthropology Newsletter):*

1. Can there be a conflict between the responsibility to the individuals studied and to the culture studied? If so, how ought the anthropologist resolve such a conflict?

2. How ought the anthropologist resolve conflicts between her/his own ethics/the laws of his/her society and the ethics and laws of the people and culture being studied? Which set of ethics applies in the field?

3. How ought the anthropologist respond to acts which are "crimes" or unacceptable behaviors in his/her society (i.e., murder, rape, genital mutilation) but are acceptable in the culture being studied?

4. How does the practicing anthropologist determine how an employer might use his/her fieldwork sometime in the future? (Givens, 1993)

This quagmire of uncertainty emerged because a pair of fundamental principles of anthropological interpretation were not as soundly based as we used to think. Ethnocentrism and cultural relativity require that in work relating to another culture anthropologists respect their values and practices (relativity) rather than judge them in terms of our own values and practices (ethnocentrism). I hasten to add that these are good principles as a basic orientation to take when involved in multiculturalism. However, they fail to provide guidelines in some situations. For example, does your commitment to cultural relativism require you to approve of and provide moral support for a policy of ethnic cleansing carried out in a society where nationals believe it is appropriate and justified? Do you feel that it is child abuse for adults to subject a girl or boy to a painful genital surgery that will interfere with sexual and reproductive function in adult years?

In trying to sort out these issues, Paul Turner points out that the value positions of other societies are just as capable of being wrong as are our own. What we need are value positions that have universal application (Turner, 1982). He describes two. One suggested by Laura Thompson grounds universal ethics in the idea of a universal ecosystem (Thompson, 1979). Health and human welfare can be evaluated in terms of what works best to preserve human and natural resources on a global scale. This would require societies to rise above their own self-interest, and anthropologists ought to have contributions to make to an ethical ecology on every level from public policy to field activism. However, many ethical issues cannot be framed in ecological terms, including the issue of ethnic cleansing or child abuse.

The other value position mentioned by Turner grew out of the Vicos Project. This development program was carried out in a rural locality in Peru by anthropologists and others from the University of Cornell just a few years before the Cornell–Navajo Project described in Chapter 7. Its goals were to stimulate development in the areas of economy and technology, education, and community organization, as well as nutrition and health. The project appears to have succeeded in many ways. As concerns health, Allan Holmberg reported that pinworm and roundworm infections along with amoebic dysentery were almost eliminated as a result of public health measures (Holmberg, 1960).

The Vicos Project contributed to efforts in the 1950s to develop an American policy for foreign aid to developing nations. In that project, the American team also faced up to issues of ethnocentrism, cultural relativism, and the need for agreeing on cross-culturally valid values as guidelines to foreign policy. Holmberg phrased the need in this way:

> In our dealings with Latin Americans we North Americans often fail to realize
> that the ways of life of many of our southern neighbors are grounded in
> assumptions and imperatives which differ in many important respects from

those of our own society. It is difficult for us to realize, for example, that the "American dream" of equal opportunity for everyone, of peace, prosperity, and happiness for all, does not have the same appeal everywhere. For a great many Latin Americans these goals have never been highly valued. Indeed, for many they are completely outside of the range of their experience. A widespread ignorance of each other's cultures has led on both sides to many misunderstandings and has left behind many distorted images. (Holmberg, 1960, p. 63)

With this nod to cultural relativism, the social scientists who designed and administered the Vicos Project apparently decided that, like it or not, the American dream should be taken as a universal value system. What else can one think when we find that they justified their intervention on the Vicos hacienda in terms of the following definitions of value sharing proposed by Harold Lasswell, an American sociologist, and taken here from his later essay on policy sciences:

- *shared power,* that is, authoritative and controlling participation in the making of important decisions
- *shared enlightenment,* that is, access to the intelligence required for the discovery of common interest
- *shared skill,* that is, opportunity to acquire, exercise, and achieve excellence in the arts, crafts, and professions
- *shared wealth,* that is, access to the benefits of production
- *shared well-being,* that is, enjoyment of safety, health, and comfort
- *shared affection,* that is, enjoyment of congenial and intimate human relations and love of inclusive groups
- *shared rectitude,* that is, a common demand to act responsibly on behalf of human dignity (Lasswell, 1968)

Turner, drawing on the work of others, believes we should also add security, liberty, equality, and growth to Lasswell's list.

Further, Turner urges us to retrieve this list of proposed universal values from the neglect they have suffered, asserting that they seem adequate as an alternative to cultural relativism for the evaluation of public policies. So what is the problem?

Basically, we need to go back to that quotation from Holmberg. These are American dream values. It is tempting to close one's eyes to philosophical and logical niceties and simply take these values as working premises. Problems arise, however, when one actually tries to apply them to concrete problems. Consider the need to make cost-benefit assessments. Which is the higher value if one has to lessen well-being (health and safety) in order to increase wealth (goods and services)? Again, how do these values conform with praxis (practice) as an anthropological theory of how people should be empowered to act on behalf of themselves in order to liberate themselves, as Karl Marx advocated, from alienation and exploitation (Warry, 1992)? In Latin America, members of different racial, ethnic, and SES groups would never be able to agree on which kind of praxis (actions) would be ethically responsible and also politically desirable and effective.

Richard Shweder describes the ethnocentrism inherent in even the most enlightened efforts to identify universal values to justify policy decisions (Shweder, 1991; pp. 167-174). He points out that ethical standards can be fundamentally either rights-based or duty-based. Where duty-based codes of ethics prevail, "The code itself takes precedence over individuals, their appetites, wants, or habits. In a duty-based culture, the individual must conform to the code" (Shweder, 1991, p. 168). Can this be reconciled with Lasswell's universal values? Again, societies differ as to whether their ethical codes are person-centered or role-centered. If role-centered, again, the needs and wants of the individual are subordinated to those of others.

Here, then, is the paradox of ethical standards. We have failed to identify universal standards of what is good and right, yet we must have standards, so we do the best we can. The same is true within the American medical community. The struggles of anthropologists are paralleled by those of clinicians (Pellegrino, 1993). From a center for health policy and ethics, Charles Dougherty proposes six key values that should inform health care policy in the United States. Clearly, they are culture-specific in the sense that they are Judeo-Christian or Enlightenment in origin and not at all universal in concept. Three are intrinsic values:

- respect for the dignity of persons
- caring in therapeutic relationships
- protection of the least well-off

Another three are instrumental values:

- service to the common good
- containment of health care costs
- simplicity in the system of health care provision (Dougherty, 1992)

Like those of Lasswell, Dougherty's ethical values raise as many questions as they answer. But let us not neglect this important final observation. In anthropology and in medicine a commitment to ethical policies is imperative, no matter how confusing and difficult. That commitment in itself is an important achievement.

THE CHALLENGE OF MEDICAL ANTHROPOLOGY

Modern science does not have answers to many of the serious problems that plague humanity. Of course. However, it is able to contribute greatly to the human potential for living long lives in good health. In terms of scientific knowledge and discovery methods, modern medical science is without precedent, both in what it can accomplish now, and in what it should be able to achieve in the future.

Medical heroes of the past included brave, selfless warriors against disease, such as Chief Kako in Africa. Laura Bohannan, an anthropologist, captured the alarm and dread of smallpox as an episode in her novel *Return to Laughter* (written under the pen name Elenore Smith Bowen). The horror of a smallpox epidemic, spreading over the countryside like a rogue fire, surrounded Kako's village. Then, what could not be avoided took place. A villager dragged himself along the path leading into the village, his pox-covered body a sure sign that evil had arrived. A scream of terror filled the air.

> While the boy's terrified voice still shrilled danger, Kako came running back out to face it. In his right hand he had his most powerful magic; he swung the heavy, soot-blackened pot before him like a censer. In his left he bore a frond of the leafy plant that protects against witchcraft. Running, Kako went to turn back danger. He was afraid, but he ran forward, shouting hoarsely, "I forbid you to enter. By that which I carry, I forbid you to enter." (Bohannan, 1964, p. 269)

Heroes like Kako still risk their lives in the fight against suffering, disease, and death. Whether with modern or traditional technology, they will be found where people are overwhelmed by natural disasters and human cruelty. But heroics are not enough. The greater need is for minds and bodies disciplined and skilled in the medical sciences, and that includes medical anthropology. Indeed, the medical anthropologist has a very important role to play.

Consider, for example, that of all medical scientists, it is the anthropologist who is qualified to document what Kako did, and to make sense of it. It is the anthropologist who is trained to develop educational programs to help individuals like Kako work more effectively in fighting disease in their communities. It is they, too, who can best help to integrate traditional and alternative healers into modern settings.

Conversely, anthropologists are trained to mediate between the practitioners of high technology medicine and the clients medicine is supposed to serve. Perhaps that is obvious, but it may not be so obvious that anthropologists experienced in participant observervation are also uniquely qualified to mediate relations among professionals in health care settings. Making multidisciplinarity work requires talking across the subcultures of medical specialties, nursing, physical therapy, social work, pastoral care, and the behavioral sciences. Communication and cooperation almost never happen easily and quickly.

The most challenging task, no doubt, is on the level of theory. It is to bring intellectual skills, training, and experience to bear on vertical thinking in matters of health. We have seen that the contemporary physician-scientist has a good orientation to vertical thinking, but tends to limit attention to basic sciences at the lower end of the hierarchy. Medical anthropologists, equally well oriented to vertical thinking, tend to address higher levels in the hierarchy. Who should take the lead in uniting these two approaches? Well, it could be by mutual rapprochement, to be sure. But it will happen sooner and, I would argue, better, if medical anthropologists take the initiative in this. They, rather than physicians, are products of a discipline with a long history of research based on cross-cultural and holistic thinking. They, rather than physicians, are trained to work with the often baffling data of the human sciences, data which rank high on Kline's complexity index. Finally, the medical anthropologist possesses a theoretical orientation well suited for this great challenge, that of the biocultural paradigm.

As stated at the outset, no one discipline has all of the answers for achieving good health for all. Physicians and surgeons have been the featured marquee players in this drama for most of the twentieth century. But that has changed. The world of medicine is now far more egalitarian. The stage, if you will, is no longer a setting for virtuoso actors. It is more like a three-ring circus in which many different kinds of actors display their skills, each with some moments in the spotlight, but all with contributions that are essential. Among these performers, medical anthropologists will increasingly be found. They are as well suited to stardom as any, but for the most part they will serve as team players along with the rest. The rewards will not be in spotlights, but in the personal satisfaction of solving puzzles and helping make this a better world for all.

CONCLUSION

The potential of medical anthropology is there, but it can be actualized only by those who have jobs. Based on the obsolete Comtean notion that the theoretical sciences were more important than engineering and other fields of application, most early medical anthropologists were employed in university settings. With growing maturity, jobs in applied fields have gained in importance. "Anthropology is changing," Thomas Johnson recently stated, as president of the Society for Medical Anthropology. "Medical anthropology is the largest and most rapidly growing subfield within anthropology, and it is likely that a majority of medical anthropologists are currently applied, not academic" (Johnson, 1994). Much of what has been discussed in this book has derived from medical anthropologists employed in international public health, disease prevention programs in the United States, the training of physicians, and as members of multidisciplinary health care teams in medical centers. They get paid for data acquisition and analysis, as clinical anthropologists, and as administrators. Yet, the field is still young. Much of the public has never heard of medical anthropologists, or if they have, are very unclear about what they do. Many physicians are equally uninformed. It is reasonable to expect that as awareness increases, so too will job opportunities. Let us hope that it will be so, because the ultimate task of the medical anthropologist is to make a contribution to humanizing health services and to helping make life better for people like Mary, who was cured of a painful limp, and Karen, whose spiritual growth was nurtured, it would seem, by incurable pain.

REFERENCES

Anderson, R. (1991). The efficacy of ethnomedicine: Research methods in trouble. *Medical Anthropology, 13,* 1–17.

Anderson, R. (1992). Comfrey in the Chinese materia medica. *Asian Medicine Newsletter, 2,* 7–11.

Bohannan, L. (E. S. Bowen). (1964). *Return to laughter.* Published in cooperation with the American Museum of Natural History. Garden City, NY: Doubleday. (Original work published 1954)

Brink, P. J. (1990). Introduction. In P. J. Brink (Ed.), *Transcultural nursing: A book of readings.* Prospect Heights, IL: Waveland Press. (Original work published 1976)

Bronstein, J. M. (1993). Commentary: On the work of medical anthropologists. *Anthropology Newsletter, 34* (1), 19.

Cassell, J. (1991). *Expected miracles: Surgeons at work.* Philadelphia: Temple University Press.

Chrisman, N. J., & Johnson, T. M. (1990). Clinically applied anthropology. In T. M. Johnson & C. F. Sargent (Eds.), *Medical anthropology: Contemporary theory and method.* New York: Praeger.

Chrisman, N. J., & Maretzki, T. W. (1982). Preface. In N. J. Chrisman & T. W. Maretzki (Eds.), *Clinically applied anthropology: Anthropologists in health science settings* (pp. vii-viii). Dordrecht: D. Reidel.

Donaldson, S., & Crowley, D. (1978). The discipline of nursing. *Nursing Outlook, 26,* 113–120.

Dougherty, C. J. (1992). Ethical values at stake in health care reform. *Journal of the American Medical Association, 268,* 2409–2412

Engel, G. L. (1977). The need for a new medical model: A challenge for biomedicine. *Science, 196,* 129–136.

Foster, G. M., & Anderson, B. G. (1978). *Medical anthropology.* New York: John Wiley & Sons.

Fox, R. (1959). *Experiment perilous.* Philadelphia: University of Pensylvania Press.

Friedman, E. (1990). Nursing: Breaking the bonds? *Journal of the American Medical Association, 264,* 3117–3122.

Galanti, G. A. (1991). *Caring for patients from different cultures: Case studies from American hospitals.* Philadelphia: University of Pennsylvania Press.

Gibbs, J. L., Jr. (1982). Anthropology as a policy science: Some limitations. In E. A. Hoebel, R. Currier, & S. Kaiser (Eds.), *Crisis in anthropology: View from Spring Hill 1980* (pp. 363–378). New York: Garland.

Givens, D. (1993). The ethics of fieldwork. *American Anthropology Newsletter, 34* (5), 2.

Hinshaw, R. E. (1980). Anthropology, administration, and public policy. *Annual Review of Anthropology, 9,* 497–522.

Holmberg, A. R. (1960). Changing community attitudes and values in Peru: A case study in guided change. In R. N. Adams, O. Lewis, J. P. Gillin, R. W. Patch, A. R. Holmberg, & C. Wagley (Eds.), *Social change in Latin America today: Its implications for United States policy* (pp. 63–107). New York: Vintage Books.

Hoy, D. (1985). Jacques Derrida. In Q. Skinner (Ed.), *The return of grand theory in the human sciences* (pp. 41–64). Cambridge: Cambridge University Press.

Johnson, T. (1994). Presidential message: On paradigm shifts in medical anthropology. *Anthropology Newsletter, 35* (5), 31-32.

Katz, P. (1981). Ritual in the operating room. *Ethnology, 20,* 335-350.

Katz, P. (1985). How surgeons make decisions. In R. A. Hahn & A. D. Gaines (Eds.), *Physicians of Western medicine: Anthropological approaches to theory and practice* (pp. 155-175). Dordrecht: D. Reidel.

Kimball, S. T. (1978). Anthropology as a policy science. In E. M. Eddy & W. L. Partridge (Eds.), *Applied anthropology in America.* New York: Columbia University Press.

Kleinman, A. (1989). Preface. In R. A. Hahn & A. D. Gaines (Eds.), *Physicians of Western medicine: Anthropological approaches to theory and practice.* Dordrecht: D. Reidel.

Konner, M. (1991). The promise of medical anthropology: An invited commentary. *Medical Anthropology Quarterly, 5,* 78-82.

Lasswell, H. D. (1968). Policy sciences. *International encyclopedia of the social sciences* (Vol 12), 181-189.

Last, M. (1990). Professionalization of indigenous healers. In T. M. Johnson & C. F. Sargent (Eds.), *Medical anthropology: Contemporary theory and method.* New York: Praeger.

Leininger, M. M. (Ed.). (1991). *Culture care diversity and universality: A theory of nursing.* (Publication No. 15-2402). New York: National League for Nursing Press.

Leslie, C. (Ed.) (1976). *Asian medical systems: A comparative study.* Berkeley: University of California Press.

Lock, M. (1988). Introduction. In M. Lock & E. Gordon (Eds.), *Biomedicine examined.* Dordrecht: Kluwer Academic Publishers.

Mullings, L. (1989). Gender and the application of anthropological knowledge to public policy in the United States. In S. Morgen (Ed.), *Gender and anthropology: Critical reviews for research and teaching* (pp. 360-381). Washington, DC: American Anthropological Association.

Osborne, O. (1990). Anthropology and nursing: Some common traditions and interests. In P. J. Brink (Ed.), *Transcultural nursing: A book of readings.* Prospect Heights, IL: Waveland Press. (Original work published in 1976).

Pellegrino, E. D. (1993). The metamorphosis of medical ethics: A 30-year retrospective. *Journal of the American Medical Association, 269,* 1158-1162.

Reverby, S. (1987). *Ordered to care.* New York: Cambridge University Press.

Romanucci-Ross, L., & Moerman, D. E. (1991). The extraneous factor in Western medicine. In L. Romanucci-Ross, D. E. Moerman, & L. R. Tancredi (Eds.), *The anthropology of medicine: From culture to method* (pp. 6-15). New York: Bergin & Garvey.

Romanucci-Ross, L., Moerman, D. E., & Tancredi L. R. (Eds.). (1991). *The anthropology of medicine: From culture to method.* New York: Bergin & Garvey.

Ryan, M. (1994). *Efficacy of the Tibetan treatment for arthritis.* Paper presented at the 93rd annual meeting of the American Anthropological Association, Atlanta, GA.

Shweder, R. A. (1991). *Thinking through cultures: Expeditions in cultural psychology.* Cambridge, MA: Harvard University Press.

Starr, P. (1982). *The social transformation of American medicine.* New York: Basic Books, Inc.

Stein, L. I., Watts, D. T., & Howell, T. (1990). The doctor-nurse game revisited. *New England Journal of Medicine, 322,* 546-549.

Thompson, L. (1979). Validity and relativism in ethnology. *Humanities, 40,* 59-75.

Turner, P. R. (1982). Anthropological value positions. *Human Organization, 41,* 76-80.

Unschuld, P. U. (1985). *Medicine in China: A history of ideas.* University of California Press.

Warry, W. (1992). The eleventh thesis: Applied anthropology as praxis. *Human Organization, 51,* 155-163.

Weaver, T. (1985a). Anthropology as a policy science: Part I, A Critique. *Human Organization, 44,* 97-105.

Weaver, T. (1985b). Anthropology as a policy science: Part II, Development and training. *Human Organization, 44,* 197-205.

Weidman, H. H. (1982). Research strategies, structural alterations and clinically applied anthropology. In N. J. Chrisman & T. W. Maretzki (Eds.), *Clinically applied anthropology: Anthropologists in health science settings* (pp. 201-241). Boston, MA: D. Reidel Publishing Co.

INDEX

Abkhazia. *See* Soviet Union
Ableness, and health, 302-304
Ablon, J., 303, 304
Abrams, W. B., 337, 338
Acculturation, 155-156. *See also* Navajo
    Cornell project
    documenting, 156-159
Ackerknecht, E., 34, 58, 162, 360, 391
Acupressure, 13
Acupuncture, 13, 393, 417
Acute health problems, 8
Adair, J., 165, 166, 168, 171, 173
Adams, W., 20
Adaptation
    cultural, 197-200
    to mild to moderate malnutrition, 281-282
    physiological, 192-195, 196
    sickle cell anemia as, 192-195
Adelson, P., 36
Adolescents
    lesbian health, 329
    medical diagnosis of, 3-5
    mental health of, 233-234
Aesculapius, 388-389
Aesthetics, in biomedical hierarchy, 36
Africa
    beer in, 237-238
    death rates in, 39
    malaria in, 192-195, 260-261
    medical discourse in, 148-149
    medical patient treatment in, 3-4
    menstruation in, 326
    midwife in, 395
    race and malaria in, 260-261
    shaman in, 5-6, 7, 348-349
    skull surgery in, 360
    smallpox in, 214-215
    Turkana of, 221-223

African-Americans. *See also* Africa; Blacks
    cardiovascular disease among, 266-267
    health beliefs and practices of, 49-50
Age and aging. *See also* Menopause; Old
    age
    child abuse and, 293-294
    childhood trauma and, 293
    dimensions of, 286
    elder neglect and, 296-298
    immunization of children and, 286-292
    levels in Soviet Union, 301-302
    old age, 294-295
Age-area hypothesis, 74
Aggression explanations, of disease causation,
    92
AIDS (acquired immunodeficiency syndrome),
    305-310
    and promiscuity, 308-310
    transmission of, 306-307
AIDS project, 18-19
Alcohol and alcoholism
    consciousness and, 235
    in Native American communities, 241
    among New York Puerto Ricans, 268
    in Old World, 236-239
    socioeconomic status and, 268-271
Alexander, L., 133-134
Alland, A., 160, 205-206, 222
Allison, A. C., 193
Allopathic medicine, 404
Altamira, Spain, prehistoric evidence in, 62-64
Altered states of consciousness (ASC), 234
    shamanism as, 346-348
Alternative healers, in biomedical settings, 416-
    419
Alternative medicine, 384. *See also* Body-
    oriented healers
    for back pain, 13

homeopathy as, 7, 380-385
naturopathy as, 379-380
Amazon, shamans in, 51
Amenorrhea, 328-329
American Anthropological Association (AAA)
ethics statement of, 420-422
gays and, 305
American Indians. *See* Native Americans
American Psychiatric Association, gays and,
305
Americas, hallucinogens in, 234. *See also*
New World
smallpox in, 215-216
Anal explanations, of disease causation, 91
Anarchy, Comte on, 24
Anatomy, 204-205, 207
of female, 322
Ancestry. *See* Genetics; Race
Andaman Islanders, The (Radcliffe-
Brown), 129
Anderson, B., 159, 298, 299, 300, 302
Anderson, E. N., 393
Anderson, K. O., 325
Anderson, M. L., 393
Anderson, R., 11, 76, 79, 93, 288, 290, 291,
293, 371, 375, 387, 392, 418
Anderson, S., 55, 352, 354
Anderson, and Quesalid, 113-114
Andritzky, W., 392
Animism
in Aztec medicine, 66
as etic term, 78
and healing, 46-47
Tylor on, 83
Animistic causation theories, 86
Anopheline mosquitoes, 193
Anorexia, 328
Anthropological linguistics, 20
Anthropologists
chronic illness and, 11-15
clinical, 413-416
methods of, 3-4
Anthropology. *See also* Medical anthropology
alternative medicine and, 13
applied, 159-161
body-oriented healers and, 376-378
four-field, 20-22
hierarchies of disciplines in, 39-41
human body and, 28-29
as isolated field, 79
of medicine, 403-429
multidisciplinarity with medicine, 163-172

nutritional, 276-282
as positivist science, 29-30
practices of, 45-46
scientific approach of, 27
study of complex societies by, 155
time dimension of, 45-69
women as subjects of, 314-315
after World War II, 154
Antigen types, 192-193
Applied anthropology, 159-161
Applied science, 25-26
Arachnoiditis, 12
Archeology, prehistoric, 55-58
Arensberg, C. M., 159, 238
Argonauts of the Western Pacific
(Malinowski), 129
Armelagos, G. J., 62, 206, 207
Art, symbolism of, 136-137
Arthritis, homeopathic treatment of, 383-384
ASC. *See* Altered states of consciousness
Ascorbic acid. *See* Vitamin C hypothesis
Asia
cholera in, 210-212, 213-214
World War II and, 154
Atherosclerosis, and aging, 338
Athletes, female, 328-329
Atlas of World Cultures (Murdock), 83
Atropine, 235
Australia
core culture in, 182
magic in, 48
Ayurveda, 386
joint manipulation and, 392
Aztec medicine, 66-69, 378
religious practices and, 68

Baer, H. A., 285, 379
Baffin Island, Inuits on, 187
Baker, B., J., 62
Balanced polymorphism, 195
Bali, structural theory and, 140-141
Bands
energy flow in, 187
and sociocultural integration, 182-183
Bantu, 194
Barclay, H. B., 318
Barnett, C., 165, 166, 168, 170, 171, 173, 191
Barnouw, V., 243
Barrett, K., 76-77
Barrett, R. J., 252
Barriers, to cultural change, 160-161
Barton, A. H., 220
Barua, D., 211

Basehart, H., 240
Baseline cultures, 167
Bastian, A., 162
Bastien, J. W., 368, 395, 344, 360, 372, 379, 396
Batchelder, W., 121
Bates, B., 144
Bates, M., 324-325, 326
Bateson, G., 250-252, 288
    on males and females in society, 314
Beall, C., 295, 297
Beals, A. R., 390
Beard, G., 247
Beauty, size and, 328
Becher, T., 77
Becker, G., 304
Beer
    in Africa, 237-238
    in Irish community, 238-239
Begay, M., 171
Bell, D., 327
Benedict, R., 109, 314
    on shamans, 345-346
Benet, S., 301
Beringia, movement across, 234-235
Berkow, R., 245, 249, 337, 338
Berlin, B., 175
Berlin, E. A., 175
Bergman's Rule, 221
Bernard, H. R., 117
Berwick, D. M., 259
Bias, supernatural causation and, 85-86
Biggs, B., 372
Biggs, H., 163
Billings, F., 291
Binary oppositions, 142
    and structural method, 137
Biochemistry, in biomedical hierarchy, 35
Biocultural model, 204-229
    environmental disasters and, 223-226
    evolutionary model, 20
    infectious epidemics and, 208-219
    medical ecology and, 220-223
Biocultural studies, 191
Biofeedback, 367
Biological anthropology and anthropologists, 20, 190-191
Biomedical approaches, herbalists and, 372-375
Biomedical diagnoses, 79
Biomedical settings, traditional and alternative healers in, 416-419

Biomedicine, 404
    Virchow and, 162
Birdsell, J. B., 56
Birdwistell, R., 394
Birth. See also Women
    attendants for, 395-396
    health and, 332-336
Blackie, M. G., 380
Blacks, racial traits and, 260-261. See also Africa; African-Americans
Blazer, D. G., II, 246
Blindness, 303
Blois, M. S., 34-35, 38
Blood types
    race and, 260-261
    research on, 192-193
Boas, F., 117, 162
    and Quesalid, 111-112, 113, 114
    shift to anthropolgy and, 162
Body
    female, and culture, 320-323
    pain perception in, 323-326
Body/mind dualism, 321
    physical laws and, 33
    Taussig on, 51
Body-oriented healers, 371-402
    anthropological approaches and, 376-378
    ethnomedical models, herbalism, and, 378-385
    herbalists as, 372-375
Body politic, women and, 322-323
Body type, and climate, 221-222
Bogin, B., 60
Bohannan, L., 215, 425
Bohannan, P., 73
Bolos, A. M., 270
Bolton, R., 305, 308-309
Bonesetting, 391-392
Bonner, V., 309
Book, first medical anthropology, 74-81
    second medical anthropology, 81-83, 84, 159, 248
Bourguignon, E., 94, 95, 234
Bowen, E. S., 215
Boyer, B., 240
Boyer, R., 240
Brady, I., 233
Brain surgery, 360-361
Brazil, shaman in, 349. See also Shamanism; Shamans
Breast disease, 336. See also Women
Breasted, J. H., 388
Breidenbach, G., 215

Breo, D. L., 163
Bride, health of, 330-331. *See also* Women
Bride-burning, 331
Brink, P., 411, 412
Brodwin, P., 321
Brody, H., 240
Bronstein, J., 415-416
Brough, R., 170
Brown, B., 316-317
Brown, P. J., 60, 62, 196, 197-198, 199, 200, 201, 274
Browner, C., 395
Buckley, T., 321, 326, 327
Bulimia, 328
Bunzel, R., 314
Burkina Faso, mortality rates in, 39, 40
Burson-Tolpin, A., 145
Byrd, R., 382

California, Mexican-American community in, 117-119
Cameron, E., 59, 60
Campbell, B. G., 65
Campbell, D., 115
Cancer, of breast, 336
Cancer specialist, interview with, 145-150
Capoeira, 394
Carbohydrate deficiency, 282
Carlson, K. J., 317
Carr, J. E., 246
Carrier, J. M., 305, 307
Cassell, J., 17-18, 19, 102, 409
Cassidy, C., 328, 330
Cassidy, J. D., 11
Caste, in India, 158. *See also* India
    cultural differentiation, 288, 318. *See also*
        Schismogenesis
Caudill, W., 22
Causation
    animistic theories of, 86
    child rearing and beliefs about disease, 90-94
    magical, 86
Causation theories
    mystical, 86
    naturalism as, 84-85
    supernatural and, 85
Caves
    at Altamira, Spain, 62-64
    at Lascaux, France, 65
    at Les-Trois-Frères, France, 64
Cell/crypt model, of colon cancer, 38-39
Cellular Pathology (Virchow), 162
Central African Republic, mortality rates in, 39.
    See also Africa

Ceremonies, of Navajo, 165
Chadwick, J., 381
Chagnon, N. A., 240
Change
    cultural barriers to, 160
    psychological barriers to, 161
    social barriers to, 160-161
Channa, V. C., 331
Chase, A., 218-219
Chavira-Prado, A., 337
Chemistry, in biomedical hierarchy, 35
Chess, S., 30, 31
Chiefdoms, health conditions and, 183-184
Child, I. L., 96, 118
    on Freudian explanations and disease causa-
        tion, 90
Child abuse, 293-294
Childbirth, 332-336
    midwives, birth attendants, and, 395-396
Childhood
    mortality, of bands, 183
    trauma in, 293
Child rearing, and beliefs about disease causa-
    tion, 90-94
Children. *See also* Child abuse; Childhood;
    Family; Mothers
    birth weight and, 281
    culture and, 30-31
    immunization of, 286-290
China. *See also* Acupuncture
    abortions of female embryos in, 315-316
    bonesetters in, 392
    dietary therapy in, 394
    joint manipulation in, 392
    medicine in, 387, 405, 417
    neurasthenia in, 247
Chinantec, study of, 117
Chiropractors, 13
    explanatory model of, 292
    opposition to vaccines, 287-290, 292
Chitwood, D. D., 308
Cholera
    in America, 212-214
    in Asia, 210-214
    control of, 219
Chrisman, N., 413-414, 415
Chronic health problems, 8
    anthropologist and, 11-15
    pain as, 9-10
Cigarettes, deaths from, 240
Circumcision, female
    in Africa, 318-320
    in U.S., 316-318
Clark, M., 117, 298, 299, 300, 302

Class
  and alcoholism, 268-271
  in India, 158
  and obesity, 271-276
Clatt, M., 308
Clements, C. J., 286
Clements, F. E., 81-83, 84, 159, 248
Clifford, J., 110
Clifton, A. C., 159
Climacteric, 337
Climates, medical ecology and, 220-224
Clinical anthropologists, 413-416
Clinical depression. *See* Depression
Clinical gaze, 323
Clinical language. *See* Discourse analysis
Clitoridectomies, 316-318. *See also*
    Circumcision, female
Cluster analysis, 107-110, 121-122
Cockburn, T. A., 55, 56
Code of Ethics, 420
Codes, mediation and, 139
Cohen, F. L., 331
Cohen, L., 296
Cohen, M. N., 58, 56, 57
Cohen, Y. A., 96
Coimbra, C. E. A., Jr., 192, 200
Collado-Ardón, R., 117-119
Collective stress situations, 220
Colley, F., 288
Colon cancer, vertical reasoning and, 36-37
Columbus, C., 62
Coming of Age in Samoa (Mead), 3, 326
Coming of Old Age in Samoa (Holmes),
    295
Comite, A., 132
Communication
  in acculturation project, 170-171
  triads and, 143
Community
  needs and acculturation project, 169
  schizophrenia and, 252-255
Community based design, rapid ethnographic
    assessment and, 124. *See also* Fieldwork;
    Susto study
Comparative method, 21-22, 82-83
  Mead and, 233
Comparison. *See* Comparative method;
    Triangulation
Computer
  simulations, 186
  statistics and, 120
Comte, A., 23, 24, 32, 47, 322
Condoms, AIDS and, 308-310
Conibo people, 351, 355

Conner, L., 140-141
Conrad, P., 304
Consciousness
  altered states of, 234
  shamanic state of, 347
Consensus, measures of, 122-123
Contagion, measurement of, 123
Contagious magic, 48-49
  Aztec medicine and, 66, 67
Contrast sets, 104-105
Conversation analysis, 149-150
Cook, T. D., 117, 120
Corbett, K. K., 14
Corbin, J., 120
Cordell, D., 39
Core culture, 181-182
Coreil, J., ORT therapy and, 174-176
Cornell University Medical College, Navajo
    project with, 163-172
Correlational analysis, and theory, 89-90
Correlational studies, HRAF for, 87-90. *See also*
    Human Relations Area Files (HRAF)
Cosmopolitan medicine, 403-404
Cosmos, shamanic, 350-351
Cost, justification of, 419
Costanzo, R., 92
Coumarin, 372-373
Cowpox, 217
Cree people, herbalism and, 374-375
Cro-Magnon art, 63
Crosby, A. W., Jr., 215, 216
Cross-cultural perspective
  categories and, 82
  comparisons, 21-22
  on obesity, 274-275
  on women, 314
Cross-cultural sample, 84
  selecting, 96
Cross-cultural studies
  adding new cultures to, 96
  language and, 145
  sample for, 96
  of Whiting, 89-90
Cruz, N. I., 372
Csordas, T., 39
Cultural adaptation
  malaria in Europe, 197-200
  malaria in South America, 195
Cultural anthropologists, 155, 191
Cultural barriers, to change, 160
Cultural bias, in Navajo-Cornell project, 165-
    167
Cultural consensus, 124
Cultural diversity

healing and, 7-8
  prehistory, health, and, 61-62
Cultural ecology, 182. *See also* Medical
  ecology
  ecosystem concept and, 185-187
  medical ecology and, 206
Cultural evolutionary theory, 73
Cultural relativism, female circumcision and,
  319-320
Cultural traits, 73-74
  generalizing about, 117
Culture
  of anthropologist, 45
  baseline, 167
  body and, 320-323
  childbirth and, 332-336
  compared with language, 136-137
  concept of, 21
  cores of, 181-182
  depression and, 246
  documentation of, 83
  emic and etic descriptions of, 76-79
  geographic dimension of, 74
  hierarchies in, 189-190
  independent evolution of, 75
  influence of, 109
  male and female subcultures in, 314-315
  in 1960s, 355
  nonhealth-related aspects of, 132
  pain perception and, 323-325
  reality of, 29
  susto and, 118-119
  of target community, 164-165
  as text, 141-144
  time as dimension of, 73-74
  traditional and alternative healers in, 417-418
  understanding of, 45
  universal characteristics of, 78
Culture-bound psychiatric syndromes
  pibloktoq as, 242-243
  startle matching taxon and, 244-245
Culture change, 155. *See also*
  Acculturation; Navajo-Cornell project
  theory of, 154-179, 181
Cupping, 392-393
Curative principle, 24
Cures
  magic and, 50
  personalistic beliefs and practices as,
  80-81
Customs, health-promoting, 197-200
Cutner, L. P., 316
Cybernetic concepts, 186

Dance, 394
D'Andrade, R. G., 39, 96
Danger, Lévi-Strauss on, 140
Database, HRAF methodology and, 95
Davis, M., 384
Davis-Floyd, R., 17, 332, 333-334, 395
Death, from cigarettes, 240. *See also*
  Mortality
Decision making
  model of, 109
  in Navajo-Cornell project, 169-170
Deconstruction and deconstructionists, 29,
  403
Dedifferentiation, 248
Dengue, 177
Dengue hemorrhagic fever, 177
Denzin, N. K., 45, 46, 120
Department of Health, Education and Welfare
  (DHEW), 172
Dependence explanations, of disease causa-
  tion, 91
Depression, 245-246
  and culture, 246
  neurasthenia and, 247
  soul loss and, 248
Derrida, J., 29, 403
Descriptive questions technique, 104-106
Descriptive statistics, 119
Deshen, S., 303
Desjarlais, R., 28, 29
Deuschle, K. W., 165, 166, 168, 171, 173
Devereux, G., 53
DeVore, Irven, 182
De Waal Malefijt, A., 45
DHEW. *See* Department of Health, Education
  and Welfare
Diabetes, anthropological approaches to, 263-
  266
Diagnosis, 79
  anthropological, 4-5
  medical, 3-4
  by shaman, 5-6
Dialog. *See* Discourse analysis
Diarrhea. *See* Oral rehydration therapy
  (ORT)
Diet, 393-394
  of bands, 182-183
  in early urban societies, 58
  growth and, 280-281
  in Mesolithic period, 56
Dietary fiber, colon cancer and, 36
Differentiation, between males and females,

·   314
Differently abled, 302-304
Diffusionism, 77, 180
Disability, and health, 302-304
Disability and Culture (Whyte and Ingstad), 303
Disasters, environmental, 223-226
Discordance hypothesis, 60-61
Discourse analysis, 144-150
Discrimination, race and, 259
Disease. *See also* Health
   and Aztec medicine
   biomedical model of, 34
   of breast, 336
   causation of, 84-85
   child rearing and beliefs about, 90-94
   cultural responses to, 197-200
   diagnosing, 3-4
   immunization and, 286-290
   malnutrition and, 279
   among Navajo, 164
   personalistic vs. naturalistic medical systems and, 52-54
   population movement and, 61-62
   regional infectious, 192-200
   seasonal change as cause of, 198
   sexually transmitted (STDs), 331
Disengagement, aging and, 298, 300
Distinctive feature analysis, Jacobson on, 136
Distortions, 110
Divale, W. T., 315
DNA
   race and, 260
   sickle cell anemia and, 194
Doan, R., 337
Doctor, traditional, 3-4, 6
Documentation
   of naturalistic medical systems, 84-86
   objectivity in, 100-101
   in Susto study, 118
Dossey, L., 382
Dougherty, C., 424
Douglas, R. G., 41
Dow, J., 39
Dow, M. M., 95
Dowry, 331
Dreams, shamanism and, 348
Dressler, W., 267
Drinking. *See* Alcohol and Alcoholism
Drugs. *See also* Herbalism and herbalists;
Mental illness; Psychopharmacology
   alcohol, 236-239
   contemporary substances abuse and, 240-241

   hallucinogens as, 234
   in 1960s, 355
   psychiatric, 361-363
   psychopharmacology of traditional healers and, 363-365
   psychotropic, 361
   tobacco, 239-240
Dualism, 29
Dual-level control
   concept of, 32-33
   mild to moderate malnutrition and, 281-282
DuBois, C., 314
Duffy, J., 217, 379, 380
Duffy, M., 120
Dunn, F. L., 56, 215, 403
Durham, J. D., 331
Durkin-Longley, M., S., 390
Dyads, patient-doctor, 149
Dyaks, spirits and, 52

East Africa, Turkana of, 221-223. *See also* Africa
Eating disorders, 328
   obesity and, 275-277
Eaton, B., 60
Ecology. *See also* Medical ecology
   ecosystem, 185-187
   malaria spread and, 193-194
   medical, 180-203
   regional, 192-200
Economics, in biomedical hierarchy, 36
Ecosystem
   concept of, 185
   levels in, 190-191
   research, 188-189
Ecosystem ecology, in anthropology, 185-187
Ecstasy, and shamanism, 347
Edelstein, S. J., 260
Edens, 395
Edgerton, R., 303
Edwards, W. T., 325, 326
Egypt, 18
   female circumcision in, 318, 320
Einstein, A., 32
Eisenberg, D., 393, 394
El Dareer, A., 318
Elderly. *See* Age and aging; Old age
Eli, S. R., 209
Eliade, M., 345, 346, 347, 353
Emic statements, 78-79
Empirical medicine, 385-394
Empiricism, 27
Energy flow

in band, 187
in ecosystem ecology, 186-187
in tribe, 188-189
Engel, G. L., 34, 411, 405
Enstrom, J. E., 60
Environment. *See also* Ecology
    and borrowed cultural traits, 180-181
    disasters in, 223-226
    malaria spread and, 193-194
Environmental hazards, medical ecology and,
    220
Epidemics, 208-219
    cholera as, 219-214
    fighting, 219
    plague as, 209-210
    smallpox as, 214-219
Epidemiological model, colon cancer and, 37
Epidemiology, 10-11
Epilepsy, 303
    drugs and, 363
Equilibrium (functional) model, 131-132
Erasmus, C. J., 159
Erikson, E., developmental stages and, 299
Erogenous zone, 90
Erzinger, S., 150
Esthetics. *See* Aesthetics
Estroff, S., 303, 362-363
Ethics, medical anthroplogy and, 420-424
Ethnic groups
    pain perception and, 323-325
    schizophrenia in, 253-254
Ethnicity
    race and, 259-267
    as unclear category, 262-263
Ethnographic methods
    Lowenberg and, 134
    and medical beliefs, 54, 55
    new questioning technique, 103-110
    participant observation, 102-103
    postmodernist critique, 110-116
    and quantitative methods, 116-119
    postpositivism and methodological triangula-
      tion, 120-123
    rapid ethnographic assessment, 123-125
    statistics, 119-120
Ethnography, good enough method, 115-116
Ethnomedical models
    and herbalism, 378-385
    homeopathy and, 380-385
    naturopathy and, 379-380
    small-scale communities and, 378-379
Ethnomedicine, 79, 405
    Clements and, 81-82

as ethnotherapy, 406
    Murdock and, 84
    Rivers and, 79-81
Ethnopsychiatry, 366-367
Ethnoscience, 103
Etic categories, 76-78, 82
Etkin, N. L., 376, 378
Europe. *See also* Western entries
    malaria in, 196-200
    plague in, 209-210
European Americans, Type A behavior and,
    267
Evans-Pritchard, E. E., 215
Evolution
    independent, 75
    interdisciplinarity of, 21
    multilinear, 181-185
Evolutionary model, of Winkelman, 95
Evolutionary stages
    of Frazer, 74-75
    of Rivers, 75-76, 180
Evolutionary theory, 20
    applied, 58-61
    discordance hypothesis and, 60-61
    vitamin C hypothesis and, 59-60
Exorcism, 7-8
Expertise, measures of, 122-123
Extinction, 56

Fagan, B. M., 65
Family. *See also* Old age
    malnutrition and, 282
    relationships in, 101
    and schizophrenia, 250-252
FAO. *See* United Nations Food and
    Agriculture Organization
Farberou, N. L., 251
Farmer, P., 307
Farquhar, J., 387, 390, 393
Fate, 86
Fathers. *See* Family; Mothers
Fay, R. E., 305
Featherstone, M., 28
Feinberg, R., 233
Feldenkreis healing, 13
Females. *See also* Women
    circumcision in Africa, 318-320
    circumcision in U.S., 316-318
    skeletons of, 322
    as subculture, 314
Feminist scholarship, 315
Feminist theory, sick role and, 135
Feminization of poverty, 336-337

Ferreira, A., 251
Fertility, prehistoric evidence of, 63-64
Fetish, 50
Fetishistic (supernatural) view, 24
Field ethnography, 103-104. *See also*
    Questioning techniques
Field reports, of cultural ecologists, 185
Fieldwork, 5, 22, 100. *See also*
    Ethnographic methods
    ethnographic, 54, 55
    participant observation, quantitative meth-
    ods, and, 116-119
    time, money, and work quality, 109
Fishbein, M., 379
Fisher, L. E., 76
Fitzgerald, M., 333
Fixations, disease and, 90-94
Flaws, 387, 393
Fleming-Moran, M., 200
Fletcher, A. J., 245, 249, 337, 338
Flow of energy. *See* Energy flow
Focal infection theory, 290-292
Focused Ethnographic Studies manual, 124-125
Folk medicine, 386, 390
Food areas, 181
Foods. *See also* Eating disorders; Health;
    Malnutrition; Starvation
    diabetes and, 265-266
    fads in, 328
    in Mesolithic period, 56
Forge, A., 136-137
Foster, G. M., 53, 130-131, 159, 160, 172, 173,
    386, 390, 394
Foster, M., 130
Foucault, M., 10, 322-323
Foulks, E., 243
Four-field anthropology, 20-22
    shared concepts and methods in, 22
Four-function paradigm, of Parsons, 272
Fox, R., 132
Frake, C., 104, 106
Frame questioning technique, 106-110
France, prehistoric caves in, 64
Frank, A., 27, 28, 275-276
Frank, J., 366-367
Frankenberg, R., 10
Fraser, D.W., 10
Frayer, D. W., 56
Frayser, S. G., 304
Frazer, J. G., 47-51, 54, 65, 84, 100, 101, 129,
    354
    etic and emic terms and, 78
    and religion, 52

Rivers and evolutionary stages of, 74-75
    science and, 68
Frederick, V., religious healing beliefs and, 93
Freed, R. S., 395
Freed, S.A., 395
Free-listing technique, 121
Freeman, D., 233
Freeman, W., 361
Free thinker, Northwest Coast Indian shaman
    as, 104
Frei, B., 60
Freudian psychoanalytic theory, 90
Frontal lobotomy, 359, 36-361
Fuller, N., 17
Functionalism, cultural ecology and, 185
Functional theory, 129-132. *See also*
    Structural theory
    Malinowski and, 130
Furst, P. T., 234

Galenic medicine, 385, 386
Gallagher, C., 320
Gallus, A., 53
Galton, F., 96, 117
Gardner, R., 215
Garhi, K., 161, 164, 176
Garrity, J., 39
Garro, L., 134
    Pichátaro, Mexico, work in, 106-110
Gay lifestyle, and health, 304-305
Geertz, C., 27, 139
Gender
    cultural adaptation to malaria and, 199-200
    culture and, 314-315
Genetics
    and alcoholism, 270-271
    blood types and, 193
    cardiovascular disease and, 266-267
    diabetes and, 263-266
    malaria, race, and, 260-261
    malaria in Africa and, 192-195
    malaria in Europe, 196-197
    malaria in South America and, 195-196
Geographic dimension of culture, 74
Geographic regions, diffusion in, 181
German anthropologists
    Bastian, 162
    Virchow, 162
Gerontology. *See* Age and aging; Old age
Gibbs, J. L., Jr., 420, 421
Gibson, R. G., 383
Giddens, A., 27
Ginsburg, F., 320, 332, 335

Girls
from birth to puberty, 315-316
infanticide and, 315-316
Glasgow Homeopathic Hospital, research at, 383-384
Glasser, M., 93
Glittenberg, J. A. (Jody), 226
Goffman, E., 251, 303, 305
Golden Bough, The (Frazer), 47-48
etic and emic terms in, 78
scientific medicine in, 54
Goldin, C., 304
Goldschmidt, W., 162
Goldstein, M., 295
Good, B. J., 10, 77, 386, 390
Good, M. J. D., 10, 77, 386, 390
Goodby, C. S., 263
Goode, W. J., 50
Gordon, D., 318, 319
Gordon, J. S., 21
Gottlieb, A., 321, 326, 327
Gould, S. J., 262
Goulet, J. G., 356
Gove, S., 124
GPS (global positioning system), 186
Graham, G., 277
Graham, S. B., 60, 328-329
Gray, S., 222
Greco-Roman medicine, 385, 386
Greece, medicine in, 388-389
Greenbaum, L. S., 94, 95
Greenbough, W. B., 211
Greenfield, S., 353, 354
Gregory, J., 39
Growth, MMM and, 280-281
G-6-Pd deficiency, 196-197
Guba, E. G., 120
Gunby, P., 287
Guthrie, D., 213, 217

Haddon, A. C., 74, 101
Hahn, R., 262
Hahnemann, S., 380, 381
Haiti, ORT program in, 174-175
Halifax, J., 350
Hallowell, I., 82
Hallucinogens, 234-235
and Amazonian shamans, 51
in Americas, 234-235
Harner on, 355-356
Halverson, J., 62
Hankinson, S. E., 60
Hanna, J. L., 394

Hardin, M., 242
Harner, M. J., 102, 103, 234, 235, 347, 350, 351, 353, 355-356, 359
Harrall, B., 327
Harris, A., 288
Harris, H., 215
Harris, M., 45, 73, 315
Hart, C. V., 386
Hasselkus, B., 146-147
Hayes, R. O., 318
Hazan, H., 297, 298, 299
Headaches, skull surgery and, 360
Healers
body-oriented, 371-402
culture-specific, 78
in general, 78
mind-oriented, 8, 344-370
and ORT, 175-176
as shamans, 346
Healing
animism and, 46-47
magic and, 47-51
religion and, 52
science and, 54
Health. *See also* Immunizations; Mental health
ableness and, 302-304
body-oriented healers and, 371-402
and climate, 222
clinical anthropology and, 413-416
customs enhancing, 197-200
discordance hypothesis and, 60-61
in early urban societies, 57-58
of female athletes, 328-329
gays and, 304-305
international, 173-177
of lesbians, 329-330
lifestyle and, 328
maintenance of, 6
menopausal and post-menopausal, 337-338
in Mesolithic period, 56
mild to moderate malnutrition and, 278-282
mind-oriented healers and, 344-370
Navajo exposure to physician methods, 168
in Neolithic period, 57
obstetrical practices and, 332-336
and old age, 294-295
Paiute and, 89-90
in Paleolithic period, 55-56
prehistoric archeology and, 55-58
prehistory, cultural diversity, and, 61-62
reproductive, 331-332
short-term (acute) vs. long-term (chronic), 8

of technologically simple societies, 182-183
  Vitamin C and, 59-60
  of women, 314-341
Health conditions
  in bands, 182-183
  in tribes and chiefdoms, 183-184
  in peasant villages, 184-185
Hearing impaired, 303-304
Hearn, W., 384
Heidel, W. A., 388
Helman, C., 132
Hemoglobin, as racial trait, 260-261
Henry, J., 294-295
Herbalism and herbalists, 372-375
  ethnomedical models and, 378-385
Herbal medicines, 364-365
Hernesniemi, A., 392
Hierarchies, 189-190
  in anthropology, 39-41
  in biomedicine, 34
Hierarchy of resort, 109
Hiernaux, J., 193
Hill, T. W., 241
Hilton-Simpson, M. W., 386
Hinshaw, R., 420
Hippocrates, 388
  principle of contraries, 381
Hirsch, J., 275
Hirsch, S., 362
Historical particularism, 73
HIV (human immunodeficiency virus), 305-
    306. See also AIDS
  lesbian health and, 331
Hogarty, G. E., 362
Holism, 21
  of nursing, 411-412
Holistic health, shamans and, 359
Holistic model, 4
  alcoholism and, 269-270
  biocultural model as, 208
Holmberg, A., 422
Holmes, J., 296
Holmes, L. D., 233, 295, 296, 301
Home births, 395-396
Homeopathic doctor, 7
Homeopathic magic, 47, 50
Homeopathy, 380-385
  research study on, 383-384
  Homo erectus, 57
  Homo sapiens, 55
Homosexuals
  health of lesbians, 329-330
  STDs and, 331

Honduras, 176
Hong Kong, 393
Hopkins, D. R., 217
Horn, J. S., 392
Houston, B. K., 267
Howell, N., 327
Howells, W., 352
Hoy, D., 403
HRAF. See Human Relations Area Files
Hsu, F. L. K., 211-212
Hsu, K., 11
Huber, B. R., 371
Hughes, C., 359
Human behavior, positivist models of, 31-32
Human body, study of, 27-29
Human Relations Area Files (HRAF)
  child rearing, disease causation, and, 91-94
  for correlational studies, 87-90
  defined, 83
  recent research, 94-95
  and theories of illness, 82-86
Humoral theory, 389-390, 393
Hunger, nutritional anthropology and, 277-282
Hunt, E. E., Jr., 160
Hunt, G., 111, 121
  and Quesalid, 112-113
Hunter, D. E., 50
Hurston, Z. N., 314
Hutchinson, J., 308, 309
Hysterectomies, 317-318
Hysteria, Inuit and, 242-243

Iatmul people, 314
Ice Age, 55
Ideal types, 135
Illness. See also Disease; Sickness; Sick
    role
  HRAF and theories of, 83-84
  middle-class model of, 134
  as soul loss, 248
  theories of, 84-85
Imitative (homeopathic) magic, 47-48. See also
    Homeopathic magic
  Aztec medicine and, 66
Immunity, 62
Immunizations. See also Inoculation;
    Vaccination
  of children, 286-290
  in Haiti, 175
Imperato, P. J., 360, 372, 391
India, 391
  elderly in, 296
  medicine in, 386-387

newly wed women in, 331
  schizophrenia in, 254-255
  Western vs. traditional medicine in, 156
Indians, American. *See* Native Americans
Indonesia, magic and religion in, 52
Infancy, disease causation and, 90-94
Infant, culture and, 30. *See also* Children
Infanticide, 315
Infant mortality, of bands, 185
Infection
  focal, 291
  theories of, 85
Infectious diseases, 176-177
  epidemics, 208-221
  genetic adaptation to, 193
  malaria in Africa and, 192-195
  malaria in South America and, 195-196
  population movement and, 61-62
  regional ecology and, 192-200
Inferential statistics, 119-120
Inferiority, of women, 321-322. *See also*
  Women
Informants, 104-106
  distortions and, 110
  free-listing technique with, 121
  use of, 121
Ingram, G., 374
Ingstad, B., 303
Inhorn, M. C., 62, 196
Initiation, to shamanism, 347
Injectionists, and ORT, 176
Inoculation, against smallpox, 217. *See also*
  Immunization; Vaccination
Intellectual evolution, Comte on, 214-25
Interdisciplinarity, 19-20, 41-42
International Biological Program, 220
International Council of Scientific Unions, 220
International health, 173-177
Interviews, therapeutic, 365-366
Intuitive knowledge, 13
Intuitive magic, 67
Inuit
  Kemp study of, 187
  pibloktoq and, 242-243
Ireland
  beer and whiskey in, 238-239
  schizophrenia and, 252, 253-254
Irish-Americans, attitude toward pain, 323-324
Irish Countryman, The (Arensberg), 238
Italian-Americans, attitude toward pain of, 324
Italians, schizophrenia and, 252-253
Italy. *See* Italian-Americans; Italians; Sardinia
Iyengar, B. K. S., 394

Jackson, J., 263
Jackson, M., 110
Jacobs, J., 384
Jacobs, S. E., 329-330
Jacobson, R., 136, 141
Jaffre, Y., 396
Janzen, J. M., 106, 157
Japan
  hygiene in, 139-140
  menopause in, 338
  structural theory in, 137
Jarcho, S., 61
Jay, M., 323
Jeffery, P., 395
Jeffery, R., 395
Jeffrey, P., 214
Jenner, E., 217-218
Jews
  attitude toward pain of, 324
  elderly neglect and, 297-298
Jivaro people, 352, 355
Johnson, T. M., 25, 271, 414, 415
Joint manipulation, 392
Jones, D. E., 347, 354, 366, 371, 372
Jones, R. A., 46
Jordan, B., 17, 19, 332, 395
Jorgensen, J., 95

Kaboré, A., 279
Kaczmarski, R. J., 328
Kako (Chief), 425
Kallawaya people, 379
Kang-Wang, J. F., 336, 395
Karasu, T., 367
Karve, I., 314
Kates, R. W., 277, 278
Katz, M. M., 254
Katz, P., 391, 409-410
Kaufman, S., 300
Keefe, S., 262, 263
Kemp, W., 187, 189
Kendall, C., 176, 177
Kennedy, K. A. R., 56
Kenya, South Turkana Ecosystem Project of,
  221-223
Kiev, A., 160
Kimball, S. T., 420
Kinsey, A., 304-305
Kinship practices, 101
Kipling, R., 21
Kirby, D. G., 336
Kirean (prophet), 215
Klein, J., 19

Klein, N., 152, 160, 170, 382, 399
Kleinman, A., 86, 206, 247, 255, 290, 359, 367, 387, 407
Kline, S. J., 30, 31, 33, 39
Koch, R., 210, 213
Komarovsky, M., 315
Konner, M., 60, 274, 335, 410
Kosch, S., 336
Kottak, C., 293
Kozloff, M. A., 132
Krehbiel, R., 264
Kroeber, A. L., 74, 239
Kuhn, T., 29-30, 73, 74
Kuipers, J., 150
!Kung San people, 316
    menopause and, 337-338
    menstruation among, 327
Kutchins, H., 359
Kwakiutl people, 357-358
    Quesalid the Shaman, 104, 111-115, 357
Kühn, H., 62

La Barre, W., 234, 236
Laderman, C., 386
Ladino (mestizo), study of, 117
Laennac, 385
Lambek, M., structural theory and, 141-144
Lambert, E. D., 291
Lamphere, L., 328
Lancaster, J. B., 327, 332
Landes, R., 314
Landsteiner blood types, 192
Landy, D., 160, 208, 243, 276
Lane, S., 18, 19, 173-174
Lang, G. C., 264, 265, 266
Lang, N. G., 307
Langer, W. L., 209
Language, physicians' use of, 144-150. *See also* Linguistics
Laqueur, T., 320
Lascaux cave, 65
Lasswell, H. D., 423, 424
Last, M., 417
Latah, 244
Latin America, 389-390. *See also* Mexico; South America
    cholera in, 213
Latu Lama, 28
Lauro, P., 344
Law of Contact, 51
Law of Similarity, 51
Leach, E., 136
Leatherman, T., 206

Lee, R. B., 182
Leeches, use of term, 78, 79
Legacé, R. O., 96
Leibel, R. L., 275
Leininger, M. M., 412-413
Leininger's model of nursing, 412-413
Leonard, T., 308
Leonard, T. L., 309
Lerner, D., 159
Lesbians. *See also* Gay lifestyle
    health of, 329-330
    STDs and, 331
Leslie, C., 387, 403, 405
Les-Trois-Frères, France, prehistoric caves in, 64
Levine, S., 133
Levinson, D., 96
Lévi-Strauss, C., 104
    and Quesalid, 111, 113, 114
Lévy-Bruhl, L., 23, 79
    on aging, 302
    structural theory and, 136, 140, 142
Lewes, G. H., 23
Lewis, I. M., 135
Lewis, L., 394
Licensed practical nurse (LPN), 411
Licensed vocational nurse (LVN), 411
Life expectancy, in Neolithic period, 57
Lifstyle, weight and, 328
Light, and shamanism, 351
Lightfoot-Klein, H., 317, 318
Lincoln, Y. S., 45, 46, 120
Linguistic anthropology, 20
Linguistics, 104. *See also* Literary theory; Text
    impact of, 136
    Jacobson and, 141
Literary theory. *See also* Linguistics; Text
    structuralism and, 144
Literature, in biomedical hierarchy, 36
Little, M., 220, 222
Livingstone, F., 193, 194
Lobotomy, 359
Lock, M., 29, 320, 321, 338, 407
Loewen, J., 80
Logan, M. H., 160, 377-378
Lowenberg, J. S., 133, 134
Lowie, R. H., 79, 239
LPN. *See* Licensed practical nurse
Lugbara people, 237-238
Luhrmann, T. M., 359
LVN. *See* Licensed vocational nurse
Lynaugh, J. E., 144

MacCormack, C. P., 395, 407
Macrobiotic diets, 404
Magic
  Age of, 47
  in Aztec medicine, 66-67
  body-oriented healers and, 371
  as etic term, 78
  as evolutionary stage, 75
  evolution of, 81
  Malinowski and, 130
  mind-oriented healers and, 344
  in obstetrical practices, 334
  origins and, 50
  personalistic medicine and, 53
  prehistoric evidence for, 62-63
  sickness, healing, and, 47-51
  surgeons and, 408
Magical causation, 86
Magical medicine, in India, 157-159
Magicians, roles of, 54
Maher, V., 336
Malaria
  control of, 219
  cultural response in Europe, 197-200
  cultural response in South America, 195
  physiological response in Africa, 192-195
  physiological response in South America, 196
  physiologic and cultural defenses against,
    194
  race and, 260-261
  as regional disease, 192-195
  sickle cell anemia as genetic defense against,
    194-195
  in South America, 195-196
  traditional belief about, 198-199
  among Turkana, 222
Malaysia
  magic in, 48
  sick role in, 134-135
Males, as subculture, 314
Malinowski, B., 39, 101, 102, 155
  functional theory and, 129-130
Malnutrition
  in early urban societies, 58
  mild to moderate (MMM), 278-282
Manic-depression, drugs and, 362
Manipulations, 391-393
Mann, W. N., 381
Manus peoples, 109
Marcus, G. E., 110
Marcus, J., 21
Maretzki, T. W., 379, 413-414, 415
Maring society, 189

Marks, J., 65
Marriott, M., 160, 176
  on Western vs. traditional medicine in India,
  156-159
Martial arts, 394
Martin, C. E., 304
Martorell, R., 280
Marwick, C., 287
Marx, K., 423
Marxism
  alcoholism, class, and, 268-269
  class, obesity, and, 271
Massage, 391
Masturbation, clitoridectomies and, 316-317
Mattson, P., 359
Mayotte Island, 141
McCay, B., 189, 220
McConnell, R., 374
McCown, T., 205
McElroy, A., 191, 206, 276
McGee, R. J., 235
McGrane, B., 77
McGrath, J. W., 307
McKenna, J. J., 60
McNeill, W. H., 55, 61, 62, 211
Mead, M., 3, 101-102, 109, 154, 235, 295, 314,
    315, 326
  natural experiment and, 232-234
Mediation, 143
  structural theory and, 139-140
Medical anthropologists, methods of, 3-4
Medical anthropology
  discipline of, 8
  ecology and, 191, 200-201
  ecosystem studies and, 189
  field of, 17-42
  growth of field, 205-208
  interdisciplinarity of, 19-20
  as policy science, 420-424
  Primitive Concepts of Disease
    (Clements) and, 81-82
Medical Anthropology, 159
Medical anthropology, *Medicine, Magic, and
Religion* (Rivers) as first book in, 74-81
Medical diagnosis, 3-5, 9-10
Medical ecology, 180-203
  and biocultural model, 204-229
  and environmental hazards, 220
  in extreme climates, 220-224
  higher levels of analysis, 189-191
Medicaments, 388-391
Medications, 362-363. *See also* Drugs
Medicinal herbs. *See* Herbs and herbalism;

Herbal medicines

Medicine. *See also* Drugs; Health; Physicians;
Psychopharmacology
allopathic, 404
and anthropology, 8
anthropology of, 403-429
Aztec, 66-69
biomedicine as, 404-405
cosmopolitan, 403-404
diets and regimens in, 393-394
ethnomedicine, 405-407
hierarchy of disciplines in, 34
homeopathy and, 7
as isolated field, 79
magical, 157-159
manipulations and, 391-393
medicaments and, 388-391
and mental health, 359-365
methods of, 3-4
multidisciplinarity with anthropology, 163-
172
old world empirical, 385-394
personalistic vs. naturalistic, 52-54
physicians and surgeons in, 407-410
prehistoric art and, 62-65
undesirable side effects in, 418-419
vertical reasoning in, 36-39, 41
Western, 405
Medicine, Magic, and Religion, 74
Mees, L. F. C., 79-80
Melanisians, Rivers on, 78-79
Memory culture, 101
Men. *See also* Males; Women
gay lifestyle and, 304-305
osteoporisis and age in, 338
Menarche, 316
Menopause, health and, 337-338
Menstruation, 326-327. *See also*
Menarche; Menopause
Mental health, 232-258. *See also* Drugs;
Mind-oriented healers
alcohol and, 236-239
contemporary substance abuse and, 240-241
culture-bound psychiatric syndromes and,
241-245
depression and, 245-246
ethnopsychiatry and, 366-367
hallucinogens and, 234-236
Mead and, 233
medical and surgical approaches to, 359-365
reductionism and, 30
schiozphrenia and, 249-252
therapeutic interview and, 365-366

tobacco and, 239-240
Merbs, C. F., 56
Mescal bean, 235
Mescalero Apache, 240
Mesolithic period, 56
Messer, E., 282
Messing, S. D., 318
Metabolic levels, obesity and, 275-276
Metaphoric relations, 137, 140, 144
Metaphysical (transitional) view, 23-24
Metaphysics, sciences and, 32
Metcalf, A., 241
Methodological triangulation, postpositivism
and, 120-123
Methodology
cross-cultural sample, 96
HRAF and, 95-96
Metonymic relations, 137
Metraux, R., 154
Metzger, D., 106, 107
Mexican-Americans
diabetes and, 264
study of, 117
Mexico
body-oriented healers in, 371
dietary therapy in, 394
folkmedicine in, 390
home births in, 395-396
ORT therapy and, 175, 176
Pichátaro, 106-110
Susto study and, 117-119
Middleton, J., 237
Midwifery. *See also* Childbirth; Women
and birth attendants, 395-396
in U.S., 335-336
Migration, health and, 61-62
Mild to moderate malnutrition (MMM), 278-
282
and vertical thinking, 280-281
Miller, B., 394
Mind, healers and, 344-370. *See also*
Mental health
Mind-altering substances, 240. *See also*
Drugs
Mind/body dualism, 252
Mind-oriented healers, 8
Mintz, S., 268
Miracle, A. W., 21
Miracles, staging, 111-112
Mishler, E., 147
MMM. *See* Mild to moderate malnutrition
Modernism, 26-27
Moerman, D. E., 376, 377, 407

Moniz, E., 359, 361
Monotheism, 46
Montagu, A., 262
Montague (Lady), 217
Morain, C., 336
Moran, E. F., 185-186, 187, 190
Morgan, L. H., 101
Morocco, magic in, 48
Morse, J. M., 373-374, 375
Mortality
  of bands, 185
  behavior and, 200
  evaluation of African, 39-41
  in peasant villages, 184-185
Mosko, S., 60
Mothers, malnutrition and, 282. *See also*
  Childbirth; Children; Family; Females; Men;
  Women
Mull, D. S., 392
Mull, J. D., 392
Mullings, L., 336, 420
Multidimensional scaling, 122
Multidisciplinarity, 8, 19, 22-25, 41-42
  anthropology and medicine, 163-172
  chiropractors, vaccinations, and, 289-290
  current, 173-177
  events leading up to, 161-162
  metaphysical (transitional) view and, 23-24
  positive (scientific) view, 24-25
  and side effects, 418-419
  theological (supernatural) view and, 23
Multidisciplinary research, lack of, 79-81
Multilinear evolution, 181-185
Murdock, G. P., 83, 84-85, 96
  religious healing beliefs and, 93
Murphy, H. B. M., 244
Murphy, R., 103, 303
Murphy, Y., 103
Mutchler, K., 308
Mystical causation theories, 86
Mystical experience. *See* Shamanism;
  Shamans
Mystical retribution, 86, 88

Naroll, R., 96, 293
Native American Church, 236
  healing and, 39
Native Americans, 101
  alcoholism and, 241
  cultural traits of, 180-181
  diabetes in, 263-266
  herbs of, 376-378
  peyote and, 235

Sanapia and, 347-348
  therapeutic interview and, 365-366
  tobacco and, 239
Natural experiment, in research design, 232-234
Naturalism
  and Aztec medicine, 68-69
  and efficacy, 93-94
  as evolutionary stage, 75
Naturalistic medicine, 52-54, 356, 363-364. *See
  also* Psychopharmacology
  as causation theory, 84
  documentation problems for, 84-86
  healers and, 344-345
  Whiting and, 87-88
Naturopathy, 379-380
Navajo
  culture and, 314
  religious healing and, 39
Navajo-Cornell project, 161
  assessment of, 172-173
  baseline cultures and, 167
  communication in, 170-171
  community needs and, 169
  cultural bias and, 165-166
  decision making in, 169-170
  knowledge of target community, 164-165
  multidisciplinarity and, 163-172
  planner culture and, 165-167
  previous social relations and, 167-168
  relations within target community, 171-172
N.D. degree (Doctor of Naturopathy), 379
Ndembu peoples, 356
Neel, J. V., 263
Negative fixation, 92
  and disease, 93
Negroes. *See* Africa; African-Americans;
  Blacks
Neolithic period, 57
Neoshamanism, 354-359
Nepal
  embodied awareness in, 28-29
  trauma in, 293
Ness, S. A., 28, 394
Netting, R., 188
Neugarten, B. L., 300
Neumann, A. K., 344
Neurasthenia, 247
Newborn, sympathetic magic and, 48-49
Newman, L. F., 58
New World, 61-62. *See also* Americas
  diabetes in, 264
  hallucinogens in, 234

Nichols, D. H., 317
Nichter, Mark, 328
Nichter, Mimi, 328
Nicotine, 239
NIDDM. *See* Noninsulin-dependent dia-
    betes mellitus
Niehoff, A. H., 159
Nigeria, schizophrenia in, 254-255
Nogami, A. H., 270
Nomads, health of, 222-223
Noninsulin-dependent diabetes mellitus
    (NIDDM), 263-266
Notes and Queries in Anthropology, 101
Novack, C. J., 394
NSAIDs (nonsteroidal anti-inflmmatory drugs),
    383-384
Nuer people, 215
Nurse anthropologists, nurses and, 410-413
Nurses, 410-413
Nursing homes, 294
Nutritional anthropology, 276-282
Nyani, 52

OAM. *See* Office of Alternative Medicine
Obesity, class and, 271-276
Obeyesekere, G., 390
Objectivism, 26-27
Objectivity
    difficulty of obtaining, 110
    standards of, 100
Observation, participant, 102-103
Obstetrical practices, 332. *See also*
    Childbirth; Midwives; Women
    in United States, 333-336
Office of Alternative Medicine (OAM), 384
Ohnuki-Tierney, E., 137, 138
Ojibway Indian, magic and, 47-48
Old age, 294-295. *See also* Age and aging
    in Samoa, 295-296
    in San Francisco, 298-300
Old Stone Age, shamanism in, 62-65
Old World, 61-62, 236-239
Olkes, C., 358 , 102
On Airs, Waters and Place (Hippocrates),
    389
O'Neale, L., 314
O'Nell, Carl, Susto study and, 117-119
Ong, A., 134-135, 336, 387
On Winds (Hippocrates), 389
Oöphorectomies, 318
Opler, M., 253, 254
Oppositions. *See also* Transformations
    binary, 137

mediation and, 139-140
Oral explanations
    of disease causation, 91
    statistical pitfalls in, 92
Oral rehydration therapy (ORT), 174-176
Orellana, S. L., 372
Orion, L., 359
ORT. *See* Oral rehydration therapy
Orthomolecular medicine, 404
Ortiz de Montellano, B. R., 66-68, 131, 378,
    386
Ortner, D. J., 55
Osborne, O., 411
Osteoporisis, and aging, 338
Otterbein, K. F., 96
Outline of Cultural Materials (Murdock),
    83
Out-of-body sensations, shamanism as, 350-354
Overfield, T., 279

Page, J. B., 308
Pago Pago. *See* Samoa
Pain, 133
    control of, 9-10
    culture, gender, and perception of, 323-326
    epidemiology and, 10-11
    surgery for, 9-12
Paintings, Paleolithic, 62-63
Paiute Indians, culture core of, 181-182
    health, politics, and, 89-90
    naturalistic medicine and, 87-88
    personalistic medicine and, 88
    sorcery and illness in, 132
Paiute Sorcery (Whiting), 87
Paleolithic period, 55-56. *See also* Stone
    Age
Panama, 80
Pandemic, AIDS as, 307
Paradigmatic relations, 137, 144
Paradigm shifts. *See also* paradigms by
    name
    cultural evolutionary theory and, 73
    ecology and, 180-181
    in ethnographic methods, 100
Parent
    and child development, 31. *See also*
    Family
    malnutrition and, 282
Parker, R., 307
Parker, S., 21
Parsons, T., 132, 271
Participant observation, 102-103
    and quantitative methods, 116-119

Past, identifying in acculturation project, 167-168

Pasteur, L., 213

Pathophysiology, 418
  diagnosis and, 93
  etic prognosis and, 80

Patient, diagnosis of, 3-4

Patterns of Culture (Benedict), 345

Paul, B. D., 159, 392, 395

Paul, L., 395

Pauling, L., 59, 60, 192-193

Paz, O., 136

Peasants, health conditions of, 184-185

Pellegrino, E. D., 424

Pelto, G. H., 119, 124, 278

Pelto, P. J., 119, 278

Penicillin, 373

Peoples' Republic of China. *See* China

Personalistic medicine, 52-54, 88
  healers, 344-345

Peters, L., 350, 356

Peyote, 235-236
  Sanapia and, 347-348

Pharmacology. *See* Drugs; Herbalism and
    herbalists; Herbal medicine;
    Psychopharmacology

Philippines, psychic surgeons in, 12, 13

Phoenix, S., 333

Phonemics, 136

Phonetics, 136

Physical anthropology, 204-205
  Virchow and, 162

Physicians. *See also* Nurses
  anthropologist cooperation with, 172-177
  language use among, 144-150
  surgeons and, 407-410

Physics, in biomedical hierarchy, 35

Physiological adaptation
  in Africa, 192-195
  malaria in Europe, 196-197
  in South America, 195-196

Physiological/biomedical models, colon cancer
    and, 37-38

Physiological responses. *See* Malaria

Physiology, in biomedical hierarchy, 35

Pibloktoq, and Inuit, 242-243

Pichátaro, Mexico, 106-110

Piché, V., 39

Pike, K., 76

Pile-sort techniques, 121-122

Pine Ridge Indian Reservation, Singer at, 77

Pipes, and American Indians, 239

Pi-Sunyer, F. X., 328

Plague, as infectious epidemic, 209-210

Plants. *See* Herbalism and herbalists;
    Herbal medicine

Pleistocene period, 55

Polanyi, M., 33

Polgar, S., 22, 23

Policy, medical anthroplogy and, 420-424

Polio, immunization and, 287

Political science, in biomedical hierarchy, 36

Politics
  Paiute and, 89-90
  and starvation, 277

Pomeroy, W. B., 304

Popkin, B., 337

Positive fixation, and disease, 93

Positive (scientific) view, 24

Positivism
  high modernity and, 27-29
  limits of, 31-32
  modernism and, 27
  postmodernism and, 29

Positivist science, anthropology as, 29-30

Possession. *See* Shamanism

Postmodernism, 29, 110-116
  defined, 110

Postpositivism
  and dual-level control concept, 32-33
  and methodological triangulation, 120-123

Potentization, 381-382

Potter, J., 36-37, 38-39

Poverty. *See also* Foods; Malnutrition;
    Starvation
  feminization of, 336-337
  and size, 280-281

Powdermaker, H., 314

Pragmatism, 93-94

Prague School, 136

Prayer, 383

Predictive value, of statistics, 120

Prehistoric archeology, 20
  and health conditions, 55-58

Prehistoric art, 62-65

Prehistory
  cultural diversity, health, and, 61-62
  shamanism in, 62-65

Preston, S., 171

Prevention
  magic and, 50
  and public health, 173

Price-Williams, D., 350

Primatology, 55

Prince, R., 363, 364

Principles of Professional Responsiiblity (AAA),

420-422
Prognosis, 79
Prolixin, 362
Promiscuity, AIDS and, 308-310
Protein, consumption of, 280-281
Prual, A., 396
Psoriasis, herbal treatment of, 373-375
Psychiatric drugs, 361-363
Psychiatric syndromes, culture-bound, 241-245
Psychiatry, 359
Psychic surgeons, in Philippines, 12, 13
Psychic unity, 96
Psychoactive plants, 234
Psychological barriers, to change, 161
Psychology, in biomedical hierarchy, 35
Psychopharmacology, of traditional healers,
    363-365. See also Drugs
Psychoses, shamans and, 345-346
Psychotropic drugs, 361
Puberty, women and, 316
Public health. See also Navajo-Cornell project;
    U.S. Public Health Service
  cholera and, 212
  clinical anthropology and, 415
  prevention and, 173
Puerto Ricans, 268
Pugh, J. F., 386
Putschar, W. G. J., 55
Pygmies, 194

Qualitative methods, 22
Quality Control Sample, 96
Quantitative methods, 22
  participant observation and, 116-119
Quesalid the Shaman, 104, 111-115, 357
  Hunt and, 112-113
Questioning techniques, 103-110
  descriptive questions, 104-106
  frame techniques, 107-110

Rabinow, P., 110
Race
  and cardiovascular disease among African
Americans, 266-267
  diabetes and, 263-266
  and ethnicity, 259-267
  hemoglobin as trait, 260-261
  malnutrition and, 278-279
  social, political factors and, 265
  as unclear category, 262
Radcliffe-Brown, A. R., 129, 101
  structural-functional theory and, 132
Randall, T., 296, 302

Randomized controlled trial, herbalism and,
    375
Rapid ethnographic assessment, 123-125
Rapp, R., 332, 335
Rappaport, R., 45-46, 73, 188, 189
Rather, L. J., 163
Ravussin, E., 275
Reality, religion, magic, and, 53
Reasoning, vertical, 35-36
Redfield, R., 184
Reductionism, error of, 30-31
Regimens, 393-394
Regional ecology, infectious diseases and, 192-
    200
Registered nurses (RNs), 410, 411
Reichardt, C. S., 117, 120
Religion. See also Magic; Shamans
  Age of, 47
  animism and, 46-47
  as etic term, 78
  as evolutionary stage, 75
  prehistoric evidence for, 62-63
  shamanism as, 356
  sickness, healing, and, 52
Renaissance, 27
Renolds, D. K., 251
Reproductive health, 331-332
Reproductive years, 327-337
Research. See also Correlational studies
  on AIDS, 305-308
  ecosystem, 188-189
  into medicinal herbs, 376-378
  recent HRAF-based, 94-95
  women-centered, 337
Reservations. See Navajo-Cornell project
Reston, J., 417
Retribution, mystical, 86, 88
Return to Laugher (Smith [Bohannan]),
    425
Reverby, S., 411
Rheumatic arthritis, homeopathic treatment of,
    383-384
Ricoeur, P., 144
Ries, L. A. G., 336
Ritenbaugh, C., 263, 276, 328
Rituals
  birth and, 395
  of Navajo, 165, 167-168
Rivers, W. H. R., 74-76, 84, 101, 159, 161-162,
    163
  diagnosis, prognosis, and, 79-80
  etic and emic terms of, 78
  evolutionary development stages of, 75-76

RNs. *See* Registered nurses
Roberts, C., 275, 329-330
Robinson, D., 279
Rodriguez-Bigas, M., 372
Rogers, Z. R., 261
Rogge, A. E., 73
Roles, sick, 132-135
Romanucci-Ross, L., 109, 406
Romney, A. K., 121
Roosevelt, A. C., 57
Rosaldo, M., 328
Royce, A. P., 394
Rubel, A. J., 116
    Susto study and, 117-119
Rubinstein, R., 173-174
Ryan, M., 206, 418

Sadove, A. M., 391
St. Hoyme, L. E., 61
Samoa
    girls in, 314
    health and old age in, 295-296
    Mead in, 233
    menstruation in, 326
Samples, targeting, 124
Sanapia, 347-348, 353-354, 371
    interviews by, 365-366
San Francisco, aging in, 298-300
San people, 233-234
Sardinia
    malaria eradication in, 200-201
    malaria in, 196-200
Sargent, C., 395
Schechner, R., 29
Scheper-Hughes, N., 29, 115, 238, 239, 240,
    251, 282, 293, 321
Schiebinger, L., 322
Schiff, I., 317
Schiffmann, A., 392
Schiller, C. A., 55
Schiller, N., 307
Schismogenesis, 288, 314
Schizophrenia, 249-252. *See also* Mental
    health
    culture-bound nature of, 253-254
    drugs and, 362
    family and, 250-252
    national perspective on, 252
    in Nigeria and India, 254-255
    organic pathology of, 249-250
Schneider, K., 304
Schoepf, B., 308
Schultes, R. E., 373

Schweder, R. A., 31, 424
Science(s). *See also* Medicine
    Age of, 47
    anthropology and, 27
    complexity of system in, 32
    Comte on, 24-25
    sickness, healing, and, 54
    Turkana health and, 223
Scientific theories, replacement of, 73
Seaman, B., 318
Seaman, G., 318
Seasonal change, as disease causation, 198
Seckler, D., 278
Segar, J., 363
Seidler, E., 379
Seligman, C.G., 101
Service, E. R., 182, 183
SES. *See* Socioeconomic status
Sex. *See* Females; Gender; Girls; Males; Men;
    Sexual explanations; Women
    *Sex and Temperament in Three Primitive
        Societies* (Mead), 315
Sexual explanations
    of disease causation, 91
    statistical pitfalls in, 92
Sexual intercourse. *See* Circumcision,
    female
Sexuality, ovulation-associated, 327-337
Sexually transmitted diseases (STDs), 331
Shamanic state of consciousness (SSC), 347
Shamanism. *See also* Shamans
    as altered state of consciousness, 346-348
    cosmos of, 350-351
    neoshamanism and, 354-359
    as out-of-body sensations, 350-354
    in prehistory, 62-65
    technology of, 351-354
    as trance possession, 348-349
Shamans, 7. *See also* Shamanism
    African, 348-349
    Brazilian, 349
    fraud of, 111-112
    healers as, 346
    in New World, 234-235
    prayer and, 383
    Quesalid as, 104, 111-115
    role of African, 5-6
    Sanapia as, 347-348
    societies found in, 94
    symptoms of, 345-346
    trickery of, 352-354
    in urban America, 359
Shapiro, H. L., 204

Shilling, C., 28
Shipley, M., 384, 390
Shirokogoroff, S. M., 345, 347
Shostak, M., 60, 233, 316, 326, 337, 395
Shutler, M. E., 372
Shweder, R. A., 92, 248
Sibley, L., 206
Sibthorpe, B., 310
Sickle cell anemia, 193
    as malaria defense, 194-195
Sickness. *See also* Disease; Health
    magic and, 47-51
    Parsons and, 132-133
    religion and, 52
    science and, 54
Sick role
    concept of, 132-135
    in Mexican village, 134
Silver, G. A., 162
Similia, 380
Simon, A., 298
Simons, R. C., 242
Singer, M., 18-19, 32, 268, 269, 271, 307
Singer, P., 77, 393
Singleton, 357, 358
Sioux, ethnicity and diabetes among, 264-266.
    See also Native Americans
Size
    and climate, 221-222
    female beauty and, 328
Skeleton, female, 322
Skin color. *See* Race
Skin disease terminology, 104-106
Skrimshaw, N. S., 280, 282
Skull surgery, 360
Sleep paralysis taxon, 359
Smallpox. *See also* Disease
    in Africa, 214-215
    in Americas, 215-216
    control of, 219
    vaccine against, 216-219
Smith, P. C., 308
Smoking. *See* Tobacco
Smuts, J-C, 21
Snow, J., 213
Snow, L., 49-50
Snuff, and possession, 349
Sobal, J., 271, 272-274
Sobo, E., 321
Social barriers, to change, 160-161
Social body, women and, 321-322
Social science, reductionist nature of, 26
Society

complex, 155
    male and female subcultures in, 315
Society for Applied Anthropology, 154, 420
Society for Medical Anthropology, 17
Sociocultural anthropology, 20
Sociocultural integration, 182
Socioeconomic status, 268-276
    and alcoholism, 268-271
    and obesity, 271-276
Sociology
    in biomedical hierarchy, 35
    human body and, 28
    use of term, 25
Songhay people, 358
Sorcery, 86
    prayer and, 383
Soul loss, 248
Sound, and shamanism, 351
South Africa, menstratuion in, 326
South America
    malaria in, 195-196
    tobacco in, 239-240
South Turkana Ecosystem Project, 221-223
Soviet Union, old age levels in, 301-302
Space, dimension of, 180-181
Spain, prehistoric evidence in, 62-64
Spinal adjusting. *See* Chiropractors
Spindler, G., 15, 19, 237
Spindler, L., 15, 237
Spirits, 52. *See also* Magic; Religion
    chasing away, 7-8
    healing and, 352
    mystical retribution and, 88
Spiritualism, animism and, 46-47
Spiro, M. E., 115
Spradley, J. P., 104
Spring, A., 336
SSC. *See* Shamanic state of consciousness
Standard Cross-Cultural Sample, 84, 96
Starr, P., 212, 385, 404
Starvation, 277. *See also* Malnutrition
Staski, E., 65
Statistics, 119-120
    for describing findings, 107-110
STDs. *See* Sexually transmitted diseases
Stebbins, K., 241
Stein, L. I., 411
Stereotypes, of pain perception, 324-325
Stern, G., 73
Stevens, P. E., 331
Steward, J. H., 180, 185
    cultural cores and, 181-182
    culture change theory and, 181

Stewart, O. C., 154
Stewart, T. D., 61
Stigma (Goffman), 303
Stocking, G. W., Jr., 39
Stoeckle, M. Y., 41
Stoller, P., 102, 358, 359, 383
Stone Age, 56, 60
Strauss, A., 120
Streptomycin, 373
Structural anthropology, 136. *See also*
    Functional theory; Structural theory
Structural linguistics, 136
Structural theory, 136-141. *See also*
    Functional theory
    Lambek's use of, 141-144
Suarez, A., 372
Subanum informants, 104-106
Substance abuse, contemporary, 240-241
Sudan, female circumcision in, 318, 319
Suddath, R. L., 249, 250
Suffering, spiritual purpose of, 13. *See
    also* Pain
Sullivan, L. R., 204
Sumaria, 388
Sunrise model, 412, 413
Supernatural and supernaturalism, 26, 53, 85.
    See also Magic; Mind-oriented healers;
    Personalistic medicine
    and Aztec medicine, 68
Surgeons, physicians and, 407-410. *See
    also* Medicine; Surgery
Surgery
    for back pain, 9-12
    on brain, 360-361
    and mental health, 359-365
    on skull, 360
Susto study, 117-119
Sutro, L., 241
Sutro, L. D., 241
Swartz, L., 116, 148, 374
Swiss Alpine village, ecosystem of, 188
Symbols and symbolism, 141. *See also*
    Linguistics
    birth and, 395
    culture and, 137
    of menstruation, 327
    in obstetrical practice, 334-335
Sympathetic magic, 47-48
Syntagmatic relations, 137
Systems, complexity of, 31-32
Szathmary, E. J. E., 265

Taboos, and menstruation, 327
Taiwan, midwives in, 336

Target community, culture of, 164-165
Target samples, 124
Taussig, M., 50
Taussig, T. T., 184
Tautology, 186-187
Taxonomic categories, 182
Taxons, sleep paralysis as, 359
Teamwork, 19, 22-23
Technology. *See also* Science(s)
    applied anthropology and, 159
    of shamanism, 351-354
Temkin, O., 388
Terminology, 144
Terms, collecting, 104-106
Texeira, J., 349, 351, 352, 353, 354
Text. *See also* Linguistics; Literary theory
    culture as, 141-144
    events as, 144
Thalassemia, 196
Theological (supernatural) view, 23. *See
    also* Religion
Theology, sciences and, 32. *See also*
    Religion
Theoretical science, 26
Theories. *See* theories by name
Therapeutic interview, 365-366
Therapy, ethnopsychiatry as, 366-367
Therapy management group, of Janzen, 157
Thick description, 139
Thinness, 328. *See also* Body
Third World
    health in, 417
    tobacco sales in, 241
Thomas, D., 119
Thompson, L., 314, 422
Thomson, S., 379
Thorazine, 361
Thorwald, J., 55
Time, as dimension of culture, 73-74
Tiv people, 215
Tobacco, 239-240
    cigarette deaths and, 240
    transnational sales of, 241
Toda, culture and, 314
Torres Straits Expedition, 74, 101
Torrey, E. F., 366, 367
Torun, 282
Toubia, N., 319
Townsend, P., 191, 206
Traditional birth attendant, 395
Traditional healers, in biomedical settings, 416-
    419
Traditional medicine
    in China, 387

in India, 157-159
Trager healing, 13
Traits
  geographical distribution of, 73, 74
  racial, 259-261
Trances, surgery during, 354. *See also*
  Shamanism
Transcultural nursing, 412-413
Transformations, 142
  and structural theory, 137-139
Trauma, childhood, 293
Trawick, M., 393
Trephination, 359, 360-361
Triads, 143-144
Triangles, 143-144
Triangulation
  postpositivism and, 120-123
  and rapid ethnographic assessment, 124
Tribes. *See also* peoples by name
  energy flow in, 188-189
  health conditions in, 183-184
Trickery, of shamans, 111-112, 352-354
Trobriand Islanders, Malinowski and, 100, 129
Trotter, R. T. H., 377-378
Trubetzkoy, N., 136
Tsembaga, energy flow and, 188, 189
Tuberculosis. *See* Navajo-Cornell project
Tungus peoples, 345, 346
Turkana, of East Africa, 221-223
Turner, E., 356-357, 358, 359, 383
Turner, M., 298
Turner, P., 422, 423
Turner, V., 356-357
Twigg, G., 209
Tylor, E. B., 46, 65, 82, 346, 354
Tylor, E. G., 101
Type A behavior pattern, 266-267
Type II diabetes mellitus, 263-266
Tzintzuntzan culture, 130-131, 314

Unani Tibb, 386, 390, 405
United Nations Food and Agriculture
Organization (FAO), 277
United States. *See also* Americas; New
  World; Western entries
  cholera in, 212-213
  obstetrics in, 333-336
U.S. Public Health Service
  and anthropologists, 172-177
  Navajo-Cornell project and, 163
Unschuld, P. U., 405
Urban medicine. *See* Cosmopolitan
  medicine
Urbanowicz, C. F., 25

Urban societies, early, 57-58
Urdaneta, M. L., 264, 265

Vaccination. *See also* Immunization
  cowpox, 217-218
  against smallpox, 216-219
Vaccines, chiropractor opposition to, 287-290
Valenstein, E. S., 360
Valley Zapotec, study of, 117
Values. *See* Ethics
Van Willigen, J., 331
Vayda, A., 189, 220
Vedas, 386
Vertical reasoning, 35-36
  in anthropology, 39-41
  in medicine, 36-39
  mild to moderate malnutrition and, 280-281
  of Parsons, 272
Vertical transformations, 137
Vesalius, 385
Vicos Project, 422
Vinblastine, 373
Vincristine, 373
Virchow, R., 34, 162-163, 209, 268, 411
Virilocality, 330
Vision impaired, 303, 304
Vitaliano, P. P., 246
Vitamin C hypothesis, evolutionary theory and,
  59-60
Viteri, 282
Vivelo, F. R., 116
Vocabulary, 144. *See also* Linguistics

Waitzkin, H., 147-148
Wall, L. L., 393
Wallace, A. F. C., 243, 245, 347, 356
Wallerstein, E., 316-317
Walsh, R. N., 346, 347, 350, 351
Ward, R. E., 391
Warner, R., 252
Warry, W., 423
Wasson, R. G., 235
Water systems, cholera and, 213, 214
Wax, M., 50
Wax, R., 50, 154
Way of the Shaman, The (Harner), 355-
  356
Weaver, T., 420
Wedge, J. H., 11
Weibel-Orlando, J., 241, 242
Weiner, N., 272
Weiss, K. M., 263, 264, 265
Weller, S. C., 121, 122
Werner, O., 76

West, C., 147
Western Hemisphere, movement into, 61
Western medicine, 405. *See also*
  Discourse analysis
  ethnomedicine and, 406
  image vs. reality, 156-157
  in non-Western society, 156
  power of, 156
Western Regional Center, multidisciplinary
  team at, 14
Whiskey, in Irish community, 238-239
White, A. H., 11, 12
White, D., 96
White, L. A., 186
Whiting, B. B., 90, 95, 132
  Paiute studies by, 87-90
  statistics and, 119, 120
Whiting, J. W. M., 96, 118
  on Freudian explanations and disease causa-
    tion, 90-94
Whitten, P., 50
WHO. *See* World Health Organization
Whyte, S., 303
Wilbert, J., 239
Wilden, A., 26
Williams, G., 106, 107
Wilson, J. A., 388
Wilson, M., 314
Wilson, P., 303
Wilson, R., 80
Wilson, S. F., religious healing beliefs and, 93
Winick, C., 356
Winkelman, M. J., 94, 95, 96
Wiser, C., 395
Wiser, W., 395
Wissler, C., 180
Witchcraft, 86
  shamanism and, 359
Withington, E. T., 389
Wives, health of young, 330-331
Wizard of Les-Trois-Frères, 64
Wolinsky, F. D., 133
Wolinsky, S. R., 133
Women. *See also* Children; Females;
Mothers
  AIDS, condom use, and, 310
  body, culture, and, 320-323
  childbirth and, 332-336
  development of girls and, 315-316
  gay lifestyle and, 304-305
  health of, 314-341
  menarche and, 316
  ovulation-associated sexuality and, 327-337

pain perception in, 325-326
  perception as inferior creatures, 321-322
  poverty and, 336-337
  reproductive health of, 331-332
  shamanistic curing of, 357
  underfed, 281
Wood, J. W., 55
Woodrow, K. M., 325
Word magic, 50
World Health Organization (WHO)
  AIDS and, 307
  meeting of, 416
  smallpox eradication by, 218
World War II, anthropological contributions
  and, 154-155

Yoruba
  culture and, 314
  healers and, 363-364
Young, A., 81, 320
Young, D. E., 356, 373-374, 375
Young, J., 134
Young, J. C., Pichátaro, Mexico, work of, 106-
  110
Young, V. R., 280, 282
YPLL-65, 266
Yucatan, 17

"Zations," 296-298
Zborowski, M., 323, 324
Zimbabwe
  magic in, 49
  medical discourse in, 148-149
  shamans in, 351
Zimmerman, F., 388
Zimmermann, F., 394
Zinsser, H., 209
Zivanovic, S., 55
Zuni peoples, 170